WIRELESS COMMUNICATION NETWORKS AND SYSTEMS

Cory Beard

University of Missouri-Kansas City

William Stallings

PEARSON

Boston • Columbus • Hoboken • Indianapolis • New York • San Francisco
Amsterdam • Cape Town • Dubai • London • Madrid • Milan • Munich • Paris • Montreal
Toronto • Delhi • Mexico City • São Paulo • Sydney • Hong Kong • Seoul • Singapore • Taipei • Tokyo

Vice President and Editorial Director, ECS:
  Marcia J. Horton
Executive Editor: *Tracy Johnson (Dunkelberger)*
Editorial Assistant: *Kelsey Loanes*
Program Manager: *Carole Snyder*
Director of Product Management: *Erin Gregg*
Team Lead Product Management: *Scott Disanno*
Project Manager: *Robert Engelhardt*
Media Team Lead: *Steve Wright*
R&P Manager: *Rachel Youdelman*
R&P Senior Project Manager: *Timothy Nicholls*
Procurement Manager: *Mary Fischer*
Senior Specialist, Program Planning and Support:
  Maura Zaldivar-Garcia

Inventory Manager: *Bruce Boundy*
VP of Marketing: *Christy Lesko*
Director of Field Marketing: *Demetrius Hall*
Product Marketing Manager: *Bram van Kempen*
Marketing Assistant: *Jon Bryant*
Cover Designer: *Marta Samsel*
Cover Art: © *John Lund / Getty Images*
Full-Service Project Management:
  Mahalatchoumy Saravanan, Jouve India
Printer/Binder: *RR Donnelley / Crawfordsville*
Cover Printer: *RR Donnelley / West Bend*
Typeface: *Times Ten LT Std 10/12*

Pearson Education Ltd., *London*
Pearson Education Australia Ply. Ltd., *Sydney*
Pearson Education Singapore, Pte. Ltd.
Pearson Education North Asia Ltd., *Hong Kong*
Pearson Education Canada, Inc., *Toronto*
Pearson Education de Mexico, S.A. de C.V.
Pearson Education–Japan, *Tokyo*
Pearson Education Malaysia, Pte. Ltd.
Pearson Education, Inc., *Hoboken, New Jersey*

Library of Congress Cataloging-in-Publication Data
Stallings, William.
    Wireless communication networks and systems / William Stallings, Cory Beard, University of Missouri-Kansas City. — First edition.
        pages cm
    Includes bibliographical references and index.
    ISBN 978-0-13-359417-1 — ISBN 0-13-359417-3   1. Wireless communication systems.   2. Wireless LANs.   I.   Beard, Cory.   II. Title.
    TK5103.2.S828 2015
    621.39'81 — dc23
                                                                                2014046683

10 9 8 7 6 5 4 3 2 1

www.pearsonhighered.com

ISBN 10: 0-13-359417-3
ISBN 13: 978-0-13-359417-1

For my loving wife, Tricia

—WS

*For Michelle, Ryan, and Jonathan,
gifts from God to me*

—CB

CONTENTS

PREFACE

Wireless technology has become the most exciting area in telecommunications and networking. The rapid growth of mobile telephone use, various satellite services, the wireless Internet, and now wireless smartphones, tablets, 4G cellular, apps, and the Internet of Things are generating tremendous changes in telecommunications and networking. It is not an understatement to say that wireless technology has revolutionized the ways that people work, how they interact with each other, and even how social structures are formed and transformed. This book provides a unified overview of the broad field of wireless communications. It comprehensively covers all types of wireless communications from satellite and cellular to local and personal area networks. Along with the content, the book provides over 150 animations, online updates to technologies after the book was published, and social networking tools to connect students with each other and instructors with each other.

The organization of the book reflects an attempt to break this massive subject into comprehensible parts and to build, piece by piece, a survey of the state of the art. The title conveys a focus on all aspects of wireless systems—wireless communication techniques, protocols and medium access control to form wireless networks, then the deployment and system management to coordinate the entire set of devices (base stations, routers, smartphones, sensors) that compose successful wireless systems. The best example of an entire wireless system is 4G Long Term Evolution (LTE).

For those new to the study of wireless communications, the book provides comprehension of the basic principles and topics of fundamental importance concerning the technology and architecture of this field. Then it provides a detailed discussion of leading-edge topics, including Gigabit Wi-Fi, the Internet of Things, ZigBee, and 4G LTE-Advanced.

The following basic themes serve to unify the discussion:

- **Technology and architecture:** There is a small collection of ingredients that serves to characterize and differentiate wireless communication and networking, including frequency band, signal encoding technique, error correction technique, and network architecture.
- **Network type:** This book covers the important types of wireless networks, including wireless LANs, wireless personal area networks, cellular, satellite, and fixed wireless access.
- **Design approaches:** The book examines alternative principles and approaches to meeting specific communication requirements. These considerations provide the reader with comprehension of the key principles that will guide wireless design for years to come.
- **Standards:** The book provides a comprehensive guide to understanding specific wireless standards, such as those promulgated by ITU, IEEE 802, and 3GPP, as well as standards developed by other organizations. This emphasis reflects the importance of such standards in defining the available products and future research directions in this field.
- **Applications:** A number of key operating systems and applications (commonly called "apps") have captivated the attention of consumers of wireless devices. This book examines the platforms and application development processes to provide apps that make wireless devices easily accessible to users.

The book includes an extensive online glossary, a list of frequently used acronyms, and a bibliography. Each chapter includes problems and suggestions for further reading. Each chapter also includes, for review, a list of key words and a number of review questions.

INTENDED AUDIENCES

This book is designed to be useful to a wide audience of readers and students interested in wireless communication networks and systems. Its development concentrated on providing flexibility for the following.

- **Variety of disciplines:** The book provides background material and depth so those from several disciplines can benefit.

  - Those with **computer science** and **information technology** backgrounds are provided with accessible and sufficient background on signals and systems. In addition to learning about all of the wireless systems, they can especially study complete systems like the Evolved Packet System that supports LTE and mobile device operating systems and programming.

  - Those from **electrical engineering**, **computer engineering**, and **electrical engineering technology** (and even other areas of engineering) are given what they need to know about networking and protocols. Then this book provides material sufficient for a senior undergraduate communications course with no prerequisite of another communication course. It provides substantial depth in Chapters 6 through 10 on wireless propagation, modulation techniques, OFDM, CDMA, and error control coding. The technologies in the later chapters of the book can then be used as examples of these techniques. This book not only provides fundamentals but also understanding of how they are used in current and future wireless technologies.

- **Ranges of experience:** Those who are novices with wireless communications, or even communication technologies themselves, are led through the knowledge they need to become proficient. And those with existing knowledge learn about the latest advances in wireless networking.

- **Levels of depth:** This book offers options for the level of depth used to cover different topics. Most notably Chapter 5, entitled Overview of Wireless Communications, provides tutorial-level coverage of the important wireless concepts needed to understand the rest of the book. For those needing more detailed understanding, however, Chapters 6 through 10 cover the same topics in more depth for fuller understanding. This again makes the book accessible to those with a variety of interests, level of prior knowledge, and expertise.

PLAN OF THE TEXT

The objective of this book is to provide a comprehensive technical survey of wireless communications fundamentals, wireless networks, and wireless applications. The book is organized into four parts as illustrated in Figure P.1.

Part One, Technical Background: Provides background material on the process of data and packet communications, as well as protocol layers, TCP/IP, and data networks.

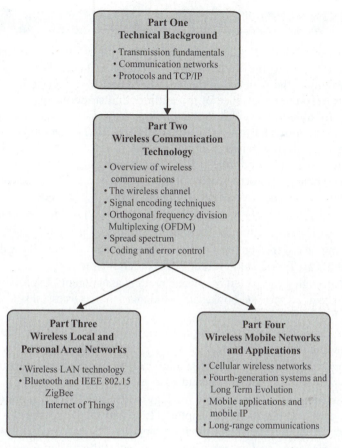

Figure P.1 Wireless Topics

Part Two, Wireless Communication Technology: Covers all of the relevant information about the process of sending a wireless signal and combating the effects of the wireless channel. The material can be covered briefly with Chapter 5, Overview of Wireless Communications, or through five chapters on the wireless channel (antennas and propagation), signal encoding, OFDM, spread spectrum, and error control coding.

Part Three, Wireless Local and Personal Area Networks: Provides details on IEEE 802.11, IEEE 802.15, Bluetooth, the Internet of Things, and ZigBee.

Part Four, Wireless Mobile Networks and Applications: Provides material on mobile cellular systems principles, LTE, smartphones, and mobile applications. It also covers long-range communications using satellite, fixed wireless, and WiMAX.

The book includes a number of pedagogic features, including the use of over 150 animations and numerous figures and tables to clarify the discussions. More details are given below. Each chapter also includes a list of key words, review questions, homework problems, and suggestions for further reading. The book also includes an extensive online glossary, a list of frequently used acronyms, and a reference list.

ORDER OF COVERAGE

With a comprehensive work such as this, careful planning is required to cover those parts of the text most relevant to the students and the course at hand. The book provides some flexibility. For example, the material in the book need not be studied sequentially. As a matter of fact, it has been the experience of the authors that students and instructors are more engaged if they are able to dive into the technologies themselves as soon as possible. One of the authors in his courses has routinely studied IEEE 802.11 (Chapter 11) before concentrating on the full details of wireless communications. Some physical layer details may need to be skipped at first (e.g., temporarily skipping Sections 11.5 and 11.6), but students are more engaged and able to perform projects if they've studied the actual technologies earlier.

The following are suggestions concerning paths through the book:

- Chapter 5, Overview of Wireless Communications, can be substituted for Chapters 6 through 10. Conversely, Chapter 5 should be omitted if using Chapters 6 through 10.
- Part Three can be covered before Part Two, omitting some physical layer details to be revisited later. Part Two should precede Part Four, however.
- Chapters 2 through 4 can be left as outside reading assignments. Especially by using animations provided with the book, some students can be successful studying these topics on their own.
- Within Part Three, the chapters are more or less independent and can be studied in either order depending on level of interest.
- The chapters in Part Four can also be studied in any order, except Chapters 13 and 14 on cellular systems and LTE should be studied as a unit.
- Computer science and information technology courses could focus more on Wi-Fi, IEEE 802.15, and mobile applications in Chapters 11, 12, and 15, then proceed with projects on MAC protocols and mobile device programming.
- Electrical engineering and engineering technology students can focus on Chapters 6 through 10 and proceed with projects related to the modulation and error control coding schemes used for IEEE 802.11 and LTE.

ANIMATIONS

Animations provide a powerful tool for understanding the complex mechanisms discussed in this book, including forward error correction, signal encoding, and protocols. Over 150 Web-based animations are used to illustrate many of the data communications and protocol concepts in this book.

The animations progressively introduce parts of diagrams and help to illustrate data flow, connection setup and maintenance procedures, error handling, encapsulation, and the ways technologies perform in different scenarios. For example, see Figure P.2 and its animation. This is actually Figure 13.7. From the ebook version, one can simply touch or click on the figure to bring up the animation. From the print version, the animations can also be accessed through the QR code next to the figure or through the book's Premium Web site discussed below. Walking step-by-step through the animation can be accomplished with a click or tap on the animation. This figure shows possible choices of handoff decisions at different locations between two base stations. The original figure might be difficult for the reader to first understand, but the animations give good enhanced understanding by showing the figure piece-by-piece with extra explanation. These animations provide significant help to the reader to understand the purpose behind each part of the figure.

INSTRUCTOR SUPPORT MATERIALS

The major goal of this text is to make it as effective a teaching tool for this exciting and fast-moving subject as possible. This goal is reflected both in the structure of the book and in the supporting material. The text is accompanied by the following supplementary material to aid the instructor:

- **Solutions manual:** Solutions to all end-of-chapter Review Questions and Problems.
- **Supplemental problems:** More problems beyond those offered in the text.
- **Projects manual:** Suggested project assignments for all of the project categories listed in the next section.
- **PowerPoint slides:** A set of slides covering all chapters, suitable for use in lecturing.
- **PDF files:** Reproductions of all figures and tables from the book.
- **Wireless courses:** Links to home pages for courses based on this book. These pages may be useful to other instructors in providing ideas about how to structure their course.
- **Social networking:** Links to social networking sites that have been established for instructors using the book, such as on Facebook and LinkedIn, where instructors can interact.

All of these support materials are available at the **Instructor Resource Center (IRC)** for this textbook, which can be reached through the publisher's Web site

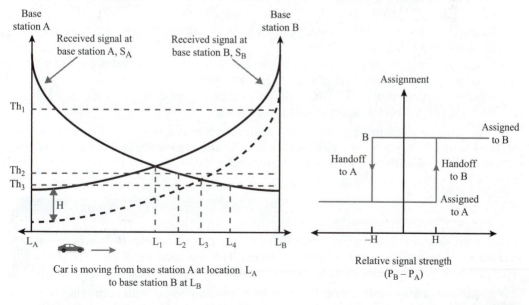

(a) Handoff decision as a function of handoff scheme   (b) Hysteresis mechanism

Figure P.2   Handoff Between Two Cells

www.pearsonhighered.com/stallings. To gain access to the IRC, please contact your local Pearson sales representative via pearsonhighered.com/educator/replocator/requestSales Rep.page or call Pearson Faculty Services at 1-800-526-0485.

The **Companion Web site**, at www.corybeardwireless.com, includes technology updates, Web resources, etc. This is discussed in more detail below in the section about student resources.

PROJECTS AND OTHER STUDENT EXERCISES

For many instructors, an important component of a wireless networking course is a project or set of projects by which students get hands-on experience to reinforce concepts from the text. This book provides an unparalleled degree of support for including a projects component in the course. The IRC not only provides guidance on how to assign and structure the projects but also includes a set of User's Manuals for various project types plus specific assignments, all written especially for this book. Instructors can assign work in the following areas:

- **Practical exercises:** Using network commands, students gain experience in network connectivity.
- **Wireshark projects:** Wireshark is a protocol analyzer that enables students to study the behavior of protocols. A video tutorial is provided to get students started, in addition to a set of Wireshark assignments.
- **Simulation projects:** Students can use different suggested simulation packages to analyze network behavior. The IRC includes a number of student assignments.
- **Performance modeling projects:** Multiple performance modeling techniques are introduced. The IRC includes a number of student assignments.
- **Research projects:** The IRC includes a list of suggested research projects that would involve Web and literature searches.
- **Interactive assignments:** Twelve interactive assignments have been designed to allow students to give a specific set of steps to invoke, or devise a sequence of steps to achieve a desired result. The IRC includes a set of assignments, plus suggested solutions, so that instructors can assess students' work.

This diverse set of projects and other student exercises enables the instructor to use the book as one component in a rich and varied learning experience and to tailor a course plan to meet the specific needs of the instructor and students.

RESOURCES FOR STUDENTS

A substantial amount of original supporting material for students has been made available online, at two Web locations. The **Companion Web site**, at www.corybeardwireless.com, includes the following.

- **Social networking tools**: Students using the book can interact with each other to share questions and insights and develop relationships. Throughout the lifetime of the book, various social networking tools may become prevalent; new social networking sites will be developed and then links and information about them will be made available here.

- **Useful Web sites:** There are links to other relevant Web sites which provide extensive help in studying these topics. Links to these are provided.
- **Errata sheet:** An errata list for this book will be maintained and updated as needed. Please e-mail any errors that you spot from the link at corybeardwireless.com. Errata sheets for other William Stallings books are at WilliamStallings.com.
- **Documents:** These include a number of documents that expand on the treatment in the book. Topics include standards organizations and the TCP/IP checksum.
- **Wireless courses:** There are links to home pages for courses based on this book. These pages may be useful to other instructors in providing ideas about how to structure their course.

Purchasing this textbook new also grants the reader six months of access to the **Premium Content site**, which includes the following:

- **Animations:** Those using the print version of the book can access the animations by going to this Web site. The QR codes next to the book figures give more direct access to these animations. The ebook version provides direct access to these animations by clicking or tapping on a linked figure.
- **Glossary:** List of key terms and definitions.
- **Appendices:** Three appendices to the book are available on traffic analysis, Fourier analysis, and data link control protocols.
- **Technology updates:** As new standards are approved and released, new chapter sections will be developed. They will be released here before a new edition of the text is published. The book will therefore not become outdated in the same way that is common with technology texts.

To access the Premium Website, click on the *Premium Website* link at pearsonhighered.com/stallings and enter the student access code found on the card in the front of the book.

William Stallings also maintains the Computer Science Student Resource Site, at computersciencestudent.com. The purpose of this site is to provide documents, information, and useful links for computer science students and professionals. Links are organized into four categories:

- **Math:** Includes a basic math refresher, a queuing analysis primer, a number system primer, and links to numerous math sites
- **How-to:** Advice and guidance for solving homework problems, writing technical reports, and preparing technical presentations
- **Research resources:** Links to important collections of papers, technical reports, and bibliographies
- **Miscellaneous:** A variety of useful documents and links

ACKNOWLEDGMENTS

This book has benefited from review by a number of people, who gave generously of their time and expertise. The following professors and instructors provided reviews: Alex Wije-sIinha (Towson University), Dr. Ezzat Kirmani (St. Cloud State University), Dr. Feng Li (Indiana University-Purdue University Indianapolis), Dr. Guillermo A. Francia III (Jacksonville State University), Dr. Kamesh Namuduri (University of North Texas), Dr. Melody Moh (San Jose State University), Dr. Wuxu Peng (Texas State University), Frank E. Green (University of Maryland, Baltimore County), Gustavo Vejarano (Loyola Marymount University), Ilker Demirkol (Rochester Institute of Tech), Prashant Krishnamurthy (University of Pittsburgh), and Russell C. Pepe (New Jersey Institute of Technology).

Several students at the University of Missouri-Kansas City provided valuable contributions in the development of the figures and animations. Bhargava Thondapu and Siva Sai Karthik Kesanakurthi provided great creativity and dedication to the animations. Pedro Tonhozi de Oliveira, Rahul Arun Paropkari, and Naveen Narasimhaiah also devoted themselves to the project and provided great help.

Kristopher Micinski contributed most of the material on mobile applications in Chapter 15.

Finally, we thank the many people responsible for the publication of the book, all of whom did their usual excellent job. This includes the staff at Pearson, particularly our editor Tracy Johnson, program manager Carole Snyder, and production manager Bob Engelhardt. We also thank Mahalatchoumy Saravanan and the production staff at Jouve India for an excellent and rapid job. Thanks also to the marketing and sales staffs at Pearson, without whose efforts this book would not be in front of you.

ABOUT THE AUTHORS

 Dr. William Stallings has authored 17 textbooks, and counting revised editions, over 40 books on computer security, computer networking, and computer architecture. In over 30 years in the field, he has been a technical contributor, a technical manager, and an executive with several high-technology firms. Currently he is an independent consultant whose clients have included computer and networking manufacturers and customers, software development firms, and leading-edge government research institutions. He has 13 times received the award for the best Computer Science textbook of the year from the Text and Academic Authors Association.

He created and maintains the Computer Science Student Resource Site at ComputerScienceStudent.com. This site provides documents and links on a variety of subjects of general interest to computer science students (and professionals). He is a member of the editorial board of Cryptologia, a scholarly journal devoted to all aspects of cryptology.

Dr. Stallings holds a PhD from MIT in computer science and a BS from Notre Dame in electrical engineering.

Dr. Cory Beard is an Associate Professor of Computer Science and Electrical Engineering at the University of Missouri-Kansas City (UMKC). His research areas involve the prioritization of communications for emergency purposes. This work has involved 3G/4G cellular networks for public safety groups, MAC layer performance evaluation, call preemption and queuing, and Internet traffic prioritization. His work has included a National Science Foundation CAREER Award.

He has received multiple departmental teaching awards and has chaired degree program committees for many years. He maintains a site for book-related social networking and supplemental materials at corybeardwireless.com.

CHAPTER 1

INTRODUCTION

LEARNING OBJECTIVES

After studying this chapter, you should be able to:

- Describe how wireless communications have developed.
- Explain the purposes of various generations of cellular technology.
- Describe the ways mobile devices have revolutionized and will continue to revolutionize society.
- Identify and describe future trends.

This book is a survey of the technology of wireless communication networks and systems. Many factors, including increased competition, the introduction of digital technology, mobile device user interface design, video content, and social networking have led to unprecedented growth in the wireless market. In this chapter, we discuss some of the key factors driving this wireless networking revolution.

1.1 WIRELESS COMES OF AGE

Guglielmo Marconi invented the wireless telegraph in 1896.[1] In 1901, he sent telegraphic signals across the Atlantic Ocean from Cornwall to St. John's Newfoundland, a distance of about 3200 km. His invention allowed two parties to communicate by sending each other alphanumeric characters encoded in an analog signal. Over the last century, advances in wireless technologies have led to the radio, the television, communications satellites, mobile telephone, and mobile data. All types of information can now be sent to almost every corner of the world. Recently, a great deal of attention has been focused on wireless networking, cellular technology, mobile applications, and the Internet of Things.

Communications satellites were first launched in the 1960s; today satellites carry about one-third of the voice traffic and all of the television signals between countries. Wireless networking allows businesses to develop WANs, MANs, and LANs without a cable plant. The IEEE 802.11 standard for wireless LANs (also known as Wi-Fi) has become pervasive. Industry consortiums have also provided seamless short-range wireless networking technologies such as ZigBee, Bluetooth, and Radio Frequency Identification tags (RFIDs).

The cellular or mobile telephone started with the objective of being the modern equivalent of Marconi's wireless telegraph, offering two-party, two-way communication. Early generation wireless phones offered voice and limited data services through bulky devices that gradually became more portable. Current third and

---

[1]The actual invention of radio communications more properly should be attributed to Nikola Tesla, who gave a public demonstration in 1893. Marconi's patents were overturned in favor of Tesla in 1943 [ENGE00].

fourth generation devices are for voice, texting, social networking, mobile applications, mobile Web interaction, and video streaming. These devices also include cameras and a myriad of sensors to support the device applications. The areas of coverage for newer technologies are continually being expanded and focused on key user populations.

The impact of wireless communications has been and will continue to be profound. Very few inventions have been able to "shrink" the world in such a manner, nor have they been able to change the way people communicate as significantly as the way wireless technology has enabled new forms of social networking. The standards that define how wireless communications devices interact are quickly converging, providing a global wireless network that delivers a wide variety of services.

Figure 1.1 highlights some of the key milestones in the development of wireless communications.[2] Wireless technologies have gradually migrated to higher frequencies. As will be seen in later chapters, higher frequencies enable the support of greater data rates and throughput but require higher power, are more affected by obstructions, and have shorter effective range.

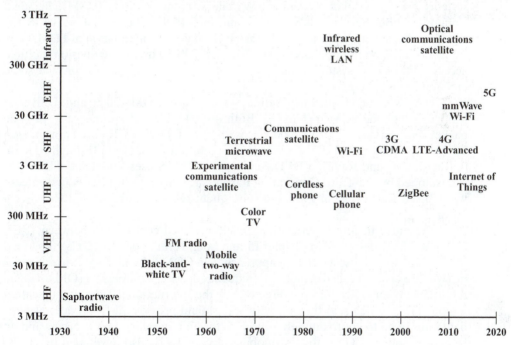

Figure 1.1 Some Milestones in Wireless Communications

---

[2]Note the use of a log scale for the *y*-axis. A basic review of log scales is in the math refresher document at the Computer Science Student Resource Site at computersciencestudent.com.

1.2 THE GLOBAL CELLULAR NETWORK

The cellular revolution is apparent in the growth of the mobile phone market alone. In 1990, the number of users was approximately 11 million [ECON99]. Today, according to 4G Americas, that number is over seven billion. There are a number of reasons for the dominance of mobile devices. Mobile devices are convenient; they move with people. In addition, by their nature, they are location aware. Mobile cellular devices communicate with regional base stations that are at fixed locations. In many geographic areas, mobile telephones are the only economical way to provide phone service to the population. Operators can erect base stations quickly and inexpensively when compared with digging up ground to lay cables in harsh terrain.

Today there is no single cellular network. Devices support several technologies and generally work only within the confines of a single operator's network. To move beyond this model, work is being done to define and implement standards.

The dominant first-generation wireless network in North America was the Advanced Mobile Phone System (AMPS). The key second generation wireless systems are the Global System for Mobile Communications (GSM), Personal Communications Service (PCS) IS-136, and PCS IS-95. The PCS standard IS-136 uses time division multiple access (TDMA); GSM uses a combination of TDMA and frequency division multiple access (FDMA), and IS-95 uses code division multiple access (CDMA). 2G systems primarily provide voice services, but also provide some moderate rate data services.

The two major third-generation systems are CDMA2000 and Universal Mobile Telephone Service (UMTS). Both use CDMA and are meant to provide packet data services. CDMA2000 released 1xRTT (1 times Radio Transmission Technology) and then 1xEV-DO (1 times Evolution-Data Only) through Release 0, Revision A, and Revision B. The competing UMTS uses Wideband CDMA. It is developed by the Third Generation Partnership Project (3GPP); its first release was labeled Release 99 in 1999, but subsequent releases were labeled Releases 4 onward.

The move to fourth generation mainly involved competition between IEEE 802.16 WiMAX, described in Chapter 15, and Long Term Evolution (LTE), described in Chapter 14. Both use a different approach than CDMA for high spectral efficiency in a wireless channel called orthogonal frequency division multiplexing (OFDM). The requirements for 4G came from directives by the International Telecommunication Union (ITU), which said that 4G networks should provide all-IP services at peak data rates of up to approximately 100 Mbps for high-mobility mobile access and up to approximately 1 Gbps for low-mobility access. LTE, also developed by 3GPP, ended up the predominant technology for 4G, and 3GPP Release 8 was its first release. Although LTE Release 8 does not meet the ITU requirements (even though marketers have called it "4G LTE"), the later Release 10 achieves the goals and is called LTE-Advanced. There are a wide number of Release 8 deployments so far but much fewer Release 10 upgrades.

1.3 THE MOBILE DEVICE REVOLUTION

Technical innovations have contributed to the success of what were originally just mobile phones. The prevalence of the latest devices, with multi-megabit Internet access, mobile apps, high megapixel digital cameras, access to multiple types of wireless networks (e.g., Wi-Fi, Bluetooth, 3G, and 4G), and several on-board sensors, all add to this momentous achievement. Devices have become increasingly powerful while staying easy to carry. Battery life has increased (even though device energy usage has also expanded), and digital technology has improved reception and allowed better use of a finite spectrum. As with many types of digital equipment, the costs associated with mobile devices have been decreasing.

The first rush to wireless was for voice. Now, the attention is on data; some wireless devices are only rarely used for voice. A big part of this market is the wireless Internet. Wireless users use the Internet differently than fixed users, but in many ways no less effectively. Wireless smartphones have limited displays and input capabilities compared with larger devices such as laptops or PCs, but mobile apps give quick access to intended information without using Web sites. Because wireless devices are location aware, information can be tailored to the geographic location of the user. Information finds users, instead of users searching for information. Tablet devices provide a happy medium between the larger screens and better input capabilities of PCs and the portability of smartphones.

Examples of wireless technologies that are used for long distance are cellular 3G and 4G, Wi-Fi IEEE 802.11 for local areas, and Bluetooth for short distance connections between devices. These wireless technologies should provide sufficient data rates for the intended uses, ease of connectivity, stable connections, and other necessary quality of service performance for services such as voice and video. There are still improvements needed to meet these requirements in ways that are truly invisible to end users.

For many people, wireless devices have become a key part of how they interact with the world around them. Currently, this involves interaction with other people through voice, text, and other forms of social media. They also interact with various forms of multimedia content for business, social involvement, and entertainment. In the near future, many envision advanced ways for people to interact with objects and machines around them (e.g., the appliances in a home) and even for the devices themselves to perform a more active role in the world.

1.4 FUTURE TRENDS

As 4G LTE-Advanced and higher speed Wi-Fi systems are now being deployed, many see great future untapped potential to be realized. Great potential exists for Machine to Machine (MTM) communications, also called the Internet of Things (IoT). The basic idea is that devices can interact with each other in areas such as healthcare, disaster recovery, energy savings, security and surveillance, environmental awareness, education, inventory and product management, manufacturing, and many others. Today's current smart devices could interact with myriads of objects equipped with wireless networking capabilities. This could start with information dissemination to enable data mining and decision support, but could also involve capabilities for automated remote adaptation and control. For example, a residential home could have sensors to monitor temperature, humidity, and airflow to assess human comfort levels. These sensors could also collaborate with home appliances, heating and air conditioning systems, lighting systems, electric vehicle charging stations, and utility companies to provide homeowners with advice or even automated control to optimize energy consumption. This would adjust when homeowners are at home conducting certain activities or away from home. Eventually these wirelessly equipped objects could interact in their own forms of social networking to discover, trust, and collaborate.

Future wireless networks will have to significantly improve to enable these capabilities. Some envision a 100-fold increase in the number of communication devices. And the type of communication would involve many short messages, not the type of communication supported easily by the current generations of the technologies studied in this book. If these communications were to involve control applications between devices, the real-time delay requirements would be much more stringent than that required in human interaction.

Also, the demands for capacity will greatly increase. The growth in the number of subscribers and per-user throughput gives a prediction of a 1000-fold increase in data traffic by 2020. This has caused the development of the following technologies for what may be considered 5G (although the definition of 5G has not been formalized). Some of these will be better understood after studying the topics in this book, but we provide them here to set the stage for learning expectations.

- **Network densification** will use many small transmitters inside buildings (called femtocells) and outdoors (called picocells or relays) to reuse the same carrier frequencies repeatedly.

- **Device-centric architectures** will provide connections that focus on what a device needs for interference reduction, throughput, and overall service quality.

- **Massive multiple-input multiple-output (MIMO)** will use 10 or more than 100 antennas (both on single devices and spread across different locations) to focus antenna beams toward intended devices even as the devices move.

- **Millimeter wave (mmWave)** frequencies in the 30 GHz to 300 GHz bands have much available bandwidth. Even though they require more transmit power and have higher attenuation due to obstructions and atmosphere, massive MIMO can be used to overcome those limitations.

- **Native support for mobile to mobile (MTM) communication** will accommodate low data rates, a massive number of devices, sustained minimum rates, and very low delays.

Throughout this book, the reader will see the methods by which technologies such as Wi-Fi have expanded and improved. We will review the foundational technologies and see the ways in which new directions such as OFDM and LTE-Advanced have created dramatic improvements. This provides excellent preparation so that researchers and practitioners will be ready to participate in these future areas.

1.5 THE TROUBLE WITH WIRELESS

Wireless is convenient and often less expensive to deploy than fixed services, but wireless is not perfect. There are limitations, political and technical difficulties, that may ultimately hamper wireless technologies from reaching their full potential. Two issues are the wireless channel and spectrum limitations.

The delivery of a wireless signal does not always require a free line-of-sight path, depending on the frequency. Signals can also be received through transmission through objects, reflections off objects, scattering of signals, and diffraction around the edges of objects. Unfortunately, reflections can cause multiple copies of the signal to arrive at the receiver at different times with different attenuations. This creates the problem of **multipath fading** when the signals add together and can cause the signal to be significantly degraded. Wireless signals also suffer from noise, interference from other users, and Doppler shifting caused by movement of devices.

A series of approaches are used to combat these problems of wireless transmission. All are discussed in this book.

- **Modulation** sends digital data in a signal format that sends as many bits as possible for the current wireless channel.

- **Error control coding**, also known as channel coding, adds extra bits to a signal so that errors can be detected and corrected.

- **Adaptive modulation and coding** dynamically adjusts the modulation and coding to measurements of the current channel conditions.

- **Equalization** counteracts the multipath effects of the channel.

- **Multiple-input multiple-output** systems use multiple antennas to point signals strongly in certain directions, send simultaneous signals in multiple directions, or send parallel streams of data.

- **Direct sequence spread spectrum** expands the signal over a wide bandwidth so that problems in parts of the bandwidth are overcome because of the wide bandwidth.

- **Orthogonal frequency division multiplexing** breaks a signal into many lower rate bit streams where each is less susceptible to multipath problems.

Spectrum regulations also affect the capabilities of wireless communications. Governmental regulatory agencies allocate spectrum to various types of uses, and wireless communications companies frequently spend large amounts of money to acquire spectrum. These agencies also give rules related to power and spectrum sharing approaches. All of this limits the bandwidth available to wireless communications. Higher frequencies have more available bandwidth but are harder to use effectively due to obstructions. They also inherently require more transmission power. Transition from today's 1 GHz to 5 GHz bands to millimeter wave (mmWave) bands in the 30 GHz to 300 GHz range is of increasing interest since they have more bandwidth available.

PART ONE

Technical Background

CHAPTER 2

TRANSMISSION FUNDAMENTALS

LEARNING OBJECTIVES

After studying this chapter, you should be able to:

- Distinguish between digital and analog information sources.
- Explain the various ways in which audio, data, image, and video can be represented by electromagnetic signals.
- Discuss the characteristics of analog and digital waveforms.
- Explain the roles of frequencies and frequency components in a signal.
- Identify the factors that affect channel capacity.
- Compare and contrast various forms of wireless transmission.

The purpose of this chapter is to make this book self-contained for the reader with little or no background in data communications. For the reader with greater interest, references for further study are supplied at the end of the chapter.

2.1 SIGNALS FOR CONVEYING INFORMATION

In this book, we are concerned with electromagnetic signals used as a means to transmit information. An electromagnetic signal is a function of time, but it can also be expressed as a function of frequency; that is, the signal consists of components of different frequencies. It turns out that the **frequency domain** view of a signal is far more important to an understanding of data transmission than a **time domain** view. Both views are introduced here.

Time Domain Concepts

Viewed as a function of time, an electromagnetic signal can be either analog or digital. An **analog signal** is one in which the signal intensity varies in a smooth fashion over time. In other words, there are no breaks or discontinuities in the signal. A **digital signal** is one in which the signal intensity maintains a constant level for some period of time and then changes to another constant level.[1] Figure 2.1 shows examples of both kinds of signals. The analog signal might represent speech, and the digital signal might represent binary 1s and 0s.

The simplest sort of signal is a **periodic signal**, in which the same signal pattern repeats over time. Figure 2.2 shows an example of a periodic analog signal (sine wave) and a periodic digital signal (square wave). Mathematically, a signal $s(t)$ is defined to be periodic if and only if

$$s(t + T) = s(t) \quad -\infty < t < +\infty$$

where the constant T is the period of the signal (T is the smallest value that satisfies the equation). Otherwise, a signal is **aperiodic**.

---

[1]This is an idealized definition. In fact, the transition from one voltage level to another will not be instantaneous, but there will be a small transition period. Nevertheless, an actual digital signal approximates closely the ideal model of constant voltage levels with instantaneous transitions.

Amplitude
(volts)

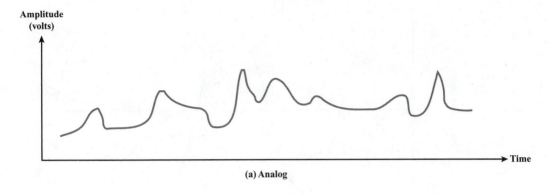

(a) Analog

Amplitude
(volts)

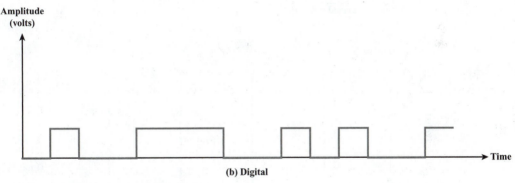

(b) Digital

Figure 2.1 Analog and Digital Waveforms

The sine wave is the fundamental analog signal. A general sine wave can be represented by three parameters: peak amplitude (A), frequency (f), and phase (ϕ). The **peak amplitude** is the maximum value or strength of the signal over time; typically, this value is measured in volts. The **frequency** is the rate [in cycles per second, or Hertz (Hz)] at which the signal repeats. An equivalent parameter is the **period** (T) of a signal, which is the amount of time it takes for one repetition; therefore, $T = 1/f$. **Phase** is a measure of the relative position in time within a single period of a signal, as illustrated later.

The general sine wave can be written as

$$s(t) = A \sin (2\pi ft + \phi) \tag{2.1}$$

A function with the form of Equation (2.1) is known as a **sinusoid**. Figure 2.3 shows the effect of varying each of the three parameters. In part (a) of the figure, the frequency is 1 Hz; thus the period is $T = 1$ second. Part (b) has the same frequency and phase but a peak amplitude of 0.5. In part (c) we have $f = 2$, which is equivalent to $T = 0.5$. Finally, part (d) shows the effect of a phase shift of $\pi/4$ radians, which is 45 degrees (2π radians $= 360° = 1$ period).

In Figure 2.3 the horizontal axis is time; the graphs display the value of a signal at a given point in space as a function of time. These same graphs, with a change of

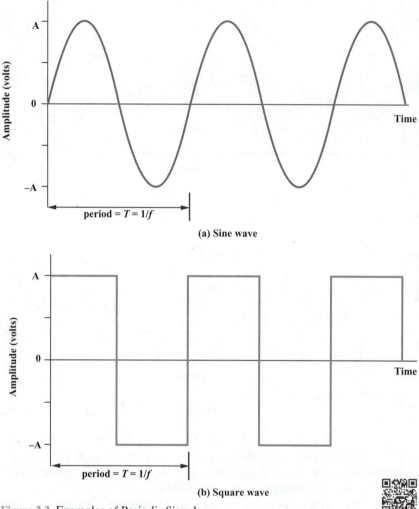

Figure 2.2 Examples of Periodic Signals

scale, can apply with horizontal axes in space. In that case, the graphs display the value of a signal at a given point in time as a function of distance. For example, for a sinusoidal transmission (e.g., an electromagnetic radio wave some distance from a radio antenna or sound some distance from loudspeaker) at a particular instant of time, the intensity of the signal varies in a sinusoidal way as a function of distance from the source.

There is a simple relationship between the two sine waves, one in time and one in space. The **wavelength** (λ) of a signal is the distance occupied by a single cycle, or, put another way, the distance between two points of corresponding phase of two consecutive cycles. Assume that the signal is traveling with a velocity v. Then the wavelength is related to the period as follows: $\lambda = vT$. Equivalently, $\lambda f = v$. Of particular relevance to this discussion is the case where $v = c$, the speed of light in free space, which is approximately 3×10^8 m/s.

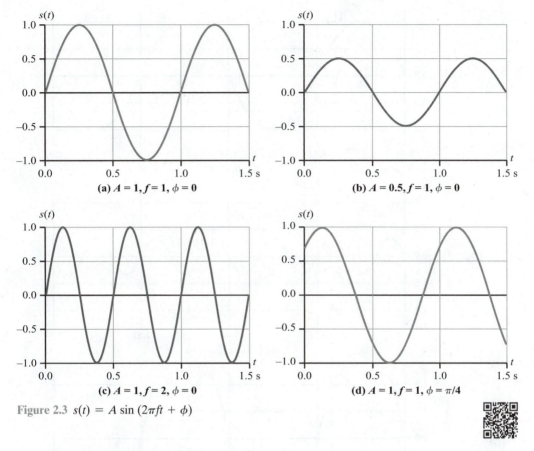

Figure 2.3 $s(t) = A \sin (2\pi ft + \phi)$

Frequency Domain Concepts

In practice, an electromagnetic signal will be made up of many frequencies. For example, the signal

$$s(t) = (4/\pi) \times (\sin(2\pi ft) + (1/3) \sin (2\pi(3f)t))$$

is shown in Figure 2.4c. The components of this signal are just sine waves of frequencies f and $3f$; parts (a) and (b) of the figure show these individual components. There are two interesting points that can be made about this figure:

- The second frequency is an integer multiple of the first frequency. When all of the frequency components of a signal are integer multiples of one frequency, the latter frequency is referred to as the **fundamental frequency**. The other components are called **harmonics**.
- The period of the total signal is equal to the period of the fundamental frequency. The period of the component $\sin(2\pi ft)$ is $T = 1/f$, and the period of $s(t)$ is also T, as can be seen from Figure 2.4c.

It can be shown, using a discipline known as Fourier analysis, that any signal is made up of components at various frequencies, in which each component is a sinusoid. By adding together enough sinusoidal signals, each with the appropriate

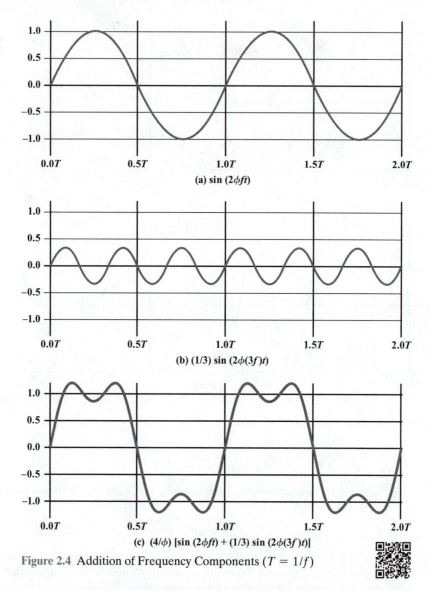

Figure 2.4 Addition of Frequency Components ($T = 1/f$)

amplitude, frequency, and phase, any electromagnetic signal can be constructed. Put another way, any electromagnetic signal can be shown to consist of a collection of periodic analog signals (sine waves) at different amplitudes, frequencies, and phases. The importance of being able to look at a signal from the frequency perspective (frequency domain) rather than a time perspective (time domain) should become clear as the discussion proceeds. For the interested reader, the subject of Fourier analysis is introduced in online Appendix B.

The **spectrum** of a signal is the range of frequencies that it contains. For the signal of Figure 2.4c, the spectrum extends from f to $3f$. The **absolute bandwidth** of a signal is the width of the spectrum. In the case of Figure 2.4c, the bandwidth is $3f - f = 2f$. Many signals have an infinite bandwidth, but with most of the energy contained in a relatively narrow band of frequencies. This band is referred to as the **effective bandwidth**, or just **bandwidth**.

Relationship between Data Rate and Bandwidth

There is a direct relationship between the information-carrying capacity of a signal and its bandwidth: The greater the bandwidth, the higher the information-carrying capacity. As a very simple example, consider the square wave of Figure 2.2b. Suppose that we let a positive pulse represent binary 0 and a negative pulse represent binary 1. Then the waveform represents the binary stream 0101.... The duration of each pulse is $1/(2f)$; thus the data rate is $2f$ bits per second (bps). What are the frequency components of this signal? To answer this question, consider again Figure 2.4. By adding together sine waves at frequencies f and $3f$, we get a waveform that begins to resemble the square wave. Let us continue this process by adding a sine wave of frequency $5f$, as shown in Figure 2.5a, and then adding a sine wave of frequency $7f$, as shown in Figure 2.5b. As we add additional odd multiples of f, suitably scaled, the resulting waveform approaches that of a square wave more and more closely.

Indeed, it can be shown that the frequency components of the square wave with amplitudes A and $-A$ can be expressed as follows:

$$s(t) = A \times \frac{4}{\pi} \times \sum_{k \text{ odd}, k=1}^{\infty} \frac{\sin (2\pi kft)}{k}$$

This waveform has an infinite number of frequency components and hence an infinite bandwidth. However, the peak amplitude of the kth frequency component, kf, is only $1/k$, so most of the energy in this waveform is in the first few frequency components. What happens if we limit the bandwidth to just the first three frequency components? We have already seen the answer, in Figure 2.5a. As we can see, the shape of the resulting waveform is reasonably close to that of the original square wave.

We can use Figures 2.4 and 2.5 to illustrate the relationship between data rate and bandwidth. Suppose that we are using a digital transmission system that is capable of transmitting signals with a bandwidth of 4 MHz. Let us attempt to transmit a sequence of alternating 0s and 1s as the square wave of Figure 2.5c. What data rate can be achieved? We look at three cases.

Case I. Let us approximate our square wave with the waveform of Figure 2.5a. Although this waveform is a "distorted" square wave, it is sufficiently close to the square wave that a receiver should be able to discriminate between a binary 0 and a binary 1. If we let $f = 10^6$ cycles/second $= 1$ MHz, then the bandwidth of the signal

$$s(t) = \frac{4}{\pi} \times \left[\sin ((2\pi \times 10^6)t) + \frac{1}{3} \sin ((2\pi \times 3 \times 10^6)t) + \frac{1}{5} \sin ((2\pi \times 5 \times 10^6)t) \right]$$

is $(5 \times 10^6) - 10^6 = 4$ MHz. Note that for $f = 1$ MHz, the period of the fundamental frequency is $T = 1/10^6 = 10^{-6} = 1$ μs. If we treat this waveform as a bit string of 1s and 0s, one bit occurs every 0.5 μs, for a data rate of $2 \times 10^6 = 2$ Mbps. Thus, for a bandwidth of 4 MHz, a data rate of 2 Mbps is achieved.

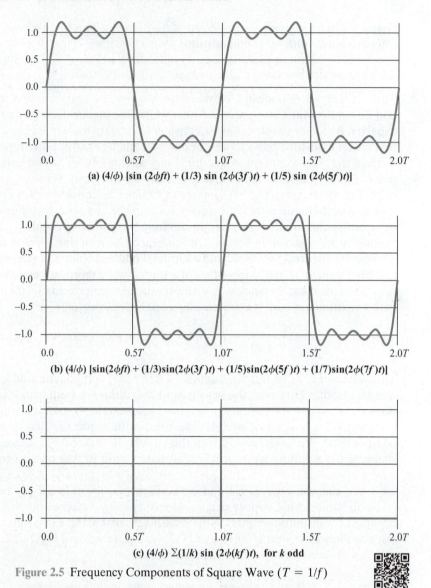

Figure 2.5 Frequency Components of Square Wave ($T = 1/f$)

Case II. Now suppose that we have a bandwidth of 8 MHz. Let us look again at Figure 2.5a, but now with $f = 2$ MHz. Using the same line of reasoning as before, the bandwidth of the signal is $(5 \times 2 \times 10^6) - (2 \times 10^6) = 8$ MHz. But in this case $T = 1/f = 0.5\,\mu s$. As a result, one bit occurs every 0.25 μs for a data rate of 4 Mbps. Thus, other things being equal, by doubling the bandwidth, we double the potential data rate.

Case III. Now suppose that the waveform of Figure 2.4c is considered adequate for approximating a square wave. That is, the difference between a positive and negative pulse in Figure 2.4c is sufficiently distinct that the waveform can be used successfully to represent a sequence of 1s and 0s. Assume as in Case II that

$f = 2\,\text{MHz}$ and $T = 1/f = 0.5\,\mu s$, so that one bit occurs every $0.25\,\mu s$ for a data rate of 4 Mbps. Using the waveform of Figure 2.4c, the bandwidth of the signal is $(3 \times 2 \times 10^6) - (2 \times 10^6) = 4\,\text{MHz}$. Thus, a given bandwidth can support various data rates depending on the ability of the receiver to discern the difference between 0 and 1 in the presence of noise and other impairments.

To summarize,

- **Case I:** Bandwidth = 4 MHz; data rate = 2 Mbps
- **Case II:** Bandwidth = 8 MHz; data rate = 4 Mbps
- **Case III:** Bandwidth = 4 MHz; data rate = 4 Mbps

We can draw the following conclusions from the preceding discussion. In general, any digital waveform using rectangular pulses will have infinite bandwidth. If we attempt to transmit this waveform as a signal over any medium, the transmission system will limit the bandwidth that can be transmitted. Furthermore, for any given medium, the greater the bandwidth transmitted, the greater the cost. Thus, on the one hand, economic and practical reasons dictate that digital information be approximated by a signal of limited bandwidth. On the other hand, limiting the bandwidth creates distortions, which makes the task of interpreting the received signal more difficult. The more limited the bandwidth, the greater the distortion and the greater the potential for error by the receiver.

2.2 ANALOG AND DIGITAL DATA TRANSMISSION

The terms *analog* and *digital* correspond, roughly, to *continuous* and *discrete*, respectively. These two terms are used frequently in data communications in at least three contexts: data, signals, and transmission.

Briefly, we define **data** as entities that convey meaning, or information. **Signals** are electric or electromagnetic representations of data. **Transmission** is the communication of data by the propagation and processing of signals. In what follows, we try to make these abstract concepts clear by discussing the terms *analog* and *digital* as applied to data, signals, and transmission.

Analog and Digital Data

The concepts of analog and digital data are simple enough. **Analog data** take on continuous values in some interval. For example, voice and video are continuously varying patterns of intensity. Most data collected by sensors, such as temperature and pressure, are continuous valued. **Digital data** take on discrete values; examples are text and integers.

The most familiar example of analog data is **audio**, which, in the form of acoustic sound waves, can be perceived directly by human beings. Figure 2.6 shows the acoustic spectrum for human speech and for music. Frequency components of typical speech may be found between approximately 100 Hz and 7 kHz. Although much of the energy in speech is concentrated at the lower frequencies, tests have shown that frequencies below 600 or 700 Hz add very little to the intelligibility of speech

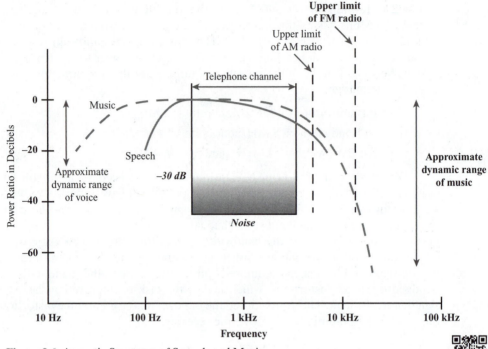

Figure 2.6 Acoustic Spectrum of Speech and Music

to the human ear. Typical speech has a dynamic range of about 25 dB[2]; that is, the power produced by the loudest shout may be as much as 300 times greater than that of the least whisper.

Analog and Digital Signaling

In a communications system, data are propagated from one point to another by means of electromagnetic signals. An **analog signal** is a continuously varying electromagnetic wave that may be propagated over a variety of media, depending on frequency; examples are copper wire media, such as twisted pair and coaxial cable; fiber optic cable; and atmosphere or space propagation (wireless). A **digital signal** is a sequence of voltage pulses that may be transmitted over a copper wire medium; for example, a constant positive voltage level may represent binary 0 and a constant negative voltage level may represent binary 1.

The principal advantages of digital signaling are that it is generally cheaper than analog signaling and is less susceptible to noise interference. The principal disadvantage is that digital signals suffer more from attenuation than do analog signals. Figure 2.7 shows a sequence of voltage pulses, generated by a source using two voltage levels, and the received voltage some distance down a conducting medium. Because of the attenuation, or reduction, of signal strength at higher frequencies, the pulses become rounded and smaller. It should be clear that this attenuation can lead rather quickly to the loss of the information contained in the propagated signal.

---

[2]The concept of decibels is explained in Appendix 2A.

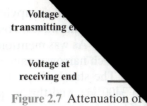

Both analog and digital data can
either analog or digital signals. This is ill
data are a function of time and occupy a li

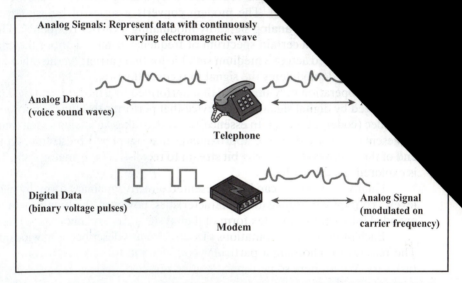

Analog Signals: Represent data with continuously varying electromagnetic wave

Analog Data
(voice sound waves)

Telephone

Digital Data
(binary voltage pulses)

Modem

Analog Signal
(modulated on
carrier frequency)

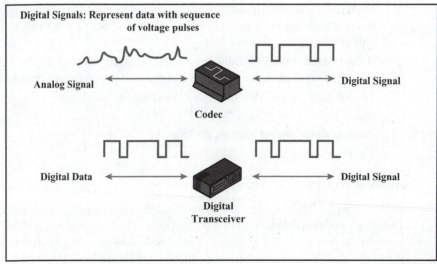

Digital Signals: Represent data with sequence of voltage pulses

Analog Signal

Codec

Digital Signal

Digital Data

Digital
Transceiver

Digital Signal

Figure 2.8 Analog and Digital Signaling of Analog and Digital Data

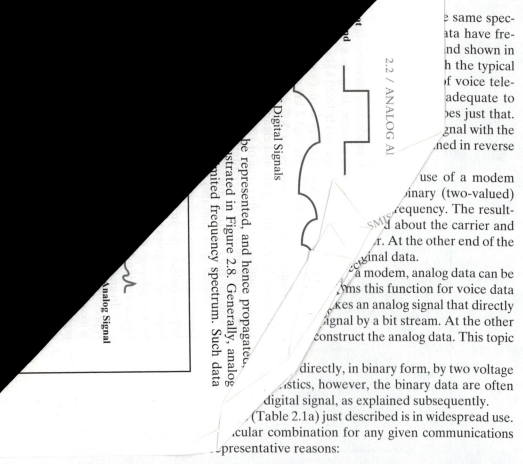

e same spec-
...ata have fre-
...nd shown in
...h the typical
...f voice tele-
...adequate to
...bes just that.
...gnal with the
...ned in reverse

...use of a modem
...inary (two-valued)
...requency. The result-
...d about the carrier and
...r. At the other end of the
...riginal data.

...a modem, analog data can be
...rms this function for voice data
...kes an analog signal that directly
...ignal by a bit stream. At the other
...construct the analog data. This topic

...directly, in binary form, by two voltage
...istics, however, the binary data are often
...digital signal, as explained subsequently.

...(Table 2.1a) just described is in widespread use.
...cular combination for any given communications
...presentative reasons:

- **Digital data, digital signal:** In general, the equipment for encoding digital data into a digital signal is less complex and less expensive than digital-to-analog equipment.
- **Analog data, digital signal:** Conversion of analog data to digital form permits the use of modern digital transmission and switching equipment for analog data.
- **Digital data, analog signal:** Some transmission media, such as optical fiber and satellite, will only propagate analog signals.
- **Analog data, analog signal:** Analog data are easily converted to an analog signal.

Analog and Digital Transmission

Both analog and digital signals may be transmitted on suitable transmission media. The way these signals are treated is a function of the transmission system. Table 2.1b summarizes the methods of data transmission. **Analog transmission** is a means of transmitting analog signals without regard to their content; the signals may represent analog data (e.g., voice) or digital data (e.g., data that pass through a modem). In either case, the analog signal will suffer attenuation that limits the length of the

Table 2.1 Analog and Digital Transmission

(a) Data and Signals

	Analog Signal	Digital Signal
Analog Data	Two alternatives: (1) signal occupies the same spectrum as the analog data; (2) analog data are encoded to occupy a different portion of spectrum.	Analog data are encoded using a codec to produce a digital bit stream.
Digital Data	Digital data are encoded using a modem to produce analog signal.	Two alternatives: (1) signal consists of two voltage levels to represent the two binary values; (2) digital data are encoded to produce a digital signal with desired properties.

(b) Treatment of Signals

	Analog Transmission	Digital Transmission
Analog Signal	Is propagated through amplifiers; same treatment whether signal is used to represent analog data or digital data.	Assumes that the analog signal represents digital data. Signal is propagated through repeaters; at each repeater, digital data are recovered from inbound signal and used to generate a new analog outbound signal.
Digital Signal	Not used	Digital signal represents a stream of 1s and 0s, which may represent digital data or may be an encoding of analog data. Signal is propagated through repeaters; at each repeater, stream of 1s and 0s is recovered from inbound signal and used to generate a new digital outbound signal.

transmission link. To achieve longer distances, the analog transmission system includes amplifiers that boost the energy in the signal. Unfortunately, the amplifier also boosts the noise components. With amplifiers cascaded to achieve long distance, the signal becomes more and more distorted. For analog data, such as voice, quite a bit of distortion can be tolerated and the data remain intelligible. However, for digital data transmitted as analog signals, cascaded amplifiers will introduce errors.

Digital transmission, in contrast, is concerned with the content of the signal. We have mentioned that a digital signal can be propagated only a limited distance before attenuation endangers the integrity of the data. To achieve greater distances, repeaters are used. A repeater receives the digital signal, recovers the pattern of ones and zeros, and retransmits a new signal. Thus, the attenuation is overcome.

The same technique may be used with an analog signal if the signal carries digital data. At appropriately spaced points, the transmission system has retransmission devices rather than amplifiers. The retransmission device recovers the digital data from the analog signal and generates a new, clean analog signal. Thus, noise is not cumulative.

2.3 CHANNEL CAPACITY

A variety of impairments can distort or corrupt a signal. A common impairment is **noise**, which is any unwanted signal that combines with and hence distorts the signal intended for transmission and reception. Noise and other impairments are discussed in Chapter 6. For the purposes of this section, we simply need to know that noise is something that degrades signal quality. For digital data, the question that then arises is to what extent these impairments limit the data rate that can be achieved. The maximum rate at which data can be transmitted over a given communication path, or channel, under given conditions is referred to as the **channel capacity**.

There are four concepts here that we are trying to relate to one another:

- **Data rate:** This is the rate, in bits per second (bps), at which data can be communicated.
- **Bandwidth:** This is the bandwidth of the transmitted signal as constrained by the transmitter and the nature of the transmission medium, expressed in cycles per second, or Hertz.
- **Noise:** For this discussion, we are concerned with the average level of noise over the communications path.
- **Error rate:** This is the rate at which errors occur, where an error is the reception of a 1 when a 0 was transmitted or the reception of a 0 when a 1 was transmitted.

The problem we are addressing is this: Communications facilities are expensive and, in general, the greater the bandwidth of a facility, the greater the cost. Furthermore, all transmission channels of any practical interest are of limited bandwidth. The limitations arise from the physical properties of the transmission medium or from deliberate limitations at the transmitter on the bandwidth to prevent interference from other sources. Accordingly, we would like to make as efficient use as possible of a given bandwidth. For digital data, this means that we would like to get as high a data rate as possible at a particular limit of error rate for a given bandwidth. The main constraint on achieving this efficiency is noise.

Nyquist Bandwidth

To begin, let us consider the case of a channel that is noise free. In this environment, the limitation on data rate is simply the bandwidth of the signal. A formulation of this limitation, due to Nyquist, states that if the rate of signal transmission is $2B$, then a signal with frequencies no greater than B is sufficient to carry the signal rate. The converse is also true: Given a bandwidth of B, the highest signal rate that can be carried is $2B$. This limitation is due to the effect of intersymbol interference, such as is produced by delay distortion.[3] The result is useful in the development of digital-to-analog encoding schemes.

Note that in the preceding paragraph, we referred to signal rate. If the signals to be transmitted are binary (take on only two values), then the data rate that can be

---

[3]Delay distortion of a signal occurs when the propagation delay for the transmission medium is not constant over the frequency range of the signal.

supported by B Hz is $2B$ bps. As an example, consider a voice channel being used, via modem, to transmit digital data. Assume a bandwidth of 3100 Hz. Then the capacity, C, of the channel is $2B = 6200$ bps. However, as we shall see in Chapter 7, signals with more than two levels can be used; that is, each signal element can represent more than one bit. For example, if four possible voltage levels are used as signals, then each signal element can represent two bits. With multilevel signaling, the Nyquist formulation becomes

$$C = 2\,B\log_2 M$$

where M is the number of discrete signal elements or voltage levels. Thus, for $M = 8$, a value used with some modems, a bandwidth of $B = 3100$ Hz yields a capacity $C = 18,600$ bps.

So, for a given bandwidth, the data rate can be increased by increasing the number of different signal elements. However, this places an increased burden on the receiver: Instead of distinguishing one of two possible signal elements during each signal time, it must distinguish one of M possible signals. Noise and other impairments on the transmission line will limit the practical value of M.

Shannon Capacity Formula

Nyquist's formula indicates that, all other things being equal, doubling the bandwidth doubles the data rate. Now consider the relationship among data rate, noise, and error rate. The presence of noise can corrupt one or more bits. If the data rate is increased, then the bits become "shorter" in time, so that more bits are affected by a given pattern of noise. Thus, at a given noise level, the higher the data rate, the higher the error rate.

Figure 2.9 is an example of the effect of noise on a digital signal. Here the noise consists of a relatively modest level of background noise plus occasional larger spikes of noise. The digital data can be recovered from the signal by sampling the received waveform once per bit time. As can be seen, the noise is occasionally sufficient to change a 1 to a 0 or a 0 to a 1.

All of these concepts can be tied together neatly in a formula developed by the mathematician Claude Shannon. As we have just illustrated, the higher the data rate, the more damage that unwanted noise can do. For a given level of noise, we would expect that a greater signal strength would improve the ability to receive data correctly in the presence of noise. The key parameter involved in this reasoning is the signal-to-noise ratio (SNR, or S/N),[4] which is the ratio of the power in a signal to the power contained in the noise that is present at a particular point in the transmission. Typically, this ratio is measured at a receiver, because it is at this point that an attempt is made to process the signal and eliminate the unwanted noise. For convenience, this ratio is often reported in **decibels (dB)**:

$$\text{SNR}_{\text{dB}} = 10\log_{10}\frac{\text{signal power}}{\text{noise power}}$$

---

[4]Some of the literature uses SNR; others use S/N. Also, in some cases the dimensionless quantity is referred to as SNR or S/N and the quantity in decibels is referred to as SNR_{db} or $(\text{S/N})_{\text{db}}$. Others use just SNR or S/N to mean the dB quantity. This text uses SNR and SNR_{db}.

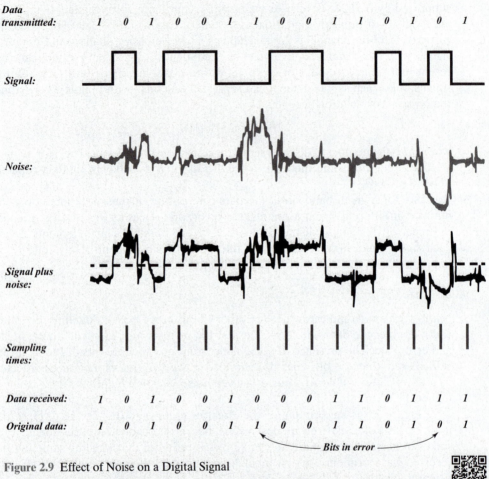

Figure 2.9 Effect of Noise on a Digital Signal

This expresses the amount, in decibels, that the intended signal exceeds the noise level. A high SNR will mean a high-quality signal.

The signal-to-noise ratio is important in the transmission of digital data because it sets the upper bound on the achievable data rate. Shannon's result is that the maximum channel capacity, in bits per second, obeys the equation

$$C = B \log_2(1 + \text{SNR})$$

where C is the capacity of the channel in bits per second and B is the bandwidth of the channel in Hertz. The Shannon formula represents the theoretical maximum that can be achieved. In practice, however, only much lower rates are achieved. One reason for this is that the formula assumes white noise (thermal noise). Impulse noise is not accounted for, nor are attenuation distortion or delay distortion. Various types of noise and distortion are discussed in Chapter 6.

The capacity indicated in the preceding equation is referred to as the error-free capacity. Shannon proved that if the actual information rate on a channel is less

Example 2.1 Let us consider an example that relates the Nyquist and Shannon formulations. Suppose that the spectrum of a channel is between 3 MHz and 4 MHz and $SNR_{dB} = 24$ dB. Then

$$B = 4 \text{ MHz} - 3 \text{ MHz} = 1 \text{ MHz}$$

$$SNR_{dB} = 24 \text{ dB} = 10 \log_{10}(SNR)$$

$$SNR = 251$$

Using Shannon's formula,

$$C = 10^6 \times \log_2(1 + 251) \approx 10^6 \times 8 = 8 \text{ Mbps}$$

This is a theoretical limit and, as we have said, is unlikely to be reached. But assume we can achieve the limit. Based on Nyquist's formula, how many signaling levels are required? We have

$$C = 2B \log_2 M$$

$$8 \times 10^6 = 2 \times (10^6) \times \log_2 M$$

$$4 = \log_2 M$$

$$M = 16$$

than the error-free capacity, then it is theoretically possible to use a suitable signal code to achieve error-free transmission through the channel. Shannon's theorem unfortunately does not suggest a means for finding such codes, but it does provide a yardstick by which the performance of practical communication schemes may be measured.

Several other observations concerning the preceding equation may be instructive. For a given level of noise, it would appear that the data rate could be increased by increasing either signal strength or bandwidth. However, as the signal strength increases, so do the effects of nonlinearities in the system, leading to an increase in intermodulation noise. Note also that, because noise is assumed to be white, the wider the bandwidth, the more noise is admitted to the system. Thus, as B increases, SNR decreases.

2.4 TRANSMISSION MEDIA

In a data transmission system, the **transmission medium** is the physical path between transmitter and receiver. Transmission media can be classified as guided or unguided. In both cases, communication is in the form of electromagnetic waves. With **guided media**, the waves are guided along a solid medium, such as copper twisted pair, copper coaxial cable, or optical fiber. The atmosphere and outer space are examples of **unguided media**, which provide a means of transmitting electromagnetic signals but do not guide them; this form of transmission is usually referred to as **wireless transmission**.

The characteristics and quality of a data transmission are determined both by the characteristics of the medium and the characteristics of the signal. In the case of guided media, the medium itself is usually more important in determining the limitations of transmission. For unguided media, the bandwidth of the signal produced by the transmitting antenna is usually more important than the medium in determining transmission characteristics. One key property of signals transmitted by antenna is directionality. In general, signals at lower frequencies are omnidirectional; that is, the signal propagates in all directions from the antenna. At higher frequencies, it is possible to focus the signal into a directional beam.

Figure 2.10 depicts the electromagnetic spectrum and indicates the frequencies at which various guided media and unguided transmission techniques operate. In the remainder of this section, we provide a brief overview of unguided, or wireless, media.

For unguided media, transmission and reception are achieved by means of an antenna. For transmission, the antenna radiates electromagnetic energy into the medium (usually air), and for reception, the antenna picks up electromagnetic waves from the surrounding medium. There are basically two types of configurations for wireless transmission: directional and omnidirectional. For the directional configuration, the transmitting antenna puts out a focused electromagnetic beam; the transmitting and receiving antennas must therefore be carefully aligned. In the omnidirectional case, the transmitted signal spreads out in all directions and can be received by many antennas.

Three general ranges of frequencies are of interest in our discussion of wireless transmission. Frequencies in the range of about 1 GHz (gigahertz = 10^9Hz) to 100 GHz are referred to as **microwave frequencies**. At these frequencies, highly directional beams are possible, and microwave is quite suitable for point-to-point transmission. Microwave is also used for satellite communications. Frequencies in the range 30 MHz to 1 GHz are suitable for omnidirectional applications. We refer to this range as the radio range.

Another important frequency range, for local applications, is the infrared portion of the spectrum. This covers, roughly, from 3×10^{11} to 2×10^{14}Hz. Infrared is useful in local point-to-point and multipoint applications within confined areas, such as a single room.

Terrestrial Microwave

Physical Description The most common type of microwave antenna is the parabolic "dish." A typical size is about 3 m in diameter. The antenna is fixed rigidly and focuses a narrow beam to achieve line-of-sight transmission to the receiving antenna. Microwave antennas are usually located at substantial heights above ground level to extend the range between antennas and to be able to transmit over intervening obstacles. To achieve long-distance transmission, a series of microwave relay towers is used, and point-to-point microwave links are strung together over the desired distance.

Applications A primary use for **terrestrial microwave** systems is in long-haul telecommunications service, as an alternative to coaxial cable or optical fiber. The microwave facility requires far fewer amplifiers or repeaters than coaxial cable over

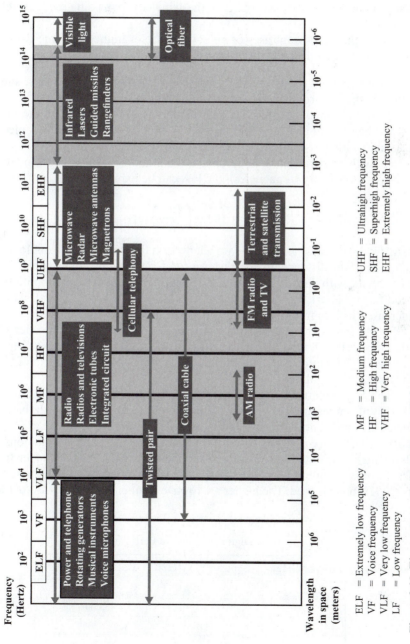

Frequency (Hertz)

ELF | VF | VLF | LF | MF | HF | VHF | UHF | SHF | EHF

10^2 10^3 10^4 10^5 10^6 10^7 10^8 10^9 10^{10} 10^{11} 10^{12} 10^{13} 10^{14} 10^{15}

Power and telephone
Rotating generators
Musical instruments
Voice microphones

Radio
Radios and televisions
Electronic tubes
Integrated circuit

Microwave
Radar
Microwave antennas
Magnetrons

Infrared
Lasers
Guided missiles
Rangefinders

Visible light

Optical fiber

Twisted pair

Coaxial cable

Cellular telephony

AM radio

FM radio and TV

Terrestrial and satellite transmission

Wavelength in space (meters)

10^6 10^5 10^4 10^3 10^2 10^1 10^0 10^{-1} 10^{-2} 10^{-3} 10^{-4} 10^{-5} 10^{-6}

ELF = Extremely low frequency
VF = Voice frequency
VLF = Very low frequency
LF = Low frequency

MF = Medium frequency
HF = High frequency
VHF = Very high frequency

UHF = Ultrahigh frequency
SHF = Superhigh frequency
EHF = Extremely high frequency

Figure 2.10 Electromagnetic Spectrum for Telecommunications

27

the same distance but requires line-of-sight transmission. Microwave is commonly used for both voice and television transmission.

Another increasingly common use of microwave is for short point-to-point links between buildings. This can be used for closed-circuit TV or as a data link between local area networks. Short-haul microwave can also be used for the so-called bypass application. A business can establish a microwave link to a long-distance telecommunications facility in the same city, bypassing the local telephone company.

Two other important uses of microwave are examined in some detail in Part Three: cellular systems and fixed wireless access.

Transmission Characteristics Microwave transmission covers a substantial portion of the electromagnetic spectrum. Common frequencies used for transmission are in the range 2 to 40 GHz. The higher the frequency used, the higher the potential bandwidth and therefore the higher the potential data rate. Table 2.2 indicates bandwidth and data rate for some typical systems.

As with any transmission system, a main source of loss is attenuation. For microwave (and radio frequencies), the loss can be expressed as

$$L = 10 \log \left(\frac{4\pi d}{\lambda} \right)^2 \text{dB} \tag{2.2}$$

where d is the distance and λ is the wavelength, in the same units. Thus, loss varies as the square of the distance. In contrast, for twisted pair and coaxial cable, loss varies exponentially with distance (linear in decibels). Thus repeaters or amplifiers may be placed farther apart for microwave systems—10 to 100 km is typical. Attenuation is increased with rainfall. The effects of rainfall become especially noticeable above 10 GHz. As frequency increases, λ decreases and loss increases. Another source of impairment is interference. With the growing popularity of microwave, transmission areas overlap and interference is always a danger. Thus the assignment of frequency bands is strictly regulated.

The most common bands for long-haul telecommunications are the 4- to 6-GHz bands. With increasing congestion at these frequencies, the 11-GHz band is now coming into use. The 12-GHz band is used as a component of cable TV systems. Microwave links are used to provide TV signals to local CATV installations; the signals are then distributed to individual subscribers via coaxial cable. Higher-frequency microwave is being used for short point-to-point links between buildings; typically, the 22-GHz band is used. The higher microwave frequencies are less useful for longer

Table 2.2 Typical Digital Microwave Performance

Band (GHz)	Bandwidth (MHz)	Data Rate (Mbps)
2	7	12
6	30	90
11	40	135
18	220	274

distances because of increased attenuation but are quite adequate for shorter distances. In addition, at the higher frequencies, the antennas are smaller and cheaper.

Satellite Microwave

Physical Description A communication satellite is, in effect, a microwave relay station. It is used to link two or more ground-based microwave transmitter/receivers, known as earth stations, or ground stations. The satellite receives transmissions on one frequency band (uplink), amplifies or repeats the signal, and transmits it on another frequency (downlink). A single orbiting satellite will operate on a number of frequency bands, called *transponder channels*, or simply *transponders*.

Applications The communication satellite is a technological revolution as important as fiber optics. Among the most important applications for satellites are

- Television distribution
- Long-distance telephone transmission
- Private business networks

Because of their broadcast nature, satellites are well suited to television distribution and are being used extensively in the United States and throughout the world for this purpose. In its traditional use, a network provides programming from a central location. Programs are transmitted to the satellite and then broadcast down to a number of stations, which then distribute the programs to individual viewers. One network, the Public Broadcasting Service (PBS), distributes its television programming almost exclusively by the use of satellite channels. Other commercial networks also make substantial use of satellite, and cable television systems are receiving an ever-increasing proportion of their programming from satellites. The most recent application of satellite technology to television distribution is direct broadcast satellite (DBS), in which satellite video signals are transmitted directly to the home user. The dropping cost and size of receiving antennas have made DBS economically feasible, and DBS is now commonplace. DBS is discussed in Chapter 16.

Satellite transmission is also used for point-to-point trunks between telephone exchange offices in public telephone networks. It is the optimum medium for high-usage international trunks and is competitive with terrestrial systems for many long-distance intranational links.

Finally, there are a number of business data applications for satellite. The satellite provider can divide the total capacity into a number of channels and lease these channels to individual business users. A user equipped with antennas at a number of sites can use a satellite channel for a private network. Traditionally, such applications have been quite expensive and limited to larger organizations with high-volume requirements.

Transmission Characteristics The optimum frequency range for satellite transmission is in the range 1 to 10 GHz. Below 1 GHz, there is significant noise from natural sources, including galactic, solar, and atmospheric noise, and human-made interference from various electronic devices. Above 10 GHz, the signal is severely attenuated by atmospheric absorption and precipitation.

Most satellites providing point-to-point service today use a frequency band-width in the range 5.925 to 6.425 GHz for transmission from earth to satellite (uplink) and a bandwidth in the range 3.7 to 4.2 GHz for transmission from satellite to earth (downlink). This combination is referred to as the 4/6-GHz band. Note that the uplink and downlink frequencies differ. For continuous operation without interference, a satellite cannot transmit and receive on the same frequency. Thus signals received from a ground station on one frequency must be transmitted back on another.

The 4/6-GHz band is within the optimum zone of 1 to 10 GHz but has become saturated. Other frequencies in that range are unavailable because of sources of inter-ference operating at those frequencies, usually terrestrial microwave. Therefore, the 12/14-GHz band has been developed (uplink: 14 to 14.5 GHz; downlink: 11.7 to 12.2 GHz). At this frequency band, attenuation problems must be overcome. However, smaller and cheaper earth-station receivers can be used. It is anticipated that this band will also saturate, and use is projected for the 20/30-GHz band (uplink: 27.5 to 30.0 GHz; downlink: 17.7 to 20.2 GHz). This band experiences even greater attenu-ation problems but will allow greater bandwidth (2500 MHz versus 500 MHz) and even smaller and cheaper receivers.

Several properties of satellite communication should be noted. First, because of the long distances involved, there is a propagation delay of about a quarter second from transmission from one earth station to reception by another earth station. This delay is noticeable in ordinary telephone conversations. It also introduces problems in the areas of error control and flow control, which we discuss in later chapters. Second, **satellite microwave** is inherently a broadcast facility. Many stations can transmit to the satellite, and a transmission from a satellite can be received by many stations.

Broadcast Radio

Physical Description The principal difference between broadcast radio and microwave is that the former is omnidirectional and the latter is directional. Thus broadcast radio does not require dish-shaped antennas, and the antennas need not be rigidly mounted to a precise alignment.

Applications *Radio* is a general term used to encompass frequencies in the range of 3 kHz to 300 GHz. We are using the informal term *broadcast radio* to cover the VHF and part of the UHF band: 30 MHz to 1 GHz. This range covers FM radio and VHF television. This range is also used for a number of data networking applications.

Transmission Characteristics The range 30 MHz to 1 GHz is an effective one for broadcast communications. Unlike the case for lower-frequency electromagnetic waves, the ionosphere is transparent to radio waves above 30 MHz. Thus transmis-sion is limited to the line of sight, and distant transmitters will not interfere with each other due to reflection from the atmosphere. Unlike the higher frequencies of the mi-crowave region, broadcast radio waves are less sensitive to attenuation from rainfall.

As with microwave, the amount of attenuation due to distance for radio obeys Equation (2.2), namely $10 \log\left(\dfrac{4\pi d}{\lambda}\right)^2$ dB. Because of the longer wavelength, radio waves suffer relatively less attenuation.

A prime source of impairment for broadcast radio waves is multipath interference. Reflection from land, water, and natural or human-made objects can create multiple paths between antennas. This effect is frequently evident when TV reception displays multiple images as an airplane passes by.

Infrared

Infrared communications is achieved using transmitters/receivers (transceivers) that modulate noncoherent infrared light. Transceivers must be within the line of sight of each other either directly or via reflection from a light-colored surface such as the ceiling of a room.

One important difference between infrared and microwave transmission is that the former does not penetrate walls. Thus the security and interference problems encountered in microwave systems are not present. Furthermore, there is no frequency allocation issue with infrared, because no licensing is required.

2.5 MULTIPLEXING

In both local and wide area communications, it is almost always the case that the capacity of the transmission medium exceeds the capacity required for the transmission of a single signal. To make efficient use of the transmission system, it is desirable to carry multiple signals on a single medium. This is referred to as *multiplexing*.

Figure 2.11 depicts the multiplexing function in its simplest form. There are *n* inputs to a multiplexer. The multiplexer is connected by a single data link to a demultiplexer. The link is able to carry *n* separate channels of data. The multiplexer combines (multiplexes) data from the *n* input lines and transmits over a higher-capacity data link. The demultiplexer accepts the multiplexed data stream, separates (demultiplexes) the data according to channel, and delivers them to the appropriate output lines.

The widespread use of multiplexing in data communications can be explained by the following:

1. The higher the data rate, the more cost-effective the transmission facility. That is, for a given application and over a given distance, the cost per kbps declines with an increase in the data rate of the transmission facility. Similarly, the cost

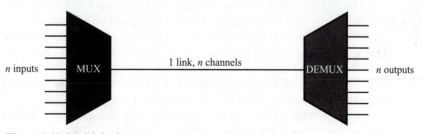

Figure 2.11 Multiplexing

of transmission and receiving equipment, per kbps, declines with increasing data rate.

2. Most individual data communicating devices require relatively modest data rate support.

The preceding statements were phrased in terms of data communicating devices. Similar statements apply to voice communications. That is, the greater the capacity of a transmission facility, in terms of voice channels, the less the cost per individual voice channel, and the capacity required for a single voice channel is modest.

Two techniques for multiplexing in telecommunications networks are in common use: **frequency division multiplexing (FDM)** and **time division multiplexing (TDM)**.

FDM takes advantage of the fact that the useful bandwidth of the medium exceeds the required bandwidth of a given signal. A number of signals can be carried simultaneously if each signal is modulated onto a different carrier frequency and the carrier frequencies are sufficiently separated so that the bandwidths of the signals do not overlap. Figure 2.12a depicts a simple case. Six signal sources are fed into a multiplexer that modulates each signal onto a different frequency ($f_1, \ldots, f_6$). Each signal requires a certain bandwidth centered on its carrier frequency, referred to as a **channel**. To prevent interference, the channels are separated by **guard bands**, which are unused portions of the spectrum (not shown in the figure).

An example is the multiplexing of voice signals. We mentioned that the useful spectrum for voice is 300 to 3400 Hz. Thus, a bandwidth of 4 kHz is adequate to carry the voice signal and provide a guard band. For both North America (AT&T standard) and internationally (International Telecommunication Union Telecommunication Standardization Sector [ITU-T] standard), a standard voice multiplexing scheme is twelve 4-kHz voice channels from 60 to 108 kHz. For higher-capacity links, both AT&T and ITU-T define larger groupings of 4-kHz channels.

TDM takes advantage of the fact that the achievable bit rate (sometimes, unfortunately, called bandwidth) of the medium exceeds the required data rate of a digital signal. Multiple digital signals can be carried on a single transmission path by interleaving portions of each signal in time. The interleaving can be at the bit level or in blocks of bytes or larger quantities. For example, the multiplexer in Figure 2.12b has six inputs that might each be, say, 9.6 kbps. A single line with a capacity of 57.6 kbps could accommodate all six sources. Analogously to FDM, the sequence of time slots dedicated to a particular source is called a channel. One cycle of time slots (one per source) is called a frame.

The TDM scheme depicted in Figure 2.12b is also known as **synchronous TDM**, referring to the fact that time slots are preassigned and fixed. Hence the timing of transmission from the various sources is synchronized. In contrast, asynchronous TDM allows time on the medium to be allocated dynamically. Unless otherwise noted, the term *TDM* will be used to mean synchronous TDM.

A generic depiction of a synchronous TDM system is provided in Figure 2.13. A number of signals [$m_i(t), i = 1, n$] are to be multiplexed onto the same transmission medium. The signals carry digital data and are generally digital signals. The incoming data from each source are briefly buffered. Each buffer is typically one bit or one character in length. The buffers are scanned sequentially to form a composite

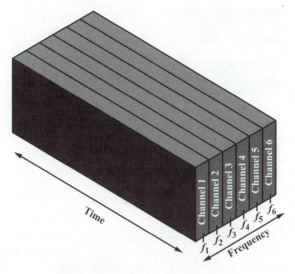

(a) Frequency division multiplexing

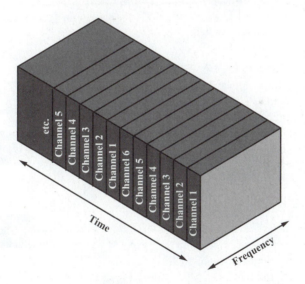

(b) Time division multiplexing

Figure 2.12 FDM and TDM

digital data stream $m_c(t)$. The scan operation is sufficiently rapid so that each buffer is emptied before more data can arrive. Thus, the data rate of $m_c(t)$ must at least equal the sum of the data rates of the $m_i(t)$. The digital signal $m_c(t)$ may be transmitted directly, or passed through a modem so that an analog signal is transmitted. In either case, transmission is typically synchronous.

The transmitted data may have a format something like Figure 2.13b. The data are organized into frames. Each frame contains a cycle of time slots. In each frame,

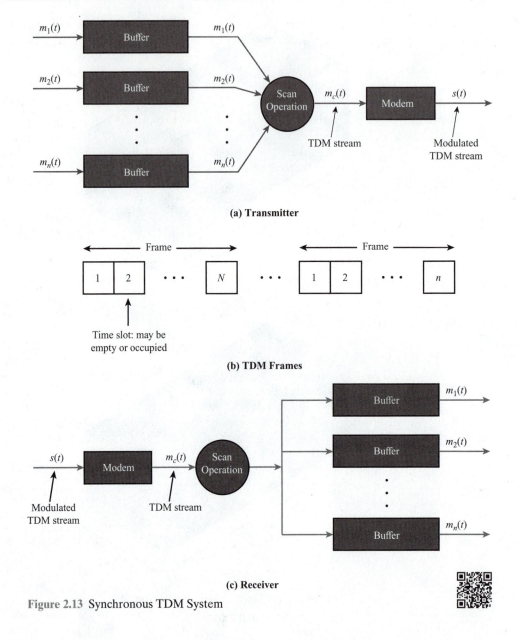

Figure 2.13 Synchronous TDM System

one or more slots are dedicated to each data source. The sequence of slots dedicated to one source, from frame to frame, is called a channel. The slot length equals the transmitter buffer length, typically a bit or a byte (character).

The byte-interleaving technique is used with asynchronous and synchronous sources. Each time slot contains one character of data. Typically, the start and stop bits of each character are eliminated before transmission and reinserted by the receiver, thus improving efficiency. The bit-interleaving technique is used with synchronous sources and may also be used with asynchronous sources. Each time slot contains just one bit.

At the receiver, the interleaved data are demultiplexed and routed to the appropriate destination buffer. For each input source $m_i(t)$, there is an identical output source that will receive the input data at the same rate at which it was generated.

Synchronous TDM is called synchronous not because synchronous transmission is used but because the time slots are preassigned to sources and fixed. The time slots for each source are transmitted whether or not the source has data to send. This is, of course, also the case with FDM. In both cases, capacity is wasted to achieve simplicity of implementation. Even when fixed assignment is used, however, it is possible for a synchronous TDM device to handle sources of different data rates. For example, the slowest input device could be assigned one slot per cycle, while faster devices are assigned multiple slots per cycle.

One example of TDM is the standard scheme used for transmitting PCM voice data, known in AT&T parlance as T1 carrier. Data are taken from each source, one sample (7 bits) at a time. An eighth bit is added for signaling and supervisory functions. For T1, 24 sources are multiplexed, so there are $8 \times 24 = 192$ bits of data and control signals per frame. One final bit is added for establishing and maintaining synchronization. Thus a frame consists of 193 bits and contains one 7-bit sample per source. Since sources must be sampled 8000 times per second, the required data rate is $8000 \times 193 = 1.544$ Mbps. As with voice FDM, higher data rates are defined for larger groupings.

TDM is not limited to digital signals. Analog signals can also be interleaved in time. Also, with analog signals, a combination of TDM and FDM is possible. A transmission system can be frequency divided into a number of channels, each of which is further divided via TDM.

2.6 RECOMMENDED READING

[STAL14] covers all of the topics in this chapter in greater detail. [FREE05] is also a readable and rigorous treatment of the topics of this chapter. A thorough treatment of both analog and digital communication is provided in [COUC13].

COUC13 Couch, L. *Digital and Analog Communication Systems*. Upper Saddle River, NJ: Pearson, 2013.

FREE05 Freeman, R. *Fundamentals of Telecommunications*. New York: Wiley, 2005.

STAL14 Stallings, W. *Data and Computer Communications, Tenth Edition*. Upper Saddle River, NJ: Pearson, 2014.

2.7 KEY TERMS, REVIEW QUESTIONS, AND PROBLEMS

Key Terms

analog data	aperiodic	channel capacity
analog signal	bandwidth	decibel (dB)
analog transmission	broadcast radio	digital data

(continued)

digital signal	microwave	synchronous TDM
digital transmission	multiplexing	terrestrial microwave
frequency	noise	time division multiplexing
frequency division	peak amplitude	(TDM)
multiplexing (FDM)	period	time domain
frequency domain	periodic	transmission media
fundamental frequency	phase	unguided media
guided media	radio	wavelength
harmonics	satellite microwave	wireless
infrared	spectrum	

Review Questions

2.1 Differentiate between an analog and a digital electromagnetic signal.

2.2 What are three important characteristics of a periodic signal?

2.3 How many radians are there in a complete circle of 360 degrees?

2.4 What is the relationship between the wavelength and frequency of a sine wave?

2.5 What is the relationship between a signal's spectrum and its bandwidth?

2.6 What is attenuation?

2.7 Define channel capacity.

2.8 What key factors affect channel capacity?

2.9 Differentiate between guided media and unguided media.

2.10 What are some major advantages and disadvantages of microwave transmission?

2.11 What is direct broadcast satellite?

2.12 Why must a satellite have distinct uplink and downlink frequencies?

2.13 Indicate some significant differences between broadcast radio and microwave.

2.14 Why is multiplexing so cost-effective?

2.15 How is interference avoided by using frequency division multiplexing?

2.16 Explain how synchronous time division multiplexing works.

Problems

2.1 A signal has a fundamental frequency of 1000 Hz. What is its period?

2.2 Express the following in the simplest form you can:
a. $\sin(2\pi ft - \pi) + \sin(2\pi ft + \pi)$
b. $\sin 2\pi ft + \sin(2\pi ft - \pi)$

2.3 Sound may be modeled as sinusoidal functions. Compare the wavelength and relative frequency of musical notes. Use 330 m/s as the speed of sound and the following frequencies for the musical scale.

Note	C	D	E	F	G	A	B	C
Frequency	264	297	330	352	396	440	495	528

2.4 If the solid curve in Figure 2.14 represents $\sin(2\pi t)$, what does the dotted curve represent? That is, the dotted curve can be written in the form $A \sin(2\pi ft + \phi)$; what are A, f, and ϕ?

2.5 Decompose the signal $(1 + 0.1 \cos 5t)\cos 100t$ into a linear combination of sinusoidal function, and find the amplitude, frequency, and phase of each component. *Hint*: Use the identity for cos a cos b.

2.6 Find the period of the function $f(t) = (10 \cos t)^2$.

2.7 Consider two periodic functions $f_1(t)$ and $f_2(t)$, with periods T_1 and T_2, respectively. Is it always the case that the function $f(t) = f_1(t) + f_2(t)$ is periodic? If so, demonstrate this fact. If not, under what conditions is $f(t)$ periodic?

2.8 Figure 2.5 shows the effect of eliminating higher-harmonic components of a square wave and retaining only a few lower harmonic components. What would the signal look like in the opposite case; that is, retaining all higher harmonics and eliminating a few lower harmonics?

2.9 What is the channel capacity for a teleprinter channel with a 300-Hz bandwidth and a signal-to-noise ratio of 3 dB?

2.10 A digital signaling system is required to operate at 9600 bps.
   a. If a signal element encodes a 4-bit word, what is the minimum required bandwidth of the channel?
   b. Repeat part (a) for the case of 8-bit words.

2.11 Study the works of Shannon and Nyquist on channel capacity. Each places an upper limit on the bit rate of a channel based on two different approaches. How are the two related?

2.12 Given the narrow (usable) audio bandwidth of a telephone transmission facility, a nominal SNR of 56 dB (400,000), and a distortion level of <0.2%,
   a. What is the theoretical maximum channel capacity (kbps) of traditional telephone lines?
   b. What is the actual maximum channel capacity?

2.13 Given a channel with an intended capacity of 20 Mbps, the bandwidth of the channel is 3 MHz. What signal-to-noise ratio is required to achieve this capacity?

2.14 Show that doubling the transmission frequency or doubling the distance between transmitting antenna and receiving antenna attenuates the power received by 6 dB.

2.15 Fill in the missing elements in the following table of approximate power ratios for various dB levels.

Decibels	1	2	3	4	5	6	7	8	9	10
Losses			0.5							0.1
Gains			2							10

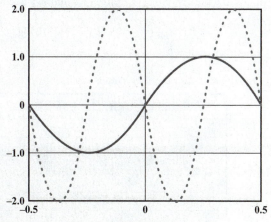

Figure 2.14 Figure for Problem 2.4

2.16 If an amplifier has a 30 dB voltage gain, what voltage ratio does the gain represent?

2.17 An amplifier has an output of 20 W. What is its output in dBW?

APPENDIX 2A DECIBELS AND SIGNAL STRENGTH

An important parameter in any transmission system is the signal strength. As a signal propagates along a transmission medium, there will be a loss, or *attenuation*, of signal strength. To compensate, amplifiers may be inserted at various points to impart a gain in signal strength.

It is customary to express gains, losses, and relative levels in decibels because

- Signal strength often falls off exponentially, so loss is easily expressed in terms of the decibel, which is a logarithmic unit.

- The net gain or loss in a cascaded transmission path can be calculated with simple addition and subtraction.

The decibel is a measure of the ratio between two signal levels. The decibel gain is given by

$$G_{dB} = 10 \log_{10} \frac{P_{out}}{P_{in}}$$

where

G_{dB} = gain, in decibels

P_{in} = input power level

P_{out} = output power level

$\log_{10}$ = logarithm to the base 10 (from now on, we will simply use log to mean $\log_{10}$)

Table 2.3 shows the relationship between decibel values and powers of 10.

There is some inconsistency in the literature over the use of the terms *gain* and *loss*. If the value of G_{dB} is positive, this represents an actual gain in power. For example, a gain of 3 dB means that the power has doubled. If the value of G_{dB} is negative, this represents an actual loss in power. For example a gain of -3 dB means that the power has halved, and this is a loss of power. Normally, this is expressed by saying there is a loss of 3 dB. However, some of the literature would say that this is a loss of -3 dB. It makes more sense to say that a negative gain corresponds to a positive loss. Therefore, we define a decibel loss as

$$L_{dB} = -10 \log_{10} \frac{P_{out}}{P_{in}} = 10 \log_{10} \frac{P_{in}}{P_{out}} \qquad (2.3)$$

Table 2.3 Decibel Values

Power Ratio	dB	Power Ratio	dB
10^1	10	10^{-1}	−10
10^2	20	10^{-2}	−20
10^3	30	10^{-3}	−30
10^4	40	10^{-4}	−40
10^5	50	10^{-5}	−50
10^6	60	10^{-6}	−60

> **Example 2.2**   If a signal with a power level of 10 mW is inserted onto a transmission line and the measured power some distance away is 5 mW, the loss can be expressed as
> $L_{dB} = 10 \log(10/5) = 10(0.3) = 3\ dB$.

Note that the decibel is a measure of relative, not absolute, difference. A loss from 1000 mW to 500 mW is also a loss of 3 dB.

The decibel is also used to measure the difference in voltage, taking into account that power is proportional to the square of the voltage:

$$P = \frac{V^2}{R}$$

where

P = power dissipated across resistance R
V = voltage across resistance R

Thus

$$L_{dB} = 10 \log \frac{P_{in}}{P_{out}} = 10 \log \frac{V_{in}^2/R}{V_{out}^2/R} = 20 \log \frac{V_{in}}{V_{out}}$$

> **Example 2.3**   Decibels are useful in determining the gain or loss over a series of transmission elements. Consider a series in which the input is at a power level of 4 mW, the first element is a transmission line with a 12-dB loss (−12 dB gain), the second element is an amplifier with a 35-dB gain, and the third element is a transmission line with a 10-dB loss. The net gain is (−12 + 35 − 10) = 13 dB. To calculate the output power P_{out},
>
> $$G_{db} = 13 = 10 \log(P_{out}/4\ mW)$$
> $$P_{out} = 4 \times 10^{1.3}\ mW = 79.8\ mW$$

Decibel values refer to relative magnitudes or changes in magnitude, not to an absolute level. It is convenient to be able to refer to an absolute level of power or voltage in decibels so that gains and losses with reference to an initial signal level may be calculated easily. The **dBW (decibel-Watt)** is used extensively in microwave applications. The value of 1 W is selected as a reference and defined to be 0 dBW. The absolute decibel level of power in dBW is defined as

$$\text{Power}_{dBW} = 10 \log \frac{\text{Power}_W}{1\ W}$$

> **Example 2.4**   A power of 1000 W is 30 dBW, and a power of 1 mW is −30 dBW.

Another common unit is the **dBm (decibel-milliWatt)**, which uses 1 mW as the reference. Thus 0 dBm = 1 mW. The formula is

$$\text{Power}_{dBm} = 10 \log \frac{\text{Power}_{mW}}{1\ mW}$$

Note the following relationships:

$$+30\ dBm = 0\ dBW$$
$$0\ dBm = -30\ dBW$$

CHAPTER 3

COMMUNICATION NETWORKS

LEARNING OBJECTIVES

After studying this chapter, you should be able to:

- Explain the roles and scope of wide, local, and metropolitan area networks.
- Define circuit switching and describe the key elements of circuit-switching networks.
- Define packet switching and describe the key elements of packet-switching technology.
- Discuss the relative merits of circuit switching and packet switching and analyze the circumstances for which each is most appropriate.

This chapter provides an overview of various approaches to communication networking. The chapter begins with a survey of different type of networks based on geographic extent. Then circuit-switching and packet-switching networks are examined.

3.1 LANS, MANS, AND WANS

Local area networks (LANs), **metropolitan area networks (MANs)**, and **wide area networks (WANs)** are all examples of communications networks. Figure 3.1 illustrates these categories, plus some special cases. By way of contrast, the typical range of parameters for a multiple-processor computer is also depicted.

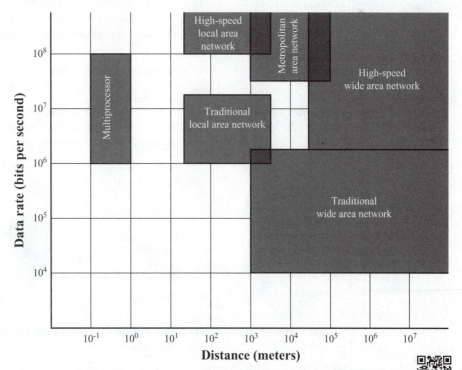

Figure 3.1 Comparison of Multiprocessor Systems, LANs, MANs, and WANs

Wide Area Networks

WANs cover a large geographical area, may require the crossing of public right-of-ways, and may rely at least in part on circuits provided by a common carrier. Typically, a WAN consists of a number of interconnected switching nodes. A transmission from any one device is routed through these internal nodes to the specified destination device.

Traditionally, WANs have been implemented using one of two technologies: circuit switching and packet switching. Subsequently, frame relay and asynchronous transfer mode (ATM) assumed major roles. While ATM and, to some extent, frame relay are still widely used, their use is gradually being supplanted by services based on gigabit Ethernet and Internet Protocol technologies.

Local Area Networks

As with WANs, a LAN is a communications network that interconnects a variety of devices and provides a means for information exchange among those devices. There are several key distinctions between LANs and WANs:

1. The scope of the LAN is small, typically a single building or a cluster of buildings. This difference in geographic scope leads to different technical solutions.

2. It is usually the case that the LAN is owned by the same organization that owns the attached devices. For WANs, this is less often the case, or at least a significant fraction of the network assets are not owned. This has two implications. First, care must be taken in the choice of LAN, since there may be a substantial capital investment (compared with charges for WANs) for both purchase and maintenance. Second, the network management responsibility for a LAN falls solely on the user.

3. The internal data rates of LANs are typically much greater than those of WANs.

A simple example of a LAN that highlights some of its characteristics is shown in Figure 3.2. All of the devices are attached to a shared transmission medium. A transmission from any one device can be received by all other devices attached to the same network.

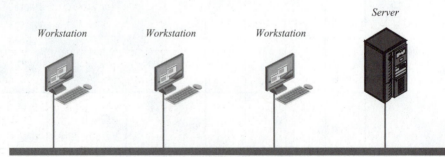

Server

Workstation   *Workstation*   *Workstation*

Shared transmission medium

Figure 3.2 A Simple Local Area Network

Traditional LANs provided data rates in a range from about 1 to 20 Mbps. These data rates, though substantial, were inadequate with the proliferation of devices, the growth in multimedia applications, and the increased use of the client–server architecture. As a result, much of the effort in LAN development has been in the development of high-speed LANs, with data rates of 100 Mbps to 100 Gbps.

Metropolitan Area Networks

As the name suggests, a MAN occupies a middle ground between LANs and WANs. Interest in MANs has come about as a result of a recognition that the traditional point-to-point and switched network techniques used in WANs may be inadequate for the growing needs of organizations. There is a requirement now for both private and public networks that provide high capacity at low costs over a large area. The high-speed shared-medium approach of the LAN standards provides a number of benefits that can be realized on a metropolitan scale. As Figure 3.1 indicates, MANs cover greater distances at higher data rates than LANs, although there is some overlap in geographical coverage.

The primary market for MANs is the customer that has high-capacity needs in a metropolitan area. A MAN is intended to provide the required capacity at lower cost and greater efficiency than obtaining an equivalent service from the local telephone company.

3.2 SWITCHING TECHNIQUES

For transmission of data beyond a local area, communication is typically achieved by transmitting data from source to destination through a network of intermediate switching nodes; this switched network design is typically used to implement LANs and MANs as well. The switching nodes are not concerned with the content of the data; rather their purpose is to provide a switching facility that will move the data from node to node until they reach their destination. Figure 3.3 illustrates a sample network. The end devices that wish to communicate may be referred to as stations. The stations may be computers, terminals, telephones, or other communicating devices. We will refer to the switching devices whose purpose is to provide communication as *nodes*. The nodes are connected to each other in some topology by transmission links. Each station attaches to a node, and the collection of nodes is referred to as a *communication network*.

> **Example 3.1** Consider Figure 3.3. Signals entering the network from a station are routed to the destination by being switched from node to node. For example, information from station A intended for station F is sent to node 4. It may then be routed via nodes 5 and 6 or nodes 7 and 6 to the destination. Several observations are in order:
>
> 1. Some nodes connect only to other nodes (e.g., 5 and 7). Their sole task is the internal (to the network) switching of information. Other nodes have one or more stations attached as well; in addition to their switching functions, such nodes accept information from and deliver information to the attached stations.

(continued)

2. Node-station links are generally dedicated point-to-point links. Node-node links are usually multiplexed links, using either frequency division multiplexing (FDM) or some form of time division multiplexing (TDM).

3. Usually, the network is not fully connected; that is, there is not a direct link between every possible pair of nodes. However, it is always desirable to have more than one possible paths through the network for each pair of stations. This enhances the reliability of the network.

Two quite different technologies are used in wide area switched networks: circuit switching and packet switching. These two technologies differ in the way the nodes switch information from one link to another on the way from source to destination.

3.3 CIRCUIT SWITCHING

In the past, **circuit switching** was the dominant technology for both voice and data communications. Communication via circuit switching implies that there is a dedicated communication path between two stations. That path is a connected

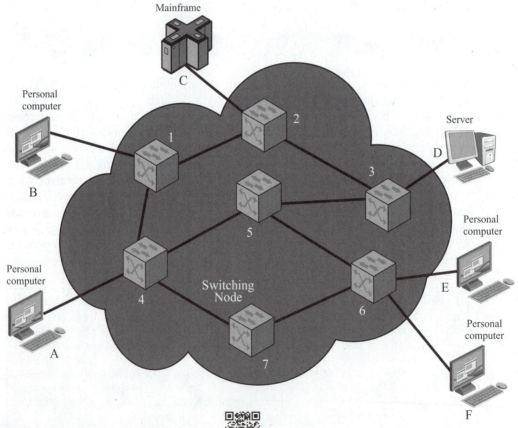

Figure 3.3 Simple Switching Network

sequence of links between network nodes. On each link, a physical or logical channel is dedicated to the connection. The most common example of circuit switching is the telephone network.

Communication via circuit switching involves three phases, which can be explained with reference to Figure 3.3.

1. **Circuit establishment.** Before any signals can be transmitted, an end-to-end (station-to-station) circuit must be established. For example, station A sends a request to node 4 requesting a connection to station E. Typically, the link from A to 4 is a dedicated line, so that part of the connection already exists. Node 4 must find the next leg in a route leading to E. Based on routing information and measures of availability and perhaps cost, node 4 selects the link to node 5, allocates a free channel (using frequency division multiplexing, FDM, or time division multiplexing, TDM) on that link, and sends a message requesting connection to E. So far, a dedicated path has been established from A through 4 to 5. Because a number of stations may attach to 4, it must be able to establish internal paths from multiple stations to multiple nodes. How this is done is discussed later in this section. The remainder of the process proceeds similarly. Node 5 dedicates a channel to node 6 and internally ties that channel to the channel from node 4. Node 6 completes the connection to E. In completing the connection, a test is made to determine if E is busy or is prepared to accept the connection.

2. **Information transfer.** Information can now be transmitted from A through the network to E. The transmission may be analog voice, digitized voice, or binary data, depending on the nature of the network. The path is A-4 link, internal switching through 4, 4-5 channel, internal switching through 5, 5-6 channel, internal switching through 6, 6-E link. Generally, the connection is full duplex, and signals may be transmitted in both directions simultaneously.

3. **Circuit disconnect.** After some period of information transfer, the connection is terminated, usually by the action of one of the two stations. Signals must be propagated to nodes 4, 5, and 6 to deallocate the dedicated resources.

Note that the connection path is established before data transmission begins. Thus, channel capacity must be reserved between each pair of nodes in the path and each node must have available internal switching capacity to handle the requested connection. The switches must have the intelligence to make these allocations and to devise a route through the network.

Circuit switching can be rather inefficient. Channel capacity is dedicated for the duration of a connection, even if no data are being transferred. For a voice connection, utilization for each direction may be about 40%, with the other 20% of the time spent on pauses between directions of the conversation. For a terminal-to-computer connection, the capacity may be idle during most of the time of the connection. In terms of performance, there is a delay prior to signal transfer for call establishment. However, once the circuit is established, the network is effectively transparent to the users. Information is transmitted at a fixed data rate with no delay other than the propagation delay through the transmission links. The delay at each node is negligible.

Circuit switching was developed to handle voice traffic but is now also used for data traffic. The best-known example of a circuit-switching network is the public telephone network (Figure 3.4). This is actually a collection of national networks

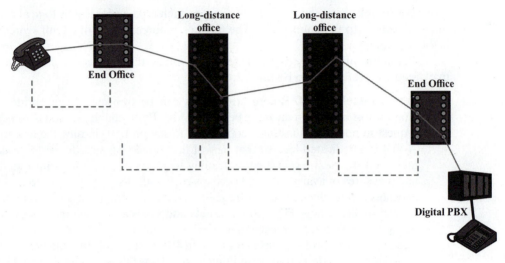

Figure 3.4 Example Connection Over a Public Circuit-Switching Network

interconnected to form the international service. Although originally designed and implemented to service analog telephone subscribers, it handles substantial data traffic via modem and is well on its way to being converted to a digital network. Another well-known application of circuit switching is the private branch exchange (PBX), used to interconnect telephones within a building or office. Circuit switching is also used in private networks. Typically, such a network is set up by a corporation or other large organization to interconnect its various sites. Such a network usually consists of PBX systems at each site interconnected by dedicated, leased lines obtained from one of the carriers, such as AT&T. A final common example of the application of circuit switching is the data switch. The data switch is similar to the PBX but is designed to interconnect digital data processing devices, such as terminals and computers.

In wireless cellular systems, a similar concept to circuit switching is commonly used. Before communication occurs, a mobile user negotiates with a base station for a connection with certain characteristics, sometimes with dedicated time slots and bandwidth.

In the wired public switched telephone network, the public telecommunications network can be described using four generic architectural components:

- **Subscribers:** The devices that attach to the network. Many subscriber devices connected to public telecommunications networks are still telephones, but the percentage of data traffic increases year by year.

- **Subscriber line:** The link between the subscriber and the network, also referred to as the local loop. Almost all subscriber line connections use twisted pair wire. The length of a subscriber line is typically in a range from a few kilometers to a few tens of kilometers. The subscriber line is also known as a **subscriber loop**, or a **local loop**.

- **Exchanges:** The switching centers in the network. A switching center that directly supports subscribers is known as an end office. Typically, an end office will support many thousands of subscribers in a localized area. There are over

19,000 end offices in the United States, so it is clearly impractical for each end office to have a direct link to each of the other end offices; this would require on the order of 2×108 links. Rather, intermediate switching nodes are used.

- **Trunks:** Trunks are the branches between exchanges. Trunks carry multiple voice-frequency circuits using either FDM or synchronous TDM. Earlier, these were referred to as carrier systems.

Subscribers connect directly to an end office, which switches traffic between subscribers and between a subscriber and other exchanges. The other exchanges are responsible for routing and switching traffic between end offices. This distinction is shown in Figure 3.5. To connect two subscribers attached to the same end office, a circuit is set up between them in the same fashion as described before. If two subscribers connect to different end offices, a circuit between them consists of a chain of circuits through one or more intermediate offices. In Figure 3.5, a connection is established between lines a and b by simply setting up the connection through the end office. The connection between c and d is more complex. In c's end office, a connection is established between line c and one channel on a TDM trunk to the intermediate switch. In the intermediate switch, that channel is connected to a channel on a TDM trunk to d's end office. In that end office, the channel is connected to line d.

Circuit-switching technology has been driven by its use to carry voice traffic. One of the key requirements for voice traffic is that there must be virtually no transmission delay and certainly no variation in delay. A constant signal transmission

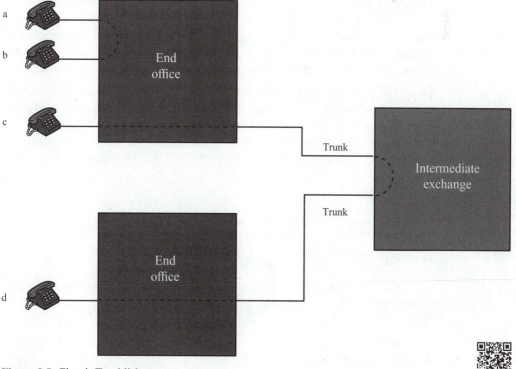

Figure 3.5 Circuit Establishment

rate must be maintained, because transmission and reception occur at the same signal rate. These requirements are necessary to allow normal human conversation. Further, the quality of the received signal must be sufficiently high to provide, at a minimum, intelligibility.

Circuit switching achieved its widespread, dominant position because it is well suited to the analog transmission of voice signals. In today's digital world, its inefficiencies are more apparent. However, despite the inefficiency, circuit switching is and will remain an attractive choice for both local area and wide area networking. One of its key strengths is that it is transparent. Once a circuit is established, it appears like a direct connection to the two attached stations; no special networking logic is needed at the station.

3.4 PACKET SWITCHING

Long-haul circuit-switching telecommunications networks were originally designed to handle voice traffic, and a large percentage of traffic on these networks continues to be voice. A key characteristic of circuit-switching networks is that resources within the network are dedicated to a particular call. For voice connections, the resulting circuit will enjoy a high percentage of utilization since, most of the time, one party or the other is talking. However, as the circuit-switching network began to be used increasingly for data connections, two shortcomings became apparent:

- In a typical terminal-to-host data connection, much of the time the line is idle. Thus, with data connections, a circuit-switching approach is inefficient.

- In a circuit-switching network, the connection provides for transmission at a constant data rate. Thus, each of the two devices that are connected must transmit and receive at the same data rate as the other, which limits the utility of the network in interconnecting a variety of host computers and workstations.

To understand how **packet switching** addresses these problems, let us briefly summarize packet-switching operation. Data are transmitted in blocks, called **packets**. A typical upper bound on packet length is 1500 octets (bytes). If a source has a longer message to send, the message is broken up into a series of packets (Figure 3.6). Each packet consists of a portion of the data (or all of the data for a short message)

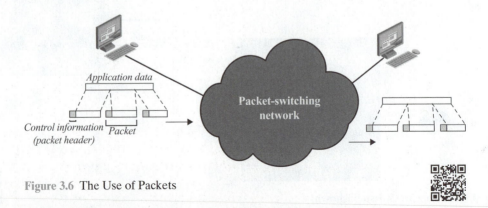

Figure 3.6 The Use of Packets

that a station wants to transmit, plus a packet **header** that contains control information. The control information, at a minimum, includes the information that the network requires in order to be able to route the packet through the network and deliver it to the intended destination. At each node en route, the packet is received, stored briefly, and passed on to the next node.

Figure 3.7 illustrates the basic operation. A transmitting computer or other device sends a message as a sequence of packets (a). Each packet includes control information indicating the destination station (computer, terminal, etc.). The packets are initially sent to the node to which the sending station attaches. As each packet arrives at this node, it stores the packet briefly, determines the next leg of the route, and queues the packet to go out on that link. Each packet is transmitted to the next node (b) when the link is available. All of the packets eventually work their way through the network and are delivered to the intended destination.

The packet-switching approach has a number of advantages over circuit switching:

- Line efficiency is greater, since a single node-to-node link can be dynamically shared by many packets over time. The packets are queued up and transmitted as rapidly as possible over the link. By contrast, with circuit switching, time on a node-to-node link is preallocated using synchronous time division multiplexing. Much of the time, such a link may be idle because a portion of its time is dedicated to a connection that is idle.

- A packet-switching network can carry out data-rate conversion. Two stations of different data rates can exchange packets, since each connects to its node at its proper data rate.

- When traffic becomes heavy on a circuit-switching network, some calls are blocked; that is, the network refuses to accept additional connection requests until the load on the network decreases. On a packet-switching network, packets are still accepted, but delivery delay increases.

- Priorities can be used. Thus, if a node has a number of packets queued for transmission, it can transmit the higher-priority packets first. These packets will therefore experience less delay than lower-priority packets.

Packet switching also has disadvantages relative to circuit switching:

- Each time a packet passes through a packet-switching node it incurs a delay not present in circuit switching. At a minimum, it incurs a transmission delay equal to the length of the packet in bits divided by the incoming channel rate in bits per second; this is the time it takes to absorb the packet into an internal buffer. In addition, there may be a variable delay due to processing and queuing in the node.

- Because the packets between a given source and destination may vary in length, may take different routes, and may be subject to varying delay in the switches they encounter, the overall packet delay can vary substantially. This phenomenon, called jitter, may not be desirable for some applications (e.g., in real-time applications, including telephone voice and real-time video).

- To route packets through the network, overhead information, including the address of the destination, and often sequencing information must be added to each packet, which reduces the communication capacity available for carrying user data. This is not needed in circuit switching once the circuit is set up.

- More processing is involved in the transfer of information using packet switching than in circuit switching at each node. In the case of circuit switching, there is virtually no processing at each switch once the circuit is set up.

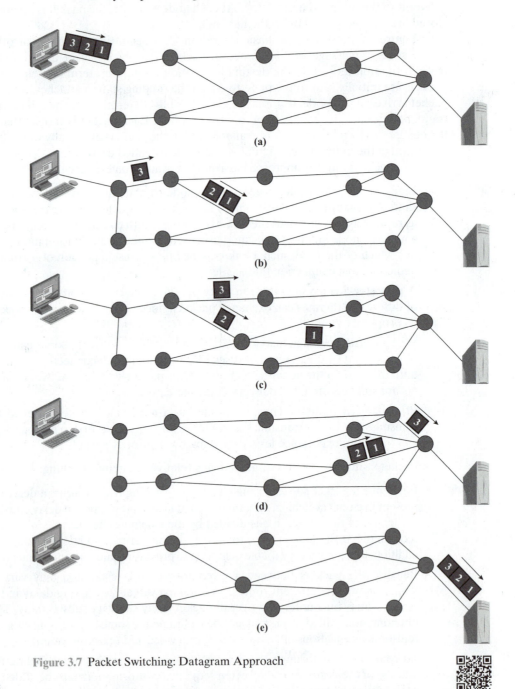

Figure 3.7 Packet Switching: Datagram Approach

Basic Operation

A station has a message to send through a packet-switching network that is of greater length than the maximum packet size. It therefore breaks the message into packets and sends these packets, one at a time, to the network. A question arises as to how the network will handle this stream of packets as it attempts to route them through the network and deliver them to the intended destination. Two approaches are used in contemporary networks: datagram and virtual circuit.

In the **datagram** approach, each packet is treated independently, with no reference to packets that have gone before. This approach is illustrated in Figure 3.7. Each node chooses the next node on a packet's path, taking into account information received from neighboring nodes on traffic, line failures, and so on. So the packets, each with the same destination address, do not all follow the same route (c), and they may arrive out of sequence at the exit point (d). In this example, the exit node restores the packets to their original order before delivering them to the destination (e). In some datagram networks, it is up to the destination rather than the exit node to do the reordering. Also, it is possible for a packet to be destroyed in the network. For example, if a packet-switching node crashes momentarily, all of its queued packets may be lost. Again, it is up to either the exit node or the destination to detect the loss of a packet and decide how to recover it. In this technique, each packet, treated independently, is referred to as a datagram.

In the **virtual circuit** approach, a preplanned route is established before any packets are sent. Once the route is established, all the packets between a pair of communicating parties follow this same route through the network. This is illustrated in Figure 3.8. Because the route is fixed for the duration of the logical connection, it is somewhat similar to a circuit in a circuit-switching network and is referred to as a virtual circuit. Each packet contains a virtual circuit identifier as well as data. Each node on the preestablished route knows where to direct such packets; no routing decisions are required. At any time, each station can have more than one virtual circuit to any other station and can have virtual circuits to more than one station.

So the main characteristic of the virtual circuit technique is that a route between stations is set up prior to data transfer. Note that this does not mean that this is a dedicated path, as in circuit switching. A packet is still buffered at each node and queued for output over a line. The difference from the datagram approach is that, with virtual circuits, the node need not make a routing decision for each packet. It is made only once for all packets using that virtual circuit.

If two stations wish to exchange data over an extended period of time, there are certain advantages to virtual circuits. First, the network may provide services related to the virtual circuit, including sequencing and error control. Sequencing refers to the fact that, because all packets follow the same route, they arrive in the original order. Error control is a service that assures not only that packets arrive in proper sequence, but also that all packets arrive correctly. For example, if a packet in a sequence from node 4 to node 6 fails to arrive at node 6, or arrives with an error, node 6 can request a retransmission of that packet from node 4 (Figure 3.3). Another advantage is that packets should transit the network more rapidly with a virtual circuit; it is not necessary to make a routing decision for each packet at each node.

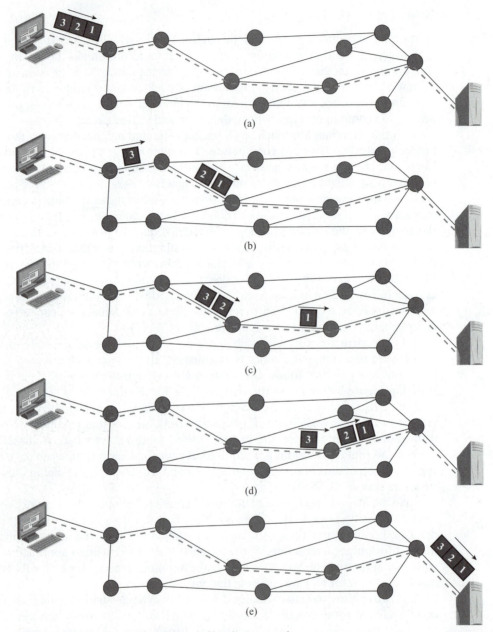

Figure 3.8 Packet Switching: Virtual-Circuit Approach

One advantage of the datagram approach is that the call setup phase is avoided. Thus, if a station wishes to send only one or a few packets, datagram delivery will be quicker. Another advantage of the datagram service is that, because it is more primitive, it is more flexible. For example, if congestion develops in one part of the network, incoming datagrams can be routed away from the congestion. With the use of virtual circuits, packets follow a predefined route, and thus it is more difficult for the network to adapt to congestion. A third advantage is that datagram delivery is inherently more reliable. With the use of virtual circuits, if a node fails, all virtual circuits that pass through that node are lost. With datagram delivery, if a node fails, subsequent packets may find an alternate route that bypasses that node.

Packet Size

There is a significant relationship between packet size and transmission time, as shown in Figure 3.9. In this example, it is assumed that there is a virtual circuit

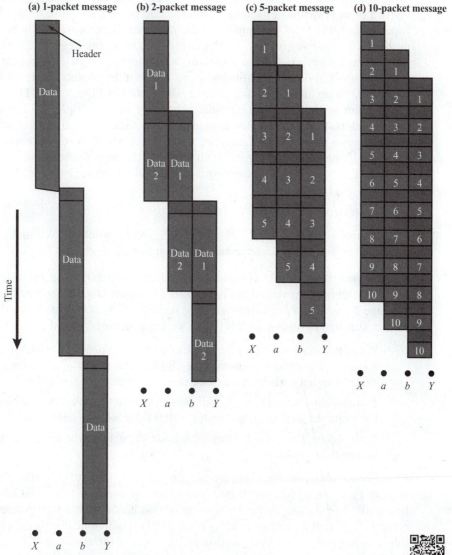

Figure 3.9 Effect of Packet Size on Transmission Time

from station A through nodes 4 and 1 to station B (Figure 3.3). The message to be sent comprises 40 octets, and each packet contains 3 octets of control information, which is placed at the beginning of each packet and is referred to as a header. If the entire message is sent as a single packet of 43 octets (3 octets of header plus 40 octets of data), then the packet is first transmitted from station A to node 4 (Figure 3.9a). When the entire packet is received, it can then be transmitted from 4 to 1. When the entire packet is received at node 1, it is then transferred to station B. Ignoring switching time, total transmission time is 129 octet-times (43 octets × 3 packet transmissions).

Suppose now that we break the message up into two packets, each containing 20 octets of the message and, of course, 3 octets each of header, or control information. In this case, node 4 can begin transmitting the first packet as soon as it has arrived from A, without waiting for the second packet. Because of this overlap in transmission, the total transmission time drops to 92 octet-times. By breaking the message up into five packets, each intermediate node can begin transmission even sooner and the savings in time is greater, with a total of 77 octet-times for transmission. However, this process of using more and smaller packets eventually results in increased, rather than reduced, delay as illustrated in Figure 3.9d. This is because each packet contains a fixed amount of header, and more packets mean more of these headers. Furthermore, the example does not show the processing and queuing delays at each node. These delays are also greater when more packets are handled for a single message. However, we shall see in the next section that an extremely small packet size (53 octets) can result in an efficient network design.

Comparison of Circuit Switching and Packet Switching

We can now compare packet switching with circuit switching. We first look at the important issue of performance and then examine other characteristics.

Performance A simple comparison of circuit switching and the two forms of packet switching is provided in Figure 3.10. The figure depicts the transmission of a message across four nodes, from a source station attached to node 1 to a destination station attached to node 4. In this figure, we are concerned with three types of delay:

- **Propagation delay:** The time it takes a signal to propagate from one node to the next. This time is generally negligible. The speed of electromagnetic signals through a wire medium, for example, is typically 2×10^8 m/s.
- **Transmission time:** The time it takes for a transmitter to send out a block of data. For example, it takes 1 s to transmit a 10,000-bit block of data onto a 10-kbps line.
- **Node delay:** The time it takes for a node to perform the necessary processing as it switches data.

For circuit switching, there is a certain amount of delay before the message can be sent. First, a Call Request signal is sent through the network, to set up a connection to the destination. If the destination station is not busy, a Call Accepted signal returns. Note that a processing delay is incurred at each node during the call request; this time is spent at each node setting up the route of the connection. On the return, this processing is not needed because the connection is already set up. After the connection is set up, the message is sent as a single block, with no noticeable delay at the switching nodes.

Virtual circuit packet switching appears quite similar to circuit switching. A virtual circuit is requested using a Call Request packet, which incurs a delay at each node. The virtual circuit is accepted with a Call Accept packet. In contrast to the circuit-switching case, the call acceptance also experiences node delays, even though the virtual circuit route is now established. The reason is that this packet is queued at each node and must wait its turn for transmission. Once the virtual circuit is established, the message is transmitted in packets. It should be clear that this phase of the operation can be no faster than circuit switching for comparable networks. This is because circuit switching is an essentially transparent process, providing a constant data rate across the network. Packet switching involves some delay at each node in the path. Worse, this delay is variable and will increase with increased load.

Datagram packet switching does not require a call setup. Thus, for short messages, it will be faster than virtual circuit packet switching and perhaps circuit switching. However, because each individual datagram is routed independently, the processing for each datagram at each node may be longer than for virtual circuit packets. Thus, for long messages, the virtual circuit technique may be superior.

Figure 3.10 is intended only to suggest what the relative performance of the techniques might be; actual performance depends on a host of factors, including the

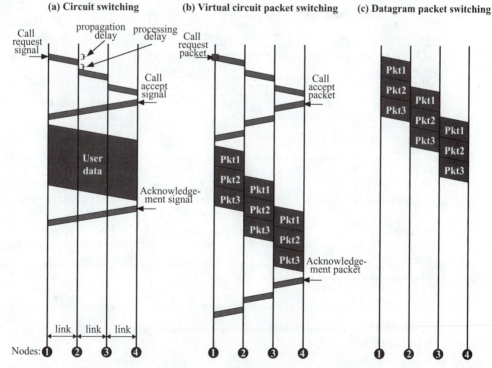

Figure 3.10 Event Timing for Circuit Switching and Packet Switching

size of the network, its topology, the pattern of load, and the characteristics of typical exchanges.

Other Characteristics Besides performance, there are a number of other characteristics that may be considered in comparing the techniques we have been discussing. Table 3.1 summarizes the most important of these. Most of these characteristics have already been discussed. A few additional comments follow. As was mentioned, circuit switching is essentially a transparent service. Once a connection is established, a constant data rate is provided to the connected stations. This is not the case with packet switching, which typically introduces variable delay, so that data arrive in a choppy manner. Indeed, with datagram packet switching, data may arrive in a different order than they were transmitted.

An additional consequence of transparency is that there is no overhead required to accommodate circuit switching. Once a connection is established, the analog or digital data are passed through, as is, from source to destination. For packet switching, analog data must be converted to digital before transmission; in addition, each packet includes overhead bits, such as the destination address.

Table 3.1 Comparison of Communication Switching Techniques

Circuit Switching	Datagram Packet Switching	Virtual Circuit Packet Switching
Dedicated transmission path	No dedicated path	No dedicated path
Continuous transmission of data	Transmission of packets	Transmission of packets
Fast enough for interactive	Fast enough for interactive	Fast enough for interactive
Messages are not stored	Packets may be stored until delivered	Packets stored until delivered
The path is established for entire conversation	Route established for each packet	Route established for entire conversation
Call setup delay; negligible transmission delay	Packet transmission delay	Call setup delay; packet transmission delay
Busy signal if called party busy	Sender may be notified if packet not delivered	Sender notified of connection denial
Overload may block call setup; no delay for established calls	Overload increases packet delay	Overload may block call setup; increases packet delay
Electromechanical or computerized switching nodes	Small switching nodes	Small switching nodes
User responsible for message loss protection	Network may be responsible for individual packets	Network may be responsible for packet sequences
Usually no speed or code conversion	Speed and code conversion	Speed and code conversion
Fixed bandwidth	Dynamic use of bandwidth	Dynamic use of bandwidth
No overhead bits after call setup	Overhead bits in each packet	Overhead bits in each packet

3.5 QUALITY OF SERVICE

Quality of service (QoS) in packet-switching networks usually pertains to the performance of a stream of related packets. For example, these packets can be related to each other by being part of a common stream of video, coming from the same file, or being from a series of interactions by the same user. The following categories of traffic are typically considered.

Voice, Audio, and Video Traffic

Packets may all be part of a stream of packets from a common voice, audio, or multimedia (i.e., video) presentation. This type of traffic requires steady delivery of packets, which translates into requirements for delay, delay variation (also called jitter), and some amount of throughput to meet the data rate of the presentation. While voice is of course audio, it has been given special attention, especially for cellular telephone networks. Additional specific requirements can typically be broken into three categories, each of which we will consider in the context of video.

- **Streaming live video** comes from occasions such as live sporting events. This is one-way video. Some expectation of recency, say within a few second delay, is expected. People would not enjoy hearing neighbors celebrate an important score when they had not seen it yet.

- **Streaming stored video** comes from sites such as YouTube where a presentation has been stored and is played to the recipient of the data stream. The recency of the data stream is not important, so several seconds of video can be buffered to overcome irregularities in traffic delivery.

- **Video conferencing** involves two-way communication. Traditionally this has involved voice, but video is now very common for both professional and personal use. In such traffic, there is an expectation of bounded round trip delay between when a person speaks and when a response would be expected in normal human interaction.

Video conferencing has strong constraints on delay, typically on the order of 200 to 300 ms round trip delay. Wireless communication links are typically the first and last of many hops between two wireless users. Therefore, they will have lower requirements; for example, LTE traffic types require less than 100 ms for conversational voice and 150 ms for conversational video.

Voice, audio, and video traffic can be generalized under the term of **real-time traffic**, in which delay and delay variation constraints are of paramount importance. Interestingly, however, this type of traffic sometimes can have a *less* stringent requirement on packet loss. If a voice over IP packet stream is 50 packets per second, losing 2% (1 packet per second) might be imperceptible, or at least tolerable.

There is a balance between compression and packet loss with voice, audio, and video. High levels of compression are always used for this traffic in wireless networks. Instead of carrying voice using compact-disk quality audio (44.1 ksamples/sec with 16 bits per sample = 705,600 bits/s), compression schemes discussed in Chapter 7 can achieve as low as 1 to 2 kbps with acceptable quality; a factor of 700 times compression. But loss of single packets causes tremendous impact in these methods, since the compression schemes have large dependencies between packets. Instead, most cellular voice communications uses compression rates 7 to 13 kbps to strike a reasonable balance between packet loss rate requirements and delay requirements.

Data Traffic

While some packet loss is tolerable for real-time traffic, data traffic requires packets to eventually arrive free from error. They can be retransmitted or corrected, as discussed in Chapter 10, so they need not be entirely free from errors at first transmission. One might also categorize data traffic in two categories.

- **Interactive data traffic** exists when people wait for data to be delivered before proceeding with anything else. This might include waiting for a Web page to load or for an online transaction to complete.
- **Non-interactive data traffic** occurs in the background while people are performing other activities. This would involve electronic mail or other types of batch processing or downloading activities.

For data traffic, throughput is somewhat more important than delay, although they are certainly related. And interactive data traffic would have more expectation of steady provision of this throughput.

Data traffic is also considered **elastic**. Data is typically delivered in files and it is the final delivery time of those files which is important, not the steady delivery of bits in the middle. This is in definite contrast to real-time traffic, so data traffic is also commonly called **non-real-time traffic**.

Example 3.2   Consider the delivery of a 10 Mbyte audio file over an LTE connection with an average rate of 2 Mbps.

The expected delivery time would be

$$(10 \times 10^6 \text{ bytes})(8 \text{ bits/byte})/(2 \times 10^6 \text{ bits/s}) = 40 \text{ s}$$

Here are three of many ways this could be delivered.

1. Steady 2 Mbps for 40 s
2. 10 Mbps for 4 s, 0.5 Mbps for 20 s, 0 Mbps for 26 s, 3 Mbps for the last 10 s.
3. 0 Mbps for 38 s, 40 Mbps for 2 s.

As long as a person watching the download does think something is wrong and quits the download early, all are acceptable.

This elastic property has been used to great advantage in data networks. Several protocols, especially TCP discussed in the next chapter, dynamically adjust their sending rates based on traffic conditions. This avoids exacerbated congestion from nodes trying to retransmit when network conditions might already be poor.

Wireless protocols can also adapt their sending rates to the changes in the wireless channel to avoid undue packet loss.

Provision of QoS

There are three basic methods by which different technologies provide support for QoS.

- **Overprovisioning** delivers sufficiently high data rates and low congestion for a very large percentage of the time. Therefore, no explicit knowledge of QoS requirements or control of resources to meet QoS is necessary. Commonly discussed along with overprovisioning is the concept of **best effort** traffic. The network does nothing special with particular traffic, but does its best to make timely deliveries.

- **Prioritization without guarantees** is a scheme where certain types of users (such as emergency users or high paying users) have their packets marked higher priority. Scheduling schemes give those packets higher priority when making decisions. But if there is congestion, the higher priority packet will receive relatively better service, but degraded service nonetheless.

- **Prioritization with guarantees** provides numerical bounds on performance, also possibly with some statistical reliability. For example, packets might receive delay less than 100 ms 99.9% of the time.

Different communication systems will use their own terminology to describe the concepts and traffic types above. They also will provide a combination of the QoS provisioning approaches as well. Typically user traffic is tagged in different categories. Some might simply be best effort; packets receive resources as the network finds them available and those users are generally content. Users with more stringent demands can tag their packets in categories that are provided prioritization with or without guarantees. They also agree to limit the amount of such traffic they provide to the network. One way the network could provide guarantees is to give a traffic stream a regularly occurring schedule of time slots. In other cases, traffic might be scheduled according to a complex combination of considerations for delay, QoS requirements, channel conditions, fairness, user priority, etc.

For wireless systems, communication commonly occurs over one hop between a node and a base station or access point. Therefore, it might seem that the discussion of circuit switching and packet switching is somewhat irrelevant. But circuit-switching concepts are important for another reason, and that is to provide mechanisms to establish QoS relationships between packets, streams of packets, and the network mechanisms to provide that QoS.

3.6 RECOMMENDED READING

As befits its age, circuit switching has inspired a voluminous literature. Two good books on the subject are [BELL00] and [FREE04]. The literature on packet switching is also enormous. [BERT92] provides a good treatment.

[STAL14] covers all of the topics in this chapter in greater detail.

BELL00 Bellamy, J. *Digital Telephony.* New York: Wiley, 2000.

BERT92 Bertsekas, D., and Gallager, R. *Data Networks.* Englewood Cliffs, NJ: Prentice Hall, 1992.

FREE04 Freeman, R. *Telecommunication System Engineering.* New York: Wiley, 2004.

STAL14 Stallings, W. *Data and Computer Communications, Tenth Edition.* Upper Saddle River, NJ: Pearson, 2014.

3.7 KEY TERMS, REVIEW QUESTIONS, AND PROBLEMS

Key Terms

best effort	local loop	packet switching
circuit switching	metropolitan area network	real-time traffic
datagram	(MAN)	subscriber loop
elastic traffic	non-real-time traffic	wide area network
header	overprovisioning	(WAN)
local area network (LAN)	packets	

Review Questions

3.1 Differentiate between WANs and LANs.

3.2 Why is it useful to have more than one possible path through a network for each pair of stations?

3.3 What is the principal application that has driven the design of circuit-switching networks?

3.4 Distinguish between static and alternate routing in a circuit-switching network.

3.5 What is a semipermanent connection?

3.6 Explain the difference between datagram and virtual circuit operation.

3.7 What are some of the limitations of using a circuit-switching network for data transmission?

3.8 If people are receiving poor quality video, what QoS requirements might not be being met?

Problems

3.1 Define the following parameters for a switching network:

N = number of hops between two given end systems
L = message length in bits
B = data rate, in bits per second (bps), on all links
P = fixed packet size, in bits
H = overhead (header) bits per packet
S = call setup time (circuit switching or virtual circuit) in seconds
T = call teardown time (circuit switching or virtual circuit) in seconds
D = propagation delay per hop in seconds

   a. For $N = 4, L = 3000, B = 9600, P = 1080, H = 80, S = 0.2, T = 0.02, D = 0.001$, compute the end-to-end delay for circuit switching, virtual circuit packet switching, and datagram packet switching. Assume that there are no acknowledgments. Ignore processing delay at the nodes. Assume no header for circuit switching.

   b. Derive general expressions for the three techniques of part (a), taken two at a time (three expressions in all), showing the conditions under which the delays are equal.

3.2   What value of P, as a function of N, L, and H, results in minimum end-to-end delay on a datagram network? Assume that L is much larger than P, and D is zero.

3.3   For Problem 3.1, the main cost for datagram switching is waiting at each node for the full packet to arrive before it can be sent onward. For circuit switching, the main cost is the setup time. Given the same parameters as Figure 3.1, for what range of the number of hops N would circuit switching have lower end-to-end delay than datagram switching? Here use setup time $S = 0.35$ s and teardown time $T = 0.02$ s.

3.4   Use the scenario from Problem 3.1a, except there is a nonzero processing delay for both virtual circuit switching (T_{VC}) and datagram switching (T_D). Processing delay is always defined as the time per node to process a packet. This processing delay is only incurred for the nodes which send packets, which includes processing time at the first node. The processing delay for datagram switching is always larger, since the node has to make routing decisions instead of just switching decisions for getting the packet to its destination. Assume the processing delay for a virtual circuit switched packet at each node is $T_{VC} = 0.0035$ s. Now compare with datagram packet switching. Find the range of processing delays (T_D) for which virtual circuit switching has a lower end-to-end delay than datagram packet switching.

3.5   Given now is the scenario from Problem 3.4, but $T_D = 14.5$ ms and $T_{VC} = 3$ ms. Assume the number of packets to transfer is unknown. For what range numbers of packets would the end-to-end delay to transfer all of the packets be less for virtual circuit switching than the datagram approach? For what range of sizes of the total message length does this correspond?

3.6   Consider a simple telephone network consisting of two end offices and one intermediate switch with a 1-MHz full-duplex trunk between each end office and the intermediate switch. The average telephone is used to make four calls per 8-hour workday, with a mean call duration of six minutes. Ten percent of the calls are long distance. What is the maximum number of telephones an end office can support?

3.7   Explain the flaw in the following reasoning: Packet switching requires control and address bits to be added to each packet. This introduces considerable overhead in packet switching. In circuit switching, a transparent circuit is established. No extra bits are needed. Therefore, there is no overhead in circuit switching, and, because there is no overhead in circuit switching, line utilization must be more efficient than in packet switching.

3.8   Assuming no malfunction in any of the stations or nodes of a network, is it possible for a packet to be delivered to the wrong destination?

3.9   Consider a packet-switching network of N nodes, connected by the following topologies:

   a. Star: One central node with no attached station; all other nodes attach to the central node.

   b. Loop: Each node connects to two other nodes to form a closed loop.

   c. Fully connected: Each node is directly connected to all other nodes.

   For each case, give the average number of hops between stations.

CHAPTER 4

Protocols and the TCP/IP Suite

LEARNING OBJECTIVES

After studying this chapter, you should be able to:

- Describe the importance and objectives of a layered protocol architecture.
- Explain the process of protocol encapsulation where PDUs are handed to different layers and headers are added for control purposes.
- Describe the TCP/IP architecture and explain the functioning of each layer.
- Explain the need for internetworking.
- Describe the operation of a router within the context of TCP/IP to provide internetworking.

We begin this chapter by introducing the concept of a layered protocol architecture. We then examine the most important such architecture, the TCP/IP protocol suite. TCP/IP is an Internet-based concept and is the framework for developing a complete range of computer communications standards. Virtually all computer vendors now provide support for this architecture. Another well-known architecture is the Open Systems Interconnection (OSI) reference model. OSI is a standardized architecture that is often used to describe communications functions but that is now rarely implemented.

Following a discussion of protocol architectures, the important concept of internetworking is examined. Inevitably, an organization will require the use of more than one communication network. Some means of interconnecting these networks is required, and this raises issues that relate to the protocol architecture.

4.1 THE NEED FOR A PROTOCOL ARCHITECTURE

When computers, terminals, and/or other data-processing devices exchange data, the procedures involved can be quite complex. Consider, for example, the transfer of a file between two computers. There must be a data path between the two computers, either directly or via a communication network. But more is needed. Typical tasks to be performed are

1. The source system must either activate the direct data communication path or inform the communication network of the identity of the desired destination system.

2. The source system must ascertain that the destination system is prepared to receive data.

3. The file transfer application on the source system must ascertain that the file management program on the destination system is prepared to accept and store the file for this particular user.

4. If the file formats used on the two systems are incompatible, one or the other system must perform a format translation function.

It is clear that there must be a high degree of cooperation between the two computer systems. Instead of implementing the logic for this as a single module, the task is broken up into subtasks, each of which is implemented separately. In a **protocol architecture**, the modules are arranged in a vertical stack. Each layer in the stack performs a related subset of the functions required to communicate with another system. It relies on the next lower layer to perform more primitive functions and to conceal the details of those functions. It provides services to the next higher layer. Ideally, layers should be defined so that changes in one layer do not require changes in other layers.

Of course, it takes two to communicate, so the same set of layered functions must exist in two systems. Communication is achieved by having the corresponding, or *peer*, layers in two systems communicate. The peer layers communicate by means of formatted blocks of data that obey a set of rules or conventions known as a ***protocol***. The key features of a protocol are

- Syntax: Concerns the format of the data blocks
- Semantics: Includes control information for coordination and error handling
- Timing: Includes speed matching and sequencing

4.2 THE TCP/IP PROTOCOL ARCHITECTURE

The TCP/IP protocol architecture is a result of protocol research and development conducted on the experimental packet-switched network, ARPANET, funded by the Defense Advanced Research Projects Agency (DARPA), and is generally referred to as the TCP/IP protocol suite. This protocol suite consists of a large collection of protocols that have been issued as Internet standards by the Internet Architecture Board (IAB).

The TCP/IP Layers

In general terms, communications can be said to involve three agents: applications, computers, and networks. Examples of applications include file transfer and electronic mail. The applications that we are concerned with here are distributed applications that involve the exchange of data between two computer systems. These applications, and others, execute on computers that can often support multiple simultaneous applications. Computers are connected to networks, and the data to be exchanged are transferred by the network from one computer to another. Thus, the transfer of data from one application to another involves first getting the data to the computer in which the application resides and then getting the data to the intended application within the computer.

With these concepts in mind, it appears natural to organize the communication task into five relatively independent layers:

- Physical layer
- Network access layer
- Internet layer
- Host-to-host, or transport layer
- Application layer

The **physical layer** covers the physical interface between a data transmission device (e.g., workstation, computer) and a transmission medium or network. This layer is concerned with specifying the characteristics of the transmission medium, the nature of the signals, the data rate, and related matters.

The **network access layer** is concerned with the exchange of data between an end system (server, workstation, etc.) and the network to which it is attached. The sending computer must provide the network with the address of the destination computer, so that the network may route the data to the appropriate destination. The sending computer may wish to invoke certain services, such as priority, that might be provided by the network. The specific software used at this layer depends on the type of network to be used; different standards have been developed for circuit switching, packet switching (e.g., ATM), LANs (e.g., Ethernet), and others. Thus it makes sense to separate those functions having to do with network access into a separate layer. By doing this, the remainder of the communications software, above the network access layer, need not be concerned about the specifics of the network to be used. The same higher-layer software should function properly regardless of the particular network to which the computer is attached.

The network access layer is concerned with access to and routing data across a network for two end systems attached to the same network. In those cases where two devices are attached to different networks, procedures are needed to allow data to traverse multiple interconnected networks. This is the function of the **internet layer**. The **Internet Protocol (IP)** is used at this layer to provide the routing function across multiple networks. This protocol is implemented not only in the end systems but also in routers. A router is a processor that connects two networks and whose primary function is to relay data from one network to the other on its route from the source to the destination end system.

Regardless of the nature of the applications that are exchanging data, there is usually a requirement that data be exchanged reliably. That is, we would like to be assured that all of the data arrive at the destination application and that the data arrive in the same order in which they were sent. As we shall see, the mechanisms for providing reliability are essentially independent of the nature of the applications. Thus, it makes sense to collect those mechanisms in a common layer shared by all applications; this is referred to as the **host-to-host layer**, or **transport layer**. The **Transmission Control Protocol (TCP)** is the most commonly used protocol to provide this functionality.

Finally, the **application layer** contains the logic needed to support the various user applications. For each different type of application, such as file transfer, a separate module is needed that is peculiar to that application.

Operation of TCP and IP

Figure 4.1 indicates how these protocols are configured for communications. To make clear that the total communications facility may consist of multiple networks, the constituent networks are usually referred to as *subnetworks*. Some sort of network access protocol, such as the Ethernet logic, is used to connect a computer to a subnetwork. This protocol enables the host to send data across the subnetwork to another host or, in the case of a host on another subnetwork,

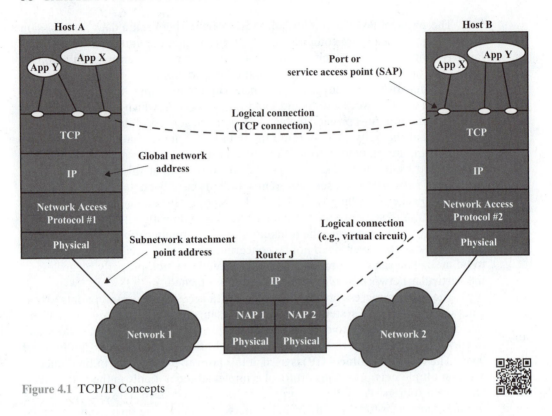

Figure 4.1 TCP/IP Concepts

to a router. IP is implemented in all of the end systems and the routers. It acts as a relay to move a block of data from one host, through one or more routers, to another host. TCP is implemented only in the end systems; it keeps track of the blocks of data to assure that all are delivered reliably to the appropriate application.

For successful communication, every entity in the overall system must have a unique address. Actually, two levels of addressing are needed. Each host on a subnetwork must have a unique global internet address; this allows the data to be delivered to the proper host. Each process with a host must have an address that is unique within the host; this allows the host-to-host protocol (TCP) to deliver data to the proper process. These latter addresses are known as **ports**.

Let us trace a simple operation. Suppose that a process, associated with port 1 at host A, wishes to send a message to another process, associated with port 3 at host B. The process at A hands the message down to TCP with instructions to send it to host B, port 3. TCP hands the message down to IP with instructions to send it to host B. Note that IP need not be told the identity of the destination port. All it needs to know is that the data are intended for host B. Next, IP hands the message down to the network access layer (e.g., Ethernet logic) with instructions to send it to router J (the first hop on the way to B).

To control this operation, control information as well as user data must be transmitted, as suggested in Figure 4.2. Let us say that the sending process generates

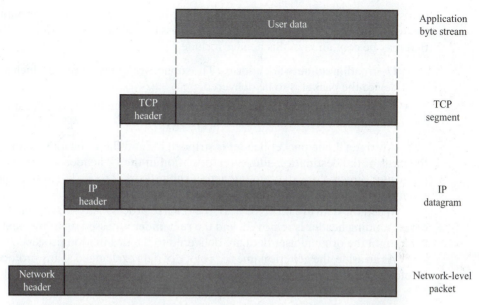

Figure 4.2 Protocol Data Units (PDUs) in the TCP/IP Architecture

a block of data and passes it to TCP. TCP may break this block into smaller pieces to make it more manageable. To each of these pieces, TCP appends control information known as the **TCP header**, forming a *TCP segment*. The control information is to be used by the peer TCP protocol entity at host B. Examples of items in this header include

- **Destination port:** When the TCP entity at B receives the segment, it must know to whom the data are to be delivered.

- **Sequence number:** TCP numbers the segments that it sends to a particular destination port sequentially, so that if they arrive out of order, the TCP entity at B can reorder them.

- **Checksum:** The sending TCP includes a code that is a function of the contents of the remainder of the segment. The receiving TCP performs the same calculation and compares the result with the incoming code. A discrepancy results if there has been some error in transmission.

Next, TCP hands each segment over to IP, with instructions to transmit it to B. These segments must be transmitted across one or more subnetworks and relayed through one or more intermediate routers. This operation, too, requires the use of control information. Thus, IP appends a header of control information to each segment to form an *IP datagram*. An example of an item stored in the IP header is the destination host address (in this example, B).

Finally, each IP datagram is presented to the network access layer for transmission across the first subnetwork in its journey to the destination. The network access layer appends its own header, creating a packet, or frame. The packet is transmitted across the subnetwork to router J. The packet header contains the information that the subnetwork needs to transfer the data across the subnetwork. Examples of items that may be contained in this header include

- **Destination subnetwork address:** The subnetwork must know to which attached device the packet is to be delivered.
- **Facilities requests:** The network access protocol might request the use of certain subnetwork facilities, such as priority.

At router J, the packet header is stripped off and the IP header examined. On the basis of the destination address information in the IP header, the IP module in the router directs the datagram out across subnetwork 2 to B. To do this, the datagram is again augmented with a network access layer header.

When the data are received at B, the reverse process occurs. At each layer, the corresponding header is removed, and the remainder is passed on to the next higher layer, until the original user data are delivered to the destination process.

As an aside, the generic name for a block of data exchanged at any protocol level is referred to as a **protocol data unit (PDU)**. Thus, a TCP segment is a TCP PDU.

TCP/IP Applications

A number of applications have been standardized to operate on top of TCP. We mention three of the most common here.

The **Simple Mail Transfer Protocol (SMTP)** provides a basic electronic mail facility. It provides a mechanism for transferring messages among separate hosts. Features of SMTP include mailing lists, return receipts, and forwarding. SMTP does not specify the way in which messages are to be created; some local editing or native electronic mail facility is required. Once a message is created, SMTP accepts the message and makes use of TCP to send it to an SMTP module on another host. The target SMTP module will make use of a local electronic mail package to store the incoming message in a user's mailbox.

The **File Transfer Protocol (FTP)** is used to send files from one system to another under user command. Both text and binary files are accommodated, and the protocol provides features for controlling user access. When a user wishes to engage in file transfer, FTP sets up a TCP connection to the target system for the exchange of control messages. This connection allows user ID and password to be transmitted and allows the user to specify the file and file actions desired. Once a file transfer is approved, a second TCP connection is set up for the data transfer. The file is transferred over the data connection, without the overhead of any headers or control information at the application level. When the transfer is complete, the control connection is used to signal the completion and to accept new file transfer commands.

The **Hypertext Transfer Protocol (HTTP)** is the foundation protocol of the World Wide Web. It is a protocol for transmitting information by making use of hypertext jumps. The data transferred by the protocol can be plaintext, hypertext, audio, images, or any Internet-accessible information. HTTP is a transaction-oriented client/server protocol. The most typical use of HTTP is between a Web browser and a Web server. To provide reliability, HTTP makes use of TCP. Nevertheless, HTTP is a stateless protocol: Each transaction is treated independently. Accordingly, a typical implementation will create a new TCP connection between client and server for each transaction and then terminate the connection as soon as the transaction completes.

4.3 THE OSI MODEL

The Open Systems Interconnection (OSI) reference model was developed by the International Organization for Standardization (ISO)[1] as a model for a computer protocol architecture and as a framework for developing protocol standards. The OSI model consists of seven layers:

- Application
- Presentation
- Session
- Transport
- Network
- Data link
- Physical

Figure 4.3 illustrates the OSI model and provides a brief definition of the functions performed at each layer. The intent of the OSI model is that protocols be developed to perform the functions of each layer.

The designers of OSI assumed that this model and the protocols developed within this model would come to dominate computer communications, eventually replacing proprietary protocol implementations and rival multivendor models such as TCP/IP. This has not happened. Networking technologies are still commonly described relative to the layers of the OSI model, however. Although many useful protocols have been developed in the context of OSI, the overall seven-layer model has not flourished. Instead, the TCP/IP architecture has come to dominate. There are a number of reasons for this outcome. Perhaps the most important is that the key TCP/IP protocols were mature and well tested at a time when similar OSI protocols were in the development stage. When businesses began to recognize the need for interoperability across networks, only TCP/IP was available and ready to go. Another reason is that the OSI model is unnecessarily complex, with seven layers to accomplish what TCP/IP does with fewer layers.

Figure 4.4 illustrates the layers of the TCP/IP and OSI architectures, showing roughly the correspondence in functionality between the two.

---

[1]ISO is not an acronym (in which case it would be IOS), but a word, derived from the Greek *isos*, meaning *equal*.

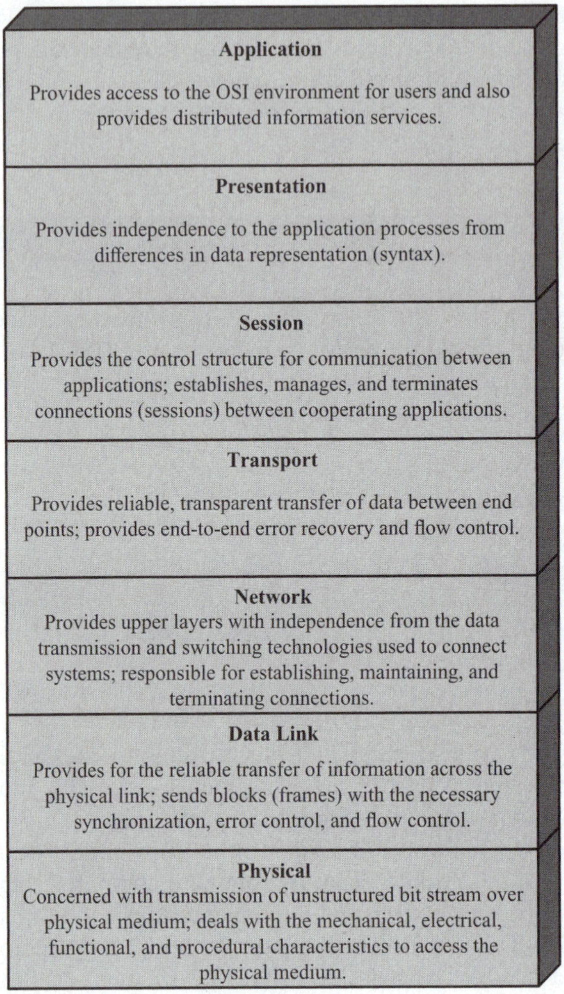

Application Provides access to the OSI environment for users and also provides distributed information services.
Presentation Provides independence to the application processes from differences in data representation (syntax).
Session Provides the control structure for communication between applications; establishes, manages, and terminates connections (sessions) between cooperating applications.
Transport Provides reliable, transparent transfer of data between end points; provides end-to-end error recovery and flow control.
Network Provides upper layers with independence from the data transmission and switching technologies used to connect systems; responsible for establishing, maintaining, and terminating connections.
Data Link Provides for the reliable transfer of information across the physical link; sends blocks (frames) with the necessary synchronization, error control, and flow control.
Physical Concerned with transmission of unstructured bit stream over physical medium; deals with the mechanical, electrical, functional, and procedural characteristics to access the physical medium.

Figure 4.3 The OSI Layers

4.4 INTERNETWORKING

In most cases, a LAN or WAN is not an isolated entity. An organization may have more than one type of LAN at a given site to satisfy a spectrum of needs. An organization may have multiple LANs of the same type at a given site to accommodate performance or security requirements. And an organization may have LANs at various sites and need them to be interconnected via WANs for central control of distributed information exchange.

Table 4.1 lists some commonly used terms relating to the interconnection of networks, or **internetworking**. An interconnected set of networks, from a user's point of view, may appear simply as a larger network. However, if each of the constituent

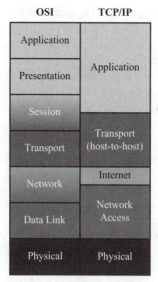

Figure 4.4 A Comparison of the OSI and TCP/IP Protocol Architectures

Table 4.1 Internetworking Terms

Communication Network

A facility that provides a data transfer service among devices attached to the network.

Internet

A collection of communication networks interconnected by bridges and/or routers.

Intranet

An internet used by a single organization that provides the key Internet applications, especially the World Wide Web. An intranet operates within the organization for internal purposes and can exist as an isolated, self-contained internet, or may have links to the Internet.

End System (ES)

A device attached to one of the networks of an internet that is used to support end-user applications or services.

Intermediate System (IS)

A device used to connect two networks and permit communication between end systems attached to different networks.

Bridge

An IS used to connect two LANs that use similar LAN protocols. The bridge acts as an address filter, picking up packets from one LAN that are intended for a destination on another LAN and passing those packets on. The bridge does not modify the contents of the packets and does not add anything to the packet. The bridge operates at layer 2 of the OSI model.

Router

An IS used to connect two networks that may or may not be similar. The router employs an internet protocol present in each router and each end system of the network. The router operates at layer 3 of the OSI model.

networks retains its identity, and special mechanisms are needed for communicating across multiple networks, then the entire configuration is often referred to as an **internet**. The most important example of an internet is referred to simply as the Internet. As the Internet has evolved from its modest beginnings as a research-oriented packet-switching network, it has served as the basis for the development of internetworking technology and as the model for private internets within organizations. These latter are also referred to as **intranets**.

Each constituent subnetwork in an internet supports communication among the devices attached to that subnetwork; these devices are referred to as **end systems** (ESs). In addition, subnetworks are connected by devices referred to in the ISO documents as **intermediate systems** (ISs). ISs provide a communications path and perform the necessary relaying and routing functions so that data can be exchanged between devices attached to different subnetworks in the internet.

Two types of ISs of particular interest are bridges and routers. The differences between them have to do with the types of protocols used for the internetworking logic. In essence, a **bridge** operates at layer 2 of the OSI seven-layer architecture and acts as a relay of frames between like networks. A **router** operates at layer 3 of the OSI architecture and routes packets between potentially different networks. Both the bridge and the router assume that the same upper-layer protocols are in use.

The roles and functions of routers were introduced in the context of IP earlier in this chapter. However, because of the importance of routers in the overall networking scheme, it is worth providing additional comment in this section.

Routers

Internetworking among dissimilar subnetworks is achieved by using routers to interconnect the subnetworks. Essential functions that the router must perform include the following:

1. Provide a link between networks.
2. Provide for the routing and delivery of data between processes on end systems attached to different networks.
3. Provide these functions in such a way as not to require modifications of the networking architecture of any of the attached subnetworks.

The third point implies that the router must accommodate a number of differences among networks, such as

- **Addressing schemes:** The networks may use different schemes for assigning addresses to devices. For example, an IEEE 802 LAN uses 48-bit binary addresses for each attached device; an ATM network typically uses 15-digit decimal addresses (encoded as 4 bits per digit for a 60-bit address). Some form of global network addressing must be provided, as well as a directory service.

- **Maximum packet sizes:** Packets from one network may have to be broken into smaller pieces to be transmitted on another network, a process known as **segmentation** or **fragmentation**. For example, Ethernet imposes a maximum packet size of 1500 bytes; a maximum packet size of 1000 bytes is common on X.25 packet-switching networks. A packet that is transmitted on an Ethernet system and picked up by a router for retransmission on an X.25 network may have to be fragmented into two smaller ones.

- **Interfaces:** The hardware and software interfaces to various networks differ. The concept of a router must be independent of these differences.

- **Reliability:** Various network services may provide anything from a reliable end-to-end virtual circuit to an unreliable service. The operation of the routers should not depend on an assumption of network reliability.

The preceding requirements are best satisfied by an internetworking protocol, such as IP, that is implemented in all end systems and routers.

Internetworking Example

Figure 4.5 depicts a configuration that we will use to illustrate the interactions among protocols for internetworking. In this case, we focus on a server attached to an ATM WAN and a workstation attached to an IEEE 802 LAN, with a router connecting the two networks.[2] The router will provide a link between the server and the

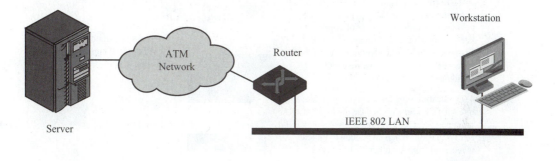

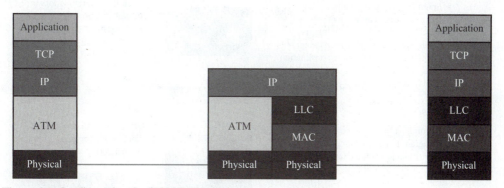

Figure 4.5 Configuration for TCP/IP Example

---

[2]Chapter 11 describes the IEEE 802 protocol architecture. For now, you need to know that the architecture consists of a physical layer; a medium access control (MAC) layer concerned with addressing and error control, and a logical link control (LLC) layer, concerned with logical connections and identifying the user of LLC.

workstation that enables these end systems to ignore the details of the intervening networks.

Figures 4.6 (sender), 4.7 (router), and 4.8 (receiver) outline typical steps in the transfer of a block of data, such as a file or a Web page, from the server, through an internet, and ultimately to an application in the workstation. In this example, the message passes through just one router. Before data can be transmitted, the application and transport layers in the server establish, with the corresponding layer

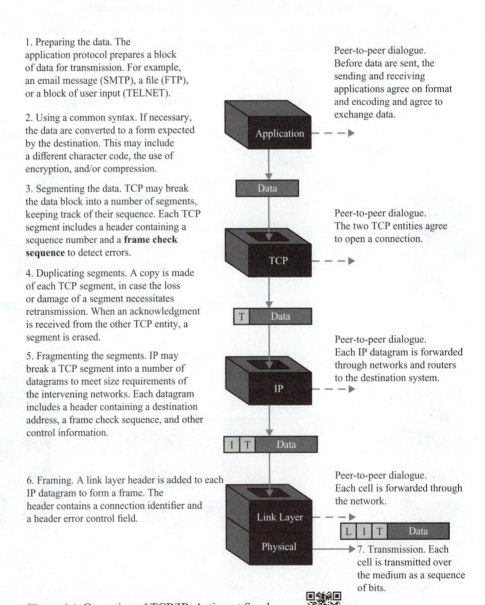

1. Preparing the data. The application protocol prepares a block of data for transmission. For example, an email message (SMTP), a file (FTP), or a block of user input (TELNET).

2. Using a common syntax. If necessary, the data are converted to a form expected by the destination. This may include a different character code, the use of encryption, and/or compression.

3. Segmenting the data. TCP may break the data block into a number of segments, keeping track of their sequence. Each TCP segment includes a header containing a sequence number and a **frame check sequence** to detect errors.

4. Duplicating segments. A copy is made of each TCP segment, in case the loss or damage of a segment necessitates retransmission. When an acknowledgment is received from the other TCP entity, a segment is erased.

5. Fragmenting the segments. IP may break a TCP segment into a number of datagrams to meet size requirements of the intervening networks. Each datagram includes a header containing a destination address, a frame check sequence, and other control information.

6. Framing. A link layer header is added to each IP datagram to form a frame. The header contains a connection identifier and a header error control field.

Peer-to-peer dialogue. Before data are sent, the sending and receiving applications agree on format and encoding and agree to exchange data.

Peer-to-peer dialogue. The two TCP entities agree to open a connection.

Peer-to-peer dialogue. Each IP datagram is forwarded through networks and routers to the destination system.

Peer-to-peer dialogue. Each cell is forwarded through the network.

7. Transmission. Each cell is transmitted over the medium as a sequence of bits.

Figure 4.6 Operation of TCP/IP: Action at Sender

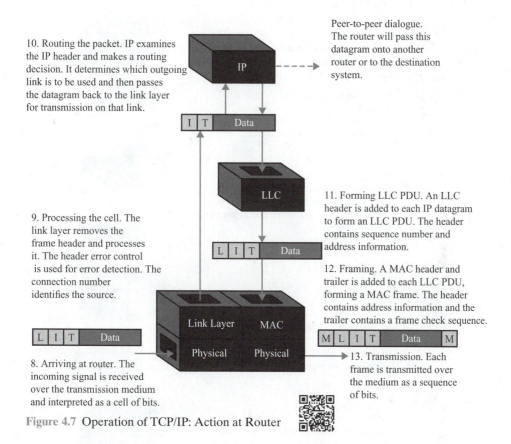

10. Routing the packet. IP examines the IP header and makes a routing decision. It determines which outgoing link is to be used and then passes the datagram back to the link layer for transmission on that link.

Peer-to-peer dialogue. The router will pass this datagram onto another router or to the destination system.

9. Processing the cell. The link layer removes the frame header and processes it. The header error control is used for error detection. The connection number identifies the source.

11. Forming LLC PDU. An LLC header is added to each IP datagram to form an LLC PDU. The header contains sequence number and address information.

12. Framing. A MAC header and trailer is added to each LLC PDU, forming a MAC frame. The header contains address information and the trailer contains a frame check sequence.

8. Arriving at router. The incoming signal is received over the transmission medium and interpreted as a cell of bits.

13. Transmission. Each frame is transmitted over the medium as a sequence of bits.

Figure 4.7 Operation of TCP/IP: Action at Router

in the workstation, the applicable ground rules for a communication session. These include character code to be used, error-checking method, and the like. The protocol at each layer is used for this purpose and then is used in the transmission of the message.

4.5 RECOMMENDED READING

[STAL14] provides a detailed description of the TCP/IP model and of the standards at each layer of the model. For the reader interested in greater detail on TCP/IP, [COME14] is considered a definitive source.

COME14 Comer, D. *Internetworking with TCP/IP, Volume I: Principles, Protocols, and Architecture*. Upper Saddle River, NJ: Pearson, 2014.

STAL14 Stallings, W. *Data and Computer Communications, Tenth Edition*. Upper Saddle River: NJ: Pearson, 2014.

20. Delivering the data. The application performs any needed transformations, including decompression and decryption, and directs the data to the appropriate file or other destination.

19. Reassembling user data. If TCP has broken the user data into multiple segments, these are reassembled and the block is passed up to the application.

18. Processing the TCP segment. TCP removes the header. It checks the frame check sequence and acknowledges if there is a match and discards for mismatch. Flow control is also performed.

17. Processing the IP datagram. IP removes the header. The frame check sequence and other control information are processed.

16. Processing the LLC PDU. The LLC layer removes the header and processes it. The sequence number is used for flow and error control.

15. Processing the frame. The MAC layer removes the header and trailer and processes them. The frame check sequence is used for error detection.

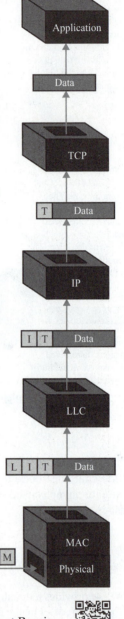

14. Arriving at destination. The incoming signal is received over the transmission medium and interpreted as a frame of bits.

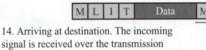

Figure 4.8 Operation of TCP/IP: Action at Receiver

4.6 KEY TERMS, REVIEW QUESTIONS, AND PROBLEMS

Key Terms

application layer	internetworking	router
checksum	network layer	service access point (SAP)
frame check sequence (FCS)	physical layer	Transmission Control
header	port	Protocol (TCP)
internet	protocol	transport layer
Internet Protocol (IP)	protocol architecture protocol	User Datagram Protocol
intranet IPv6	data unit (PDU)	(UDP)

Review Questions

4.1 What is the major function of the network access layer?

4.2 What tasks are performed by the transport layer?

4.3 What is a protocol?

4.4 What is a protocol data unit (PDU)?

4.5 What is a protocol architecture?

4.6 What is TCP/IP?

4.7 What are some advantages to layering as seen in the TCP/IP architecture?

4.8 What is a router?

Problems

4.1 Using the layer models in Figure 4.9, describe the ordering and delivery of a pizza, indicating the interactions at each level.

4.2 a. The French and Chinese prime ministers need to come to an agreement by telephone, but neither speaks the other's language. Further, neither has on hand a translator that can translate to the language of the other. However, both prime ministers have English translators on their staffs. Draw a diagram similar to · Figure 4.9 to depict the situation, and describe the interaction and each level.

   b. Now suppose that the Chinese prime minister's translator can translate only to Japanese and that the French prime minister has a German translator available. A translator between German and Japanese is available in Germany. Draw a

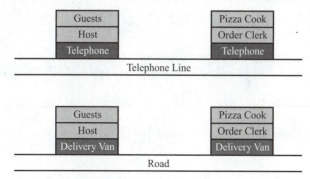

Figure 4.9 Architecture for Problem 4.1

new diagram that reflects this arrangement and describe the hypothetical phone conversation.

4.3   List the major disadvantages with the layered approach to protocols.

4.4   Two blue armies are each poised on opposite hills preparing to attack a single red army in the valley. The red army can defeat either of the blue armies separately but will fail to defeat both blue armies if they attack simultaneously. The blue armies communicate via an unreliable communications system (a foot soldier). The commander with one of the blue armies would like to attack at noon. His problem is this: If he sends a message to the other blue army, ordering the attack, he cannot be sure it will get through. He could ask for acknowledgment, but that might not get through. Is there a protocol that the two blue armies can use to avoid defeat?

4.5   A broadcast network is one in which a transmission from any one attached station is received by all other attached stations over a shared medium. Examples are a bus-topology local area network, such as Ethernet, and a wireless radio network. Discuss the need or lack of it for a network layer (OSI layer 3) in a broadcast network.

4.6   Among the principles used by ISO to define the OSI layers were
   • The number of layers should be small enough to avoid unwieldy design and implementation, but large enough so that separate layers handle functions that are different in process or technology.
   • Layer boundaries should be chosen to minimize the number and size of interactions across boundaries.
   Based on these principles, design an architecture with eight layers and make a case for it. Design one with six layers and make a case for that.

4.7   In Figure 4.2, exactly one protocol data unit (PDU) in layer N is encapsulated in a PDU at layer $(N - 1)$. It is also possible to break one N-level PDU into multiple $(N - 1)$-level PDUs (segmentation) or to group multiple N-level PDUs into one $(N - 1)$-level PDU (blocking).
   a.   In the case of segmentation, is it necessary that each $(N - 1)$-level segment contain a copy of the N-level header?
   b.   In the case of blocking, is it necessary that each N-level PDU retain its own header, or can the data be consolidated into a single N-level PDU with a single N-level header?

4.8   A TCP segment consisting of 1500 bits of data and 160 bits of header is sent to the IP layer, which appends another 160 bits of header. This is then transmitted through two networks, each of which uses a 24-bit packet header. The destination network has a maximum packet size of 800 bits. How many bits, including headers, are delivered to the network layer protocol at the destination?

4.9   Why is UDP needed? Why can't a user program directly access IP?

4.10 IP, TCP, and UDP all discard a packet that arrives with a checksum error and do not attempt to notify the source. Why?

4.11 Why does the TCP header have a header length field while the UDP header does not?

APPENDIX 4A INTERNET PROTOCOL

Within the TCP/IP protocol suite, perhaps the most important protocol is the Internet Protocol (IP). The version that has been used for decades is known as IPv4. Recently, a new version, **IPv6**, has been standardized. IPv4 is first discussed, then IPv6.

IPv4

Figure 4.10a shows the IPv4 header format, which is a minimum of 20 octets, or 160 bits. The fields are

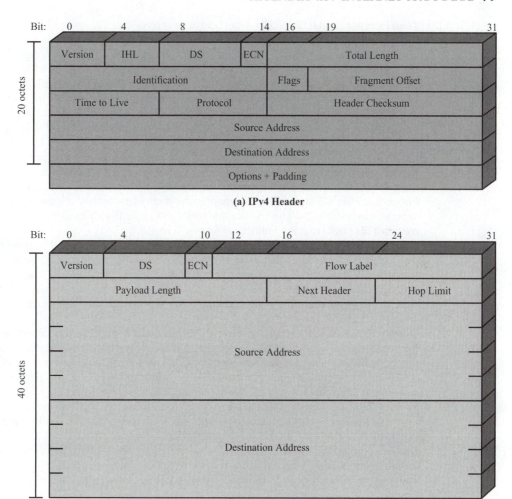

Figure 4.10 IP Headers

DS = Differentiated Services field
ECN = Explicit Congestion Notification field

Note: The 8-bit DS/ECN fields were formerly known as the Type of Service field in the IPv4 header and the Traffic Class field in the IPv6 header.

- **Version (4 bits):** Indicates version number, to allow evolution of the protocol; the value is 4.
- **Internet Header Length (IHL) (4 bits):** Length of header in 32-bit words. The minimum value is five, for a minimum header length of 20 octets.
- **DS/ECN (8 bits):** Prior to the introduction of differentiated services, this field was referred to as the **Type of Service** field and specified reliability, precedence, delay, and throughput parameters. This interpretation has now been superseded. The first 6 bits of the TOS field are now referred to as the DS (differentiated services) field. The DS field supports a quality-of-service (QoS) capability for the Internet. The remaining 2 bits are reserved for an ECN (explicit congestion notification) field, which provides congestion control functionality for the Internet.

- **Total Length (16 bits):** Total IP packet length, in octets.
- **Identification (16 bits):** A sequence number that, together with the source address, destination address, and user protocol, is intended to identify a packet uniquely. Thus, the identifier should be unique for the packet's source address, destination address, and user protocol for the time during which the packet will remain in the internet.
- **Flags (3 bits):** Only two of the bits are currently defined. When a packet is fragmented, the More bit indicates whether this is the last fragment in the original packet. The Don't Fragment bit prohibits fragmentation when set. This bit may be useful if it is known that the destination does not have the capability to reassemble fragments. However, if this bit is set, the packet will be discarded if it exceeds the maximum size of an en route subnetwork. Therefore, if the bit is set, it may be advisable to use source routing to avoid subnetworks with small maximum packet size.
- **Fragment Offset (13 bits):** Indicates where in the original packet this fragment belongs, measured in 64-bit units. This implies that fragments other than the last fragment must contain a data field that is a multiple of 64 bits in length.
- **Time to Live (8 bits):** Specifies how long, in seconds, a packet is allowed to remain in the internet. Every router that processes a packet must decrease the TTL by at least one, so the TTL is somewhat similar to a hop count.
- **Protocol (8 bits):** Indicates the next higher level protocol, which is to receive the data field at the destination; thus, this field identifies the type of the next header in the packet after the IP header.
- **Header Checksum (16 bits):** An error-detecting code applied to the header only. Because some header fields may change during transit (e.g., time to live, segmentation-related fields), this is reverified and recomputed at each router. The checksum field is the 16-bit ones complement addition of all 16-bit words in the header. For purposes of computation, the checksum field is itself initialized to a value of zero.[3]
- **Source Address (32 bits):** Coded to allow a variable allocation of bits to specify the network and the end system attached to the specified network, as discussed subsequently.
- **Destination Address (32 bits):** Same characteristics as source address.
- **Options (variable):** Encodes the options requested by the sending user; these may include security label, source routing, record routing, and timestamping.
- **Padding (variable):** Used to ensure that the packet header is a multiple of 32 bits in length.

The source and destination address fields in the IP header each contain a 32-bit global internet address, generally consisting of a network identifier and a host identifier. The address is coded to allow a variable allocation of bits to specify network and host, as depicted in Figure 4.11. This encoding provides flexibility in assigning addresses to hosts and allows a mix of network sizes on an internet. The three principal network classes are best suited to the following conditions:

- **Class A:** Few networks, each with many hosts
- **Class B:** Medium number of networks, each with a medium number of hosts
- **Class C:** Many networks, each with a few hosts

In a particular environment, it may be best to use addresses all from one class. For example, a corporate internetwork that consists of a large number of departmental local area networks may need to use Class C addresses exclusively. However, the format of the addresses is such that it is possible to mix all three classes of addresses on the same internetwork; this

---

[3]A discussion of this checksum is contained in a supporting document at this book's Web site.

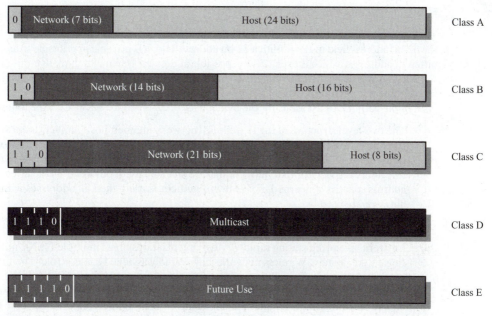

Figure 4.11 IP Address Formats

is what is done in the case of the Internet itself. A mixture of classes is appropriate for an internetwork consisting of a few large networks, many small networks, plus some medium-sized networks.

IP addresses are usually written in what is called *dotted decimal notation*, with a decimal number representing each of the octets of the 32-bit address. For example, the IP address 11000000 11100100 00010001 00111001 is written as 192.228.17.57.

Note that all Class A network addresses begin with a binary 0. Network addresses with a first octet of 0 (binary 00000000) and 127 (binary 01111111) are reserved, so there are 126 potential Class A network numbers, which have a first dotted decimal number in the range 1 to 126. Class B network addresses begin with a binary 10, so that the range of the first decimal number in a Class B address is 128 to 191(binary 10000000 to 10111111). The second octet is also part of the Class B address, so that there are $2^{14} = 16,384$ Class B addresses. For Class C addresses, the first decimal number ranges from 192 to 223 (11000000 to 11011111). The total number of Class C addresses is $2^{21} = 2,097,152$.

IPv6

IPv4 has been the foundation of the Internet and virtually all multivendor private internetworks. This protocol is reaching the end of its useful life and a new protocol, known as IPv6 (IP version 6), has been defined to ultimately replace IP.[4]

We first look at the motivation for developing a new version of IP and then examine some of its details.

---

[4]The currently deployed version of IP is IP version 4; previous versions of IP (1 through 3) were successively defined and replaced to reach IPv4. Version 5 is the number assigned to the Stream Protocol, a connection-oriented internet-layer protocol. Hence the use of label version 6.

IP Next Generation

The driving motivation for the adoption of a new version of IP was the limitation imposed by the 32-bit address field in IPv4. With a 32-bit address field, it is possible in principle to assign 2^{32} different addresses, which is over 4 billion possible addresses. One might think that this number of addresses was more than adequate to meet addressing needs on the Internet. However, in the late 1980s it was perceived that there would be a problem, and this problem began to manifest itself in the early 1990s. Reasons for the inadequacy of 32-bit addresses include the following:

- The two-level structure of the IP address (network number, host number) is convenient but wasteful of the address space. Once a network number is assigned to a network, all of the host-number addresses for that network number are assigned to that network. The address space for that network may be sparsely used, but as far as the effective IP address space is concerned, if a network number is used, then all addresses within the network are used.
- The IP addressing model generally requires that a unique network number be assigned to each IP network whether or not it is actually connected to the Internet.
- Networks are proliferating rapidly. Most organizations boast multiple LANs, not just a single LAN system. Wireless networks have rapidly assumed a major role. The Internet itself has grown explosively for years.
- Growth of TCP/IP usage into new areas will result in a rapid growth in the demand for unique IP addresses. Examples include using TCP/IP to interconnect electronic point-of-sale terminals and for cable television receivers.
- Typically, a single IP address is assigned to each host. A more flexible arrangement is to allow multiple IP addresses per host. This, of course, increases the demand for IP addresses.

So the need for an increased address space dictated that a new version of IP was needed. In addition, IP is a very old protocol, and new requirements in the areas of address configuration, routing flexibility, and traffic support had been defined.

In response to these needs, the Internet Engineering Task Force (IETF) issued a call for proposals for a next generation IP (IPng) in July of 1992. A number of proposals were received, and by 1994 the final design for IPng emerged. A major milestone was reached with the publication of Request for Comments (RFC) 1752, "The Recommendation for the IP Next Generation Protocol," issued in January 1995. RFC documents are the TCP/IP standards documents. RFC 1752 outlines the requirements for IPng, specifies the PDU formats, and highlights the IPng approach in the areas of addressing, routing, and security. A number of other Internet documents defined details of the protocol, now officially called IPv6; these include an overall specification of IPv6 (RFC 2460), an RFC dealing with addressing structure of IPv6 (RFC 4291), and numerous others.

IPv6 includes the following enhancements over IPv4:

- **Expanded address space:** IPv6 uses 128-bit addresses instead of the 32-bit addresses of IPv4. This is an increase of address space by a factor of 2^{96}. It has been pointed out [HIND95] that this allows on the order of 6×10^{23} unique addresses per square meter of the surface of the Earth. Even if addresses are very inefficiently allocated, this address space seems inexhaustible.
- **Improved option mechanism:** IPv6 options are placed in separate optional headers that are located between the IPv6 header and the transport-layer header. Most of these optional headers are not examined or processed by any router on the packet's path. This simplifies and speeds up router processing of IPv6 packets compared to IPv4 datagrams.[5] It also makes it easier to add additional options.

---

[5]The protocol data unit for IPv6 is referred to as a packet rather than a datagram, which is the term used for IPv4 PDUs.

- **Address autoconfiguration:** This capability provides for dynamic assignment of IPv6 addresses.
- **Increased addressing flexibility:** IPv6 includes the concept of an anycast address, for which a packet is delivered to just one of a set of nodes. The scalability of multicast routing is improved by adding a scope field to multicast addresses.
- **Support for resource allocation:** IPv6 enables the labeling of packets belonging to a particular traffic flow for which the sender requests special handling. This aids in the support of specialized traffic such as real-time video.

All of these features are explored in the remainder of this section.

IPv6 Structure

An IPv6 protocol data unit (known as a packet) has the following general form.

```
<—40 octets—>   <———————   0 or more   ———————>
┌─────────────┬─────────────┬─────┬─────────────┬─────────────┐
│ IPv6 header │  Extension  │ ••• │  Extension  │ Transport-  │
│             │   header    │     │   header    │ level PDU   │
└─────────────┴─────────────┴─────┴─────────────┴─────────────┘
```

The only header that is required is referred to simply as the IPv6 header. This is of fixed size with a length of 40 octets, compared to 20 octets for the mandatory portion of the IPv4 header. Details on the IPv6 header format are given in Figure 4.10b. The following extension headers have been defined:

- **Hop-by-Hop Options header:** Defines special options that require hop-by-hop processing
- **Routing header:** Provides extended routing, similar to IPv4 source routing
- **Fragment header:** Contains fragmentation and reassembly information
- **Authentication header:** Provides packet integrity and authentication
- **Encapsulating Security Payload header:** Provides privacy
- **Destination Options header:** Contains optional information to be examined by the destination node

The IPv6 standard recommends that when multiple extension headers are used, the IPv6 headers appear in the following order:

1. IPv6 header: Mandatory, must always appear first
2. Hop-by-Hop Options header
3. Destination Options header: For options to be processed by the first destination that appears in the IPv6 Destination Address field plus subsequent destinations listed in the Routing header
4. Routing header
5. Fragment header
6. Authentication header
7. Encapsulating Security Payload header
8. Destination Options header: For options to be processed only by the final destination of the packet

Figure 4.12 shows an example of an IPv6 packet that includes an instance of each header, except those related to security. Note that the IPv6 header and each extension header include a Next Header field. This field identifies the type of the immediately following header. If the next header is an extension header, then this field contains the type identifier of that header. Otherwise, this field contains the protocol identifier of the upper-layer protocol using IPv6

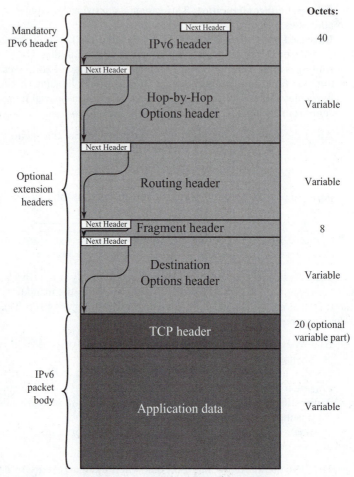

Figure 4.12 IPv6 Packet with Extension Headers (containing a TCP segment)

(typically a transport-level protocol), using the same values as the IPv4 Protocol field. In Figure 4.12, the upper-layer protocol is TCP; thus, the upper-layer data carried by the IPv6 packet consist of a TCP header followed by a block of application data.

We first look at the main IPv6 header and then examine each of the extensions in turn.

IPv6 Header

The IPv6 header has a fixed length of 40 octets, consisting of the following fields (Figure 4.10b):

- **Version (4 bits):** Internet protocol version number; the value is 6.
- **DS/ECN (8 bits):** Available for use by originating nodes and/or forwarding routers for differentiated services and congestion functions, as described for the IPv4 DS/ECN field. This 8-bit field was originally referred to as the Traffic Class field, but the 6-bit DS and 2-bit ECN designation is now used.
- **Flow Label (20 bits):** May be used by a host to label those packets for which it is requesting special handling by routers within a network, discussed subsequently.

- **Payload Length (16 bits):** Length of the remainder of the IPv6 packet following the header, in octets. In other words, this is the total length of all of the extension headers plus the transport-level PDU.
- **Next Header (8 bits):** Identifies the type of header immediately following the IPv6 header; this will either be an IPv6 extension header or a higher-layer header, such as TCP or UDP.
- **Hop Limit (8 bits):** The remaining number of allowable hops for this packet. The Hop Limit is set to some desired maximum value by the source and decremented by 1 by each node that forwards the packet. The packet is discarded if Hop Limit is decremented to zero. This is a simplification over the processing required for the Time to Live field of IPv4. The consensus was that the extra effort in accounting for time intervals in IPv4 added no significant value to the protocol. In fact, IPv4 routers, as a general rule, treat the Time to Live field as a Hop Limit field.
- **Source Address (128 bits):** The address of the originator of the packet.
- **Destination Address (128 bits):** The address of the intended recipient of the packet. This may not in fact be the intended ultimate destination if a Routing header is present, as explained subsequently.

Although the IPv6 header is longer than the mandatory portion of the IPv4 header (40 octets versus 20 octets), it contains fewer fields (8 versus 12). Thus, routers have less processing to do per header, which should speed up routing.

Flow Label

RFC 3697 defines a flow as a sequence of packets sent from a particular source to a particular (unicast, anycast, or multicast) destination for which the source desires special handling by the intervening routers. A flow is uniquely identified by the combination of a source address, destination address, and a nonzero 20-bit flow label. Thus, all packets that are to be part of the same flow are assigned the same flow label by the source.

From the source's point of view, a flow typically will be a sequence of packets that are generated from a single application instance at the source and that have the same transfer service requirements. A flow may comprise a single TCP connection or even multiple TCP connections; an example of the latter is a file transfer application, which could have one control connection and multiple data connections. A single application may generate a single flow or multiple flows. An example of the latter is multimedia conferencing, which might have one flow for audio and one for graphic windows, each with different transfer requirements in terms of data rate, delay, and delay variation.

From the router's point of view, a flow is a sequence of packets that share attributes that affect how these packets are handled by the router. These include path, resource allocation, discard requirements, accounting, and security attributes. The router may treat packets from different flows differently in a number of ways, including allocating different buffer sizes, giving different precedence in terms of forwarding, and requesting different quality of service from networks.

There is no special significance to any particular flow label. Instead, the special handling to be provided for a packet flow must be declared in some other way. For example, a source might negotiate or request special handling ahead of time from routers by means of a control protocol, or at transmission time by information in one of the extension headers in the packet, such as the Hop-by-Hop Options header. Examples of special handling that might be requested include some sort of nondefault quality of service and some form of real-time service.

In principle, all of a user's requirements for a particular flow could be defined in an extension header and included with each packet. If we wish to leave the concept of flow open to include a wide variety of requirements, this design approach could result in very large packet headers. The alternative, adopted for IPv6, is the flow label, in which the flow requirements are defined prior to flow commencement and a unique flow label is assigned to the flow. In this case, the router must save flow requirement information about each flow.

The following rules apply to the flow label:

1. Hosts or routers that do not support the Flow Label field must set the field to zero when originating a packet, pass the field unchanged when forwarding a packet, and ignore the field when receiving a packet.

2. All packets originating from a given source with the same nonzero Flow Label must have the same Destination Address, Source Address, Hop-by-Hop Options header contents (if this header is present), and Routing header contents (if this header is present). The intent is that a router can decide how to route and process the packet by simply looking up the flow label in a table and without examining the rest of the header.

3. The source assigns a flow label to a flow. New flow labels must be chosen (pseudo-) randomly and uniformly in the range 1 to $2^{20} - 1$, subject to the restriction that a source must not reuse a flow label for a new flow within the lifetime of the existing flow. The zero flow label is reserved to indicate that no flow label is being used.

This last point requires some elaboration. The router must maintain information about the characteristics of each active flow that may pass through it, presumably in some sort of table. To forward packets efficiently and rapidly, table lookup must be efficient. One alternative is to have a table with 2^{20} (about 1 million) entries, one for each possible flow label; this imposes an unnecessary memory burden on the router. Another alternative is to have one entry in the table per active flow, include the flow label with each entry, and require the router to search the entire table each time a packet is encountered. This imposes an unnecessary processing burden on the router. Instead, most router designs are likely to use some sort of hash table approach. With this approach a moderate-sized table is used, and each flow entry is mapped into the table using a hashing function on the flow label. The hashing function might simply be the low-order few bits (say 8 or 10) of the flow label or some simple calculation on the 20 bits of the flow label. In any case, the efficiency of the hash approach typically depends on the flow labels being uniformly distributed over their possible range, hence requirement number 3 in the preceding list.

IPv6 Addresses

IPv6 addresses are 128 bits in length. Addresses are assigned to individual interfaces on nodes, not to the nodes themselves.[6] A single interface may have multiple unique unicast addresses. Any of the unicast addresses associated with a node's interface may be used to uniquely identify that node.

The combination of long addresses and multiple addresses per interface enables improved routing efficiency over IPv4. In IPv4, addresses generally do not have a structure that assists routing, and therefore a router may need to maintain huge table of routing paths. Longer Internet addresses allow for aggregating addresses by hierarchies of network, access provider, geography, corporation, and so on. Such aggregation should make for smaller routing tables and faster table lookups. The allowance for multiple addresses per interface would allow a subscriber that uses multiple access providers across the same interface to have separate addresses aggregated under each provider's address space.

---

[6]In IPv6, a node is any device that implements IPv6; this includes hosts and routers.

IPv6 allows three types of addresses:

- **Unicast:** An identifier for a single interface. A packet sent to a unicast address is delivered to the interface identified by that address.
- **Anycast:** An identifier for a set of interfaces (typically belonging to different nodes). A packet sent to an anycast address is delivered to one of the interfaces identified by that address (the "nearest" one, according to the routing protocols' measure of distance).
- **Multicast:** An identifier for a set of interfaces (typically belonging to different nodes). A packet sent to a multicast address is delivered to all interfaces identified by that address.

IPv6 addresses are represented by treating the 128-bit address as a sequence of eight 16-bit numbers, and representing this in the form of eight hexadecimal numbers divided by colons, for example:

2001:0DB8:0055:0000:CD23:0000:0000:0205

APPENDIX 4B TRANSMISSION CONTROL PROTOCOL

For most applications that make use of the TCP/IP protocol suite, the application relies on TCP to assure reliable delivery of data; TCP in turn relies on IP to handle addressing and routing chores.

We begin with a discussion of one of the central mechanisms of TCP: flow control. The functionality of TCP is then summarized by discussing the elements in the TCP header.

TCP Flow Control

As with most protocols that provide flow control, TCP uses a form of sliding-window mechanism. It differs from the mechanism used in many other protocols, such as LLC, HDLC, and X.25, in that it decouples acknowledgment of received data units from the granting of permission to send additional data units.

The flow control mechanism used by TCP is known as a credit allocation scheme. For the credit scheme, each individual octet of data that is transmitted is considered to have a sequence number. In addition to data, each transmitted segment includes in its header three fields related to flow control: the sequence number (SN) of the first data byte in the segment, acknowledgment number (AN), and window (W). When a transport entity sends a segment, it includes the sequence number of the first octet in the segment data field. A transport entity acknowledges an incoming segment with a return segment that includes ($AN = i, W = j$), with the following interpretation:

- All octets through sequence number $SN = i - 1$ are acknowledged; the next expected octet has sequence number i.
- Permission is granted to send an additional window of $W = j$ octets of data; that is, the j octets corresponding to sequence numbers i through $i + j - 1$.

Figure 4.13 illustrates the mechanism. For simplicity, we show data flow in one direction only and assume that 200 octets of data are sent in each segment. Initially, through the connection establishment process, the sending and receiving sequence numbers are synchronized and A is granted an initial credit allocation of 1400 octets, beginning with octet number 1001. After sending 600 octets in three segments, A has shrunk its window to a size of 800 octets (numbers 1601 through 2400). Following receipt of these segments, B acknowledges receipt of all octets through 1601 and issues a credit of 1000 octets. This means that A can send octets 1601 through 2600 (5 segments). However, by the time that B's message has arrived at A, A

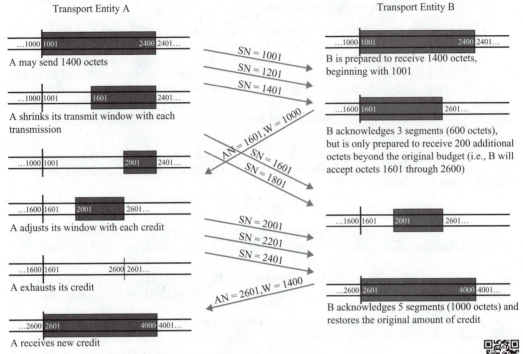

Figure 4.13 Example of TCP Credit Allocation Mechanism

has already sent two segments, containing octets 1601 through 2000 (which was permissible under the initial allocation). Thus, A's remaining credit at this point is only 400 octets (2 segments). As the exchange proceeds, A advances the trailing edge of its window each time that it transmits and advances the leading edge only when it is granted credit.

The credit allocation mechanism is quite flexible. For example, consider that the last message issued by B was ($AN = i, W = j$) and that the last octet of data received by B was octet number $i - 1$. Then

- To increase credit to an amount $k(k > j)$ when no additional data have arrived, B issues ($AN = i, W = k$).
- To acknowledge an incoming segment containing m octets of data ($m < j$) without granting additional credit, B issues ($AN = i + m, W = j - m$).

TCP Segment Format

TCP uses only a single type of protocol data unit, called a TCP segment. The header is shown in Figure 4.14a. Because one header must serve to perform all protocol mechanisms, it is rather large, with a minimum length of 20 octets. The fields are

- **Source Port (16 bits):** Source TCP user.
- **Destination Port (16 bits):** Destination TCP user.
- **Sequence Number (32 bits):** Sequence number of the first data octet in this segment except when the SYN flag is set. If SYN is set, this field contains the initial sequence number (ISN) and the first data octet in this segment has sequence number ISN + 1.

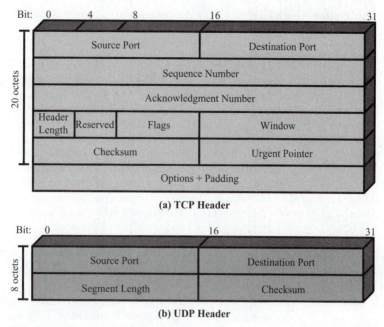

(a) TCP Header

(b) UDP Header

Figure 4.14 TCP and UDP Headers

- **Acknowledgment Number (32 bits):** A piggybacked acknowledgment. Contains the sequence number of the next data octet that the TCP entity expects to receive.
- **Header Length (4 bits):** Number of 32-bit words in the header.
- **Reserved (6 bits):** Reserved for future use.
- **Flags (6 bits):** For each flag, if set to 1, the meaning is
    CWR: congestion window reduced

    ECE: ECN-Echo; the CWR and ECE bits, defined in RFC 3168, are used for the explicit congestion notification function

    URG: urgent pointer field significant

    ACK: acknowledgment field significant

    PSH: push function

    RST: reset the connection

    SYN: synchronize the sequence numbers

    FIN: no more data from sender
- **Window (16 bits):** Flow control credit allocation, in octets. Contains the number of data octets, beginning with the sequence number indicated in the acknowledgment field that the sender is willing to accept.
- **Checksum (16 bits):** The ones complement of the ones complement sum modulo of all the 16-bit words in the segment plus a pseudoheader, described subsequently.[7]
- **Urgent Pointer (16 bits):** This value, when added to the segment sequence number, contains the sequence number of the last octet in a sequence of urgent data. This allows the receiver to know how much urgent data are coming.

---

[7]A discussion of this checksum is contained in a supporting document at this book's Web site.

- **Options (Variable):** An example is the option that specifies the maximum segment size that will be accepted.

The *sequence number* and *acknowledgment number* are bound to octets rather than to entire segments. For example, if a segment contains sequence number 1001 and includes 600 octets of data, the sequence number refers to the first octet in the data field; the next segment in logical order will have sequence number 1601. Thus, TCP is logically stream oriented: It accepts a stream of octets from the user, groups them into segments as it sees fit, and numbers each octet in the stream.

The *checksum* field applies to the entire segment plus a pseudoheader prefixed to the header at the time of calculation (at both transmission and reception). The pseudoheader includes the following fields from the IP header: source and destination internet address and protocol, plus a segment length field. By including the pseudoheader, TCP protects itself from misdelivery by IP. That is, if IP delivers a segment to the wrong host, even if the segment contains no bit errors, the receiving TCP entity will detect the delivery error.

APPENDIX 4C USER DATAGRAM PROTOCOL

In addition to TCP, there is one other transport-level protocol that is in common use as part of the TCP/IP protocol suite: the **User Datagram Protocol (UDP)**, specified in RFC 768. UDP provides a connectionless service for application-level procedures. Thus, UDP is basically an unreliable service; delivery and duplicate protection are not guaranteed. However, this does reduce the overhead of the protocol and may be adequate in many cases.

The strengths of the connection-oriented approach are clear. It allows connection-related features such as flow control, error control, and sequenced delivery. Connectionless service, however, is more appropriate in some contexts. At lower layers (internet, network), connectionless service is more robust. An example of this is the datagram approach to packet switching, discussed in Chapter 3. When each packet is treated independently and routed independently, the impact of congestion or loss in the network is less than if there is a pre-defined route or connection over which all packets travel.

In addition, a connectionless service represents a "least common denominator" of service to be expected at higher layers. Further, even at transport and above there is justification for a connectionless service. There are instances in which the overhead of connection establishment and maintenance is unjustified or even counterproductive. Some examples include the following:

- **Inward data collection:** Involves the periodic active or passive sampling of data sources, such as sensors, and automatic self-test reports from security equipment or network components. In a real-time monitoring situation, the loss of an occasional data unit would not cause distress, because the next report should arrive shortly.
- **Outward data dissemination:** Includes broadcast messages to network users, the announcement of a new node or the change of address of a service, and the distribution of real-time clock values.
- **Request-response:** Applications in which a transaction service is provided by a common server to a number of distributed transport service users, and for which a single request-response sequence is typical. Use of the service is regulated at the application level, and lower-level connections are often unnecessary and cumbersome.
- **Real-time applications:** Such as voice and telemetry, involving a degree of redundancy and/or a real-time transmission requirement. These must not have connection-oriented functions such as retransmission.

Thus, there is a place at the transport level for both a connection-oriented and a connectionless type of service.

UDP sits on top of IP. Because it is connectionless, UDP has very little to do. Essentially, it adds a port addressing capability to IP. This is best seen by examining the UDP header, shown in Figure 4.14b. The header includes a source port and destination port. The Length field contains the length of the entire UDP segment, including header and data. The checksum is the same algorithm used for TCP and IP. For UDP, the checksum applies to the entire UDP segment plus a pseudoheader prefixed to the UDP header at the time of calculation and is the same pseudoheader used for TCP. If an error is detected, the segment is discarded and no further action is taken.

The Checksum field in UDP is optional. If it is not used, it is set to zero. However, it should be pointed out that the IP checksum applies only to the IP header and not to the Data field, which in this case consists of the UDP header and the user data. Thus, if no checksum calculation is performed by UDP, then no check is made on the user data.

PART TWO

Wireless Communication Technology

CHAPTER 5

OVERVIEW OF WIRELESS COMMUNICATION

LEARNING OBJECTIVES

After studying this chapter, you should be able to:

- Explain the importance of unlicensed frequencies.
- Compute path loss for free space and real-world environments using the path loss exponent.
- Characterize the multipath and Doppler spreading characteristics of channels.
- Describe the approaches used to correct channel impairments.
- Describe the three major ways digital data can be encoded onto an analog signal.
- Determine performance of modulation schemes from E_b/N_0 curves.
- Describe and compare error recovery processes for error detection, retransmission/ARQ, and error correction.
- Describe the capabilities and bandwidth efficiency of codes in terms of their coding rate, Hamming distance, and coding gain.
- Present an overview of OFDM and OFDMA.
- Explain the value of orthogonal carriers.
- Describe the operation of the two major forms of spread spectrum: frequency hopping and direct sequence.

This chapter is a condensed version of Chapters 6-10. It provides a complete coverage of the wireless physical medium but at less depth for quicker coverage. It covers the same material and uses many of the same figures as the subsequent five chapters. If more depth is desired for a particular topic, the corresponding later chapter can be consulted.

5.1 SPECTRUM CONSIDERATIONS

The proper choice of the range of wireless frequencies over which a technology is to operate (i.e., its **spectrum**) is vital to its success. Some frequencies travel better over long distances; others penetrate obstacles such as buildings and walls more effectively. Wireless frequencies need to be shared with multiple types of users.

Regulation

The wireless medium is shared by a myriad of different types of users, applications, and traffic types. These are controlled by regulatory bodies to provide fair use while also meeting the key demands of society. The following differentiates signals from each other.

- Carrier Frequency: Each signal is shifted from its base frequency up to a carrier frequency. For example, a 22 MHz IEEE 802.11 signal might be shifted up to be centered at a carrier frequency of 2.412 GHz, so that it would occupy 2.401 to 2.423 GHz.
- Signal Power: Signals are limited in their propagation range by the allowed transmission power. At sufficient distances from each other, multiple users and groups can reuse the same spectrum.
- Multiple Access Scheme: Multiple users within a same spectrum range can share the spectrum by each having their own small slice of time or frequency;

this is known as Time Division Multiple Access (TDMA) or Frequency Division Multiple Access (FDMA). They might also encode their signals in different ways while sharing the same time and frequency; this is known as **Code Division Multiple Access (CDMA)**.

In the United States, the Federal Communications Commission (FCC) regulates these issues for different types of groups to share the wireless spectrum. Similar bodies operate throughout the world. In most cases, a license is required by the FCC to operate. In some cases, auctions are conducted for the purchase of these licenses. The FCC regulates which frequencies are government exclusive, nongovernment exclusive, or government/nongovernment shared. They provide for a variety of services, including the following:

- Aeronautical
- Amateur
- Broadcasting
- Maritime
- Meteorological
- Mobile
- Satellite
- Space

An illustration of the spectrum allocations by the FCC can be seen on the book Web site at corybeardwireless.com. FCC licenses are allocated for different uses so that there are no conflicts. This frequently causes spectrum to be underutilized, so researchers are exploring a new concept known as **dynamic spectrum access**. Here users would share spectrum among primary and secondary users. If primary users are not active, secondary users could use the spectrum but release the spectrum as soon as primary users need it. A technology known as **cognitive radio** would be implemented in the devices to scan wide bands of frequency to sense when spectrum is being used.

Within a given spectrum band, it is possible for frequencies to be allocated among multiple services. FCC licenses are allocated for these different services so that there are no conflicts. Frequency bands used for the technologies covered in this textbook are relatively narrow compared to the overall wide spectrum. Several technologies (e.g., IEEE 802.11 and 802.15) use the industrial, scientific, and medical (ISM) bands because those frequencies can be used without a license as long the transmitters stay within power limitations and use a spread spectrum technique. Some of these ISM bands are 915 $\pm$ 13 MHz, 2450 $\pm$ 50 MHz, 5.8 $\pm$ 0.75 GHz, and 57–64 GHz.

Propagation Modes

A signal radiated from an antenna travels along one of three routes: ground wave, sky wave, or line of sight (LOS). Figure 5.1 illustrates each type.

- **Ground wave propagation** (Figure 5.1a) more or less follows the contour of the earth and can propagate considerable distances, well over the visual horizon. This effect is found in frequencies up to about 3 MHz. Electromagnetic

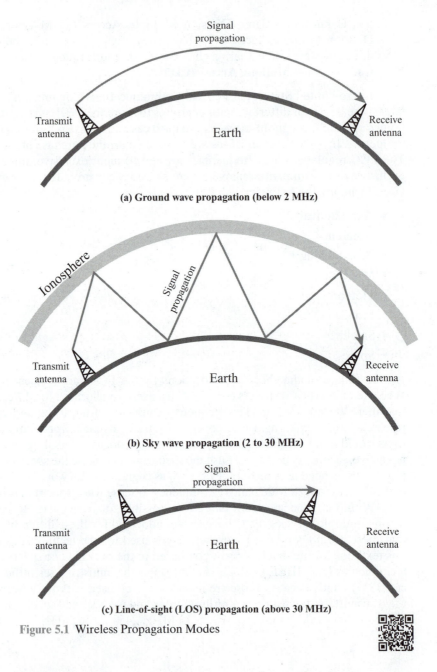

(a) Ground wave propagation (below 2 MHz)

(b) Sky wave propagation (2 to 30 MHz)

(c) Line-of-sight (LOS) propagation (above 30 MHz)

Figure 5.1 Wireless Propagation Modes

waves in this frequency range are scattered by the atmosphere in such a way that they do not penetrate the upper atmosphere. The best-known example of ground wave communication is AM radio.

- With **sky wave propagation** (Figure 5.1b), a signal from an earth-based antenna is *refracted* from the ionized layer of the upper atmosphere (ionosphere) back down to earth. A sky-wave signal can travel through a number of hops, bouncing back and forth between the ionosphere and the earth's surface. With this propagation mode, a signal can be picked up thousands of kilometers from the transmitter. Sky waves generally operate between 3 and 30 MHz.

- **Line-of-sight propagation (LOS)** (Figure 5.1c) is necessary when neither ground wave nor sky wave propagation modes can operate. This generally occurs above 30 MHz. Most of the technologies we will discuss operate from 100s of MHz to a few GHz, so they operate in a line-of-sight mode. This does not mean that line of sight always requires complete free space between transmitters and receivers, however. Different frequencies will be attenuated by atmospheric effects or have capabilities for penetrating through surfaces (e.g., through walls, buildings, cars, etc.). For most materials, the ability to transmit through an object significantly degrades as frequency increases.

5.2 LINE-OF-SIGHT TRANSMISSION

With any communications system, the signal that is received will differ from the signal that is transmitted, due to various transmission impairments. For analog signals, these impairments introduce various random modifications that degrade the signal quality. For digital data, bit errors are introduced: A binary 1 is transformed into a binary 0, and vice versa. In this section, we examine the various impairments and comment on their effect on the information-carrying capacity of a communications link. Our concern in this book is mainly with LOS wireless transmission frequencies, and in this context, the most significant impairments are

- Attenuation and attenuation distortion
- Free space loss
- Noise
- Atmospheric absorption
- Multipath
- **Refraction**

Five Basic Propagation Mechanisms

There are five different mechanisms by which electromagnetic signals can transfer information from a transmitter to a receiver:

1. **Free-space propagation** transmits a wave when there are no obstructions. The signal strength decays as a function of distance.
2. **Transmission** propagates a signal as it penetrates in and through a medium. The signal is refracted at the surface of the medium to a different angle of transmission.
3. **Reflections** occur when electromagnetic waves impinge upon surfaces that are large relative to the wavelength of a signal.

4. **Diffraction** occurs when a signal is obstructed by an object with sharp edges. Secondary waves are then present behind the sharp edges to deliver the signal to a possibly shadowed receiver.

5. **Scattering** is involved when a signal interacts with large numbers of objects that are small relative to its wavelength. This can involve rough surfaces, foliage, street signs, etc. in a typical communication system.

The last four involve interacting objects. The dielectric and conducting properties of these objects affect the strength and angle of signal propagation when these interactions occur.

Antennas

Before examining free-space propagation, first it is important to have some understanding of antennas. An **antenna** can be defined as an electrical conductor or system of conductors used either for radiating electromagnetic energy or for collecting electromagnetic energy. For transmission of a signal, radio-frequency electrical energy from the transmitter is converted into electromagnetic energy by the antenna and radiated into the surrounding environment (atmosphere, space, water). For reception of a signal, electromagnetic energy impinging on the antenna is converted into radio-frequency electrical energy and fed into the receiver.

An antenna will radiate power in all directions but, typically, does not perform equally well in all directions. A common way to characterize the performance of an antenna is the **radiation pattern**, which is a graphical representation of the radiation properties of an antenna as a function of space coordinates. The simplest pattern is produced by an idealized antenna known as the isotropic antenna. An **isotropic antenna** is a point in space that radiates power in all directions equally. The actual radiation pattern for the isotropic antenna is a sphere with the antenna at the center. However, radiation patterns are almost always depicted as a two-dimensional cross section of the three-dimensional pattern. The pattern for the isotropic antenna is shown in Figure 5.2a. The distance from the antenna to each point on the radiation pattern is proportional to the power radiated from the antenna in that direction.

Figure 5.2b shows an actual directional antenna pattern produced from an array of antennas spaced apart by half of a wavelength and placed in a linear array. If weights are optimized, this pattern can be produced with a main lobe that is 60° wide. This requires four antennas. In this example, the main strength of the antenna is in the x direction. Notice that some energy is sent to the sides and back of the antenna in what are called the *sidelobes*. There are also, however, *nulls* in the patterns where very little signal energy is sent in those directions.

The actual size of a radiation pattern is arbitrary. What is important is the *relative* distance from the antenna position in each direction. The relative distance determines the relative power. To determine the relative power in a given direction, a line is drawn from the antenna position at the appropriate angle, and the point of intercept with the radiation pattern is determined. Figure 5.2 shows a comparison of two transmission angles, A and B, drawn on the two radiation patterns. The

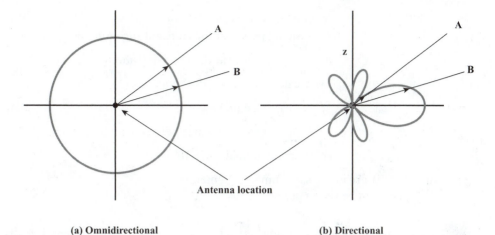

(a) Omnidirectional   (b) Directional

Figure 5.2 Antenna Radiation Patterns

isotropic antenna produces an omnidirectional radiation pattern of equal strength in all directions, so the A and B vectors are of equal length. For the antenna pattern shown in Figure 5.2b, the B vector is longer than the A vector, indicating that more power is radiated in the B direction than in the A direction, and the relative lengths of the two vectors are proportional to the amount of power radiated in the two directions. Please note that this type of diagram shows relative ***antenna gain*** in each direction, not relative distance of coverage, although they are of course related.

Free Space Loss

For any type of wireless communication, the signal disperses with distance and causes **attenuation**. Energy dispersal can be viewed as radiating in a sphere with a receiver on the surface extracting energy on part of the surface area. A larger and larger sphere occurs as distance from the transmitter increases, so there is less energy per each unit of surface area. Therefore, an antenna with a fixed area will receive less signal power the farther it is from the transmitting antenna. For satellite communication, this is the primary mode of signal loss. Even if no other sources of attenuation or impairment are assumed, a transmitted signal attenuates over distance because the signal is being spread over a larger and larger area. This form of attenuation is known as **free space loss**, which can be expressed in terms of the ratio of the radiated power P_t to the power P_r received by the antenna or, in decibels, by taking 10 times the log of that ratio. For the ideal isotropic antenna, free space loss is

$$\frac{P_t}{P_r} = \frac{(4\pi d)^2}{\lambda^2} = \frac{(4\pi f d)^2}{c^2} \tag{5.1}$$

where

$$P_t = \text{signal power at the transmitting antenna}$$

$$P_r = \text{signal power at the receiving antenna}$$

$$\lambda = \text{carrier wavelength}$$

$$f = \text{carrier frequency}$$

$$d = \text{propagation distance between antennas}$$

$$c = \text{speed of light } (3 \times 10^8 \text{ m/s})$$

and d and λ are in the same units (e.g., meters).

This can be recast in decibels as

$$L_{dB} = 10\log\frac{P_t}{P_r} = 20\log\left(\frac{4\pi d}{\lambda}\right) = -20\log(\lambda) + 20\log(d) + 21.98 \text{ dB}$$

$$= 20\log\left(\frac{4\pi f d}{c}\right) = 20\log(f) + 20\log(d) - 147.56 \text{ dB} \tag{5.2}$$

Figure 5.3 shows plots of curves from the free space loss equation.[1]

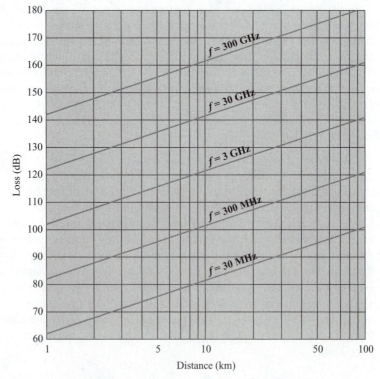

Figure 5.3 Free Space Loss

---

[1]As was mentioned in Appendix 2A, there is some inconsistency in the literature over the use of the terms *gain* and *loss*. Equation (5.2) follows the convention of Equation (2.2) in Section 2.4.

For other antennas, we must take into account the gain of the antenna, which yields the following free space loss equation:

$$\frac{P_t}{P_r} = \frac{(4\pi)^2(d)^2}{G_rG_t\lambda^2} = \frac{(\lambda d)^2}{A_rA_t} = \frac{(cd)^2}{f^2\,A_rA_t}$$

where

G_t = gain of the transmitting antenna

G_r = gain of the receiving antenna

A_t = effective area of the transmitting antenna

A_r = effective area of the receiving antenna

The effective area of an antenna is related to the physical size of the antenna and to its shape.

We can recast this equation as

$$L_{dB} = 20\log(\lambda) + 20\log(d) - 10\log(A_tA_r)$$
$$= -20\log(f) + 20\log(d) - 10\log(A_tA_r) + 169.54\text{ dB} \qquad (5.3)$$

Thus, for the same antenna dimensions and separation, the longer the carrier wavelength (lower the carrier frequency f), the higher is the free space path loss. It is interesting to compare Equations (5.2) and (5.3). Equation (5.2) indicates that as the frequency increases, the free space loss also increases, which would suggest that at higher frequencies, losses become more burdensome. However, Equation (5.3) shows that we can easily compensate for this increased loss with antenna gains. Since Equation (5.1) says there is increased gain at higher frequencies, in fact there is a net gain at higher frequencies, other factors remaining constant. Equation (5.2) shows that at a fixed distance an increase in frequency results in an increased loss measured by $20\log(f)$. However, if we take into account antenna gain, and fix antenna area, then the change in loss is measured by $-20\log(f)$; that is, there is actually a decrease in loss at higher frequencies.

Example 5.1 Determine the isotropic free space loss at 4 GHz for the shortest path to a synchronous satellite from earth (35,863 km). At 4 GHz, the wavelength is $(3 \times 10^8)/(4 \times 10^9) = 0.075$ m. Then,

$$L_{dB} = -20\log(0.075) + 20\log(35.853 \times 10^6) + 21.98 = 195.6\text{ dB}$$

Now consider the antenna gain of both the satellite- and ground-based antennas. Typical values are 44 dB and 48 dB, respectively. The free-space loss is:

$$L_{dB} = 195.6 - 44 - 48 = 103.6\text{ dB}$$

Now assume a transmit power of 250 W at the earth station. What is the power received at the satellite antenna? A power of 250 W translates into 24 dBW, so the power at the receiving antenna is $24 - 103.6 = -79.6$ dBW, where dBW is the decibel-watt, defined in Appendix 2A. This signal is approximately 10^{-8} W, still useable by receiver circuitry.

Path Loss Exponent in Practical Systems

Practical systems involve many types of obstructions that cause reflections, scattering, etc. Both theoretical and measurement-based models have shown that beyond a certain distance the average received signal power decreases logarithmically with distance according to a $10n \log(d)$ relationship where n is known as the **path loss exponent** [RAPP02]. Such models have been used extensively. Both Equations (5.2) and (5.3) showed a $20 \log(d)$ term which came from a d^2 distance relationship, hence a path-loss exponent of $n = 2$. These should be replaced with the more general $10n \log(d)$ term as follows:

$$\frac{P_t}{P_r} = \left(\frac{4\pi}{\lambda}\right)^2 d^n = \left(\frac{4\pi f}{c}\right)^2 d^n$$

$$L_{dB} = 10 \log\frac{P_t}{P_r} = 10 \log\left(\left(\frac{4\pi}{\lambda}\right)^2 d^n\right) = -20 \log(\lambda) + 10n \log(d) + 21.98 \, \text{dB}$$

$$= 10 \log\left(\left(\frac{4\pi f}{c}\right)^2 d^n\right) = 20 \log(f) + 10n \log(d) - 147.56 \, \text{dB} \tag{5.4}$$

Using effective areas and the general path loss exponent, n,

$$L_{dB} = 20 \log(\lambda) + 10n \log(d) - 10 \log(A_t A_r)$$

$$= -20 \log(f) + 10n \log(d) - 10 \log(A_t A_r) + 169.54 \, \text{dB} \tag{5.5}$$

Table 5.1 shows typical path loss exponents obtained for various environments. Note that in a building, LOS can be better than $n = 2$ (e.g., in hallways) since reflections help keep the signal stronger than if it decayed with distance as in free space.

Example 5.2 Compare the path loss in dB for two possible cellular environments where there is (1) free space between mobiles and base stations, and (2) urban area cellular radio with $n = 3.1$. Use 1.9 GHz at a distance of 1.5 km and assume isotropic antennas.

For free space using $n = 2.0$

$$L_{dB} = 20 \log(1.9 \times 10^9) + 10 \times 2.0 \log(1.5 \times 10^3) - 147.56 = 101.53 \, \text{dB}$$

For urban cellular radio using $n = 3.1$

$$L_{dB} = 20 \log(1.9 \times 10^9) + 10 \times 3.1 \log(1.5 \times 10^3) - 147.56 = 136.47 \, \text{dB}$$

Table 5.1 Path Loss Exponents for Different Environments [RAPP02]

Environment	Path Loss Exponent, n
Free space	2
Urban area cellular radio	2.7 to 3.5
Shadowed cellular radio	3 to 5
In building line-of-sight	1.6 to 1.8
Obstructed in building	4 to 6
Obstructed in factories	2 to 3

Example 5.3 Compare the range of coverage for two possible cellular environments where there is (1) free space between mobiles and base stations, and (2) urban area cellular radio with $n = 3.1$. Use 1.9 GHz and assume isotropic antennas. Assume the transmit power is 2 W and the received power must be above -110 dBW.

P_t in dB $= 10 \log (2) = 3.0$

Requirement is, therefore, $L_{dB} < 113$ dB

For free space using $n = 2.0$

$$L_{dB} = 20 \log(1.9 \times 10^9) + 10 \times 2.0 \log(d) - 147.56 < 113 \text{ dB}$$
$$10 \times 2.0 \log(d) < 74.99 \text{ dB}$$
$$d < 5.61 \text{ km}$$

For free space using $n = 2.0$

$$L_{dB} = 20 \log(1.9 \times 10^9) + 10 \times 3.1 \log(d) - 147.56 < 113 \text{ dB}$$
$$10 \times 3.1 \log(d) < 74.99 \text{ dB}$$
$$d < 262 \text{ m}$$

Models Derived from Empirical Measurements

In designing a wireless system, the communications engineer must take account of various propagation effects, the desired maximum transmit power level at the base station and the mobile units, the typical height of the mobile unit antenna, and the available height of the BS antenna. These factors will determine the coverage area of a wireless system. Unfortunately, the propagation effects are dynamic and difficult to predict. The best that can be done is to come up with a model based on empirical data and to apply that model to a given environment to develop guidelines. One of the most widely used models was developed by Okumura et al. [OKUM68] and subsequently refined by Hata [HATA80], commonly called the Okumura-Hata model. The original was a detailed analysis of the Tokyo area and produced path loss information for an urban environment. The Okumura-Hata model is an empirical formulation that takes into account a variety of environments and conditions. For an urban environment, predicted path loss is

$$L_{dB} = 69.55 + 26.16 \log f_c - 13.82 \log h_t - A(h_r) + (44.9 - 6.55 \log h_t) \log d \quad (5.6)$$

where

f_c = carrier frequency in MHz from 150 to 1500 MHz

h_t = height of transmitting antenna (base station) in m, from 30 to 300 m

h_r = height of receiving antenna (mobile unit) in m, from 1 to 10 m

d = propagation distance between antennas in km, from 1 to 20 km

$A(h_r)$ = correction factor for mobile unit antenna height

For a small or medium-sized city, the correction factor is given by

$$A(h_r) = (1.1 \log f_c - 0.7) h_r - (1.56 \log f_c - 0.8) \text{ dB}$$

And for a large city it is given by

$$A(h_r) = 8.29 \, [\log(1.54 \, h_r)]^2 - 1.1 \text{ dB} \qquad \text{for } f_c \leq 300 \text{ MHz}$$

$$A(h_r) = 3.2 \, [\log(11.75 \, h_r)]^2 - 4.97 \text{ dB} \qquad \text{for } f_c \geq 300 \text{ MHz}$$

To estimate the path loss in a suburban area, the formula for urban path loss in Equation (10.1) is modified as

$$L_{dB}(\text{suburban}) = L_{dB}(\text{urban small/medium city}) - 2[\log (f_c/28)]^2 - 5.4$$

And for the path loss in open or rural areas, the formula is modified as

$$L_{dB}(\text{open}) = L_{dB}(\text{urban small/medium city}) - 4.78 \, (\log f_c)^2$$
$$- 18.733 \, (\log f_c) - 40.98$$

The Okumura/Hata model is considered to be among the best in terms of accuracy in path loss prediction and provides a practical means of estimating path loss in a wide variety of situations [FREE07, RAPP02].

Example 5.4 Let $f_c = 900$ MHz, $h_t = 40$ m, $h_r = 5$ m, and $d = 10$ km. Estimate the path loss for a medium-sized city.

$$A(h_r) = (1.1 \log 900 - 0.7) \, 5 - (1.56 \log 900 - 0.8) \text{ dB}$$
$$= 12.75 - 3.8 = 8.95 \text{ dB}$$

$$L_{dB} = 69.55 + 26.16 \log 900 - 13.82 \log 40 - 8.95 + (44.9 - 6.55 \log 40) \log 10$$
$$= 69.55 + 77.28 - 22.14 - 8.95 + 34.4 = 150.14 \text{ dB}$$

Noise

For any data transmission event, the received signal will consist of the transmitted signal, modified by the various distortions imposed by the transmission system, plus additional unwanted signals that are inserted somewhere between transmission and reception. These unwanted signals are referred to as **noise**. Noise is the major limiting factor in communications system performance.

Noise may be divided into four categories:

- **Thermal noise** is due to thermal agitation of electrons. It is present in all electronic devices and transmission media and is a function of temperature. Thermal noise is uniformly distributed across the frequency spectrum and hence is often referred to as *white noise*. Thermal noise cannot be eliminated and therefore places an upper bound on communications system performance.

- When signals at different frequencies share the same transmission medium, the result may be **intermodulation noise**. Intermodulation noise produces signals at a frequency that is the sum or difference of the two original frequencies or multiples of those frequencies.

- **Crosstalk** has been experienced by anyone who, while using the telephone, has been able to hear another conversation; it is an unwanted coupling between signal paths.

- **Impulse noise**, however, is unpredictable and noncontinuous, consisting of irregular pulses or noise spikes of short duration and of relatively high amplitude. It is generated from a variety of causes, including external electromagnetic disturbances, such as lightning, and faults and flaws in the communications system. Impulse noise is the primary source of error in digital data transmission. For example, a sharp spike of energy of 0.01 s duration would barely be noticed for voice conversation but would wash out about 10,000 bits of data being transmitted at 1 Mbps.

The Expression E_b/N_0

Chapter 2 introduced the **signal-to-noise ratio (SNR)**. There is a parameter related to SNR that is more convenient for determining digital data rates and error rates and that is the standard quality measure for digital communication system performance. The parameter is the ratio of signal *energy* per bit to noise power density per Hertz, E_b/N_0. The ratio E_b/N_0 is important because the bit error rate (BER) for digital data is a (decreasing) function of this ratio. Figure 5.4 illustrates the typical shape of a plot of BER versus E_b/N_0. Such plots are commonly found in the literature and several examples appear in this text. For any particular curve, as the signal strength relative to the noise increases (increasing E_b/N_0), the BER performance at the receiver decreases.

This makes intuitive sense. However, there is not a single unique curve that expresses the dependence of BER on E_b/N_0. Instead the performance of a transmission/reception system, in terms of BER versus E_b/N_0, also depends on the way in which the data is encoded onto the signal. Thus, Figure 5.4 shows two curves, one of which gives better performance than the other. A curve below and to the left of another curve defines superior performance. At the same BER for two signals, the

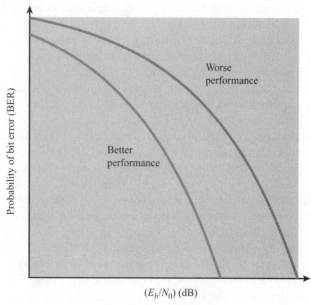

Figure 5.4 General Shape of BER vs E_b/N_0 Curves

curve to the left uses less E_b/N_0 to achieve that BER. For two signals using the same E_b/N_0, the curve below achieves a better BER. Chapter 7 explores the relationship of signal encoding with performance. A more detailed discussion of E_b/N_0 can be found in [SKLA01].

5.3 FADING IN THE MOBILE ENVIRONMENT

Perhaps the most challenging technical problem facing communications systems engineers is **fading** in a mobile environment. The term *fading* refers to the time variation of received signal power caused by changes in the transmission medium or path(s). In a fixed environment, fading is affected by changes in atmospheric conditions, such as rainfall. But in a mobile environment, where one of the two antennas is moving relative to the other, the relative location of various obstacles changes over time, creating complex transmission effects. Sometimes these variations can be quite rapid.

Multipath Propagation

One of the key effects causing fading is multipath propagation. For wireless facilities where there is a relatively free choice of where antennas are to be located, they can be placed so that if there are no nearby interfering obstacles, there is a direct line-of-sight path from transmitter to receiver. This is generally the case for many satellite facilities and for point-to-point microwave. In other cases, such as mobile telephony, there are obstacles in abundance. The signal can be reflected by such obstacles so that multiple copies of the signal with varying delays can be received. In fact, in extreme cases, the receiver might capture only reflected signals and not the direct signal. Depending on the differences in the path lengths of the direct and reflected waves, the composite signal can be either larger or smaller than the direct signal. Reinforcement and cancellation of the signal can occur, resulting from copies of the signal added together following multiple paths.

Three propagation mechanisms, illustrated in Figure 5.5, play a role. **Reflection** occurs when an electromagnetic signal encounters a surface that is large relative to the wavelength of the signal. For example, suppose a ground-reflected wave near the mobile unit is received. The ground-reflected wave and the line-of-sight (LOS) wave may tend to cancel, resulting in high signal loss. Further, because the mobile antenna is lower than most human-made structures in the area, multipath interference occurs. These reflected waves may interfere constructively or destructively at the receiver.

Diffraction occurs at the edge of an impenetrable body that is large compared to the wavelength of the radio wave. When a radio wave encounters such an edge, waves propagate in different directions with the edge as the source. Thus, signals can be received even when there is no unobstructed LOS from the transmitter.

If the size of an obstacle is on the order of the wavelength of the signal or less, **scattering** occurs. An incoming signal is scattered into several weaker outgoing signals. At typical cellular microwave frequencies, there are numerous objects, such as lamp posts and traffic signs, that can cause scattering. Thus, scattering effects are difficult to predict.

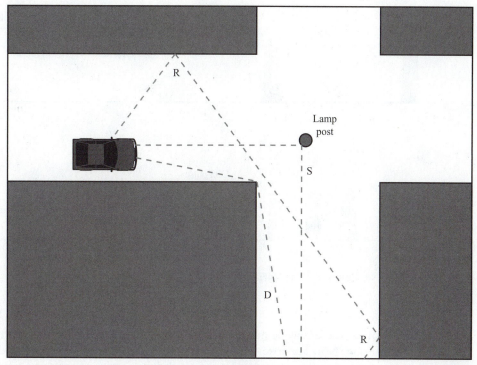

Figure 5.5 Sketch of Three Important Propagation Mechanisms: Reflection (R), Scattering (S), and Diffraction (D)

These three propagation effects influence system performance in various ways depending on local conditions and as the mobile unit moves within a cell. If a mobile unit has a clear LOS to the transmitter, then diffraction and scattering are generally minor effects, although reflection may have a significant impact. If there is no clear LOS, such as in an urban area at street level, then diffraction and scattering are the primary means of signal reception.

The Effects of Multipath Propagation As multipath signals add together, the resulting signal power can be stronger, but can also be lower by a factor of 100 or 1000 (20 or 30 dB). The signal level relative to noise declines, making signal detection at the receiver more difficult.

A second phenomenon, of particular importance for digital transmission, is intersymbol interference (ISI). Consider that we are sending a narrow pulse at a given frequency across a link between a fixed antenna and a mobile unit. Figure 5.6 shows what the channel may deliver to the receiver if the impulse is sent at two different times. The upper line shows two pulses at the time of transmission. The lower line shows the resulting pulses at the receiver. In each case the first received pulse is the desired LOS signal. The magnitude of that pulse may change because of changes in atmospheric attenuation. Further, as the mobile unit moves farther away from the fixed antenna, the amount of LOS attenuation increases. But in addition to this

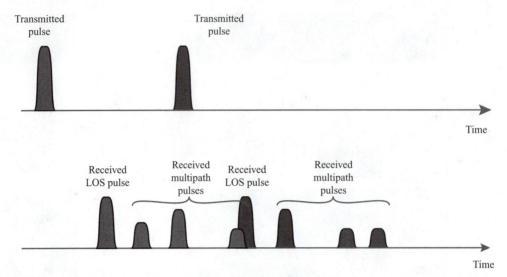

Figure 5.6 Two Pulses in Time Variant Multipath

primary pulse, there may be multiple secondary pulses due to reflection, diffraction, and scattering. Now suppose that this pulse encodes one or more bits of data. In that case, one or more delayed copies of a pulse may arrive at the same time as the primary pulse for a subsequent bit. These delayed pulses act as a form of noise to the subsequent primary pulse, making recovery of the bit information more difficult.

As the mobile antenna moves, the location of various obstacles changes; hence the number, magnitude, and timing of the secondary pulses change. This makes it difficult to design signal processing techniques that will filter out multipath effects so that the intended signal is recovered with fidelity.

Types of Fading Fading effects in a mobile environment can be classified as either small-scale or large-scale. Referring to Figure 5.5, as the mobile unit moves down a street in an urban environment, as the mobile user covers distances well in excess of a wavelength, the urban environment changes as the user passes buildings of different heights, vacant lots, intersections, and so forth. Over these longer distances, there is a change in the average received power. This change is mainly caused by shadowing and differences in distance from the transmitter. This is indicated by the slowly changing waveform in Figure 5.7 and is referred to as **large-scale fading**.

However, rapid variations in signal strength also occur over distances of about one-half a wavelength. At a frequency of 900 MHz, which is typical for mobile cellular applications, a wavelength is 0.33 m. The rapidly changing waveform in Figure 5.7 shows an example of the spatial variation of received signal amplitude at 900 MHz in an urban setting. Note that changes of amplitude can be as much as 20 or 30 dB over a short distance. This type of rapidly changing fading phenomenon, known as **small-scale fading**, affects not only mobile phones in automobiles, but even a mobile phone user walking down an urban street.

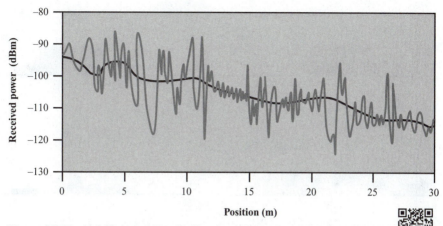

Figure 5.7 Typical Slow and Fast Fading in an Urban Mobile Environment

There are two distinct types of small-scale fading effects.

- **Doppler spread** causes signal performance to change with time due to the movement of mobiles and obstacles.

- **Multipath fading** causes the signal to vary with location due to the combination of delayed multipath signal arrivals.

Regarding Doppler spread, a channel may change over a very short time span. This is characterized by the channel's **coherence time**, T_c, which is the time over which the channel stays relatively constant. Coherence times for a pedestrian might be 70 ms, whereas times might be 5 ms for a vehicle moving at highway speeds.[2] This might have a significant effect on a signal, depending on its bit rate, r_b bits/s. This signal would have a bit time $T_b = 1/r_b$ s/bit. If the coherence time T_c is much, much longer than the bit time T_b, then the channel could be called **slow fading**. The channel changes very slowly during the time to transmit each bit. If, however, this is not true, the channel is undergoing **fast fading**. Therefore, for our purposes in this book we consider a channel to be fast fading if the coherence time T_c is less than, approximately equal, or even slightly greater than the bit time T_b, since in all cases the coherence time is not much, much greater than the bit time.

The other small-scale effect, multipath fading, can cause distortion and inter-symbol interference. **Flat fading** is that type of fading in which all frequency components of the received signal fluctuate in the same proportions simultaneously. Multipath fading can be characterized by a **coherence bandwidth**, B_C, which is the range of frequencies over which the channel response is relatively constant. Therefore, if the coherence bandwidth is much, much greater than the signal bandwidth, then flat fading occurs. If a signal bandwidth can be approximated as $B_S \approx r_b$, then B_C must be much, much greater than B_S. In contrast, **frequency selective fading** occurs when flat fading is not present. It affects unequally the different spectral

---

[2]A common formula is $T_c = 0.423c/vf$, where c is the speed of light, v is the velocity of movement, and f is the frequency [RAPP02].

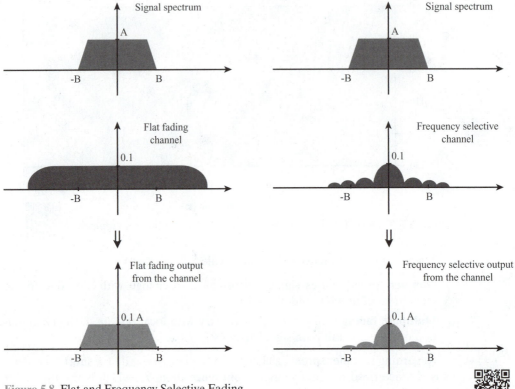

Figure 5.8 Flat and Frequency Selective Fading

components of a radio signal. If attenuation occurs over only a portion of the bandwidth of the signal the fading is considered to be frequency selective. Figure 5.8 illustrates a flat fading channel versus a frequency selective channel relative to the bandwidth of a signal.

These characterizations for Doppler spread and multipath fading do not depend on each other. Therefore, four combinations can occur: fast-flat, slow-flat, fast-frequency selective, and slow-frequency selective fading.

Example 5.5 Suppose that a pedestrian is moving through an urban environment that has a wireless channel with a coherence time of 70 and a coherence bandwidth of 150 kHz. The bit rate of the signal being used is 100 kbps.

a. How would the channel be characterized regarding Doppler spread and multipath fading?

To check for slow fading, test the following, using a factor of 10 for much, much greater.

$$T_b = 1/r_S = 10\,\mu s$$

$$T_C \gg T_b?$$

$$T_C > 10T_b?$$

Test condition: $70\,ms > 100\,\mu s$?

This is true, so *slow fading*.
To check for flat fading, test the following.

$$\text{Assume } B_S \approx r_S = 100 \, kHz$$

$$B_C \gg B_S?$$

$$B_C > 10B_S?$$

$$\textit{Test condition}: 150 \, kHz > 1 \, Mbps?$$

This is not true, so *frequency selective fading*.
This channel is slow and frequency selective.
b. What range of bit rates can be supported to have flat fading?
This is the requirement

$$B_C \gg B_S$$

$$B_C > 10B_S$$

$$150 \, kHz > 10B_S$$

$$B_S < 15 \, kHz$$

$$r_b < 15 \, \text{kbps}$$

5.4 CHANNEL CORRECTION MECHANISMS

The efforts to compensate for the errors and distortions introduced by multipath fading fall into four general categories: forward error correction, adaptive equalization, adaptive modulation and coding, and diversity techniques with multiple-input multiple-output (MIMO). In the typical mobile wireless environment, techniques from all three categories are combined to combat the error rates encountered.

Forward Error Correction

Forward error correction is applicable in digital transmission applications: those in which the transmitted signal carries digital data or digitized voice or video data. The term *forward* refers to procedures whereby a receiver, using only information contained in the incoming digital transmission, corrects bit errors in the data. This is in contrast to backward error correction, in which the receiver merely detects the presence of errors and then sends a request back to the transmitter to retransmit the data in error. Backward error correction is not practical in many wireless applications. For example, in satellite communications, the amount of delay involved makes retransmission undesirable. In mobile communications, the error rates are often so high that there is a high probability that the retransmitted block of bits will also contain errors. In these applications, forward error correction is required. In essence, forward error correction is achieved as follows:

1. Using a coding algorithm, the transmitter adds a number of additional, redundant bits to each transmitted block of data. These bits form an ***error-correcting code*** and are calculated as a function of the data bits.

2. For each incoming block of bits (data plus error-correcting code), the receiver calculates a new error-correcting code from the incoming data bits. If the calculated code matches the incoming code, then the receiver assumes that no error has occurred in this block of bits.

3. If the incoming and calculated codes do not match, then one or more bits are in error. If the number of bit errors is below a threshold that depends on the length of the code and the nature of the algorithm, it is possible for the receiver to determine the bit positions in error and correct all errors.

Typically in mobile wireless applications, the ratio of total bits sent to data bits sent is between 2 and 3. This may seem an extravagant amount of overhead, in that the capacity of the system is cut to one-half or one-third of its potential, but the mobile wireless environment is such a challenging medium that such levels of redundancy are necessary.

Section 5.6 and Chapter 10 examine forward error correction techniques in more detail.

Adaptive Equalization

Adaptive equalization can be applied to transmissions that carry analog information (e.g., analog voice or video) or digital information (e.g., digital data, digitized voice or video) and is used to combat intersymbol interference. The process of equalization involves some method of gathering the dispersed symbol energy back together into its original time interval.

Diversity Techniques and MIMO

Diversity is based on the fact that individual channels experience independent fading events. For example, multiple antennas that are spaced far enough apart will have independent fading. We can therefore compensate for error effects by providing multiple logical channels in some sense between transmitter and receiver and sending part of the signal over each channel. This technique does not eliminate errors but it does reduce the error rate, since we have spread the transmission out to avoid being subjected to the highest error rate that might occur. The other techniques (equalization, forward error correction) can then cope with the reduced error rate.

Some diversity techniques involve the physical transmission path and are referred to as *space diversity*. For example, multiple nearby antennas, if spaced far enough apart, may be used to receive the message with the signals combined in some fashion to reconstruct the most likely transmitted signal. Another example is the use of collocated multiple directional antennas, each oriented to a different reception angle with the incoming signals again combined to reconstitute the transmitted signal.

With *frequency diversity*, the signal is spread out over a larger frequency bandwidth or carried on multiple frequency carriers. The most important examples of this approach are orthogonal frequency division multiplexing (OFDM) and spread spectrum.

Time diversity techniques aim to spread the data out over time so that a noise burst affects fewer bits. This can be accomplished with interleaving or through a Rake receiver.

When these multiple signals are received, there are two basic ways they can be used:

1. **Selection diversity:** Choose one signal that is acceptable or the best.

2. **Diversity combining:** Combine the best signal with the other signals. Adjust the gain and phase so they add together to improve the overall output signal.

Example 5.6. Suppose a wireless channel has two possible quality levels. It has an 80% probability of having a bit error rate of 10^{-6}, but a 20% probability of having a bit error rate of 0.1. Assume independently varying signals can be received through two antennas, and the system uses selection diversity to choose the best signal. How does the overall performance improve?

For one signal, the performance is

$$P_b = Pr\{poor\} * (P_b \ for \ poor) + Pr\{good\} * (P_b \ for \ good)$$
$$P_b = 0.2(0.1) + 0.8(10^{-6}) \approx 0.02$$

For two diversity branches, the only case of poor performance would occur if both branches would be poor so no good signal could be found. The probability of both being poor is 0.2^2, so

$$P_b = 0.2^2(0.1) + (1 - 0.2^2)(10^{-6}) \approx 0.004$$

For k signals, $P_b \approx 0.2^k(0.1)$. This means that P_b drops one order of magnitude for each additional diversity branch.

Multiple-Input Multiple-Output (MIMO) Antennas If a transmitter and receiver implement a system with multiple antennas, this is called a **multiple-input multiple-output (MIMO)** system. These allow several of the mechanisms discussed in this chapter to be implemented as illustrated in Figure 5.9.

1. **Diversity:** Diversity can be accomplished to have multiple received signals through multiple transmit and/or receive antennas.

2. **Beam-forming:** Multiple antennas can be configured to create directional antenna patterns to focus and increase energy to intended recipients.

3. **Multi-user MIMO (MU-MIMO):** With enough MIMO antennas, directional antenna beams can be established to multiple users simultaneously.

4. **Multilayer transmission:** Multiple, parallel data streams can flow between a pair of transmit and receive antennas.

Modern systems implement up to 4×4 (4 input, 4 output) and 8×8 MIMO configurations. Antenna systems have been approved in specifications for as many as 8 per antenna array, and two-dimensional arrays of 64 antennas or more are being envisioned for future technologies.

The MIMO antenna architecture has become a key technology in evolving high-speed wireless networks, including IEEE 802.11 Wi-Fi LANs and Long Term Evolution (LTE) fourth-generation cellular. Together, MIMO and OFDM technologies are the cornerstone of emerging broadband wireless networks.

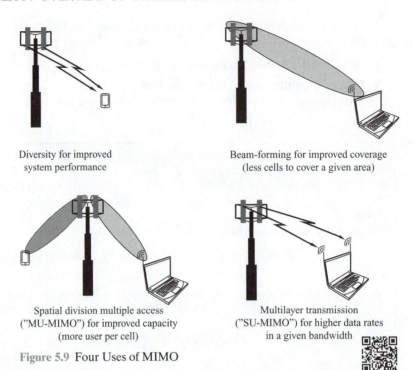

Diversity for improved
system performance

Beam-forming for improved coverage
(less cells to cover a given area)

Spatial division multiple access
("MU-MIMO") for improved capacity
(more user per cell)

Multilayer transmission
("SU-MIMO") for higher data rates
in a given bandwidth

Figure 5.9 Four Uses of MIMO

Spread Spectrum and OFDM

Traditional communications, wireline or wireless, simply modulate a baseband signal up to a required transmission channel and frequency. No change to the original signal occurs. Two methods, however, have been used to overcome wireless channel impairments; the signals are significantly modified for transmission.

- **Orthogonal Frequency Division Multiplexing (OFDM)** splits a signal into many lower bit rate streams that are transmitted over carefully spaced frequencies. This can overcome frequency selective fading by using significantly lower bandwidth per stream with longer bit times. Each of these frequencies can then be amplified separately. This is briefly discussed later in this chapter, and Chapter 8 provides a thorough examination.

- **Spread spectrum** makes a signal use 100 times or more wider bandwidth, with lower energy density at each frequency. This can overcome frequency selective situations; even if some frequencies are poor, good overall average performance is achieved. This is examined briefly later in this chapter and in Chapter 9.

The remainder of the chapter provides an overview of signal encoding and error control techniques. Then it introduces more information about OFDM and spread spectrum.

Adaptive Modulation and Coding

Since the characteristics of a wireless channel can change 100s of times per second due to fading (e.g., 200 times/s for a 5 ms coherence time), modern systems use adaptive modulation and coding (AMC) to adjust their schemes just as quickly. Modulation and coding are discussed more in this chapter in Sections 5.5 and 5.6, in more depth in Chapters 7 and 10. They essentially create signals that send as much information as possible for a given received signal strength and noise, then they detect and correct the errors. To adapt 100's of times per second, two features must be present in the protocols for a system.

1. Mechanisms to measure the quality of the wireless channel. These might include monitoring packet loss rates or sending special pilot signals expressly for measurement purposes.

2. Messaging mechanisms to communicate the signal quality indicators between transmitters and receivers, and also to communicate the new modulation and coding formats.

Bandwidth Expansion

All of the above correction mechanisms seek to increase the efficient use of the bandwidth of a channel, commonly measured in an efficiency of bps/Hz. But according to Shannon's theory there is a limit to this efficiency for a given signal to noise ratio. If throughput requirements are beyond what can be achieved in a given bandwidth, a series of bandwidth expansion approaches are used.

- **Carrier aggregation** combines multiple channels. For example, 802.11n and 802.11ac combine the 20 MHz channels from earlier 802.11 standards into 40, 80, or 160 MHz channels.

- **Frequency reuse** allows the same carrier frequencies to be reused when devices are sufficiently far enough away so the signal-to-interference ratio is low enough. This has traditionally been provided by breaking a cellular coverage area into large cells, called *macro cells*, of several kilometers in diameter. Cells far enough away can reuse the frequencies. But now **small cells** with limited power and range are being used for the same frequency reuse objectives. Indoor small cells are commonly called **femtocells** and outdoor cells are provided by *relays* or **picocells**. These are discussed in conjunction with LTE in Chapter 14. This approach is called *network densification* because it allows frequencies to be reused many times.

- **Millimeter wave (mmWave)** bands are higher frequencies in the 30 GHz to 300 GHz bands that have more bandwidth available in wider bandwidth channels. Recall that $\lambda = c/f$, so 30 to 300 GHz has wavelengths of 10 to 1 mm. This is an example of using different carrier frequencies to achieve higher bandwidth, given spectrum regulations. mmWave bands are more difficult to use, however, since they are more susceptible to attenuation by obstructions and **atmospheric absorption**. IEEE 802.11ad uses mmWave bands within a single room. Future technologies, however, may use them for wider range communication, in conjunction with higher gain MIMO configurations.

5.5 DIGITAL SIGNAL ENCODING TECHNIQUES

A variety of methods are used to encode analog and digital data onto analog and digital signals. Many of these techniques are examined in Chapter 7, which is dedicated to signal encoding topics. Here, we only discuss the encoding of digital data onto analog signals, since most of today's wireless communication is the transmission of digital data.

The basis for analog signals is a continuous constant-frequency signal known as the carrier signal. This is represented by a sinusoidal function as follows.

$$s(t) = A \cos(2\pi f_c t + \theta) \tag{5.7}$$

This signal has an amplitude, A, a frequency, f, and a phase, θ. The frequency, f_c, that is used here is called the carrier frequency. This is chosen to be compatible with the transmission medium being used. In the case of wireless communication, frequencies and signal powers must also be used as specified by regulatory agencies.

Data is transmitted using a carrier signal by modulation. Modulation is the process of encoding source data onto the carrier signal. All modulation techniques involve sending information by changing one or more of the three fundamental frequency domain parameters: amplitude, frequency, and phase. Accordingly, there are three basic encoding or modulation techniques for transforming digital data into analog signals, as illustrated in Figure 5.10: amplitude-shift keying (ASK),

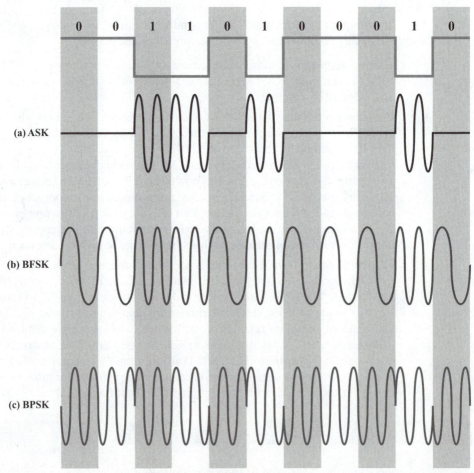

Figure 5.10 Modulation of Analog Signals for Digital Data

frequency-shift keying (FSK), and phase-shift keying (PSK). In all these cases, the resulting signal occupies a bandwidth centered on the carrier frequency.

- In **amplitude-shift keying (ASK)** the two binary values are represented by two different amplitudes of the carrier frequency. Commonly, one of the amplitudes is zero; that is, one binary digit is represented by the presence, at constant amplitude, of the carrier, the other by the absence of the carrier (Figure 5.10a).

$$\textbf{ASK} \qquad s(t) = \begin{cases} A\cos(2\pi f_c\, t) & \text{binary 1} \\ 0 & \text{binary 0} \end{cases} \qquad (5.8)$$

- The most common form of **frequency-shift keying (FSK)** is binary FSK (BFSK), in which the two binary values are represented by two different frequencies near the carrier frequency (Figure 5.10b).

$$\textbf{BFSK} \qquad Bs(t) = \begin{cases} A\cos(2\pi f_1 t) & \text{binary 1} \\ A\cos(2\pi f_2 t) & \text{binary 0} \end{cases} \qquad (5.9)$$

- In **phase-shift keying (PSK)**, the phase of the carrier signal is shifted to represent data. The simplest scheme uses two phases to represent the two binary digits (Figure 5.10c) and is known as binary phase-shift keying.

$$\textbf{BPSK} \qquad s(t) = \begin{cases} A\cos(2\pi f_c t) \\ A\cos(2\pi f_c t + \pi) \end{cases} = \begin{cases} A\cos(2\pi f_c t) & \text{binary 1} \\ A\cos(2\pi f_c t) & \text{binary 0} \end{cases} \qquad (5.10)$$

With two values of amplitude, frequency, or phase, one bit of information can be transmitted at a time. If, for example, four frequencies where used for FSK (which would then be called multilevel FSK or MFSK), two bits of information could be transmitted at a time. Each frequency could correspond to a two-bit sequence. This would effectively double the bit rate of the information transfer. If a scheme used M levels (M would always be a power of 2), the bit rate would increase by a factor of $L = \log_2(M)$ bits. If the same amount of transmitted power were still used, however, the bit error rate of the signal generally would also increase, creating a tradeoff between increased bit rates but also increased error rates.

> **Example 5.7** With $f_c = 250\,\text{kHz}$ and $M = 8$ ($L = 3$ bits), we can have the following frequency assignments for each of the 8 possible 3-bit data combinations if the frequencies are spaced apart by 50 kHz.
>
> $f_1 = 75\,\text{kHz}\ 000$ $f_2 = 125\,\text{kHz}\ 001$ $f_3 = 175\,\text{kHz}\ 010$ $f_4 = 225\,\text{kHz}\ 011$
>
> $f_5 = 275\,\text{kHz}\ 100$ $f_6 = 325\,\text{kHz}\ 101$ $f_7 = 375\,\text{kHz}\ 110$ $f_8 = 425\,\text{kHz}\ 111$

When using a multilevel scheme, more than one of the signal characteristics can be changed. For example, 16-level Quadrature Amplitude Modulation (16QAM) uses various combinations of amplitudes and phases to create 16 different combinations. This would transmit four bits at a time. Figure 5.11 illustrates 16QAM in what is known as a constellation diagram. The amplitude of the signal will be the distance from the origin. For example, symbol 1111 would be transmitted with an amplitude of $\sqrt{1^2 + 1^2} = \sqrt{2}$. The phase of the signal would be the angle of the point in the

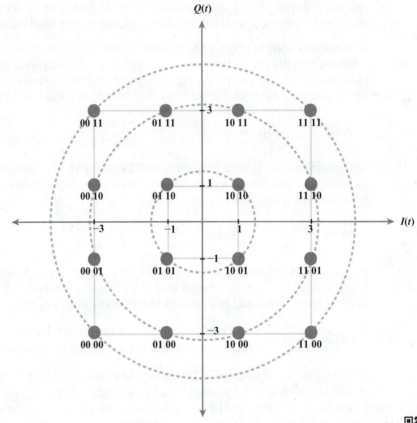

Figure 5.11 16QAM Constellation Diagram

constellation, which for 1111 would be $\tan^{-1}(1/1) = 45°$. By looking carefully at the constellation, we can see that there would be three different possible amplitudes, and 12 different possible phases. The frequencies are the same every time. Some modulation schemes used in communication systems involve 64QAM or 256QAM.

Figure 5.12 shows the received E_b/N_0 versus bit error rate curves for multilevel FSK in Figure 5.12a and QPSK (called quadrature phase-shift keying, which is really a version of 4QAM), 16QAM, and 64QAM in Figure 5.12b. Even though 64QAM will allow more data to be packed into each symbol, and hence a higher data rate, the bit error rate is worse for the same E_b/N_0. Note again that this is the *received* E_b/N_0, so if the wireless channel is good, then the E_b/N_0 will be higher and a constellation like 64QAM might be used to achieve a high data rate. If, however, the received signal strength is low, then E_b/N_0 would be too low and the 64QAM BER would be unacceptable. Only 16QAM or QPSK might be possible. It is very useful, therefore, to have **adaptive modulation and coding (AMC)**, because we know that received signal strength can vary greatly from one coherence time to the next. The system could monitor channel conditions and use QPSK for a period of time then switch to 64QAM later.

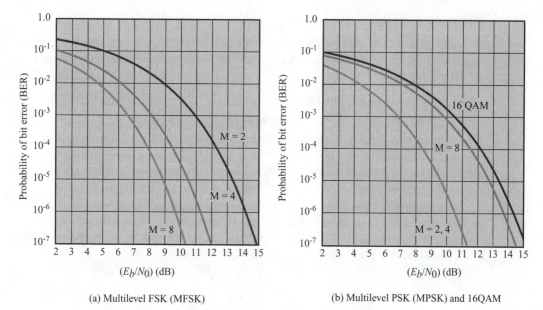

(a) Multilevel FSK (MFSK) (b) Multilevel PSK (MPSK) and 16QAM

Figure 5.12 Theoretical Bit Error Rate for Multilevel FSK, PSK, and QAM

Chapter 7 provides more details on these schemes and illustrates error rate performance. It also discusses modulation of analog data and the encoding of voice signals.

5.6 CODING AND ERROR CONTROL

In earlier sections, we talked about transmission impairments and the effect of data rate and signal-to-noise ratio on bit error rate. Regardless of the design of the transmission system, there will be errors, resulting in the change of one or more bits in a transmitted frame.

Three approaches are in common use for coping with data transmission errors:

- Error detection codes
- Error correction codes, also called **forward error correction (FEC)** codes
- Automatic repeat request (ARQ) protocols

An **error detection** code simply detects the presence of an error. Typically, such codes are used in conjunction with a protocol at the data link or transport level that uses an ARQ scheme. With an ARQ scheme, a receiver discards a block of data in which an error is detected and the transmitter retransmits that block of data. FEC codes are designed not just to detect but correct errors, avoiding the need for retransmission. FEC schemes are frequently used in wireless transmission, where retransmission schemes are highly inefficient and error rates may be high. Some wireless protocols use Hybrid ARQ, which is a combination of FEC and ARQ.

Error Detection

In what follows, we assume that data are transmitted as one or more contiguous sequences of bits, called *frames*. Let us define these probabilities with respect to errors in transmitted frames:

P_b: Probability of a single bit error; also known as the bit error rate (BER)

P_1: Probability that a frame arrives with no bit errors

P_2: Probability that, with an error detection algorithm in use, a frame arrives with one or more undetected errors

P_3: Probability that, with an error detection algorithm in use, a frame arrives with one or more detected bit errors but no undetected bit errors

First consider the case when no means are taken to detect errors. Then the probability of detected errors (P_3) is zero. To express the remaining probabilities, assume the probability that any bit is in error (P_b) is constant and independent for each bit. Then, we have

$$P_1 = (1 - P_b)^F$$

$$P_2 = 1 - P_1$$

where F is the number of bits per frame. In words, the probability that a frame arrives with no bit errors decreases when the probability of a single bit error increases, as you would expect. Also, the probability that a frame arrives with no bit errors decreases with increasing frame length; the longer the frame, the more bits it has and the higher the probability that one of these is in error.

Example 5.8 A system has a defined objective for connections that the BER should be less than 10^{-6} on at least 90% of observed 1-minute intervals. Suppose now that we have the rather modest user requirement that on average one frame with an undetected bit error should occur per day on a continuously used 1 Mbps channel, and let us assume a frame length of 1000 bits. The number of frames that can be transmitted in a day comes out to 8.64×10^7, which yields a required frame error rate of $P_2 = 1/(8.64 \times 10^7) = 1.16 \times 10^{-8}$. But if we assume a value of P_b of 10^{-6}, then $P_1 = (0.999999)^{1000} = 0.999$ and therefore $P_2 = 10^{-3}$, which is about five orders of magnitude too large to meet our requirement. This means that $(8.64 \times 10^7)*P_2 = 86,400$ frames with undetected bit errors would occur per day for P_b of 10^{-6}.

This is the kind of result that motivates the use of error detection techniques. All of these techniques operate on the following principle (Figure 5.13). For a given frame of bits, the transmitter adds additional bits that constitute an error-detecting code. This code is calculated as a function of the other transmitted bits. Typically, for a data block of k bits, the error detection algorithm yields an error detection code of $n - k$ bits, where $(n - k) < k$. The error detection code, also referred to as the **check bits**, is appended to the data block to produce a frame of n bits, which is then transmitted. The receiver separates the incoming frame into the k bits of data and $(n - k)$ bits of the error detection code. The receiver performs the same error detection calculation on the data bits and compares this value with the value of the incoming error detection code. A detected error occurs if and only if there is a mismatch. Thus, P_3 is the probability that a frame contains errors and that the error

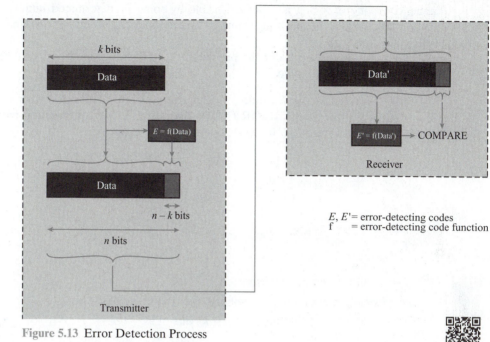

Figure 5.13 Error Detection Process

detection scheme will detect that fact. P_2 is known as the *residual error rate* and is the probability that an error will be undetected despite the use of an error detection scheme.

Parity Check The simplest error detection scheme is to append a parity bit to the end of a block of data. A typical example is character transmission, in which a parity bit is attached to each 7-bit character. The value of this bit is selected so that the character has an even number of 1s (even parity) or an odd number of 1s (odd parity).

> **Example 5.9** If the transmitter is transmitting 1110001 and using odd parity, it will append a 1 and transmit 11110001. The receiver examines the received character and, if the total number of 1s is odd, assumes that no error has occurred. If one bit (or any odd number of bits) is erroneously inverted during transmission (e.g., 11100001), then the receiver will detect an error.

Note, however, that if two (or any even number) of bits are inverted due to error, an undetected error occurs. Typically, even parity is used for synchronous transmission and odd parity for asynchronous transmission.

The use of the parity bit is not foolproof, as noise impulses are often long enough to destroy more than one bit, especially at high data rates.

Cyclic Redundancy Check One of the most common, and one of the most powerful, error-detecting codes is the **cyclic redundancy check (CRC)**, which can be described as follows. Given a k-bit block of bits, or message, the transmitter generates an $(n - k)$-bit sequence, known as a frame check sequence (FCS), such that the resulting frame, consisting of n bits, is exactly divisible by some predetermined number. The receiver then divides the incoming frame by that number and, if there is no remainder, assumes there was no error.[3]

To clarify this, we present the procedure in three ways: modulo 2 arithmetic, polynomials, and digital logic.

Modulo 2 Arithmetic Modulo 2 arithmetic uses binary addition with no carries, which is just the exclusive-OR (XOR) operation. Binary subtraction with no carries is also interpreted as the XOR operation: For example:

$$
\begin{array}{r}
1111 \\
+\ 1010 \\
\hline
0101
\end{array}
\qquad
\begin{array}{r}
1111 \\
-0101 \\
\hline
1010
\end{array}
\qquad
\begin{array}{r}
11001 \\
\times\ 11 \\
\hline
11001 \\
11001 \\
\hline
101011
\end{array}
$$

Now define:

$T = n$-bit frame to be transmitted

$D = k$-bit block of data, or message, the first k bits of T

$F = (n - k)$-bit FCS, the last $(n - k)$ bits of T

$P = $ pattern of $n - k + 1$ bits; this is the predetermined divisor

We would like T/P to have no remainder. It should be clear that

$$T = 2^{n-k}D + F$$

That is, by multiplying D by 2^{n-k}, we have in effect shifted it to the left by $n - k$ bits and padded out the result with zeroes. Adding F yields the concatenation of D and F, which is T. We want T to be exactly divisible by P. Suppose that we divide $2^{n-k}D$ by P:

$$\frac{2^{n-k}D}{P} = Q + \frac{R}{P} \tag{5.11}$$

There is a quotient and a remainder. Because division is modulo 2, the remainder is always at least one bit shorter than the divisor. We will use this remainder as our FCS. Then,

$$T = 2^{n-k}D + R \tag{5.12}$$

Does this R satisfy our condition that T/P have no remainder? To see that it does, consider

$$\frac{T}{P} = \frac{2^{n-k}D + R}{P} = \frac{2^{n-k}D}{P} + \frac{R}{P}$$

Substituting Equation (5.11), we have

$$\frac{T}{R} = Q + \frac{R}{P} + \frac{R}{P}$$

---

[3]This procedure is slightly different from that of Figure 5.13. As shall be seen, the CRC process could be implemented as follows. The receiver could perform a division operation on the incoming k data bits and compare the result to the incoming $(n - k)$ check bits.

However, any binary number added to itself modulo 2 yields zero. Thus,

$$\frac{T}{P} = Q + \frac{R + R}{P} = Q$$

There is no remainder, and therefore T is exactly divisible by P. Thus, the FCS is easily generated: Simply divide $2^{n-k}D$ by P and use the $(n - k)$-bit remainder as the FCS. On reception, the receiver will divide T by P and will get no remainder if there have been no errors.

Example 5.10

1. Given

$$\text{Message } D = 1010001101 \text{ (10 bits)}$$
$$\text{Pattern } P = 110101 \text{ (6 bits)}$$
$$\text{FCS } R = \text{to be calculated (5 bits)}$$

Thus, $n = 15$, $k = 10$, and $(n-k) = 5$.

2. The message is multiplied by 2^5, yielding 101000110100000.

3. This product is divided by P:

```
                              1 1 0 1 0 1 0 1 1 0 ← Q
        P→1 1 0 1 0 1 / 1 0 1 0 0 0 1 1 0 1 0 0 0 0 0 ← 2ⁿ⁻ᵏD
                        1 1 0 1 0 1
                        1 1 1 0 1 1
                        1 1 0 1 0 1
                            1 1 1 0 1 0
                            1 1 0 1 0 1
                                1 1 1 1 1 0
                                1 1 0 1 0 1
                                    1 0 1 1 0 0
                                    1 1 0 1 0 1
                                        1 1 0 0 1 0
                                        1 1 0 1 0 1
                                            0 1 1 1 0 ← R
```

4. The remainder is added to $2^5 D$ to give $T = 101000110101110$, which is transmitted.

5. If there are no errors, the receiver receives T intact. The received frame is divided by P:

```
                              1 1 0 1 0 1 0 1 1 0 ← Q
        P→1 1 0 1 0 1 / 1 0 1 0 0 0 1 1 0 1 0 1 1 1 0 ← T
                        1 1 0 1 0 1
                        1 1 1 0 1 1
                        1 1 0 1 0 1
                            1 1 1 0 1 0
                            1 1 0 1 0 1
                                1 1 1 1 1 0
                                1 1 0 1 0 1
                                    1 0 1 1 1 1
                                    1 1 0 1 0 1
                                        1 1 0 1 0 1
                                        1 1 0 1 0 1
                                            0 ← R
```

Because there is no remainder, it is assumed that there have been no errors.

The pattern P is chosen to be one bit longer than the desired FCS, and the exact bit pattern chosen depends on the type of errors expected. At minimum, both the high- and low-order bits of P must be 1.

There is a concise method for specifying the occurrence of one or more errors. An error results in the reversal of a bit. This is equivalent to taking the XOR of the bit and 1 (modulo 2 addition of 1 to the bit): $0 + 1 = 1; 1 + 1 = 0$. Thus, the errors in an n-bit frame can be represented by an n-bit field with 1s in each error position. The resulting frame T_r can be expressed as

$$T_r = T \oplus E$$

where

$$T = \text{transmitted frame}$$

$$E = \text{error pattern with 1s in positions where errors occur}$$

$$T_r = \text{received frame}$$

If there is an error ($E \neq 0$), the receiver will fail to detect the error if and only if T_r is divisible by P, which is equivalent to E divisible by P. Intuitively, this seems an unlikely occurrence.

Polynomials A second way of viewing the CRC process is to express all values as polynomials in a dummy variable X, with binary coefficients. The coefficients correspond to the bits in the binary number. Arithmetic operations are again modulo 2. The CRC process can now be described as

$$\frac{X^{n-k}D(X)}{P(X)} = Q(X) + \frac{R(X)}{P(X)}$$

$$T(X) = X^{n-k}D(X) + R(X)$$

Compare these equations with Equations (5.11) and (5.12).

An error $E(X)$ will only be undetectable if it is divisible by $P(X)$. It can be shown [PETE61, RAMA88] that all of the following errors are not divisible by a suitably chosen $P(X)$ and hence are detectable:

- All single-bit errors, if $P(X)$ has more than one nonzero term
- All double-bit errors, as long as $P(X)$ has a factor with at least three terms
- Any odd number of errors, as long as $P(X)$ contains a factor $(X + 1)$
- Any burst error[4] for which the length of the burst is less than or equal to $n - k$; that is, less than or equal to the length of the FCS
- A fraction of error bursts of length $n - k + 1$; the fraction equals $1 - 2^{-(n-k-1)}$
- A fraction of error bursts of length greater than $n - k + 1$; the fraction equals $1 - 2^{-(n-k)}$

In addition, it can be shown that if all error patterns are considered equally likely, then for a burst error of length $r + 1$, the probability of an undetected error [i.e., $E(X)$ is divisible by $P(X)$] is $1/2^{r-1}$ and for a longer burst, the probability is $1/2^r$,

---

[4]A burst error of length B is a contiguous sequence of B bits in which the first and last bits and any number of intermediate bits are received in error.

Example 5.11 Continuing with Example 5.10, for $D = 1010001101$, we have $D(X) = X^9 + X^7 + X^3 + X^2 + 1$, and for $P = 110101$, we have $P(X) = X^5 + X^4 + X^2 + 1$. We should end up with $R = 01110$, which corresponds to $R(X) = X^3 + X^2 + X$. Figure 5.14 shows the polynomial division that corresponds to the binary division in the preceding example.

$$
\begin{array}{r}
X^9 + X^8 + X^6 + X^4 + X^2 + X \quad \leftarrow Q(X) \\
P(X) \rightarrow X^5 + X^4 + X^2 + 1 \, \big/ \, X^{14} \qquad X^{12} \qquad\qquad X^8 + X^7 + \quad X^5 \quad \leftarrow X^5 D(X) \\
X^{14} + X^{13} + \quad X^{11} + \quad X^9 \\
\hline
X^{13} + X^{12} + X^{11} + \quad X^9 + X^8 \\
X^{13} + X^{12} + \quad X^{10} + \quad X^8 \\
\hline
X^{11} + X^{11} + X^9 + \quad X^7 \\
X^{11} + X^{10} + \quad X^8 + \quad X^6 \\
\hline
X^9 + X^8 + X^7 + X^6 + X^5 \\
X^9 + X^8 + \quad X^6 + \quad X^4 \\
\hline
X^7 + \quad X^5 + X^4 \\
X^7 + X^6 + \quad X^4 + \quad X^2 \\
\hline
X^6 + X^5 + \qquad X^2 \\
X^6 + X^5 + \quad X^3 + \quad X \\
\hline
X^3 + X^2 + X \quad \leftarrow R(X)
\end{array}
$$

Figure 5.14 Polynomial Division for Example 5.10

where r is the length of the FCS. This means there are 2^r possible error patterns, and only one of those patterns will go undetected.

Four versions of $P(X)$ have been widely used:

$$\text{CRC-12} = X^{12} + X^{11} + X^3 + X^2 + X + 1$$

$$\text{CRC-16} = X^{16} + X^{15} + X^2 + 1$$

$$\text{CRC-CCITT} = X^{16} + X^{12} + X^5 + 1$$

$$\text{CRC-32} = X^{32} + X^{26} + X^{23} + X^{22} + X^{16} + X^{12} + X^{11}$$
$$+ X^{10} + X^8 + X^7 + X^5 + X^4 + X^2 + X + 1$$

The CRC-12 system is used for transmission of streams of 6-bit characters and generates a 12-bit FCS. Both CRC-16 and CRC-CCITT are popular for 8-bit characters, in the United States and Europe, respectively, and both result in a 16-bit FCS. This would seem adequate for most applications, although CRC-32 is specified as an option in some point-to-point synchronous transmission standards.

Block Error Correction Codes

Error detection is a useful technique, found in data link control protocols, such as high-level data link control (HDLC), and in transport protocols, such as TCP. However, correction of errors using an error detection code requires that block of data be retransmitted, using the ARQ discipline explained in detail in Section 10.4. For wireless applications, this approach is inadequate for two reasons.

1. The bit error rate on a wireless link can be quite high, which would result in a large number of retransmissions.

2. In some cases, especially satellite links, the propagation delay is very long compared to the transmission time of a single frame. The result is a very inefficient system. As is discussed in Section 10.4, the common approach to retransmission is to retransmit the frame in error plus all subsequent frames. With a long data link, an error in a single frame necessitates retransmitting many frames.

Instead, it would be desirable to enable the receiver to correct errors in an incoming transmission on the basis of the bits in that transmission. Figure 5.15 shows in general how this is done. On the transmission end, each k-bit block of data is mapped into an n-bit block ($n > k$) called a **codeword**, using an FEC encoder. The codeword is then transmitted; in the case of wireless transmission a modulator produces an analog signal for transmission. During transmission, the signal is subject to noise, which may produce bit errors in the signal. At the receiver, the incoming signal is demodulated to produce a bit string that is similar to the original codeword but may contain errors. This block is passed through an FEC decoder, with one of five possible outcomes:

1. If there are no bit errors, the input to the FEC decoder is identical to the original codeword, and the decoder produces the original data block as output.

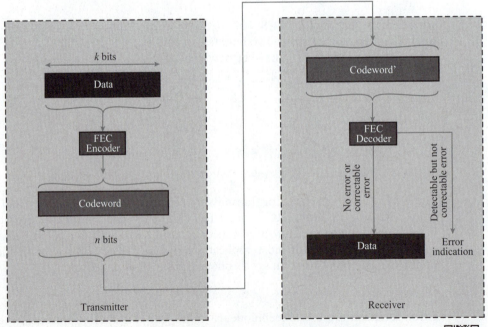

Figure 5.15 Forward Error Correction Process

2. For certain error patterns, it is possible for the decoder to detect and correct those errors. Thus, even though the incoming data block differs from the transmitted codeword, the FEC decoder is able to map this block into the original data block.

3. For certain error patterns, the decoder can detect but not correct the errors. In this case, the decoder simply reports an uncorrectable error.

4. For certain, typically rare, error patterns, the decoder detects an error, but does not correct it properly. It assumes a certain block of data was sent when in reality of different one was sent.

5. For certain even more rare error patterns, the decoder does not detect that any errors have occurred and maps the incoming n-bit data block into a k-bit block that differs from the original k-bit block.

How is it possible for the decoder to correct bit errors? In essence, error correction works by adding redundancy to the transmitted message. Consider an example where a binary 0 or 1 were to be sent, but instead the codewords that were sent were either 0000 or 1111. The redundancy makes it possible for the receiver to deduce what the original message was, even in the face of a certain level of error rate. If a 0010 were received, we could assume that a 0000 was sent corresponding to the original binary 0, since only one bit change would have occurred to make this happen. There is, however, a much more unlikely yet possible scenario were a 1111 was sent. The decoder would then make a mistake by assuming a 0 was sent. Consider if another received codeword were 0011. In this case, the decoder would not be able to decide since it would be equally likely that 0000 or 1111 was sent.

In this section, we look at a widely used form of error correction code known as a block error correction code. We begin with a discussion of general principles. Before proceeding, we note that in many cases, the error correction code follows the same general layout as shown for error detection codes in Figure 5.13. That is, the FEC algorithm takes as input a k-bit block and adds $(n - k)$ check bits to that block to produce an n-bit block; all of the bits in the original k-bit block show up in the n-bit block. For some FEC algorithms, such as the convolutional code, the FEC algorithm maps the k-bit input into an n-bit codeword in such a way that the original k bits do not appear in the codeword.

Block Code Principles

To begin, we define a term that shall be of use to us. The **Hamming distance** $d(v_1, v_2)$ between two n-bit binary sequences v_1 and v_2 is the number of bits in which v_1 and v_2 disagree. For example, if

$$v_1 = 011011, \qquad v_2 = 110001$$

then

$$d(v_1, v_2) = 3$$

Suppose we wish to transmit blocks of data of length k bits. Instead of transmitting each block as k bits, we map each k-bit sequence into a unique n-bit codeword.

Example 5.12 For $k = 2$ and $n = 5$, we can make the following assignment:

Data block	Codeword
00	00000
01	00111
10	11001
11	11110

Now, suppose that a codeword block is received with the bit pattern 00100. This is not a valid codeword and so the receiver has detected an error. Can the error be corrected? We cannot be sure which data block was sent because 1, 2, 3, 4, or even all 5 of the bits that were transmitted may have been corrupted by noise. However, notice that it would require only a single bit change to transform the valid codeword 00000 into 00100. It would take two bit changes to transform 00111 to 00100, three bit changes to transform 11110 to 00100, and it would take four bit changes to transform 11001 into 00100. Thus, we can deduce that the most likely codeword that was sent was 00000 and that therefore the desired data block is 00. This is error correction. In terms of Hamming distances, we have

$$d(00000, 00100) = 1; d(00111, 00100) = 2;$$
$$d(11001, 00100) = 4; d(11110, 00100) = 3$$

So the rule we would like to impose is that if an invalid codeword is received, then the valid codeword that is closest to it (minimum distance) is selected. This will only work if there is a unique valid codeword at a minimum distance from each invalid codeword.

For our example, it is not true that for every invalid codeword there is one and only one valid codeword at a minimum distance. There are $2^5 = 32$ possible codewords of which 4 are valid, leaving 28 invalid codewords. For the invalid codewords, we have the following:

Invalid Codeword	Minimum Distance	Valid Codeword	Invalid Codeword	Minimum Distance	Valid Codeword
00001	1	00000	10000	1	00000
00010	1	00000	10001	1	11001
00011	1	00111	10010	2	00000 or 11110
00100	1	00000	10011	2	00111 or 11001
00101	1	00111	10100	2	00000 or 11110
00110	1	00111	10101	2	00111 or 11001
01000	1	00000	10110	1	11110
01001	1	11001	10111	1	00111
01010	2	00000 or 11110	11000	1	11001
01011	2	00111 or 11001	11010	1	11110
01100	2	00000 or 11110	11011	1	11001
01101	2	00111 or 11001	11100	1	11110
01110	1	11110	11101	1	11001
01111	1	00111	11111	1	11110

There are eight cases in which an invalid codeword is at a distance 2 from two different valid codewords. Thus, if one such invalid codeword is received, an error in 2 bits could have caused it and the receiver has no way to choose between the two alternatives. An error is detected but cannot be corrected. The only remedy is retransmission. However, in every case in which a single bit error occurs, the resulting codeword is of distance 1 from only one valid codeword and the decision can be made. This code is therefore capable of correcting all single-bit errors but cannot correct double bit errors. Another way to see this is to look at the pairwise distances between valid codewords:

$$d(00000, 00111) = 3; \quad d(00000, 11001) = 3; \quad d(00000, 11110) = 4;$$
$$d(00111, 11001) = 4; \quad d(00111, 11110) = 3; \quad d(11001, 11110) = 3;$$

The minimum distance between valid codewords is 3. Therefore, a single bit error will result in an invalid codeword that is a distance 1 from the original valid codeword but a distance at least 2 from all other valid codewords. As a result, the code can always correct a single-bit error. Note that the code also will always detect a double-bit error.

The preceding example illustrates the essential properties of a block error-correcting code. An (n, k) block code encodes k data bits into n-bit codewords. Thus the design of a block code is equivalent to the design of a function of the form $\mathbf{v_c} = f(\mathbf{v_d})$, where $\mathbf{v_d}$ is a vector of k data bits and $\mathbf{v_c}$ is a vector of n codeword bits.

With an (n, k) block code, there are 2^k valid codewords out of a total of 2^n possible codewords. The ratio of redundant bits to data bits, $(n - k)/k$, is called the **redundancy** of the code, and the ratio of data bits to total bits, k/n, is called the **code rate**. The code rate is a measure of how much additional bandwidth is required to carry data at the same data rate as without the code. For example, a code rate of 1/2 requires double the bandwidth of an uncoded system to maintain the same data rate. Our example has a code rate of 2/5 and so requires a bandwidth 2.5 times the bandwidth for an uncoded system. For example, if the data rate input to the encoder is 1 Mbps, then the output from the encoder must be at a rate of 2.5 Mbps to keep up.

For a code consisting of the codewords $\mathbf{w}_1, \mathbf{w}_2, \ldots, \mathbf{w}_s$, where $s = 2^k$, the minimum distance d_{min} of the code is defined as

$$d_{min} = \min_{i \neq j} \lfloor d(\mathbf{w}_i, \mathbf{w}_j) \rfloor$$

It can be shown that the following conditions hold. For a given positive integer t, if a code satisfies $d_{min} \geq 2t + 1$, then the code can correct all bit errors up to and including errors of t bits. If $d_{min} \geq 2t$, then all errors $\leq t - 1$ bits can be corrected and errors of t bits can be detected but not, in general, corrected. Conversely, any code for which all errors of magnitude $\leq t$ are corrected must satisfy $d_{min} \geq 2t + 1$, and any code for which all errors of magnitude $\leq t - 1$ are corrected and all errors of magnitude t are detected must satisfy $d_{min} \geq 2t$.

Another way of putting the relationship between d_{min} and t is to say that the maximum number of guaranteed correctable errors per codeword satisfies

$$t = \left\lfloor \frac{d_{min} - 1}{2} \right\rfloor$$

where $\lfloor x \rfloor$ means the largest integer not to exceed x (e.g., $\lfloor 6.3 \rfloor = 6$). Furthermore, if we are concerned only with error detection and not error correction, then the number of errors, t, that can be detected satisfies

$$t = d_{min} - 1$$

To see this, consider that if d_{min} errors occur, this could change one valid codeword into another. Any number of errors less than d_{min} cannot result in another valid codeword.

The design of a block code involves a number of considerations:

1. For given values of n and k, we would like the largest possible value of d_{min}.

2. The code should be relatively easy to encode and decode, requiring minimal memory and processing time.

3. We would like the number of extra bits, $(n - k)$, to be small, to reduce bandwidth.

4. We would like the number of extra bits, $(n - k)$, to be large, to reduce error rate.

Clearly, the last two objectives are in conflict, and trade-offs must be made.

Let us examine Figure 5.16. The literature on error-correcting codes frequently includes graphs of this sort to demonstrate the effectiveness of various encoding schemes. Recall from earlier in this section that modulation schemes can be chosen to reduce the required E_b/N_0 value to achieve a given bit error rate. Modulation has to do with the definition of signal elements to represent bits. This modulation also has an effect on E_b/N_0. In Figure 5.16, the curve on the right is for an uncoded modulation system; the shaded region represents the area in which potential improvement can be achieved. In this region, a smaller BER is achieved for a given E_b/N_0, and conversely, for a given BER, a smaller E_b/N_0 is required. The other curve is a typical result of a code rate of one-half (equal number of data and check bits). Note that at an error rate of 10^{-6}, the use of coding allows a reduction in E_b/N_0 of 2.77 dB. This reduction is referred to as the **coding gain**, which is defined as the reduction, in decibels, in the required E_b/N_0 to achieve a specified BER of an error-correcting coded system compared to an uncoded system using the same modulation.

It is important to realize that the BER for the second rate 1/2 curve refers to the rate of uncorrected errors and that the E_b value refers to the energy per data bit. Because the rate is 1/2, there are two bits on the channel for each data bit, effectively reducing the data throughput by 1/2 as well. The energy per coded bit is half that of the energy per data bit, or a reduction of 3 dB. If we look at the energy per coded bit for this system, then we see that the channel bit error rate is about 2.4×10^{-2}, or 0.024.

Finally, note that below a certain threshold of E_b/N_0, the coding scheme actually degrades performance. In our example of Figure 5.16, the threshold occurs at about 5.4 dB. Below the threshold, the extra check bits add overhead to the system that reduces the energy per data bit causing increased errors. Above the threshold, the error-correcting power of the code more than compensates for the reduced E_b, resulting in a coding gain.

Commonly used error correction block codes are Hamming, Cyclic, BCH, and Reed-Solomon codes. Chapter 10 provides details on these specific block error correction codes.

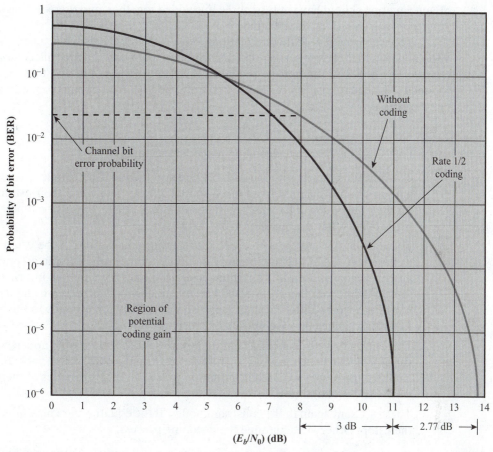

Figure 5.16 How Coding Improves System Performance

Low-Density Parity-Check Codes

For decades, researchers were not able to approach the Shannon limit for data capacity for a given channel bandwidth, at least not within practical computational hardware constraints. There were some capacity-approaching codes developed in the 1960s, called low-density parity-check (LDPC) codes, which were rediscovered in the 1990s. They only then became of practical use, since their computational complexity was at first prohibitive. They have since been enhanced and become popular, for example in the latest generation of IEEE 802.11 standards.

LDPC uses very long block codes, normally longer than 1000 bits. To check for errors among these bits, a series of parity equations are implemented, usually organized in an **H** matrix. For example, one might require the following:

$$b_{10} + b_{13} + b_{45} + b_{192} = 0$$

Each equation should have at least three bits added together, and there will be hundreds of such equations for 1000 bits.

To visualize a few of these equations, see Figure 5.17. This is a Tanner graph. The nodes in the top row correspond to each of the data bits and are called *variable nodes*. The nodes in the bottom row are called *constraint nodes*, and these correspond to the equations. For example, constraint node c_1 corresponds to the following equation:

$$v_3 + v_4 + v_5 + v_6 = 0$$

LDPC uses an iterative decoding procedure as follows:

1. The procedure starts with the variable nodes at the top. These nodes use external information, mainly from the demodulator, to determine their estimates for their bit values. If they use a soft decoding approach, they also estimate the probabilities that the bits should be 0 or 1.

2. These estimates are then sent to the constraint nodes to see if the estimated values satisfy all of the equations. If so, the decoding stops since an acceptable answer has been found. If not, the constraint nodes combine the information sent to them from their connected variable nodes to determine which bits are most likely to be different than their estimates. This corresponds to the most likely bit changes that are needed to satisfy the equations.

3. The estimates from the constraint nodes are sent to the variable nodes. Since variable nodes are connected to multiple constraint nodes, the variable nodes combine the newly acquired information to update their estimates of their bit values and probabilities.

4. These are sent again to the constraint nodes. If the equations are now satisfied, then stop. Otherwise, continue the decoding process.

This decoding procedure is known as *message passing* or *belief propagation*. The performance of LDPC codes can be impressive, approaching Shannon capacity within a fraction of a dB when using long codes.

Convolutional Codes

Block codes are one of the two widely used categories of error correction codes for wireless transmission; the other is convolutional codes. A (n, k) block code processes data in blocks of k bits at a time, producing a block of n bits $(n > k)$ as output

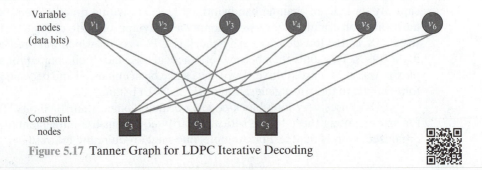

Figure 5.17 Tanner Graph for LDPC Iterative Decoding

for every block of k bits as input. If data are transmitted and received in a more or less continuous stream, a block code, particularly one with a large value of n, may not be as convenient as a code that generates redundant bits continuously so that error checking and correcting are carried out continuously. This is the function of convolutional codes.

A convolutional code is defined by three parameters: n, k, and K. An (n, k, K) code processes input data k bits at a time and produces an output of n bits for each incoming k bits. So far this is the same as the block code. In the case of a convolutional code, n and k are generally quite small numbers. The difference is that convolutional codes have memory, which is characterized by the *constraint factor K*. In essence, the current n-bit output of an (n, k, K) code depends not only on the value of the current block of k input bits but also on the previous $K - 1$ blocks of k input bits. Hence, the current output of n bits is a function of the last $K \times k$ input bits.

Convolutional codes are best understood by looking at a specific example. We use the example shown in Figure 5.18. There are two alternative representations of the code shown in the figure. Figure 5.18a is a shift register, which is most convenient for describing and implementing the encoding process. Figure 5.18b is an equivalent representation that is useful in discussing the decoding process.

For an (n, k, K) code, the shift register contains the most recent $K \times k$ input bits; the register is initialized to all zeros.[5] The encoder produces n output bits, after

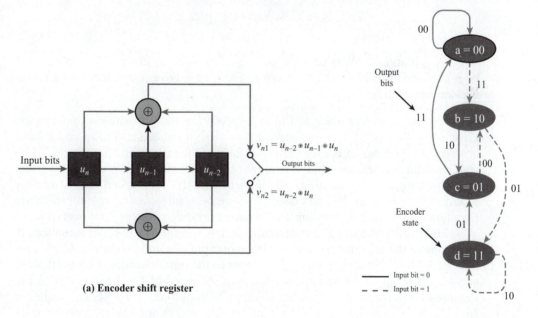

(a) Encoder shift register

(b) Encoder state diagram

Figure 5.18 Convolutional Encoder with $(n, k, K) = (2, 1, 3)$

---

[5]In some of the literature, the shift register is shown with one less storage cell and with the input bits feeding the XOR circuits as well as a storage cell; the depictions are equivalent.

which the oldest k bits from the register are discarded and k new bits are shifted in. Thus, although the output of n bits depends on $K \times k$ input bits, the rate of encoding is n output bits per k input bits. As in a block code, the code rate is therefore k/n. The most commonly used binary encoders have $k = 1$ and hence a shift register length of K. Our example is of a $(2, 1, 3)$ code (Figure 5.18a). The shift register holds $K \times k = 3 \times 1$ *bits* u_n, u_{n-1}, and u_{n-2}. For each new input bit u_n, two output bits v_{n1} and v_{n2} are produced using the three most recent bits. The first output bit produced here is from the upper logic circuit ($v_{n1} = u_n \oplus u_{n-1} \oplus u_{n-2}$), and the second output bit from the lower logic circuit ($v_{n2} = u_n \oplus u_{n-2}$).

For any given input of k bits, there are $2^{k(K-1)}$ different functions that map the k input bits into n output bits. Which function is used depends on the history of the previous $(K - 1)$ input blocks of k bits each. We can therefore represent a convolutional code using a finite-state machine. The machine has $2^{k(K-1)}$ states, and the transition from one state to another is determined by the most recent k bits of inputs and produces n output bits. The initial state of the machine corresponds to the all-zeros state. For our example (Figure 5.18b) there are four states, one for each possible pair of values for the previous two bits. The next input bit causes a transition and produces an output of two bits. For example, if the last two bits were 10 ($u_{n-1} = 1$, $u_{n-2} = 0$) and the next bit is 1 ($u_n = 1$), then the current state is state b (10) and the next state is d (11). The output is

$$v_{n1} = u_{n-2} \oplus u_{n-1} \oplus u_n = 0 \oplus 1 \oplus 1 = 0$$

$$v_{n2} = 0 \oplus 1 = 1$$

Convolutional codes provide good performance in noisy channels where a high proportion of the bits are in error. Thus, they have found increasing use in wireless applications.

Turbo Coding   As higher and higher speeds are used in wireless applications, error correction continues to pose a major design challenge. **Turbo codes** have emerged as a popular choice for third- and fourth-generation wireless systems. Turbo codes exhibit performance, in terms of bit error probability, that is very close to the Shannon limit and can be efficiently implemented for high-speed use. A number of different turbo encoders and decoders have been introduced, most of which are based on convolutional encoding. In this subsection, we give a general overview.

Figure 5.19a depicts a turbo encoder. In this scheme, the encoder is replicated. One copy of the encoder receives a stream of input bits and produces a single output check bit C_1 for each input bit. The input to the other encoder is an interleaved version of the input bit stream, producing a sequence of C_2 check bits. The initial input bit plus the two check bits are then multiplexed to produce the sequence $I_1 C_{11} C_{21} I_2 C_{12} C_{22} \ldots$, that is, the first input bit followed by the first bit from encoder one, followed by the first bit from encoder 2, and so on. The resulting sequence has a code rate of 1/3. A code rate of 1/2 can be achieved by taking only half of the check bits, alternating between outputs from the two encoders; this process is called *puncturing*. Rates of 1/3 and 1/2 are both found in third- and fourth-generation systems.

Note that each encoder only produces a single check bit for each input bit and that the input bit is preserved. In the convolutional encoders we have discussed so far (e.g., Figure 5.18a), the input bits are not preserved, and there are multiple output

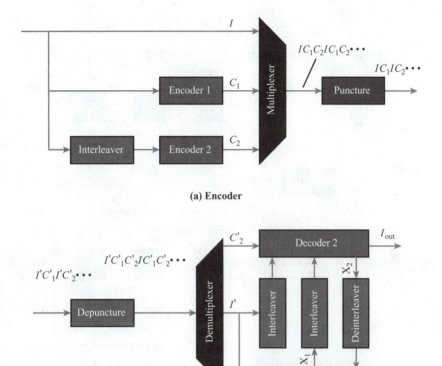

(a) Encoder

(b) Decoder

Figure 5.19 Turbo Encoding and Decoding

bits (*n* output check bits for *k* input bits). For turbo coding, a variation of the convolutional code, known as a recursive systematic convolutional code (RSC), is used. Figure 5.20 shows how a turbo encoder can be implemented using two RSC coders.

Figure 5.19b is a general diagram of a turbo decoder. The received data is depunctured, if necessary, by estimating the missing check bits or by setting the missing bits to 0. Decoder 1 operates first, using the estimated I' and C_1' values received from the demodulator. These values are not simply 0 or 1, but rather are larger or smaller values given the demodulator's confidence in its decision. This is called *soft decision decoding*. Decoder 1 then produces correction (X_1) values. The I' and X_1 values are fed into decoder 2, together with the C_2' values. Interleaving must be performed to align bits properly. Decoder 2 uses all of its input to produce correction values X_2. These are fed back to Decoder 1 for a second iteration of the decoding algorithm, being first deinterleaved for alignment. After sufficient iterations to produce a high level of confidence, an output bit is generated. This may take several iterations to produce a good result, which could cause significant delay. Turbo coding's use of interleaving, parallel encoding, puncturing, soft decision decoding, and feedback gives it high performance.

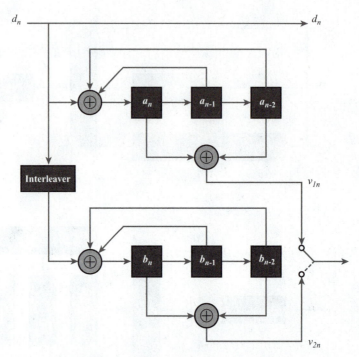

Figure 5.20 Parallel Concatenation of Two RSC Encoders

Automatic Repeat Request

Automatic repeat request (ARQ) is a mechanism used in data link control and transport protocols and relies on the use of an error detection code, such as the cyclic redundancy check (CRC) described earlier in this section. In what follows, we refer to the block of data that is transmitted from one protocol entity to another as a protocol data unit (PDU); this term was introduced in Chapter 4.

Error control mechanisms detect and correct errors that occur in the transmission of PDUs. The model that we will use, which covers the typical case, is illustrated in Figure 5.21b. Data are sent as a sequence of PDUs; PDUs arrive in the same order in which they are sent; and each transmitted PDU suffers an arbitrary and variable amount of delay before reception. In addition, we admit the possibility of two types of errors:

- **Lost PDU:** A PDU fails to arrive at the other side. For example, a noise burst may damage a PDU to the extent that the receiver is not aware that a PDU has been transmitted.

- **Damaged PDU:** A recognizable PDU does arrive, but some of the bits are in error (have been altered during transmission) and cannot be corrected.

The most common techniques for error control are based on some or all of the following ingredients:

- **Error detection:** The receiver detects errors and discards PDUs that are in error.

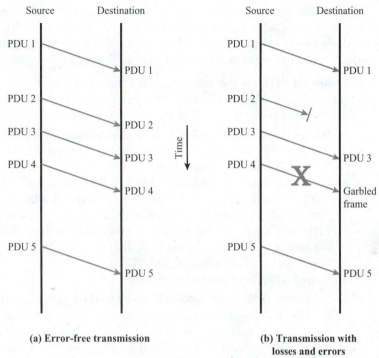

Figure 5.21 Model of PDU Transmission

- **Positive acknowledgment:** The destination returns a positive acknowledgment to successfully received, error-free PDUs.

- **Retransmission after timeout:** The source retransmits a PDU that has not been acknowledged after a predetermined amount of time.

- **Negative acknowledgment and retransmission:** The destination returns a negative acknowledgment to PDUs in which an error is detected. The source retransmits such PDUs.

Collectively, these mechanisms are all referred to as **automatic repeat request (ARQ)**; the effect of ARQ is to turn an unreliable data link into a reliable one. The most commonly used version of ARQ is known as go-back-N ARQ. In go-back-N ARQ, a station may send a series of PDUs sequentially numbered modulo some maximum value. The number of unacknowledged PDUs outstanding is determined by window size, using the sliding-window flow control technique. When no errors occur, the destination will acknowledge incoming PDUs with RR = receive ready or with a piggybacked acknowledgment on a data PDU. If the destination station detects an error in a PDU, it sends a negative acknowledgment (REJ = reject) for that PDU. The destination station will discard that PDU and all future incoming PDUs until the PDU in error is correctly received. Thus the source station, when it receives a REJ, must retransmit the PDU in error plus all succeeding PDUs that had been transmitted in the interim. Hence, the name go-back-N to retransmit these PDUs.

Consider that station A is sending PDUs to station B. After each transmission, A sets an acknowledgment timer for the PDU just transmitted. Suppose that B has previously successfully received PDU ($i - 1$) and A has just transmitted PDU i. The go-back-N technique takes into account the following contingencies:

1. **Damaged PDU.** If the received PDU is invalid (i.e., B detects an error), B discards the PDU and takes no further action as the result of that PDU. There are two subcases:

   a. Within a reasonable period of time, A subsequently sends PDU ($i + 1$). B receives PDU ($i + 1$) out of order since it is expecting PDU (i) and sends a REJ i. A must retransmit PDU i and all subsequent PDUs.

   b. A does not soon send additional PDUs. B receives nothing and returns neither an RR nor a REJ. When A's timer expires, it transmits an RR PDU that includes a bit known as the P bit, which is set to 1. B interprets the RR PDU with a P bit of 1 as a command that must be acknowledged by sending an RR indicating the next PDU that it expects, which is PDU i. When A receives the RR, it retransmits PDU i.

2. **Damaged RR.** There are two subcases:

   a. B receives PDU i and sends RR ($i + 1$), which suffers an error in transit. Because acknowledgments are cumulative (e.g., RR 6 means that all PDUs through 5 are acknowledged), it may be that A will receive a subsequent RR to a subsequent PDU and that it will arrive before the timer associated with PDU i expires.

   b. If A's timer expires, it transmits an RR command as in Case 1b. It sets another timer, called the P-bit timer. If B fails to respond to the RR command, or if its response suffers an error in transit, then A's P-bit timer will expire. At this point, A will try again by issuing a new RR command and restarting the P-bit timer. This procedure is tried for a number of iterations. If A fails to obtain an acknowledgment after some maximum number of attempts, it initiates a reset procedure.

3. **Damaged REJ.** If a REJ is lost, this is equivalent to Case 1b.

Figure 5.22 is an example of the PDU flow for go-back-N ARQ. It sends RRs only for even numbered PDUs. Because of the propagation delay on the line, by the time that an acknowledgment (positive or negative) arrives back at the sending station, it has already sent two additional PDUs beyond the one being acknowledged. Thus, when a REJ is received to PDU 5, not only PDU 5 but PDUs 6 and 7 must be retransmitted. Thus, the transmitter must keep a copy of all unacknowledged PDUs.

Hybrid Automatic Repeat Request In practical wireless system implementation, neither FEC nor ARQ is an adequate one-size-fits-all solution. FEC may add unnecessary redundancy (i.e., use extra bandwidth) if channel conditions are good and ARQ with error detection may cause excessive delays from retransmissions in poor channel conditions. Therefore, a solution known as *Hybrid Automatic Repeat Request (HARQ)* has been widely implemented in today's systems; it uses a combination of FEC to correct the most common errors and ARQ for retransmission when FEC cannot make corrections. Going beyond this basic concept, the following additional approaches may be implemented.

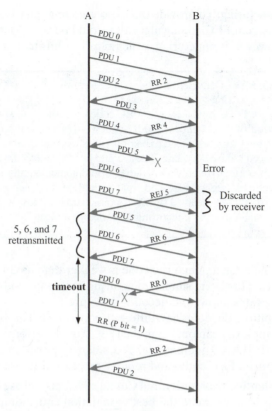

Figure 5.22 Go-back-N ARQ

- **Soft Decision Decoding:** The decoding process can provide not just an assessment of a bit being 0 or 1, but also levels of confidence in those results.

- **Chase Combining:** Previous frames that were not corrected by FEC need not be discarded. The soft decision information can be stored and then combined with soft decision information from retransmissions. If using turbo coding as seen in Figure 5.19, the decoders in the receivers now use information from multiple frames not just the current frame. This will result in stronger FEC capabilities. In *chase combining*, the exact same frames are retransmitted each time and soft combined.

- **Incremental Redundancy:** Each time a sender retransmits, different coding information can be provided. This can accomplish two goals.

    1. Lower Overhead. The initial packets can include less coding; if enough, then the packet can be successful and overhead can be avoided. For example, the first frame may only include a few bytes of an error detection code like CRC, with later frames then including FEC after the first frame has errors.

    2. Stronger Correction. The retransmissions can provide different coding at the same coding rates or stronger coding at lower coding rates. If adapted to the current wireless channel environment, this will increase the probability of a successful transmission by the second or third frames.

- **Puncturing:** To provide the various coding rates for incremental redundancy, a different FEC coding algorithm could be used each time. A simpler approach, however, is puncturing, which removes bits to increase the coding rate.

Example 5.13   Consider an FEC coder that produces a 1/3 rate code that is punctured to become a 1/2 rate code. Say there are 100 bits of data that become a 300 bit FEC codeword. To become a 1/2 rate FEC codeword, there need to be 2 bits of codeword for every 1 bit of data, hence a 200-bit codeword. This means 100 bits, 1 of every 3 bits of the original FEC code, need to be punctured. At the receiver, the missing 100 bits would be replaced before decoding. These could just be replaced with random numbers, which would mean that roughly 50 of those would coincidentally be correct and the other 50 incorrect. The original FEC code may actually still be plenty effective enough to correct those errors if the received signal-to-noise ratio is relatively good. If not, a later retransmission might use less puncturing or puncture different bits.

In general, a punctured code is weaker than an unpunctured code at the same rate. However, simply puncturing the same code to achieve different coding rates allows the decoder structure to remain the same, instead of having multiple decoders for different code rates. The benefits of this reduction in complexity can outweigh the reduction in performance from puncturing. Used with HARQ incremental redundancy, puncturing will take a single output from an FEC coder and remove more or different bits each time.

- **Adaptive Modulation and Coding:** Systems will use channel quality information (CQI) to estimate the best modulation and coding to work with HARQ. For example, LTE uses the CQI to determine the highest modulation and coding rate that would provide a 10% block error rate for the first HARQ transmission. Also, if the CQI changes in the middle of an HARQ process, the modulation and coding might be adapted.

- **Parallel HARQ Processes:** Some systems wait until the HARQ process finishes for one frame before sending the next frame; this is known as a stop-and-wait protocol. The process of waiting for an ACK or NACK, followed by possible multiple retransmissions can be time consuming, however. Therefore, some HARQ implementations allow for multiple open HARQ operations to be occurring at the same time. This is known as an *N-channel Stop-and-Wait* protocol.

5.7 ORTHOGONAL FREQUENCY DIVISION MULTIPLEXING (OFDM)

This section looks at OFDM-based techniques that have created great expansion in the capacity of wireless networks. The main air interface technology to move from third to fourth-generation cellular is OFDM. OFDM also allowed the expansion of IEEE 802.11 data rates. We first look at the basic mechanisms of OFDM, namely orthogonal carriers and transmitter design based on the inverse fast Fourier transform. Then we look at the ways OFDM is used in practical systems for multiple access.

OFDM Basics

OFDM, also called *multicarrier modulation*, uses multiple carrier signals at different frequencies, sending some of the bits on each channel. This is similar to FDM. However, in the case of OFDM, many **subcarriers** are dedicated to a single data source.

Figure 5.23 illustrates a conceptual understanding of OFDM. Actual transmitter operation is simplified, but the basic concept can first be understood here.

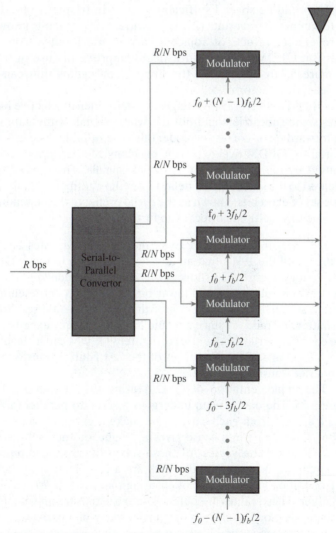

Figure 5.23 Conceptual Understanding of Orthogonal Frequency-Division Multiplexing

Suppose we have a binary data stream operating at R bps and an available bandwidth of Nf_b, centered at f_0. The entire bandwidth could be used to send the data stream, in which case each bit duration would be $1/R$. The alternative is to split the data stream into N substreams, using a serial-to-parallel converter. Each substream has a data rate of R/N bps and is transmitted on a separate subcarrier, with a spacing between adjacent subcarriers of f_b. Now the bit duration is N/R, which is substantially longer and creates special capabilities to overcome multipath fading.

OFDM relies on a principle known as *orthogonality*. If two subcarriers are placed at just that right spacing, each subcarrier signal can be retrieved at the receiver even if the signals overlap. The result is shown in Figure 5.24b; it looks like the signals are packed too close together because they overlap substantially. Previous FDM approaches are illustrated in Figure 5.24c, which assumed signals should be spaced sufficiently apart in frequency to (1) avoid overlap in the frequency bands and (2) to provide extra spacing known as *guard bands* to prevent the effects of adjacent carrier interference from out-of-band emissions. But OFDM is able to drastically improve the use of frequency spectrum. In Figure 5.24b over 5.24c, the number of signals that can be supported has increased by a factor of 6!

OFDM has several advantages. First, frequency selective fading only adversely affects some subcarriers and not the whole signal. If the data stream is protected by a forward error correction code, this type of fading is easily handled. But more importantly, OFDM overcomes the problems of intersymbol interference (ISI) that is caused by the multitude of multipath signals. The symbol times are very long compared to the spread of the delays from the multipath signals. In addition, OFDM adds a set of extra bits, known as the cyclic prefix, to the beginning of each set of bits to reduce this multipath effect even further.

OFDM Implementation Even though OFDM dates back some 40 years, it was only until the 1990s that an advance was made to make OFDM an economical technology. Figure 5.23 showed a conceptual understanding of OFDM where a data stream is split into many lower bit rate streams and then modulated on many different subcarriers. Such an approach, however, would result in a very expensive transmitter and receiver since it would have some many expensive oscillators to generate each subcarrier frequency. Fortunately, OFDM can instead be implemented by taking advantage of the properties of the **fast Fourier transform (FFT)** and **inverse fast Fourier transform (IFFT)**.

The implementation of OFDM using the FFT and IFFT is illustrated in Figure 5.25. The data stream undergoes a serial to parallel (S/P) operation, which takes a sample from each carrier and make a group of samples called an **OFDM symbol**. Each value in a sense gives a weight for each subcarrier. Then the IFFT (not FFT) takes the values for these subcarriers and computes the time domain data stream to be transmitted, which are a combination of these subcarriers. The IFFT operation has the effect of ensuring that the subcarriers do not interfere with each other. These values are put back into a serial stream with a P/S operation, then the stream is modulated onto the carrier using one oscillator. At the receiver, the reverse operation is conduced. An FFT module is used to map the incoming signal back to the M subcarriers, from which the data streams are recovered as the weights for each subcarrier are retrieved for each sample.

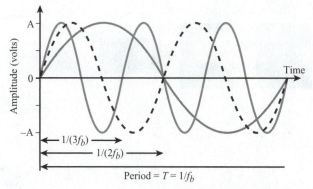

(a) Three subcarriers in time domain

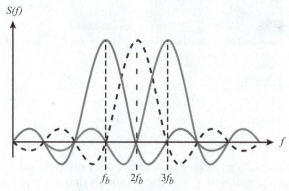

(b) Three orthogonal subcarriers in frequency domain

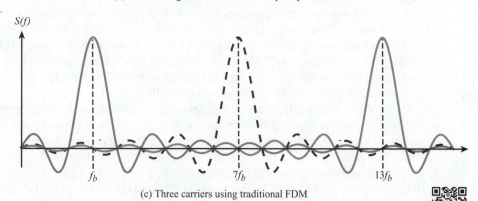

(c) Three carriers using traditional FDM

Figure 5.24 Illustration of Orthogonality of OFDM

Orthogonal Frequency Division Multiple Access (OFDMA)

Multiple access strategies share a wireless channel by making use of scheduled times (time division multiple access), random access times (carrier sense multiple access), scheduled use of frequencies (frequency division multiple access), coded spreading of signals (direct sequence spread spectrum), and/or coded frequency hopping of signals (frequency hopping spread spectrum). Throughout this text, one of the

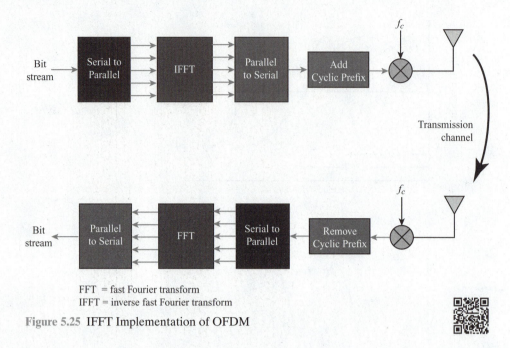

FFT = fast Fourier transform
IFFT = inverse fast Fourier transform

Figure 5.25 IFFT Implementation of OFDM

defining attributes of a technology is how it accomplishes multiple access, both in terms of the approaches just mentioned and the protocols that are used for mobile devices to cooperate.

OFDMA uses a combination of FDMA and TDMA by allowing different users to use a subset of the subcarriers at different times. All technologies that use OFDM do not use OFDMA. For example, some forms of 802.11 use OFDM for the signal transmission, but CSMA for multiple access. The transmitter uses the full set of subcarriers when transmitting. LTE only uses OFDMA on the downlink, but instead uses a single-carrier approach on the uplink.

OFDMA uses OFDM, which employs multiple closely spaced subcarriers, but the subcarriers are divided into groups of subcarriers since it would not be computationally feasible (because of hundreds of subcarriers) or sufficient (since each subcarrier only carries a small capacity) to schedule by individual subcarrier. Each group is named a subchannel. In the downlink, a subchannel may be intended for different receivers. Figure 5.26 contrasts OFDM and OFDMA; in the OFDMA case the use of adjacent subcarriers to form a subchannel is illustrated. Depending on the technology and specifics of an expected wireless channel characteristic, subchannels can be formed using adjacent subcarriers, regularly spaced subcarriers, or randomly spaced subcarriers.

Single-carrier FDMA (SC-FDMA) is a relatively recently developed multiple access technique which has similar structure and performance to OFDMA. One prominent advantage of SC-FDMA over OFDMA is the lower peak-to-average power ratio (PAPR) of the transmit waveform, which benefits the mobile user in terms of battery life, power efficiency, and lower cost.

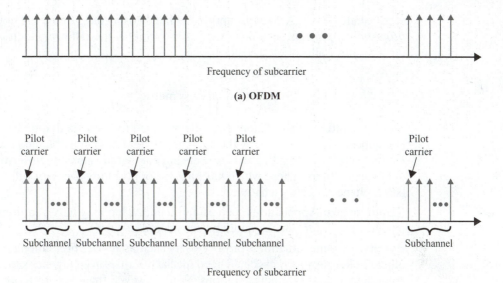

Figure 5.26 OFDM and OFDMA

Opportunistic Scheduling

Subchannelization defines subchannels, called *Resource Blocks* by LTE, which can be allocated to subscriber stations (SSs) depending on their channel conditions and data requirements. Particular power levels could also be prescribed to those stations in order to optimize throughput and limit interference.

One might think that the time varying and multipath nature of wireless communications would limit the ability for effective use of the wireless channel, but the opposite is actually true. Such variations provide opportunities that can be exploited. Since channel conditions change and are expected to change, resource allocations can adjust in a dynamic fashion. Hence, the term **opportunistic scheduling** has been used. Particular implementations and equipment providers can approach this problem in ways that provide them competitive advantage, since most standards do not prescribe OFDMA scheduling approaches. There are a variety of considerations when scheduling such subchannels.

- **Efficiency:** One could schedule subchannels based on the users with the highest signal-to-interference-plus-noise ratio (SINR) for that time slot. Those users could use adaptive modulation and coding to obtain much higher throughput than others with poorer SINR. The total efficiency and capacity would be highest; the time-varying nature of the channel would be exploited to the highest benefit.

- **Fairness:** If scheduling is only based on efficiency, however, some users (likely those far from base stations) would receive little or no throughput. Fairness could also be a consideration. A completely fair allocation might give the same number of subchannels or the same throughput to all users, but this could sacrifice efficiency. A popular approach that finds a compromise is known as *proportional fairness*, in which every user computes the following metric during a resource allocation decision.

$$\text{Proportional fairness metric} = \frac{r_i}{\bar{r}_i}$$

This is the ratio of the rate that could be obtained for user i in that time slot for that subchannel, r_i, divided by the average rate that has been obtained for user i in that subchannel, $\bar{r}_i$. In essence, users are compared against themselves and not against others. Those which have a good opportunity *for them* will have a better chance at being scheduled.

- **Requirements:** Applications such as audio and video may have requirements on delay and jitter. These should be considered.
- **Priority:** In some situations, priority users such as police, fire, ambulance, or other public safety workers could need special priorities in emergency situations, regardless of their channel conditions. Note, however, that even for those users their channel conditions may improve significantly within a few milliseconds.

5.8   SPREAD SPECTRUM

An important form of communications is known as **spread spectrum**. The spread spectrum technique was developed initially for military and intelligence requirements. The essential idea is to spread the information signal over a wider bandwidth to make jamming and interception more difficult. The first type of spread spectrum developed is known as frequency hopping.[6] A more recent type of spread spectrum is direct sequence. Both of these techniques are used in various wireless communications standards and products, most notably 2G and 3G cellular, Bluetooth, and earlier generations of IEEE 802.11 WLANs. Spread spectrum approaches are mandated in many unlicensed spectrum allocations, like the ISM bands at 2.4 GHz and 5 GHz that are used for these technologies. This is because many users can share the same frequencies using spread spectrum with minimal impact on each other and without a need for any central control.

After a brief overview, we look at the two spread spectrum techniques. We then examine the code division multiple access technique that is based on spread spectrum.

The Concept of Spread Spectrum

Figure 5.27 highlights the key characteristics of any spread spectrum system. Input is fed into a channel encoder that produces an analog signal with a relatively narrow bandwidth around some center frequency. This signal is further modulated using

---

[6]Spread spectrum (using frequency hopping) was invented, believe it or not, by Hollywood screen siren Hedy Lamarr in 1940 at the age of 26. She and a partner who later joined her effort were granted a patent in 1942 (U.S. Patent 2,292,387; August 11, 1942). Lamarr considered this her contribution to the war effort and never profited from her invention.

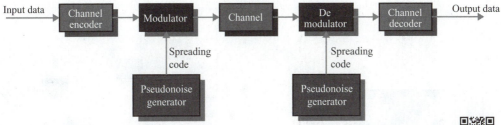

Figure 5.27 General Model of Spread Spectrum Digital Communication System

a sequence of digits known as a spreading code or spreading sequence. Typically, but not always, the spreading code is generated by a pseudonoise, or pseudorandom number, generator. The effect of this modulation is to increase significantly the bandwidth (spread the spectrum) of the signal to be transmitted. On the receiving end, the same digit sequence is used to demodulate the spread spectrum signal. Finally, the signal is fed into a channel decoder to recover the data.

Several things can be gained from this apparent waste of spectrum:

- The signals gains immunity from various kinds of noise and multipath distortion. The earliest applications of spread spectrum were military, where it was used for its immunity to jamming.

- It can also be used for hiding and encrypting signals. Only a recipient who knows the spreading code can recover the encoded information.

- Several users can independently use the same higher bandwidth with very little interference. This property is used in cellular telephony applications with a technique known as code division multiplexing (CDM) or code division multiple access (CDMA).

Frequency Hopping Spread Spectrum

With **frequency hopping spread spectrum** (FHSS), the signal is broadcast over a seemingly random series of radio frequencies, hopping from frequency to frequency at fixed intervals. A receiver, hopping between frequencies in synchronization with the transmitter, picks up the message. Would-be eavesdroppers hear only unintelligible blips. Attempts to jam the signal on one frequency succeed only at knocking out a few bits of it.

Figure 5.28 shows an example of a frequency hopping (FH) signal. A number of channels, C, are allocated for the FH signal. For example, IEEE 802.15.1, Bluetooth, uses $C = 80$. The spacing between carrier frequencies and hence the width of each channel usually corresponds to the bandwidth of the input signal. The transmitter operates in one channel at a time for a fixed interval; for example, the IEEE 802.15.1 Bluetooth standard uses a 0.625-ms interval. During that interval, some number of bits (possibly a fraction of a bit, as discussed subsequently) is transmitted using some encoding scheme. A spreading code dictates the sequence of channels used. Both the transmitter and receiver use the same code to tune into a sequence of channels in synchronization.

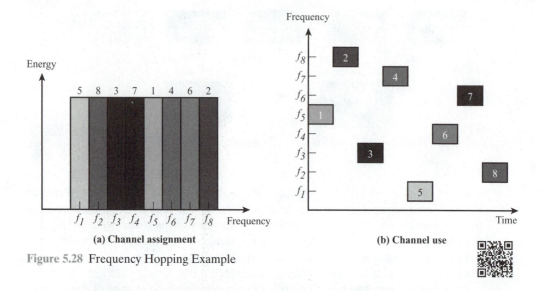

(a) Channel assignment   **(b) Channel use**

Figure 5.28 Frequency Hopping Example

A typical block diagram for a frequency hopping system is shown in Figure 5.29. For transmission, binary data are fed into a modulator using some digital-to-analog encoding scheme, such as frequency-shift keying (FSK) or binary phase-shift keying (BPSK). The resulting signal $s_d(t)$ is centered on some base frequency. A pseudo-noise (PN), or pseudorandom number, source serves as an index into a table of frequencies; this is the spreading code referred to previously. At each successive interval (each k PN bits), a new carrier frequency $c(t)$ is selected. This frequency is then modulated by the signal produced from the initial modulator to produce a new signal $s(t)$ with the same shape but now centered on the selected carrier frequency. On reception, the spread spectrum signal is demodulated using the same sequence of PN-derived frequencies and then demodulated to produce the output data.

FHSS Performance Considerations Typically, a large number of frequencies are used in FHSS so that the total FHSS bandwidth W_s is much larger than the bandwidth of each individual channel, W_d. One benefit of this is that a large value of k results in a system that is quite resistant to noise and jamming. For example, suppose we have a transmitter with bandwidth W_d and noise jammer of the same bandwidth and fixed power S_j on the signal carrier frequency. Then we have a ratio of signal energy per bit to jammer interference power density per hertz of

$$\frac{E_b}{I_j} = \frac{E_b}{S_j/W_d} = \frac{E_b W_d}{S_j}$$

If frequency hopping is used, the jammer must jam all C frequencies. With a fixed power, this reduces the jamming power in any one frequency band to S_j/C. The gain in signal-to-noise ratio, or processing gain, is

$$G_P = C = \frac{W_s}{W_d} \tag{5.13}$$

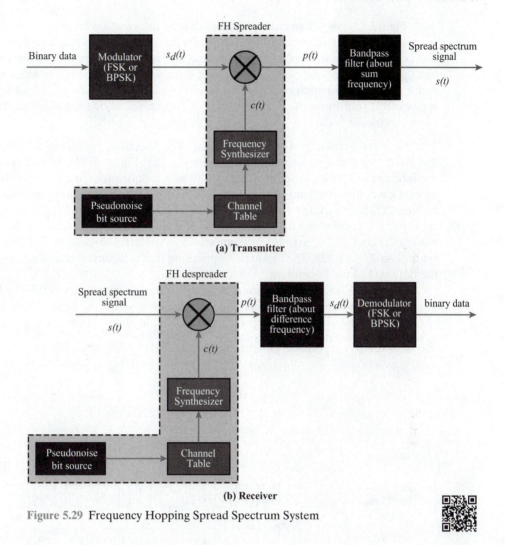

Figure 5.29 Frequency Hopping Spread Spectrum System

Direct Sequence Spread Spectrum

For **direct sequence spread spectrum** (DSSS), each bit in the original signal is represented by multiple bits in the transmitted signal, using a spreading code. The spreading code spreads the signal across a wider frequency band in direct proportion to the number of bits used. Therefore, a 10-bit spreading code spreads the signal across a frequency band that is 10 times greater than a 1-bit spreading code. Since the bits in the PN sequence are much smaller, they are sometimes called *chips*; the sequence is then called the *chip sequence*.

One technique for direct sequence spread spectrum is to combine the digital information stream with the spreading code bit stream using an exclusive-OR (XOR). The XOR obeys the following rules:

$$0 \oplus 0 = 0 \quad 0 \oplus 1 = 1 \quad 1 \oplus 0 = 1 \quad 1 \oplus 1 = 0$$

Figure 5.30 shows an example. Note that an information bit of one inverts the spreading code bits in the combination, while an information bit of zero causes the spreading code bits to be transmitted without inversion. The combination bit stream has the data rate of the original spreading code sequence, so it has a wider bandwidth than the information stream. In this example, the spreading code bit stream is clocked at four times the information rate. Figure 5.31 shows the implementation of this approach.

DSSS Performance Considerations The spectrum spreading achieved by the direct sequence technique is easily determined (Figure 5.32). In our example, the information signal has a bit width of T, which is equivalent to a data rate of $1/T$. In that case, the spectrum of the signal, depending on the encoding technique, is roughly $2/T$. Similarly, the spectrum of the PN signal is $2/T_c$. Figure 5.32c shows the resulting spectrum spreading. The total spectrum is $2/T_c + 2/T$, which is approximately $2/T_c$, since $2/T$ is small in comparison. One technology uses 128 chips per symbol, so $T/T_c = 128$. The amount of spreading that is achieved is a direct result of the data rate of the PN stream.

As with FHSS, we can get some insight into the performance of DSSS by looking at its effectiveness against jamming. The jamming power is reduced by a factor of (T_c/T) through the use of spread spectrum. The inverse of this factor is the gain in signal-to-noise ratio for the transmitted signal:

$$G_P = \frac{T}{T_c} = \frac{R_c}{R} \approx \frac{W_s}{W_d} \tag{5.14}$$

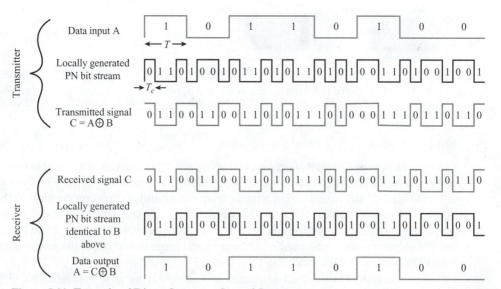

Figure 5.30 Example of Direct Sequence Spread Spectrum

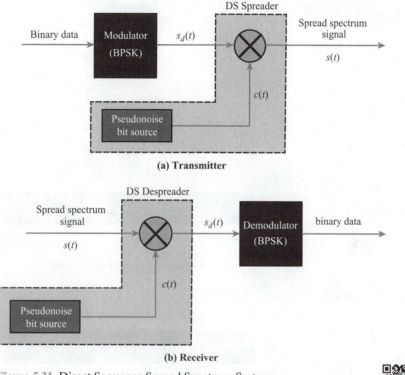

(a) Transmitter

(b) Receiver

Figure 5.31 Direct Sequence Spread Spectrum System

where R_c is the spreading bit rate, R is the data rate, W_d is the signal bandwidth, and W_s is the spread spectrum signal bandwidth.

Code Division Multiple Access

CDMA is a multiplexing technique used with spread spectrum to share the wireless medium. It simply uses different PN sequences for different users. For frequency hopping the result is easy to understand, since the data can only be retrieved if the receiver knows the PN hopping sequence.

For DSSS, consider again Figure 5.31. The receiver will detect a signal that has a combination of many users utilizing different code. Using ideal codes (called "orthogonal codes"), only the desired signal will be retrieved after accomplishing the despreading multiplication operation. All other signals will be canceled to zero. Such codes are very nice to have but there are not all that many of them. Therefore, practical systems will use codes that are non-ideal. The result out of the despreader will be the desired signal but with what looks like a level of noise from the other users.

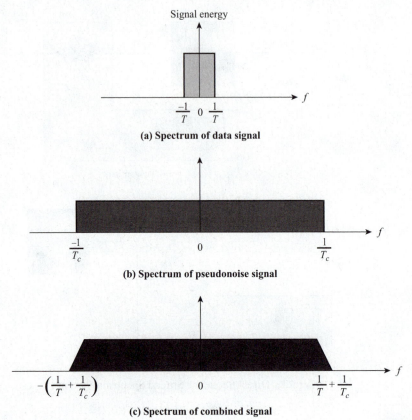

Signal energy

$\dfrac{-1}{T}$ 0 $\dfrac{1}{T}$

f

(a) Spectrum of data signal

$\dfrac{-1}{T_c}$ 0 $\dfrac{1}{T_c}$

f

(b) Spectrum of pseudonoise signal

$-\left(\dfrac{1}{T}+\dfrac{1}{T_c}\right)$ 0 $\dfrac{1}{T}+\dfrac{1}{T_c}$

f

(c) Spectrum of combined signal

Figure 5.32 Approximate Spectrum of Direct Sequence Spread Spectrum Signal

In practice, the CDMA receiver can filter out the contribution from unwanted users or they appear as low-level noise. However, if there are many users competing for the channel with the user the receiver is trying to listen to, or if the signal power of one or more competing signals is too high, perhaps because it is very near the receiver (the "near/far" problem), the system breaks down. Many CDMA systems use tight power control of transmitting devices so none of the competing signals can be too strong.

The limit on the number of users in the system is derived from this understanding. A common measurement for a CDMA system is the **rise-over-thermal**, which compares the total contribution of this noise from the users in the system to the background thermal noise of the environment. One system uses 7 dB rise-over-thermal as a key performance metric to limit additional users.

5.9 RECOMMENDED READING

For references on specific topics, please consult the chapters that cover those topics in more detail.

5.10 KEY TERMS, REVIEW QUESTIONS, AND PROBLEMS

Key Terms

adaptive modulation and coding (AMC)	flat fading	multi-user MIMO (MU-MIMO)
amplitude-shift keying (ASK)	forward error correction (FEC)	orthogonal frequency division multiple access (OFDMA)
antenna	free space loss	
antenna gain	frequency hopping spread spectrum	parity check
atmospheric absorption	frequency selective fading	phase-shift keying (PSK)
attenuation	frequency-shift keying (FSK)	picocells
code division multiple access (CDMA)	ground wave propagation	radiation pattern
code rate	Hamming distance	reflections
codeword	hybrid automatic repeat request (H-ARQ)	refraction
coding gain	isotropic antenna	scattering
cyclic redundancy check (CRC)	large-scale fading	signal-to-noise ratio (SNR)
diffraction	line of sight (LOS)	small cells
direct sequence spread spectrum	mmWave	small-scale fading
diversity	multiple-input multiple-output (MIMO)	sky wave propagation
Doppler spread		slow fading
error detection	multipath	spectrum
fading	noise	spread spectrum
fast fading	orthogonal frequency division multiplexing (OFDM)	subcarriers
femtocells		thermal noise
		turbo coding

Review Questions

5.1 What is an isotropic antenna?

5.2 What information is available from a radiation pattern?

5.3 What is fading?

5.4 What is the difference between diffraction and scattering?

5.5 What is the difference between fast and slow fading?

5.6 What is the difference between flat and selective fading?

5.7 Indicate three major advantages of digital transmission over analog transmission.

5.8 How are binary values represented in amplitude-shift keying?

5.9 What is QAM?

5.10 What is a parity bit?

5.11 What is the CRC?

5.12 Why would you expect a CRC to detect more errors than a parity bit?

5.13 What two key elements comprise error control?

5.14 Explain how Go-back-N ARQ works.

5.15 Briefly define OFDM, OFDMA, and SC-FDMA.

5.16 What is the relationship between the bandwidth of a signal before and after it has been encoded using spread spectrum?

5.17 List three benefits of spread spectrum.

5.18 What is frequency hopping spread spectrum?

5.19 What is direct sequence spread spectrum?

5.20 What is CDMA?

Problems

5.1 For radio transmission in free space, signal power is reduced in proportion to the square of the distance from the source, whereas in wire transmission, the attenuation is a fixed number of dB per kilometer. The following table is used to show the dB reduction relative to some reference for free-space radio and uniform wire. Fill in the missing numbers to complete the table.

Distance (km)	Radio (dB)	Wire (dB)
1	−6	−3
2		
4		
8		
16		

5.2 It turns out that the depth in the ocean to which airborne electromagnetic signals can be detected grows with the wavelength. Therefore, the military got the idea of using very long wavelengths corresponding to about 30 Hz to communicate with submarines throughout the world. If we want to have an antenna that is about one-half wavelength long, how long would that be?

5.3 The audio power of the human voice is concentrated at about 300 Hz. Antennas of the appropriate size for this frequency are impracticably large, so that to send voice by radio the voice signal must be used to modulate a higher (carrier) frequency for which the natural antenna size is smaller.
   a. What is the length of an antenna one-half wavelength long for sending radio at 300 Hz?
   b. An alternative is to use a modulation scheme for transmitting the voice signal by modulating a carrier frequency, so that the bandwidth of the signal is a narrowband centered on the carrier frequency. Suppose we would like a half-wave antenna to have a length of 1 m. What carrier frequency would we use?

5.4 Stories abound of people who receive radio signals in fillings in their teeth. Suppose you have one filling that is 2.5 mm (0.0025 m) long that acts as a radio antenna. That is, it is equal in length to one-half the wavelength. What frequency do you receive?

5.5 It is often more convenient to express distance in km rather than m and frequency in MHz rather than Hz. Rewrite Equation (5.1) using these dimensions.

5.6 Suppose a transmitter produces 50 W of power.
   a. Express the transmit power in units of dBm and dBW.
   b. If the transmitter's power is applied to a unity gain antenna with a 900 MHz carrier frequency, what is the received power in dBm at a free space distance of 100 m?
   c. Repeat (b) for a distance of 10 km.
   d. Repeat (c) but assume a receiver antenna gain of 2.

5.7 Show that doubling the transmission frequency or doubling the distance between transmitting antenna and receiving antenna attenuates the power received by 6 dB.

5.8 What is the purpose of using modulo 2 arithmetic rather than binary arithmetic in computing an FCS?

5.9 Consider a frame consisting of two characters of four bits each. Assume that the probability of bit error is 10^{-3} and that it is independent for each bit.

  a. What is the probability that the received frame contains at least one error?
  b. Now add a parity bit to each character. What is the probability?

5.10 Using the CRC-CCITT polynomial, generate the 16-bit CRC code for a message consisting of a 1 followed by 15 0s. Use long division.

5.11 For $P = 110011$ and $M = 11100011$, find the CRC.

5.12 Calculate the pairwise Hamming distances among the following codewords:
  a. 00000, 10101, 01010
  b. 000000, 010101, 101010, 110110

5.13 For a given positive integer t, if a code satisfies $d_{min} \geq 2t + 1$, then the code can correct all bit errors up to and including errors of t bits. Prove this assertion. *Hint:* Start by observing that for a codeword **w** to be decoded as another codeword **w'**, the received sequence must be at least as close to **w'** as to **w**.

5.14 The simplest form of flow control, known as **stop-and-wait flow control**, works as follows. A source entity transmits a frame. After the destination entity receives the frame, it indicates its willingness to accept another frame by sending back an acknowledgment to the frame just received. The source must wait until it receives the acknowledgment before sending the next frame. The destination can thus stop the flow of data simply by withholding acknowledgment. Consider a half-duplex point-to-point link using a stop-and-wait scheme, in which a series of messages is sent, with each message segmented into a number of frames. Ignore errors and frame overhead.
  a. What is the effect on line utilization of increasing the message size so that fewer messages will be required? Other factors remain constant.
  b. What is the effect on line utilization of increasing the number of frames for a constant message size?
  c. What is the effect on line utilization of increasing frame size?

5.15 For an 18 Mbps LTE data stream with a symbol time of 66.67 μs, how many subcarriers are created?

5.16 LTE assigns subcarriers in *resource blocks* of 180 kHz. Given the information in Problem 5.15, how many subcarriers are in a resource block? Approximate $B_S \approx r_b$.

5.17 The following table illustrates the operation of an FHSS system for one complete period of the PN sequence.

Time	0	1	2	3	4	5	6	7	8	9	10	11
Input data	0	1	1	1	1	1	1	0	0	0	1	0
Frequency	f_1		f_3		f_{23}		f_{22}		f_8		f_{10}	
PN sequence	001				110				011			

Time	12	13	14	15	16	17	18	19
Input data	0	1	1	1	1	0	1	0
Frequency	f_1		f_3		f_2		f_2	
PN sequence	001				001			

  a. The system makes use of a form of FSK. What form of FSK is it?
  b. What is the number of bits per signal element (symbol)?
  c. What is the number of FSK frequencies?
  d. What is the length of a PN sequence per hop?
  e. Is this a slow or fast FH system?
  f. What is the total number of possible carrier frequencies?
  g. Show the variation of the base, or demodulated, frequency with time.

CHAPTER 6

THE WIRELESS CHANNEL

LEARNING OBJECTIVES

After studying this chapter, you should be able to:

- Describe antenna patterns and the operation of MIMO directional antennas.
- Explain the importance of unlicensed frequencies.
- Compute path loss for free space and real-world environments using the path loss exponent.
- Compute path loss based on the Okumura–Hata model.
- Characterize the multipath and Doppler spreading characteristics of channels.
- Describe the approaches used to correct channel impairments.

Wireless communication presents several unique challenges over using other types of communication media. Channel attenuation decays strongly with distance and also fluctuates wildly over short distances due to multipath propagation. Sharing scarce wireless spectrum and coping with user mobility are also very important. Modern systems, however, have developed several creative and effective methods to provide good coverage and high data rates.

This chapter provides some fundamental background for wireless transmission. We begin with an overview of antennas and then look at spectrum considerations, signal propagation, fading, and channel correction.

6.1 ANTENNAS

An **antenna** can be defined as an electrical conductor or a system of conductors used either for radiating electromagnetic energy or for collecting electromagnetic energy. For transmission of a signal, radio-frequency electrical energy from the transmitter is converted into electromagnetic energy by the antenna and radiated into the surrounding environment (atmosphere, space, water). For reception of a signal, electromagnetic energy impinging on the antenna is converted into radio-frequency electrical energy and fed into the receiver.

In two-way communication, the same antenna can be and often is used for both transmission and reception. This is possible because any antenna transfers energy from the surrounding environment to its input receiver terminals with the same efficiency that it transfers energy from the output transmitter terminals into the surrounding environment, assuming that the same frequency is used in both directions. Put another way, antenna characteristics are essentially the same whether an antenna is sending or receiving electromagnetic energy.

Radiation Patterns

An antenna will radiate power in all directions but, typically, does not perform equally well in all directions. A common way to characterize the performance of an antenna is the **radiation pattern**, which is a graphical representation of the radiation properties of an antenna as a function of space coordinates. The simplest pattern is produced by an idealized antenna known as the isotropic antenna. An **isotropic**

antenna is a point in space that radiates power in all directions equally. The actual radiation pattern for the isotropic antenna is a sphere with the antenna at the center. However, radiation patterns are almost always depicted as a two-dimensional cross section of the three-dimensional pattern. The pattern for the isotropic antenna is shown in Figure 6.1a. The distance from the antenna to each point on the radiation pattern is proportional to the power radiated from the antenna in that direction. Figure 6.1b shows the radiation pattern of another idealized antenna. This is a **directional antenna** in which the preferred direction of radiation is along one axis.

The actual size of a radiation pattern is arbitrary. What is important is the *relative* distance from the antenna position in each direction. The relative distance determines the relative power. To determine the relative power in a given direction, a line is drawn from the antenna position at the appropriate angle, and the point of intercept with the radiation pattern is determined. Figure 6.1 shows a comparison of two transmission angles, A and B, drawn on the two radiation patterns. The isotropic antenna produces an omnidirectional radiation pattern of equal strength in all directions, so the **A** and **B** vectors are of equal length. For the antenna pattern of Figure 6.1b, the **B** vector is longer than the **A** vector, indicating that more power is radiated in the B direction than in the **A** direction, and the relative lengths of the two vectors are proportional to the amount of power radiated in the two directions. Please note that this type of diagram shows relative *antenna gain* in each direction, not relative distance of coverage, although they are of course related.

The radiation pattern provides a convenient means of determining the **beam width** of an antenna, which is a common measure of the directivity of an antenna. The beam width, also referred to as the half-power beam width, is the angle within which the power radiated by the antenna is at least half of what it is in the most preferred direction.

When an antenna is used for reception, the radiation pattern becomes a **reception pattern**. The longest section of the pattern indicates the best direction for reception.

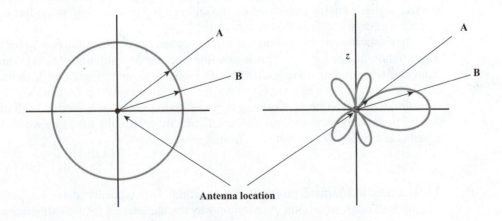

(a) Omnidirectional   (b) Directional

Figure 6.1 Antenna Radiation Patterns

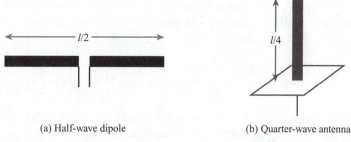

(a) Half-wave dipole   (b) Quarter-wave antenna

Figure 6.2 Simple Antennas

Antenna Types

Dipoles Two of the simplest and most basic antennas are the half-wave **dipole,** or **Hertz antenna** (Figure 6.2a) and the quarter-wave vertical, or *Marconi antenna* (Figure 6.2b). The half-wave dipole consists of two straight collinear conductors of equal length, separated by a small gap. The length of the antenna is one-half the wavelength of the signal that can be transmitted most efficiently. A vertical quarter-wave antenna is the type commonly used for automobile radios and portable radios.

A half-wave dipole has a uniform or omnidirectional radiation pattern in one dimension and a figure eight pattern in the other two dimensions (Figure 6.3a). This means the energy is directed along the ground. Much less energy is expended vertically (and lost) as compared to an isotropic antenna.

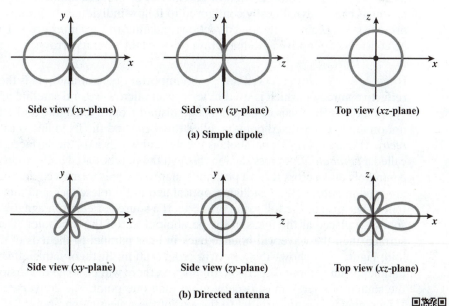

Figure 6.3 Radiation Patterns in Three Dimensions

Directional Antennas If multiple antennas are configured in an array of antennas, these multiple antennas can produce a directional beam. The radiation of electric field from a single antenna is

$$E = \frac{E_0}{d} \operatorname{Re}\left[\exp\left(j\left(\omega t - \frac{2\pi d}{\lambda}\right)\right)\right] = \frac{E_0}{d} \cos\left(\omega t - \frac{2\pi d}{\lambda}\right) \tag{6.1}$$

With multiple antennas, the signals to each antenna can be adjusted with complex weights z_i to impose certain phases, amplitudes, and time delays such that the sum of the antenna patterns sends or listens more strongly in a certain direction. This results in

$$E = \operatorname{Re}\left[E_0 \exp\left(j\omega t\right) \sum_{i=1}^{N} z_i \frac{1}{d_k} \exp\left(-\frac{j2\pi d_k}{\lambda}\right)\right] \tag{6.2}$$

where d_k is the distance from each antenna element to the receiver. The weights are optimized according to different criteria. For example, if antennas are placed in a **linear antenna array**, a typical directional radiation pattern is shown in Figure 6.3b. This pattern produces a main lobe that is 60° wide. This requires four antennas and is produced from a linear array where the antennas are each spaced apart by a half of a wavelength. In this example, the main strength of the antenna is in the x direction. Notice that some energy is sent to the sides and back of the antenna in what are called the **sidelobes**. There are also, however, *nulls* in the patterns were very little signal energy is sent in those directions.

Directional antennas are becoming increasingly practical and useful in modern systems, but actually have been used for many years. For example, a typical cellular coverage area is split into three, 120° sectors using three sets of directional antennas in a triangular configuration of antennas. For modern applications, directional antennas can be dynamically configured to follow individuals or groups of users to provide strong gain in intended directions and nulls toward interferers. These would be considered adaptive antenna arrays or switched antenna arrays.

Parabolic Reflective Antenna An important type of antenna is the **parabolic reflective antenna**, which is used in terrestrial microwave and satellite applications. A parabola is the locus of all points equidistant from a fixed line and a fixed point not on the line. The fixed point is called the *focus* and the fixed line is called the *directrix* (Figure 6.4a). If a parabola is revolved about its axis, the surface generated is called a *paraboloid*. A cross section through the paraboloid parallel to its axis forms a parabola and a cross section perpendicular to the axis forms a circle. Such surfaces are used in automobile headlights, optical and radio telescopes, and microwave antennas because of the following property: If a source of electromagnetic energy (or sound) is placed at the focus of the paraboloid, and if the paraboloid is a reflecting surface, then the wave will bounce back in lines parallel to the axis of the paraboloid; Figure 6.4b shows this effect in cross section. In theory, this effect creates a parallel beam without dispersion. In practice, there will be some dispersion, because the source of energy must occupy more than one point. The converse is also true. If incoming waves are parallel to the axis of the reflecting paraboloid, the resulting signal will be concentrated at the focus.

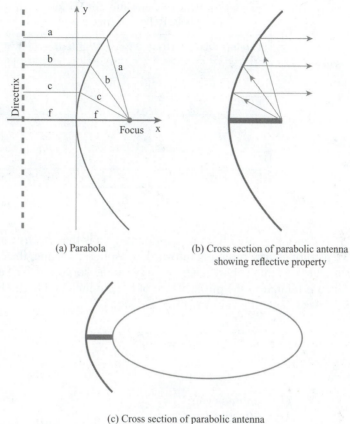

(a) Parabola

(b) Cross section of parabolic antenna
showing reflective property

(c) Cross section of parabolic antenna
showing radiation pattern

Figure 6.4 Parabolic Reflective Antenna

Figure 6.4c shows a typical radiation pattern for the parabolic reflective antenna, and Table 6.1 lists beam widths for antennas of various sizes at a frequency of 12 GHz. Note that the larger the diameter of the antenna, the more tightly directional is the beam.

Antenna Gain

Antenna gain is a measure of the directionality of an antenna. Antenna gain is defined as the power output, in a particular direction, compared to that produced in any direction by a perfect omnidirectional antenna (isotropic antenna). For example, if an antenna has a gain of 3 dB, the antenna improves upon the isotropic antenna in that direction by 3 dB, or a factor of 2. The increased power radiated in a given direction is at the expense of other directions. In effect, increased power is radiated in one direction by reducing the power radiated in other directions. It is important to note that antenna gain does not refer to obtaining more output power than input power but rather to directionality.

Table 6.1 Antenna Beamwidths for Various Diameter
Parabolic Reflective Antennas at $f = 12\,\text{GHz}$

Antenna Diameter (m)	Beam Width (degrees)
0.5	3.5
0.75	2.33
1.0	1.75
1.5	1.166
2.0	0.875
2.5	0.7
5.0	0.35

A concept related to that of antenna gain is the ***effective area*** of an antenna. If we picture energy radiating outward in a spherical shape, the effective area is the surface area on that sphere where energy can be harvested. The effective area of an antenna is related to the physical size of the antenna and to its shape. The relationship between antenna gain and effective area is

$$G = \frac{4\pi A_e}{\lambda^2} = \frac{4\pi f^2 A_e}{c^2} \tag{6.3}$$

where

$$
\begin{aligned}
G &= \text{antenna gain} \\
A_e &= \text{effective area} \\
f &= \text{carrier frequency} \\
c &= \text{speed of light } (\approx 3 \times 10^8 \text{ m/s}) \\
\lambda &= \text{carrier wavelength}
\end{aligned}
$$

Table 6.2 shows the antenna gain and effective area of some typical antenna shapes.

Table 6.2 Antenna Gains and Effective Areas

Type of Antenna	Effective Area A_e (m^2)	Power Gain (relative to isotropic)
Isotropic	$\lambda^2/4\pi$	1
Infinitesimal dipole or loop	$1.5\,\lambda^2/4\pi$	1.5
Half-wave dipole	$1.64\,\lambda^2/4\pi$	1.64
Horn, mouth area A	$0.81\,A$	$10A/\lambda^2$
Parabolic, face area A	$0.56\,A$	$7A/\lambda^2$
Turnstile (two crossed, perpendicular dipoles)	$1.15\,\lambda^2/4\pi$	1.15

Example 6.1 For a parabolic reflective antenna with a diameter of 2 m, operating at 12 GHz, what is the effective area and the antenna gain? According to Table 6.2, for a parabolic antenna we use the face area, which is circular. We have an area of $A = \pi r^2 = \pi$ and an effective area of $A_e = 0.56\pi$. The wavelength is $\lambda = c/f = (3 \times 10^8)/(12 \times 10^9) = 0.025$ m. Then

$$G = (7A)/\lambda^2 = (7 \times \pi)/(0.025)^2 = 35{,}186$$

$$G_{dB} = 45.46 \text{ dB}$$

6.2 SPECTRUM CONSIDERATIONS

The proper choice of the range of wireless frequencies over which a technology is to operate (i.e., its spectrum) is vital to its success. Some frequencies travel better over long distances; others penetrate obstacles such as buildings and walls more effectively. And wireless frequencies need to be shared with multiple types of users.

Regulation

The wireless medium is shared by a myriad of different types of users, applications, and traffic types. These are controlled by regulatory bodies to provide fair use while also meeting the key demands of society. The following differentiates signals from each other.

- **Carrier frequency:** Each signal is shifted from its base frequency up to a carrier frequency. For example, a 22 MHz IEEE 802.11 signal might be shifted up to a carrier frequency of 2.412 GHz, so that it would occupy 2.401 to 2.423 GHz.
- **Signal power:** Signals are limited in their propagation range by the allowed transmission power. At sufficient distances from each other, multiple users and groups can use the same spectrum.
- **Multiple access scheme:** Multiple users within a same spectrum range can share the spectrum by each having their own small slice of time or frequency; this is known as Time Division Multiple Access (TDMA) or Frequency Division Multiple Access (FDMA). They might also encode their signals in different ways while sharing the same time and frequency; this is known as Code Division Multiple Access (CDMA).

In the United States, the Federal Communications Commission (FCC) regulates these issues for different types of groups to share the wireless spectrum. Similar bodies operate throughout the world. In most cases, a license is required by the FCC to operate. In some case, auctions are conducted for the purchase of these licenses. The FCC regulates which frequencies are government exclusive, nongovernment exclusive, or government/nongovernment shared. They provide for a variety of services, including the following:

- Aeronautical
- Amateur

- Broadcasting
- Maritime
- Meteorological
- Mobile
- Satellite
- Space

An illustration of the spectrum allocations by the FCC can be seen on the book Web site at corybeardwireless.com. FCC licenses are allocated for different uses so that there are no conflicts. This frequently causes spectrum to be underutilized, so researchers are exploring a new concept known as **dynamic spectrum access**. Here, users would share spectrum among primary and secondary users. If primary users are not active, secondary users could use the spectrum but release the spectrum as soon as primary users need it. A technology known as **cognitive radio** would be implemented in the devices to scan wide bands of frequency to sense when spectrum is being used.

Frequency bands used for the technologies in this textbook are relatively narrow compared to the overall wide spectrum. Several technologies (e.g., IEEE 802.11 and 802.15) use the industrial, scientific, and medical (ISM) bands because those frequencies can be used without a license as long the transmitters stay within power limitations and use a spread spectrum technique. Some of these ISM bands are 915 $\pm$ 13 MHz, 2450 $\pm$ 50 MHz, 5.8 $\pm$ 0.75 GHz, and 57–64 GHz.

Propagation Modes

A signal radiated from an antenna travels along one of three routes: ground wave, sky wave, or **line of sight** (LOS). Table 6.3 shows in which frequency range each predominates. In this book, we are almost exclusively concerned with LOS communication, but a short overview of each mode is given in this section.

Table 6.3   Frequency Bands

Band	Frequency Range	Free Space Wavelength Range	Propagation Characteristics	Typical Use
ELF (extremely low frequency)	30 to 300 Hz	10,000 to 1,000 km	GW	Power line frequencies; used by some home control systems.
VF (voice frequency)	300 to 3000 Hz	1,000 to 100 km	GW	Used by the telephone system for analog subscriber lines.
VLF (very low frequency)	3 to 30 kHz	100 to 10 km	GW; low attenuation day and night; high atmospheric noise level	Long-range navigation; submarine communication
LF (low frequency)	30 to 300 kHz	10 to 1 km	GW; slightly less reliable than VLF; absorption in daytime	Long-range navigation; marine communication radio beacons

MF (medium frequency)	300 to 3000 kHz	1,000 to 100 m	GW and night SW; attenuation low at night, high in day; atmospheric noise	Maritime radio; direction finding; AM broadcasting.
HF (high frequency)	3 to 30 MHz	100 to 10 m	SW; quality varies with time of day, season, and frequency.	Amateur radio; international broadcasting, military communication; long-distance aircraft and ship communication
VHF (very high frequency)	30 to 300 MHz	10 to 1 m	LOS; scattering because of temperature inversion; cosmic noise	VHF television; FM broadcast and two-way radio, AM aircraft communication; aircraft navigational aids
UHF (ultra high frequency)	300 to 3000 MHz	100 to 10 cm	LOS; cosmic noise	UHF television; cellular telephone; radar; microwave links; personal communications systems
SHF (super high frequency)	3 to 30 GHz	10 to 1 cm	LOS; rainfall attenuation above 10 GHz; atmospheric attenuation due to oxygen and water vapor	Satellite communication; radar; terrestrial microwave links; wireless local loop
EHF (extremely high frequency)	30 to 300 GHz	10 to 1 mm	LOS; atmospheric attenuation due to oxygen and water vapor	Experimental; wireless local loop
Infrared	300 GHz to 400 THz	1 mm to 770 nm	LOS	Infrared LANs; consumer electronic applications
Visible light	400 THz to 900 THz	770 to 330 nm	LOS	Optical communication

Ground Wave Propagation **Ground wave propagation** (Figure 6.5a) more or less follows the contour of the earth and can propagate considerable distances, well over the visual horizon. This effect is found in frequencies up to about 2 MHz. Several factors account for the tendency of electromagnetic wave in this frequency band to follow the earth's curvature. One factor is that the electromagnetic wave induces a current in the earth's surface, the result of which is to slow the wavefront near the earth, causing the wavefront to tilt downward and hence follow the earth's curvature. Another factor is diffraction, which is a phenomenon having to do with the behavior of electromagnetic waves in the presence of obstacles.

Electromagnetic waves in this frequency range are scattered by the atmosphere in such a way that they do not penetrate the upper atmosphere.

The best-known example of ground wave communication is AM radio.

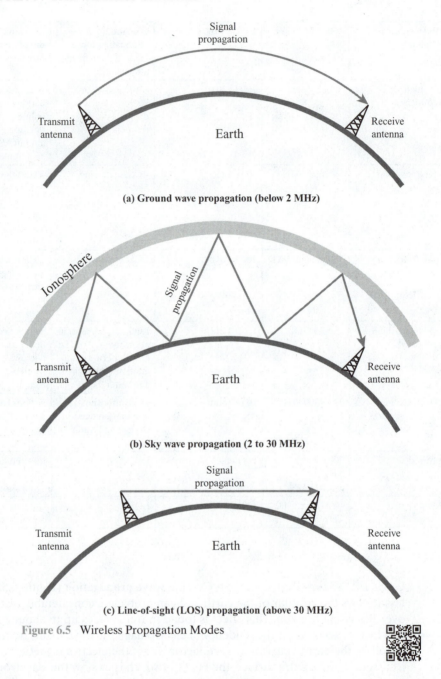

Figure 6.5 Wireless Propagation Modes

Sky Wave Propagation **Sky wave propagation** is used for amateur radio, CB radio, and international broadcasts such as BBC and Voice of America. With sky wave propagation, a signal from an earth-based antenna can be viewed as being reflected from the ionized layer of the upper atmosphere (ionosphere) back down to earth. Although it appears that the wave is reflected from the ionosphere as if the ionosphere were a hard reflecting surface, the effect is in fact caused by refraction. Refraction is described subsequently.

A sky wave signal can travel through a number of hops, bouncing back and forth between the ionosphere and the earth's surface (Figure 6.5b). With this propagation mode, a signal can be picked up thousands of kilometers from the transmitter.

Line-of-Sight Propagation Above 30 MHz, neither ground wave nor sky wave propagation modes operate and communication must be by line of sight (Figure 6.5c). For satellite communication, a signal above 30 MHz is not reflected by the ionosphere and therefore can be transmitted between an earth station and a satellite overhead that is not beyond the horizon. For ground-based communication, the transmitting and receiving antennas must be within an *effective* line of sight of each other. The term *effective* is used because microwaves are bent or refracted by the atmosphere. The amount and even the direction of the bend depend on conditions, but generally microwaves are bent with the curvature of the earth and will therefore propagate farther than the optical line of sight.

Refraction Before proceeding, a brief discussion of refraction is warranted. **Refraction** occurs because the velocity of an electromagnetic wave is a function of the density of the medium through which it travels. In a vacuum, an electromagnetic wave (such as light or a radio wave) travels at approximately 3×10^8 m/s. This is the constant, c, commonly referred to as the speed of light, but actually referring to the speed of light in a vacuum. In air, water, glass, and other transparent or partially transparent media, electromagnetic waves travel at speeds less than c.

When an electromagnetic wave moves from a medium of one density to a medium of another density, its speed changes. The effect is to cause a one-time bending of the direction of the wave at the boundary between the two media. This is illustrated in Figure 6.6. If moving from a less dense to a more dense medium, the wave will bend toward the more dense medium. This phenomenon is easily observed by partially immersing a stick in water. The result will look much like Figure 6.6, with the stick appearing shorter and bent.

The index of refraction of one medium relative to another is the sine of the angle of incidence, θ_i, divided by the sine of the angle of refraction, θ_r. The index of refraction is also equal to the ratio of the respective velocities in the two media. The absolute index of refraction of a medium is calculated in comparison with that of a vacuum. Refractive index varies with wavelength, so that refractive effects differ for signals with different wavelengths.

Although Figure 6.6 shows an abrupt, one-time change in direction as a signal moves from one medium to another, a continuous, gradual bending of a signal will occur if it is moving through a medium in which the index of refraction gradually changes. Under normal propagation conditions, the refractive index of the atmosphere decreases with height so that radio waves travel more slowly near the ground than at higher altitudes. The result is a slight bending of the radio waves toward the earth. With sky waves, the density of the ionosphere and its gradual change in density cause the waves to be refracted back toward the earth.

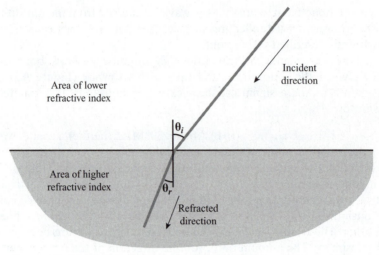

Incident
direction

Area of lower
refractive index

θ_i

Area of higher
refractive index

θ_r

Refracted
direction

Figure 6.6 Refraction of an Electromagnetic Wave

Optical and Radio Line of Sight With no intervening obstacles, the **optical line of sight** is influenced by the curvature of the earth and can be expressed as

$$d = 3.57\sqrt{h}$$

where d is the distance between an antenna and the horizon in kilometers and h is the antenna height in meters. The effective, or **radio, line of sight** to the horizon is expressed as (Figure 6.7)

$$d = 3.57\sqrt{Kh}$$

where K is an adjustment factor to account for the refraction. A good rule of thumb is K = 4/3. Thus, the maximum distance between two antennas for LOS propagation is $3.57(\sqrt{Kh_1} + \sqrt{Kh_2})$, where h_1 and h_2 are the heights of the two antennas.

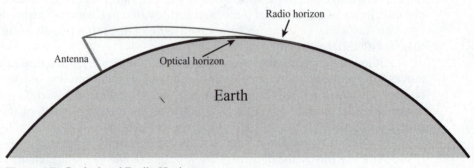

Radio horizon

Antenna

Optical horizon

Earth

Figure 6.7 Optical and Radio Horizons

Example 6.2 The maximum distance between two antennas for LOS transmission if one antenna is 100 m high and the other is at ground level is

$$d = 3.57\sqrt{Kh} = 3.57\sqrt{133} = 41 \text{ km}$$

Now suppose that the receiving antenna is 10 m high. To achieve the same distance, how high must the transmitting antenna be? The result is

$$41 = 3.57(\sqrt{Kh_1} + \sqrt{13.3})$$

$$\sqrt{Kh_1} = \frac{41}{3.57} - \sqrt{13.3} = 7.84$$

$$h_1 = 7.84^2/1.33 = 46.2 \text{ m}$$

This is a savings of over 50 m in the height of the transmitting antenna. This example illustrates the benefit of raising receiving antennas above ground level to reduce the necessary height of the transmitter.

Transmission and Reflection Properties

An electromagnetic wave interacts with an object with a combination of transmission through, reflection off, and absorption into the object. This is dependent on the permittivity of the material, which is dependent on several factors, including signal frequency. This means that certain frequencies may pass effectively through an object where others might not. For example, roadway bridges affect AM radio frequencies not those for FM radio. This affects the design of a network of wireless indoor devices, depending on the propagation through the building materials used for floors and walls.

Table 6.4 shows the attenuation that can be seen for different frequencies through a variety of materials [NIST97]. In most cases, attenuation significantly worsens as frequency increases.

Table 6.4 Signal Attenuation through Materials [NIST97]

Materials	0.5 GHz (dB)	1 GHz (dB)	2 GHz (dB)	5.8 GHz (dB)	8 GHz (dB)
Brick 89 mm	−0.5	−3.7	−5.4	−15.5	−16.0
Brick 267 mm	−3.8	−6.9	−10.6	−38.0	−27.2
Composite Brick 90 mm/Concrete Wall 203 mm	−20.7	−25.0	−33.0	−73.8	−82.4
Masonry 203 mm	−9.5	−11.5	−11.3	−15.5	−18.4
Masonry 610 mm	−26.3	−28.0	−30.0	−47.2	−38.8
Drywall 16 mm	−0.1	−0.3	−0.6	−0.3	−1.0
Concrete 102 mm	−9.7	−12.2	−14.9	−24.1	−27.8
Concrete 305 mm	−32.3	−34.8	−36.0	−74.9	−90.0
Glass 6 mm	−0.2	−0.8	−1.4	−1.0	−1.5
Glass 19 mm	−2.3	−3.1	−3.9	−0.4	−1.0

(Continued)

Table 6.4 (*Continued*)

Materials	0.5 GHz (dB)	1 GHz (dB)	2 GHz (dB)	5.8 GHz (dB)	8 GHz (dB)
Plywood (dry) 6 mm	−0.07	−0.49	−0.93	−0.1	−1.0
Plywood (dry) 32 mm	−0.73	−1.4	−2.0	−0.9	−1.0
Reinforced concrete 203 mm/1% steel	−22.3	−27.3	−31.0	−56.7	−69

6.3 LINE-OF-SIGHT TRANSMISSION

With any communications system, the signal that is received will differ from the signal that is transmitted, due to various transmission impairments. For analog signals, these impairments introduce various random modifications that degrade the signal quality. For digital data, bit errors are introduced: A binary 1 is transformed into a binary 0, and vice versa. In this section, we examine the various impairments and comment on their effect on the information-carrying capacity of a communications link. Our concern in this book is with LOS wireless transmission frequencies, and in this context, the most significant impairments are

- Attenuation and attenuation distortion
- Free space loss
- Noise
- Atmospheric absorption
- Multipath
- Refraction

Five Basic Propagation Mechanisms

There are five different mechanisms by which electromagnetic signals can transfer information from a transmitter to a receiver.

1. **Free-space propagation** transmits a wave when there are no obstructions. The signal strength decays as a function of distance.
2. **Transmission** propagates a signal as it penetrates in and through a medium.
3. **Reflections** occur when electromagnetic waves impinge upon surfaces that are large relative to the wavelength of a signal.
4. **Diffraction** occurs when a signal is obstructed by an object with sharp edges. Secondary waves are then present behind the sharp edges to deliver the signal to a possibly shadowed receiver.
5. **Scattering** is involved when a signal interacts with large numbers of objects that are small relative to its wavelength. This can involve rough surfaces, foliage, street signs, etc., in a typical communications system.

The last four involve interacting objects. The dielectric and conducting properties of these objects affect the strength and angle of signal propagation when these interactions occur.

Attenuation

The strength of a signal falls off with distance over any transmission medium. For guided media, this reduction in strength, or **attenuation**, is generally exponential and thus is typically expressed as a constant number of decibels per increase in distance by a factor of 10. For unguided media, attenuation is a more complex function of distance and the makeup of the atmosphere. Attenuation introduces three factors for the transmission engineer:

1. A received signal must have sufficient strength so that the electronic circuitry in the receiver can detect and interpret the signal.

2. The signal must maintain a level sufficiently higher than noise to be received without error.

3. Attenuation is greater at higher frequencies, resulting in distortion because signals typically comprise many frequency components.

The first and second factors are dealt with by attention to signal strength and the use of amplifiers or repeaters. For a point-to-point transmission (one transmitter and one receiver), the signal strength of the transmitter must be strong enough to be received intelligibly, but not so strong as to overload the circuitry of the transmitter or receiver, which would cause distortion. Regulatory requirements will also limit transmission power. Beyond a certain distance, the attenuation becomes unacceptably great, and repeaters or amplifiers are used to boost the signal at regular intervals. These problems are more complex when there are multiple receivers, where the distance from transmitter to receiver is variable.

The third factor is known as attenuation distortion. Because the attenuation varies as a function of frequency, the received signal is distorted, reducing intelligibility. Specifically, the frequency components of the received signal have different relative strengths than the frequency components of the transmitted signal. To overcome this problem, techniques are available for equalizing attenuation across a band of frequencies. One approach is to use amplifiers that amplify high frequencies more than lower frequencies.

Free Space Loss

For any type of wireless communication, the signal disperses with distance. Energy dispersal can be viewed as radiating in a sphere with a receiver on the surface extracting energy on part of the surface area. A larger and larger sphere occurs as distance from the transmitter increases, so there is less energy per each unit of surface area. Therefore, an antenna with a fixed area will receive less signal power the farther it is from the transmitting antenna. For satellite communication, this is the primary mode of signal loss. Even if no other sources of attenuation or impairment are assumed, a transmitted signal attenuates over distance because the signal is being spread over a larger and larger area. This form of attenuation is known as **free space loss**, which can be expressed in terms of the ratio of the radiated power P_t to the power P_r received by the antenna or, in decibels, by taking 10 times the log of that ratio. For the ideal isotropic antenna, free space loss is

$$\frac{P_t}{P_r} = \frac{(4\pi d)^2}{\lambda^2} = \frac{(4\pi f d)^2}{c^2}$$

where

P_t = signal power at the transmitting antenna
P_r = signal power at the receiving antenna
λ = carrier wavelength
f = carrier frequency
d = propagation distance between antennas
c = speed of light (3×10^8 m/s)

where d and λ are in the same units (e.g., meters).

This can be recast in decibels as

$$L_{dB} = 10 \log \frac{P_t}{P_r} = 20 \log \left(\frac{4\pi d}{\lambda} \right) = -20 \log (\lambda) + 20 \log (d) + 21.98 \, \text{dB}$$

$$= 20 \log \left(\frac{4\pi f d}{c} \right) = 20 \log (f) + 20 \log (d) - 147.56 \, \text{dB} \tag{6.4}$$

Figure 6.8 illustrates the free space loss equation.[1]

For other antennas, we must take into account the gain of the antenna, which yields the following free space loss equation:

$$\frac{P_t}{P_r} = \frac{(4\pi)^2(d)^2}{G_r G_t \lambda^2} = \frac{(\lambda d)^2}{A_r A_t} = \frac{(cd)^2}{f^2 A_r A_t}$$

where

G_t = gain of the transmitting antenna
G_r = gain of the receiving antenna
A_t = effective area of the transmitting antenna
A_r = effective area of the receiving antenna

The third fraction is derived from the second fraction using the relationship between antenna gain and effective area defined in Equation (6.3). We can recast this equation as

$$L_{dB} = 20 \log (\lambda) + 20 \log (d) - 10 \log (A_t A_r)$$
$$= -20 \log (f) + 20 \log (d) - 10 \log (A_t A_r) + 169.54 \, \text{dB} \tag{6.5}$$

Thus, for the same antenna dimensions and separation, the longer the carrier wavelength (lower the carrier frequency f), the higher is the free space path loss. It is interesting to compare Equations (6.4) and (6.5). Equation (6.4) indicates that as the frequency increases, the free space loss also increases, which would suggest that at higher frequencies, losses become more burdensome. However, Equation (6.5) shows that we can easily compensate for this increased loss with antenna gains. As Equation (6.3) indicates, there is increased gain at higher frequencies, in fact there is a net gain at higher frequencies, other factors remaining constant. Equation (6.4) shows that at a fixed distance an increase in frequency results in an increased loss measured by $20 \log(f)$. However, if we take into account antenna gain, and fix antenna area, then the change in loss is measured by $-20 \log(f)$; that is, there is actually a decrease in loss at higher frequencies.

---

[1]As was mentioned in Appendix 2A, there is some inconsistency in the literature over the use of the terms *gain* and *loss*. Equation (6.4) follows the convention of Equation (2.2) in Section 2.4.

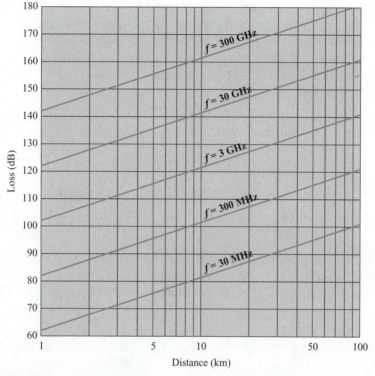

Figure 6.8 Free Space Loss

Example 6.3 Determine the isotropic free-space loss at 4 GHz for the shortest path to a synchronous satellite from earth (35,863 km). At 4 GHz, the wavelength is $(3 \times 10^8)/(4 \times 10^9) = 0.075$ m. Then,

$$L_{dB} = -20 \log (0.075) + 20 \log(35.853 \times 10^6) + 21.98 = 195.6 \text{ dB}$$

Now consider the antenna gain of both the satellite- and ground-based antennas. Typical values are 44 dB and 48 dB, respectively. The free space loss is:

$$L_{dB} = 195.6 - 44 - 48 = 103.6 \text{ dB}$$

Now assume a transmit power of 250 W at the earth station. What is the power received at the satellite antenna? A power of 250 W translates into 24 dBW, so the power at the receiving antenna is $24 - 103.6 = -79.6$ dBW, where dBW is decibel-watt, defined in Appendix 2A. This signal is approximately 10^{-8} W, but still usable by receiver circuitry.

Path Loss Exponent in Practical Systems

Practical systems involve many types of obstructions that cause reflections, scattering, etc. Both theoretical and measurement-based models have shown that beyond a certain distance the average received signal power decreases by a factor of $1/d^n$, also seen as logarithmically decreasing with distance according to a $10n \log(d)$ relationship where n is known as the **path loss exponent** [RAPP02]. Such models have been used extensively. Both Equations (6.4) and (6.5) showed a 20 log(d) term that came from a d^2 distance relationship, hence a path loss exponent of $n = 2$. These should be replaced with the more general $10n$ log(d) term as follows:

$$\frac{P_t}{P_r} = \left(\frac{4\pi}{\lambda}\right)^2 d^n = \left(\frac{4\pi f}{c}\right)^2 d^n$$

$$L_{dB} = 10 \log \frac{P_t}{P_r} = 10 \log\left(\left(\frac{4\pi}{\lambda}\right)^2 d^n\right) = -20 \log(\lambda) + 10n \log(d) + 21.98 \text{ dB}$$

$$= 10 \log\left(\left(\frac{4\pi f}{c}\right)^2 d^n\right) = 20 \log(f) + 10n \log(d) - 147.56 \text{ dB} \quad (6.6)$$

Using effective areas and the general path loss exponent, n,

$$L_{dB} = 20 \log(\lambda) + 10n \log(d) - 10 \log(A_t A_r)$$
$$= -20 \log(f) + 10n \log(d) - 10 \log(A_t A_r) + 169.54 \text{ dB} \quad (6.7)$$

Table 6.5 shows typical path-loss exponents obtained for various environments. Note that in-building LOS can be better than $n = 2$ (e.g., in hallways) because reflections help keep the signal stronger than if it decayed with distance as in free space.

Example 6.4 Compare the path loss in dB for two possible cellular environments where there is (1) free space between mobiles and base stations, and (2) urban area cellular radio with $n = 3.1$. Use 1.9 GHz at a distance of 1.5 km and assume isotropic antennas.

For free space using $n = 2.0$,

$$L_{dB} = 20 \log(1.9 \times 10^9) + 10 \times 2.0 \log(1.5 \times 10^3) - 147.56 = 101.53 \text{ dB}$$

For urban cellular radio using $n = 3.1$,

$$L_{dB} = 20 \log(1.9 \times 10^9) + 10 \times 3.1 \log(1.5 \times 10^3) - 147.56 = 136.47 \text{ dB}$$

Example 6.5 Compare the range of coverage for two possible cellular environments where there is (1) free space between mobiles and base stations, and (2) urban area cellular radio with $n = 3.1$. Use 1.9 GHz and assume isotropic antennas. Assume the transmit power is 2 W and the received power must be above -110 dBW.

P_t in dB = $10 \log(2) = 3.0$

The requirement is, therefore, $L_{dB} < 113$ dB

For free space using $n = 2.0$,

$$L_{dB} = 20 \log(1.9 \times 10^9) + 10 \times 2.0 \log(d) - 147.56 < 113 \text{ dB}$$
$$10 \times 2.0 \log(d) < 74.99 \text{ dB}$$
$$d < 5.61 \text{ km}$$

For urban area using $n = 3.1$,

$$L_{dB} = 20 \log(1.9 \times 10^9) + 10 \times 3.1 \log(d) - 147.56 < 113 \text{ dB}$$
$$10 \times 3.1 \log(d) < 74.99 \text{ dB}$$
$$d < 262 \text{ m}$$

Table 6.5 Path Loss Exponents for Different
Environments [RAPP02]

Environment	Path Loss Exponent, n
Free space	2
Urban area cellular radio	2.7 to 3.5
Shadowed cellular radio	3 to 5
In building line-of-sight	1.6 to 1.8
Obstructed in building	4 to 6
Obstructed in factories	2 to 3

Models Derived from Empirical Measurements

In designing a wireless system, the communications engineer must take account of various propagation effects, the desired maximum transmit power level at the base station and the mobile units, the typical height of the mobile unit antenna, and the available height of the BS antenna. These factors will determine the coverage area of wireless system. Unfortunately, the propagation effects are dynamic and difficult to predict. The best that can be done is to come up with a model based on empirical data and to apply that model to a given environment to develop guidelines. One of the most widely used models was developed by Okumura et al. [OKUM68] and subsequently refined by Hata [HATA80], commonly called the **Okumura-Hata model**. The original was a detailed analysis of the Tokyo area and produced path loss information for an urban environment. The Okumura–Hata model is an empirical formulation that takes into account a variety of environments and conditions. For an urban environment, predicted path loss is

$$L_{dB} = 69.55 + 26.16 \log f_c - 13.82 \log h_t - A(h_r)$$
$$+ (44.9 - 6.55 \log h_t) \log d \qquad (6.8)$$

where

f_c = carrier frequency in MHz from 150 to 1500 MHz
h_t = height of transmitting antenna (base station) in m, from 30 to 300 m
h_r = height of receiving antenna (mobile unit) in m, from 1 to 10 m
d = propagation distance between antennas in km, from 1 to 20 km
$A(h_r)$ = correction factor for mobile unit antenna height

For a small or medium-sized city, the correction factor is given by

$$A(h_r) = (1.1 \log f_c - 0.7) h_r - (1.56 \log f_c - 0.8) \text{ dB}$$

And for a large city, it is given by

$$A(h_r) = 8.29 [\log(1.54 h_r)]^2 - 1.1 \text{ dB} \qquad \text{for } f_c \leq 300 \text{ MHz}$$

$$A(h_r) = 3.2 [\log(11.75 h_r)]^2 - 4.97 \text{ dB} \qquad \text{for } f_c \geq 300 \text{ MHz}$$

To estimate the path loss in a suburban area, the formula for urban path loss in Equation (6.8) is modified as

$$L_{dB}(\text{suburban}) = L_{dB}(\text{urban small/medium city}) - 2[\log (f_c/28)]^2 - 5.4$$

And for the path loss in open or rural areas, the formula is modified as

$$L_{dB}(\text{open}) = L_{dB}(\text{urban small/medium city}) - 4.78 (\log f_c)^2$$
$$- 18.733 (\log f_c) - 40.98$$

The Okumura–Hata model is considered to be among the best in terms of accuracy in path loss prediction and provides a practical means of estimating path loss in a wide variety of situations [FREE07, RAPP02].

Example 6.6 Let $f_c = 900$ MHz, $h_t = 40$ m, $h_r = 5$ m, and $d = 10$ km. Estimate the path loss for a medium-sized city.

$A(h_r) = (1.1 \log 900 - 0.7) 5 - (1.56 \log 900 - 0.8)$ dB

$\qquad = 12.75 - 3.8 = 8.95$ dB

$L_{dB} = 69.55 + 26.16 \log 900 - 13.82 \log 40 - 8.95 + (44.9 - 6.55 \log 40) \log 10$

$\qquad = 69.55 + 77.28 - 22.14 - 8.95 + 34.4 = 150.14$ dB

Noise

For any data transmission event, the received signal will consist of the transmitted signal, modified by the various distortions imposed by the transmission system, plus additional unwanted signals that are inserted somewhere between transmission and reception. These unwanted signals are referred to as **noise**. Noise is the major limiting factor in communications system performance.

Noise may be divided into four categories:

- Thermal noise
- Intermodulation noise
- Cross talk
- Impulse noise

Thermal noise is due to thermal agitation of electrons. It is present in all electronic devices and transmission media and is a function of temperature. Thermal noise is uniformly distributed across the frequency spectrum and hence is often referred to as *white noise*. Thermal noise cannot be eliminated and therefore places an upper bound on the performance of the communications system. Because of the weakness of the signal received by satellite earth stations, thermal noise is particularly significant for satellite communication.

The amount of thermal noise to be found in a bandwidth of 1 Hz in any device or conductor is

$$N_0 = kT(\text{W/Hz})$$

where[2]

N_0 = noise power density in watts per 1 Hz of bandwidth
k = Boltzmanns constant = 1.38×10^{-23} J/K
T = temperature, in kelvins (absolute temperature)

Example 6.7 Room temperature is usually specified as $T = 17°C$, or 290 K. At this temperature, the thermal noise power density is

$$N_0 = (1.3803 \times 10^{-23}) \times 290 = 4 \times 10^{-21} \text{ W/Hz} = -204 \text{ dBW/Hz}$$

The noise is assumed to be independent of frequency. Thus, the thermal noise in watts present in a bandwidth of B Hertz can be expressed as

$$N = kTB$$

or, in decibel-watts

$$N = 10 \log k + 10 \log T + 10 \log B$$
$$= -228.6 \text{ dBW} + 10 \log T + 10 \log B$$

Example 6.8 Given a receiver with an effective noise temperature of 294 K and a 10-MHz bandwidth, the thermal noise level at the receiver's output is

$$N = -228.6 \text{ dBW} + 10 \log(294) + 10 \log 10^7$$
$$= -228.6 + 24.7 + 70$$
$$= -133.9 \text{ dBW}$$

When signals at different frequencies share the same transmission medium, the result may be **intermodulation noise**. Intermodulation noise produces signals at a frequency that is the sum or difference of the two original frequencies or multiples of those frequencies. For example, the mixing of signals at frequencies f_1 and f_2 might produce energy at the frequency $f_1 + f_2$. This derived signal could interfere with an intended signal at the frequency $f_1 + f_2$.

Intermodulation noise is produced when there is some nonlinearity in the transmitter, receiver, or intervening transmission system. Normally, these components behave as linear systems; that is, the output is equal to the input times a constant. In a nonlinear system, the output is a more complex function of the input. Such nonlinearity can be caused by component malfunction, the use of excessive signal strength, or just the nature of the amplifiers used. It is under these circumstances that the sum and difference frequency terms occur.

---

[2]A Joule (J) is the International System (SI) unit of electrical, mechanical, and thermal energy. A watt is the SI unit of power, equal to one joule per second. The kelvin (K) is the SI unit of thermodynamic temperature. For a temperature in degrees kelvin of T, the corresponding temperature in degrees Celsius is equal to $T - 273.15$.

Cross talk has been experienced by anyone who, while using the telephone, has been able to hear another conversation; it is an unwanted coupling between signal paths. It can occur by electrical coupling between nearby twisted pairs or, rarely, coax cable lines carrying multiple signals. Cross talk can also occur when unwanted signals are picked up by microwave antennas; although highly directional antennas are used, microwave energy does spread during propagation. Typically, cross talk is of the same order of magnitude as, or less than, thermal noise. However, in the unlicensed ISM bands, cross talk often dominates.

All of the types of noise discussed so far have reasonably predictable and relatively constant magnitudes. Thus it is possible to engineer a transmission system to cope with them. **Impulse noise**, however, is noncontinuous, consisting of irregular pulses or noise spikes of short duration and of relatively high amplitude. It is generated from a variety of causes, including external electromagnetic disturbances, such as lightning, and faults and flaws in the communications system.

Impulse noise is generally only a minor annoyance for analog data. For example, voice transmission may be corrupted by short clicks and crackles with no loss of intelligibility. However, impulse noise is the primary source of error in digital data transmission. For example, a sharp spike of energy of 0.01 s duration would barely be noticed for voice conversation but would wash out about 10,000 bits of data being transmitted at 1 Mbps.

The Expression E_b/N_o

Chapter 2 introduced the signal-to-noise ratio (SNR). There is a parameter related to SNR that is more convenient for determining digital data rates and error rates and that is the standard quality measure for digital communications system performance. The parameter is the ratio of signal *energy* per bit to noise power density per Hertz, E_b/N_0. Consider a signal, digital or analog, that contains binary digital data transmitted at a certain bit rate R. Recalling that 1 watt $= 1$ J/s, the energy per bit in a signal is given by $E_b = ST_b$, where S is the signal power and T_b is the time required to send one bit. The data rate R is just $R = 1/T_b$. Thus,

$$\frac{E_b}{N_0} = \frac{S/R}{N_0} = \frac{S}{kTR} \tag{6.9}$$

or, in decibel notation,

$$\left(\frac{E_b}{N_0}\right)_{dB} = S_{dBW} - 10\log R - 10\log k - 10\log T$$
$$= S_{dBW} - 10\log R + 228.6 \text{ dBW} - 10\log T$$

The ratio E_b/N_0 is important because the bit error rate (BER) for digital data is a (decreasing) function of this ratio. Figure 6.9 illustrates the typical shape of a plot of BER versus E_b/N_0. Such plots are commonly found in the literature and several examples appear in this text. For any particular curve, as the signal strength relative to the noise increases (increasing E_b/N_0), the BER performance at the receiver decreases. This makes intuitive sense. However, there is not a single unique curve

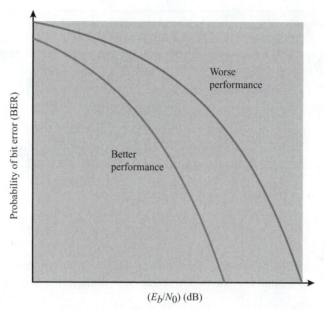

Figure 6.9 General Shape of BER versus E_b/N_0 Curves

that expresses the dependence of BER on E_b/N_0. Instead the performance of a transmission/reception system, in terms of BER versus E_b/N_0, also depends on the way in which the data is encoded onto the signal. Thus, Figure 6.9 shows two curves, one of which gives better performance than the other. A curve below and to the left of another curve defines superior performance. At the same BER for two signals, the curve to the left shows how much less E_b/N_0 is needed (really E_b since N_0 is constant) to achieve that BER. For two signals using the same E_b/N_0, the curve shows the better BER. Chapter 7 explores the relationship of signal encoding to performance. A more detailed discussion of E_b/N_0 is found in [SKLA01].

Given a value of E_b/N_0 needed to achieve a desired error rate, the parameters in Equation (6.9) may be selected. Note that as the bit rate R increases, the transmitted signal power S, relative to noise, must increase to maintain the required E_b/N_0.

Let us try to grasp this result intuitively by considering again Figure 2.9. The signal here is digital, but the reasoning would be the same for an analog signal. In several instances, the noise is sufficient to alter the value of a bit. If the data rate were doubled, the bits would be more tightly packed together, and the same passage of noise might destroy two bits. Thus, for constant signal and noise strength, an increase in data rate increases the error rate. Also, some decoding schemes average out the noise effects over the bit period; if the bit period is shorter, there is less time and effectiveness of this averaging process.

The advantage of E_b/N_0 compared to SNR is that the latter quantity depends on the bandwidth.

Example 6.9   Suppose a signal encoding technique requires that $E_b/N_0 = 8.4$ dB for a bit error rate of 10^{-4} (one bit error out of every 10,000). If the effective noise temperature is 290 K (room temperature) and the data rate is 100 kbps, what received signal level is required to overcome thermal noise?

We have

$$8.4 = S_{\text{dBW}} - 10 \log 100000 + 228.6 \text{ dBW} - 10 \log 290$$
$$= S_{\text{dBW}} - (10)(5) + 228.6 - (10)(2.46)$$
$$S = -145.6 \text{ dBW}$$

We can relate E_b/N_0 to SNR as follows. We have

$$\frac{E_b}{N_0} = \frac{S}{N_0 R}$$

The parameter N_0 is the noise power density in watts/hertz. Hence, the noise in a signal with bandwidth B is $N = N_0 B$. Substituting, we have

$$\frac{E_b}{N_0} = \frac{S}{N} \frac{B}{R} \tag{6.10}$$

Another formulation of interest relates to E_b/N_0 spectral efficiency. Recall, from Chapter 2, Shannon's result that the maximum channel capacity, in bits per second, obeys the equation

$$C = B \log_2(1 + S/N)$$

where C is the capacity of the channel in bits per second and B is the bandwidth of the channel in hertz. This can be rewritten as

$$\frac{S}{N} = 2^{C/B} - 1$$

Using Equation (6.10), and R with C, we have

$$\frac{E_b}{N_0} = \frac{B}{C}(2^{C/B} - 1)$$

This is a useful formula that relates the achievable spectral efficiency C/B to E_b/N_0.

Example 6.10.   Suppose we want to find the minimum E_b/N_0 required to achieve a spectral efficiency of 6 bps/Hz. Then, $E_b/N_0 = (1/6)(2^6 - 1) = 10.5 = 10.21$ dB.

Atmospheric Absorption

An additional loss between the transmitting and receiving antennas is **atmospheric absorption**. Water vapor and oxygen contribute most to attenuation. A peak attenuation occurs in the vicinity of 22 GHz due to water vapor. At frequencies below

15 GHz, the attenuation is less. The presence of oxygen results in an absorption peak in the vicinity of 60 GHz but contributes less at frequencies below 30 GHz. Rain and fog (suspended water droplets) cause scattering of radio waves that results in attenuation. This can be a major cause of signal loss. Thus, in areas of significant precipitation, either path lengths have to be kept short or lower-frequency bands should be used.

Multipath

For wireless facilities where there is a relatively free choice of where antennas are to be located, they can be placed so that if there are no nearby interfering obstacles, there is a direct line-of-sight path from transmitter to receiver. This is generally the case for many satellite facilities and for point-to-point microwave. In other cases, such as mobile telephony, there are obstacles in abundance. The signal can be reflected by such obstacles so that multiple copies of the signal with varying delays can be received. In fact, in extreme cases, the receiver my capture only reflected signals and not the direct signal. Depending on the differences in the path lengths of the direct and reflected waves, the composite signal can be either larger or smaller than the direct signal. Reinforcement and cancellation of the signal resulting from the signal following multiple paths can be controlled for communication between fixed, well-sited antennas, and between satellites and fixed ground stations. One exception is when the path goes across water, where the wind keeps the reflective surface of the water in motion. For mobile telephony and communication to antennas that are not well sited, multipath considerations can be paramount.

Figure 6.10 illustrates in general terms the types of multipath interference typical in terrestrial, fixed microwave, and in mobile communications. For fixed

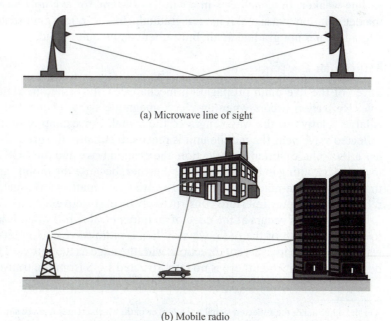

(a) Microwave line of sight

(b) Mobile radio

Figure 6.10 Examples of Multipath Interference

microwave, in addition to the direct line of sight, the signal may follow a curved path through the atmosphere due to refraction and the signal may also reflect from the ground. For mobile communications, structures and topographic features provide reflection surfaces.

Refraction

Radio waves are refracted (or bent) when they propagate through the atmosphere. The refraction is caused by changes in the speed of the signal with altitude or by other spatial changes in the atmospheric conditions. Normally, the speed of the signal increases with altitude, causing radio waves to bend downward. However, on occasion, weather conditions may lead to variations in speed with height that differ significantly from the typical variations. This may result in a situation in which only a fraction or no part of the line-of-sight wave reaches the receiving antenna.

6.4 FADING IN THE MOBILE ENVIRONMENT

Perhaps the most challenging technical problem facing communications systems engineers is **fading** in a mobile environment. The term *fading* refers to the time variation of received signal power caused by changes in the transmission medium or path(s). In a fixed environment, fading is affected by changes in atmospheric conditions, such as rainfall. But in a mobile environment, where one of the two antennas is moving relative to the other, the relative location of various obstacles changes over time, creating complex transmission effects.

In regular vernacular, the term "fading" usually relates to a gradual process of getting weaker. In some cases in a wireless system, for example large-scale fading, the degradation of a signal is indeed gradual. However, for small-scale fading, signal degradation is not gradual at all, but rather can be quite rapid.

Multipath Propagation

Three of the five main propagation mechanisms, illustrated in Figure 6.11, play a role. **Reflection** occurs when an electromagnetic signal encounters a surface that is large relative to the wavelength of the signal. For example, suppose a ground-reflected wave near the mobile unit is received. Because the ground-reflected wave has a 180°-phase shift after reflection, the ground wave and the LOS wave may tend to cancel, resulting in high signal loss.[3] Further, because the mobile antenna is lower than most human-made structures in the area, multipath interference occurs. These reflected waves may interfere constructively or destructively at the receiver.

Diffraction occurs at the edge of an impenetrable body that is large compared to the wavelength of the radio wave. When a radio wave encounters such an edge, waves propagate in different directions with the edge as the source. Thus, signals can be received even when there is no unobstructed LOS from the transmitter.

---

[3]On the other hand, the reflected signal has a longer path, which creates a phase shift due to delay relative to the unreflected signal. When this delay is equivalent to half a wavelength, the two signals are back in phase.

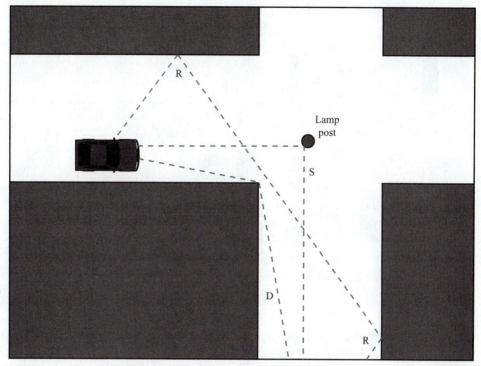

Figure 6.11 Sketch of Three Important Propagation Mechanisms:
Reflection (R), Scattering (S), and Diffraction (D)

If the size of an obstacle is on the order of the wavelength of the signal or less, **scattering** occurs. An incoming signal is scattered into several weaker outgoing signals. At typical cellular microwave frequencies, there are numerous objects, such as lamp posts and traffic signs, that can cause scattering. Thus, scattering effects are difficult to predict.

These three propagation effects influence system performance in various ways depending on local conditions and as the mobile unit moves within a cell. If a mobile unit has a clear LOS to the transmitter, then diffraction and scattering are generally minor effects, although reflection may have a significant impact. If there is no clear LOS, such as in an urban area at street level, then diffraction and scattering are the primary means of signal reception.

The Effects of Multipath Propagation As just noted, one unwanted effect of multipath propagation is that multiple copies of a signal may arrive at different signal phases. If these phases add destructively, the resulting signal power can be lower by a factor of 100 or 1000 (20 or 30 dB). The signal level relative to noise declines, making signal detection at the receiver more difficult.

A second phenomenon, of particular importance for digital transmission, is intersymbol interference (ISI). Consider that we are sending a narrow pulse at a given frequency across a link between a fixed antenna and a mobile unit. Figure 6.12 shows what the channel may deliver to the receiver if the impulse is sent at two

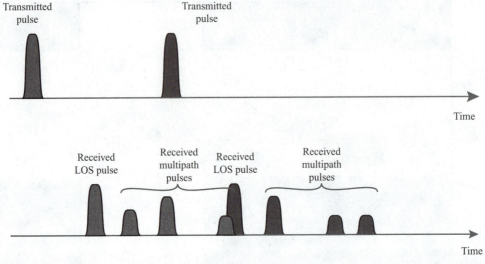

Figure 6.12 Two Pulses in Time Variant Multipath

different times. The upper line shows two pulses at the time of transmission. The lower line shows the resulting pulses at the receiver. In each case the first received pulse is the desired LOS signal. The magnitude of that pulse may change because of changes in atmospheric attenuation. Further, as the mobile unit moves farther away from the fixed antenna, the amount of LOS attenuation increases. But in addition to this primary pulse, there may be multiple secondary pulses due to reflection, diffraction, and scattering. Now suppose that this pulse encodes one or more bits of data. In that case, one or more delayed copies of a pulse may arrive at the same time as the primary pulse for a subsequent bit. These delayed pulses act as a form of noise to the subsequent primary pulse, making recovery of the bit information more difficult.

As the mobile antenna moves, the location of various obstacles changes; hence the number, magnitude, and timing of the secondary pulses change. This makes it difficult to design signal processing techniques that will filter out multipath effects so that the intended signal is recovered with fidelity.

Types of Fading Fading effects in a mobile environment can be classified as either small scale or large scale. Referring to Figure 6.11, as the mobile unit moves down a street in an urban environment, as the mobile user covers distances well in excess of a wavelength, the urban environment changes as the user passes buildings of different heights, vacant lots, intersections, and so forth. Over these longer distances, there is a change in the average received power. This change is mainly caused by shadowing and differences in distance from the transmitter. This is indicated by the slowly changing waveform in Figure 6.13 and is referred to as **large-scale fading**.

However, rapid variations in signal strength also occur over distances of about one-half a wavelength. At a frequency of 900 MHz, which is typical for mobile cellular applications, a wavelength is 0.33 m. The rapidly changing waveform in Figure 6.13 shows an example of the spatial variation of received signal amplitude at

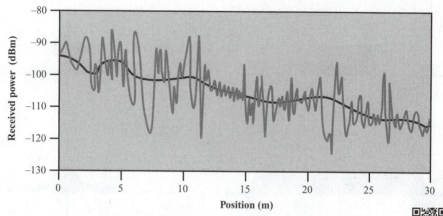

Figure 6.13 Typical Slow and Fast Fading in an Urban Mobile Environment

900 MHz in an urban setting. Note that changes of amplitude can be as much as 20 or 30 dB over a short distance. This type of rapidly changing fading phenomenon, known as **small-scale fading**, affects not only mobile phones in automobiles, but even a mobile phone user walking down an urban street.

There are two distinct types of small-scale fading effects.

- **Doppler spread** causes signal performance to change with time due to movement of mobiles and obstacles.

- **Multipath fading** causes the signal to vary with location due to the combination of delayed multipath signal arrivals.

Regarding Doppler spread, a channel may change over a short time span. This is caused by movement of mobiles and surrounding objects. This is characterized by the channel's **coherence time**, T_c, which is the time over which the channel stays relatively constant. Coherence times for a pedestrian might be 70 ms, whereas times might be 5 ms for a vehicle moving at highway speeds.[4] This might have a significant effect on a signal, depending on its bit rate, r_b bits/second. This signal would have a bit time $T_b = 1/r_b$ second/bit. If the coherence time T_c is much, much longer than the bit time T_b, then the channel could be called **slow fading**; The channel changes very slowly during the time to transmit each bit. If, however, this is not true, the channel is undergoing **fast fading**. Therefore, for our purposes in this book, we consider a channel to be fast fading if the coherence time T_c is less than, approximately equal, or even slightly greater than the bit time T_b, because in all cases the coherence time is not much, much greater than the bit time.

The other small-scale effect, multipath fading, can cause distortion and inter-symbol interference. **Flat fading** is that type of fading in which all frequency components of the received signal fluctuate in the same proportions simultaneously. Multipath fading can be characterized by a **coherence bandwidth**, B_C, which is the range of frequencies over which the channel response is relatively constant.

---

[4]A common formula is $T_c = 0.423c/vf$, where c is the speed of light, v is the velocity of movement, and f is the frequency [RAPP02].

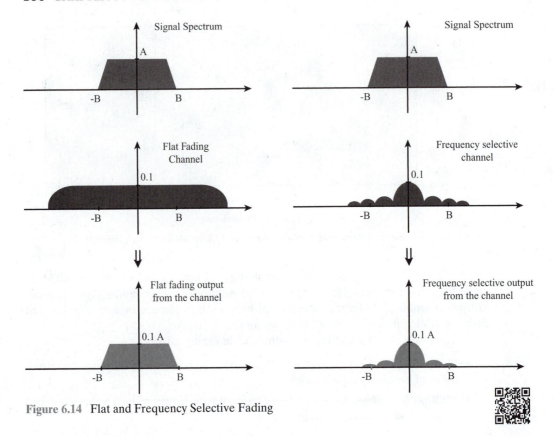

Figure 6.14   Flat and Frequency Selective Fading

Therefore, if the coherence bandwidth is much, much greater than the signal bandwidth, then flat fading occurs. If a signal bandwidth can be approximated as $B_S \approx r_b$, then B_C must be much, much greater than B_S. In contrast, **frequency selective fading** occurs when flat fading is not present. It affects unequally the different spectral components of a radio signal. If attenuation occurs over only a portion of the bandwidth of the signal the fading is considered to be frequency selective. Figure 6.14 illustrates a flat fading channel versus a frequency selective channel relative to the bandwidth of a signal.

These characterizations for Doppler spread and multipath fading do not depend on each other. Therefore, four combinations can occur: fast-flat, slow-flat, fast-frequency selective, and slow-frequency selective fading.

Example 6.11.   Suppose that a pedestrian is moving in an urban environment that has a wireless channel with a coherence time of 70 ms and a coherence bandwidth of 150 kHz. The bit rate of the signal being used is 100 kbps.

a. How would the channel be characterized regarding Doppler spread and multipath fading?

To check for slow fading, test the following, using a factor of 10 for much, much greater.

$$T_b = 1/r_S = 10 \ \mu s$$

$$T_C \gg T_b?$$

$$T_C > 10T_b?$$

Test condition: $70 \ ms > 100 \ \mu s$?

This is true, so *slow fading*.
To check for flat fading, test the following:

Assume $B_S \approx r_S = 100 \ kHz$

$$B_C \gg B_S?$$

$$B_C > 10B_S?$$

Test condition: $150 \ kHz > 1 \ Mbps$?

This is not true, so *frequency selective fading*.
This channel is slow and frequency selective.
b. What range of bit rates can be supported to have flat fading?
This is the requirement

$$B_C \gg B_S$$

$$B_C > 10B_S$$

$$150 \ kHz > 10B_S$$

$$B_S < 15 \ kHz$$

$$r_b < 15 \ kbps$$

The Fading Channel In designing a communications system, the communications engineer needs to estimate the effects of multipath fading and noise on the mobile channel. The simplest channel model, from the point of view of analysis, is the *additive white Gaussian noise (AWGN)* channel. In this channel, the desired signal is degraded by thermal noise associated with the physical channel itself as well as electronics at the transmitter and receiver (and any intermediate amplifiers or repeaters). This model is fairly accurate in some cases, such as space communications and some wire transmissions, such as coaxial cable. For terrestrial wireless transmission, particularly in the mobile situation, AWGN is not a good guide for the designer.

Rayleigh fading occurs when there are multiple indirect paths between the transmitter and the receiver and no distinct dominant path, such as an LOS path. This represents a worst case scenario. Fortunately, Rayleigh fading can be dealt with analytically, providing insights into performance characteristics that can be used in difficult environments, such as downtown urban settings.

Rician fading best characterizes a situation where there is a direct LOS path in addition to a number of indirect multipath signals. The Rician model is often applicable in an indoor environment whereas the Rayleigh model characterizes outdoor settings. The Rician model also becomes more applicable in smaller cells or in more open outdoor environments. The channels can be characterized by a parameter K, defined as follows:

$$K = \frac{\text{power in the dominant path}}{\text{power in the scattered paths}}$$

When $K = 0$, the channel is Rayleigh (i.e., numerator is zero) and when $K = \infty$, the channel is AWGN (i.e., denominator is zero). Figure 6.15, based on [FREE98a] and [SKLA01], shows system performance in the presence of noise. Here, bit error rate is plotted as a function of the ratio E_b/N_0. Of course, as that ratio increases, the bit error rate drops. The figure shows that with a reasonably strong signal, relative to noise, an AWGN exhibit provides fairly good performance, as do Rician channels with larger values of K, roughly corresponding to microcells or an open country environment. The performance would be adequate for a digitized voice application, but for digital data transfer efforts to compensate would be needed. The Rayleigh channel provides relatively poor performance; this is likely to be seen for flat fading and for slow fading; in these cases, error compensation mechanisms become more desirable. Finally, some environments produce fading effects worse than the so-called worst case of Rayleigh. Examples are fast fading in

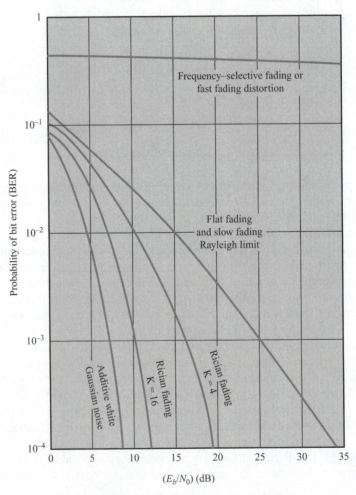

Figure 6.15 Theoretical Bit Error Rate for Various Fading Conditions

an urban environment and the fading within the affected band of a selective fading channel. In these cases, no level of E_b/N_0 will help achieve the desired performance, and compensation mechanisms are mandatory. We turn to a discussion of those mechanisms next.

6.5 CHANNEL CORRECTION MECHANISMS

The efforts to compensate for the errors and distortions introduced by multipath fading fall into four general categories: forward error correction, adaptive equalization, adaptive modulation and coding, diversity techniques (especially with MIMO), orthogonal frequency division multiplexing (OFDM), and spread spectrum. In the typical mobile wireless environment, techniques from many of the categories are combined to combat the error rates encountered.

Forward Error Correction

Forward error correction is applicable in digital transmission applications: those in which the transmitted signal carries digital data or digitized voice or video data. The term *forward* refers to procedures whereby a receiver, using only information contained in the incoming digital transmission, corrects bit errors in the data. This is in contrast to backward error correction, in which the receiver merely detects the presence of errors and then sends a request back to the transmitter to retransmit the data in error. Backward error correction is not practical in many wireless applications. For example, in satellite communications, the amount of delay involved makes retransmission undesirable. In mobile communications, the error rates are often so high that there is a high probability that the retransmitted block of bits will also contain errors. In these applications, forward error correction is required. In essence, forward error correction is achieved as follows:

1. Using a coding algorithm, the transmitter adds a number of additional, redundant bits to each transmitted block of data. These bits form an ***error-correcting code*** and are calculated as a function of the data bits.

2. For each incoming block of bits (data plus error-correcting code), the receiver calculates a new error-correcting code from the incoming data bits. If the calculated code matches the incoming code, then the receiver assumes that no error has occurred in this block of bits.

3. If the incoming and calculated codes do not match, then one or more bits are in error. If the number of bit errors is below a threshold that depends on the length of the code and the nature of the algorithm, it is possible for the receiver to determine the bit positions in error and correct all errors.

Typically in mobile wireless applications, the ratio of total bits sent to data bits sent is between 2 and 3. This may seem an extravagant amount of overhead, in that the capacity of the system is cut to one-half or one-third of its potential, but the mobile wireless environment is so difficult that such levels of redundancy are necessary.

Chapter 10 examines forward error correction techniques in detail.

Adaptive Equalization

Adaptive equalization can be applied to transmissions that carry analog information (e.g., analog voice or video) or digital information (e.g., digital data, digitized voice or video) and is used to combat intersymbol interference. The process of equalization involves some method of gathering the dispersed symbol energy back together into its original time interval. Equalization is a broad topic; techniques include the use of so-called lumped analog circuits as well as sophisticated digital signal processing algorithms. Here we give a flavor of the digital signal processing approach.

Figure 6.16 illustrates a common approach using a linear equalizer circuit. In this specific example, for each output symbol, the input signal is sampled at five uniformly spaced intervals of time, separated by a delay τ. These samples are individually weighted by the coefficients C_i and then summed to produce the output. The circuit is referred to as adaptive because the coefficients are dynamically adjusted. Typically, the coefficients are set using a *training sequence*, which is a known sequence of bits. The training sequence is transmitted. The receiver compares the received training sequence with the expected training sequence and on the basis of the comparison calculates suitable values for the coefficients. Periodically, a new training sequence is sent to account for changes in the transmission environment.

For Rayleigh channels, or worse, it may be necessary to include a new training sequence with every single block of data. Again, this represents considerable overhead but is justified by the error rates encountered in a mobile wireless environment.

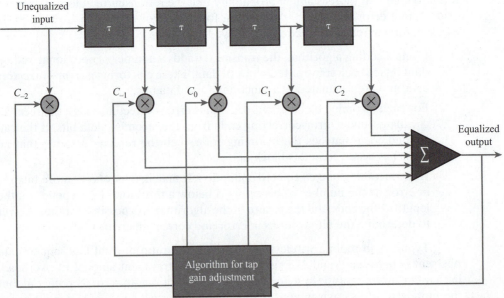

Figure 6.16 Linear Equalizer Circuit

Adaptive Modulation and Coding

Because the characteristics of a wireless channel can change 100s of times per second due to fading and Doppler shifting (e.g., roughly 200 times/second for a 5 ms coherence time), modern systems use **adaptive modulation and coding** (AMC) to adjust their schemes just as quickly. Modulation and coding are discussed in depth in Chapters 7 and 10. They essentially create signals that send as much information as possible (within a bit error probability constraint) for a given received signal strength and noise, then they detect and correct the errors. To adapt 100s of times per second, two features must be present in the protocols for a system.

1. Mechanisms to measure the quality of the wireless channel. These might include monitoring packet loss rates or sending special pilot signals expressly for measurement purposes.

2. Messaging mechanisms to communicate the signal quality indicators between transmitters and receivers, and also to communicate the new modulation and coding formats.

3G and 4G cellular systems, such as Long Term Evolution (LTE), use AMC extensively. Chapter 14 discusses LTE in depth, including its AMC protocols.

Diversity Techniques and MIMO

Diversity is based on the fact that individual channels experience independent fading events. For example, multiple antennas that are spaced far enough apart will have independent fading. We can therefore compensate for error effects by providing multiple logical channels between transmitter and receiver and sending part of the signal over each channel. This technique does not eliminate errors but it does reduce the error rate, because we have spread the transmission out to avoid being subjected to the highest error rate that might occur. The other techniques (equalization, forward error correction) can then cope with the reduced error rate.

Some diversity techniques involve the physical transmission path and are referred to as *space diversity*. For example, multiple antennas, if spaced far enough apart, may be used to receive the message with the signals combined in some fashion to reconstruct the most likely transmitted signal. Another example is the use of collocated multiple directional antennas, each oriented to a different reception angle with the incoming signals again combined to reconstitute the transmitted signal.

With *frequency diversity*, the signal is spread out over a larger frequency bandwidth or carried on multiple frequency carriers. The most important example of this approach is spread spectrum, which is examined in Chapter 9.

Time diversity techniques aim to spread the data out over time so that a noise burst affects fewer bits. This can be accomplished with interleaving as discussed in Chapter 10, as seen in Figure 6.17. It could also be accomplished through a Rake receiver as discussed in Chapter 9.

When these multiple signals are received, there are two basic ways they can be used.

1. **Selection Diversity:** Choose one signal that is acceptable or the best.

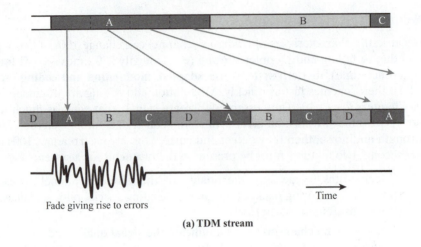

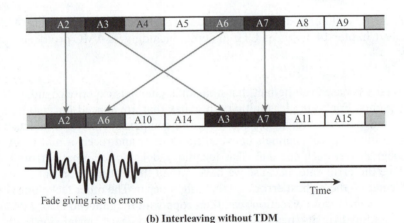

(a) TDM stream

(b) Interleaving without TDM

Figure 6.17 Interleaving Data Blocks to Spread the Effects of Error Bursts

2. **Diversity Combining:** Combine the best signal with the other signals. Adjust the gain and phase so they add together to improve the overall output signal.

Example 6.12. Suppose a wireless channel has two possible quality levels. It has an 80% probability of having a bit error rate of 10^{-6}, but a 20% probability of having a bit error rate of 0.1. Assume independently varying signals can be received through two antennas, and the system uses selection diversity to choose the best signal. How does the overall performance improve?

For one signal, the performance is

$$P_b = Pr\{poor\}*(P_b \text{ for poor}) + Pr\{good\}*(P_b \text{ for good})$$
$$P_b = 0.2(0.1) + 0.8(10^{-6}) \approx 0.02$$

For two diversity branches, the only case of poor performance would occur if both branches would be poor so no good signal could be found. The probability of both being poor is 0.2^2, so

$$P_b = 0.2^2(0.1) + (1 - 0.2^2)(10^{-6}) \approx 0.004$$

For k signals, $P_b \approx 0.2^k(0.1)$. This means that P_b drops two orders of magnitude for each additional diversity branch.

Multiple-Input Multiple-Output (MIMO) Antennas If a transmitter and receiver implement a system with multiple antennas, this is called a **multiple-input multiple-output (MIMO)** system. These allow several of the mechanisms discussed in this chapter to be implemented. Earlier, we saw how an array of antennas can be used to provide a directional antenna pattern. Three other important uses of antenna arrays are also possible. These are all illustrated in Figure 6.18.

1. **Diversity:** Space diversity can be accomplished to have multiple received signals through multiple transmit and/or receive antennas. If spacing cannot be achieved for full signal independence, some benefits of space diversity can still be achieved.

2. **Multiple streams:** Multiple, parallel data streams can flow between pairs of transmit and receive antennas.

3. **Beam-forming:** Multiple antennas can be configured to create directional antenna patterns to focus and increase energy to intended recipients.

4. **Multi-user MIMO:** With enough MIMO antennas, directional antenna beams can be established to multiple users simultaneously.

Diversity for improved
system performance

Beam-forming for improved coverage
(less cells to cover a given area)

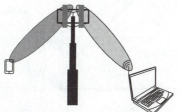

Spatial division multiple access
("MU-MIMO") for improved capacity
(more user per cell)

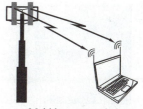

Multi layer transmission
("SU-MIMO") for higher data rates
in a given bandwidth

Figure 6.18 Four Uses of MIMO

Modern systems implement up to 4 x 4 (4 input, 4 output) and 8 x 8 MIMO configurations. Antenna systems have been approved in specifications for as many as 8 per antenna array, and two-dimensional arrays of 64 antennas or more are being envisioned for future technologies.

The MIMO antenna architecture has become a key technology in evolving high-speed wireless networks, including IEEE 802.11 Wi-Fi LANs and LTE. MIMO exploits the space dimension to improve wireless systems in terms of capacity, range, and reliability. Together, MIMO and OFDM technologies are the cornerstone of emerging broadband wireless networks.

MIMO Principles In a MIMO scheme, the transmitter and receiver employ multiple antennas. The source data stream is divided into n substreams, one for each of the n transmitting antennas. The individual substreams are the input to the transmitting antennas (multiple input). At the receiving end, m antennas receive the transmissions from the n source antennas via a combination of line-of-sight transmission and multipath (Figure 6.19). The output signals from all of the m receiving antennas (multiple outputs) are combined. With a lot of complex math, the result is a much better receiver signal than can be achieved with either a single antenna or multiple frequency channels. Note that the terms *input* and *output* refer to the input to the transmission channel and the output from the transmission channel, respectively.

MIMO systems are characterized by the number of antennas at each end of the wireless channel. Thus an 8×4 MIMO system has eight antennas at one end of the channel and four at the other end. In configurations with a base station, the first number typically refers to the number of antennas at the base station. There are two types of MIMO transmission schemes:

- **Spatial diversity:** The same data is coded and transmitted through multiple antennas, which effectively increases the power in the channel proportional to the number of transmitting antennas. This improves signal-to-noise (SNR) for cell edge performance. Further, diverse multipath fading offers multiple "views" of the transmitted data at the receiver, thus increasing robustness. In a multipath scenario where each receiving antenna would experience a different

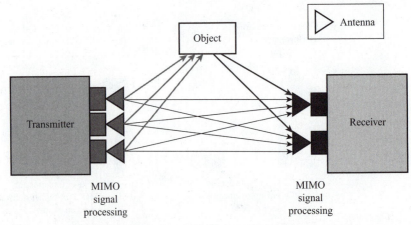

Figure 6.19 MIMO Scheme

interference environment, there is a high probability that if one antenna is suffering a high level of fading, another antenna has sufficient signal level.

- **Spatial multiplexing:** A source data stream is divided among the transmitting antennas. The gain in channel capacity is proportional to the available number of antennas at the transmitter or receiver, whichever is less. Spatial multiplexing can be used when transmitting conditions are favorable and for relatively short distances compared to spatial diversity. The receiver must do considerable signal processing to sort out the incoming substreams, all of which are transmitting in the same frequency channel, and to recover the individual data streams.

For spatial multiplexing, there is a multilink channel that can be expressed as $\mathbf{y} = \mathbf{Hc} + \mathbf{n}$, where $\mathbf{y}$ is the vector of received signals, $\mathbf{c}$ is the vector of transmitted signals, $\mathbf{n}$ is an additive noise component, and $\mathbf{H} = [h_{ij}]$ is an $r \times t$ channel matrix, with r being the number of receiving antennas and t the number of transmitting antennas. The number of spatial data streams is $\min[r, t]$. For a channel with three transmitters and four receivers, the equation is

$$\begin{bmatrix} y_1 \\ y_2 \\ y_3 \\ y_4 \end{bmatrix} = \begin{bmatrix} h_{11} & h_{12} & h_{13} \\ h_{21} & h_{22} & h_{23} \\ h_{31} & h_{32} & h_{33} \\ h_{41} & h_{42} & h_{43} \end{bmatrix} \begin{bmatrix} c_1 \\ c_2 \\ c_3 \end{bmatrix} + \begin{bmatrix} n_1 \\ n_2 \\ n_3 \end{bmatrix}$$

The h_{ij} are complex numbers $x + jz$ that represent both the mean amplitude attenuation (x) over the channel and the path dependent phase shift (z), and the n_i are additive noise components. The receiver measures the channel gains based on training fields containing known patterns in the packet preamble, and can estimate the transmitted signal with the following equation:

$$\begin{bmatrix} \hat{c}_1 \\ \hat{c}_2 \\ \hat{c}_3 \end{bmatrix} = \mathbf{H}^{-1} \begin{bmatrix} y_1 \\ y_2 \\ y_3 \\ y_4 \end{bmatrix}$$

Multi-User MIMO Multi-user MIMO (MU-MIMO) extends the basic MIMO concept to multiple end points, each with multiple antennas. The advantage of MU-MIMO compared to single-user MIMO is that the available capacity can be shared to meet time-varying demands. MU-MIMO techniques are used in both Wi-Fi and 4G cellular networks.

There are two applications of MU-MIMO:

- **Uplink—Multiple Access Channel (MAC):** Multiple end users transmit simultaneously to a single base station.

- **Downlink—Broadcast Channel (BC):** The base station transmits separate data streams to multiple independent users.

MIMO-MAC is used on the uplink channel to provide multiple access to subscriber stations. In general, MIMO-MAC systems outperform point-to-point MIMO, particularly if the number of receiver antennas is greater than the number of transmit antennas at each user. A variety of multiuser detection techniques are used to separate the signals transmitted by the users.

MIMO-BC is used on the downlink channel to enable the base station to transmit different data streams to multiple users over the same frequency band. MIMO-BC is more challenging to implement. The techniques employed involve processing of the data symbols at the transmitter to minimize interuser interference.

OFDM and Spread Spectrum

Traditional communications, wireline or wireless, simply modulate a baseband signal up to a required transmission channel and frequency. No change to the original signal occurs. Two methods, however, have been used to overcome wireless channel impairments; the signals are significantly modified for transmission.

- **Orthogonal frequency division multiplexing (OFDM)** splits a signal into many lower bit rate streams that are transmitted over precisely spaced frequencies. This can overcome frequency selective fading by using significantly lower bandwidth per stream with longer bit times. Each of these frequencies can then be amplified separately. Chapter 8 provides a thorough examination.
- **Spread spectrum** makes a signal use 100 times or more wider bandwidth, with lower energy density at each frequency. This can overcome frequency selective situations; even if some frequencies are poor, good overall average performance is achieved. This is examined in Chapter 9.

Bandwidth Expansion

All of the above correction mechanisms seek to increase the efficient use of the bandwidth of a channel, commonly measured in an efficiency of bps/Hz. But according to Shannon's theory there is a limit to this efficiency for a given signal-to-noise ratio. If throughput requirements are beyond what can be achieved in a given bandwidth, a series of bandwidth expansion approaches are used.

- **Carrier aggregation** combines multiple channels. For example, 802.11n and 802.11ac combine the 20 MHz channels from earlier 802.11 standards into 40, 80 or 160 MHz channels.
- **Frequency reuse** allows the same carrier frequencies to be reused when devices are sufficiently far enough away so the signal-to-interference ratio is low enough. This has traditionally been provided by breaking a cellular coverage area into large cells, called *macro cells*, of several kilometers in diameter. Cells far enough away can reuse the frequencies. But now *small cells* with limited power and range are being used for the same frequency reuse objectives. Indoor small cells are commonly called *femtocells* and outdoor cells are provided by *relays* or *picocells*. These are discussed in conjunction with LTE in Chapter 14. This approach is called *network densification* because it allows frequencies to be reused many times.
- **Millimeter wave (mmWave)** bands are higher frequencies in the 30 to 300 GHz bands that have more bandwidth available in wider bandwidth channels. Recall that $\lambda = c/f$, so 30 to 300 GHz has wavelengths of 10 to 1 mm. This is

an example of using different carrier frequencies to achieve higher bandwidth, given spectrum regulations. mmWave bands are more difficult to use, however, because they are more susceptible to attenuation by obstructions and atmospheric absorption. IEEE 802.11ad uses mmWave bands within a single room. Future technologies, however, may use them for wider range communication, in conjunction with higher gain MIMO configurations.

6.6 RECOMMENDED READING

[FREE07] and [RAPP02] provide good coverage of all of the topics in this chapter. A rigorous treatment of antennas and propagation is found in [BERT00]. [THUR00] provides an exceptionally clear discussion of antennas.

BERT00 Bertoni, H. *Radio Propagation for Modern Wireless Systems*. Upper Saddle River, NJ: Prentice Hall, 2000.

FREE07 Freeman, R. *Radio System Design for Telecommunications*. New York: Wiley, 2007.

RAPP02 Rappaport, T. *Wireless Communications: Principles and Practice*. Upper Saddle River, NJ: Prentice Hall, 2002.

THUR00 Thurwachter, C. *Data and Telecommunications: Systems and Applications*. Upper Saddle River, NJ: Prentice Hall, 2000.

6.7 KEY TERMS, REVIEW QUESTIONS, AND PROBLEMS

Key Terms

adaptive equalization	fading	multipath
adaptive modulation and coding	fast fading	noise
	flat fading	Okumura–Hata model
antenna	forward error correction (FEC)	optical line of sight
antenna gain		parabolic reflective antenna
atmospheric absorption	free space loss	path loss exponent
attenuation	frequency selective fading	radiation pattern
beam width	ground wave propagation	radio line of sight
cognitive radio	Hertz antenna	reception pattern
coherence bandwidth	impulse noise	reflection
coherence time	intermodulation noise	refraction
cross talk	isotropic antenna	scattering
diffraction	large-scale fading	sidelobe
dipole	line of sight (LOS)	small-scale fading
directional antenna	linear antenna array	sky wave propagation
diversity	multiple-input multiple-output (MIMO)	slow fading
Doppler spread		thermal noise
dynamic spectrum access	Multiuser MIMO	

Review Questions

6.1   What two functions are performed by an antenna?

6.2   What is an isotropic antenna?

6.3   Describe a directional antenna pattern and its features.

6.4   What information is available from a radiation pattern?

6.5   What is the advantage of a parabolic reflective antenna?

6.6   What factors determine antenna gain?

6.7   What is a path loss exponent?

6.8   What is the primary cause of signal loss in satellite communications?

6.9   Name and briefly define four types of noise.

6.10   What is refraction?

6.11   What is multipath fading?

6.12   What is the difference between diffraction and scattering?

6.13   What is the difference between fast and slow fading?

6.14   What is the difference between flat and selective fading?

6.15   Name and briefly define three diversity techniques.

Problems

6.1   For radio transmission in free space, signal power is reduced in proportion to the square of the distance from the source, whereas in wire transmission, the attenuation is a fixed number of dB per kilometer. The following table is used to show the dB reduction relative to some reference for free space radio and uniform wire. Fill in the missing numbers to complete the table.

Distance (km)	Radio (dB)	Wire (dB)
1	−6	−3
2		
4		
8		
16		

6.2   Find the optimum wavelength and frequency for a half-wave dipole of length 10 m.

6.3   The audio power of the human voice is concentrated at about 300 Hz. Antennas of the appropriate size for this frequency are impracticably large, so that to send voice by radio the voice signal must be used to modulate a higher (carrier) frequency for which the natural antenna size is smaller.

   a.   What is the length of an antenna one-half wavelength long for sending radio at 300 Hz?

   b.   An alternative is to use a modulation scheme, as described in Chapter 7, for transmitting the voice signal by modulating a carrier frequency, so that the bandwidth of the signal is a narrow band centered on the carrier frequency. Suppose we would like a half-wave antenna to have a length of 1 m. What carrier frequency would we use?

6.4   Section 6.1 states that if a source of electromagnetic energy is placed at the focus of the paraboloid, and if the paraboloid is a reflecting surface, then the wave will bounce back in lines parallel to the axis of the paraboloid. To demonstrate this, consider the parabola $y^2 = 2px$ shown in Figure 6.20. Let $P(x_1, y_1)$ be a point on the parabola, and PF be the line from P to the focus. Construct the line L through P parallel to the x axis and the line M tangent to the parabola at P. The angle between L and M is β, and the angle between PF and M is α. The angle α is the angle at which a ray from F strikes the parabola at P. Because the angle of incidence equals the angle of reflection, the ray reflected from P must be at an angle α to M. Thus, if we can show that $\alpha = \beta$, we have demonstrated that rays reflected from the parabola starting at F will be parallel to the x axis.

    a. First show that $\tan \beta = (p/y_1)$. *Hint:* Recall from trigonometry that the slope of a line is equal to the tangent of the angle the line makes with the positive x direction. Also recall that the slope of the line tangent to a curve at a given point is equal to the derivative of the curve at that point.

    b. Now show that $\tan \alpha = (p/y_1)$, which demonstrates that $\alpha = \beta$. *Hint:* Recall from trigonometry that the formula for the tangent of the difference between two angles α_1 and α_2 is $\tan (\alpha_2 - \alpha_1) = (\tan \alpha_2 - \tan \alpha_1) = (\tan \alpha_2 - \tan \alpha_1)/(1 + \tan \alpha_2 \times \tan \alpha_1)$.

6.5 It is often more convenient to express distance in km rather than m and frequency in MHz rather than Hz. Rewrite Equation (6.4) using these dimensions.

6.6 Suppose a transmitter produces 50 W of power.

    a. Express the transmit power in units of dBm and dBW.

    b. If the transmitter's power is applied to a unity gain antenna with a 900-MHz carrier frequency, what is the received power in dBm at a free space distance of 100 m?

    c. Repeat (b) for a distance of 10 km.

    d. Repeat (c) but assume a receiver antenna gain of 2.

6.7 Instead of assuming a free space environment in Problem 6.6, assume an urban area cellular radio scenario. Use a path loss exponent of $n = 3.1$ and a transmitter power of 50 W.

    a. What is the range of path loss exponents for this environment?

    b. If the transmitter's power is applied to a unity gain antenna with a 900-MHz carrier frequency, what is the received power in dBm at a free space distance of 100 m?

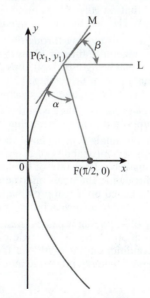

Figure 6.20 Parabolic Reflection

    c. Repeat (b) for a distance of 10 km.

    d. Repeat (c) but assume a receiver antenna gain of 2.

 6.8 What is the range of path loss exponents that will satisfy the following requirements?
- Transmitter power = 2 W
- Received power = −105 dBm
- Unity gain transmit and receive antennas
- Carrier frequency = 1.8 GHz
- Distance of 5.2 km

6.9 A microwave transmitter has an output of 0.1 W at 2 GHz. Assume that this transmitter is used in a microwave communications system where the transmitting and receiving antennas are parabolas, each 1.2 m in diameter.

    a. What is the gain of each antenna in decibels?

    b. Taking into account antenna gain, what is the effective radiated power of the transmitted signal?

    c. If the receiving antenna is located 24 km from the transmitting antenna over a free space path, find the available signal power out of the receiving antenna in dBm units.

6.10 Show that doubling the transmission frequency or doubling the distance between transmitting antenna and receiving antenna attenuates the power received by 6 dB.

6.11 Use the Okumura–Hata model to compute the path loss in dB for a suburban environment, with $f_c = 900$ MHz, $h_t = 45$ m, $h_r = 3$ m, and $d = 5$ km.

6.12 Determine the height of an antenna for a TV station that must be able to reach customers up to 80 km away. Use the Okumura–Hata model for a rural environment with $f_c = 76$ MHz and $h_r = 1.5$ m. Transmit power is 150 kW and received power must be greater than 10^{-13} W.

6.13 What is the thermal noise level of a channel with a bandwidth of 10 kHz carrying 1000 watts of power operating at 50°C? Compare the noise level to the operating power.

6.14 The square wave of Figure 2.5c, with $T = 1$ ms, is passed through a low-pass filter that passes frequencies up to 8 kHz with no attenuation.

    a. Find the power in the output waveform.

    b. Assuming that at the filter input there is a thermal noise voltage with $N_0 = 0.1 \ \mu$W/Hz, find the output signal to noise ratio in dB.

6.15 Suppose that a car is moving through a suburban environment that has a wireless channel with a coherence time of 10 ms and a coherence bandwidth of 600 kHz. The bit rate of the signal being used is 50 kbps. Characterize the channel.

    a. Is the channel slow or fast fading?

    b. Is the channel flat or frequency-selective fading?

6.16 Suppose a wireless channel has a coherence bandwidth of 100 kHz. What range of bit rates can be supported to have flat fading?

6.17 Consider again Example 6.12. Suppose a wireless channel has two possible quality levels. It has an 85% probability of having a bit error rate of 10^{-6}, but a 15% probability of having a bit error rate of 0.1. Assume independently varying signals can be received through k antennas, and the system uses selection diversity to choose the best signal. Based on the approximation approach in Example 6.12, how many branches are needed to achieve a bit error probability of 10^{-4}?

6.18 Suppose a ray of visible light passes from the atmosphere into water at an angle to the horizontal of 30°. What is the angle of the ray in the water? *Note:* At standard atmospheric conditions at the earth's surface, a reasonable value for refractive index is 1.0003. A typical value of refractive index for water is 4/3.

CHAPTER 7

SIGNAL ENCODING TECHNIQUES

LEARNING OBJECTIVES

After studying this chapter, you should be able to:

- Describe the three major ways digital data can be encoded onto an analog signal.
- Explain the trade-offs between phase- and frequency-shift keying.
- Determine performance of modulation schemes from E_b/N_0 curves.
- Recognize a modulation scheme by its waveform.
- Describe methods of modulating analog waveforms.
- Contrast waveform encoders and vocoders.

In Chapter 2, a distinction was made between analog and digital data and analog and digital signals. Figure 2.8 suggested that either form of data could be encoded into either form of signal.

Figure 7.1 is another depiction that emphasizes the process involved. For **_digital signaling_**, a data source $g(t)$, which may be either digital or analog, is encoded into a digital signal $x(t)$. The actual form of $x(t)$ depends on the encoding technique and is chosen to optimize use of the transmission medium. For example, the encoding may be chosen to conserve bandwidth or to minimize errors.

The basis for **_analog signaling_** is a continuous constant-frequency signal known as the carrier signal. The frequency of the carrier signal is chosen to be compatible with the transmission medium being used. In the case of wireless communication, frequencies must also be used as specified by regulatory agencies. Data may be transmitted using a carrier signal by **modulation**. Modulation is the process of encoding source data onto a carrier signal with frequency f_c. All modulation techniques involve sending information by changing one or more of the three fundamental frequency domain parameters: amplitude, frequency, and phase.

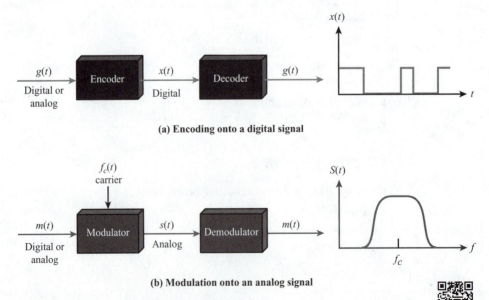

(a) Encoding onto a digital signal

(b) Modulation onto an analog signal

Figure 7.1 Encoding and Modulation Techniques

The input signal $m(t)$ may be analog or digital and is called the modulating signal or baseband signal. The result of modulating the carrier signal is called the modulated signal $s(t)$. As Figure 7.1b indicates, $s(t)$ is a bandlimited (bandpass) signal. The location of the bandwidth on the spectrum is related to f_c and is often centered on f_c. Again, the actual form of the encoding is chosen to optimize some characteristic of the transmission.

Figure 7.1 suggests four different mappings, or encodings, as was discussed in Chapter 2: digital-to-digital, digital-to-analog, analog-to-analog, and analog-to-digital. The latter three techniques are most relevant in the context of wireless communication and are in widespread use in that context:

- **Digital-to-analog:** Digital data and digital signals must be converted to analog signals for wireless transmission.
- **Analog-to-analog:** Typically, a baseband analog signal, such as voice or video, must be modulated onto a higher-frequency carrier for transmission.
- **Analog-to-digital:** It is common to digitize voice signals prior to transmission over either guided or unguided media to improve quality and to take advantage of TDM schemes. For wireless transmission, the resulting digital data must be modulated onto an analog carrier.

These three techniques are examined in this chapter. First we look at some criteria that can be used in evaluating various approaches in each category. Chapters 8 and 9 examine orthogonal frequency division multiplexing (OFDM) and spread spectrum, which combine techniques from several categories.

7.1 SIGNAL ENCODING CRITERIA

To begin, we need to define some terms. Recall that a digital signal is a sequence of discrete, discontinuous voltage pulses. Each pulse is a signal element. Binary data are transmitted by encoding each data bit into signal elements. In the simplest case, there is a one-to-one correspondence between bits and signal elements. An example is shown in Figure 2.9, in which binary 0 is represented by a higher voltage level and binary 1 by a lower voltage level. Similarly, a digital bit stream can be encoded onto an analog signal as a sequence of signal elements, with each signal element being a pulse of constant frequency, phase, and amplitude. Modern systems shape the pulses to not be so rectangular, but the concept is clear. There may be a one-to-one correspondence between data elements (bits) and analog signal elements. For both analog and digital signals, there may be a one-to-multiple or multiple-to-one correspondence between data elements and signal elements, as will be shown.

The data signaling rate, or just **data rate**, of a signal is the rate, in bits per second, that data are transmitted. The duration or length of a bit is the amount of time it takes for the transmitter to emit the bit; for a data rate R, the bit duration is $1/R$. The **modulation rate**, in contrast, is the rate at which the signal level is changed. This will depend on the nature of the encoding, as explained later. The modulation rate is expressed in baud, which means signal elements (or *symbols*) per second. Table 7.1 summarizes key terms; these should be clearer when we see an example later in this chapter.

Table 7.1 Key Data Transmission Terms

Term	Units	Definition
Data element	Bits	A single binary one or zero
Data rate	Bits per second (bps)	The rate at which data elements are transmitted
Signal element	Digital: a voltage pulse of constant amplitude Analog: a pulse of constant frequency, phase, and amplitude	That part of a signal that occupies the shortest interval of a signaling code
Signaling rate or modulation rate	Signal elements per second (baud)	The rate at which signal elements are transmitted

The tasks involved in interpreting digital signals at the receiver can be summarized by again referring to Figure 2.9. First, the receiver must know the timing of each bit. That is, the receiver must know with some accuracy when a bit begins and ends. Second, the receiver must determine whether the signal level for each bit position is high (0) or low (1). In Figure 2.9, these tasks can be performed by sampling each bit position in the middle of the interval and comparing the value to a threshold. Because of noise and other impairments, there will be errors, as shown.

What factors determine how successful the receiver will be in interpreting the incoming signal? We saw in Chapter 2 that three factors are important: the signal-to-noise ratio (or, better, E_b/N_0), the data rate, and the bandwidth. With other factors held constant, the following statements are true:

- An increase in data rate increases **bit error rate (BER)**.[1]
- An increase in signal-to-noise ratio (SNR) decreases bit error rate.
- An increase in bandwidth allows an increase in data rate.

There is another factor that can be used to improve performance, and that is the encoding scheme. The encoding scheme is simply the mapping from data bits to signal elements. A variety of approaches are in use. Before describing these techniques, let us consider the following ways of evaluating or comparing the various techniques.

- **Signal spectrum:** Several aspects of the signal spectrum are important. A lack of high-frequency components means that less bandwidth is required for transmission. In addition, lack of a direct current (dc) component is also desirable. With a dc component to the signal, there must be direct physical attachment of transmission components. With no dc component, alternating current (ac) coupling via transformer is possible; this provides excellent electrical isolation, reducing interference. Finally, the magnitude of the effects of signal distortion and interference depend on the spectral properties of the transmitted signal. In practice, it usually happens that the transfer function of a channel is worse near the band

---

[1]The BER is the most common measure of error performance on a data circuit and is defined as the probability that a bit is received in error. It is also called the *bit error ratio*. This latter term is clearer, because the term *rate* typically refers to some quantity that varies with time. Unfortunately, most books and standards documents refer to the R in BER as *rate*. Figures here use both "BER" "and bit error probability" as labels.

edges. Therefore, a good signal design should concentrate the transmitted power toward the middle of the transmission bandwidth. In such a case, less distortion should be present in the received signal. To meet this objective, codes can be designed with the aim of shaping the spectrum of the transmitted signal.

- **Clocking:** The receiver must determine the beginning and end of each bit position. This is no easy task. One rather expensive approach is to provide a separate clock channel to synchronize the transmitter and receiver. The alternative is to provide some synchronization mechanism that is based on the transmitted signal. This can be achieved with suitable encoding.
- **Signal interference and noise immunity:** Certain codes exhibit superior performance in the presence of noise. This is usually expressed in terms of BER.
- **Cost and complexity:** Although digital logic continues to drop in price, this factor should not be ignored. In particular, the higher the signaling rate to achieve a given data rate, the greater the cost. We will see that some codes require a signaling rate that is in fact greater than the actual data rate.

We now turn to a discussion of various techniques.

7.2 DIGITAL DATA, ANALOG SIGNALS

We start with the case of transmitting digital data using analog signals. A familiar use of this transformation is for transmitting digital data through the public telephone network. The telephone network is designed to receive, switch, and transmit analog signals in the voice-frequency range of about 300 to 3400 Hz. Digital devices are attached to the telephone network via a modem (modulator-demodulator), which converts digital data to analog signals, and vice versa.

For the telephone network, modems are used that produce signals in the voice-frequency range. The same basic techniques are used for modems that produce signals at higher frequencies (e.g., microwave). This section introduces these techniques and provides a brief discussion of the performance characteristics of the alternative approaches.

We mentioned that modulation involves operation on one or more of the three characteristics of a carrier signal: amplitude, frequency, and phase. Accordingly, there are three basic encoding or modulation techniques for transforming digital data into analog signals, as illustrated in Figure 7.2: **amplitude-shift keying (ASK)**, **frequency-shift keying (FSK)**, and **phase-shift keying (PSK)**. In all these cases, the resulting signal occupies a bandwidth centered on the **carrier frequency**.

Amplitude-Shift Keying

In ASK, the two binary values are represented by two different amplitudes of the carrier frequency. Commonly, one of the amplitudes is zero; that is, one binary digit is represented by the presence, at constant amplitude, of the carrier, the other by the absence of the carrier (Figure 7.2a). The resulting transmitted signal for one bit time is

$$\textbf{ASK} \qquad s(t) = \begin{cases} A \cos\left(2\pi f_c t\right) & \text{binary 1} \\ 0 & \text{binary 0} \end{cases} \qquad (7.1)$$

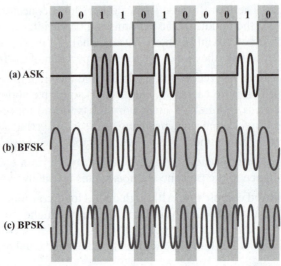

Figure 7.2 Modulation of Analog Signals for Digital Data

where the carrier signal is $A \cos (2\pi f_c t)$. ASK is susceptible to sudden gain changes and is a rather inefficient modulation technique.

The ASK technique is used to transmit digital data over optical fiber. For light-emitting diode (LED) transmitters, Equation (7.1) is valid. That is, one signal element is represented by a light pulse while the other signal element is represented by the absence of light. Laser transmitters normally have a fixed "bias" current that causes the device to emit a low light level. This low level represents one signal element, while a higher-amplitude light wave represents another signal element.

Frequency–Shift Keying

The most common form of FSK is binary FSK (BFSK), in which the two binary values are represented by two different frequencies near the carrier frequency (Figure 7.2b). The resulting transmitted signal for one bit time is

$$\textbf{BFSK} \qquad s(t) = \begin{cases} A \cos (2\pi f_1 t) & \text{binary 1} \\ A \cos (2\pi f_2 t) & \text{binary 0} \end{cases} \qquad (7.2)$$

where f_1 and f_2 are typically offset from the carrier frequency f_c by equal but opposite amounts.

Figure 7.3 shows an example of the use of BFSK for full-duplex operation over a voice-grade line. The figure is a specification for the Bell System 108 series modems. A voice-grade line will pass frequencies in the approximate range of 300 to 3400 Hz. *Full duplex* means that signals are transmitted in both directions at the same time. To achieve full-duplex transmission, this bandwidth is split. In one direction (transmit or receive), the frequencies used to represent 1 and 0 are centered on 1170 Hz, with a shift of 100 Hz on either side. The effect of alternating between those two

Signal strength

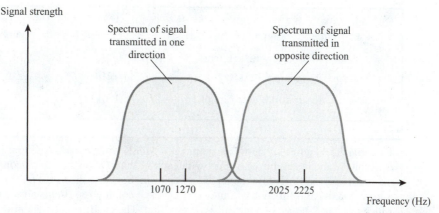

Spectrum of signal
transmitted in one
direction

Spectrum of signal
transmitted in
opposite direction

1070 1270   2025 2225

Frequency (Hz)

Figure 7.3 Full-Duplex FSK Transmission on a Voice-Grade Channel

frequencies is to produce a signal whose spectrum is indicated as the shaded area on the left in Figure 7.3. Similarly, for the other direction (receive or transmit), the modem uses frequencies shifted 100 Hz to each side of a center frequency of 2125 Hz. This signal is indicated by the shaded area on the right in Figure 7.3. Note that there is little overlap and thus little interference.

BFSK is less susceptible to error than ASK. On voice-grade lines, it is typically used up to 1200 bps. It is also commonly used for high-frequency (3 to 30 MHz) radio transmission. It can also be used at even higher frequencies on local area networks that use coaxial cable.

A signal that is less susceptible to error is multilevel FSK (MFSK). In this signal more than two frequencies are used. In this case each signaling element represents more than one bit. The transmitted MFSK signal for one signal element time can be defined as follows:

$$\textbf{MFSK} \qquad s_i(t) = A \cos 2\pi f_i t, \qquad 1 \le i \le M \qquad (7.3)$$

where

$$f_i = f_c + (2i - 1 - M)f_d$$
$$f_c = \text{the carrier frequency}$$
$$f_d = \text{the difference frequency}$$
$$M = \text{number of different signal elements} = 2^L$$
$$L = \text{number of bits per signal element}$$

To match the data rate of the input bit stream, each output signal element is held for a period of $T_s = LT$ seconds, where T is the bit period (data rate $= 1/T$). Thus, one signal element, which is a constant-frequency tone, encodes L bits. For example, each of $M = 8$ signal elements can represent $L = 3$ bits of information. The total bandwidth required is approximately $2Mf_d$. It can be shown that the minimum frequency separation required is $2f_d = 1/T_s$. Therefore, the modulator requires a bandwidth of $W_d = 2Mf_d = M/T_s$

Example 7.1 With $f_c = 250$ kHz, $f_d = 25$ kHz, and $M = 8$ ($L = 3$ bits), we have the following frequency assignments for each of the eight possible 3-bit data combinations:

$f_1 = 75$ kHz 000 $f_2 = 125$ kHz 001 $f_3 = 175$ kHz 010 $f_4 = 225$ kHz 011

$f_5 = 275$ kHz 100 $f_6 = 325$ kHz 101 $f_7 = 375$ kHz 110 $f_8 = 425$ kHz 111

This scheme can support a data rate of $1/T = 2Lf_d = 150$ kbps.

Example 7.2 Figure 7.4 shows an example of MFSK with $M = 4$. An input bit stream of 20 bits is encoded 2 bits at a time, with each of the four possible 2-bit combinations transmitted as a different frequency. The display in the figure shows the frequency transmitted (y-axis) as a function of time (x-axis). Each column represents a time unit T_s in which a single 2-bit signal element is transmitted. The shaded rectangle in the column indicates the frequency transmitted during that time unit.

Phase–Shift Keying

In PSK, the phase of the carrier signal is shifted to represent data.

Two–Level PSK The simplest scheme uses two phases to represent the two binary digits (Figure 7.2c) and is known as binary phase-shift keying. The resulting transmitted signal for one bit time is

$$\textbf{BPSK} \quad s(t) = \begin{cases} A\cos(2\pi f_c t) \\ A\cos(2\pi f_c t + \pi) \end{cases} = \begin{cases} A\cos(2\pi f_c t) & \text{binary 1} \\ -A\cos(2\pi f_c t) & \text{binary 0} \end{cases} \quad (7.4)$$

Because a phase shift of $180°(\pi)$ is equivalent to flipping the sine wave or multiplying it by -1, the rightmost expressions in Equation (7.4) can be used. This leads to a convenient formulation. If we have a bit stream, and we define $d(t)$ as the discrete function that takes on the value of $+1$ for one bit time if the corresponding bit in the bit stream is 1 and the value of -1 for one bit time if the corresponding bit in the bit stream is 0, then we can define the transmitted signal as

$$\textbf{BPSK} \qquad s_d(t) = A\,d(t)\cos(2\pi f_c t) \qquad (7.5)$$

An alternative form of two-level PSK is **differential PSK (DPSK)**. Figure 7.5 shows an example. In this scheme, a binary 0 is represented by sending a signal burst

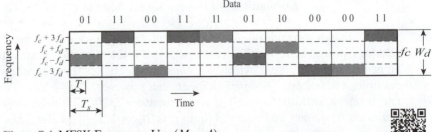

Figure 7.4 MFSK Frequency Use ($M = 4$)

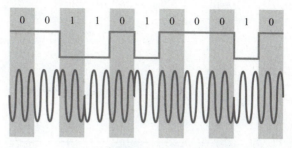

Figure 7.5 Differential Phase-Shift Keying (DPSK)

of the same phase as the previous signal burst sent. A binary 1 is represented by sending a signal burst of opposite phase to the preceding one. This term *differential* refers to the fact that the phase shift is with reference to the previous bit transmitted rather than to some constant reference signal. In differential encoding, the information to be transmitted is represented in terms of the changes between successive data symbols rather than the signal elements themselves. DPSK avoids the requirement for an accurate local oscillator phase at the receiver that is matched with the transmitter. As long as the preceding phase is received correctly, the phase reference is accurate. The BER performance of DPSK is worse than BPSK, however, as will be seen in Figure 7.9.

Four-Level PSK More efficient use of bandwidth can be achieved if each signaling element represents more than one bit. For example, instead of a phase shift of 180°, as allowed in PSK, a common encoding technique, known as **quadrature phase-shift keying (QPSK)**, uses phase shifts separated by multiples of $\pi/2(90°)$.

$$
\textbf{QPSK} \qquad s(t) = \begin{cases} A \cos\left(2\pi f_c t + \dfrac{\pi}{4}\right) & 11 \\[2ex] A \cos\left(2\pi f_c t + \dfrac{3\pi}{4}\right) & 01 \\[2ex] A \cos\left(2\pi f_c t - \dfrac{3\pi}{4}\right) & 00 \\[2ex] A \cos\left(2\pi f_c t - \dfrac{\pi}{4}\right) & 10 \end{cases} \qquad (7.6)
$$

Thus, each signal element represents two bits rather than one. We refer to such signal element as a *symbol* with a corresponding symbol time and symbol rate. The relationship between symbol rate and bit rate can be easily found; for example, the bit rate here would be twice the symbol rate. If 1 million symbols/second were transmitted, this would correspond to 2 million bits/second since each symbol would be sending two bits.

Modulation schemes are commonly represented using a ***constellation diagram*** as seen in Figure 7.6. Each point shows the combination of $I(t)$ and $Q(t)$ that are used for each symbol.

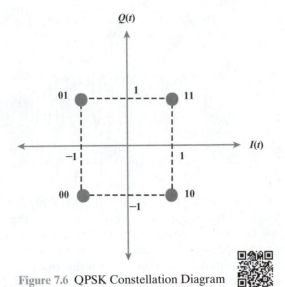

Figure 7.6 QPSK Constellation Diagram

Figure 7.7 shows the QPSK modulation scheme in general terms. The input is a stream of binary digits with a data rate of $R = 1/T_b$, where T_b is the width of each bit. This stream is converted into two separate bit streams of $R/2$ bps each, by taking alternate bits for the two streams. The two data streams are referred to as the I (in-phase) and Q (quadrature phase) streams. In the diagram, the upper stream is modulated on a carrier of frequency f_c by multiplying the bit stream by the carrier. For convenience of modulator structure, we map binary 1 to $\sqrt{1/2}$ and binary 0 to $-\sqrt{1/2}$. Thus, a binary 1 is represented by a scaled version of the carrier wave and a binary 0 is represented by a scaled version of the negative of the carrier wave, both at a constant amplitude. This same carrier wave is shifted by 90°, which makes it a sine wave, and is used for modulation of the lower binary stream. The two

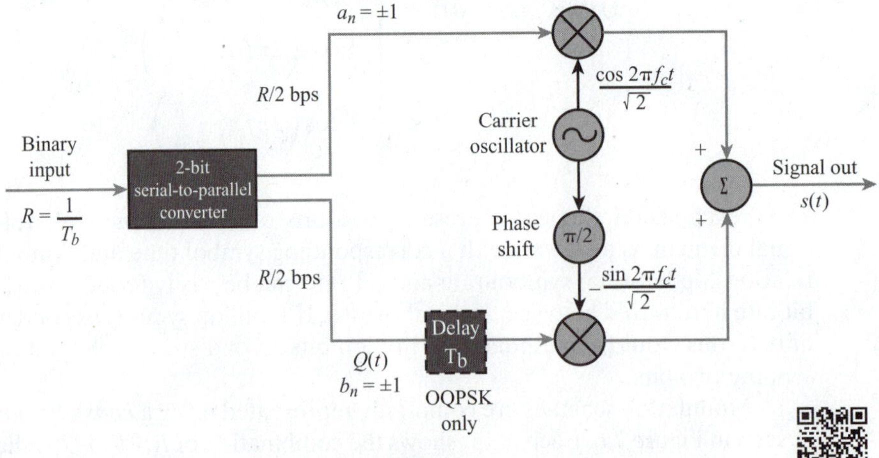

Figure 7.7 QPSK and OQPSK Modulators

modulated signals are then added together and transmitted. The transmitted signal can be expressed as follows:

QPSK $$s(t) = \frac{1}{\sqrt{2}}I(t) \cos 2\pi f_c t - \frac{1}{\sqrt{2}}Q(t) \sin 2\pi f_c t$$

Figure 7.8 shows an example of QPSK coding. Each of the two modulated streams is a BPSK signal at half the data rate of the original bit stream. Thus, the combined signals have a symbol rate that is half the input bit rate. This reduces the bandwidth that is needed. Note that from one symbol time to the next, a phase change of as much as 180°(π) is possible.

Figure 7.8 also shows a variation of QPSK known as offset QPSK (OQPSK), or orthogonal QPSK. The difference is that a delay of one bit time (one half of a symbol time) is introduced in the Q stream, resulting in the following signal:

OQPSK $$s(t) = \frac{1}{\sqrt{2}}I(t) \cos 2\pi f_c t - \frac{1}{\sqrt{2}}Q(t - T_b) \sin 2\pi f_c t$$

Because OQPSK differs from QPSK only by the delay in the Q stream, its spectral characteristics and bit error performance are the same as that of QPSK. From Figure 7.7, we can observe that only one of two bits in the pair can change sign at any time and thus the phase change in the combined signal never exceeds 90°($\pi/2$). This can be an advantage because physical limitations on phase modulators make large phase shifts at high transition rates difficult to perform. OQPSK also provides superior error performance when the transmission channel (including transmitter and receiver) has significant nonlinear components. The effect of nonlinearities is a spreading of the signal bandwidth, which may result in adjacent channel

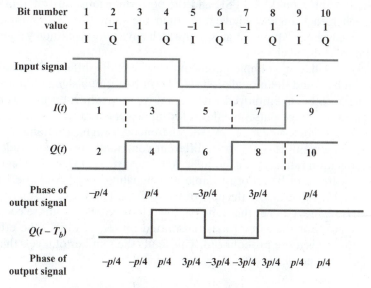

Figure 7.8 Example of QPSK and OQPSK Waveforms

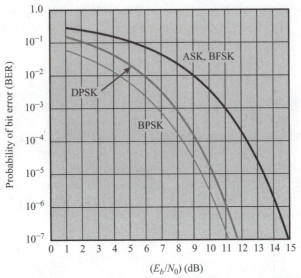

Figure 7.9 Theoretical Bit Error Rate for Various Encoding Schemes

interference. It is easier to control this spreading if the phase changes are smaller, hence the advantage of OQPSK over QPSK.

Multilevel PSK The use of multiple levels can be extended beyond taking bits two at a time. It is possible to transmit bits three at a time using eight different phase angles. This would be 8 PSK and the performance is illustrated later in Figure 7.10. Further, each angle can have more than one amplitude. For example, one could send a signal using 12 phase angles, 4 of which have two amplitude values, for a total of 16 different signal elements.

This latter example points out very well the difference between the data rate R (in bps) and the modulation rate D (in baud) of a signal. Let us assume that this scheme is being employed with digital input in which each bit is represented by a constant voltage pulse, one level for binary one and one level for binary zero. The data rate is $R = 1/T_b$. However, the encoded signal contains $L = 4$ bits in each signal element using $M = 16$ different combinations of amplitude and phase. The modulation rate can be seen to be $R/4$, because each change of signal element communicates four bits. For example, the signaling speed could be 1 million symbols/ second (1 Mbaud), but the data rate is 4 Mbps. This is the reason that higher bit rates can be achieved over the same bandwidth by employing more complex modulation schemes. For the same total transmitted power, however, the effect of noise and distortion is more pronounced. This limits the number of levels that can be used.

In general,

$$D = \frac{R}{L} = \frac{R}{\log_2 M} \qquad (7.7)$$

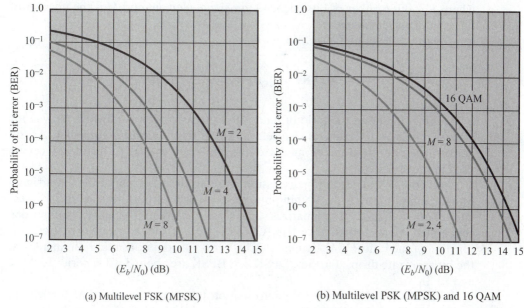

(a) Multilevel FSK (MFSK)

(b) Multilevel PSK (MPSK) and 16 QAM

Figure 7.10 Theoretical Bit Error Rate for Multilevel FSK, PSK, and QAM

where

D = modulation rate, baud (symbols/second)

R = data rate, bps

M = number of different signal elements $= 2^L$

L = number of bits per signal element

Performance

In looking at the performance of various digital-to-analog modulation schemes, the first parameter of interest is the bandwidth of the modulated signal. This depends on a variety of factors, including the definition of bandwidth used and the filtering technique used to create the bandpass signal. We will use some straightforward results from [COUC12].

The transmission bandwidth B_T for ASK is of the form

$$\textbf{ASK} \qquad B_T = (1 + r)R \qquad (7.8)$$

where R is the bit rate and r is related to the technique by which the signal is filtered to establish a bandwidth for transmission; typically $0 < r < 1$. Thus the bandwidth is directly related to the bit rate. The preceding formula is also valid for PSK and, under certain assumptions, FSK.

With MPSK, significant improvements in bandwidth can be achieved. In general,

$$\textbf{MPSK} \qquad B_T = \left(\frac{1 + r}{L}\right)R = \left(\frac{1 + r}{\log_2 M}\right)R \qquad (7.9)$$

where L is the number of bits encoded per signal element and M is the number of different signal elements.

For multilevel FSK (MFSK), we have

$$\textbf{MFSK} \qquad B_T = \left(\frac{(1 + r)M}{\log_2 M}\right)R \qquad (7.10)$$

Table 7.2 shows the ratio of data rate to transmission bandwidth (R/B_T) for various schemes. This ratio is also referred to as the **bandwidth efficiency**. As the name suggests, this parameter measures the efficiency with which bandwidth can be used to transmit data.

Of course, the preceding discussion refers to the spectrum of the input signal to a communications line. Nothing has yet been said of performance in the presence of noise. Figure 7.9 summarizes some results based on reasonable assumptions concerning the transmission system [COUC12]. Here, bit error rate is plotted as a function of the ratio E_b/N_0 defined in Chapter 6. Of course, as that ratio increases, the bit error rate drops. Further, DPSK and BPSK are about 3 dB superior to ASK and BFSK.

Figure 7.10 shows the same information for various levels of M for MFSK and MPSK. There is an important difference. For MFSK, the error probability for a given value E_b/N_0 decreases as M increases, while the opposite is true for MPSK. On the other hand, comparing Equations (7.9) and (7.10), the bandwidth efficiency of MFSK decreases as M increases, while the opposite is true of MPSK. Thus, in both cases, there is a trade-off between bandwidth efficiency and error performance: an increase in bandwidth efficiency results in an increase in error probability. The fact that these trade-offs move in opposite directions with respect to the number

Table 7.2 Bandwidth Efficiency (R/B_T) for Various Digital-to-Analog Encoding Schemes

	$r = 0$	$r = 0.5$	$r = 1$
ASK	1.0	0.67	0.5
FSK	0.5	0.33	0.25
Multilevel FSK			
$M = 4, L = 2$	0.5	0.33	0.25
$M = 8, L = 3$	0.375	0.25	0.1875
$M = 16, L = 4$	0.25	0.167	0.125
$M = 32, L = 5$	0.156	0.104	0.078
PSK	1.0	0.67	0.5
Multilevel PSK			
$M = 4, L = 2$	2.00	1.33	1.00
$M = 8, L = 3$	3.00	2.00	1.50
$M = 16, L = 4$	4.00	2.67	2.00
$M = 32, L = 5$	5.00	3.33	2.50

of levels M for MFSK and MPSK can be derived from the underlying equations. A discussion of the reasons for this difference is beyond the scope of this book. See [SKLA01] for a full treatment.

Example 7.3 What is the bandwidth efficiency for FSK, ASK, PSK, and QPSK for a bit error rate of 10^{-7} on a channel with an SNR of 12 dB?

Using Equation (6.9), we have

$$\left(\frac{E_b}{N_0}\right)_{dB} = \left(\frac{S/R}{N/B_T}\right)_{dB} = \left(\frac{S}{N}\right)_{dB} - \left(\frac{R}{B_T}\right)_{dB} = 12\,dB - \left(\frac{R}{B_T}\right)_{dB}$$

For FSK and ASK, from Figure 7.9,

$$\left(\frac{E_b}{N_0}\right)_{dB} = 14.8\,dB$$

$$\left(\frac{R}{B_T}\right)_{dB} = -2.8\,dB$$

$$\frac{R}{B_T} = 0.53$$

For PSK, from Figure 7.9

$$\left(\frac{E_b}{N_0}\right)_{dB} = 11.2\,dB$$

$$\left(\frac{R}{B_T}\right)_{dB} = 0.8\,dB$$

$$\frac{R}{B_T} = 1.2$$

The result for QPSK must take into account that the baud rate $D = R/2$. Thus,

$$\frac{R}{B_T} = 2.4$$

As the preceding example shows, ASK and FSK exhibit the same bandwidth efficiency, PSK is better, and even greater improvement can be achieved with multilevel signaling.

Minimum-Shift Keying

More advanced versions of the above modulation schemes are commonly used today. Minimum-shift keying (MSK) is a form of modulation that is found in some mobile communications systems. It provides superior bandwidth efficiency to BFSK with only a modest decrease in error performance. MFSK can be considered to be a form of BFSK. For MFSK, the transmitted signal for one bit time is

$$\textbf{MSK} \qquad s(t) = \begin{cases} \sqrt{\dfrac{2E_b}{T_b}} \cos\left(2\pi f_1 t + \theta(0)\right) & \text{binary 1} \\[2mm] \sqrt{\dfrac{2E_b}{T_b}} \cos\left(2\pi f_2 t + \theta(0)\right) & \text{binary 0} \end{cases}$$

where E_b is the transmitted signal energy per bit and T_b is the bit duration. The phase $\theta(0)$ denotes the value of the phase at time $t = 0$. An important characteristic of MSK is that it is a form of FSK known as continuous-phase FSK (CPFSK), in which the phase is continuous during the transition from one bit time to the next. The BFSK signal shown in Figure 7.2b is in fact an example of CPFSK. Note that the signal is smooth between bit times. In contrast, in Figure 7.2c, there is sometimes an abrupt change in phase.

For MSK, the two frequencies satisfy the following equations:

$$f_1 = f_c + \frac{1}{4T_b} \qquad f_2 = f_c - \frac{1}{4T_b}$$

It can be shown that this spacing between the two frequencies is the minimum that can be used and permit successful detection of the signal at the receiver. This is the reason for the term *minimum* in MSK.

It can also be shown that MSK can be thought of as a special case of OQPSK. In OQPSK, the carrier is multiplied by either $I(t)$ or $Q(t)$, both of which are rectangular pulse functions, taking on the values $+1$ and -1. For MSK, the carrier is multiplied by a sinusoidal function, as follows:

$$\textbf{MSK} \qquad s(t) = I(t) \cos\left(\frac{\pi t}{2T_b}\right) \cos 2\pi f_c t + Q(t - T_b) \sin\left(\frac{\pi t}{2T_b}\right) \sin 2\pi f_c t$$

An analysis of MSK is beyond the scope of this book. For more details, see [PASU79] and [XION94].

Quadrature Amplitude Modulation

Quadrature amplitude modulation (QAM) is a popular analog signaling technique that is used in some wireless standards. This modulation technique is a combination of ASK and PSK. QAM can also be considered a logical extension of QPSK. QAM takes advantage of the fact that it is possible to send two different signals simultaneously on the same carrier frequency, by using two copies of the carrier frequency, one shifted by 90° with respect to the other. The two independent signals are simultaneously transmitted over the same medium. At the receiver, the two signals are demodulated and the results combined to produce the original binary input.

Figure 7.12 shows the QAM modulation scheme in general terms. The input is a stream of binary digits arriving at a rate of R bps. This stream is converted into two separate bit streams of $R/2$ bps each, by taking alternate bits for the two streams. These bits are converted to a_n and b_n values as specified by the type of QAM. In the diagram, the upper stream is modulated on a carrier of frequency f_c by multiplying the a_n values by the carrier. This same carrier wave is shifted by 90° and used for modulation of the b_n values on the lower binary stream. The two modulated signals are then added together and transmitted. The transmitted signal can be expressed as follows:

QAM $\qquad s(t) = a_n(t) \cos 2\pi f_c t + b_n(t)\sin 2\pi f_c t$

Figure 7.11 shows a 16QAM constellation, which illustrates the amplitudes of the independent cosine and sine functions.

If two levels are used, then each of the two streams can be in one of two states and the combined stream can be in one of $4 = 2 \times 2$ states. This is essentially QPSK. If four levels are used (i.e., four different amplitude levels), then the combined stream can be in one of $16 = 4 \times 4$ states as seen in Figure 7.11. Systems using 64 and even 256 states have been implemented and commonly used, especially where noise effects are low. The greater the number of states, the higher the data rate that is possible within a given bandwidth. The greater the number of states, however, the higher the potential error rate due to noise and attenuation.

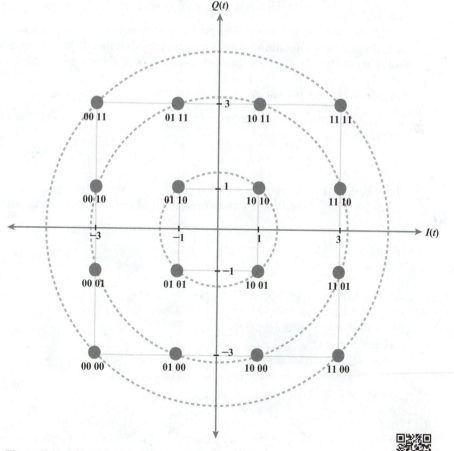

Figure 7.11 16QAM Constellation Diagram

7.3 ANALOG DATA, ANALOG SIGNALS

Modulation has been defined as the process of combining an input signal $m(t)$ and a carrier at frequency f_c to produce a signal $s(t)$ whose bandwidth is (usually) centered on f_c. For digital data, the motivation for modulation should be clear: When only analog transmission facilities are available, modulation is required to convert the digital data to analog form. The motivation when the data are already analog is less clear. After all, voice signals are transmitted over telephone lines at their original spectrum (referred to as baseband transmission). There are three principal reasons for analog modulation of analog signals:

- A higher frequency may be needed for effective transmission. For unguided transmission, it is virtually impossible to transmit baseband signals; the required antennas would be many kilometers in diameter.
- Modulation permits frequency division multiplexing, an important technique that was discussed in Chapter 2.
- For wireless transmission, regulations require use of specified carrier frequencies for different purposes (e.g., commercial, military, or amateur).

In this section, we look at the principal techniques for modulation using analog data: **amplitude modulation (AM)**, **frequency modulation (FM)**, and **phase modulation (PM)**. As before, the three basic characteristics of a signal are used for modulation.

Amplitude Modulation

Amplitude modulation is depicted in Figure 7.13. Mathematically, the process can be expressed as

$$\mathbf{AM} \qquad s(t) = [1 + n_a x(t)]\cos 2\pi f_c t \qquad (7.11)$$

where $\cos 2\pi f_c t$ is the carrier and $x(t)$ is the input signal (carrying data), both normalized to unity amplitude. The parameter n_a, known as the modulation index, is

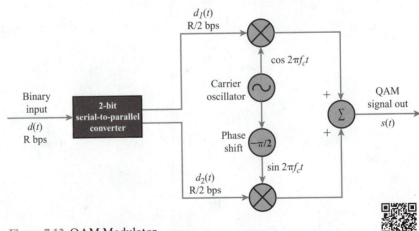

Figure 7.12 QAM Modulator

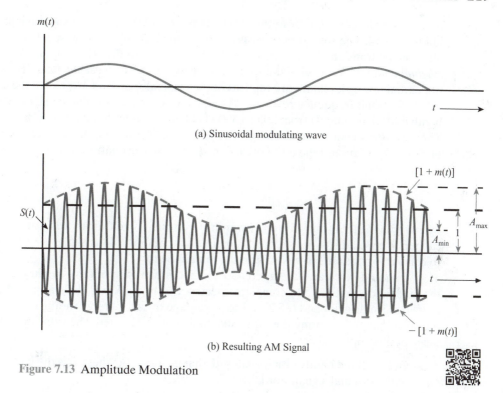

(a) Sinusoidal modulating wave

(b) Resulting AM Signal

Figure 7.13 Amplitude Modulation

the ratio of the amplitude of the input signal to the carrier. Corresponding to our previous notation, the input signal is $m(t) = n_a x(t)$. The "1" in Equation (7.11) is a dc component that prevents loss of information, as explained subsequently. This scheme is also known as double sideband transmitted carrier (DSBTC).

Example 7.4 Derive an expression for $s(t)$ if $x(t)$ is the amplitude-modulating signal $\cos 2\pi f_m t$.

We have

$$s(t) = [1 + n_a \cos 2\pi f_m t] \cos 2\pi f_c t$$

By trigonometric identity, this may be expanded to

$$s(t) = \cos 2\pi f_c t + \frac{n_a}{2} \cos 2\pi (f_c - f_m)t + \frac{n_a}{2} \cos 2\pi (f_c + f_m)t$$

The resulting signal has a component at the original carrier frequency plus a pair of components each spaced f_m hertz from the carrier.

From Equation (7.11) and Figure 7.13, it can be seen that AM involves the multiplication of the input signal by the carrier. The envelope of the resulting signal is $[1 + n_a x(t)]$ and, as long as $n_a < 1$, the envelope is an exact reproduction of the original signal. If $n_a > 1$, the envelope will cross the time axis and information is lost.

It is instructive to look at the spectrum of the AM signal. An example is shown in Figure 7.14. The spectrum consists of the original carrier plus the spectrum of the input signal translated to f_c. The portion of the spectrum for $|f| > |f_c|$ is the *upper sideband*, and the portion of the spectrum for $|f| < |f_c|$ is *lower sideband*. Both the upper and lower sidebands are replicas of the original spectrum $M(f)$, with the lower sideband being frequency reversed. As an example, consider a voice signal with a bandwidth that extends from 300 to 3000 Hz being modulated on a 60-kHz carrier. The resulting signal contains an upper sideband of 60.3 to 63 kHz, a lower sideband of 57 to 59.7 kHz, and the 60-kHz carrier. An important relationship is

$$P_t = P_c\left(1 + \frac{n_a^2}{2}\right)$$

where P_t is the total transmitted power in $s(t)$ and P_c is the transmitted power in the carrier. We would like n_a as large as possible so that most of the signal power is used to carry information. However, n_a must remain below 1.

It should be clear that $s(t)$ contains unnecessary components, because each of the sidebands contains the complete spectrum of $m(t)$. A popular variant of AM, known as single sideband (SSB), takes advantage of this fact by sending only one of the sidebands, eliminating the other sideband and the carrier. The principal advantages of this approach are

- Only half the bandwidth is required, that is, $B_T = B$, where B is the bandwidth of the original signal. For DSBTC, $B_T = 2B$.

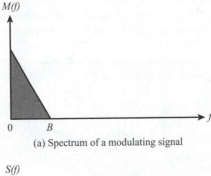

(a) Spectrum of a modulating signal

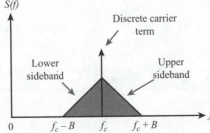

(b) Spectrum of an AM signal with carrier at f_c

Figure 7.14 Spectrum of an AM Signal

• Less power is required because no power is used to transmit the carrier or the other sideband. Another variant is double sideband suppressed carrier (DSBSC), which filters out the carrier frequency and sends both sidebands. This saves some power but uses as much bandwidth as DSBTC.

The disadvantage of suppressing the carrier is that the carrier can be used for synchronization purposes. For example, suppose that the original analog signal is an ASK waveform encoding digital data. The receiver needs to know the starting point of each bit time to interpret the data correctly. A constant carrier provides a clocking mechanism by which to time the arrival of bits. A compromise approach is vestigial sideband (VSB), which uses one sideband and a reduced-power carrier.

Angle Modulation

Frequency modulation and phase modulation are special cases of **angle modulation**. The modulated signal is expressed as

$$\textbf{Angle modulation} \qquad s(t) = A_c \cos\left[2\pi f_c t + \phi(t)\right] \qquad (7.12)$$

For phase modulation, the phase is proportional to the modulating signal:

$$\textbf{PM} \qquad \phi(t) = n_p m(t) \qquad (7.13)$$

where n_p is the phase modulation index.

For *frequency modulation*, the derivative of the phase is proportional to the modulating signal:

$$\textbf{FM} \qquad \phi'(t) = n_f m(t) \qquad (7.14)$$

where n_f is the frequency modulation index.

For those who wish a more detailed mathematical explanation of the preceding, consider the following. The phase of $s(t)$ at any instant is just $2\pi f_c t + \phi(t)$. The instantaneous phase deviation from the carrier signal is $\phi(t)$. In PM, this instantaneous phase deviation is proportional to $m(t)$. Because frequency can be defined as the rate of change of phase of a signal, the instantaneous frequency of $s(t)$ is

$$2\pi f_i(t) = \frac{d}{dt}[2\pi f_c t + \phi(t)]$$

$$f_i(t) = f_c + \frac{1}{2\pi}\phi'(t)$$

and the instantaneous frequency deviation from the carrier frequency is $\phi'(t)$, which in FM is proportional to $m(t)$.

Figure 7.15 illustrates amplitude, phase, and frequency modulation by a sine wave. The shapes of the FM and PM signals are very similar. Indeed, it is impossible to tell them apart without knowledge of the modulation function.

Several observations about the FM process are in order. The peak deviation ΔF can be seen to be

$$\Delta F = \frac{1}{2\pi}n_f A_m\,\text{Hz}$$

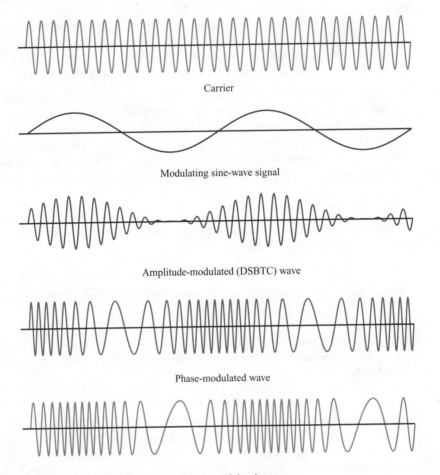

Carrier

Modulating sine-wave signal

Amplitude-modulated (DSBTC) wave

Phase-modulated wave

Frequency-modulated wave

Figure 7.15 Amplitude, Phase, and Frequency Modulations of a Sine-Wave Carrier by a Sine-Wave Signal

where A_m is the maximum value of $m(t)$. Thus an increase in the magnitude of $m(t)$ will increase ΔF, which, intuitively, should increase the transmitted bandwidth B_T. However, as should be apparent from Figure 7.15, this will not increase the average power level of the FM signal, which is $A_c^2/2$. This is distinctly different from AM, where the level of modulation affects the power in the AM signal but does not affect its bandwidth.

Example 7.5 Derive an expression for $s(t)$ if $\phi(t)$ is the phase-modulating signal $n_p\cos 2\pi f_m t$. Assume that $A_c = 1$. This can be seen directly to be

$$s(t) = \cos[2\pi f_c t + n_p\cos 2\pi f_m t]$$

The instantaneous phase deviation from the carrier signal is $n_p \cos 2\pi f_m t$. The phase angle of the signal varies from its unmodulated value in a simple sinusoidal fashion, with the peak phase deviation equal to n_p.

Because the preceding has a sinusoid inside a sinusoid, the expression can be expanded using Bessel's trigonometric identities:

$$s(t) = \sum_{n=-\infty}^{\infty} J_n(n_p) \cos\left(2\pi f_c t + 2\pi n f_m t + \frac{n\pi}{2}\right)$$

where $J_n(n_p)$ is the nth-order Bessel function of the first kind. Using the property

$$J_{-n}(x) = (-1)^n J_n(x)$$

this can be rewritten as

$$s(t) = J_0(n_p) \cos 2\pi f_c t +$$

$$\sum_{n=1}^{\infty} J_n(n_p) \left[\cos\left(2\pi(f_c + n f_m)t + \frac{n\pi}{2}\right) + \cos\left(2\pi(f_c - n f_m)t + \frac{(n+2)\pi}{2}\right)\right]$$

The resulting signal has a component at the original carrier frequency plus a set of sidebands displaced from f_c by all possible multiples of f_m. For $n_p \ll 1$, the higher-order terms fall off rapidly.

Example 7.6 Derive an expression for $s(t)$ if $\phi'(t)$ is the frequency-modulating signal $-n_f \sin 2\pi f_m t$. The form of $\phi'(t)$ was chosen for convenience. We have

$$\phi(t) = -\int n_f \sin 2\pi f_m t\, dt = \frac{n_f}{2\pi f_m} \cos 2\pi f_m t$$

Thus,

$$s(t) = \cos\left[2\pi f_c t + \frac{n_f}{2\pi f_m} \cos 2\pi f_m t\right]$$

$$= \cos\left[2\pi f_c t + \frac{\Delta F}{f_m} \cos 2\pi f_m t\right]$$

The instantaneous frequency deviation from the carrier signal is $-n_f \sin 2\pi f_m t$. The frequency of the signal varies from its unmodulated value in a simple sinusoidal fashion, with the peak frequency deviation equal to n_f radians/second.

The equation for the FM signal has the identical form as for the PM signal in Example 7.5, with $\Delta F / f_m$ substituted for n_p. Thus the Bessel expansion is the same.

As with AM, both FM and PM result in a signal whose bandwidth is centered at f_c. However, we can now see that the magnitude of that bandwidth is very different. Amplitude modulation is a linear process and produces frequencies that are the sum and difference of the carrier signal and the components of the modulating signal. Hence, for AM,

$$B_T = 2B$$

However, angle modulation includes a term of the form $\cos(\phi(t))$, which is nonlinear and will produce a wide range of frequencies. In essence, for a modulating sinusoid of frequency f_m, $s(t)$ will contain components at $f_c + f_m$, $f_c + 2f_m$, and so on. In the most general case, infinite bandwidth is required to transmit an FM or PM signal. As a practical matter, a very good rule of thumb, known as Carson's rule [COUC12], is

$$B_T = 2(\beta + 1)B$$

where

$$\beta = \begin{cases} n_p A_m & \text{for PM} \\ \dfrac{\Delta F}{B} = \dfrac{n_f A_m}{2\pi B} & \text{for FM} \end{cases}$$

We can rewrite the formula for FM as

$$B_T = 2\Delta F + 2B \tag{7.15}$$

Thus, both FM and PM require greater bandwidth than AM.

7.4 ANALOG DATA, DIGITAL SIGNALS

In this section, we examine the process of transforming analog data into digital signals. Strictly speaking, it might be more correct to refer to this as a process of converting analog data into digital data; this process is known as digitization. Once analog data have been converted into digital data, a number of things can happen. The three most common are as follows:

1. The digital data can be transmitted using NRZ-L.[2] In this case, we have in fact gone directly from analog data to a digital signal.

2. The digital data can be encoded as a digital signal using a code other than NRZ-L. Thus an extra step is required.

3. The digital data can be converted into an analog signal for bandpass transmission, using one of the modulation techniques discussed in Section 6.2.

This last, seemingly curious, procedure is illustrated in Figure 7.16, which shows voice data that are digitized and then converted to an analog ASK signal. This allows digital transmission in the sense defined in Chapter 2. The voice data,

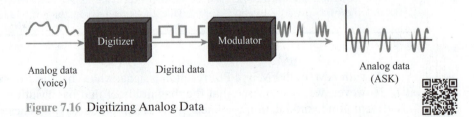

Analog data (voice) Digital data Analog data (ASK)

Figure 7.16 Digitizing Analog Data

---

[2] NRZ-L (nonreturn to zero, level) is the most common, and easiest, way to transmit digital signals. It uses two different voltage levels for the two binary digits: a negative voltage represents binary 1 and a positive voltage represents binary 0. NRZ-L is generally the code used to generate or interpret digital data by terminals and other devices. If a different code is to be used for transmission, it is typically generated from an NRZ-L signal by the transmission system.

because they have been digitized, can be treated as digital data, even though transmission requirements (e.g., use of microwave) dictate that an analog signal be used.

The device used for converting analog data into digital form for transmission, and subsequently recovering the original analog data from the digital, is known as a codec (coder-decoder).

Codecs can use two principal approaches: **waveform encoding** or **model-based encoding**. Waveform encoding seeks to capture the shape of the analog waveform. Model-based encoding captures knowledge of features of the source of the analog signal and how it has generated the sound. When applied to a voice signal, a **vocoder** accomplishes this by capturing how the vocal cords, mouth, lips, and nasal cavity have shaped the sound. We will look at each approach and then close with a discussion of comparative performance.

Waveform Encoding

In this section, we examine the principal waveform encoding techniques used in codecs, pulse code modulation, delta modulation, and differential pulse code modulation.

Pulse Code Modulation **Pulse code modulation (PCM)** is based on the sampling theorem, which states that

> If a signal $f(t)$ is sampled at regular intervals of time and at a rate higher than twice the highest signal frequency, then the samples contain all the information of the original signal. The function $f(t)$ may be reconstructed from these samples by the use of a low-pass filter.

For the interested reader, a proof is provided in a supporting document at this book's Web site. If voice data are limited to frequencies below 4000 Hz, a conservative procedure for intelligibility, 8000 samples per second would be sufficient to characterize the voice signal completely. Note, however, that these are analog samples, called *pulse amplitude modulation (PAM)* samples with a continuous range of possible amplitudes. To convert to digital, each of these analog samples must be assigned a binary code.

Figure 7.17 shows an example in which the original signal is assumed to be band-limited with a bandwidth of B. PAM samples are taken at a rate of $2B$, or once every $T_s = 1/2B$ seconds. Each PAM sample is approximated by being *quantized* into one of 16 different levels. Each sample can then be represented by 4 bits. But because the quantized values are only approximations, it is impossible to recover the original signal exactly. By using an 8-bit sample, which allows 256 quantizing levels, the quality of the recovered voice signal is comparable with that achieved via analog transmission. Note that this implies that a data rate of (8000 samples per second) $\times$ (8 bits per sample) $=$ 64 kbps is needed for a single voice signal.

Thus, PCM starts with a continuous-time, continuous-amplitude (analog) signal, from which a digital signal is produced. The digital signal consists of blocks of n bits, where each n-bit number corresponds to the amplitude of a PCM pulse. On reception, the process is reversed to reproduce the analog signal. Notice, however, that this process violates the terms of the sampling theorem. By quantizing the PAM pulse, the original signal is now only approximated and cannot be recovered exactly.

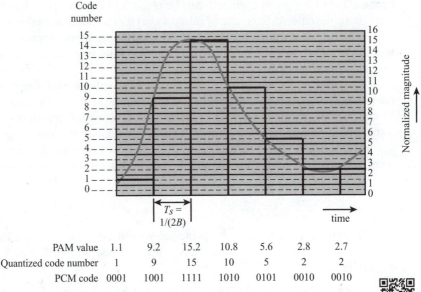

	PAM value	1.1	9.2	15.2	10.8	5.6	2.8	2.7
Quantized code number		1	9	15	10	5	2	2
	PCM code	0001	1001	1111	1010	0101	0010	0010

Figure 7.17 Pulse-Code Modulation Example

This effect is known as quantizing error or quantizing noise. The signal-to-noise ratio for quantizing noise can be expressed as [GIBS93]

$$\text{SNR}_{\text{dB}} = 20 \log 2^n + 1.76 \text{ dB} = 6.02n + 1.76 \text{ dB}$$

where n is the number of quantization bits. Thus each additional bit used for quantizing increases SNR by about 6 dB, which is a factor of 4.

Typically, the PCM scheme is refined using a technique known as nonlinear encoding, which means, in effect, that the quantization levels are not equally spaced. The problem with equal spacing is that the mean absolute error for each sample is the same, regardless of signal level. Consequently, lower amplitude values are relatively more distorted. By using a greater number of quantizing steps for signals of low amplitude and a smaller number of quantizing steps for signals of large amplitude, a marked reduction in overall signal distortion is achieved (e.g., see Figure 7.18).

The same effect can be achieved by using uniform quantizing but companding (compressing-expanding) the input analog signal. Companding is a process that compresses the intensity range of a signal by imparting more gain to weak signals than to strong signals on input. At output, the reverse operation is performed. Figure 7.19 shows typical companding functions. Note that the effect on the input side is to compress the sample so that the higher values are reduced with respect to the lower values. Thus, with a fixed number of quantizing levels, more levels are available for lower-level signals. On the output side, the compander expands the samples so the compressed values are restored to their original values.

Nonlinear encoding can significantly improve the PCM-SNR ratio. For voice signals, improvements of 24 to 30 dB have been achieved.

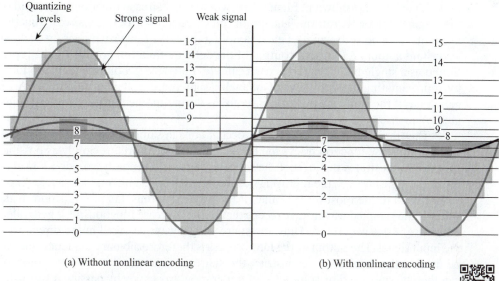

Figure 7.18 Effect of Nonlinear Coding

Delta Modulation (DM) A variety of techniques have been used to improve the performance of PCM or to reduce its complexity. One of the most popular alternatives to PCM is **delta modulation (DM)**.

With delta modulation, an analog input is approximated by a staircase function that moves up or down by one quantization level (δ) at each sampling interval

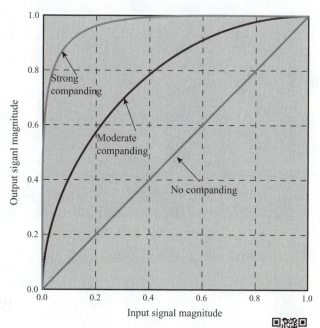

Figure 7.19 Typical Companding Functions

(T_s). An example is shown in Figure 7.20, where the staircase function is overlaid on the original analog waveform. The important characteristic of this staircase function is that its behavior is binary: At each sampling time, the function moves up or down a constant amount δ. Thus, the output of the delta modulation process can be represented as a single binary digit for each sample. In essence, a bit stream is produced by approximating the derivative of an analog signal rather than its amplitude: A 1 is generated if the staircase function is to go up during the next interval; a 0 is generated otherwise.

The transition (up or down) that occurs at each sampling interval is chosen so that the staircase function tracks the original analog waveform as closely as possible. Figure 7.21 illustrates the logic of the process, which is essentially a feedback mechanism. For transmission, the following occurs: At each sampling time, the analog input is compared to the most recent value of the approximating staircase function. If the value of the sampled waveform exceeds that of the staircase function, a 1 is generated; otherwise, a 0 is generated. Thus, the staircase is always changed in the direction of the input signal. The output of the DM process is therefore a binary sequence that can be used at the receiver to reconstruct the staircase function. The staircase function can then be smoothed by some type of integration process or by passing it through a low-pass filter to produce an analog approximation of the analog input signal.

There are two important parameters in a DM scheme: the size of the step assigned to each binary digit, δ, and the sampling rate. As Figure 7.20 illustrates, δ

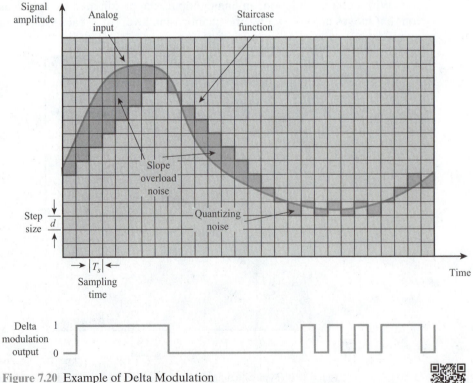

Figure 7.20 Example of Delta Modulation

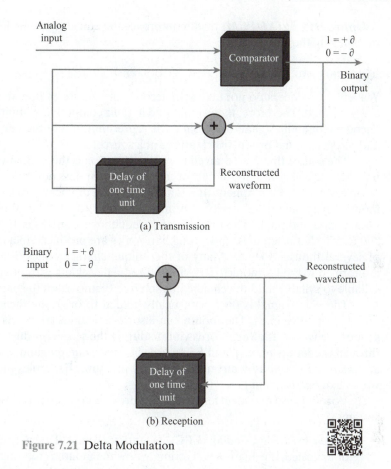

Figure 7.21 Delta Modulation

must be chosen to produce a balance between two types of errors or noise. When the analog waveform is changing very slowly, there will be quantizing noise. This noise increases as δ is increased. On the other hand, when the analog waveform is changing more rapidly than the staircase can follow, there is slope overload noise. This noise increases as δ is decreased.

It should be clear that the accuracy of the scheme can be improved by increasing the sampling rate. However, this increases the data rate of the output signal.

The principal advantage of DM over PCM is the simplicity of its implementation. In general, PCM exhibits better SNR characteristics at the same data rate.

Differential Pulse Code Modulation (DPCM) A variety of related techniques have been developed to use a combination of the PCM and DM methods. In *differential pulse code modulation (DPCM)*, the DM approach is used, but the change in the signal can be multiples of the quantization level (δ) from one sample to the next. This requires multiple bits at each sample to represent the changes, but generally requires fewer bits than PCM. DPCM also can use previous samples $m[k - 1], m[k - 2], m[k - 3]$, etc. to predict the next sample $\hat{m}[k]$. It then only transmits the prediction error $d[k] = m[k] - \hat{m}[k]$, which requires even fewer bits.

Adaptive DPCM (ADPCM) further improves the efficiency of the DPCM approach by changing the step size δ.

Model–Based Encoding and Vocoders

Waveform encoders do not take into account the nature of how the analog signals are generated. Therefore, they are limited in their compression ability. Model-based encoders for audio signals use parametric representations of the key sound qualities and physical sound production features of a source.

The source that has received the most attention is the human voice. Voice signals still are a very important part of the traffic in wireless networks and are formed by a very complex instrument that is a combination of vocal cords, trachea, tongue, mouth cavity, and nasal cavity. An intricate oscillator, the vocal cords, generates vocal sound and pitch. The fundamental frequency for males is 100 to 150 Hz and 190 to 250 Hz for females, and strong harmonics are produced in a frequency range of several thousand Hertz. Many of the unique characteristics of a person's voice are formed in the harmonics [BEAR79]. Frequency changes frequently, often from syllable to syllable, and the change in pitch is very important in some languages.

The voice signal is then acoustically guided through the throat and then the oral and nasal cavities. The mouth can also form sounds from this signal. Certain sounds are *voiced*; the vocal cords vibrate during the sound production, for example through the letters *m*, *n*, *g*, and *b* in words like *mut*, *nut*, *gut*, and *but*. Other sounds are *unvoiced*, formed by air movement and pressure. Examples are *h*, *c*, and *p* in words like *hut*, *cut*, and *put*.

Vocoders use two main approaches to provide good quality, low bit rate digital streams.

1. **Linear Prediction Coding (LPC)**: After determining if a voice segment is voiced or unvoiced, the analysis will estimate how the mouth is filtering the sound. The result will be a set of parameters for a linear filter that are transmitted. The receiver uses these parameters to create a voice-synthesized regeneration of the signal. The end-user actually hears the output of a voice-synthesizing machine.

2. **Code-Excited Linear Prediction (CELP)**: Code-excited linear prediction (CELP) vocoders use a codebook, which is a table of typical linear prediction coding (LPC) signals. Designers set these up beforehand and the transmitter searches for an entry in the codebook that best matches the sound. Then the index to that entry is transmitted. The codebook must be sufficiently large to produce good results, but the resulting data rate is still quite small. Enhancements to the CELP approach are used in most modern cellular systems.

Vocoders must be chosen to balance bandwidth and speech quality requirements. Designers must also consider end-to-end encoding delay, algorithmic complexity, power requirements, and the robustness of the code to transmission errors. The wireless medium is hostile to transmissions and the vocoders must be robust to transmission errors. At low bit rates, all information is very vital to an intelligible signal and needs to be more safely preserved. The corresponding extra error control procedures that might be needed for this protection may offset the bit rate reduction benefits that were anticipated.

Performance

Good voice reproduction via PCM can be achieved with 128 quantization levels, or 7-bit coding ($2^7 = 128$). A voice signal, conservatively, occupies a bandwidth of 4 kHz. Thus, according to the sampling theorem, samples should be taken at a rate of 8000 samples per second. This implies a data rate of $8000 \times 7 = 56$ kbps for the PCM-encoded digital data.

Consider what this means from the point of view of bandwidth requirement. An analog voice signal occupies 4 kHz. Using PCM this 4-kHz analog signal can be converted into a 56-kbps digital signal. But using the Nyquist criterion from Chapter 2, this digital signal could require on the order of 28 kHz of bandwidth. Even more severe differences are seen with higher bandwidth signals. For example, a common PCM scheme for color television uses 10-bit codes, which works out to 92 Mbps for a 4.6-MHz bandwidth signal. In spite of these numbers, digital techniques continue to grow in popularity for transmitting analog data. The principal reasons for this are as follows:

- Because repeaters are used instead of amplifiers, there is no additive noise.
- As we shall see, time division multiplexing (TDM) is used for digital signals instead of the frequency division multiplexing (FDM) used for analog signals. With TDM, there is no intermodulation noise, whereas we have seen that this is a concern for FDM.
- The conversion to digital signaling allows the use of the more efficient digital switching techniques.

Furthermore, techniques have been developed to provide more efficient codes. In the case of voice, a reasonable goal appears to be in the neighborhood of 4 kbps. LPC and CELP encoders achieve rates from 1.2 kbps to 13 kbps with differing quality scores. With video, advantage can be taken of the fact that from frame to frame, most picture elements will not change. Interframe coding techniques should allow the video requirement to be reduced to about 15 Mbps, and for slowly changing scenes, such as found in a video teleconference, down to 64 kbps or less.

As a final point, we mention that in many instances, the use of a telecommunications system will result in both digital-to-analog and analog-to-digital processing. The overwhelming majority of local terminations into the telecommunications network is analog, and the network itself uses a mixture of analog and digital techniques. Thus, digital data at a user's terminal may be converted to analog by a modem, subsequently digitized by a codec, and perhaps suffer repeated conversions before reaching its destination.

Thus, telecommunication facilities handle analog signals that represent both voice and digital data. The characteristics of the waveforms are quite different. Whereas voice signals tend to be skewed to the lower portion of the bandwidth (Figure 2.6), analog encoding of digital signals has a more uniform spectral content over the bandwidth and therefore contains more high-frequency components. Studies have shown that, because of the presence of these higher frequencies, PCM-related techniques are preferable to DM-related techniques for digitizing analog signals that represent digital data.

7.5 RECOMMENDED READING

There are many good references on analog modulation schemes for digital data. Good choices are [COUC13], [XION06], and [PROA14]; these three also provide comprehensive treatment of digital and analog modulation schemes for analog data.

An exceptionally clear exposition that covers digital-to-analog, analog-to-digital, and analog-to-analog techniques is [PEAR92]. Another comprehensive treatment of the topics in this chapter is [SKLA01].

An instructive treatment of the concepts of bit rate, baud, and bandwidth is [FREE98]. Helpful vocoder discussions are provided in [LATH09] and [RAPP02].

COUC13 Couch, L. *Digital and Analog Communication Systems.* Upper Saddle River, NJ: Pearson, 2013.

FREE98 Freeman, R. "Bits, Symbols, Baud, and Bandwidth." *IEEE Communications Magazine,* April 1998.

LATH09 Lathi, B. *Modern Digital and Analog Communication Systems.* New York: Oxford University Press, 2009.

PEAR92 Pearson, J. *Basic Communication Theory.* Englewood Cliffs, NJ: Prentice Hall, 1992.

PROA14 Proakis, J. *Fundamentals of Communication Systems.* Upper Saddle River, NJ: Pearson, 2014.

RAPP02 Rappaport, T. *Wireless Communications: Principles and Practice.* Upper Saddle River, NJ: Prentice Hall, 2002.

SKLA01 Sklar, B. *Digital Communications: Fundamentals and Applications.* Upper Saddle River, NJ: Prentice Hall, 2001.

XION06 Xiong, F. *Digital Modulation Techniques.* Boston: Artech House, 2006.

7.6 KEY TERMS, REVIEW QUESTIONS, AND PROBLEMS

Key Terms

amplitude modulation (AM)	frequency modulation (FM)	quadrature amplitude modulation (QAM)
amplitude-shift keying (ASK)	frequency-shift keying (FSK)	quadrature PSK (QPSK)
angle modulation	model-based encoding	vocoder
bit error rate (BER)	modulation	waveform encoding
carrier frequency	phase modulation (PM)	
delta modulation (DM)	phase-shift keying (PSK)	
differential PSK (DPSK)	pulse code modulation (PCM)	

Review Questions

7.1 What is differential encoding?

7.2 What function does a modem perform?

7.3 Indicate three major advantages of digital transmission over analog transmission.

7.4 How are binary values represented in amplitude-shift keying, and what is the limitation of this approach?

7.5 What is NRZ-L? What is a major disadvantage of this data encoding approach?

7.6 What is the difference between QPSK and offset QPSK?

7.7 What is QAM?

7.8 What does the sampling theorem tell us concerning the rate of sampling required for an analog signal?

7.9 What are the differences among AM, PM, and FM?

7.10 How is a vocoder different from a waveform encoder? Which typically provides a lower bit rate?

Problems

7.1 Given a bit rate of 10 Mbps and a carrier frequency of 20 MHz, draw an ASK signal for the bit sequence 10110.

7.2 Given a bit rate of 10 Mbps and a carrier frequency of 10 MHz or 20 MHz to represent a binary 0 or 1, draw an FSK signal for the bit sequence 10110.

7.3 Given a bit rate of 10 Mbps and a carrier frequency of 10 MHz, draw a QPSK signal for the bit sequence 101101 using the constellation diagram in Figure 7.6.

7.4 Given a bit rate of 20 Mbps and a carrier frequency of 10 MHz, draw a 16QAM signal for the bit sequence 1011000011001111 using the constellation diagram in Figure 7.13.

7.5 Figure 7.22 shows the QAM demodulator corresponding to the QAM modulator of Figure 7.12. Show that this arrangement does recover the two signals $d_1(t)$ and $d_2(t)$, which can be combined to recover the original input.

7.6 A sine wave is to be used for two different signaling schemes: (a) PSK; (b) QPSK. The duration of a signal element is 10^{-5} s. If the received signal is of the following form:

$$s(t) = 0.005 \sin (2\pi 10^6 t + \theta) \text{ V}$$

and if the measured noise power at the receiver is 2.5×10^{-8} W, determine the E_b/N_0 (in dB) for each case.

7.7 Derive an expression for baud rate D as a function of bit rate R for QPSK using the digital encoding techniques of Figure 7.2.

7.8 Given BER curves in Figure 7.9, how much higher E_b/N_0 (in dB) is needed to achieve a BER = 10^{-4} for DPSK and ASK as compared to BPSK?

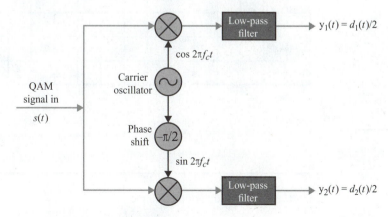

Figure 7.22 QAM Demodulator

7.9 Given your answer in Problem 7.8 and the signal amplitude of the BPSK signal is 0.01 V when using rectangular pulses, what would be the required signal amplitudes for DPSK and ASK?

7.10 What SNR ratio is required to achieve a bandwidth efficiency of 1.0 for ASK, FSK, PSK, and QPSK? Assume that the required bit error rate is 10-6.

7.11 Why should PCM be preferable to DM for encoding analog signals that represent digital data?

7.12 A signal is quantized using 10-bit PCM. Find the signal-to-quantization noise ratio.

7.13 Consider an audio signal with spectral components in the range 300 to 3000 Hz. Assume that a sampling rate of 7000 samples per second will be used to generate a PCM signal.
   a. For SNR = 30 dB, what is the number of uniform quantization levels needed?
   b. What data rate is required?

7.14 Find the step size δ required to prevent slope overload noise as a function of the frequency of the highest-frequency component of the signal. Assume that all components have amplitude A.

7.15 A PCM encoder accepts a signal with a full-scale voltage of 10 V and generates 8-bit codes using uniform quantization. The maximum normalized quantized voltage is $1 - 2^{-8}$. Determine (a) normalized step size, (b) actual step size in volts, (c) actual maximum quantized level in volts, (d) normalized resolution, (e) actual resolution, and (f) percentage resolution.

7.16 The analog waveform shown in Figure 7.23 is to be delta modulated. The sampling period and the step size are indicated by the grid on the figure. The first DM output and the staircase function for this period are also shown. Show the rest of the staircase function and give the DM output. Indicate regions where slope overload distortion exists.

7.17 Consider the angle-modulated signal

$$s(t) = 10 \cos [(10^8)\pi t + 5 \sin 2\pi(10^3)t]$$

Find the maximum phase deviation and the maximum frequency deviation.

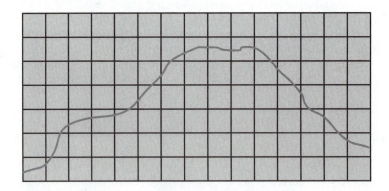

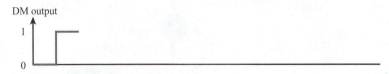

DM output

Figure 7.23 Delta Modulation Example

7.18 Consider the angle-modulated signal

$$s(t)\pi = 10 \cos [2\pi(10^6)t + 0.1 \sin (10^3)\pi t]$$

a. Express $s(t)$ as a PM signal with $n_p = 10$.
b. Express $s(t)$ as an FM signal with $n_f = 10\pi$.

7.19 Let $m_1(t)$ and $m_2(t)$ be message signals and let $s_1(t)$ and $s_2(t)$ be the corresponding modulated signals using a carrier frequency of f_c.

a. Show that if simple AM modulation is used, then $m_1(t) + m_2(t)$ produces a modulated signal equal that is a linear combination of $s_1(t)$ and $s_2(t)$. This is why AM is sometimes referred to as linear modulation.
b. Show that if simple PM modulation is used, then $m_1(t) + m_2(t)$ produces a modulated signal that is not a linear combination of $s_1(t)$ and $s_2(t)$. This is why angle modulation is sometimes referred to as nonlinear modulation.

CHAPTER 8

ORTHOGONAL FREQUENCY DIVISION MULTIPLEXING

This chapter introduces **orthogonal frequency division multiplexing (OFDM)**-based techniques that have created great expansion in the capacity of wireless networks. OFDM is the main air interface technology used to move from third- to fourth-generation cellular technologies. OFDM also allows the expansion of IEEE 802.11 data rates. Finally, OFDM is a critical technology in the development of broadband wireless Internet access for both fixed and mobile systems under the WiMAX standard. We first look at the basic mechanisms of OFDM, namely, orthogonal carriers and transmitter design based on the inverse fast Fourier transform. Then we look at the ways OFDM is used in practical systems for multiple access topics and the methods to address OFDM problems, especially peak-to-average power ratio (PAPR) and intercarrier interference issues. This chapter discusses fundamental principles; more details about the implementation of OFDM for specific technologies are given in the discussions of IEEE 802.11 Wi-Fi, LTE, and WiMAX in Chapters 11, 14, and 16.

8.1 ORTHOGONAL FREQUENCY DIVISION MULTIPLEXING

OFDM, also called *multicarrier modulation*, uses multiple carrier signals at different frequencies, sending some of the bits on each channel. This is similar to frequency division multiplexing (FDM). However, in the case of OFDM, many subcarriers are dedicated to a single data source.

Figure 8.1 illustrates a conceptual understanding of OFDM. Actual transmitter operation is simplified, but the basic concept can first be understood here. Suppose we have a binary data stream operating at R bps and an available bandwidth of Nf_b, centered at f_0. The entire bandwidth could be used to send the data stream, in which case each bit duration would be $\frac{1}{R}$. The alternative is to split the data stream into N substreams, using a serial-to-parallel converter. Each substream has a data rate of R/N bps and is transmitted on a separate subcarrier, with a spacing between adjacent subcarriers of f_b. Now the bit duration is N/R, which is substantially longer and creates special capabilities to overcome multipath fading.

Orthogonality

To gain a clearer understanding of OFDM, let us consider the scheme in terms of its base frequency, f_b. This is the lowest-frequency subcarrier. All of the other subcarriers are integer multiples of the base frequency, namely, $2f_b$, $3f_b$, and so on,

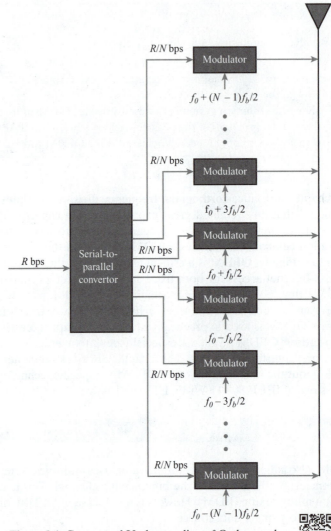

Figure 8.1 Conceptual Understanding of Orthogonal Frequency Division Multiplexing

as shown in Figure 8.2. The OFDM scheme uses advanced digital signal processing techniques to distribute the data over multiple carriers at precise frequencies. The relationship among the subcarriers is referred to as **orthogonality**. The result is shown in Figure 8.2b. It looks like the signals are packed too close together because they overlap substantially, but one property of orthogonality is that the peaks of the power spectral density of each subcarrier occur at a point at which the power of other subcarriers is zero. Previous FDM approaches are illustrated in Figure 8.2c, which assumed signals should be spaced sufficiently apart in frequency to (1) avoid overlap in the frequency bands and (2) to provide extra spacing known as *guard bands* to prevent the effects of adjacent carrier interference from out-of-band

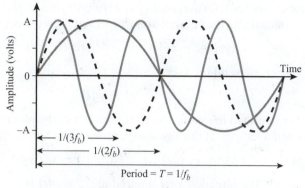

(a) Three subcarriers in time domain

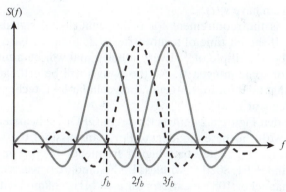

(b) Three orthogonal subcarriers in frequency domain

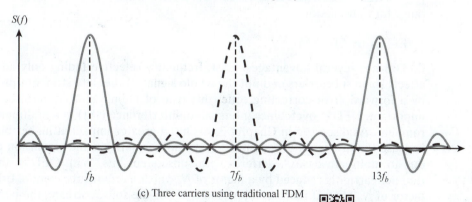

(c) Three carriers using traditional FDM

Figure 8.2 Illustration of Orthogonality of OFDM

emissions. But OFDM is able to drastically improve the use of frequency spectrum. Viewing Figure 8.2b compared to 8.2c, the number of signals that can be supported has increased by a factor of 6!

With OFDM, the subcarriers can be packed tightly together because there is minimal interference between adjacent subcarriers (zero interference if the carrier spacing is not corrupted). Orthogonality is defined by an important mathematical principle. Two signals, $s_1(t)$ and $s_2(t)$, are orthogonal if they meet this requirement.

$$\text{Average over bit time of } s_1(t)s_2(t) = 0$$

At the transmitter, we send the signal

$$s(t) = s_1(t) + s_2(t)$$

At the receiver intended to extract the $s_1(t)$ signal from the received signal, it multiplies by $s_1(t)$ and averages. If the signals are orthogonal, here is the result.

$$\text{Average over bit time of } s_1(t)s(t) = s_1(t)s_1(t) + s_1(t)s_2(t) = s_1^2(t) + 0$$

The output is only the intended $s_1(t)$ squared and the $s_2(t)$ is removed. If there are many signals that are all orthogonal, the receiver can remove all of the other signals and only again have $s_1(t)$.

Here is the requirement for orthogonal digital signals that are subcarriers of OFDM. If the bit time of a subcarrier is T, then the base frequency f_b must be chosen to be a multiple of $\frac{1}{T}$. Every other signal will be a multiple of f_b such that $Mf_b = \frac{M}{T}$ for some integer M. All the signals will be orthogonal. One example of OFDM is that used for fourth-generation cellular LTE technology which uses a subcarrier spacing of 15 kHz.

Note that Figure 8.2 depicts the set of OFDM subcarriers in a frequency band beginning with the base frequency. For transmission, the set of OFDM subcarriers is further modulated to a higher frequency band. For example, the OFDM scheme in the IEEE 802.11n wireless LAN standard consists of 48 subcarriers over a 20 MHz channel or 108 subcarriers for a 40 MHz channel with a base frequency of $f_b = 0.3125$ MHz. This set of subcarriers is then translated to 2.4-GHz or 5-GHz range for transmission.

Benefits of OFDM

OFDM has several advantages. First, frequency selective fading only adversely affects some subcarriers and not the whole signal. If the data stream is protected by a forward error-correcting code, this type of fading is easily handled. More important, OFDM overcomes intersymbol interference (ISI) in a multipath environment. As discussed in Chapter 3, ISI has a greater impact at higher bit rates; because the distance between bits, or symbols, is smaller, the expansion of time due to multipath easily interferes with subsequent bits. With OFDM, the data rate per carrier is reduced by a factor of N, which increases the symbol time by a factor of N. Thus, if the symbol period is T_s for the source stream, the period for the OFDM signals is NT_s. This dramatically reduces the effect of ISI because the symbols are substantially longer. As a design criterion, N is chosen so that NT_s is significantly greater than the root-mean-square delay spread of the channel. Even the spread in the time delays of the multipath components does not affect the signal substantially.

As a result of these considerations, with the use of OFDM, it may not be necessary to deploy equalizers to counteract ISI. Equalizers are complex and expensive devices whose complexity increases with the severity of the ISI.

OFDM Implementation

OFDM implementation has two important operations that are involved to create the benefits just described. These are use of the inverse fast Fourier transform (IFFT) and cyclic prefix (CP).

Inverse Fast Fourier Transform Even though OFDM dates back some 40 years, it was only until the 1990s that an advance was made to make OFDM an economical technology. Figure 8.1 showed a conceptual understanding of OFDM where a data stream is split into many lower bit rate streams and then modulated on many different subcarriers. Such an approach, however, would result in a very expensive transmitter and receiver because it would have some many expensive oscillators.

Fortunately, OFDM can instead be implemented by taking advantage of the properties of the **discrete Fourier transform (DFT)** which refers to any algorithm that generates a quantized Fourier transform, $X[k]$, of a discrete time-domain function, $x[n]$.

$$X[k] = \sum_{n=0}^{N-1} x[n] e^{-j\frac{2\pi kn}{N}}$$

The inverse discrete Fourier transform, which converts the frequency values back to time domain values, is as follows.

$$x[n] = \sum_{n=0}^{N-1} X[k] e^{j\frac{2\pi kn}{N}}$$

When this function is implemented using a number of data points N that is a power of two, the computational time is greatly reduced and these then are called the **fast Fourier transform (FFT)** and **inverse fast Fourier transform (IFFT)**.

The implementation of OFDM using the FFT and IFFT is illustrated in Figure 8.3. The data stream undergoes a serial to parallel (S/P) operation, which takes a sample from each carrier and makes a group of samples called an ***OFDM symbol***. Each value in a sense gives a weight for each subcarrier. Then the IFFT (not FFT) takes the values for these subcarriers and computes the time domain data stream to be transmitted, which is a combination of these subcarriers. The IFFT operation has the effect of ensuring that the subcarriers do not interfere with each other. These values are put back into a serial stream with a P/S operation, then the stream is modulated onto the carrier using one oscillator. At the receiver, the reverse operation is performed. An FFT module is used to map the incoming signal back to the M subcarriers, from which the data streams are recovered as the weights for each subcarrier are retrieved for each sample.

Note that in OFDM the term "symbol" takes on a different meaning than is used in other contexts. This might at first be confusing. In Chapter 7, we referred to a symbol as a point in a signal constellation diagram that could be used to transmit multiple bits per symbol. Here, an OFDM symbol is a group of samples, one from each subcarrier. This is the input to the IFFT operation. It is, therefore, entirely possible that if one were using a 16QAM modulation scheme and an OFDM block

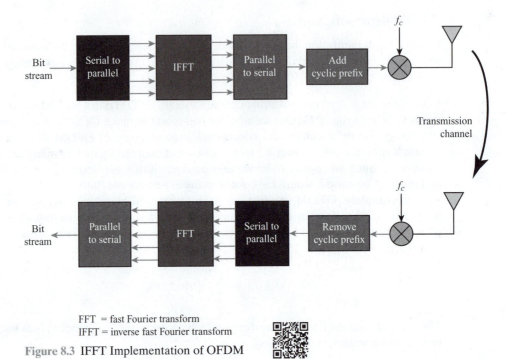

FFT = fast Fourier transform
IFFT = inverse fast Fourier transform

Figure 8.3 IFFT Implementation of OFDM

size of eight samples, one would be transmitting an OFDM symbol of 8 16 quadrature amplitude modulation (QAM) symbols!

The Cyclic Prefix Even though OFDM by definition limits ISI by using long symbol times, OFDM also uses a **cyclic prefix** which goes another step further to combat ISI and completely eliminate the need for equalizers. The cyclic prefix is illustrated in Figure 8.4. The X_i values are the OFDM symbols. This accomplishes two functions:

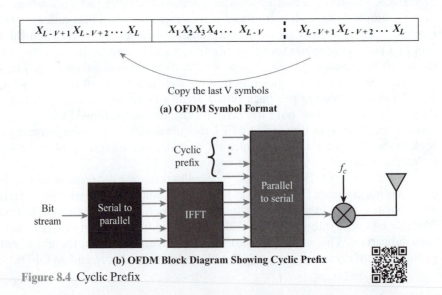

$$X_{L-V+1}X_{L-V+2}\cdots X_L \quad \mid \quad X_1 X_2 X_3 X_4 \cdots X_{L-V} \quad \mid \quad X_{L-V+1}X_{L-V+2}\cdots X_L$$

Copy the last V symbols

(a) OFDM Symbol Format

(b) OFDM Block Diagram Showing Cyclic Prefix

Figure 8.4 Cyclic Prefix

1. Additional time, known as a guard interval, is added to the beginning of the OFDM symbol before the actual data begins. This allows all residual ISI to diminish before it impacts the received data.

2. This beginning time period is packed with data that is an actual copy of the data from the *end* of the OFDM symbol which is being sent. This converts the mathematics of the signal processing into a *circular* operation instead of a linear one. This isolates the parallel subchannels and allows for simple frequency domain digital signal processing techniques.

Example 8.1 Consider an OFDM implementation in the LTE cellular standard. LTE uses 15 kHz subcarriers and can use an OFDM symbol of 1024 subcarriers. The *nominal cyclic prefix* can account for a 7% guard time; the *extended cyclic prefix* can use up to 25%. 600 subcarriers can be used for data transmission. The rest are needed for pilot and null subcarriers. The nominal CP adds $0.07 \times 1024 = 72$ guard symbols, and the extended CP adds $0.25 \times 1024 = 256$ guard symbols. For a transmission bandwidth of 10 MHz and 16 QAM modulation (4 bits/symbol), the data rate for the nominal and extended CPs would be

$$R_{nominal} = 10 \ MHz \frac{600 \ data \ subcarriers}{1024 + 72 \ total \ symbols} (4) = 21.9 \ Mbps$$

$$R_{extended} = 10 \ MHz \frac{600 \ data \ subcarriers}{1024 + 256 \ total \ symbols} (4) = 18.8 \ Mbps$$

Difficulties of OFDM

Even though OFDM has tremendous benefits and the implementation process has been highly simplified, there are still two key issues that must be addressed for successful OFDM implementation.

Peak-to-Average Power Ratio (PAPR) OFDM signals have a higher **peak-to-average power ratio (PAPR)** than single-carrier signals because, in the time domain, a multicarrier signal is the sum of many narrowband signals. At some time instances, this sum is large and at other instances it is small, which means that the peak value of the signal is substantially larger than the average value. This is one of the most important challenges for implementation of OFDM because it increases the cost of power amplifiers.

The objective of a power amplifier is to increase the amplitude of a signal by some factor K. This would result in an equation of the relationship between input and output voltage as follows:

$$V_{out} = KV_{in}$$

This is an equation of the line in Figure 8.5 labeled as the ideal amplifier. Ideally this relationship would exist for all input voltages, but instead all amplifiers have a nonlinear region where the amplifier saturates, meaning it cannot produce any higher output voltage regardless of the input voltage. This is indicated by the practical amplifier curve in Figure 8.5. Up until the input voltage is 3 V, the curve is linear,

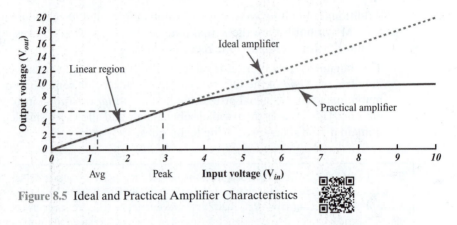

Figure 8.5 Ideal and Practical Amplifier Characteristics

but subsequently the curve becomes nonlinear and the amplifier cannot produce an output beyond 10 V regardless of the input voltage.

Figure 8.6 illustrates the effect that such an amplifier as shown in Figure 8.5 has on output signals. Figure 8.6a shows two signals with amplitudes of 20 V and 2 V, respectively. Figure 8.6b shows the output signals with the smaller signal amplified by a factor of 2 with no distortion. The larger signal, however, has experienced clipping from the amplifier. The signal has now been distorted. If such distortion is

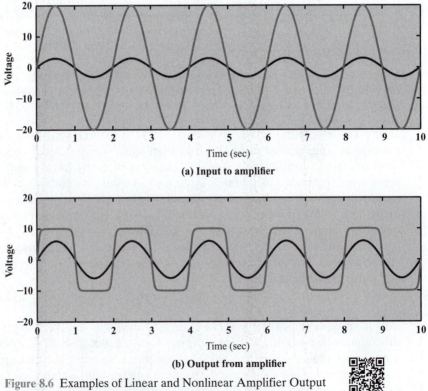

Figure 8.6 Examples of Linear and Nonlinear Amplifier Output

present in OFDM systems, the result will be loss of orthogonality, out-of-band emissions, and increased bit error rate (BER).

Using amplifiers with a long linear range is needed for signals with a wide range of amplitudes as in the OFDM PAPR problem. Such amplifiers are significantly more expensive, however. Another simplistic solution would be to limit the maximum signal amplitude within the linear range of the amplifier. This is called *input backoff*. But this would reduce the power efficiency of the system, decrease signal to interference plus noise ratio (SINR), and reduce coverage.

It is, therefore, important to instead reduce the actual PAPR in the OFDM signal. This is especially true in the uplink from a mobile to a base station. For the downlink, more expensive approaches and amplifiers could be used, because base stations are small in number, but mobiles are many in number and sensitive to cost. PAPR reduction techniques that have been suggested include specialized coding, phase adjustments, clipping using Gaussian functions, and active constellation extension. Systems like LTE have used single-carrier frequency division multiple access (SC-FMDA), which is discussed in a subsequent section.

Intercarrier Interference In order to demodulate an OFDM signal, time and frequency synchronization is necessary. Because OFDM symbol times are long, the demands on time synchronization are somewhat relaxed compared to other systems. But conversely, because OFDM frequencies are spaced as closely as possible, the frequency synchronization requirements are significantly more stringent. If not met, **intercarrier interference (ICI)** will result. Timing and frequency synchronization algorithms are the responsibility of each equipment manufacturer, and these problems are some of the most challenging for OFDM implementation.

The cyclic prefix provides an excellent way of ensuring orthogonality of carriers because it eliminates the effects of multipath. Because the CP causes a reduction in spectral efficiency, however, a certain level of ICI may be tolerated in an effort to reduce CP length. In addition, Doppler shift or mismatched oscillators of even one subcarrier can cause ICI in many adjacent subcarriers. Refer again to Figure 8.2. It is readily seen that the spacing between subcarriers has tight constraints and can be easily perturbed.

Because ICI can be a limiting factor for OFDM systems, implementations will seek to find a balance between carrier spacing and OFDM symbol length. Short symbol duration will reduce Doppler-induced ICI, but also may cause the CP to be an unacceptably large part of the OFDM symbol time. Systems may also use different OFDM pulse shapes, use self-interference cancellation by modulating information across multiple carriers to reduce ICI, and implement frequency domain equalizers.

8.2 ORTHOGONAL FREQUENCY DIVISION MULTIPLE ACCESS (OFDMA)

Multiple access strategies share a wireless channel by making use of scheduled times (time division multiple access), random access times (carrier sense multiple access), scheduled use of frequencies (frequency division multiple access), coded spreading of signals (direct sequence spread spectrum), and/or coded frequency hopping of signals (frequency hopping spread spectrum). Throughout this text, one of the defining attributes of a technology is how it accomplishes multiple access, both in terms of the approaches just mentioned and the protocols that are used for mobile devices to cooperate.

Orthogonal frequency division multiple access (OFDMA) uses a combination of FDMA and TDMA by allowing different users to use a subset of the subcarriers at different times. All technologies that use OFDM do not use OFDMA. For example, some forms of 802.11 use OFDM for the signal transmission, but CSMA for multiple access. The transmitter uses the full set of subcarriers when transmitting. LTE only uses OFDMA on the downlink, but instead uses a single-carrier approach on the uplink.

OFDMA uses OFDM, which employs multiple closely spaced subcarriers, but the subcarriers are divided into groups of subcarriers because it would not be computationally feasible (because of hundreds of subcarriers) or sufficient (because each subcarrier only carries a small capacity) to schedule by individual subcarrier. Each group is named a subchannel. In the downlink, a subchannel may be intended for different receivers. In the uplink, a transmitter may be assigned one or more subchannels. Subchannelization in the uplink can save user device transmit power because it can concentrate power only on certain subchannel(s) allocated to it. This power-saving feature is particularly useful for battery-powered user devices, the likely case in mobile 4G. Figure 8.7 contrasts OFDM and OFDMA; in the OFDMA case the use of adjacent subcarriers to form a subchannel is illustrated. Subchannels can be formed using three different methods:

- **Adjacent subcarriers:** All subcarriers could be assigned in a contiguous block of frequencies. All of the SINRs would be approximately equal. This could be a problem if those frequencies had poor performance, but this also provides

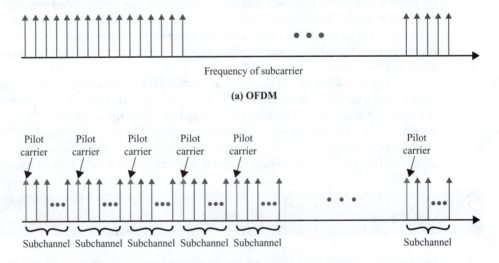

Frequency of subcarrier

(a) OFDM

Frequency of subcarrier

(b) OFDMA (adjacent subcarriers)

Figure 8.7 OFDM and OFDMA

an opportunity if the system can choose across many possible blocks to find the best allocation of blocks to different users that could optimize a balance of channel efficiency, user requirements, priority, and fairness. This approach, however, requires the system to accurately know the propagation channel over the full system bandwidth for each user, and adapt as those characteristics change. This requires pilot symbols and signals, and also prediction mechanisms because the information could already be out-of-date when it is received and fully processed. This approach can be used by LTE and WiMAX.

- **Regularly spaced subcarriers:** These can be thought of as "distributed" or "comb" allocation. This provides frequency diversity so that there are a sufficient number of good subcarriers, regardless of which are chosen. The burden of channel estimation is not as significant. This approach can also be used by LTE.

- **Randomly spaced subcarriers:** This has similar benefits to regularly spaced subcarriers, but it also has benefits from reduced adjacent-cell interference. This can also be used by WiMAX.

Opportunistic Scheduling

Subchannelization defines subchannels, called **_Resource Blocks_** by LTE, which can be allocated to subscriber stations (SSs) depending on their channel conditions and data requirements. Particular power levels could also be prescribed to those stations in order to optimize throughput and limit interference.

One might think that the time-varying and multipath nature of wireless communications would limit the ability for effective use of the wireless channel, but the opposite is actually true. Such variations provide opportunities that can be exploited. Because channel conditions change and are expected to change, resource allocations can adjust in a dynamic fashion. Hence, the term **opportunistic scheduling** has been used. Particular implementations and equipment providers can approach this problem in ways that provide them competitive advantage, because most standards do not prescribe OFDMA scheduling approaches. There are a variety of considerations when scheduling such subchannels.

- **Efficiency:** One could schedule subchannels based on the users with the highest SINR for that time slot. Those users could use adaptive modulation and coding to obtain much higher throughput than others with poorer SINR. The total efficiency and capacity would be highest; the time-varying nature of the channel would be exploited to the highest benefit.

- **Fairness:** If is scheduling only based on efficiency, however, some users (likely those far from base stations) would receive little or no throughput. Fairness could also be a consideration. A completely fair allocation might give the same number of subchannels or the same throughput to all users, but this could sacrifice efficiency. A popular approach that finds a compromise is known as **proportional fairness**, in which every user computes the following metric during a resource allocation decision:

$$\text{Proportional fairness metric} = \frac{r_i}{\overline{r_i}}$$

This is the ratio of the rate that could be obtained for user i in that time slot for that subchannel, r_i, divided by the average rate that has been obtained for user i in that subchannel, $\bar{r}_i$. In essence, users are compared against themselves and not against others. Those which have a good opportunity *for them* will have a better chance at being scheduled.

- **Requirements:** Applications such as audio and video may have requirements on delay and jitter. These should be considered.

- **Priority:** Priority users such as police, fire, ambulance, or other public safety workers could need special priorities in emergency situations, regardless of their channel conditions. Note, however, that even for those users their channel conditions may improve significantly within a few milliseconds.

8.3 SINGLE-CARRIER FDMA

Single-carrier FDMA (SC-FDMA) is a relatively recently developed multiple access technique which has similar structure and performance to OFDMA. One prominent advantage of SC-FDMA over OFDMA is the lower PAPR of the transmit waveform, which benefits the mobile user in terms of battery life, power efficiency, and lower cost. Even though the term "single-carrier FDMA" sounds similar to basic OFDM, it is not the same because it performs an extra DFT operation and frequency equalization operation on transmitter and receiver. SC-FDMA is used on the uplink and OFDMA is still used on the downlink for greater multiple access possibilities.

As shown in Figure 8.8, SC-FDMA performs a DFT prior to the IFFT operation, which spreads the data symbols over all the subcarriers carrying information and produces a virtual single-carrier structure. This then is passed through the OFDM processing modules to split the signal into subcarriers. Now, however, every data symbol is carried by every subcarrier. Figure 8.9 is an example of how the OFDM and SC-FDMA signals appear.

With Figure 8.9 in mind, we can make several observations. For OFDM, a source data stream is divided into N separate data streams and these streams are modulated and transmitted in parallel on N separate subcarriers each with bandwidth f_b. The source data stream has a data rate of R bps, and the data rate on each subcarrier is R/N bps. For SC-FDMA, it appears from Figure 8.9 that the source data stream is modulated on a single carrier (hence the SC prefix to the name) of bandwidth $N \times f_b$ and transmitted at a data rate of R bps. The data is transmitted at a higher rate, but over a wider bandwidth compared to the data rate on a single subcarrier of OFDM. However, because of the complex signal processing of SC-FDMA, the preceding description is not accurate. In effect, the source data stream is replicated N times, and each copy of the data stream is independently modulated and transmitted on a subcarrier, with a data rate on each subcarrier of R bps. Compared with OFDM, we are transmitting at a much higher data rate on each subcarrier, but because we are sending the same data stream on each subcarrier, it is still possible to reliably recover the original data stream at the receiver.

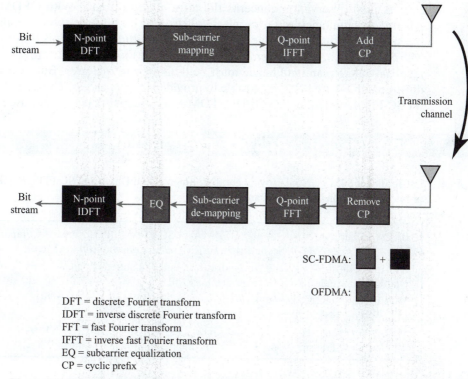

DFT = discrete Fourier transform
IDFT = inverse discrete Fourier transform
FFT = fast Fourier transform
IFFT = inverse fast Fourier transform
EQ = subcarrier equalization
CP = cyclic prefix

Figure 8.8 Simplified Block Diagram of OFDMA and SC-FDMA

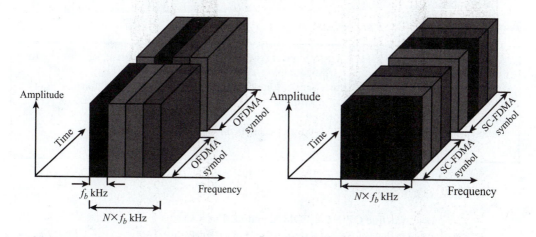

(a) OFDMA: Data symbols occupy f_b kHz for one OFDMA symbol period

(b) SC-FDMA: Data symbols occupy $N \times f_b$ kHz for $1/N$ SC-FDMA symbol period

Figure 8.9 Example of OFDMA and SC-FDMA

A final observation concerns the term *multiple access*. With OFDMA, it is possible to simultaneously transmit either from or to different users by allocating the subcarriers during any one time interval to multiple users. This is not possible with SC-FDMA: At any given point in time, all of the subcarriers are carrying the identical data stream and hence must be dedicated to one user. But over time, as illustrated in Figure 8.9, it is possible to provide multiple access. Thus, a better term for SC-FDMA might be SC-OFDM-TDMA, although that term is not used.

8.4 RECOMMENDED READING

[BERA08] and [MYUN06] provide good treatment of OFDMA and SC-FDMA. [GHOS11] provides discussion of OFDMA and LTE.

BERA08 Beradinelli, G., et al. "OFDMA vs SC-FDMA: Performance Comparison in Local Area IMT-A Scenarios." *IEEE Wireless Communications,* October 2008.

GHOS11 Ghosh, A.; Zhang, J.; Andrews J.; and Muhamed, R. *Fundamentals of LTE.* Upper Saddle River, NJ: Prentice Hall, 2011.

MOLI11 Molisch, A, *Wireless Communications,* Second Edition, West Sussex, UK: John Wiley & Sons, Ltd.

MYUN06 Myung, H.; Lim, J.; and Goodman, D. "Single Carrier FDMA for Uplink Wireless Transmission." *IEEE Vehicular Technology,* September 2006.

8.5 KEY TERMS, REVIEW QUESTIONS, AND PROBLEMS

Key Terms

cyclic prefix discrete Fourier transform (DFT) fast Fourier transform (FFT) intercarrier interference (ICI) inverse fast Fourier transform (IFFT)	opportunistic scheduling orthogonality orthogonal frequency division multiplexing (OFDM) orthogonal frequency division multiple access (OFDMA)	peak-to-average power ratio (PAPR) proportional fairness single-carrier FDMA (SC-FDMA)

Review Questions

8.1 Briefly define OFDM, OFDMA, and SC-FDMA.

8.2 What is the fundamental requirement of OFDM?

8.3 What are the main strengths of OFDM?

8.4 What are the main technical problem issues of OFDM?

8.5 What are the main differences between OFDM and OFDMA?

8.6 How does the IFFT approach affect the number of oscillators required in the transmitter? In the receiver?

8.7 How does orthogonality allow for increased capacity?

8.8 What problem does the cyclic prefix address?

8.9 OFDM creates several lower-rate (i.e., longer symbol time) subcarriers. Why is that helpful?

8.10 What are the benefits of each of the following OFDMA approaches – adjacent subcarriers, regularly spaced subcarriers, and randomly spaced subcarriers?

8.11 What is the purpose of using SC-FDMA?

Problems

8.1 For an 18 Mbps LTE data stream with a symbol time of 66.67 μs, how many subcarriers are created?

8.2 LTE assigns subcarriers in *resource blocks* of 180 kHz. Given the information in Problem 8.1, how many subcarriers are in a resource block? Approximate $B_S \approx r_b$.

8.3 Now consider a different system than described in Problems 8.1 and 8.2. Recall from Chapter 6 that a system is considered *flat fading* if the coherence bandwidth B_C is much, much greater (using a factor of 10) than the signal bandwidth B_S. A channel is found to have a coherence bandwidth of 80 kHz and to be frequency selective for a high data rate signal of 16 Mbps. How many subcarriers are needed to make each subcarrier a flat fading signal? Approximate $B_S \approx r_b$.

8.4 The cyclic prefix is intended to be long enough to encompass most significant multipath signals. Consider one of the LTE CP durations of 4.7 μs. Multipath delays come from signals traveling longer distances that the shortest path signal. If the shortest path between TX and RX is 1 km, what is the distance of the longest traveled multipath signal if the multipath delay should be much, much less (again using a factor of 10) than the CP duration? Assume signals travel at the speed of light.

8.5 Find the relationship between subcarrier frequencies f_1 and f_2 that is required for two subcarriers to be orthogonal to satisfy the following orthogonality condition. Assume f_1 and f_2 are both integer multiples of $\frac{1}{T_b}$.

$$\int_0^{T_b} \cos{(2\pi f_1 t)} \cos{(2\pi f_2 t)} \, dt = 0$$

8.6 For Problem 8.5, what is the minimum spacing that is possible to still maintain orthogonality?

CHAPTER 9

SPREAD SPECTRUM

LEARNING OBJECTIVES

After studying this chapter, you should be able to:

- Describe the operation of the two major forms of spread spectrum: frequency hopping and direct sequence.
- Illustrate how frequency hopping accomplishes a spread spectrum objective.
- Explain the relationships between bandwidth and spreading bit rate.
- Describe how the RAKE receiver takes advantage of direct sequence spread spectrum to provide time diversity to overcome multipath.

Spread spectrum is an important form of communications. This technique does not fit neatly into the categories defined in the preceding chapter, as it can be used to transmit either analog or digital data, using an analog signal.

The spread spectrum technique was developed initially for military and intelligence requirements. The essential idea is to spread the information signal over a wider bandwidth to make jamming and interception more difficult. The first type of spread spectrum developed is known as frequency hopping.[1] A more recent type of spread spectrum is direct sequence. Both of these techniques are used in various wireless communications standards and products.

After a brief overview, we look at these two spread spectrum techniques. We then examine a multiple access technique based on spread spectrum.

9.1 THE CONCEPT OF SPREAD SPECTRUM

Figure 9.1 highlights the key characteristics of any spread spectrum system. Input is fed into a channel encoder that produces an analog signal with a relatively narrow bandwidth around some center frequency. This signal is further modulated using a sequence of digits known as a **spreading code** or **spreading sequence**. Typically, but not always, the spreading code is generated by a **pseudonoise (PN)**,

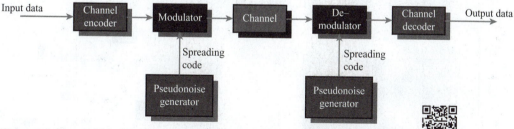

Figure 9.1 General Model of Spread Spectrum Digital Communication System

---

[1]Spread spectrum (using frequency hopping) was invented, believe it or not, by Hollywood screen siren Hedy Lamarr in 1940 at the age of 26. She and a partner who later joined her effort were granted a patent in 1942 (U.S. Patent 2,292,387; 11 August 1942). Lamarr considered this her contribution to the war effort and never profited from her invention.

or pseudorandom number, generator. The effect of this modulation is to increase significantly the bandwidth (spread the spectrum) of the signal to be transmitted. On the receiving end, the same digit sequence is used to demodulate the spread spectrum signal. Finally, the signal is fed into a channel decoder to recover the data. Several things can be gained from this apparent waste of spectrum:

- The signals gain immunity from various kinds of noise and multipath distortion. The earliest applications of spread spectrum were military, where it was used for its immunity to jamming.

- It can also be used for hiding and encrypting signals. Only a recipient who knows the spreading code can recover the encoded information.

- Several users can independently use the same higher bandwidth with very little interference. This property is used in cellular telephony applications, with a technique known as code division multiplexing (CDM) or code division multiple access (CDMA).

9.2 FREQUENCY HOPPING SPREAD SPECTRUM

With **frequency hopping spread spectrum (FHSS)**, the signal is broadcast over a seemingly random series of radio frequencies, hopping from frequency to frequency at fixed intervals. A receiver, hopping between frequencies in synchronization with the transmitter, picks up the message. Would-be eavesdroppers hear only unintelligible blips. Attempts to jam the signal on one frequency succeed only at knocking out a few bits of it.

Basic Approach

Figure 9.2 shows an example of a frequency hopping signal. A number of channels, C, are allocated for the FH signal. For example, IEEE 802.15.1, Bluetooth, uses $C = 80$. The spacing between carrier frequencies and hence the width of each channel usually corresponds to the bandwidth of the input signal. The transmitter operates in one

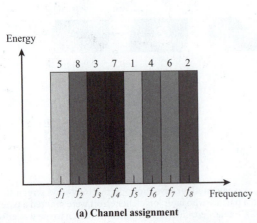

(a) Channel assignment

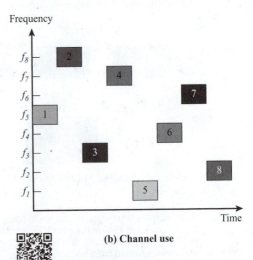

(b) Channel use

Figure 9.2 Frequency Hopping Example

channel at a time for a fixed interval; for example, the IEEE 802.15.1 Bluetooth standard uses a 0.625-ms interval. During that interval, some number of bits (possibly a fraction of a bit, as discussed subsequently) is transmitted using some encoding scheme. A spreading code dictates the sequence of channels used. Both the transmitter and the receiver use the same code to tune into a sequence of channels in synchronization.

A typical block diagram for a frequency hopping system is shown in Figure 9.3. For transmission, binary data are fed into a modulator using some digital-to-analog encoding scheme, such as frequency-shift keying (FSK) or binary phase-shift keying (BPSK). The resulting signal $s_d(t)$ is centered on some base frequency. A pseudonoise, or pseudorandom number, source serves as an index into a table of frequencies; this is the spreading code referred to previously. At each successive interval (each k PN bits), a new carrier frequency $c(t)$ is selected. This frequency is then modulated by the signal produced from the initial modulator to produce a new signal $s(t)$ with the same shape but now centered on the selected carrier frequency.

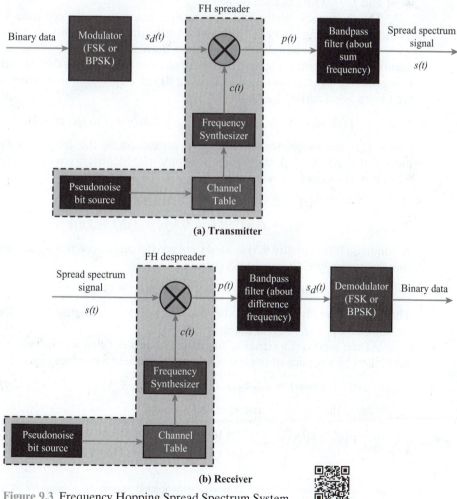

Figure 9.3 Frequency Hopping Spread Spectrum System

On reception, the spread spectrum signal is demodulated using the same sequence of PN-derived frequencies and then demodulated to produce the output data.

Figure 9.3 indicates that the two signals are multiplied. Let us give an example of how this works, using BFSK as the data modulation scheme. We can define the FSK input to the FHSS system as [compare to Equation (7.2)]

$$s_d(t) = A \cos (2\pi(f_0 + 0.5(b_i + 1)\Delta f)t) \qquad \text{for } iT < t < (i + 1)T \qquad (9.1)$$

where

A = amplitude of signal
f_0 = base frequency
b_i = value of the ith bit of data (+1 for binary 1, −1 for binary 0)
Δf = frequency separation
T = bit duration; data rate = $1/T$

Thus, during the ith bit interval, the frequency of the data signal is f_0 if the data bit is −1 and $f_0 + \Delta f$ if the data bit is +1.

The frequency synthesizer generates a constant-frequency tone whose frequency hops among a set of C frequencies, with the hopping pattern determined by a PN sequence. For simplicity, assume the duration of one hop is the same as the duration of 1 bit and we ignore phase differences between the data signal $s_d(t)$ and the spreading signal, also called a **chipping signal**, $c(t)$. Then the product signal during the ith hop (during the ith bit) is

$$p(t) = s_d(t)c(t) = A \cos (2\pi(f_0 + 0.5(b_i + 1)\Delta f)t) \cos (2\pi f_i t)$$

where f_i is the frequency of the signal generated by the frequency synthesizer during the ith hop. Using the trigonometric identity[2] $\cos (x) \cos (y) = (1/2)$ $(\cos (x + y) + \cos (x − y))$, we have

$$p(t) = 0.5A \,[\cos (2\pi(f_0 + 0.5(b_i + 1)\Delta f + f_i)t)$$
$$+ \cos (2\pi(f_0 + 0.5(b_i + 1)\Delta f − f_i)t)]$$

A bandpass filter (Figure 9.3) is used to block the difference frequency and pass the sum frequency, yielding an FHSS signal of

$$s(t) = 0.5A \cos (2\pi(f_0 + 0.5(b_i + 1)\Delta f + f_i)t) \qquad (9.2)$$

Thus, during the ith bit interval, the frequency of the data signal is $f_0 + f_i$ if the data bit is −1 and $f_0 + f_i + \Delta f$ if the data bit is +1.

At the receiver, a signal of the form $s(t)$ just defined will be received. This is multiplied by a replica of the spreading signal to yield a product signal of the form

$$p(t) = s(t)c(t) = 0.5A \cos (2\pi(f_0 + 0.5(b_i + 1)\Delta f + f_i)t) \cos (2\pi f_i t)$$

Again using the trigonometric identity, we have

$$p(t) = s(t)c(t) = 0.25A \,[\cos (2\pi(f_0 + 0.5(b_i + 1)\Delta f + f_i + f_i)t)$$
$$+ \cos (2\pi(f_0+0.5(b_i + 1)\Delta f)t)]$$

---

[2]See the math refresher document at computersciencestudent.com for a summary of trigonometric identities.

A bandpass filter (Figure 9.3) is used to block the sum frequency and pass the difference frequency, yielding a signal of the form of $s_d(t)$, defined in Equation (9.1):

$$0.25A \cos \left(2\pi(f_0 + 0.5(b_i + 1)\Delta f)t\right)$$

FHSS Using MFSK

A common modulation technique used in conjunction with FHSS is multiple FSK (MFSK). Recall from Chapter 7 that MFSK uses $M = 2^L$ different frequencies to encode the digital input L bits at a time. The transmitted signal is of the form [Equation (6.3)]:

$$s_i(t) = A \cos 2\pi f_i t, \qquad 1 \le i \le M$$

where

$f_i = f_c + (2i - 1 - M)f_d$
f_c = denotes the carrier frequency
f_d = denotes the difference frequency
M = number of different signal elements = 2^L
L = number of bits per signal element (symbol)

For FHSS, the MFSK signal is translated to a new frequency every T_c seconds by modulating the MFSK signal with the FHSS carrier signal. The effect is to translate the MFSK signal into the appropriate FHSS channel. For a data rate of R, L bits are transmitted per signal element (symbol). This means the symbol rate is $R_s = R/L$ and the symbol time is $T_s = 1/R_s$. Because each symbol transmits L bits, we can say each bit takes $T = T_s/L$ seconds. If T_c is greater than or equal to T_s, more than one symbol is transmitted at each hopping frequency and the spreading modulation is referred to as ***slow-frequency-hop spread spectrum*** (**slow FHSS**). In contrast, ***fast-frequency-hop spread spectrum*** (**fast FHSS**) switches faster than the symbol times and splits symbols across different hopping frequencies.[3] To summarize,

Slow-frequency-hop spread spectrum	$T_c \ge T_s$
Fast-frequency-hop spread spectrum	$T_c < T_s$

Example 9.1 A system transmits at 30 kbps, sending 3 bits per symbol. The time between hops for a FHSS system is 0.125 ms. Is the system using slow-frequency-hop spread spectrum or fast-frequency-hop spread spectrum?

$$R = 30 \text{ kbps} = 30 \times 10^3 \text{ bps}$$
$$R_s = R/L = 10 \times 10^3 \text{ symbols/sec}$$
$$T_s = 1/R_s = 0.1 \text{ ms/symbol}$$
$$T_c = 0.125 \text{ ms per frequency hop}$$
$$T_c < T_s$$

So, the system is using fast-frequency-hop spread spectrum.

---

[3]Some authors use a somewhat different definition (e.g., [PICK82]) of multiple hops per bit for fast frequency hop, multiple bits per hop for slow frequency hop, and one hop per bit if neither fast nor slow. The more common definition, which we use, relates hops to symbols rather than bits.

Figure 9.4 shows an example of slow FHSS, using the MFSK example from Figure 7.4. That is, $M = 4$, and the same sequence of input bits is used in both examples. The display in the figure shows the frequency transmitted (y-axis) as a function of time (x-axis). Each column represents a time unit T_s in which a single 2-bit signal element is transmitted. The shaded rectangle in the column indicates the frequency transmitted during that time unit. Each pair of columns corresponds to the selection of a frequency band based on a 2-bit PN sequence. Thus, for the first pair of columns, governed by PN sequence 00, the lowest band of frequencies is used. For the second pair of columns, governed by PN sequence 11, the highest band of frequencies is used.

Here we have $M = 4$, which means that four different frequencies are used to encode the data input 2 bits at a time. Each signal element is a discrete frequency tone, and the total MFSK bandwidth is $W_d = Mf_d$. We use an FHSS scheme with $C = 4$. That is, there are four different channels, each of width W_d. The total FHSS bandwidth is $W_s = CW_d$. Each 2 bits of a PN sequence can be used to select one of the four channels. That channel is held for a duration of two signal elements, or 4 bits ($T_c = 2T_s = 4T$) for slow frequency hopping.

Figure 9.5 shows an example of fast FHSS, using the same MFSK example. Again, $C = 4$. In this case, however, each signal element is carried by two frequency-hopping tones. Again, $W_d = Mf_d$ and $W_s = CW_d$. In this example, $T_c = T_s/2 = T$; each frequency is held for a duration of $\frac{1}{2}$ of a symbol. In general, fast FHSS provides improved performance compared to slow FHSS in the face of noise or jamming. For example, if three or more frequencies (chips) are used for each signal element, the receiver can decide which signal element was sent on the basis of a majority of the chips being correct.

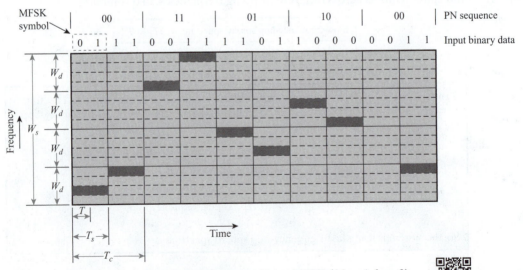

Figure 9.4 Slow Frequency Hop Spread Spectrum Using MFSK ($M = 4, k = 2$)

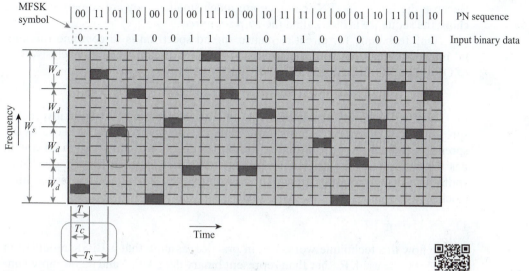

Figure 9.5 Fast Frequency Hop Spread Spectrum Using MFSK ($M = 4, k = 2$)

FHSS Performance Considerations

Typically, a large number of frequencies are used in FHSS so that W_s is much larger than W_d. One benefit of this is that a large value of k results in a system that is quite resistant to noise and jamming. For example, suppose we have an MFSK transmitter with bandwidth W_d and noise jammer of the same bandwidth and fixed power S_j on the signal carrier frequency. Then we have a ratio of signal energy per bit to jammer interference power density per Hertz of

$$\frac{E_b}{I_j} = \frac{E_b}{S_j/W_d} = \frac{E_b W_d}{S_j}$$

If frequency hopping is used, the jammer must jam all C frequencies. With a fixed power, this reduces the jamming power in any one frequency band to S_j/C. The gain in signal-to-noise ratio, or processing gain, is

$$G_P = C = \frac{W_s}{W_d} \tag{9.3}$$

9.3 DIRECT SEQUENCE SPREAD SPECTRUM

For **direct sequence spread spectrum (DSSS)**, each bit in the original signal is represented by multiple bits in the transmitted signal, using a spreading code. The spreading code spreads the signal across a wider frequency band in direct proportion to the number of bits used. Therefore, a 10-bit spreading code spreads the signal across a frequency band that is approximately 10 times greater than a 1-bit spreading code.

Because the bits in the PN sequence are much smaller, they are sometimes called **chips**; the sequence is then called the ***chip sequence***.

One technique for direct sequence spread spectrum is to combine the digital information stream with the spreading code bit stream using an exclusive-OR (XOR). The XOR obeys the following rules:

$$0 \oplus 0 = 0 \qquad 0 \oplus 1 = 1 \qquad 1 \oplus 0 = 1 \qquad 1 \oplus 1 = 0$$

Figure 9.6 shows an example. Note that an information bit of one inverts the spreading code bits in the combination, while an information bit of zero causes the spreading code bits to be transmitted without inversion. The combination bit stream has the data rate of the original spreading code sequence, so it has a wider bandwidth than the information stream. In this example, the spreading code bit stream is clocked at four times the information rate.

DSSS Using BPSK

To see how this technique works out in practice, assume that a BPSK modulation scheme is to be used. Rather than represent binary data with 1 and 0, it is more convenient for our purposes to use +1 and −1 to represent the two binary digits. In that case, a BPSK signal can be represented as was shown in Equation (7.5)

$$s_d(t) = A \, d(t) \cos (2\pi f_c t) \tag{9.4}$$

where

A = amplitude of signal

f_c = carrier frequency

$d(t)$ = the discrete function that takes on the value of +1 for one bit time if the corresponding bit in the bit stream is 1 and the value of −1 for one bit time if the corresponding bit in the bit stream is 0

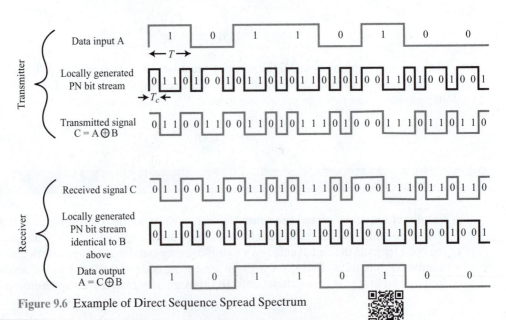

Figure 9.6 Example of Direct Sequence Spread Spectrum

To produce the DSSS signal, we multiply the preceding by $c(t)$, which is the PN sequence taking on values of $+1$ and -1:

$$s(t) = A\, d(t)c(t) \cos (2\pi f_c t) \qquad (9.5)$$

At the receiver, the incoming signal is multiplied again by $c(t)$. But $c(t) \times c(t) = 1$ and therefore the original signal is recovered:

$$s(t)c(t) = A\, d(t)c(t)c(t) \cos (2\pi f_c t) = s_d(t)$$

Equation (9.5) can be interpreted in two ways, leading to two different implementations. The first interpretation is to first multiply $d(t)$ and $c(t)$ together and then perform the BPSK modulation. That is the interpretation we have been discussing. Alternatively, we can first perform the BPSK modulation on the data stream $d(t)$ to generate the data signal $s_d(t)$. This signal can then be multiplied by $c(t)$.

An implementation using the second interpretation is shown in Figure 9.7. Figure 9.8 is an example of this approach.

DSSS Performance Considerations

The spectrum spreading achieved by the direct sequence technique is easily determined (Figure 9.9). In our example, the information signal has a bit width of T, which is equivalent to a data rate of $1/T$. In that case, the spectrum of the signal,

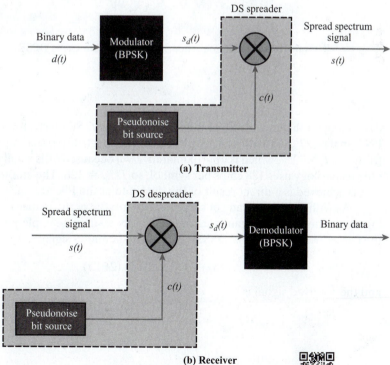

(a) Transmitter

(b) Receiver

Figure 9.7 Direct Sequence Spread Spectrum System

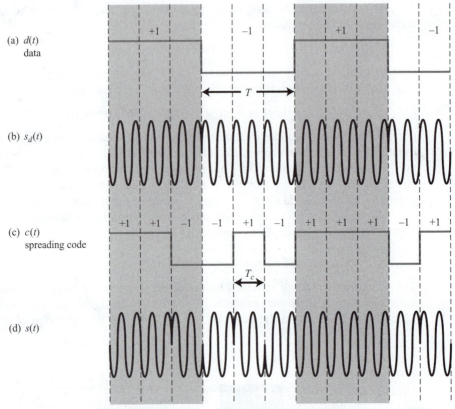

(a) $d(t)$
data

(b) $s_d(t)$

(c) $c(t)$
spreading code

(d) $s(t)$

Figure 9.8 Example of Direct Sequence Spread Spectrum Using BPSK

depending on the encoding technique, is roughly $2/T$. Similarly, the spectrum of the PN signal is $2/T_c$. Figure 9.9c shows the resulting spectrum spreading. The total spectrum is $2/T_c + 2/T$, which is approximately $2/T_c$, because $2/T$ is small in comparison. One technology uses 128 chips per symbol, so $T/T_c = 128$. The amount of spreading that is achieved is a direct result of the data rate of the PN stream.

As with FHSS, we can get some insight into the performance of DSSS by looking at its effectiveness against jamming. Let us assume a simple jamming signal at the center frequency of the DSSS system. The jamming signal has the form

$$s_j(t) = \sqrt{2S_j} \cos{(2\pi f_c t)}$$

and the received signal is

$$s_r(t) = s(t) + s_j(t) + n(t)$$

where

$s(t) =$ transmitted signal
$s_j(t) =$ jamming signal

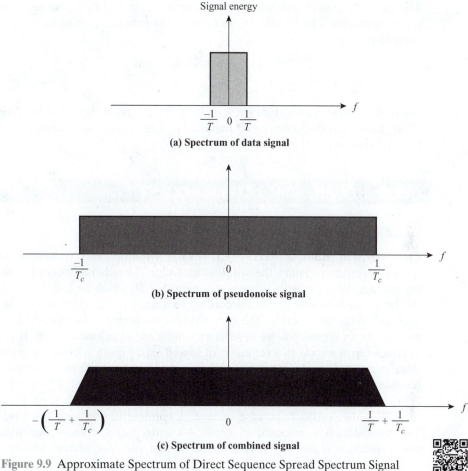

Figure 9.9 Approximate Spectrum of Direct Sequence Spread Spectrum Signal

$n(t)$ = additive white noise

S_j = jammer signal power

The despreader at the receiver multiplies $s_r(t)$ by $c(t)$, so the signal component due to the jamming signal is

$$y_j(t) = \sqrt{2S_j}\,c(t)\,\cos\,(2\pi f_c t)$$

This is simply a BPSK modulation of the carrier tone. Thus, the carrier power S_j is spread over a bandwidth of approximately $2/T_c$. However, the BPSK demodulator (Figure 9.7) following the DSSS despreader includes a bandpass filter matched to the BPSK data, with bandwidth of $2/T$. Thus, most of the jamming power is filtered. Although a number of factors come into play, as an approximation, we can say that the jamming power passed by the filter is

$$S_{jF} = S_j\,(2/T)/(2/T_c) = S_j\,(T_c/T)$$

The jamming power has been reduced by a factor of (T_c/T) through the use of spread spectrum. The inverse of this factor is the gain in signal-to-noise ratio for the transmitted signal:

$$G_P = \frac{T}{T_c} = \frac{R_c}{R} \approx \frac{W_s}{W_d} \tag{9.6}$$

where R_c is the spreading bit rate, R is the data rate, W_d is the signal bandwidth, and W_s is the spread spectrum signal bandwidth. The result is similar to the result for FHSS [Equation 9.3)].

9.4 CODE DIVISION MULTIPLE ACCESS

Basic Principles

Code Division Multiple Access (CDMA) is a multiplexing technique used with spread spectrum to share the wireless medium. The scheme works in the following manner. We start with a data signal with rate D, which we call the bit data rate. We break each bit into k chips according to a fixed pattern that is specific to each user, called the user's code. The new channel has a chip data rate of kD chips per second. As an illustration we consider a simple example[4] with $k = 6$. It is simplest to characterize a code as a sequence of 1s and -1s. Figure 9.10 shows the codes for three users, A, B, and C, each of which is communicating with the same base station receiver, R. Thus, the code for user A is $c_A = \,<1, -1, -1, 1, -1, 1>$. Similarly, user B has code $c_B = \,<1, 1, -1, -1, 1, 1>$, and user C has code $c_C = \,<1, 1, -1, 1, 1, -1>$.

We now consider the case of user A communicating with the base station. The base station is assumed to know A's code. For simplicity, we assume that communication is already synchronized so that the base station knows when to look for codes. If A wants to send a 1 bit, A transmits its code as a chip pattern $<1, -1, -1, 1, -1, 1>$. If a 0 bit is to be sent, A transmits the complement (1s and -1s reversed) of its code, $<-1, 1, 1, -1, 1, -1>$. At the base station, the receiver decodes the chip patterns. In our simple version, if the receiver R receives a chip pattern $d = \,<d1, d2, d3, d4, d5, d6>$, and the receiver is seeking to communicate with a user u so that it has at hand u's code, $<c1, c2, c3, c4, c5, c6>$, the receiver performs electronically the following decoding function:

$$S_u(d) = (d1 \times c1) + (d2 \times c2) + (d3 \times c3) + (d4 \times c4)$$
$$+ (d5 \times c5) + (d6 \times c6)$$

The subscript u on S simply indicates that u is the user that we are interested in. Let's suppose the user u is actually A and see what happens. If A sends a 1 bit, then d is $<1, -1, -1, 1, -1, 1>$ and the preceding computation using S_A becomes

$$S_A(1, -1, -1, 1, -1, 1) = [1 \times 1] + [(-1) \times (-1)] + [(-1) \times (-1)]$$
$$+ [1 \times 1] + [(-1) \times (-1)] + [1 \times 1] = 6$$

---

[4]This example was provided by Prof. Richard Van Slyke of the Polytechnic University of Brooklyn.

Code

Message "1101" Encoded

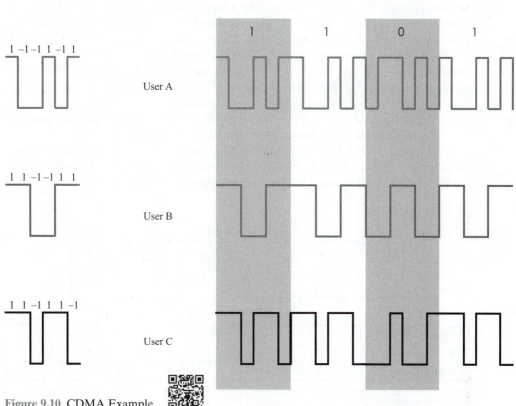

1 −1 −1 1 −1 1

User A

1 1 −1 −1 1 1

User B

1 1 −1 1 1 −1

User C

Figure 9.10 CDMA Example

If A sends a 0 bit that corresponds to $d = <-1, 1, 1, -1, 1, -1>$, we get

$$S_A(-1, 1, 1, -1, 1, -1) = [-1 \times 1] + [1 \times (-1)] + [1 \times (-1)]$$
$$+ [(-1) \times 1] + [1 \times (-1)] + [(-1) \times 1] = -6$$

Please note that it is always the case that $-6 \leq S_A(d) \leq 6$ no matter what sequence of -1s and 1s comprise d, and that the only values of d resulting in the extreme values of 6 and -6 are A's code and its complement, respectively. So if S_A produces a $+6$, we say that we have received a 1 bit from A; if S_A produces a -6, we say that we have received a 0 bit from user A; otherwise, we assume that someone else is sending information or there is an error. So why go through all this? The reason becomes clear if we see what happens if user B is sending and we try to receive it with S_A, that is, we are decoding with the wrong code, A's. If B sends a 1 bit, then $d = <1, 1, -1, -1, 1, 1>$. Then,

$$S_A(1, 1, -1, -1, 1, 1) = [1 \times 1] + [1 \times (-1)] + [(-1) \times (-1)] + [(-1) \times 1]$$
$$+ [1 \times (-1)] + [1 \times 1] = 0$$

Thus, the unwanted signal (from B) does not show up at all. You can easily verify that if B had sent a 0 bit, the decoder would produce a value of 0 for S_A again. This means that if the decoder is linear and if A and B transmit signals s_A and s_B, respectively, at the same time, then $S_A(s_A + s_B) = S_A(s_A) + S_A(s_B) = S_A(s_A)$ because the decoder ignores B when it is using A's code. The codes of A and B that have the property that $S_A(c_B) = S_B(c_A) = 0$ are called **orthogonal**. Such codes are very nice to have but there are not all that many of them. More common is the case when $S_X(c_Y)$ is small in absolute value when $X \neq Y$. Then it is easy to distinguish between the two cases when $X = Y$ and when $X \neq Y$. In our example $S_A(c_C) = S_C(c_A) = 0$, but $S_B(c_C) = S_C(c_B) = 2$. In the latter case the C signal would make a small contribution to the decoded signal instead of 0. Using the decoder, S_u, the receiver can sort out transmission from u even when there may be other users broadcasting in the same cell.

Table 9.1 summarizes the example from the preceding discussion.

In practice, the CDMA receiver can filter out the contribution from unwanted users or they appear as low-level noise. However, if there are many users competing for the channel with the user the receiver is trying to listen to, or if the signal power

Table 9.1 CDMA Example

(a) User's codes

User A	1	−1	−1	1	−1	1
User B	1	1	−1	−1	1	1
User C	1	1	−1	1	1	−1

(b) Transmission from A

Transmit (data bit = 1)	1	−1	−1	1	−1	1	
Receiver codeword	1	−1	−1	1	−1	1	
Multiplication	1	1	1	1	1	1	= 6

Transmit (data bit = 0)	−1	1	1	−1	1	−1	
Receiver codeword	1	−1	−1	1	−1	1	
Multiplication	−1	−1	−1	−1	−1	−1	= −6

(c) Transmission from B, receiver attempts to recover A's transmission

Transmit (data bit = 1)	1	1	−1	−1	1	1	
Receiver codeword	1	−1	−1	1	−1	1	
Multiplication	1	−1	1	−1	−1	1	= 0

(d) Transmission from C, receiver attempts to recover B's transmission

Transmit (data bit = 1)	1	1	−1	1	1	−1	
Receiver codeword	1	1	−1	−1	1	1	
Multiplication	1	1	1	−1	1	−1	= 2

(e) Transmission from B and C, receiver attempts to recover B's transmission

B (data bit = 1)	1	1	−1	−1	1	1	
C (data bit = 1)	1	1	−1	1	1	−1	
Combined signal	2	2	−2	0	2	0	
Receiver codeword	1	1	−1	−1	1	1	
Multiplication	2	2	2	0	2	0	= 8

of one or more competing signals is too high, perhaps because it is very near the receiver (the "near/far" problem), the system breaks down.

The limit on the number of users in the system is derived from this understanding. A common measurement for a CDMA system is the **rise-over-thermal**, which compares the total contribution of this noise from the users in the system to the background thermal noise of the environment. One system uses 7 dB rise-over-thermal as a key performance metric to limit additional users.

CDMA for Direct Sequence Spread Spectrum

Let us now look at CDMA from the viewpoint of a DSSS system using BPSK. Figure 9.11 depicts a configuration in which there are n users, each transmitting using a different, orthogonal, PN sequence (compare Figure 9.7). For each user, the data stream to be transmitted, $d_i(t)$, is BPSK modulated to produce a signal with a bandwidth of W_s and then multiplied by the spreading code for that user, $c_i(t)$. All of the signals, plus noise, are received at the receiver's antenna. Suppose that the receiver is attempting to recover the data of user 1. The incoming signal is multiplied by the spreading code of user 1 and then demodulated. The effect of this is to narrow the bandwidth of that portion of the incoming signal corresponding to user 1 to the original bandwidth of the unspread signal, which is proportional to the data rate. Incoming signals from other users are not despread by the spreading code from user 1 and hence retain their bandwidth of W_s. Thus, the unwanted signal energy remains spread over a large bandwidth and the wanted signal is concentrated in a narrow bandwidth. The bandpass filter at the demodulator can therefore recover the desired signal.

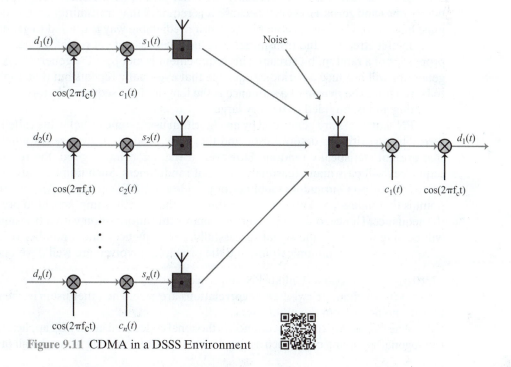

Figure 9.11 CDMA in a DSSS Environment

Generation of Spreading Sequences

As was mentioned, the spreading sequence, $c(t)$, is a sequence of binary digits shared by transmitter and receiver. Spreading consists of multiplying (XOR) the input data by the spreading sequence, where the bit rate of the spreading sequence is higher than that of the input data. When the signal is received, the spreading is removed by multiplying with the same spreading code, exactly synchronized with the received signal.

The resulting data rate is consequently that of the spreading sequence. This increases the transmitted data rate and therefore increases the required bandwidth. The redundancy of the system is also increased. The spreading codes are chosen so that the resulting signal is noise like; therefore, there should be an approximately equal number of ones and zeros in the spreading code and few or no repeated patterns. When spreading codes are used in a CDMA application, there is further requirement of lack of **correlation**. When multiple signals are received, each spread with a different spreading code, the receiver should be able to pick out any individual signal using that signal's spreading code. The spread signals should behave as if they were uncorrelated with each other, so that other signals will appear as noise and not interfere with the despreading of a particular signal. Because of the high degree of redundancy provided by the spreading operation, the despreading operation is able to cope with the interference of other signals in the same bandwidth.

Two general categories of spreading sequences have been used: PN sequences and orthogonal codes. PN sequences are the most common ones used in FHSS systems and in DSSS systems not employing CDMA. In DSSS CDMA systems, both PN and orthogonal codes have been used. We examine each of these approaches in turn.

PN Sequences An ideal spreading sequence would be a random sequence of binary ones and zeros. However, because it is required that transmitter and receiver must have a copy of the random bit stream, a predictable way is needed to generate the same bit stream at the transmitter and the receiver and yet retain the desirable properties of a random bit stream. This requirement is met by a PN generator. A PN generator will produce a periodic sequence that eventually repeats but that appears to be random. The *period* of a sequence is the length of the sequence before it starts repeating and is intended to be very large.

PN sequences are generated by an algorithm using some initial value called the *seed*. The algorithm is deterministic and therefore produces sequences of numbers that are not statistically random. However, if the algorithm is good, the resulting sequences will pass many reasonable tests of randomness. Such numbers are often referred to as **pseudorandom numbers**, or **pseudonoise PN sequences**. An important point is that unless you know the algorithm and the seed, it is impractical to predict the sequence. Hence, only a receiver that shares this information with a transmitter will be able to decode the signal successfully. PN sequences find a number of uses in computers and communications, and the principles involved are well developed.

Orthogonal Codes Unlike PN sequences, an orthogonal code is a set of sequences in which all pairwise **cross correlations** are zero. The other users in the system see no noise from the other users.

Walsh codes are the most common orthogonal codes used in CDMA applications. Orthogonal spreading codes such as the Walsh sequences can only be used if all of the users in the same CDMA channel are synchronized to the accuracy of a small fraction of one chip. Because the cross correlation between different shifts of Walsh sequences is not zero, if tight synchronization is not provided, PN sequences are needed.

Multiple Spreading When sufficient bandwidth is available, a multiple spreading technique can prove highly effective. A typical approach is to spread the data rate by an orthogonal code to provide mutual orthogonality among all users in the same cell and to further spread the result by a PN sequence to provide mutual randomness (low cross correlation) between users in different cells. In such a two-stage spreading, the orthogonal codes are referred to as ***channelization codes***, and the PN codes are referred to as ***scrambling codes***.

RAKE Receiver

In a multipath environment, which is common in wireless systems, if the multiple versions of a signal arrive more than one chip interval apart from each other, the receiver can recover the signal by correlating the chip sequence with the dominant incoming signal. The remaining signals are treated as noise. However, even better performance can be achieved if the receiver attempts to recover the signals from multiple paths and then combine them, with suitable delay adjustments. This principle is used in the RAKE receiver.

Figure 9.12 illustrates the principle of the RAKE receiver. The original binary signal to be transmitted is spread by the exclusive-OR (XOR) operation with the

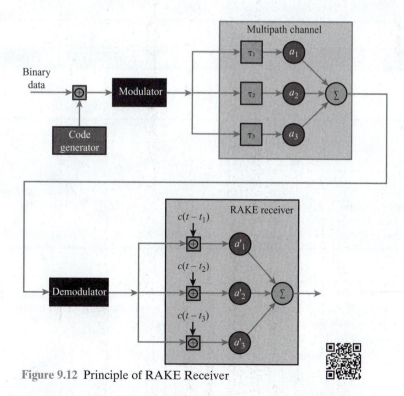

Figure 9.12 Principle of RAKE Receiver

transmitter's chipping code. The spread sequence is then modulated for transmission over the wireless channel. Because of multipath effects, the channel generates multiple copies of the signal, each with a different amount of time delay (τ_1, τ_2, etc.), and each with a different attenuation factors (a_1, a_2, etc.). At the receiver, the combined signal is demodulated. The demodulated chip stream is then fed into multiple correlators, each delayed by a different amount. These signals are then combined using weighting factors estimated from the channel.

9.5 RECOMMENDED READING

Both [PETE95] and [DIXO94] provide comprehensive treatment of spread spectrum. [TANT98] contains reprints of many important papers in the field, including [PICK82], which provides an excellent introduction to spread spectrum.

DIXO94 Dixon, R. *Spread Spectrum Systems with Commercial Applications.* New York: Wiley, 1994.

PETE95 Peterson, R.; Ziemer, R.; and Borth, D. *Introduction to Spread Spectrum Communications.* Englewood Cliffs, NJ: Prentice Hall, 1995.

PICK82 Pickholtz, R.; Schilling, D.; and Milstein, L. "Theory of Spread Spectrum Communications—A Tutorial." *IEEE Transactions on Communications*, May 1982. Reprinted in [TANT98].

TANT98 Tantaratana, S, and Ahmed, K., eds. *Wireless Applications of Spread Spectrum Systems: Selected Readings.* Piscataway, NJ: IEEE Press, 1998.

9.6 KEY TERMS, REVIEW QUESTIONS, AND PROBLEMS

Key Terms

chips	fast FHSS	rise-over-thermal
chipping signal	frequency hopping spread	slow FHSS
code division multiple access	spectrum (FHSS)	spread spectrum
(CDMA)	orthogonal	spreading code
correlation	pseudonoise (PN)	spreading sequence
cross correlation	pseudonoise (PN)	
direct sequence spread	sequence	
spectrum (DSSS)	pseudorandom numbers	

Review Questions

9.1 What is the relationship between the bandwidth of a signal before and after it has been encoded using spread spectrum?

9.2 List three benefits of spread spectrum.

9.3 What is frequency hopping spread spectrum?

9.4 Explain the difference between slow FHSS and fast FHSS.

9.5 What is direct sequence spread spectrum?

9.6 What is the relationship between the bit rate of a signal before and after it has been encoded using DSSS?

9.7 What is CDMA?

Problems

9.1 Assume we wish to transmit a 56-kbps data stream using spread spectrum.
   a. Find the channel bandwidth required to achieve a 56-kbps channel capacity when SNR = 0.1, 0.01, and 0.001.
   b. In an ordinary (not spread spectrum) system, a reasonable goal for bandwidth efficiency might be 1 bps/Hz. That is, to transmit a data stream of 56 kbps, a bandwidth of 56 kHz is used. In this case, what is the minimum SNR that can be endured for transmission without appreciable errors? Compare to the spread spectrum case.
   Hint: Review the discussion of channel capacity in Section 2.3.

9.2 An FHSS system employs a total bandwidth of $W_s = 400$ MHz and an individual channel bandwidth of 100 Hz. What is the minimum number of PN bits required for each frequency hop?

9.3 An FHSS system using MFSK with $M = 4$ employs 1000 different frequencies. What is the processing gain?

9.4 The following table illustrates the operation of an FHSS system for one complete period of the PN sequence.

Time	0	1	2	3	4	5	6	7	8	9	10	11
Input data	0	1	1	1	1	1	1	0	0	0	1	0
Frequency	f_1		f_3		f_{23}		f_{22}		f_8		f_{10}	
PN sequence	001				110				011			

Time	12	13	14	15	16	17	18	19
Input data	0	1	1	1	1	0	1	0
Frequency	f_1		f_3		f_2		f_2	
PN sequence	001				001			

   a. The system makes use of a form of FSK. What form of FSK is it?
   b. What is the number of bits per signal element (symbol)?
   c. What is the number of FSK frequencies?
   d. What is the length of a PN sequence per hop?
   e. Is this a slow or fast FH system?
   f. What is the total number of possible carrier frequencies?
   g. Show the variation of the base, or demodulated, frequency with time.

9.5 The following table illustrates the operation of an FHSS system using the same PN sequence as Problem 9.4.

Time	0	1	2	3	4	5	6	7	8	9	10	11
Input data	0	1	1	1	1	1	1	0	0	0	1	0
Frequency	f_1	f_{21}	f_{11}	f_3	f_3	f_3	f_{22}	f_{10}	f_0	f_0	f_2	f_{22}
PN sequence	001	110	011	001	001	001	110	011	001	001	001	110

Time	12	13	14	15	16	17	18	19
Input data	0	1	1	1	1	0	1	0
Frequency	f_9	f_1	f_3	f_3	f_{22}	f_{10}	f_2	f_2
PN sequence	011	001	001	001	110	011	001	001

a. The system makes use of a form of FSK. What form of FSK is it?
b. What is the number of bits per signal element (symbol)?
c. What is the number of FSK frequencies?
d. What is the length of a PN sequence per hop?
e. Is this a slow or fast FH system?
f. What is the total number of possible carrier frequencies?
g. Show the variation of the base, or demodulated, frequency with time.

9.6 Consider an MFSK scheme with $f_c = 250$ kHz, $f_d = 25$ kHz, and $M = 8$ ($L = 3$ bits)
a. Make a frequency assignment for each of the 8 possible 3-bit data combinations.
b. We wish to apply FHSS to this MFSK scheme with $k = 2$; that is, the system will hop among four different carrier frequencies. Expand the results of part (a) to show the $4 \times 8 = 32$ frequency assignments. Example from Chapter 7

CHAPTER 10

CODING AND ERROR CONTROL

273

LEARNING OBJECTIVES

After studying this chapter, you should be able to:

- Describe and compare error recovery processes for error detection, retransmission/ARQ, and error correction.
- Create and decode cyclic block codes.
- Create and decode convolutional codes.
- Describe the capabilities and bandwidth efficiency of codes in terms of their coding rate, Hamming distance, and coding gain.
- Describe the operation of LDPC and turbo codes.
- Explain the operation of H-ARQ and the options for how it could be implemented.

In earlier chapters, we talked about transmission impairments and the effect of data rate and signal-to-noise ratio on bit error rate. Regardless of the design of the transmission system, there will be errors, resulting in the change of one or more bits in a transmitted frame.

Three approaches are in common use for coping with data transmission errors:

- Error detection codes
- Error correction codes, also called forward error correction (FEC) codes
- Automatic repeat request (ARQ) protocols

An error detection code simply detects the presence of an error. Typically, such codes are used in conjunction with a protocol at the data link or transport level that uses an ARQ scheme. With an ARQ scheme, a receiver discards a block of data in which an error is detected and the transmitter retransmits that block of data. FEC codes are designed not just to detect but correct errors, avoiding the need for retransmission. FEC schemes are frequently used in wireless transmission, where retransmission schemes are highly inefficient and error rates may be high. Some wireless protocols use Hybrid ARQ, which is a combination of FEC and ARQ.

This chapter looks at all three approaches in turn.

10.1 ERROR DETECTION

In what follows, we assume that data are transmitted as one or more contiguous sequences of bits, called *frames*. Let us define these probabilities with respect to errors in transmitted frames:

P_b: Probability of a single-bit error; also known as the bit error rate (BER)

P_1: Probability that a frame arrives with no bit errors

P_2: Probability that, with an error detection algorithm in use, a frame arrives with one or more undetected errors

P_3: Probability that, with an error detection algorithm in use, a frame arrives with one or more detected bit errors but no undetected bit errors

First consider the case when no means are taken to detect errors. Then the probability of detected errors (P_3) is zero. To express the remaining probabilities, assume the probability that any bit is in error (P_b) is constant and independent for each bit. Then we have,

$$P_1 = (1 - P_b)^F$$

$$P_2 = 1 - P_1$$

where F is the number of bits per frame. In words, the probability that a frame arrives with no bit errors decreases when the probability of a single-bit error increases, as you would expect. Also, the probability that a frame arrives with no bit errors decreases with increasing frame length; the longer the frame, the more bits it has and the higher the probability that one of these is in error.

> **Example 10.1**   A system has a defined objective for connections that the BER should be less than 10^{-6} on at least 90% of observed 1-minute intervals. Suppose now that we have the rather modest user requirement that on average one frame with an undetected bit error should occur per day on a continuously used 1 Mbps channel, and let us assume a frame length of 1000 bits. The number of frames that can be transmitted in a day comes out to 8.64×10^7, which yields a required frame error rate of $P_2 = 1/(8.64 \times 10^7) = 1.16 \times 10^{-8}$. But if we assume a value of P_b of 10^{-6}, then $P_1 = (0.999999)^{1000} = 0.999$ and therefore $P_2 = 10^{-3}$, which is about five orders of magnitude too large to meet our requirement. This means that $(8.64 \times 10^7)*P_2 = 86{,}400$ frames with undetected bit errors would occur per day for P_b of 10^{-6}.

This is the kind of result that motivates the use of **error detection** techniques. All of these techniques operate on the following principle (Figure 10.1). For a given frame of bits, the transmitter adds additional bits that constitute an **error detection code**. This code is calculated as a function of the other transmitted bits. Typically, for a data block of k bits, the error detection algorithm yields an error detection code of $n - k$ bits, where $(n - k) < k$. The error detection code, also referred to as the **check bits**, is appended to the data block to produce a frame of n bits, which is then transmitted. The receiver separates the incoming frame into the k bits of data and $(n - k)$ bits of the error detection code. The receiver performs the same error detection calculation on the data bits and compares this value with the value of the incoming error detection code. A detected error occurs if and only if there is a mismatch. Thus, P_3 is the probability that a frame contains errors and that the error detection scheme will detect that fact. P_2 is known as the *residual error rate* and is the probability that an error will be undetected despite the use of an error detection scheme.

Parity Check

The simplest error detection scheme is to append a **parity bit** to the end of a block of data. A typical example is character transmission, in which a parity bit is attached to each 7-bit character. The value of this bit is selected so that the character has an even number of 1s (even parity) or an odd number of 1s (odd parity).

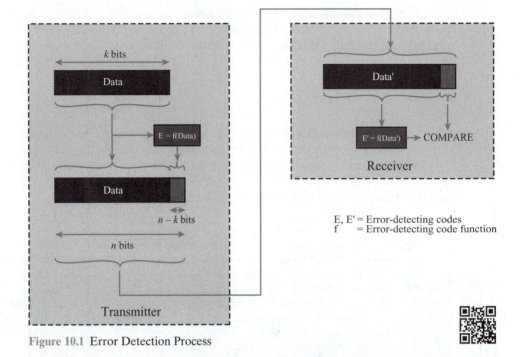

Figure 10.1 Error Detection Process

Example 10.2 If the transmitter is transmitting 1110001 and using odd parity, it will append a 1 and transmit 11110001. The receiver examines the received character to conduct a **parity check** and, if the total number of 1s is odd, assumes that no error has occurred. If one bit (or any odd number of bits) is erroneously inverted during transmission (e.g., 11100001), then the receiver will detect an error.

Note, however, that if two (or any even number) of bits are inverted due to error, an undetected error occurs. Typically, even parity is used for synchronous transmission and odd parity for asynchronous transmission.

The use of the parity bit is not foolproof, as noise impulses are often long enough to destroy more than one bit, especially at high data rates.

Cyclic Redundancy Check

One of the most common, and one of the most powerful, error-detecting codes is the **cyclic redundancy check (CRC)**, which can be described as follows. Given a k-bit block of bits, or message, the transmitter generates an $(n - k)$-bit sequence, known as a **frame check sequence (FCS)**, such that the resulting frame, consisting of n bits, is exactly divisible by some predetermined number. The receiver then divides the incoming frame by that number and, if there is no remainder, assumes there was no error.[1]

---

[1]This procedure is slightly different from that in Figure 10.1. As shall be seen, the CRC process could be implemented as follows. The receiver could perform a division operation on the incoming k data bits and compare the result to the incoming $(n - k)$ check bits.

To clarify this, we present the procedure in three ways: modulo 2 arithmetic, polynomials, and digital logic.

Modulo 2 Arithmetic Modulo 2 arithmetic uses binary addition with no carries, which is just the exclusive-OR (XOR) operation. Binary subtraction with no carries is also interpreted as the XOR operation: For example:

$$
\begin{array}{ccc}
\begin{array}{r} 1111 \\ +1010 \\ \hline 0101 \end{array} &
\begin{array}{r} 1111 \\ -0101 \\ \hline 1010 \end{array} &
\begin{array}{r} 11001 \\ \times\, 11 \\ \hline 11001 \\ 11001 \\ \hline 101011 \end{array}
\end{array}
$$

Now define:

$T = n$-bit frame to be transmitted
$D = k$-bit block of data, or message, the first k bits of T
$F = (n - k)$-bit FCS, the last $(n - k)$ bits of T
$P = $ pattern of $n - k + 1$ bits; this is the predetermined divisor

We would like T/P to have no remainder. It should be clear that

$$T = 2^{n-k}D + F$$

That is, by multiplying D by 2^{n-k}, we have in effect shifted it to the left by $n - k$ bits and padded out the result with zeroes. Adding F yields the concatenation of D and F, which is T. We want T to be exactly divisible by P. Suppose that we divide $2^{n-k}D$ by P,

$$\frac{2^{n-k}D}{P} = Q + \frac{R}{P} \tag{10.1}$$

There is a quotient and a remainder. Because division is modulo 2, the remainder is always at least one bit shorter than the divisor. We will use this remainder as our FCS. Then,

$$T = 2^{n-k}D + R \tag{10.2}$$

Does this R satisfy our condition that T/P have no remainder? To see that it does, consider

$$\frac{T}{P} = \frac{2^{n-k}D + R}{P} = \frac{2^{n-k}D}{P} + \frac{R}{P}$$

Substituting Equation (10.1), we have

$$\frac{T}{P} = Q + \frac{R}{P} + \frac{R}{P}$$

However, any binary number added to itself modulo 2 yields zero. Thus,

$$\frac{T}{P} = Q + \frac{R + R}{P} = Q$$

There is no remainder, and therefore T is exactly divisible by P. Thus, the FCS is easily generated: Simply divide $2^{n-k}D$ by P and use the $(n - k)$-bit remainder as the FCS. On reception, the receiver will divide T by P and will get no remainder if there have been no errors.

Example 10.3

1. Given

$$\text{Message } D = 1010001101 \text{ (10 bits)}$$

$$\text{Pattern } P = 110101 \text{ (6 bits)}$$

$$\text{FCS } R = \text{to be calculated (5 bits)}$$

Thus, $n = 15$, $k = 10$, and $(n - k) = 5$.

2. The message is multiplied by 2^5, yielding 101000110100000.

3. This product is divided by P:

```
                              1 1 0 1 0 1 0 1 1 0  ← Q
      P → 1 1 0 1 0 1 / 1 0 1 0 0 0 1 1 0 1 0 0 0 0 0  ← 2^(n-k)D
                       1 1 0 1 0 1
                       1 1 1 0 1 1
                       1 1 0 1 0 1
                         1 1 1 0 1 0
                         1 1 0 1 0 1
                           1 1 1 1 1 0
                           1 1 0 1 0 1
                             1 0 1 1 0 0
                             1 1 0 1 0 1
                               1 1 0 0 1 0
                               1 1 0 1 0 1
                                 0 1 1 1 0  ← R
```

4. The remainder is added to 2^5D to give $T = 101000110101110$, which is transmitted.

5. If there are no errors, the receiver receives T intact. The received frame is divided by P:

```
                              1 1 0 1 0 1 0 1 1 0  ← Q
      P → 1 1 0 1 0 1 / 1 0 1 0 0 0 1 1 0 1 0 1 1 1 0  ← T
                       1 1 0 1 0 1
                       1 1 1 0 1 1
                       1 1 0 1 0 1
                         1 1 1 0 1 0
                         1 1 0 1 0 1
                           1 1 1 1 1 0
                           1 1 0 1 0 1
                             1 0 1 1 1 1
                             1 1 0 1 0 1
                               1 1 0 1 0 1
                               1 1 0 1 0 1
                                       0  ← R
```

Because there is no remainder, it is assumed that there have been no errors.

The pattern P is chosen to be one bit longer than the desired FCS, and the exact bit pattern chosen depends on the type of errors expected. At minimum, both the high- and low-order bits of P must be 1.

There is a concise method for specifying the occurrence of one or more errors. An error results in the reversal of a bit. This is equivalent to taking the XOR of the bit and 1 (modulo 2 addition of 1 to the bit): $0 + 1 = 1; 1 + 1 = 0$. Thus, the errors in an n-bit frame can be represented by an n-bit field with 1s in each error position. The resulting frame T_r can be expressed as

$$T_r = T \oplus E$$

where

T = transmitted frame
E = error pattern with 1s in positions where errors occur
T_r = received frame

If there is an error ($E \neq 0$), the receiver will fail to detect the error if and only if T_r is divisible by P, which is equivalent to E divisible by P. Intuitively, this seems an unlikely occurrence.

Polynomials A second way of viewing the CRC process is to express all values as polynomials in a dummy variable X, with binary coefficients. The coefficients correspond to the bits in the binary number. Arithmetic operations are again modulo 2. The CRC process can now be described as

$$\frac{X^{n-k}D(X)}{P(X)} = Q(X) + \frac{R(X)}{P(X)}$$

$$T(X) = X^{n-k}D(X) + R(X)$$

Compare these equations with Equations (10.1) and (10.2).

Example 10.4 Continuing with Example 10.3, for $D = 1010001101$, we have $D(X) = X^9 + X^7 + X^3 + X^2 + 1$, and for $P = 110101$, we have $P(X) = X^5 + X^4 + X^2 + 1$. We should end up with $R = 01110$, which corresponds to $R(X) = X^3 + X^2 + X$. Figure 10.2 shows the polynomial division that corresponds to the binary division in the preceding example.

$$
\begin{array}{r}
X^9 + X^8 + X^6 + X^4 + X^2 + X \qquad \leftarrow Q(X) \\
\hline
P(X) \rightarrow X^5 + X^4 + X^2 + 1\ \overline{)\ X^{14} \quad\quad X^{12} \qquad\qquad X^8 + X^7 + \quad X^5 \quad \leftarrow X^5D(X)} \\
X^{14}+X^{13}+\quad X^{11}+\quad X^9 \\
\hline
X^{13}+X^{12}+X^{11}+\quad X^9 + X^8 \\
X^{13}+X^{12}+\quad X^{10}+\quad X^8 \\
\hline
X^{11}+X^{10}+X^9+\quad X^7 \\
X^{11}+X^{10}+\quad X^8+\quad X^6 \\
\hline
X^9 + X^8 + X^7 + X^6 + X^5 \\
X^9 + X^8 +\quad X^6+\quad X^4 \\
\hline
X^7+\quad X^5+X^4 \\
X^7 + X^6 +\quad X^4 +\quad X^2 \\
\hline
X^6 + X^5 +\quad X^2 \\
X^6 + X^5 +\quad X^3 +\quad X \\
\hline
X^3 + X^2 + X \quad \leftarrow R(X)
\end{array}
$$

 **Figure 10.2** Polynomial Division for Example 5.10

An error $E(X)$ will only be undetectable if it is divisible by $P(X)$. It can be shown [PETE61, RAMA88] that all of the following errors are not divisible by a suitably chosen $P(X)$ and hence are detectable:

- All single-bit errors, if $P(X)$ has more than one nonzero term
- All double-bit errors, as long as $P(X)$ has a factor with at least three terms
- Any odd number of errors, as long as $P(X)$ contains a factor $(X + 1)$
- Any burst error[2] for which the length of the burst is less than or equal to $n - k$; that is, less than or equal to the length of the FCS
- A fraction of error bursts of length $n - k + 1$; the fraction equals $1 - 2^{-(n-k-1)}$
- A fraction of error bursts of length greater than $n - k + 1$; the fraction equals $1 - 2^{-(n-k)}$

In addition, it can be shown that if all error patterns are considered equally likely, then for a burst error of length $r + 1$, the probability of an undetected error [i.e., $E(X)$ is divisible by $P(X)$] is $1/2^{r-1}$, and for a longer burst, the probability is $1/2^r$, where r is the length of the FCS. This means there are 2^r possible error patterns, and only one of those patterns will go undetected.

Four versions of $P(X)$ have been widely used:

$$\text{CRC} - 12 = X^{12} + X^{11} + X^3 + X^2 + X + 1 = (X + 1)(X^{11} + X^2 + 1)$$

$$\text{CRC} - 16 = X^{16} + X^{15} + X^2 + 1 = (X + 1)(X^{15} + X + 1)$$

$$\text{CRC} - \text{CCITT} = X^{16} + X^{12} + X^5 + 1 = (X + 1)(X^{15} + X^{14} + X^{13} + X^{12}$$

$$+ X^4 + X^3 + X^2 + X + 1)$$

$$\text{CRC} - 32 = X^{32} + X^{26} + X^{23} + X^{22} + X^{16} + X^{12} + X^{11}$$

$$+ X^{10} + X^8 + X^7 + X^5 + X^4 + X^2 + X + 1$$

The CRC-12 system is used for transmission of streams of 6-bit characters and generates a 12-bit FCS. Both CRC-16 and CRC-CCITT are popular for 8-bit characters in the United States and Europe, respectively, and both result in a 16-bit FCS. This would seem adequate for most applications, although CRC-32 is specified as an option in some point-to-point synchronous transmission standards.

Digital Logic The CRC process can be represented by, and indeed implemented as, a dividing circuit consisting of XOR gates and a shift register. The shift register is a string of 1-bit storage devices. Each device has an output line, which indicates the value currently stored, and an input line. At discrete time instants, known as clock times, the value in the storage device is replaced by the value indicated by its input line. The entire register is clocked simultaneously, causing a 1-bit shift along the entire register.

The circuit is implemented as follows:

1. The register contains $n - k$ bits, equal to the length of the FCS.
2. There are up to $n - k$ XOR gates.

---

[2] A burst error of length B is a contiguous sequence of B bits in which the first and last bits and any number of intermediate bits are received in error.

3. The presence or absence of a gate corresponds to the presence or absence of a term in the divisor polynomial, $P(X)$, excluding the terms 1 and X^{n-k}.

Example 10.5 The architecture of this circuit is best explained by first considering an example, which is illustrated in Figure 10.3. In this example, we use

$$\text{Data } D = 1010001101; \quad D(X) = X^9 + X^7 + X^3 + X^2 + 1$$
$$\text{Divisor } P = 110101; \quad\quad P(X) = X^5 + X^4 + X^2 + 1$$

which were used in Examples (10.3) and (10.4).

Figure 10.3a shows the shift register implementation. The process begins with the shift register cleared (all zeros). The message, or dividend, is then entered, one bit at a time, starting with the most significant bit. Figure 10.3b is a table that shows the step-by-step operation as the input is applied one bit at a time. Each row of the table shows the values currently stored in the five shift-register elements. In addition, the row shows the values that appear at the outputs of the three XOR circuits. Finally, the row shows the value of the next input bit, which is available for the operation of the next step.

Note that the XOR operation affects C_4, C_2, and C_0 on the next shift. This is identical to the binary long division process illustrated earlier. The process continues through all the bits of the message. To produce the proper output, two switches are used. The

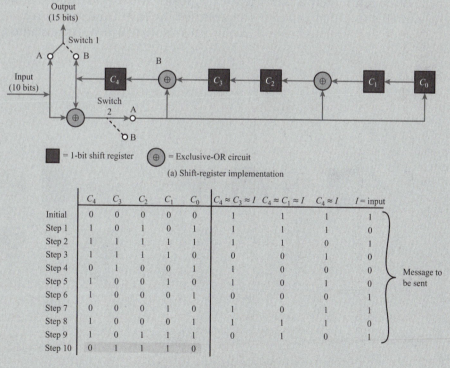

(a) Shift-register implementation

	C_4	C_3	C_2	C_1	C_0	$C_4 \oplus C_3 \approx I$	$C_4 \oplus C_1 \approx I$	$C_4 \approx I$	I = input	
Initial	0	0	0	0	0	1	1	1	1	
Step 1	1	0	1	0	1	1	1	1	0	
Step 2	1	1	1	1	1	1	1	0	1	
Step 3	1	1	1	1	0	0	0	1	0	
Step 4	0	1	0	0	1	1	0	0	0	Message to
Step 5	1	0	0	1	0	1	0	1	0	be sent
Step 6	1	0	0	0	1	0	0	0	1	
Step 7	0	0	0	1	0	1	0	1	1	
Step 8	1	0	0	0	1	1	1	1	0	
Step 9	1	0	1	1	1	0	1	0	1	
Step 10	0	1	1	1	0					

(b) Example with input of 1010001101

Figure 10.3 Circuit with Shift Registers for Dividing by the Polynomial $X^5 + X^4 + X^2 + 1$

input data bits are fed in with both switches in the A position. As a result, for the first 10 steps, the input bits are fed into the shift register and also used as output bits. After the last data bit is processed, the shift register contains the remainder (FCS) (shown shaded). As soon as the last data bit is provided to the shift register, both switches are set to the B position. This has two effects: (1) all of the XOR gates become simple pass-throughs; no bits are changed, and (2) as the shifting process continues, the 5 CRC bits are output.

At the receiver, the same logic is used. As each bit of M arrives, it is inserted into the shift register. If there have been no errors, the shift register should contain the bit pattern for R at the conclusion of M. the transmitted bits of R now begin to arrive, and the effect is to zero out the register so that, at the conclusion of reception, the register contains all 0s.

Figure 10.4 indicates the general architecture of the shift register implementation of a CRC for the polynomial $P(X) = \sum_{i=0}^{n-k} A_i X^i$, where $A_0 = A_{n-k} = 1$ and all other A_i equal either 0 or 1.[3]

10.2 BLOCK ERROR CORRECTION CODES

Error detection is a useful technique, found in data link control protocols, such as HDLC, and in transport protocols, such as TCP. However, correction of errors using an error detection code requires that block of data be retransmitted, using the

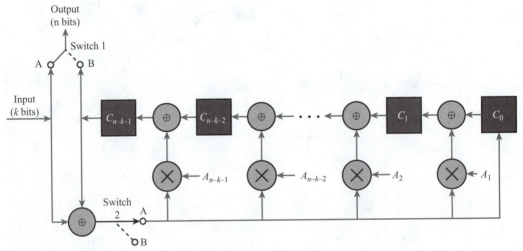

Figure 10.4 General CRC Architecture to Implement Divisor $1 + A_1 X + A_2 X^2 + \cdots + A_{n-1} X^{n-k-1} + X^{n-k}$

---

[3]It is common for the CRC register to be shown shifting to the right, which is the reverse of the analogy to binary division. Because binary numbers are usually shown with the most significant bit on the left, a left-shifting register is more appropriate.

ARQ discipline explained in Section 10.4. For wireless applications, this approach is inadequate for two reasons:

1. The bit error rate on a wireless link can be quite high, which would result in a large number of retransmissions.

2. In some cases, especially satellite links, the propagation delay is very long compared to the transmission time of a single frame. The result is a very inefficient system. As is discussed in Section 10.4, the common approach to retransmission is to retransmit the frame in error plus all subsequent frames. With a long data link, an error in a single frame necessitates retransmitting many frames.

Instead, it would be desirable to enable the receiver to correct errors in an incoming transmission on the basis of the bits in that transmission. Figure 10.5 shows in general how this is done. On the transmission end, each k-bit block of data is mapped into an n-bit block ($n > k$) called a **codeword**, using an **forward error correction (FEC)** encoder. The codeword is then transmitted; in the case of wireless transmission a modulator produces an analog signal for transmission. During transmission, the signal is subject to noise, which may produce bit errors in the signal. At the receiver, the incoming signal is demodulated to produce a bit string that is similar to the original codeword but may contain errors. This block is passed through an FEC decoder, with one of five possible outcomes:

1. If there are no bit errors, the input to the FEC decoder is identical to the original codeword, and the decoder produces the original data block as output.

2. For certain error patterns, it is possible for the decoder to detect and correct those errors. Thus, even though the incoming data block differs from the

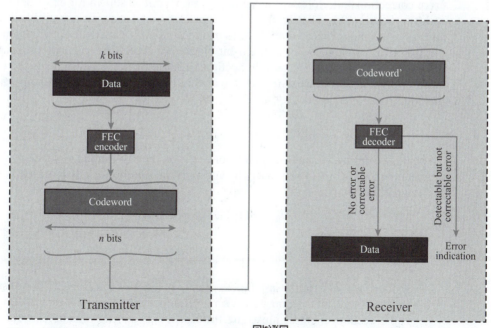

Figure 10.5 Forward Error Correction Process

transmitted codeword, the FEC decoder is able to map this block into the original data block.

3. For certain error patterns, the decoder can detect but not correct the errors. In this case, the decoder simply reports an uncorrectable error.

4. For certain, typically rare, error patterns, the decoder detects an error, but does not correct it properly. It assumes a certain block of data was sent when in reality of different one was sent.

5. For certain even more rare error patterns, the decoder does not detect that any errors have occurred and maps the incoming n-bit data block into a k-bit block that differs from the original k-bit block.

How is it possible for the decoder to correct bit errors? In essence, **error correction** works by adding redundancy to the transmitted message. Consider an example where a binary 0 or 1 were to be sent, but instead the codewords that were sent were either 0000 or 1111. The redundancy makes it possible for the receiver to deduce what the original message was, even in the face of a certain level of error rate. If a 0010 were received, we could assume that a 0000 was sent corresponding to the original binary 0, because only one bit change would have occurred to make this happen. There is, however, a much more unlikely yet possible scenario where a 1111 was sent. The decoder would then make a mistake by assuming a 0 was sent. Consider if another received codeword were 0011. In this case, the decoder would not be able to decide because it would be equally likely that 0000 or 1111 was sent.

In this section we look at a widely used form of error correction code known as a block error correction code. We begin with a discussion of general principles and then look at some specific codes. Before proceeding, we note that in many cases, the error correction code follows the same general layout as shown for error detection codes in Figure 10.1. That is, the FEC algorithm takes as input a k-bit block and adds $(n - k)$ check bits to that block to produce an n-bit block; all of the bits in the original k-bit block show up in the n-bit block. For some FEC algorithms, such as the convolutional code discussed in Section 10.3, the FEC algorithm maps the k-bit input into an n-bit codeword in such a way that the original k bits do not appear in the codeword.

Block Code Principles

To begin, we define a term that shall be of use to us. The **Hamming distance** $d(\mathbf{v}_1, \mathbf{v}_2)$ between two n-bit binary sequences $\mathbf{v}_1$ and $\mathbf{v}_2$ is the number of bits in which $\mathbf{v}_1$ and $\mathbf{v}_2$ disagree. For example, if

$$\mathbf{v}_1 = 011011, \quad \mathbf{v}_2 = 110001$$

then

$$d(\mathbf{v}_1, \mathbf{v}_2) = 3$$

Suppose we wish to transmit blocks of data of length k bits. Instead of transmitting each block as k bits, we map each k-bit sequence into a unique n-bit codeword.

The preceding example illustrates the essential properties of a block error correction code. An (n, k) block code encodes k data bits into n-bit codewords. Thus

Example 10.6 For $k = 2$ and $n = 5$, we can make the following assignment:

Data Block	Codeword
00	00000
01	00111
10	11001
11	11110

Now, suppose that a codeword block is received with the bit pattern 00100. This is not a valid codeword and so the receiver has detected an error. Can the error be corrected? We cannot be sure which data block was sent because $1, 2, 3, 4$, or even all 5 of the bits that were transmitted may have been corrupted by noise. However, notice that it would require only a single bit change to transform the valid codeword 00000 into 00100. It would take two bit changes to transform 00111 to 00100, three bit changes to transform 11110 to 00100, and it would take four bit changes to transform 11001 into 00100. Thus, we can deduce that the most likely codeword that was sent was 00000 and that therefore the desired data block is 00. This is error correction. In terms of Hamming distances, we have

$$d(00000, 00100) = 1; \ d(00111, 00100) = 2; \ d(11001, 00100) = 4;$$
$$d(11110, 00100) = 3$$

So the rule we would like to impose is that if an invalid codeword is received, then the valid codeword that is closest to it (minimum distance) is selected. This will only work if there is a unique valid codeword at a minimum distance from each invalid codeword.

For our example, it is not true that for every invalid codeword there is one and only one valid codeword at a minimum distance. There are $2^5 = 32$ possible codewords of which 4 are valid, leaving 28 invalid codewords. For the invalid codewords, we have the following:

Invalid Codeword	Minimum Distance	Valid Codeword	Invalid Codeword	Minimum Distance	Valid Codeword
00001	1	00000	10000	1	00000
00010	1	00000	10001	1	11001
00011	1	00111	10010	2	00000 or 11110
00100	1	00000	10011	2	00111 or 11001
00101	1	00111	10100	2	00000 or 11110
00110	1	00111	10101	2	00111 or 11001
01000	1	00000	10110	1	11110
01001	1	11001	10111	1	00111
01010	2	00000 or 11110	11000	1	11001
01011	2	00111 or 11001	11010	1	11110
01100	2	00000 or 11110	11011	1	11001
01101	2	00111 or 11001	11100	1	11110
01110	1	11110	11101	1	11001
01111	1	00111	11111	1	11110

There are eight cases in which an invalid codeword is at a distance 2 from two different valid codewords. Thus, if one such invalid codeword is received, an error in 2 bits could have caused it and the receiver has no way to choose between the two alternatives. An error is detected but cannot be corrected. The only remedy is retransmission. However, in every case in which a single-bit error occurs, the resulting codeword is of distance 1 from only one valid codeword and the decision can be made. This code is therefore capable of correcting all single-bit errors but cannot correct double-bit errors. Another way to see this is to look at the pairwise distances between valid codewords:

$$d(00000, 00111) = 3; \quad d(00000, 11001) = 3; \quad d(00000, 11110) = 4;$$
$$d(00111, 11001) = 4; \quad d(00111, 11110) = 3; \quad d(11001, 11110) = 3;$$

The minimum distance between valid codewords is 3. Therefore, a single-bit error will result in an invalid codeword that is a distance 1 from the original valid codeword but a distance at least 2 from all other valid codewords. As a result, the code can always correct a single-bit error. Note that the code also will always detect a double-bit error.

the design of a block code is equivalent to the design of a function of the form $\mathbf{v_c} = f(\mathbf{v_d})$, where $\mathbf{v_d}$ is a vector of k data bits and $\mathbf{v_c}$ is a vector of n codeword bits.

With an (n, k) block code, there are 2^k valid codewords out of a total of 2^n possible codewords. The ratio of redundant bits to data bits, $(n - k)/k$, is called the **redundancy** of the code, and the ratio of data bits to total bits, k/n, is called the **code rate**. The code rate is a measure of how much additional bandwidth is required to carry data at the same data rate as without the code. For example, a code rate of $\frac{1}{2}$ requires double the bandwidth of an uncoded system to maintain the same data rate. Our example has a code rate of $\frac{2}{5}$ and so requires a bandwidth 2.5 times the bandwidth for an uncoded system. For example, if the data rate input to the encoder is 1 Mbps, then the output from the encoder must be at a rate of 2.5 Mbps to keep up.

For a code consisting of the codewords $\mathbf{w}_1, \mathbf{w}_2, \ldots, \mathbf{w}_s$, where $s = 2^k$, the minimum distance d_{min} of the code is defined as

$$d_{min} = \min_{i \neq j}[d(\mathbf{w}_i, \mathbf{w}_j)]$$

It can be shown that the following conditions hold. For a given positive integer t, if a code satisfies $d_{min} \geq 2t + 1$, then the code can correct all bit errors up to and including errors of t bits. If $d_{min} \geq 2t$, then all errors $\leq t - 1$ bits can be corrected and errors of t bits can be detected but not, in general, corrected. Conversely, any code for which all errors of magnitude $\leq t$ are corrected must satisfy $d_{min} \geq 2t + 1$, and any code for which all errors of magnitude $\leq t - 1$ are corrected and all errors of magnitude t are detected must satisfy $d_{min} \geq 2t$.

Another way of putting the relationship between d_{min} and t is to say that the maximum number of guaranteed correctable errors per codeword satisfies

$$t = \left\lfloor \frac{d_{min} - 1}{2} \right\rfloor$$

where $\lfloor x \rfloor$ means the largest integer not to exceed x (e.g., $\lfloor 6.3 \rfloor = 6$). Furthermore, if we are concerned only with error detection and not error correction, then the number of errors, t, that can be detected satisfies

$$t = d_{min} - 1$$

To see this, consider that if d_{min} errors occur, this could change one valid codeword into another. Any number of errors less than d_{min} cannot result in another valid codeword.

The design of a block code involves a number of considerations.

1. For given values of n and k, we would like the largest possible value of d_{min}.
2. The code should be relatively easy to encode and decode, requiring minimal memory and processing time.
3. We would like the number of extra bits, $(n - k)$, to be small, to reduce bandwidth.
4. We would like the number of extra bits, $(n - k)$, to be large, to reduce error rate.

Clearly, the last two objectives are in conflict, and trade-offs must be made.

Before looking at specific codes, it will be useful to examine Figure 10.6. The literature on error correction codes frequently includes graphs of this sort to demonstrate the effectiveness of various encoding schemes. Recall from Chapter 7 that coding can be used to reduce the required E_b/N_0 value to achieve a given bit error rate.[4] The coding discussed in Chapter 7 has to do with the definition of signal elements to represent bits. The coding discussed in this chapter also has an effect on E_b/N_0. In Figure 10.6, the curve on the right is for an uncoded modulation system; the shaded region represents the area in which potential improvement can be achieved. In this region, a smaller BER is achieved for a given E_b/N_0, and conversely, for a given BER, a smaller E_b/N_0 is required. The other curve is a typical result of a code rate of one-half (equal number of data and check bits). Note that at an error rate of 10^{-6}, the use of coding allows a reduction in E_b/N_0 of 2.77 dB. This reduction is referred to as the ***coding gain***, which is defined as the reduction, in decibels, in the required E_b/N_0 to achieve a specified BER of an error correction coded system compared to an uncoded system using the same modulation.

It is important to realize that the BER for the second rate $\frac{1}{2}$ curve refers to the rate of uncorrected errors and that the E_b value refers to the energy per data bit. Because the rate is $\frac{1}{2}$, there are two bits on the channel for each data bit, effectively reducing the data throughput by $\frac{1}{2}$ (or requiring twice the raw data rate) as well. The energy per coded bit is half that of the energy per data bit, or a reduction of 3 dB. If we look at the energy per coded bit for this system, then we see that the channel bit error rate is about 2.4×10^{-2}, or 0.024.

Finally, note that below a certain threshold of E_b/N_0, the coding scheme actually degrades performance. In our example of Figure 10.6, the threshold occurs at about 5.4 dB. Below the threshold, the extra check bits add overhead to the system that reduces the energy per data bit causing increased errors. Above the threshold, the error-correcting power of the code more than compensates for the reduced E_b, resulting in a coding gain.

We now turn to a look at some specific block error correction codes.

---

[4] E_b/N_0 is the ratio of signal energy per bit to noise power density per hertz; it was defined and discussed in Chapter 6.

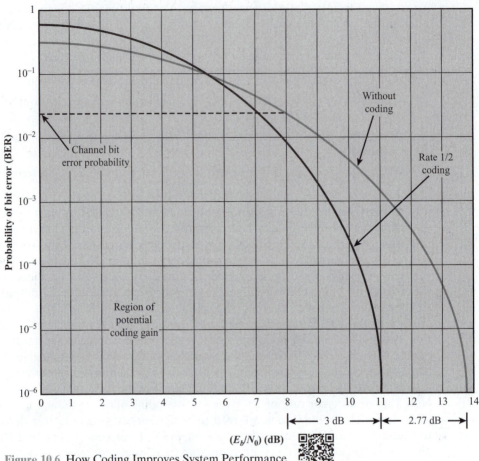

Figure 10.6 How Coding Improves System Performance

Hamming Code

Hamming codes are a family of (n, k) block error correction codes that have the following parameters:

Block length:	$n = 2^m - 1$
Number of data bits:	$k = 2^m - m - 1$
Number of check bits:	$n - k = m$
Minimum distance:	$d_{min} = 3$

where $m \geq 3$. Hamming codes are straightforward and easy to analyze but are rarely used. We begin with these codes because they illustrate some of the fundamental principles of block codes.

Hamming codes are designed to correct single-bit errors. To start, let us determine how long the code must be. The Hamming code process has the same structure as the error detection logic shown in Figure 10.1; that is, the encoding process preserves the k data bits and adds $(n - k)$ check bits. For decoding, the comparison

Table 10.1 Hamming Code Requirements

Data Bits	Single-Error Correction		Single-Error Correction/ Double-Error Detection	
	Check Bits	**% Increase**	**Check Bits**	**% Increase**
8	4	50	5	62.5
16	5	31.25	6	37.5
32	6	18.75	7	21.875
64	7	10.94	8	12.5
128	8	6.25	9	7.03
256	9	3.52	10	3.91

logic receives as input two $(n - k)$-bit values, one from the incoming codeword and one from a calculation performed on the incoming data bits. A bit-by-bit comparison is done by taking the XOR of the two inputs. The result is called the **syndrome word**. Thus, each bit of the syndrome is 0 or 1 according to whether there is or is not a match in that bit position for the two inputs.

The syndrome word is therefore $(n - k)$ bits wide and has a range between 0 and $2^{(n-k)} - 1$. The value 0 indicates that no error was detected, leaving $2^{(n-k)} - 1$ values to indicate, if there is an error, which bit was in error. Now, because an error could occur on any of the k data bits or $(n - k)$ check bits, we must have

$$2^{(n-k)} - 1 \geq k + (n - k) = n$$

This equation gives the number of bits needed to correct a single-bit error in a word containing k data bits. Table 10.1 lists the number of check bits required for various data lengths.

For convenience, we would like to generate a syndrome with the following characteristics:

- If the syndrome contains all 0s, no error has been detected.
- If the syndrome contains one and only one bit set to 1, then an error has occurred in one of the check bits. No correction is needed.
- If the syndrome contains more than one bit set to 1, then the numerical value of the syndrome indicates the position of the data bit in error. This data bit is inverted for correction.

To achieve these characteristics, the data and check bits are arranged into an n-bit block as follows. Counting from the least-significant (rightmost) position, the Hamming check bits are inserted at positions that are a power of 2 [i.e., positions $1, 2, 4, \ldots, 2^{(n-k)}$]. The remaining bits are data bits. To calculate the check bits, each data position that has a value 1 is represented by a binary value equal to its position; thus, if the 9th bit is 1, the corresponding value is 1001. All of the position values are then XORed together to produce the bits of the Hamming code. At the receiver, all bit position values where there is 1 are XORed. In this case, the XOR includes both data bits and check bits. Because the check bits occur at bit positions that are a power of 2, we can simply XOR all data bit positions with a value of 1, plus the Hamming code formed by the check bits. If the result of the XOR is zero, no error is detected. If the result is nonzero, then the result is the syndrome, and its value equals the bit position that is in error.

Example 10.7 A (12, 8) Hamming code has the assignment shown in Table 10.2. The 8-bit data block is 00111001. Four of the data bits have a value 1 (shaded in the table), and their bit position values are XORed to produce the Hamming code 0111, which forms the four check digits. The entire block that is transmitted is 001101001111. Suppose now that data bit 3, in bit position 6, sustains an error and is changed from 0 to 1. Then the received block is 001101101111. The received Hamming code is still 0111. The receiver performs an XOR of the Hamming code and all of the bit position values for nonzero data bits, with a result of 0110. The nonzero result detects an error and indicates that the error is in bit position 6.

Table 10.2 Layout of Data Bits and Check Bits

(a) Transmitted block

Bit Position	12	11	10	9	8	7	6	5	4	3	2	1
Position Number	1100	1011	1010	1001	1000	0111	0110	0101	0100	0011	0010	0001
Data Bit	D8	D7	D6	D5		D4	D3	D2		D1		
Check Bit					C8				C4		C2	C1
Transmitted Block	0	0	1	1	0	1	0	0	1	1	1	1
Codes			1010	1001		0111				0011		

(b) Check bit calculation prior to transmission

Position	Code
10	1010
9	1001
7	0111
3	0011
XOR = C8 C4 C2 C1	0111

(c) Received block

Bit Position	12	11	10	9	8	7	6	5	4	3	2	1
Position Number	1100	1011	1010	1001	1000	0111	0110	0101	0100	0011	0010	0001
Data Bit	D8	D7	D6	D5		D4	D3	D2		D1		
Check Bit					C8				C4		C2	C1
Received Block	0	0	1	1	0	1	1	0	1	1	1	1
Codes			1010	1001		0111	0110			0011		

(d) Check bit calculation after reception

Position	Code
Hamming	0111
10	1010
9	1001
7	0111
6	0110
3	0011
XOR = syndrome	0110

The code just described is known as a *single-error-correcting* (SEC) code. A variation is a single-error-correcting, double-error-detecting (SEC-DED) code. As Table 10.1 shows, such codes require one additional bit compared with SEC codes. The extra bit is a parity bit over the entire code block.

Cyclic Codes

Most of the error correction block codes that are in use are in a category called **cyclic codes**. For such codes, if the n-bit sequence $c = (c_0, c_1, \ldots, c_{n-1})$ is a valid codeword, then $(c_{n-1}, c_0, c_1, \ldots, c_{n-2})$, which is formed by cyclically shifting c one place to the right, is also a valid codeword. This class of codes can be easily encoded and decoded using linear feedback shift registers (LFSRs). Examples of cyclic codes include the Bose–Chaudhuri–Hocquenghem (BCH) and Reed–Solomon (RS) codes.

The LFSR implementation of a cyclic error correction encoder is the same as that of the CRC error detection code, illustrated in Figure 10.4. The key difference is that the CRC code takes an input of arbitrary length and produces a fixed-length CRC check code, while a cyclic error correction code takes a fixed-length input (k bits) and produces a fixed-length check code ($n - k$ bits).

Figure 10.7 shows the LFSR implementation of the decoder for a cyclic block code. Compare this to the encoder logic in Figure 10.4. Note that for the encoder, the k data bits are treated as input to produce an $(n - k)$ code of check bits in the shift register. For the decoder, the input is the received bit stream of n bits, consisting of k data bits followed by $(n - k)$ check bits. If there have been no errors, after the first k steps, the shift register contains the pattern of check bits that were transmitted. After the remaining $(n - k)$ steps, the shift register contains a syndrome code.

For decoding of a cyclic code, the following procedure is used:

1. Process received bits to compute the syndrome code in exactly the same fashion as the encoder processes the data bits to produce the check code.

2. If the syndrome bits are all zero, no error has been detected.

3. If the syndrome is nonzero, perform additional processing on the syndrome for error correction.

Received
(*n* bits)

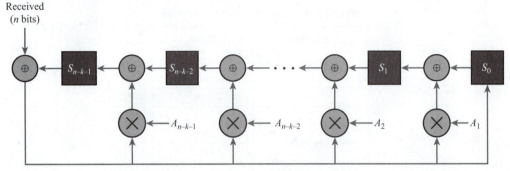

Figure 10.7 Block Syndrome Generator for Divisor $1 + A_1X + A_2X^2 + \cdots + A_{n-1}X^{n-k-1} + X^{n-k}$

To understand the significance of the syndrome, let us examine the block code using polynomials. As in the case of the CRC, a particular cyclic code can be represented by a polynomial divisor, called the generator polynomial. For an (n, k) code, the generator polynomial has the form

$$P(X) = 1 + \sum_{i=1}^{n-k-1} A_iX^i + X^{n-k}$$

where each coefficient A_i is either 0 or 1, corresponding to one bit position in the divisor. For example, for $P = 11001$, we have $P(X) = X^4 + X^3 + 1$. Similarly, the set of data bits is represented by the polynomial $D(X)$ and the check code by the polynomial $C(X)$. Recall from the CRC discussion that a check code is determined in the following way:

$$\frac{X^{n-k}D(X)}{P(X)} = Q(X) + \frac{C(X)}{P(X)}$$

That is, the data block $D(X)$ is shifted to the left by $(n - k)$ bits and divided by $P(X)$. This produces a quotient $Q(X)$ and a remainder $C(X)$ of length $(n - k)$ bits. The transmitted block is formed by concatenating $D(X)$ and $C(X)$:

$$T(X) = X^{n-k}D(X) + C(X) \tag{10.3}$$

If there is no error on reception, $T(X)$ will be exactly divisible by $P(X)$ with no remainder. This is easily demonstrated by

$$\frac{T(X)}{P(X)} = \frac{X^{n-k}D(X)}{P(X)} + \frac{C(X)}{P(X)}$$

$$= \left(Q(X) + \frac{C(X)}{P(X)}\right) + \frac{C(X)}{P(X)} = Q(X) \tag{10.4}$$

The last equality is valid because of the rules of modulo 2 arithmetic ($a + a = 0$, whether $a = 1$ or $a = 0$). Thus, if there are no errors, the division of $T(X)$ by $P(X)$ produces no remainder.

If one or more bit errors occur, then the received block $Z(X)$ will be of the form

$$Z(X) = T(X) + E(X)$$

where $E(X)$ is an n-bit error polynomial with a value of 1 in each bit position that is in error in $Z(X)$. If we pass $Z(X)$ through the LFSR of Figure 10.7, we are performing the division $Z(X)/P(X)$, which produces the $(n - k)$ bit syndrome $S(X)$:

$$\frac{Z(X)}{P(X)} = B(X) + \frac{S(X)}{P(X)} \tag{10.5}$$

where $B(X)$ is the quotient and $S(X)$ is the remainder. Thus, $S(X)$ is a function of $Z(X)$. But how does this help us perform error correction? To see this, let us expand Equation (10.5).

$$\frac{Z(X)}{P(X)} = B(X) + \frac{S(X)}{P(X)}$$

$$\frac{T(X) + E(X)}{P(X)} = B(X) + \frac{S(X)}{P(X)}$$

$$Q(X) + \frac{E(X)}{P(X)} = B(X) + \frac{S(X)}{P(X)} \tag{10.6}$$

$$\frac{E(X)}{P(X)} = [Q(X) + B(X)] + \frac{S(X)}{P(X)}$$

What we see is that $E(X)/P(X)$ produces the same remainder as $Z(X)/P(X)$. Therefore, regardless of the initial pattern of bits (transmitted value of $T(X)$), the syndrome value $S(X)$ depends only on the error bits. If we can recover the error bits, $E(X)$, from $S(X)$, then we can correct the errors in $Z(X)$ by simple addition:

$$Z(X) + E(X) = T(X) + E(X) + E(X) = T(X)$$

Because $S(X)$ depends only on $E(X)$, we can easily determine the power of a cyclic block code. The syndrome pattern consists of $n - k$ bits and therefore takes on 2^{n-k} possible values. A value of all zeros indicates no errors. Therefore, a total of $2^{n-k} - 1$ different error patterns can be corrected. To be able to correct all possible single-bit errors with an (n, k) code, we must have $n \leq (2^{n-k} - 1)$. To be able to correct all single- and double-bit errors, the relationship is $\left(n + \dfrac{n(n - 1)}{2}\right) \leq (2^{n-k} - 1)$.

The way in which $E(X)$ is recovered from $S(X)$ may depend on the specific code involved. The most straightforward approach is to develop a table of all possible values of $E(X)$ with the corresponding value of $S(X)$ of each. Then a simple table lookup is required.

BCH Codes

BCH codes are among the most powerful cyclic block codes and are widely used in wireless applications. For any positive pair of integers m and t, there is a binary (n, k) BCH code with the following parameters:

Block length:	$n = 2^m - 1$
Number of check bits:	$n - k \leq mt$
Minimum distance:	$d_{\min} \geq 2t + 1$

Example 10.8 [5]   Consider a $(7, 4)$ code with the generator polynomial $P(X) = X^3 + X^2 + 1$. We have $7 = 2^3 - 1$, so this code is capable of correcting all single-bit errors. Table 10.3a lists all of the valid codewords; note that d_{min} is 3, confirming that this is a single-error-correcting code. For example, for the data block 1010, we have $D(X) = X^3 + X$ and $X^{n-k}D(X) = X^6 + X^4$. Dividing as in Equation (10.4),

$$
\begin{array}{r}
X^3 + X^2 + 1 \quad\quad\quad\quad\quad \longleftarrow Q(X) \\[2pt]
P(X) \longrightarrow X^3 + X^2 + 1 \,\overline{\big)\, X^6 \quad\quad X^4 \quad\quad\quad\quad} \longleftarrow 2^3D(X) \\[2pt]
\underline{X^6 + X^5 + \quad\quad X^3} \\[2pt]
X^5 + X^4 + X^3 \\[2pt]
\underline{X^5 + X^4 + \quad\quad X^2} \\[2pt]
X^3 + X^2 \\[2pt]
\underline{X^3 + X^2 + \quad\quad\quad 1} \\[2pt]
1 \longleftarrow C(X)
\end{array}
$$

Then, using Equation (10.3), we have $T(X) = X^6 + X^4 + 1$, which is the codeword 1010001.

For error correction, we need to construct the syndrome table shown in Table 10.3b. For example, for an error pattern of 1000000, $E(X) = X^6$. Using the last line of Equation (10.6), we calculate:

$$
\begin{array}{r}
X^3 + X^2 + X \quad\quad\quad\quad\quad \longleftarrow Q(X) + B(X) \\[2pt]
P(X) \longrightarrow X^3 + X^2 + 1 \,\overline{\big)\, X^6 \quad\quad\quad\quad\quad\quad\quad} \longleftarrow E(X) \\[2pt]
\underline{X^6 + X^5 + \quad\quad X^3} \\[2pt]
X^5 + \quad X^3 \\[2pt]
\underline{X^5 + X^4 + \quad\quad X^2} \\[2pt]
X^4 + X^3 + X^2 \\[2pt]
\underline{X^4 + X^3 + \quad\quad X} \\[2pt]
X^2 + X \longleftarrow S(X)
\end{array}
$$

Therefore, $S = 110$. The remaining entries in Table 10.3b are calculated similarly. Now suppose the received block is 1101101, or $Z(X) = X^6 + X^5 + X^3 + X^2 + 1$. Using Equation (10.5):

$$
\begin{array}{r}
X^3 \quad\quad\quad\quad\quad\quad\quad \longleftarrow B(X) \\[2pt]
P(X) \longrightarrow X^3 + X^2 + 1 \,\overline{\big)\, X^6 + X^5 + \quad\quad X^3 + X^2 + 1} \longleftarrow Z(X) \\[2pt]
\underline{X^6 + X^5 + \quad\quad X^3} \\[2pt]
X^2 + 1 \longleftarrow S(X)
\end{array}
$$

Thus, $S = 101$. Using Table 10.3b, this yields $E = 0001000$. Then,

$$T = 1101101 \oplus 0001000 = 1100101$$

Then, from Table 10.3a, the transmitted data block is 1100.

---

[5]This example is taken from [LATH98].

Table 10.3 A Single-Error-Correcting (7, 4) Cyclic Code

(a) Table of valid codewords		(b) Table of syndromes for single-bit errors	
Data Block	**Codeword**	**Error Pattern E**	**Syndrome S**
0000	0000000	0000001	001
0001	0001101	0000010	010
0010	0010111	0000100	100
0011	0011010	0001000	101
0100	0100011	0010000	111
0101	0101110	0100000	011
0110	0110100	1000000	110
0111	0111001		
1000	1000110		
1001	1001011		
1010	1010001		
1011	1011100		
1100	1100101		
1101	1101000		
1110	1110010		
1111	1111111		

This code can correct all combinations of t or fewer errors. The generator polynomial for this code can be constructed from the factors of $(X^{2^m - 1} + 1)$. The BCH codes provide flexibility in the choice of parameters (block length, code rate) for a given number of errors to be corrected. Table 10.4 lists the BCH parameters for code lengths up to $2^8 - 1$. Table 10.5 lists some of the BCH generator polynomials.

A number of techniques have been designed for BCH decoding that require less memory than a simple table lookup. One of the simplest was proposed by Berlekamp [BERL80]. The central idea is to compute an error-locator polynomial and solve for its roots. The complexity of the algorithm increases only as the square of the number of errors to be corrected.

Reed–Solomon Codes

Reed–Solomon codes are a widely used subclass of nonbinary BCH codes. With RS codes, data are processed in chunks of m bits, called symbols. An (n, k) RS code has the following parameters:

Symbol length:	m bits per symbol
Block length:	$n = 2^m - 1$ symbols $= m(2^m - 1)$ bits
Data length:	k symbols
Size of check code:	$n - k = 2t$ symbols $= m(2t)$ bits
Minimum distance:	$d_{min} = 2t + 1$ symbols

Table 10.4 BCH Code Parameters

n	k	t	n	k	t	n	k	t	n	k	t	n	k	t
7	4	1	63	30	6	127	64	10	255	207	6	255	99	23
15	11	1		24	7		57	11		199	7		91	25
	7	2		18	10		50	13		191	8		87	26
	5	3		16	11		43	14		187	9		79	27
31	26	1		10	13		36	15		179	10		71	29
	21	2		7	15		29	21		171	11		63	30
	16	3	127	120	1		22	23		163	12		55	31
	11	5		113	2		15	27		155	13		47	42
	6	7		106	3		8	31		147	14		45	43
63	57	1		99	4	255	247	1		139	15		37	45
	51	2		92	5		239	2		131	18		29	47
	45	3		85	6		231	3		123	19		21	55
	39	4		78	7		223	4		115	21		13	59
	36	5		71	9		215	5		107	22		9	63

Table 10.5 BCH Polynomial Generators

N	k	t	P(X)
7	4	1	$X^3 + X + 1$
15	11	1	$X^4 + X + 1$
15	7	2	$X^8 + X^7 + X^6 + X^4 + 1$
15	5	3	$X^{10} + X^8 + X^5 + X^4 + X^2 + X + 1$
31	26	1	$X^5 + X^2 + 1$
31	21	2	$X^{10} + X^9 + X^8 + X^6 + X^5 + X^3 + 1$

Thus, the encoding algorithm expands a block of k symbols to n symbols by adding $n - k$ redundant check symbols. Typically, m is a power of 2; a popular value of m is 8.

Example 10.9 Let $t = 1$ and $m = 2$. Denoting the symbols as 0, 1, 2, 3, we can write their binary equivalents as $0 = 00; 1 = 01; 2 = 10; 3 = 11$. The code has the following parameters:

$$n = 2^2 - 1 = 3 \text{ symbols} = 6 \text{ bits}$$
$$(n - k) = 2 \text{ symbols} = 4 \text{ bits}$$

This code can correct any burst error that spans a symbol of 2 bits.

RS codes are well suited for burst error correction. They make highly efficient use of redundancy, and block lengths and symbol sizes can be easily adjusted to accommodate a wide range of message sizes. In addition, efficient coding techniques are available for RS codes.

Low-Density Parity-Check Codes

For decades, researchers were not able to approach the Shannon limit for data capacity for a given channel bandwidth, at least not within practical computational hardware constraints. There were some capacity-approaching codes developed in the 1960s, however, called low-density parity-check (LDPC) codes that were redis-covered in the 1990s. Only then did they become of practical use, because their computational complexity was at first prohibitive. They have since been enhanced and become popular, for example in the latest generation of IEEE 802.11 standards.

LDPC uses very long block codes, normally longer than 1000 bits. To check for errors among these bits, a series of parity equations are implemented, usually organized in an **H** matrix. For example, one might require the following:

$$b_{10} + b_{13} + b_{45} + b_{192} = 0$$

Each equation should have at least three bits added together, and there will be hun-dreds of such equations for 1000 bits.

To visualize a few of these equations, see Figure 10.8. This is a Tanner graph. The nodes in the top row correspond to each of the data bits and are called *variable nodes*. The nodes in the bottom row are called *constraint nodes*, and these corre-spond to the equations. For example, constraint node c_1 corresponds to the follow-ing equation:

$$v_3 + v_4 + v_5 + v_6 = 0$$

LDPC uses an iterative decoding procedure as follows:

1. The procedure starts with the variable nodes at the top. These nodes use exter-nal information, mainly from the demodulator, to determine their estimates for their bit values. If they use a soft decoding approach, they also estimate the probabilities that the bits should be 0 or 1.

2. These estimates are then sent to the constraint nodes to see if the estimated values satisfy all of the equations. If so, the decoding stops because an accept-able answer has been found. If not, the constraint nodes combine the informa-tion sent to them from their connected variable nodes to determine which bits

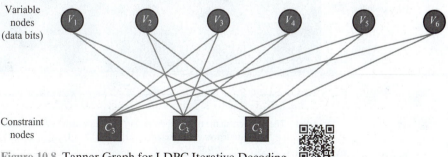

Figure 10.8 Tanner Graph for LDPC Iterative Decoding

are most likely to be different than their estimates. This corresponds to the most likely bit changes that are needed to satisfy the equations.

3. The estimates from the constraint nodes are sent to the variable nodes. Because variable nodes are connected to multiple constraint nodes, the variable nodes combine the newly acquired information to update their estimates of their bit values and probabilities.

4. These are sent again to the constraint nodes. If the equations are now satisfied, then stop. Otherwise, continue the decoding process.

This decoding procedure is known as *message passing* or *belief propagation*. The performance of LDPC codes can be impressive, approaching Shannon capacity within a fraction of a dB when using long codes.

Block Interleaving

Block interleaving is a common technique used with block codes in wireless systems; we saw an example of this in Figure 6.17. The advantage of interleaving is that a burst error that affects a sequence of bits is spread out over a number of separate blocks at the receiver so that error correction is possible. Interleaving is accomplished by reading and writing data from memory in different orders. Figure 10.9 illustrates a simple and common interleaving technique. In this case, m blocks of data to be transmitted are stored in a rectangular array in which each row consists of n bits, equal to the block size. Data are then read out one column at a time. The result is that the k data bits and their corresponding $(n - k)$ check bits, which form a single n-bit block, are spread out and interspersed with bits from other blocks. There are $m - 1$ bits from other blocks in between. At the receiver, the data are deinterleaved to recover the original order. If, during transmission, a burst of noise affects a consecutive sequence of bits, those bits belong to different blocks and hence only

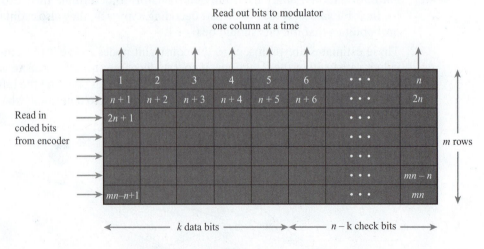

Note: The numbers in the matrix indicate the order in which bits are read in.
Interleaver output sequence: $1, n + 1, 2n + 1, \ldots$

Figure 10.9 Block Interleaving

a few of the bits in error are part of a particular block that needs to be corrected by any one set of check bits. Specifically, a burst of length $l = mb$ is broken up into m bursts of length b. Some thought should convince you of the following assertion: Suppose we have an (n, k) code that can correct all combinations of t or fewer errors, where $t = \lfloor (n - k)/2 \rfloor$. Then if we use an interleaver of degree m, then the result is an (mn, mk) code that can correct burst errors of up to mt bits.

10.3 CONVOLUTIONAL CODES

Block codes are one of the two widely used categories of error correction codes for wireless transmission; the other is **convolutional codes**. An (n, k) block code processes data in blocks of k bits at a time, producing a block of n bits $(n > k)$ as output for every block of k bits as input. If data are transmitted and received in a more or less continuous stream, a block code, particularly one with a large value of n, may not be as convenient as a code that generates redundant bits continuously so that error checking and correcting are carried out continuously. This is the function of convolution codes.

A convolutional code is defined by three parameters: n, k, and K. An (n, k, K) code processes input data k bits at a time and produces an output of n bits for each incoming k bits. So far this is the same as the block code. In the case of a convolutional code, n and k are generally quite small numbers. The difference is that convolutional codes have memory, which is characterized by the *constraint factor K*. In essence, the current n-bit output of an (n, k, K) code depends not only on the value of the current block of k input bits but also on the previous $K - 1$ blocks of k input bits. Hence, the current output of n bits is a function of the last $K \times k$ input bits.

Convolutional codes are best understood by looking at a specific example. We use the example shown in Figure 10.10. There are two alternative representations of the code shown in the figure. Figure 10.10a is a shift register, which is most convenient for describing and implementing the encoding process. Figure 10.10b is an equivalent representation that is useful in discussing the decoding process.

For an (n, k, K) code, the shift register contains the most recent $K \times k$ input bits; the register is initialized to all zeros.[6] The encoder produces n output bits, after which the oldest k bits from the register are discarded and k new bits are shifted in. Thus, although the output of n bits depends on $K \times k$ input bits, the rate of encoding is n output bits per k input bits. As in a block code, the code rate is therefore k/n. The most commonly used binary encoders have $k = 1$ and hence a shift register length of K. Our example is of a $(2, 1, 3)$ code (Figure 10.10a). The shift register holds $K \times k = 3 \times 1$ *bits* u_n, u_{n-1}, and u_{n-2}. For each new input bit u_n, two output bits v_{n1} and v_{n2} are produced using the three most recent bits. The first output bit produced here is from the upper logic circuit $(v_{n1} = u_n \oplus u_{n-1} \oplus u_{n-2})$, and the second output bit from the lower logic circuit $(v_{n2} = u_n \oplus u_{n-2})$.

For any given input of k bits, there are $2^{k(K-1)}$ different functions that map the k input bits into n output bits. Which function is used depends on the history

---

[6]In some of the literature, the shift register is shown with one less storage cell and with the input bits feeding the XOR circuits as well as a storage cell; the depictions are equivalent.

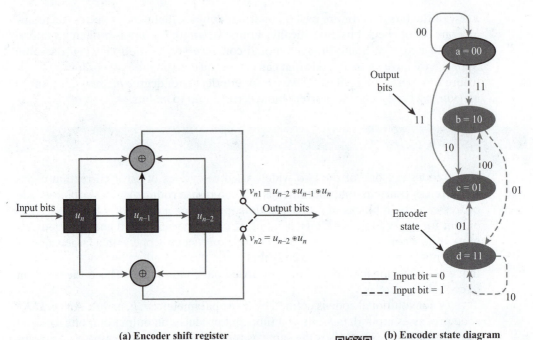

(a) Encoder shift register **(b) Encoder state diagram**

Figure 10.10 Convolutional Encoder with $(n, k, K) = (2, 1, 3)$

of the previous $(K - 1)$ input blocks of k bits each. We can therefore represent a convolutional code using a finite-state machine. The machine has $2^{k(K-1)}$ states, and the transition from one state to another is determined by the most recent k bits of inputs and produces n output bits. The initial state of the machine corresponds to the all-zeros state. For our example (Figure 10.10b) there are four states, one for each possible pair of values for the previous two bits. The next input bit causes a transition and produces an output of two bits. For example, if the last two bits were 10 ($u_{n-1} = 1, u_{n-2} = 0$) and the next bit is 1 ($u_n = 1$), then the current state is state b (10) and the next state is d (11). The output is

$$v_{n1} = u_{n-2} \oplus u_{n-1} \oplus u_n = 0 \oplus 1 \oplus 1 = 0$$
$$v_{n2} = 0 \oplus 1 = 1$$

Decoding

To understand the decoding process, it simplifies matters to expand the state diagram to show the time sequence of the encoder. If the state diagram is laid out vertically, as shown in Figure 10.10b, then the expanded diagram, called a **trellis**, is constructed by reproducing the states horizontally and showing the state transitions going from left to right corresponding to time, or data input (Figure 10.11). If the constraint length K is large, then the trellis becomes unwieldy because there would be a large number of rows. In that case, 2^{K-2} simplified trellis fragments can be used

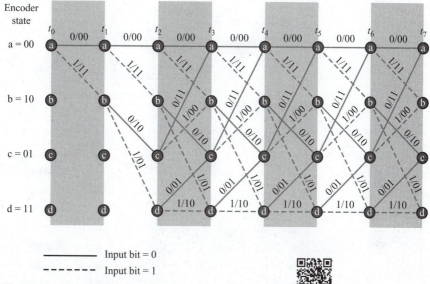

Figure 10.11 Trellis Diagram for Encoder of Figure 10.9

to depict the transitions. Figure 10.12 demonstrates this for a (2, 1, 7) code. Each of the states of the encoder is shown, along with the branch definition.

Any valid output is defined by a path through the trellis. In our example, the path a-b-c-b-d-c-a-a produces the output 11 10 00 01 01 11 00 and was generated by the input 1011000. If an invalid path occurs, such as a-c, then the decoder attempts error correction. In essence, the decoder must determine what data input was most likely to have produced the invalid output.

A number of error correction algorithms have been developed for convolutional codes. Perhaps the most important is the Viterbi algorithm. In essence, the Viterbi technique compares the received sequence with all possible transmitted sequences. The algorithm chooses a path through the trellis whose coded sequence differs from the received sequence in the fewest number of places. Once a valid path is selected as the correct path, the decoder can recover the input data bits from the most likely output code bits.

There are several variations on the Viterbi algorithm, depending on which metric is used to measure differences between received sequences and valid sequences. To give an idea of the operation of the algorithm, we use the common metric of Hamming distance. We represent a received coded sequence as the word $\mathbf{w} = w_0 w_1 w_2 \ldots$, and attempt to find the most likely valid path through the trellis. At each time i and for each state we list the *active path* (or paths) through the trellis to the state. An active path is a valid path through the trellis whose Hamming distance from the received word up to time i is minimal. We label each state at time i by the distance of its active path from the received word. The following relationship is used:

(distance of a path) = (distance of the last edge)

$$+ \text{ (distance of the last } - \text{ but } - \text{ one state)} \qquad (10.7)$$

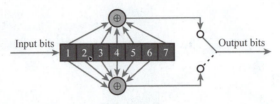

(a) Shift register diagram

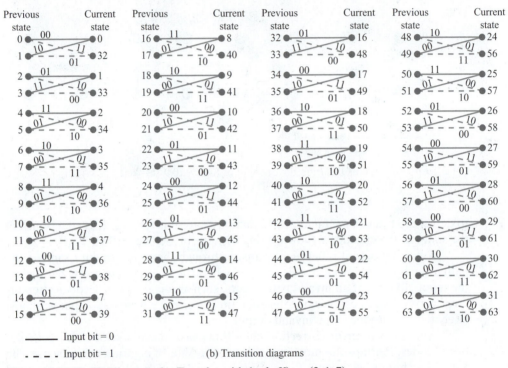

(b) Transition diagrams

Figure 10.12 Trellis Diagrams for Encoder with $(n, k, K) = (2, 1, 7)$

The algorithm proceeds in $(b + 1)$ steps, where b is a prechosen window size. For an (n, k, K) code, the first output block of n bits, $w_0 w_1 w_2 \ldots w_{n-1}$, is decoded in the following steps:

Step 0: The initial state of the trellis at time 0 is labeled 0, because there is so far no discrepancy.

Step $i + 1$: For each state S at time $i + 1$, find all active paths leading to S [using Equation (10.7)]. Label S by the distance of that path or paths.

Step b: The algorithm terminates at time b. If all the active paths at that time have the same first edge and the label of that edge is $x_0 x_1 x_2 \ldots x_{n-1}$, then the first code block $w_0 w_1 w_2 \ldots w_{n-1}$ is corrected to $x_0 x_1 x_2 \ldots x_{n-1}$. If there are two active first edges, the error is not correctable.

After accepting and, if necessary, correcting, the first code block, the decoding window is moved n bits to the right and the decoding of the next block is performed.

Example 10.10 [7]   Using the encoder defined in Figures 10.9 and 10.10, Figure 10.13 shows the application of the Viterbi algorithm to the sequence 10010100101100 . . . , with a decoding window of length $b = 7$. The animation for Figure 10.13 illustrates the following procedure. The lines in the figure represent valid paths through the trellis. The label for each lines shows the input data bit that caused that path and the output bits. The bold lines indicate the current active paths that were chosen at each step that had the minimal Hamming distance. At step 1, we have a received sequence of $w_0 w_1 = 10$. The two valid sequences are 00 for edge a-a and 11 for edge a-b as seen in Figure 10.10. For both of these sequences, there is a distance of 1 from the received sequence. Two active paths are defined, each with a state label of 1. For the next step, we have $w_2 w_3 = 01$. Using Equation (10.7), we compute the total cumulative differences to the four possible valid states (from top to bottom) as 2, 2, 3, and 1. So far, all possible valid paths are included as active paths. In Step 3, we see that some valid paths do not survive because they are not chosen as active paths. This is because each such path terminates on a state for which there is another valid path that has a smaller distance. For example, the state sequence a-a-a-a has a discrepancy of 3, while the state sequence a-b-c-a has the discrepancy of 4 and is excluded. At the conclusion of step 7, all active paths pass through the first edge a-b, which has the output 11. The algorithm corrects $w_0 w_1$ to 11 and continues with the next block $w_2 w_3$. Working backward through the trellis also decodes the original data by looking at the input bits that caused that path. Note that if the window size b was 5, the error would not have been correctable because the first edges a-a and a-b are both active.

Convolutional codes provide good performance in noisy channels where a high proportion of the bits is in error. Thus, they have found increasing use in wireless applications.

Turbo Coding

As higher and higher speeds are used in wireless applications, error correction continues to pose a major design challenge. Recently, a new class of codes, called **turbo codes**, has emerged as a popular choice for third and fourth-generation wireless systems. Turbo codes exhibit performance, in terms of bit error probability, that is very close to the Shannon limit and can be efficiently implemented for high-speed use. A number of different turbo encoders and decoders have been introduced, most of which are based on convolutional encoding. In this subsection, we give a general overview.

Figure 10.14a depicts a turbo encoder. In this scheme, the encoder is replicated. One copy of the encoder receives a stream of input bits and produces a single output check bit C_1 for each input bit. The input to the other encoder is an interleaved version of the input bit stream, producing a sequence of C_2 check bits. The initial input bit plus the two check bits are then multiplexed to produce the sequence $I_1 C_{11} C_{21} I_2 C_{12} C_{22} \ldots$, that is, the first input bit followed by the first bit from encoder 1, followed by the first bit from encoder 2, and so on. The resulting sequence has a code rate of $\frac{1}{3}$. A code rate of $\frac{1}{2}$ can be achieved by taking only half of the check bits, alternating between outputs from the two encoders; this process

---

[7]This example is based on one in [ADAM91].

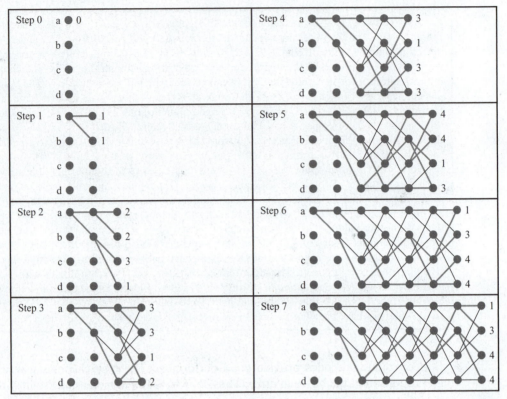

Figure 10.13 Viterbi Algorithm for $w = 10010100101100 \ldots$ with Decoding Window $b = 7$

is called *puncturing*. Rates of $\frac{1}{3}$ and $\frac{1}{2}$ are both found in third- and fourth-generation systems.

Note that each encoder only produces a single check bit for each input bit and that the input bit is preserved. In the convolutional encoders we have discussed so far (e.g., Figure 10.10a), the input bits are not preserved, and there are multiple output bits (*n* output check bits for *k* input bits). For turbo coding, a variation of the convolutional code, known as a recursive systematic convolutional code (RSC), is used. In a (2, 1, *K*) RSC encoder, which is typical, one of the two check bit calculations is fed back to the shift register, and the other check bit calculation produces an output bit (Figure 10.15). The output of the encoder consists of alternating input and check bits. The RSC encoder has the same trellis structure as a conventional convolutional encoder and similar statistical properties.

Figure 10.16 shows how a turbo encoder can be implemented using two RSC coders, where the switch is used to puncture the code, producing a code rate of $\frac{1}{2}$. Without the switch, the code rate is $\frac{1}{3}$.

Figure 10.14b is a general diagram of a turbo decoder. The received data are depunctured, if necessary, by estimating the missing check bits or by setting the missing bits to 0. Decoder 1 operates first, using the estimated I$'$ and C$'_1$ values received from the demodulator. These values are not simply 0 or 1, but rather are larger or smaller values given the demodulator's confidence in its decision. This is

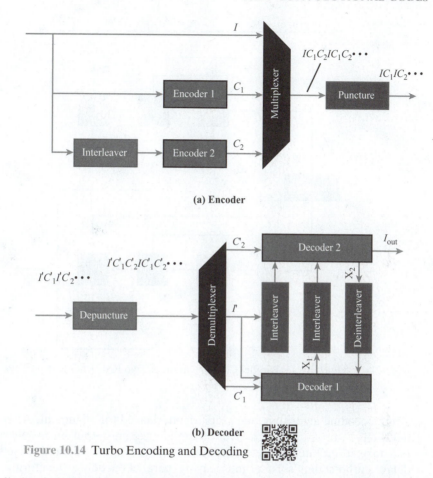

(a) Encoder

(b) Decoder

Figure 10.14 Turbo Encoding and Decoding

called *soft decision decoding*. Decoder 1 then produces correction (X_1) values. The I' and X_1 values are fed into Decoder 2, together with the C'_2 values. Interleaving must be performed to align bits properly. Decoder 2 uses all of its input to produce correction values X_2. These are fed back to Decoder 1 for a second iteration

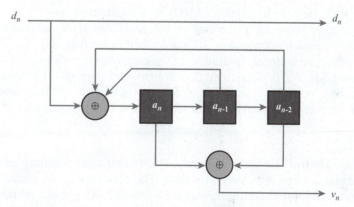

Figure 10.15 Recursive Systematic Convolutional (RSC) Encoder

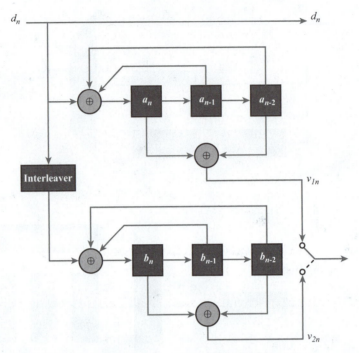

Figure 10.16 Parallel Concatenation of Two RSC Encoders

of the decoding algorithm, being first deinterleaved for alignment. After sufficient iterations to produce a high level of confidence, an output bit is generated. This may take several iterations to produce a good result, which could cause significant delay. Turbo coding's use of interleaving, parallel encoding, puncturing, soft decision decoding, and feedback gives it high performance.

10.4 AUTOMATIC REPEAT REQUEST

Automatic repeat request (ARQ) is a mechanism used in data link control and transport protocols and relies on the use of an error detection code, such as the cyclic redundancy check (CRC) described in Section 10.1. The ARQ error control mechanism is closely related to a flow control mechanism that is also a part of these protocols. We first examine flow control and then go on to look at ARQ. In what follows, we refer to the block of data that is transmitted from one protocol entity to another as a **protocol data unit (PDU)**; this term was introduced in Chapter 4.

Flow Control

Flow control is a technique for assuring that a transmitting entity does not overwhelm a receiving entity with data. The receiving entity typically allocates a data buffer of some maximum length for a transfer. When data are received, the receiver must do a certain amount of processing (e.g., examine the header and strip it off the

PDU) before passing the data to the higher-level software. In the absence of flow control, the receiver's buffer may fill up and overflow while it is processing old data.

To begin, we examine mechanisms for flow control in the absence of errors. The model we will use is depicted in Figure 10.17a, which is a vertical-time sequence diagram. It has the advantages of showing time dependencies and illustrating the correct send-receive relationship. Each arrow represents a single PDU traversing a data link between two stations. The data are sent in a sequence of PDUs, with each PDU containing a portion of the data and some control information. For now, we assume that all PDUs that are transmitted are successfully received; no PDUs are lost and none arrive with errors. Furthermore, PDUs arrive in the same order in which they are sent. However, each transmitted PDU suffers an arbitrary and variable amount of delay before reception.

Typically, when a source has a block or stream of data to transmit, the source will break up the block of data into smaller blocks and transmit the data in many PDUs. This is done for the following reasons:

- The buffer size of the receiver may be limited.
- The longer the transmission, the more likely that there will be an error, necessitating retransmission of the entire PDU. With smaller PDUs, errors are detected sooner, and a smaller amount of data needs to be retransmitted.
- On a shared medium, such as a LAN, it is usually desirable not to permit one station to occupy the medium for an extended period, thus causing long delays at the other sending stations.

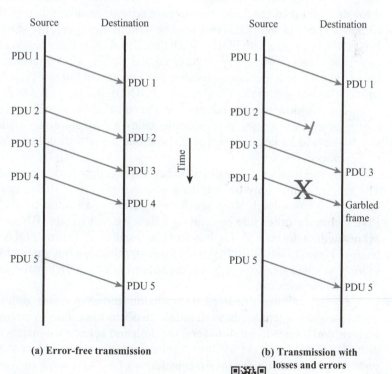

(a) Error-free transmission

(b) Transmission with losses and errors

Figure 10.17 Model of PDU Transmission

Typically, protocols that have a flow control mechanism allow multiple PDUs to be in transit at the same time. Let us examine how this might work for two stations, A and B, connected via a full-duplex link. Station B allocates buffer space for W PDUs. Thus B can accept W PDUs, and A is allowed to send W PDUs without waiting for any acknowledgments. To keep track of which PDUs have been acknowledged, each is labeled with a sequence number. B acknowledges a PDU by sending an acknowledgment that includes the sequence number of the next PDU expected. This acknowledgment also implicitly announces that B is prepared to receive the next W PDUs, beginning with the number specified. This scheme can also be used to acknowledge multiple PDUs to save network overhead. For example, B could receive PDUs 2, 3, and 4 but withhold acknowledgment until PDU 4 has arrived. By then returning an acknowledgment with sequence number 5, B acknowledges PDUs 2, 3, and 4 at one time. A maintains a list of sequence numbers that it is allowed to send, and B maintains a list of sequence numbers that it is prepared to receive. Each of these lists can be thought of as a *window* of PDUs. The operation is referred to as **sliding-window flow control**.

Several additional comments need to be made. Because the sequence number to be used occupies a field in the PDU, it is clearly of bounded size. For example, for a 3-bit field, the sequence number can range from 0 to 7. Accordingly, PDUs are numbered modulo 8; that is, after sequence number 7, the next number is 0. In general, for a k-bit field the range of sequence numbers is 0 through $2^k - 1$, and PDUs are numbered modulo 2^k.

Figure 10.18 is a useful way of depicting the sliding-window process. It assumes the use of a 3-bit sequence number, so that PDUs are numbered sequentially from 0 through 7, and then the same numbers are reused for subsequent PDUs. The shaded rectangle indicates the PDUs that may be sent; in this figure, the sender may transmit five PDUs, beginning with PDU 0. Each time a PDU is sent, the shaded window shrinks; each time an acknowledgment is received, the shaded window grows. PDUs between the vertical bar and the shaded window have been sent but not yet acknowledged. As we shall see, the sender must buffer these PDUs in case they need to be retransmitted.

The window size need not be the maximum possible size for a given sequence number length. For example, using a 3-bit sequence number, a window size of 4 could be configured for the stations using the sliding-window flow control protocol.

The mechanism so far described does indeed provide a form of flow control: The receiver must only be able to accommodate seven PDUs beyond the one it has last acknowledged. Most protocols also allow a station to cut off the flow of PDUs from the other side by sending a Receive Not Ready (RNR) message, which acknowledges former PDUs but forbids transfer of future PDUs. Thus, RNR 5 means "I have received all PDUs up through number 4 but am unable to accept any more." At some subsequent point, the station must send a normal acknowledgment to reopen the window.

So far, we have discussed transmission in one direction only. If two stations exchange data, each needs to maintain two windows, one to transmit and one to receive, and each side needs to send the data and acknowledgments to the other. To provide efficient support for this requirement, a feature known as *piggybacking* is typically provided. Each *data PDU* includes a field that holds the sequence number of that PDU plus a field that holds the sequence number used for acknowledgment.

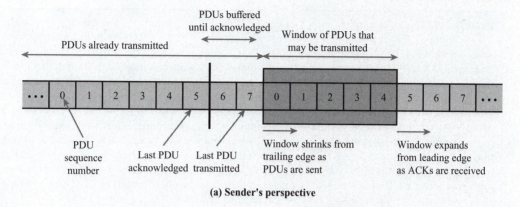

(a) Sender's perspective

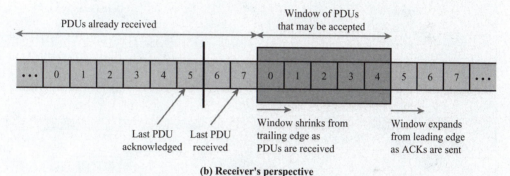

(b) Receiver's perspective

Figure 10.18 Sliding-Window Depiction

Thus, if a station has data to send and an acknowledgment to send, it sends both together in one PDU, saving communication capacity. Of course, if a station has an acknowledgment but no data to send, it sends a separate *acknowledgment PDU*. If a station has data to send but no new acknowledgment to send, it must repeat the last acknowledgment that it sent. This is because the data PDU includes a field for the acknowledgment number, and some value must be put into that field. When a station receives a duplicate acknowledgment, it simply ignores it.

Error Control

Error control refers to mechanisms to detect and correct errors that occur in the transmission of PDUs. The model that we will use, which covers the typical case, is illustrated in Figure 10.17b. As before, data are sent as a sequence of PDUs; PDUs arrive in the same order in which they are sent; and each transmitted PDU suffers an arbitrary and variable amount of delay before reception. In addition, we admit the possibility of two types of errors:

- **Lost PDU:** A PDU fails to arrive at the other side. For example, a noise burst may damage a PDU to the extent that the receiver is not aware that a PDU has been transmitted.

Example 10.11 An example is shown in Figure 10.19 and its animation. The example assumes a 3-bit sequence number field and a maximum window size of seven PDUs. Initially, A and B have windows indicating that A may transmit seven PDUs, beginning with PDU 0 (P0). After transmitting three PDUs (P0, P1, P2) without acknowledgment, A has shrunk its window to four PDUs and maintains a copy of the three transmitted PDUs. The window indicates that A may transmit four PDUs, beginning with PDU number 3. B then transmits an RR (Receive Ready) 3, which means "I have received all PDUs up through PDU number 2 and am ready to receive PDU number 3; in fact, I am prepared to receive seven PDUs, beginning with PDU number 3." With this acknowledgment, A once again has permission to transmit seven frames, still beginning with frame 3; also A may discard the buffered frames that have now been acknowledged. A proceeds to transmit PDUs 3, 4, 5, and 6. B returns RR 4, which acknowledges P3, and allows transmission of P4 through the next instance of P2. By the time this RR reaches A, it has already transmitted P4, P5, and P6, and therefore A may only open its window to permit sending four PDUs beginning with P7.

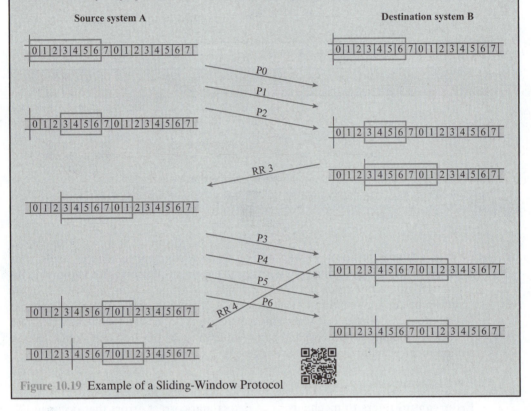

Figure 10.19 Example of a Sliding-Window Protocol

- **Damaged PDU:** A recognizable PDU does arrive, but some of the bits are in error (have been altered during transmission) and cannot be corrected.

The most common techniques for error control are based on some or all of the following ingredients:

- **Error detection:** The receiver detects errors and discards PDUs that are in error.

- **Positive acknowledgment:** The destination returns a positive acknowledgment for one or more successfully received, error-free frames.

- **Retransmission after timeout:** The source retransmits a PDU that has not been acknowledged after a predetermined amount of time.

- **Negative acknowledgment and retransmission:** The destination returns a negative acknowledgment to PDUs in which an error is detected. The source retransmits such PDUs.

Collectively, these mechanisms are all referred to as **automatic repeat request (ARQ)**; the effect of ARQ is to turn an unreliable data link into a reliable one. The most commonly used version of ARQ is known as **go-back-N ARQ**. Go-back-N ARQ is based on the sliding-window flow control mechanism just discussed.

In go-back-N ARQ, a station may send a series of PDUs sequentially numbered modulo some maximum value. The number of unacknowledged PDUs outstanding is determined by window size, using the sliding-window flow control technique. While no errors occur, the destination will acknowledge incoming PDUs as usual (RR = receive ready, or piggybacked acknowledgment). If the destination station detects an error in a PDU, it sends a negative acknowledgment (REJ = reject) for that PDU. The destination station will discard that PDU and all future incoming PDUs until the PDU in error is correctly received. Thus the source station, when it receives a REJ, must retransmit the PDU in error plus all succeeding PDUs that had been transmitted in the interim. Hence, the name go-back-N to retransmit these PDUs.

Consider that station A is sending PDUs to station B. After each transmission, A sets an acknowledgment timer for the PDU just transmitted. Suppose that B has previously successfully received PDU $(i - 1)$ and A has just transmitted PDU i. The go-back-N technique takes into account the following contingencies:

1. **Damaged PDU.** If the received PDU is invalid (i.e., B detects an error), B discards the PDU and takes no further action as the result of that PDU. There are two subcases:

   a. Within a reasonable period of time, A subsequently sends PDU $(i + 1)$. B receives PDU $(i + 1)$ out of order because it is expecting PDU (i) and sends a REJ i. A must retransmit PDU i and all subsequent PDUs.

   b. A does not soon send additional PDUs. B receives nothing and returns neither an RR nor a REJ. When A's timer expires, it transmits an RR PDU that includes a bit known as the P bit, which is set to 1. B interprets the RR PDU with a P bit of 1 as a command that must be acknowledged by sending an RR indicating the next PDU that it expects, which is PDU i. When A receives the RR, it retransmits PDU i.

2. **Damaged RR.** There are two subcases:

   a. B receives PDU i and sends RR $(i + 1)$, which suffers an error in transit. Because acknowledgments are cumulative (e.g., RR 6 means that all PDUs through 5 are acknowledged), it may be that A will receive a subsequent RR to a subsequent PDU and that it will arrive before the timer associated with PDU i expires.

   b. If A's timer expires, it transmits an RR command as in Case 1b. It sets another timer, called the P-bit timer. If B fails to respond to the RR command, or if its response suffers an error in transit, then A's P-bit timer will expire. At this point, A will try again by issuing a new RR command and restarting the P-bit timer. This procedure is tried for a number of iterations. If A fails to obtain an acknowledgment after some maximum number of attempts, it initiates a reset procedure.

3. **Damaged REJ.** If a REJ is lost, this is equivalent to Case 1b.

Figure 10.20 is an example of the PDU flow for go-back-N ARQ. It sends RRs only for even numbered PDUs. Because of the propagation delay on the line, by the time that an acknowledgment (positive or negative) arrives back at the sending station, it has already sent two additional PDUs beyond the one being acknowledged. Thus, when a REJ is received to PDU 5, not only PDU 5 but PDUs 6 and 7 must be retransmitted. Thus, the transmitter must keep a copy of all unacknowledged PDUs.

Hybrid Automatic Repeat Request

In practical wireless system implementation, neither FEC nor ARQ is an adequate one-size-fits-all solution. FEC may add unnecessary redundancy (i.e., use extra bandwidth) if channel conditions are good and ARQ with error detection may cause excessive delays from retransmissions in poor channel conditions. Therefore, a solution known as **Hybrid Automatic Repeat Request (HARQ)** has been widely implemented in today's systems; it uses a combination of FEC to correct the most common errors and ARQ for retransmission when FEC cannot make corrections. Going beyond this basic concept, the following additional approaches may be implemented.

- **Soft decision decoding:** The decoding process can provide not just an assessment of a bit being 0 or 1, but also levels of confidence in those results.

- **Chase combining:** Previous frames that were not corrected by FEC need not be discarded. The soft decision information can be stored and then combined with soft decision information from retransmissions. If using turbo coding as seen in Figure 10.14, the decoders in the receivers now use information from multiple frames not just the current frame. This will result in stronger FEC capabilities. In **chase combining** the exact same frames are retransmitted each time and soft combined.

- **Incremental redundancy:** Each time a sender retransmits, different coding information can be provided. This can accomplish two goals:

  1. Lower Overhead. The initial packets can include less coding; if enough, then the packet can be successful and overhead can be avoided. For example, the first frame may only include a few bytes of an error detection code like CRC, with later frames then including FEC after the first frame has errors.

  2. Stronger Correction. The retransmissions can provide different coding at the same coding rates or stronger coding at lower coding rates. If adapted to the current wireless channel environment, this will increase the probability of a successful transmission by the second or third frames.

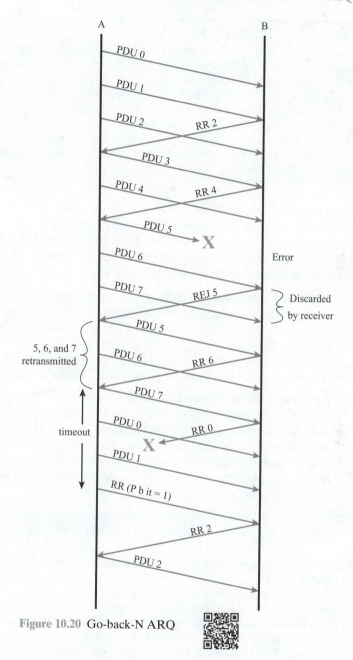

Figure 10.20 Go-back-N ARQ

- **Puncturing:** To provide the various coding rates for incremental redundancy, a different FEC coding algorithm could be used each time. A simpler approach, however, is **puncturing**, which removes bits to increase the coding rate.

In general, a punctured code is weaker than an unpunctured code at the same rate. However, simply puncturing the same code to achieve different coding

> **Example 10.12** Consider an FEC coder that produces a $\frac{1}{3}$ rate code that is punctured to become a $\frac{1}{2}$ rate code. Say, there are 100 bits of data that become a 300 bit FEC codeword. To become a $\frac{1}{2}$ rate FEC codeword, there need to be 2 bits of codeword for every 1 bit of data, hence a 200 bit codeword. This means 100 bits, 1 of every 3 bits of the original FEC code, need to be punctured. At the receiver, the missing 100 bits would be replaced before decoding. These could just be replaced with random numbers, which would mean that roughly 50 of those would coincidentally be correct and the other 50 incorrect. The original FEC code may actually still be plenty effective enough to correct those errors if the received signal-to-noise ratio is relatively good. If not, a later retransmission might use less puncturing or puncture different bits.

rates allows the decoder structure to remain the same, instead of having multiple decoders for different code rates. The benefits of this reduction in complexity can outweigh the reduction in performance from puncturing. Used with HARQ incremental redundancy, puncturing will take a single output from an FEC coder and remove more or different bits each time.

- **Adaptive modulation and coding:** Systems will use channel quality information (CQI) to estimate the best modulation and coding to work with HARQ. For example, fourth-generation cellular LTE uses the CQI to determine the highest modulation and coding rate that would provide a 10% block error rate for the first HARQ transmission. Also, if the CQI changes in the middle of an HARQ process, the modulation and coding might be adapted.

- **Parallel HARQ processes:** Some systems wait until the HARQ process finishes for one frame before sending the next frame; this is known as a stop-and-wait protocol. The process of waiting for an ACK or NACK, followed by possible multiple retransmissions can be time consuming, however. Therefore, some HARQ implementations allow for multiple open HARQ operations to be occurring at the same time. This is known as an **N-channel Stop-and-Wait** protocol.

10.5 RECOMMENDED READING

The classic treatment of error detection codes and CRC is [PETE61]. [RAMA88] is an excellent tutorial on CRC.

[ADAM91] provides comprehensive treatment of error correction codes. [SKLA01] contains a clear, well-written section on the subject. Two useful survey articles are [BERL87] and [BHAR83]. A quite readable theoretical and mathematical treatment of error correction codes is [ASH90].

Two good treatments of turbo codes are [SKLA97] and [BERR96]. A more detailed analysis is [VUCE00]. Hybrid ARQ is discussed in [GHOS11] in several places when describing LTE.

ADAM91 Adamek, J. *Foundations of Coding.* New York: Wiley, 1991.

ASH90 Ash, R. *Information Theory.* New York: Dover, 1990.

BERL87 Berlekamp, E.; Peile, R.; and Pope, S. "The Application of Error Control to Communications." *IEEE Communications Magazine,* April 1987.

BERR96 Berrou, C., and Glavieux, A. "Near Optimum Error Correcting Codes and Decoding: Turbo Codes." *IEEE Transactions on Communications,* October 1996.

BHAR83 Bhargava, V. "Forward Error Correction Schemes for Digital Communications." *IEEE Communications Magazine,* January 1983.

GHOS11 Ghosh, A.; Zhang, J.; Andrews J.; and Muhamed, R. *Fundamentals of LTE.* Upper Saddle River, NJ: Prentice Hall, 2011.

PETE61 Peterson, W., and Brown, D. "Cyclic Codes for Error Detection." *Proceedings of the IEEE,* January 1961.

RAMA88 Ramabadran, T., and Gaitonde, S. "A Tutorial on CRC Computations." *IEEE Micro,* August 1988.

SKLA97 Sklar, B. "A Primer on Turbo Code Concepts." *IEEE Communications Magazine,* December 1997.

SKLA01 Sklar, B. *Digital Communications: Fundamentals and Applications.* Upper Saddle River, NJ: Prentice Hall, 2001.

VUCE00 Vucetic, B., and Yuan, J. *Turbo Codes: Principles and Applications.* Boston: Kluwer Academic Publishers, 2000.

10.6 KEY TERMS, REVIEW QUESTIONS, AND PROBLEMS

Key Terms

automatic repeat request (ARQ)	error correction	Hybrid Automatic Repeat Request (HARQ)
block interleaving	error detection	incremental redundancy
chase combining	error detection code	N-channel Stop-and-Wait
check bits	flow control	parity bit
codeword	forward error correction (FEC)	parity check
convolutional code	frame check sequence (FCS)	protocol data unit (PDU)
cyclic code		puncturing
cyclic redundancy check (CRC)	go-back-N ARQ	sliding-window flow control
error control	Hamming code	trellis
	Hamming distance	turbo code

Review Questions

10.1 What is a parity bit?

10.2 What is the CRC?

10.3 Why would you expect a CRC to detect more errors than a parity bit?

10.4 List three different ways in which the CRC algorithm can be described.

10.5 Is it possible to design an FEC that will correct some double-bit errors but not all double-bit errors? Why or why not?

10.6 In an (n, k) block FEC, what do n and k represent?

10.7 In an (n, k, K) convolutional code, what do n, k, and K represent?

10.8 What is a trellis in the context of a convolutional code?

10.9 What two key elements comprise error control?

10.10 Explain how go-back-N ARQ works.

10.11 How does soft decision decoding improve H-ARQ?

Problems

10.1 What is the purpose of using modulo 2 arithmetic rather than binary arithmetic in computing an FCS?

10.2 Consider a frame consisting of two characters of four bits each. Assume that the probability of bit error is 10^{-3} and that it is independent for each bit.
   a. What is the probability that the received frame contains at least one error?
   b. Now add a parity bit to each character. What is the probability?

10.3 Using the CRC-CCITT polynomial, generate the 16-bit CRC code for a message consisting of a 1 followed by 15 0s.
   a. Use long division.
   b. Use the shift register mechanism shown in Figure 10.4.

10.4 Explain in words why the shift register implementation of CRC will result in all 0s at the receiver if there are no errors. Demonstrate by example.

10.5 For $P = 110011$ and $M = 11100011$, find the CRC.

10.6 A CRC is constructed to generate a 4-bit FCS for an 11-bit message. The generator polynomial is $X^4 + X^3 + 1$.
   a. Draw the shift register circuit that would perform this task (see Figure 10.4).
   b. Encode the data bit sequence 10011011100 (leftmost bit is the least significant) using the generator polynomial and give the codeword.
   c. Now assume that bit 7 (counting from the least significant bit) in the codeword is in error and show that the detection algorithm detects the error.

10.7 A modified CRC procedure is commonly used in communications standards such as HDLC. It is defined as follows:

$$\frac{X^{16}M(X) + X^k L(X)}{P(X)} = Q + \frac{R(X)}{P(X)}$$

$$\text{FCS} = L(X) + R(X)$$

where

$$L(X) = X^{15} + X^{14} + X^{13} + \cdots + X + 1$$

and k is the number of bits being checked (address, control, and information fields).
   a. Describe in words the effect of this procedure.
   b. Explain the potential benefits.
   c. Show a shift register implementation for $P(X) = X^{16} + X^{12} + X^5 + 1$.

10.8 Figure 10.21 shows a polynomial division circuit that produces a result equivalent to that of the circuit in Figure 10.4.
   a. Using this alternative structure, draw a LFSR for dividing by $X^5 + X^4 + X^2 + 1$ that is equivalent to that of Figure 10.3a.
   b. Show the sequence of steps that produces the resulting CRC, following the method of Figure 10.3. You should end up with the same pattern, 01110, in the shift register at the end of the operation. *Hint:* note that there is a delay in outputting the input bits of $(n - k)$ bits, so you need to perform $(n - k)$ additional shifts to produce the final result.
   c. An advantage of the structure in Figure 10.21, compared to that in Figure 10.4,

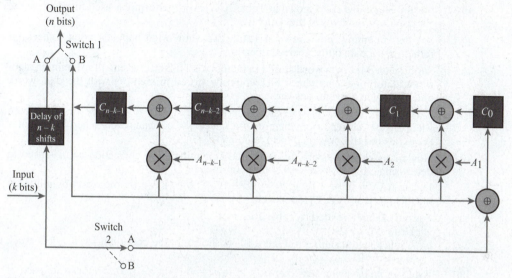

Figure 10.21 Another CRC Architecture to Implement Divisor $1 + A_1X + A_2X^2 + \cdot \cdot + A_{n-1}X^{n-k-1} + X^{n-k}$

is that it shows the correspondence with the long division process more clearly. Explain.

   d. What is a disadvantage of the structure in Figure 10.21?

10.9 Calculate the Hamming pairwise distances among the following codewords:
   a. 00000, 10101, 01010
   b. 000000, 010101, 101010, 110110

10.10 Section 10.2 discusses block error correction codes that make a decision on the basis of minimum distance. That is, given a code consisting of s equally likely codewords of length n, for each received sequence $\mathbf{v}$, the receiver selects the codeword $\mathbf{w}$ for which the distance $d(\mathbf{w}, \mathbf{v})$ is a minimum. We would like to prove that this scheme is "ideal" in the sense that the receiver always selects the codeword for which the probability of $\mathbf{w}$ given $\mathbf{v}$, $p(\mathbf{w}|\mathbf{v})$, is a maximum. Because all codewords are assumed equally likely, the code word that maximizes $p(\mathbf{w}|\mathbf{v})$ is the same as the codeword that maximizes $p(\mathbf{v}|\mathbf{w})$.
   a. In order that $\mathbf{w}$ be received as $\mathbf{v}$, there must be exactly $d(\mathbf{w}, \mathbf{v})$ errors in transmission, and these errors must occur in those bits where $\mathbf{w}$ and $\mathbf{v}$ disagree. Let β be the probability that a given bit is transmitted incorrectly and n be the length of a codeword. Write an expression for $p(\mathbf{v}|\mathbf{w})$ as a function of β, $d(\mathbf{w}, \mathbf{v})$, and n. *Hint:* the number of bits in error is $d(\mathbf{w}, \mathbf{v})$ and the number of bits not in error is $n - d(\mathbf{w}, \mathbf{v})$.
   b. Now compare $p(\mathbf{v}|\mathbf{w}_1)$ and $p(\mathbf{v}|\mathbf{w}_2)$ for two different codewords $\mathbf{w}_1$ and $\mathbf{w}_2$ by calculating $p(\mathbf{v}|\mathbf{w}_1)/p(\mathbf{v}|\mathbf{w}_2)$.
   c. Assume that $0 < \beta < 0.5$ and show that $p(\mathbf{v}|\mathbf{w}_1) > p(\mathbf{v}|\mathbf{w}_2)$ if and only if $d(\mathbf{v}, \mathbf{w}_1) < d(\mathbf{v}, \mathbf{w}_2)$. This proves that the codeword $\mathbf{w}$ that gives the largest value of $p(\mathbf{v}|\mathbf{w})$ is that word whose distance from $\mathbf{v}$ is a minimum.

10.11 Section 10.2 states that for a given positive integer t, if a code satisfies $d_{\min} \geq 2t + 1$, then the code can correct all bit errors up to and including errors of t bits. Prove this assertion. *Hint:* Start by observing that for a codeword $\mathbf{w}$ to be decoded as another codeword $\mathbf{w}'$, the received sequence must be at least as close to $\mathbf{w}'$ as to $\mathbf{w}$.

10.12 For the Hamming code shown in Table 10.2, show the formulas used to calculate the check bits as functions of the data bits.

10.13 For the Hamming code shown in Table 10.2, show what happens when a check bit rather than a data bit is received in error.

10.14 Suppose an 8-bit data word stored in memory is 11000010. Using the Hamming algorithm, determine what check bits would be stored in memory with the data word. Show how you got your answer.

10.15 For the 8-bit word 00111001, the check bits stored with it would be 0111. Suppose when the word is read from memory, the check bits are calculated to be 1101. What is the data word that was read from memory?

10.16 How many check bits are needed if the Hamming error correction code is used to detect single-bit errors in a 1024-bit data word?

10.17 Divide $f(X) = X^6 + 1$ by $g(X) = X^4 + X^3 + X + 1$. Verify the result by multiplying the quotient by $g(X)$ to recover $f(X)$.

10.18 For the example related to Table 10.3:
  a. Draw the LFSR.
  b. Using a layout similar to Figure 10.3b, show that the check bits for the data block 1010 are 001.

10.19 Using an interleaving structure of $n = 4, m = 6$ (Figure 10.9), demonstrate each of the following block interleaving characteristics:
  a. Any burst of m contiguous channel bit errors results in isolated errors at the deinterleaver output that are separated from each other by at least n bits.
  b. Any bm bursts of errors ($b > 1$) results in output bursts from the deinterleaver of no more than $\lceil b \rceil$ errors. Each output burst is separated from the other bursts by no less than $\lfloor b \rfloor$ bits. The notation $\lceil b \rceil$ means the smallest integer no less than b, and $\lfloor b \rfloor$ means the largest integer no greater than b.
  c. A periodic sequence of single-bit errors spaced m bits apart results in a single burst of errors of length n at the deinterleaver output.
  d. Not including channel propagation delay, the interleaver end-to-end delay is $2(n(m - 1) + 1)$. Only $(n(m - 1) + 1)$ cells need to be filled before transmission can begin and a corresponding number needs to be filled at the receiver before deinterleaving can begin.

10.20 Consider a convolutional encoder defined by ($v_{n1} = u_n \oplus u_{n-2}$) and ($v_{n2} = u_{n-1} \oplus u_{n-2}$).
  a. Draw a shift register implementation for this encoder similar to Figure 10.10a.
  b. Draw a state diagram for this encoder similar to Figure 10.10b.
  c. Draw a trellis diagram for this encoder similar to Figure 10.11.

10.21 For the encoder of Problem 10.20, assume that the shift register is initialized to all zeros and that after the transmission of the last information bit, two zero bits are transmitted.
  a. Why are the two extra bits needed?
  b. What is the encoded sequence corresponding to the information sequence 1101011, where the leftmost bit is the first bit presented to the encoder?

10.22 The simplest form of flow control, known as **stop-and-wait flow control**, works as follows. A source entity transmits a frame. After the destination entity receives the frame, it indicates its willingness to accept another frame by sending back an acknowledgment to the frame just received. The source must wait until it receives the acknowledgment before sending the next frame. The destination can thus stop the flow of data simply by withholding acknowledgment. Consider a half-duplex point-to-point link using a stop-and-wait scheme, in which a series of messages is sent, with each message segmented into a number of frames. Ignore errors and frame overhead.
  a. What is the effect on line utilization of increasing the message size so that fewer messages will be required? Other factors remain constant.

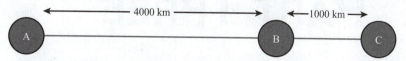

Figure 10.22 Configuration for Problem 10.22

    b. What is the effect on line utilization of increasing the number of frames for a constant message size?
    c. What is the effect on line utilization of increasing frame size?

10.23 In Figure 10.22, frames are generated at node A and sent to node C through node B. Determine the minimum data rate required between nodes B and C so that the buffers of node B are not flooded, based on the following:
- The data rate between A and B is 100 kbps.
- The propagation delay is 5 μs/km for both lines.
- There are full duplex lines between the nodes.
- All data frames are 1000 bits long; ACK frames are separate frames of negligible length.
- Between A and B, a sliding-window protocol with a window size of 3 is used.
- Between B and C, stop-and-wait is used.
- There are no errors.

    Hint: In order not to flood the buffers of B, the average number of frames entering and leaving B must be the same over a long interval.

10.24 A channel has a data rate of R bps and a propagation delay of t seconds per kilometer. The distance between the sending and receiving nodes is L kilometers. Nodes exchange fixed-size frames of B bits. Find a formula that gives the minimum sequence field size of the frame as a function of R, t, B, and L (considering maximum utilization). Assume that ACK frames are negligible in size and the processing at the nodes is instantaneous.

10.25 Two neighboring nodes (A and B) use a sliding-window protocol with a 3-bit sequence number. As the ARQ mechanism, go-back-N is used with a window size of 4. Assuming A is transmitting and B is receiving, show the window positions for the following succession of events:
    a. Before A sends any frames
    b. After A sends frames 0, 1, 2 and receives acknowledgment from B for 0 and 1
    c. After A sends frames 3, 4, and 5 and B acknowledges 4 and the ACK is received by A

10.26 Two stations communicate via a 1-Mbps satellite link with a propagation delay of 270 ms. The satellite serves merely to retransmit data received from one station to another, with negligible switching delay. Using frames of 1024 bits with 3-bit sequence numbers, what is the maximum possible data throughput; that is, what is the throughput of data bits carried in frames?

PART THREE

Wireless Local and Personal Area Networks

CHAPTER 11

WIRELESS LAN TECHNOLOGY

LEARNING OBJECTIVES

After studying this chapter, you should be able to:

- Explain the roles of the layers in the IEEE 802.11 architecture.
- Describe the services provided by IEEE 802.11.
- Explain the use of backoff, interframe spacing, point coordination, and distributed coordination for MAC layer operation of IEEE 802.11.
- Describe the main methods used to improve throughput in IEEE 802.11n, 802.11ac, and 802.11ad.
- Explain the IEEE 802.11i WLAN security procedures.

Wireless LANs (WLANs) play an important role in the local area network market. Increasingly, organizations are finding that wireless LANs are an indispensable adjunct to traditional wired LANs, to satisfy requirements for mobility, relocation, ad hoc networking, and coverage of locations difficult to wire. In addition, a plethora of wireless devices use WLANs as a replacement for cellular coverage when in range (usually indoors) or as their main source of wireless connectivity.

This chapter provides a survey of wireless LANs. We begin with an overview that looks at the motivations for using wireless LANs and summarizes the various approaches in current use.

11.1 OVERVIEW AND MOTIVATION

As the name suggests, a wireless LAN is one that makes use of a wireless transmission medium for a local area network. Figure 11.1 indicates a simple wireless LAN configuration that is typical of many environments. There is a backbone wired LAN, such as Ethernet, that supports servers, workstations, and one or more bridges or routers to link with other networks. In addition, there is a control module (CM) that acts as an interface to a wireless LAN. The control module includes either bridge or router functionality to link the wireless LAN to the backbone. It includes some sort of access control logic, such as a polling or token-passing scheme, to regulate the access from the end systems. Note that some of the end systems are stand-alone devices, such as a workstation or a server. Hubs or other user modules (UMs) that control a number of stations off a wired LAN may also be part of the wireless LAN configuration.

The configuration of Figure 11.1 can be referred to as a single-cell wireless LAN; all of the wireless end systems are within the range of a single control module. This may be true of a small office or a home. Another common configuration, suggested by Figure 11.2, is a multiple-cell wireless LAN. In this case, there are multiple control modules interconnected by a wired LAN. Each control module supports a number of wireless end systems within its transmission range. For example, with IEEE 802.11ad WLAN, transmission is limited to a single room due to its use of 60 GHz frequencies; therefore, one cell is needed for each room in an office building that requires wireless support.

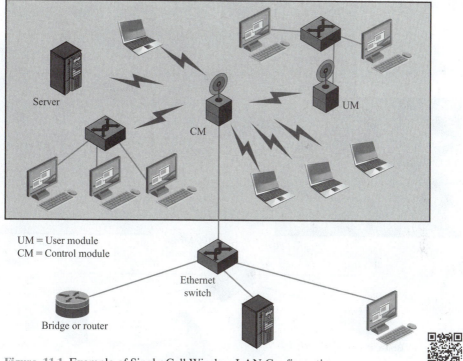

UM = User module
CM = Control module

Figure 11.1 Example of Single-Cell Wireless LAN Configuration

An **ad hoc network** is a peer-to-peer network (no centralized server) set up temporarily to meet some immediate need. For example, a group of devices in a home may connect to share multimedia content. This may be a temporary network just for the duration of the multimedia session. Figure 11.3 shows a wireless LAN configured as an ad hoc wireless LAN. A peer collection of stations within the range of each other may dynamically configure themselves into a temporary network. WLANs can provide a wireless connectivity for an ad hoc network, as may Bluetooth, ZigBee, and other technologies mentioned in Chapter 12, depending on range, throughput, and power requirements.

Motivation

WLANs are providing many important capabilities. As newer standards exceed gigabit per second throughput, the following capabilities are enhanced [VERM13]:

- **Cellular data offloading:** The spectrum available in mobile cellular networks is limited and costly to consumers. Mobile devices such as smartphones, laptops, and tablets can use higher capacity WLANs. This is especially helpful in high density locations such as shopping malls, enterprises, universities, and even sporting venues.

- **Sync/file transfer:** Multi-gigabit Wi-Fi (Wireless Fidelity) allows synchronization between devices 10 times faster than previous Wi-Fi. For example, this eliminates the need to use cables to synchronize mobile devices.

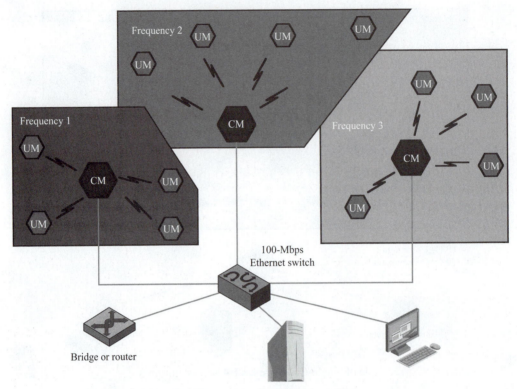

Figure 11.2 Example of Multiple-Cell Wireless LAN Configuration

Figure 11.3 Ad Hoc Wireless LAN Configuration

- **Internet Access:** Multi-gigabit Wi-Fi enables faster Internet access, eliminating any significant bottlenecks from the WLAN.

- **Multimedia Streaming:** Streaming uncompressed video can require 3 Gbps, and streaming of compressed video has issues of quality and latency. Wi-Fi can be more suitable than other proposed wireless approaches because of its larger deployment, user awareness, support for IP networking, ease of connection, and standardized security mechanism.

Wireless LAN Requirements

A WLAN must meet the same sort of requirements typical of any LAN, including high capacity, ability to cover short distances, full connectivity among attached stations, and broadcast capability. In addition, there are a number of requirements specific to the wireless LAN environment. The following are among the most important requirements for wireless LANs:

- **Throughput:** The medium access control (MAC) protocol should make as efficient use as possible of the wireless medium to maximize capacity.

- **Number of nodes:** WLANs may need to support hundreds of nodes across multiple cells.

- **Connection to backbone LAN:** In most cases, interconnection with stations on a wired backbone LAN is required. For infrastructure WLANs, this is easily accomplished through the use of control modules that connect to both types of LANs. There may also need to be accommodation for mobile users with ad hoc wireless networks.

- **Service area:** A typical coverage area for a WLAN has a diameter of 100 to 300 m.

- **Battery power consumption:** Mobile workers use battery-powered smartphones, tablets, and workstations that need to have a long battery life. This suggests that a MAC protocol that requires mobile nodes to monitor access points constantly or engage in frequent handshakes with a base station is inappropriate. Typical WLAN implementations have features to reduce power consumption, such as sleep modes, while not using the network.

- **Transmission robustness and security:** Unless properly designed, a WLAN may be especially vulnerable to interference and network eavesdropping. The design of a WLAN must permit reliable transmission even in a noisy environment and should provide security from eavesdropping.

- **Collocated network operation:** It is common for two or more wireless LANs to operate in the same area or in some area where interference between the WLANs is possible. Such interference may thwart the normal operation of a MAC algorithm and may allow unauthorized access to a particular WLAN.

- **License-free operation:** Users need to buy and operate WLAN products without having to secure a license for the frequency band used by the WLAN.

- **Handoff/roaming:** The MAC protocol used in the WLAN should enable mobile stations to move from one cell to another.

- **Dynamic configuration:** The MAC addressing and network management aspects of the WLAN should permit dynamic and automated addition, deletion, and relocation of end systems without disruption to other users.

It is instructive to compare wireless LANs to wired LANs and mobile data networks using **Kiviat graphs**,[1] as shown in Figure 11.4.

Wireless LAN Physical Layer

Wireless LANs use unlicensed spectrum. These use spread spectrum and orthogonal frequency division multiplexing (OFDM) techniques that must meet the regulatory requirements for those bands that are shared by many users and uses.

Configuration Except for quite small offices, a wireless LAN makes use of a multiple-cell arrangement, as illustrated in Figure 11.2. Adjacent cells make use of different center frequencies within the same band to avoid interference.

Within a given cell, the topology can be either hub or peer to peer. The hub topology is indicated in Figure 11.2. In a hub topology, the hub is typically mounted on the ceiling and connected to a backbone wired LAN to provide connectivity to stations attached to the wired LAN and to stations that are part of wireless LANs in other cells. The hub may also control access, as in the IEEE 802.11 point coordination function. The hub may also control access by acting as a multiport repeater with similar functionality to the multiport Ethernet repeaters. In this case, all stations in the cell transmit only to the hub and receive only from the hub. Alternatively, and regardless of access control mechanism, each station may broadcast using an omnidirectional antenna so that all other stations in the cell may receive; this corresponds to a logical bus configuration.

One other potential function of a hub is automatic handoff of mobile stations. At any time, a number of stations are dynamically assigned to a given hub based on

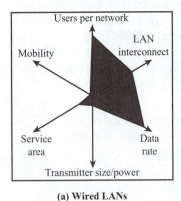

(a) Wired LANs

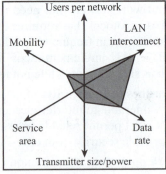

(b) Wireless LANs

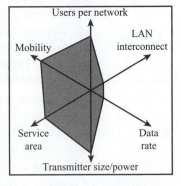

(c) Mobile data networks

Figure 11.4 Kiviat Graphs for Data Networks

---

[1]A Kiviat graph provides a pictorial means of comparing systems along multiple variables. The variables are laid out at equal angular intervals. A given system is defined by one point on each variable; these points are connected to yield a shape that is characteristic of that system.

proximity. When the hub senses a weakening signal, it can automatically hand off to the nearest adjacent hub.

A peer-to-peer topology is one in which there is no hub. A MAC algorithm such as carrier sense multiple access (CSMA) is used to control access. This topology is appropriate for ad hoc LANs.

Transmission Issues A necessary characteristic of a wireless LAN is that it be usable without having to go through a licensing procedure. The licensing regulations differ from one country to another, which complicates this objective. Within the United States, the Federal Communications Commission (FCC) has authorized two unlicensed applications within the ISM (industrial, scientific, and medical) band: spread spectrum systems, which can operate at up to 1 watt, and very low power systems, which can operate at up to 0.5 watts. Since the FCC opened up this band, its use for spread spectrum wireless LANs became popular.

In the United States, there are four microwave bands of interest to us that have been set aside for unlicensed spread spectrum use: 902–928 MHz (915 MHz band), 2.4–2.5 GHz (2.4 GHz band), 5.725–5.875 GHz (5.8 GHz band), and 58-64 GHz (60 GHz band). Of these, the 2.4 GHz is also used in this manner in Europe and Japan. The higher the frequency, the higher the potential bandwidth, so the bands are of increasing order of attractiveness from a capacity point of view. In addition, the potential for interference must be considered. There are a number of devices that operate at around 900 MHz, including cordless telephones, wireless microphones, and amateur radio. There are fewer devices operating at 2.4 GHz; one notable example is the microwave oven, which tends to have greater leakage of radiation with increasing age. At present there is less competition at the 5.8 and 60 GHz bands; however, the higher the frequency band, in general, the more expensive the equipment.

Spread spectrum wireless LANs operate using either direct sequence spread spectrum (DSSS) or OFDM. Recent advances using OFDM, along with channel bonding and multiuser multiple-input-multiple-output (MIMO), have increased channel rates to well over 1 Gbps.

11.2 IEEE 802 ARCHITECTURE

The IEEE 802.11 working group developed the most prominent specification for WLANs. We look first at the overall architecture of IEEE 802 standards and then at the specifics of IEEE 802.11.

The architecture of a LAN is best described in terms of a layering of protocols that organize the basic functions of a LAN. This section opens with a description of the standardized protocol architecture for LANs, which encompasses physical, medium access control, and logical link control (LLC) layers. We then look in more detail at medium access control and logical link control.

Protocol Architecture

Protocols defined specifically for LAN and MAN (metropolitan area network) transmission address issues relating to the transmission of blocks of data over the network. In OSI terms (see Chapter 4), higher-layer protocols (layer 3 or 4 and above) are independent of network architecture and are applicable to LANs, MANs, and WANs. Thus, a discussion of LAN protocols is concerned principally with lower layers of the OSI model.

Figure 11.5 relates the LAN protocols to the OSI architecture(Figure 4.3). This architecture was developed by the IEEE 802 committee and has been adopted by all organizations working on the specification of LAN standards. It is generally referred to as the IEEE 802 reference model.[2]

Working from the bottom up, the lowest layer of the IEEE 802 reference model corresponds to the *physical layer* of the OSI model and includes such functions as

- Encoding/decoding of signals (e.g., PSK, QAM, etc.)
- Preamble generation/removal (for synchronization)
- Bit transmission/reception

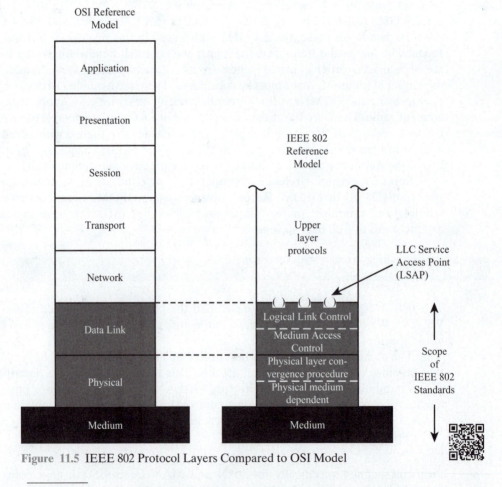

Figure 11.5 IEEE 802 Protocol Layers Compared to OSI Model

---

[2]A supporting document at this book's Web site provides an overview of the key organizations involved in developing communication and protocol standards, including the IEEE 802 Standards Committee.

In addition, the physical layer of the 802 model includes a specification of the transmission medium and the topology. Generally, this is considered "below" the lowest layer of the OSI model. However, the choice of transmission medium and topology is critical in LAN design, and so a specification of the medium is included. For some of the IEEE 802 standards, the physical layer is further subdivided into sublayers. In the case of IEEE 802.11, two sublayers are defined:

- **Physical layer convergence procedure (PLCP):** Defines a method of mapping 802.11 MAC layer protocol data units (MPDUs) into a framing format suitable for sending and receiving user data and management information between two or more stations using the associated PMD sublayer.

- **Physical medium dependent (PMD) sublayer:** Defines the characteristics of, and method of transmitting and receiving, user data through a wireless medium between two or more stations.

Above the physical layer are the functions associated with providing service to LAN users. These include

- On transmission, assemble data into a frame with address and error detection fields.

- On reception, disassemble frame and perform address recognition and error detection.

- Govern access to the LAN transmission medium.

- Provide an interface to higher layers and perform flow and error control.

These are functions typically associated with OSI layer 2. The set of functions in the last bullet item is grouped into a **logical link control (LLC)** layer. The functions in the first three bullet items are treated as a separate layer, called **medium access control (MAC)**. The separation is done for the following reasons:

- The logic required to manage access to a shared-access medium is not found in traditional layer 2 data link control.

- For the same LLC, several MAC options may be provided.

Figure 11.6 illustrates the relationship between the levels of the architecture. Higher-level data are passed down to LLC, which appends control information as a header, creating an *LLC protocol data unit (PDU)*. This control information is used in the operation of the LLC protocol. The entire LLC PDU is then passed down to the MAC layer, which appends control information at the front and back of the packet, forming a *MAC frame*. Again, the control information in the frame is needed for the operation of the MAC protocol. For context, the figure also shows the use of TCP/IP and an application layer above the LAN protocols.

MAC Frame Format

The MAC layer receives a block of data from the LLC layer and is responsible for performing functions related to medium access and for transmitting the data. As with other protocol layers, MAC implements these functions making use of a protocol data unit at its layer. In this case, the PDU is referred to as a MAC frame.

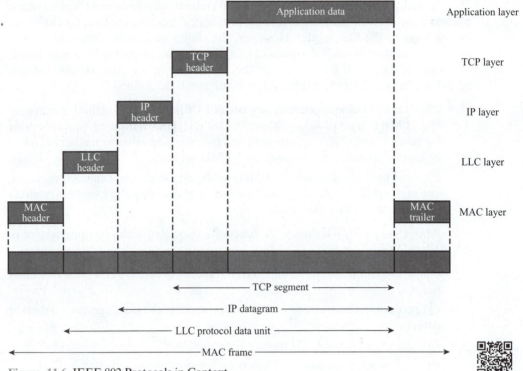

Figure 11.6 IEEE 802 Protocols in Context

The exact format of the MAC frame differs somewhat for the various MAC protocols in use. In general, all of the MAC frames have a format similar to that of Figure 11.7. The fields of this frame are as follows:

- **MAC:** This field contains any protocol control information needed for the functioning of the MAC protocol. For example, a priority level could be indicated here.

- **Destination MAC Address:** The destination physical attachment point on the LAN for this frame.

- **Source MAC Address:** The source physical attachment point on the LAN for this frame.

- **Data:** The body of the MAC frame. This may be LLC data from the next higher layer or control information relevant to the operation of the MAC protocol.

- **CRC:** The cyclic redundancy check field (also known as the frame check sequence, FCS, field). This is an error-detecting code, as described in Section 10.1. The CRC is used in virtually all data link protocols, such as high-level data link control (HDLC) (online Appendix C).

In most data link control protocols, the data link protocol entity is responsible not only for detecting errors using the CRC but for recovering from those errors by retransmitting damaged frames. In the LAN protocol architecture, these two functions are split between the MAC and LLC layers. The MAC layer is responsible for

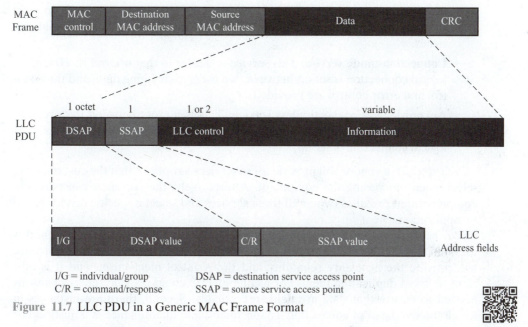

I/G = individual/group   DSAP = destination service access point
C/R = command/response   SSAP = source service access point

Figure 11.7 LLC PDU in a Generic MAC Frame Format

detecting errors and discarding any frames that are in error. The LLC layer option-ally keeps track of which frames have been successfully received and retransmits unsuccessful frames.

Logical Link Control

The LLC layer for LANs is similar in many respects to other link layers in common use. Like all link layers, LLC is concerned with the transmission of a link-level PDU between two stations, without the necessity of an intermediate switching node. LLC has two characteristics not shared by most other link control protocols:

1. It must support the multiaccess, shared-medium nature of the link (this differs from a multidrop line in that there is no primary node).

2. It is relieved of some details of link access by the MAC layer.

Addressing in LLC involves specifying the source and destination LLC users. Typically, a user is a higher-layer protocol or a network management function in the station. These LLC user addresses are referred to as service access points (SAPs), in keeping with OSI terminology for the user of a protocol layer.

We look first at the services that LLC provides to a higher-level user, and then at the LLC protocol.

LLC Services LLC specifies the mechanisms for addressing stations across the medium and for controlling the exchange of data between two users. The operation and format of this standard is based on HDLC. LLC provides three alternative ser-vices for attached devices:

- **Unacknowledged connectionless service:** This is a datagram-style service. It is a very simple service that does not involve any flow- and error-control mechanisms. Thus, the delivery of data is not guaranteed. However, in most devices, there will be some higher layer of software that deals with reliability issues.

- **Connection-mode service:** This service is similar to that offered by HDLC. A logical connection is set up between two users exchanging data, and flow control and error control are provided.

- **Acknowledged connectionless service:** This is a cross between the previous two services. It provides that datagrams are to be acknowledged, but no prior logical connection is set up.

Typically, a vendor will provide these services as options that the customer can select when purchasing the equipment. Alternatively, the customer can purchase equipment that provides two or all three services and select a specific service based on application.

The *unacknowledged connectionless service* requires minimum logic and is useful in two contexts. First, it will often be the case that higher layers of software will provide the necessary reliability and flow-control mechanism, and it is efficient to avoid duplicating them. For example, TCP could provide the mechanisms needed to ensure that data are delivered reliably. Second, there are instances in which the overhead of connection establishment and maintenance is unjustified or even counterproductive (for example, data collection activities that involve the periodic sampling of data sources, such as sensors and automatic self-test reports from security equipment or network components). In a monitoring application, the loss of an occasional data unit would not cause distress, as the next report should arrive shortly. Thus, in most cases, the unacknowledged connectionless service is the preferred option.

The *connection-mode service* could be used in very simple devices, such as remote sensors, that have little software operating above this level. In these cases, it would provide the flow control and reliability mechanisms normally implemented at higher layers of the communications software.

The *acknowledged connectionless service* is useful in several contexts. With the connection-mode service, the logical link control software must maintain some sort of table for each active connection, to keep track of the status of that connection. If the user needs guaranteed delivery but there are a large number of destinations for data, then the connection-mode service may be impractical because of the large number of tables required. An example is a process control or automated factory environment where a central site may need to communicate with a large number of processors and programmable controllers. Another use of this is the handling of important and time-critical alarm or emergency control signals in a factory. Because of their importance, an acknowledgment is needed so that the sender can be assured that the signal got through. Because of the urgency of the signal, the user might not want to take the time first to establish a logical connection and then send the data.

LLC Protocol The basic LLC protocol is modeled after HDLC and has similar functions and formats. The differences between the two protocols can be summarized as follows:

- LLC makes use of the asynchronous balanced mode of operation of HDLC, to support connection-mode LLC service; this is referred to as type 2 operation. The other HDLC modes are not employed.
- LLC supports an unacknowledged connectionless service using the unnumbered information PDU; this is known as type 1 operation.
- LLC supports an acknowledged connectionless service by using two new unnumbered PDUs; this is known as type 3 operation.
- LLC permits multiplexing by the use of LLC service access points (LSAPs).

All three LLC protocols employ the same PDU format (Figure 11.7), which consists of four fields. The destination service access point (DSAP) and source service access point (SSAP) fields each contain a 7-bit address, which specify the destination and source users of LLC, respectively. One bit of the DSAP indicates whether the DSAP is an individual or group address. One bit of the SSAP indicates whether the PDU is a command or response PDU. The format of the LLC control field is identical to that of HDLC, using extended (7-bit) sequence numbers.

For *type 1 operation*, which supports the unacknowledged connectionless service, the unnumbered information (UI) PDU is used to transfer user data. There is no acknowledgment, flow control, or error control. However, there is error detection and discard at the MAC level.

Two other PDU types, XID and TEST, are used to support management functions associated with all three types of operation. Both PDU types are used in the following fashion. An LLC entity may issue a command (C/R bit = 0) XID or TEST. The receiving LLC entity issues a corresponding XID or TEST in response. The XID PDU is used to exchange two types of information: types of operation supported and window size. The TEST PDU is used to conduct a loopback test of the transmission path between two LLC entities. Upon receipt of a TEST command PDU, the addressed LLC entity issues a TEST response PDU as soon as possible.

With *type 2 operation*, a data link connection is established between two LLC SAPs prior to data exchange. Connection establishment is attempted by the type 2 protocol in response to a request from a user. The LLC entity issues a SABME PDU[3] to request a logical connection with the other LLC entity. If the connection is accepted by the LLC user designated by the DSAP, then the destination LLC entity returns an unnumbered acknowledgment (UA) PDU. The connection is henceforth uniquely identified by the pair of user SAPs. If the destination LLC user rejects the connection request, its LLC entity returns a disconnected mode (DM) PDU.

Once the connection is established, data are exchanged using information PDUs, as in HDLC. Information PDUs include send and receive sequence numbers, for sequencing and flow control. The supervisory PDUs are used, as in HDLC,

---

[3]This stands for *set asynchronous balanced mode extended*. It is used in HDLC to choose ABM and to select extended sequence numbers of 7 bits. Both ABM and 7-bit sequence numbers are mandatory in type 2 operation.

for flow control and error control. Either LLC entity can terminate a logical LLC connection by issuing a disconnect (DISC) PDU.

With *type 3 operation*, each transmitted PDU is acknowledged. A new (not found in HDLC) unnumbered PDU, the acknowledged connectionless (AC) information PDU, is defined. User data are sent in AC command PDUs and must be acknowledged using an AC response PDU. To guard against lost PDUs, a 1-bit sequence number is used. The sender alternates the use of 0 and 1 in its AC command PDU, and the receiver responds with an AC PDU with the opposite number of the corresponding command. Only one PDU in each direction may be outstanding at any time.

11.3 IEEE 802.11 ARCHITECTURE AND SERVICES

In 1990, the IEEE 802 Committee formed a new working group, IEEE 802.11, specifically devoted to WLANs, with a charter to develop a MAC protocol and physical medium specification. The initial interest was in developing a WLAN operating in the ISM band. Since that time, the demand for WLANs, at different frequencies and data rates, has exploded. Keeping pace with this demand, the IEEE 802.11 working group has issued an ever-expanding list of standards (Table 11.1). Table 11.2 briefly defines key terms used in the IEEE 802.11 standard.

Table 11.1 IEEE 802.11 Standards

Standard	Date	Scope
IEEE 802.11	1997	Medium access control (MAC): One common MAC for WLAN applications
		Physical layer: Infrared at 1 and 2 Mbps
		Physical layer: 2.4-GHz FHSS at 1 and 2 Mbps
		Physical layer: 2.4-GHz DSSS at 1 and 2 Mbps
IEEE 802.11a	1999	Physical layer: 5-GHz OFDM at rates from 6 to 54 Mbps
IEEE 802.11b	1999	Physical layer: 2.4-GHz DSSS at 5.5 and 11 Mbps
IEEE 802.11c	2003	Bridge operation at 802.11 MAC layer
IEEE 802.11d	2001	Physical layer: Extend operation of 802.11 WLANs to new regulatory domains (countries)
IEEE 802.11e	2007	MAC: Enhance to improve quality of service and enhance security mechanisms
IEEE 802.11f	2003	Recommended practices for multivendor access point interoperability
IEEE 802.11g	2003	Physical layer: Extend 802.11b to data rates > 20 Mbps
IEEE 802.11h	2003	Physical/MAC: Enhance IEEE 802.11a to add indoor and outdoor channel selection and to improve spectrum and transmit power management

Standard	Date	Scope
IEEE 802.11i	2007	MAC: Enhance security and authentication mechanisms
IEEE 802.11j	2007	Physical: Enhance IEEE 802.11a to conform to Japanese requirements
IEEE 802.11k	2008	Radio Resource Measurement enhancements to provide interface to higher layers for radio and network measurements
IEEE 802.11m	Ongoing	This group provides maintenance of the IEEE 802.11 standard by rolling published amendments into revisions of the 802.11 standard.
IEEE 802.11n	2009	Physical/MAC: Enhancements to enable higher throughput
IEEE 802.11p	2010	Wireless Access in Vehicular Environments (WAVE)
IEEE 802.11r	2008	Fast Roaming/Fast BSS Transition
IEEE 802.11s	2011	Mesh Networking
IEEE 802.11T	Abandoned	Recommended Practice for Evaluation of 802.11 Wireless Performance
IEEE 802.11u	2011	Interworking with External Networks
IEEE 802.11v	2011	Wireless Network Management
IEEE 802.11w	2009	Protected Management Frames
IEEE 802.11y	2008	Contention Based Protocol
IEEE 802.11z	2010	Extensions to Direct Link Setup
IEEE 802.11aa	2012	Video Transport Stream
IEEE 802.11ac	Ongoing	Very High Throughput <6 GHz
IEEE 802.11ad	2012	Very High Throughput in 60 GHz
IEEE 802.11ae	2012	Prioritization of Management Frames
IEEE 802.11af	Ongoing	Wireless LAN in the TV White Space
IEEE 802.11ah	Ongoing	Sub 1 GHz
IEEE 802.11ai	Ongoing	Fast Initial Link Setup
IEEE 802.11aj	Ongoing	China Milli-Meter Wave (CMMW)
IEEE 802.11ak	Ongoing	Enhancements For Transit Links Within Bridged Networks
IEEE 802.11aq	Ongoing	Pre-Association Discovery (PAD)
IEEE 802.11ax	Ongoing	High Efficiency WLAN (HEW)

The Wi-Fi Alliance

Although 802.11 products are all based on the same standards, there is always a concern whether products from different vendors will successfully interoperate. To meet this concern, the Wireless Ethernet Compatibility Alliance (WECA), an industry consortium, was formed in 1999. This organization, subsequently renamed the Wi-Fi Alliance, created a test suite to certify interoperability for 802.11b products. The term used for certified 802.11b products is **Wi-Fi**. Wi-Fi certification has been extended to other 802.11 products.

The Wi-Fi Alliance is concerned with a range of market areas for WLANs, including enterprise, home, and hot spots.

Table 11.2 IEEE 802.11 Terminology

Access point (AP)	Any entity that has station functionality and provides access to the distribution system via the wireless medium for associated stations
Basic service set (BSS)	A set of stations controlled by a single coordination function
Coordination function	The logical function that determines when a station operating within a BSS is permitted to transmit and may be able to receive PDUs
Distribution system (DS)	A system used to interconnect a set of BSSs and integrated LANs to create an ESS
Extended service set (ESS)	A set of one or more interconnected BSSs and integrated LANs that appear as a single BSS to the LLC layer at any station associated with one of these BSSs
MAC protocol data unit (MPDU)	The unit of data exchanged between two peer MAC entities using the services of the physical layer
MAC service data unit (MSDU)	Information that is delivered as a unit between MAC users
Station	Any device that contains an IEEE 802.11 conformant MAC and physical layer

IEEE 802.11 Architecture

Figure 11.8 illustrates the model developed by the 802.11 working group. The smallest building block of a WLAN is a **basic service set (BSS)**, which consists of some number of stations executing the same MAC protocol and competing for access to the same shared wireless medium. A BSS may be isolated or it may connect to a backbone **distribution system (DS)** through an **access point (AP)**. The AP functions as a bridge and a relay point. In a BSS, client stations do not communicate directly with one another. Rather, if one station in the BSS wants to communicate with another station in the same BSS, the MAC frame is first sent from the originating station to the AP, and then from the AP to the destination station. Similarly, a MAC frame from a station in the BSS to a remote station is sent from the local station to the AP and then relayed by the AP over the DS on its way to the destination station. The BSS generally corresponds to what is referred to as a cell in the literature. The DS can be a switch, a wired network, or a wireless network.

When all the stations in the BSS are mobile stations, with no connection to other BSSs, the BSS is called an **independent BSS (IBSS)**. An IBSS is typically an ad hoc network. In an IBSS, the stations all communicate directly, and no AP is involved.

A simple configuration is shown in Figure 11.8, in which each station belongs to a single BSS; that is, each station is within wireless range only of other stations within the same BSS. It is also possible for two BSSs to overlap geographically, so that a single station could participate in more than one BSS. Further, the association between a station and a BSS is dynamic. Stations may turn off, come within range, and go out of range.

An **extended service set (ESS)** consists of two or more BSSs interconnected by a distribution system. Typically, the distribution system is a wired backbone LAN but can be any communications network. The ESS appears as a single logical LAN to the LLC level.

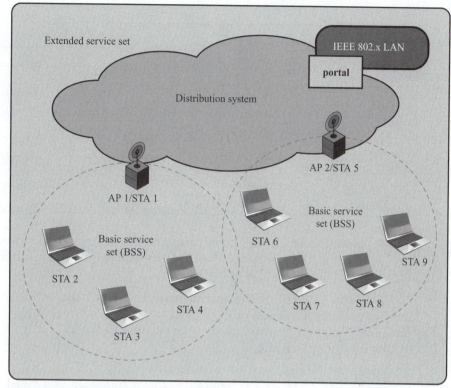

Figure 11.8 IEEE 802.11 Extended Service Set

Figure 11.8 indicates that an AP is implemented as part of a station; the AP is the logic within a station that provides access to the DS by providing DS services in addition to acting as a station. To integrate the IEEE 802.11 architecture with a traditional wired LAN, a ***portal*** is used. The portal logic is implemented in a device, such as a bridge or router, that is part of the wired LAN and that is attached to the DS.

IEEE 802.11 Services

IEEE 802.11 defines nine services that need to be provided by the wireless LAN to provide functionality equivalent to that which is inherent to wired LANs. Table 11.3 lists the services and indicates two ways of categorizing them.

1. The service provider can be either the station or the DS. Station services are implemented in every 802.11 station, including AP stations. Distribution services are provided between BSSs; these services may be implemented in an AP or in another special-purpose device attached to the distribution system.
2. Three of the services are used to control IEEE 802.11 LAN access and confidentiality. Six of the services are used to support delivery of **MAC service data units (MSDUs)** between stations. The MSDU is the block of data passed down from the MAC user to the MAC layer; typically this is an LLC PDU.

Table 11.3 IEEE 802.11 Services

Service	Provider	Used to Support
Association	Distribution system	MSDU delivery
Authentication	Station	LAN access and security
Deauthentication	Station	LAN access and security
Disassociation	Distribution system	MSDU delivery
Distribution	Distribution system	MSDU delivery
Integration	Distribution system	MSDU delivery
MSDU delivery	Station	MSDU delivery
Privacy	Station	LAN access and security
Reassocation	Distribution system	MSDU delivery

If the MSDU is too large to be transmitted in a single MAC frame, it may be fragmented and transmitted in a series of MAC frames. Fragmentation is discussed in Section 11.4.

Following the IEEE 802.11 document, we next discuss the services in an order designed to clarify the operation of an IEEE 802.11 ESS network. MSDU delivery, which is the basic service, has already been mentioned. Services related to security are discussed in Section 11.8.

Distribution of Messages within a DS The two services involved with the distribution of messages within a DS are distribution and integration. *Distribution* is the primary service used by stations to exchange MAC frames when the frame must traverse the DS to get from a station in one BSS to a station in another BSS. For example, suppose a frame is to be sent from station 2 (STA 2) to STA 7 in Figure 11.8. The frame is sent from STA 2 to STA 1, which is the AP for this BSS. The AP gives the frame to the DS, which has the job of directing the frame to the AP associated with STA 5 in the target BSS. STA 5 receives the frame and forwards it to STA 7. How the message is transported through the DS is beyond the scope of the IEEE 802.11 standard.

If the two stations that are communicating are within the same BSS, then the distribution service logically goes through the single AP of that BSS.

The *integration* service enables transfer of data between a station on an IEEE 802.11 LAN and a station on an integrated IEEE 802.x LAN. The term *integrated* refers to a wired LAN that is physically connected to the DS and whose stations may be logically connected to an IEEE 802.11 LAN via the integration service. The integration service takes care of any address translation and media conversion logic required for the exchange of data.

Association-Related Services The primary purpose of the MAC layer is to transfer MSDUs between MAC entities; this purpose is fulfilled by the distribution service. For that service to function, it requires information about stations within the ESS, which is provided by the association-related services. Before the distribution service can deliver data to or accept data from a station, that station must be *associated*.

Before looking at the concept of association, we need to describe the concept of mobility. The standard defines three transition types, based on mobility:

- **No transition:** A station of this type is either stationary or moves only within the direct communication range of the communicating stations of a single BSS.

- **BSS transition:** This is defined as a station movement from one BSS to another BSS within the same ESS. In this case, delivery of data to the station requires that the addressing capability be able to recognize the new location of the station.

- **ESS transition:** This is defined as a station movement from a BSS in one ESS to a BSS within another ESS. This case is supported only in the sense that the station can move. Maintenance of upper-layer connections supported by 802.11 cannot be guaranteed. In fact, disruption of service is likely to occur.

To deliver a message within a DS, the distribution service needs to know where the destination station is located. Specifically, the DS needs to know the identity of the AP to which the message should be delivered in order for that message to reach the destination station. To meet this requirement, a station must maintain an association with the AP within its current BSS. Three services relate to this requirement:

- **Association:** Establishes an initial association between a station and an AP. Before a station can transmit or receive frames on a WLAN, its identity and address must be known. For this purpose, a station must establish an association with an AP within a particular BSS. The AP can then communicate this information to other APs within the ESS to facilitate routing and delivery of addressed frames.

- **Reassociation:** Enables an established association to be transferred from one AP to another, allowing a mobile station to move from one BSS to another.

- **Disassociation:** A notification from either a station or an AP that an existing association is terminated. A station should give this notification before leaving an ESS or shutting down. However, the MAC management facility protects itself against stations that disappear without notification.

11.4 IEEE 802.11 MEDIUM ACCESS CONTROL

The IEEE 802.11 MAC layer covers three functional areas: reliable data delivery, access control, and security. This section covers the first two topics and Section 11.8 covers the third.

Reliable Data Delivery

As with any wireless network, a WLAN using the IEEE 802.11 physical and MAC layers is subject to considerable unreliability. Noise, interference, and other propagation effects result in the loss of a significant number of frames. Even with error-correction codes, a number of MAC frames may not successfully be received. This situation can be dealt with by reliability mechanisms at a higher layer, such as TCP. However, timers used for retransmission at higher layers are typically on the order of seconds. It is therefore more efficient to deal with errors at the MAC level. For this purpose, IEEE 802.11 includes a frame exchange protocol. When a station receives a data frame from another station, it returns an acknowledgment (ACK) frame to the source station. This exchange is treated as an atomic unit, not to be interrupted by a transmission from any other station. If the source does not receive an ACK within a short period of time, either because its data frame was damaged or because the returning ACK was damaged, the source retransmits the frame.

Thus, the basic data transfer mechanism in IEEE 802.11 involves an exchange of two frames. To further enhance reliability, a four-frame exchange may be used. In this scheme, a source first issues a request to send (RTS) frame to the destination. The destination then responds with a clear to send (CTS). After receiving the CTS, the source transmits the data frame, and the destination responds with an ACK. The RTS alerts all stations that are within reception range of the source that an exchange is under way; these stations refrain from transmission in order to avoid a collision between two frames transmitted at the same time. Similarly, the CTS alerts all stations that are within reception range of the destination that an exchange is under way. The RTS/CTS portion of the exchange is a required function of the MAC but may be disabled.

Medium Access Control

The 802.11 working group considered two types of proposals for a MAC algorithm: distributed access protocols, which, like Ethernet, distribute the decision to transmit over all the nodes using a carrier-sense mechanism; and centralized access protocols, which involve regulation of transmission by a centralized decision maker. A distributed access protocol makes sense for an ad hoc network of peer workstations (typically an IBSS) and may also be attractive in other WLAN configurations that consist primarily of bursty traffic. A centralized access protocol is natural for configurations in which a number of wireless stations are interconnected with each other and some sort of base station that attaches to a backbone wired LAN; it is especially useful if some of the data are time sensitive or high priority.

The end result for 802.11 is a MAC algorithm called DFWMAC (distributed foundation wireless MAC) that provides a distributed access control mechanism with an optional centralized control built on top of that. Figure 11.9 illustrates the architecture. The lower sublayer of the MAC layer is the **distributed coordination function (DCF)**. DCF uses a contention algorithm to provide access to all traffic. Ordinary asynchronous traffic directly uses DCF. The **point coordination function (PCF)** is a centralized MAC algorithm used to provide contention-free service. PCF is built on top of DCF and exploits features of DCF to assure access for its users. Let us consider these two sublayers in turn.

Distributed Coordination Function The DCF sublayer makes use of a simple CSMA (carrier sense multiple access) algorithm. If a station has a MAC frame to transmit, it listens to the medium. If the medium is idle, the station may transmit; otherwise the station must wait until the current transmission is complete before

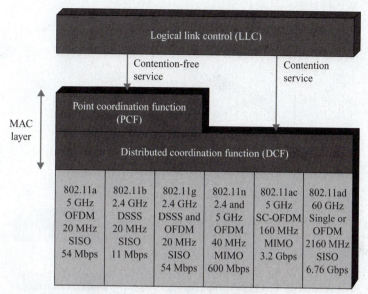

Figure 11.9 IEEE 802.11 Protocol Architecture

transmitting. The DCF does not include a collision detection function (i.e., CSMA/CD) because collision detection is not practical on a wireless network. The dynamic range of the signals on the medium is very large, so that a transmitting station cannot effectively distinguish incoming weak signals from noise and the effects of its own transmission.

To ensure the smooth and fair functioning of this algorithm, DCF includes a set of delays that amounts to a priority scheme. Let us start by considering a single delay known as an interframe space (IFS). In fact, there are three different IFS values, but the algorithm is best explained by initially ignoring this detail. Using an IFS, the rules for CSMA are as follows (Figure 11.10):

1. A station with a frame to transmit senses the medium. If the medium is idle, it waits to see if the medium remains idle for a time equal to IFS. If so, the station may transmit immediately.

2. If the medium is busy (either because the station initially finds the medium busy or because the medium becomes busy during the IFS idle time), the station defers transmission and continues to monitor the medium until the current transmission is over.

3. Once the current transmission is over, the station delays another IFS. If the medium remains idle for this period, then the station backs off a random amount of time and again senses the medium. If the medium is still idle, the station may transmit. During the backoff time, if the medium becomes busy, the backoff timer is halted and resumes when the medium becomes idle.

4. If the transmission is unsuccessful, which is determined by the absence of an acknowledgment, then it is assumed that a collision has occurred.

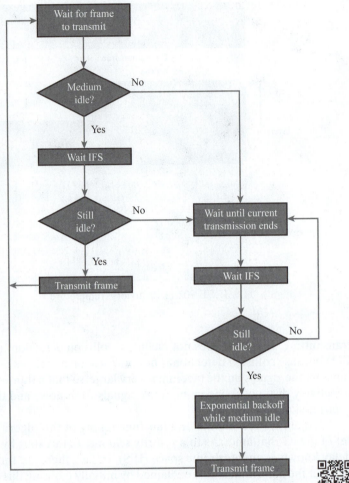

Figure 11.10 IEEE 802.11 Medium Access Control Logic

To ensure that backoff maintains stability, a technique known as **binary exponential backoff** is used. A station will attempt to transmit repeatedly in the face of repeated collisions, but after each collision, the mean value of the random delay is doubled up to some maximum value. The binary exponential backoff provides a means of handling a heavy load. Repeated failed attempts to transmit result in longer and longer backoff times, which helps to smooth out the load. Without such a backoff, the following situation could occur. Two or more stations attempt to transmit at the same time, causing a collision. These stations then immediately attempt to retransmit, causing a new collision.

The preceding scheme is refined for DCF to provide priority-based access by the simple expedient of using three values for IFS:

- **SIFS (short IFS):** The shortest IFS, used for all immediate response actions, as explained in the following discussion.

- **PIFS (point coordination function IFS):** A midlength IFS, used by the centralized controller in the PCF scheme when issuing polls.

- **DIFS (distributed coordination function IFS):** The longest IFS, used as a minimum delay for asynchronous frames contending for access.

Figure 11.11a illustrates the use of these time values. Consider first the SIFS. Any station using SIFS to determine transmission opportunity has, in effect, the highest priority, because it will always gain access in preference to a station waiting an amount of time equal to PIFS or DIFS. The SIFS is used in the following circumstances:

- **Acknowledgment (ACK):** When a station receives a frame addressed only to itself (not multicast or broadcast), it responds with an ACK frame after waiting only for an SIFS gap. This has two desirable effects. First, because collision detection is not used, the likelihood of collisions is greater than with CSMA/CD, and the MAC-level ACK provides for efficient collision recovery. Second, the SIFS can be used to provide efficient delivery of an LLC PDU that requires multiple MAC frames. In this case, the following scenario occurs. A station with a multiframe LLC PDU to transmit sends out the MAC frames one at a time. Each frame is acknowledged by the recipient after SIFS. When the source receives an ACK, it immediately (after SIFS) sends the next frame in the sequence. The result is that once a station has contended for the channel, it will maintain control of the channel until it has sent all of the fragments of an LLC PDU.

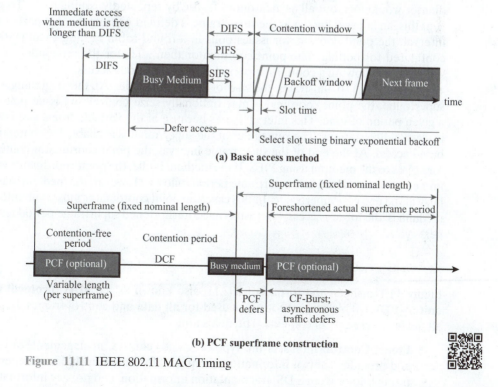

(a) Basic access method

(b) PCF superframe construction

Figure 11.11 IEEE 802.11 MAC Timing

- **Clear to send (CTS):** A station can ensure that its data frame will get through by first issuing a small RTS frame. The station to which this frame is addressed should immediately respond with a CTS frame if it is ready to receive. All other stations receive the RTS and defer using the medium.
- **Poll response:** This is explained in the following discussion of PCF.

The next longest IFS interval is the PIFS. This is used by the centralized controller in issuing polls and takes precedence over normal contention traffic. However, those frames transmitted using SIFS have precedence over a PCF poll.

Finally, the DIFS interval is used for all ordinary asynchronous traffic.

Point Coordination Function PCF is an alternative access method implemented on top of the DCF. The operation consists of polling by the centralized polling master (point coordinator). The point coordinator makes use of PIFS when issuing polls. Because PIFS is smaller than DIFS, the point coordinator can seize the medium and lock out all asynchronous traffic while it issues polls and receives responses.

As an extreme, consider the following possible scenario. A wireless network is configured so that a number of stations with time-sensitive traffic are controlled by the point coordinator while remaining traffic contends for access using CSMA. The point coordinator could issue polls in a round-robin fashion to all stations configured for polling. When a poll is issued, the polled station may respond using SIFS. If the point coordinator receives a response, it issues another poll using PIFS. If no response is received during the expected turnaround time, the coordinator issues a poll.

If the discipline of the preceding paragraph were implemented, the point coordinator would lock out all asynchronous traffic by repeatedly issuing polls. To prevent this, an interval known as the superframe is defined. During the first part of this interval, the point coordinator issues polls in a round-robin fashion to all stations configured for polling. The point coordinator then idles for the remainder of the superframe, allowing a contention period for asynchronous access.

Figure 11.11b illustrates the use of the superframe. At the beginning of a superframe, the point coordinator may optionally seize control and issue polls for a given period of time. This interval varies because of the variable frame size issued by responding stations. The remainder of the superframe is available for contention-based access. At the end of the superframe interval, the point coordinator contends for access to the medium using PIFS. If the medium is idle, the point coordinator gains immediate access and a full superframe period follows. However, the medium may be busy at the end of a superframe. In this case, the point coordinator must wait until the medium is idle to gain access; this results in a foreshortened superframe period for the next cycle.

MAC Frame

Figure 11.12a shows the format of 802.11, also known as the **MAC protocol data unit (MPDU)**. This general format is used for all data and control frames, but not all fields are used in all contexts. The fields are:

- **Frame Control:** Indicates the type of frame (control, management, or data) and provides control information. Control information includes whether the frame is to or from a DS, fragmentation information, and privacy information.

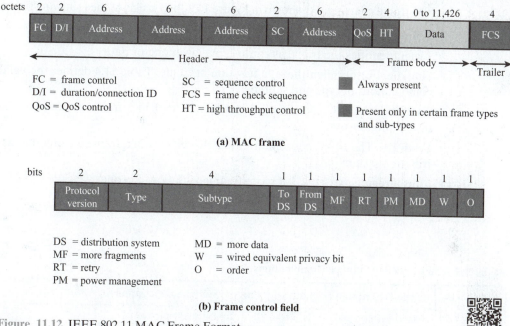

Figure 11.12 IEEE 802.11 MAC Frame Format

- **Duration/Connection ID:** If used as a duration field, indicates the time (in microseconds) the channel will be allocated for successful transmission of a MAC frame. In some control frames, this field contains an association, or connection, identifier.

- **Addresses:** The number and meaning of the 48-bit address fields depend on context. The *transmitter address* and *receiver address* are the MAC addresses of stations joined to the BSS that are transmitting and receiving frames over the WLAN. The **service set identifier (SSID)** identifies the WLAN over which a frame is transmitted. For an IBSS, the SSID is a random number generated at the time the network is formed. For a wireless LAN that is part of a larger configuration, the SSID identifies the BSS over which the frame is transmitted; specifically, the SSID is the MAC-level address of the AP for this BSS (Figure 11.8). Finally the *source address* and *destination address* are the MAC addresses of stations, wireless or otherwise, that are the ultimate source and destination of this frame. The source address may be identical to the transmitter address and the destination address may be identical to the receiver address.

- **Sequence Control:** Contains a 4-bit fragment number subfield, used for fragmentation and reassembly, and a 12-bit sequence number used to number frames sent between a given transmitter and receiver.

- **QoS Control:** Contains information relating to the IEEE 802.11 quality of service (QoS) facility.

- **High Throughput Control:** This field contains control bits related to the operation of 802.11n, 802.11ac, and 802.11ad.

- **Frame Body:** Contains an MSDU or a fragment of an MSDU. The MSDU is a LLC protocol data unit or MAC control information.

- **Frame Check Sequence:** A 32-bit cyclic redundancy check.

The frame control field, shown in Figure 11.12b, consists of the following fields:

- **Protocol Version:** 802.11 version, currently version 0.
- **Type:** Identifies the frame as control, management, or data.
- **Subtype:** Further identifies the function of frame. Table 11.4 defines the valid combinations of type and subtype.
- **To DS:** The MAC coordination sets this bit to 1 in a frame destined to the distribution system.
- **From DS:** The MAC coordination sets this bit to 1 in a frame leaving the distribution system.
- **More Fragments:** Set to 1 if more fragments follow this one.
- **Retry:** Set to 1 if this is a retransmission of a previous frame.

Table 11.4 Valid Type and Subtype Combinations

Type Value	Type Description	Subtype Value	Subtype Description
00	Management	0000	Association request
00	Management	0001	Association response
00	Management	0010	Reassociation request
00	Management	0011	Reassociation response
00	Management	0100	Probe request
00	Management	0101	Probe response
00	Management	1000	Beacon
00	Management	1001	Announcement traffic indication message
00	Management	1010	Dissociation
00	Management	1011	Authentication
00	Management	1100	Deauthentication
01	Control	1010	Power save-poll
01	Control	1011	Request to send
01	Control	1100	Clear to send
01	Control	1101	Acknowledgment
01	Control	1110	Contention-free (CF)-end
01	Control	1111	CF-end + CF-ack
10	Data	0000	Data
10	Data	0001	Data + CF-Ack
10	Data	0010	Data + CF-Poll
10	Data	0011	Data + CF-Ack + CF-Poll
10	Data	0100	Null function (no data)
10	Data	0101	CF-Ack (no data)
10	Data	0110	CF-poll (no data)
10	Data	0111	CF-Ack + CF-poll (no data)

- **Power Management:** Set to 1 if the transmitting station is in a sleep mode.

- **More Data:** Indicates that a station has additional data to send. Each block of data may be sent as one frame or a group of fragments in multiple frames.

- **WEP:** Set to 1 if the optional wired equivalent privacy is implemented. WEP is used in the exchange of encryption keys for secure data exchange. This bit also is set if the newer WPA security mechanism is employed, as described in Section 11.8.

- **Order:** Set to 1 in any data frame sent using the Strictly Ordered service, which tells the receiving station that frames must be processed in order.

We now look at the three MAC frame types.

Control Frames Control frames assist in the reliable delivery of data frames. There are six control frame subtypes:

- **Power Save-Poll (PS-Poll):** This frame is sent by any station to the station that includes the AP (access point). Its purpose is to request that the AP transmit a frame that has been buffered for this station while the station was in power-saving mode.

- **Request to Send:** This is the first frame in the four-way frame exchange discussed under the subsection on reliable data delivery at the beginning of Section 11.4. The station sending this message is alerting a potential destination, and all other stations within reception range, that it intends to send a data frame to that destination.

- **Clear to Send:** This is the second frame in the four-way exchange. It is sent by the destination station to the source station to grant permission to send a data frame.

- **Acknowledgment:** Provides an acknowledgment from the destination to the source that the immediately preceding data, management, or PS-Poll frame was received correctly.

- **Contention-Free (CF)-End:** Announces the end of a contention-free period that is part of the point coordination function.

- **CF-End + CF-Ack:** Acknowledges the CF-end. This frame ends the contention-free period and releases stations from the restrictions associated with that period.

Data Frames There are eight data frame subtypes, organized into two groups. The first four subtypes define frames that carry upper-level data from the source station to the destination station. The four data-carrying frames are as follows:

- **Data:** This is the simplest data frame. It may be used in both a contention period and a contention-free period.

- **Data + CF-Ack:** May only be sent during a contention-free period. In addition to carrying data, this frame acknowledges previously received data.

- **Data + CF-Poll:** Used by a point coordinator to deliver data to a mobile station and also to request that the mobile station send a data frame that it may have buffered.

- **Data + CF-Ack + CF-Poll:** Combines the functions of the Data + CF-Ack and Data + CF-Poll into a single frame.

The remaining four subtypes of data frames do not in fact carry any user data. The Null Function data frame carries no data, polls, or acknowledgments. It is used only to carry the power management bit in the frame control field to the AP, to indicate that the station is changing to a low-power operating state. The remaining three frames (CF-Ack, CF-Poll, CF-Ack + CF-Poll) have the same functionality as the corresponding data frame subtypes in the preceding list (Data + CF-Ack, Data + CF-Poll, Data + CF-Ack + CF-Poll) but without the data.

Management Frames Management frames are used to manage communications between stations and APs. The following subtypes are included:

- **Association Request:** Sent by a station to an AP to request an association with this BSS. This frame includes capability information, such as whether encryption is to be used and whether this station is pollable.
- **Association Response:** Returned by the AP to the station to indicate whether it is accepting this association request.
- **Reassociation Request:** Sent by a station when it moves from one BSS to another and needs to make an association with the AP in the new BSS. The station uses reassociation rather than simply association so that the new AP knows to negotiate with the old AP for the forwarding of data frames.
- **Reassociation Response:** Returned by the AP to the station to indicate whether it is accepting this reassociation request.
- **Probe Request:** Used by a station to obtain information from another station or AP. This frame is used to locate an IEEE 802.11 BSS.
- **Probe Response:** Response to a probe request.
- **Beacon:** Transmitted periodically to allow mobile stations to locate and identify a BSS.
- **Announcement Traffic Indication Message:** Sent by a mobile station to alert other mobile stations that may have been in low power mode that this station has frames buffered and waiting to be delivered to the station addressed in this frame.
- **Dissociation:** Used by a station to terminate an association.
- **Authentication:** Multiple authentication frames are used in an exchange to authenticate one station to another.
- **Deauthentication:** Sent by a station to another station or AP to indicate that it is terminating secure communications.

11.5 IEEE 802.11 PHYSICAL LAYER

Since its first introduction, the IEEE 802.11 standard has been expanded and revised a number of times. The first version of the standard, simply called IEEE 802.11, includes the MAC layer and three physical layer specifications, two in the 2.4 GHz band (ISM) and one in the infrared, all operating at 1 and 2 Mbps. This version is now obsolete and no longer in use. Table 11.5 summarizes key characteristics of the subsequent revisions. In this section, we survey 802.11b, 802.11a, 802.11g, and 802.11n. The following section deals with 802.11ac and 802.11ad, both of which provide for data rates greater than 1 Gbps.

IEEE 802.11b

One of the original 802.11 standards, now obsolete, used DSSS. It operates in the 2.4 GHz ISM band, at data rates of 1 Mbps and 2 Mbps. In the United States, the FCC requires no licensing for the use of this band. The number of channels available depends on the bandwidth allocated by the various national regulatory agencies.

IEEE 802.11b is an extension of the IEEE 802.11 DSSS scheme, providing data rates of 5.5 and 11 Mbps in the ISM band. The chipping rate is 11 MHz, which is the same as the original DSSS scheme, thus providing the same occupied bandwidth. To achieve a higher data rate in the same bandwidth at the same chipping rate, a modulation scheme known as **complementary code keying (CCK)** is used. The CCK modulation scheme is quite complex and shown in Figure 11.15, but is not examined in detail here.

An optional alternative to CCK is known as packet binary convolutional coding (PBCC). PBCC provides for potentially more efficient transmission at the cost of increased computation at the receiver. PBCC was incorporated into 802.11b in anticipation of its need for higher data rates for future enhancements to the standard.

Physical-Layer Frame Structure IEEE 802.11b defines two physical-layer frame formats, which differ only in the length of the preamble. The long preamble of 144 bits is the same as used in the original 802.11 DSSS scheme and allows

Table 11.5 IEEE 802.11 Physical Layer Standards

Standard	802.11a	802.11b	802.11g	802.11n	802.11ac	802.11ad
Year introduced	1999	1999	2003	2000	2012	2014
Maximum data transfer speed	54 Mbps	11 Mbps	54 Mbps	65 to 600 Mbps	78 Mbps to 3.2 Gbps	6.76 Gbps
Frequency band	5 GHz	2.4 GHz	2.4 GHz	2.4 or 5 GHz	5 GHz	60 GHz
Channel bandwidth	20 MHz	20 MHz	20 MHz	20, 40 MHz	40, 80, 160 MHz	2160 MHz
Highest order modulation	64 QAM	11 CCK	64 QAM	64 QAM	256 QAM	64 QAM
Spectrum usage	OFDM	DSSS	DSSS, OFDM	OFDM	SC-OFDM	SC, OFDM
Antenna configuration	1×1 SISO	1×1 SISO	1×1 SISO	Up to 4×4 MIMO	Up to 8×8 MIMO, MU-MIMO	1×1 SISO

interoperability with other legacy systems. The short preamble of 72 bits provides improved throughput efficiency. Figure 11.13b illustrates the physical layer frame format with the short preamble. The ***PLCP (physical layer convergence protocol) Preamble*** field enables the receiver to acquire an incoming signal and synchronize the demodulator. It consists of two subfields: a 56-bit ***Sync*** field for synchronization and a 16-bit start-of-frame delimiter (***SFD***). The preamble is transmitted at 1 Mbps using differential BPSK and Barker code spreading.

Following the preamble is the ***PLCP Header***, which is transmitted at 2 Mbps using DQPSK. It consists of the following subfields:

- **Signal:** Specifies the data rate at which the MPDU portion of the frame is transmitted.
- **Service:** Only 3 bits of this 8-bit field are used in 802.11b. One bit indicates whether the transmit frequency and symbol clocks use the same local oscillator. Another bit indicates whether CCK or PBCC encoding is used. A third bit acts as an extension to the Length subfield.
- **Length:** Indicates the length of the MPDU field by specifying the number of microseconds necessary to transmit the MPDU. Given the data rate, the length of the MPDU in octets can be calculated. For any data rate over 8 Mbps, the length extension bit from the Service field is needed to resolve a rounding ambiguity.

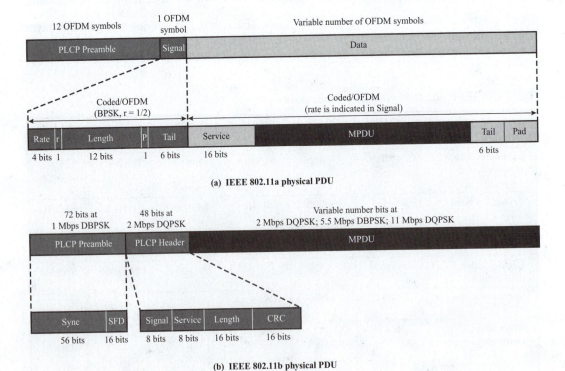

(a) IEEE 802.11a physical PDU

(b) IEEE 802.11b physical PDU

Figure 11.13 IEEE 802 Physical-Level Protocol Data Units

- **CRC:** A 16-bit error-detection code used to protect the Signal, Service, and Length fields.

The *MPDU* field consists of a variable number of bits transmitted at the data rate specified in the Signal subfield. Prior to transmission, all of the bits of the physical layer PDU are scrambled (see Appendix 11A for a discussion of scrambling).

IEEE 802.11a

Although 802.11b achieved a certain level of success, its limited data rate resulted in limited appeal. To meet the needs for a truly high-speed WLAN, *IEEE 802.11a* was developed. Even though it is now obsolete, much of its functionality has been carried over to subsequent 802.11 improvements, so we now investigate some of those details.

Channel Structure IEEE 802.11a makes use of the frequency band called the Universal Networking Information Infrastructure (UNNI), which is divided into three parts. The UNNI-1 band (5.15 to 5.25 GHz) is intended for indoor use; the UNNI-2 band (5.25 to 5.35 GHz) can be used either indoor or outdoor; and the UNNI-3 band (5.725 to 5.825 GHz) is for outdoor use.

IEEE 802.11a has several advantages over IEEE 802.11b/g:

- IEEE 802.11a utilizes more available bandwidth than 802.11b/g. Each UNNI band provides four nonoverlapping channels for a total of 12 across the allocated spectrum.

- IEEE 802.11a provides much higher data rates than 802.11b and the same maximum data rate as 802.11g.

- IEEE 802.11a uses a different, relatively uncluttered frequency spectrum (5 GHz).

Figure 11.14 shows the channel structure used by 802.11a (and also by 802.11n and 802.11ac which use the 5 GHz bands). The first part of the figure indicates a transmit spectrum mask, which is defined in 802.11b as follows: The transmitted spectrum mask shall have a 0 dBr (dB relative to the maximum spectral density of the signal) bandwidth not exceeding 18 MHz (9 MHz offset), −20 dBr at 11 MHz frequency offset, −28 dBr at 20 MHz frequency offset, and −40 dBr at 30 MHz frequency offset and above. The transmitted spectral density of the transmitted signal shall fall within the spectral mask. A typical signal spectrum is shown. The purpose of the spectrum mask is to constrain the spectral properties of the transmitted signal such that signals in adjacent channels do not interfere with one another.

Coding and Modulation Unlike the 2.4 GHz specifications, IEEE 802.11a does not use a spread spectrum scheme but rather uses OFDM. OFDM, also called multicarrier modulation, uses multiple carrier signals at different frequencies, sending some of the bits on each channel. It is discussed in Chapter 8. This is similar to FDM. However, in the case of OFDM, all of the subchannels are dedicated to a single data source.

To complement OFDM, the specification supports the use of a variety of modulation and coding alternatives. The system uses up to 48 subcarriers that are

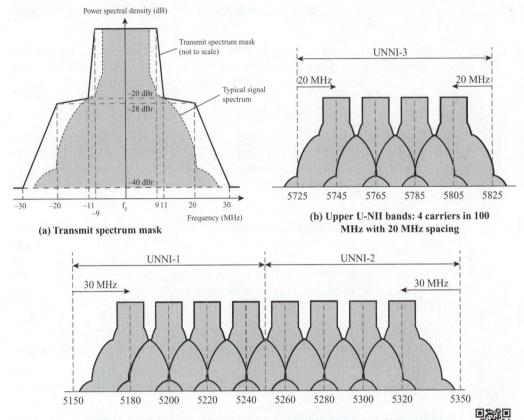

Figure 11.14 IEEE 802.11a Channel Scheme

modulated using BPSK, QPSK, 16-QAM, or 64-QAM. Subcarrier frequency spacing is 0.3125 MHz and each subcarrier transmits at a rate of 250 kbaud. A convolutional code at a rate of 1/2, 2/3, or 3/4 provides forward error correction (FEC). The combination of modulation technique and coding rate determines the data rate.

Physical-Layer Frame Structure The primary purpose of the physical layer is to transmit MPDUs as directed by the 802.11 MAC layer. The PLCP sublayer provides the framing and signaling bits needed for the OFDM transmission and the PMD sublayer performs the actual encoding and transmission operation.

Figure 11.13a illustrates the physical layer frame format. The ***PLCP Preamble*** field enables the receiver to acquire an incoming OFDM signal and synchronize the demodulator. Next is the ***Signal*** field, which consists of 24 bits encoded as a single OFDM symbol. The Preamble and Signal fields are transmitted at 6 Mbps using BPSK. The signal field consists of the following subfields:

- **Rate:** Specifies the data rate at which the data field portion of the frame is transmitted.
- **r:** reserved for future use.

- **Length:** Number of octets in the MAC PDU.
- **P:** An even parity bit for the 17 bits in the Rate, r, and Length subfields.
- **Tail:** Consists of 6 zero bits appended to the symbol to bring the convolutional encoder to zero state.

The *Data* field consists of a variable number of OFDM symbols transmitted at the data rate specified in the Rate subfield. Prior to transmission, all of the bits of the Data field are scrambled (see Appendix 11A for a discussion of scrambling). The Data field consists of four subfields:

- **Service:** Consists of 16 bits, with the first 7 bits set to zeros to synchronize the descrambler in the receiver, and the remaining 9 bits (all zeros) reserved for future use.
- **MAC PDU:** Handed down from the MAC layer. The format is shown in Figure 11.12.
- **Tail:** Produced by replacing the six scrambled bits following the MPDU end with 6 bits of all zeros; used to reinitialize the convolutional encoder.
- **Pad:** The number of bits required to make the Data field a multiple of the number of bits in an OFDM symbol (48, 96, 192, or 288).

IEEE 802.11g

IEEE 802.11g extends 802.11b to data rates above 20 Mbps, up to 54 Mbps. Like 802.11b, 802.11g operates in the 2.4 GHz range and thus the two are compatible. The standard is designed so that 802.11b devices will work when connected to an 802.11g AP, and 802.11g devices will work when connected to an 802.11b AP, in both cases using the lower 802.11b data rate.

IEEE 802.11g offers a wide array of data rate and modulation scheme options. IEEE 802.11g provides compatibility with 802.11 and 802.11b by specifying the same modulation and framing schemes as these standards for 1, 2, 5.5, and 11 Mbps. At data rates of 6, 9, 12, 18, 24, 36, 48, and 54 Mbps, 802.11g adopts the 802.11a OFDM scheme, adapted for the 2.4 GHz rate; this is referred to as ERP-OFDM, with ERP standing for extended rate physical layer. In addition, an ERP-PBCC scheme is used to provide data rates of 22 and 33 Mbps.

The IEEE 802.11 standards do not include a specification of speed versus distance objectives. Different vendors will give different values, depending on the environment. Table 11.6, based on [LAYL04], gives estimated values for a typical office environment.

IEEE 802.11n

With increasing demands being placed on WLANs, the 802.11 committee looked for ways to increase the data throughput and overall capacity of 802.11 networks. The goal of this effort was to not just increase the bit rate of the transmitting antennas but to increase the effective throughput of the network. Increasing effective throughput involves not only looking at the signal encoding scheme, but also at the antenna architecture and the MAC frame structure. The result of these efforts is

Table 11.6 Estimated Distance (m) Versus Data Rate

Data Rate (Mbps)	802.11b	802.11a	802.11g
1	90+	—	90+
2	75	—	75
5.5(b)/6(a/g)	60	60+	65
9	—	50	55
11(b)/12(a/g)	50	45	50
18	—	40	50
24	—	30	45
36	—	25	35
48	—	15	25
54	—	10	20

a package of improvements and enhancements embodied in IEEE 802.11n. This standard is defined to operate in both the 2.4 GHz and the 5 GHz bands and can therefore be made upwardly compatible with either 802.11a or 802.11b/g.

IEEE 802.11n embodies changes in three general areas: use of MIMO, enhancements in radio transmission, and MAC enhancements. We examine each of these in the following subsections.

Multiple-Input-Multiple-Output MIMO antenna architecture is a major enhancement provided by 802.11n. Discussions of MIMO are provided in Chapters 5 and 6, so we content ourselves with a brief overview. In a MIMO scheme, the transmitter employs multiple antennas. MIMO can provide multiple types of benefits, by using multiple parallel streams, beamforming, diversity, or multiuser MIMO. The first three capabilities are supported in 802.11n (some optionally), and the use of at least two parallel streams is required from the AP [PERA08].

The source data stream is divided into n substreams, one for each of the n transmitting antennas. The individual substreams are the input to the transmitting antennas (multiple input). At the receiving end, m antennas receive the transmissions from the n source antennas via a combination of line-of-sight transmission and multipath. The outputs from the m receiving antennas (multiple output) are combined. With a lot of complex math, the result is a much better received signal than can be achieved with either a single antenna or multiple frequency channels. 802.11n defines a number of different combinations for the number of transmitters and the number of receivers, from 2×1 to 4×4. Each additional transmitter or receiver in the system increases the SNR (signal-to-noise ratio). A simplified computation would say that four parallel streams would increase the total transmitted data rate approximately by a factor of 4.

Due to the inherent cost of multiple antennas, three or four spatial streams from the AP are not required, and only one spatial stream is required from the station. The standard also supports optional features such as four streams in both directions, transmit beamforming, and space-time block coding to improve diversity reliability.

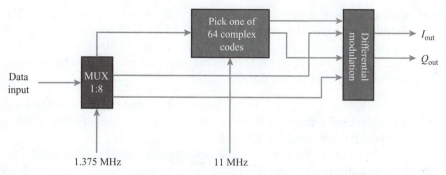

Figure 11.15 11-Mbps CCK Modulation Scheme

Radio Transmission Schemes In addition to MIMO, 802.11n makes a number of changes to the radio transmission scheme to increase capacity. The most significant of these techniques, known as channel bonding, combines two 20 MHz channels to create a 40 MHz channel. Using OFDM, this allows for a little more than twice as many subchannels, more than doubling the transmission rate. When a 40 MHz channel is created, it is formed from two adjacent 20 MHz channels. Each 20 MHz channel reserves some bandwidth at the edges to avoid interference, but when these are combined, the extra bandwidth in between the channels can be used. The effect is that 802.11n achieves slightly more than double the rate with 40 MHz channels. 802.11a and 802.11g used 48 subcarriers per 20 MHz, but 802.11n defined 108 per 40 MHz, 2.25 times the original bandwidth.

802.11a and 802.11g use OFDM symbols that last 4 μs. For the highest rate of 54 Mbps, 216 bits per symbol are spread out over 48 subcarriers. Also included is an 800 ns guard interval (used for the OFDM cyclic prefix), hopefully confining multipath effects to that time interval. This 54 Mbps rate uses 64 QAM and 72 additional error-correction bits; 216 data bits are used out of the total $216 + 72$ bits resulting in a $\frac{3}{4}$ coding rate. 802.11n continues to use this 4 μs symbol, but also allows for better channel conditions. In cases where multipath is not as significant, a 400 ns guard interval can be used, reducing the symbol time to 3.6 μs. This improves the data rate by 11%. 802.11n increases the highest encoding rate to 5/6, for another 11% increase. The final result is a maximum of 150 Mbps per 40 MHz, and 600 Mbps for 4 parallel streams.

In addition to these maximum data rates, 802.11n provides 32 different modulation and coding (MCS) combinations where the AP and the station work together to estimate channel conditions and find the best fit. There are several other MCS combinations that are also supported if the AP and station use different schemes when they transmit, because the channel quality from the AP to the station might be different than in the reverse direction.

In some cases, 802.11n devices will have to operate alongside legacy devices, in which case there will be some reductions in efficiency. First of all, 802.11n devices must sense legacy devices and might only be able to use 20 MHz if others are active. Also, the legacy devices need to recognize 802.11n, so 802.11n headers need to include extra headers that are encoded at lower data rates that legacy devices can read to recognize that 802.11n devices are using the channels and for how long. Additionally, 802.11n must send RTS/CTS or CTS-to-self messages. 802.11n also supports, however, a high throughput mode (also known as *greenfield* operation), where these headers and RTS/CTS messages do not need to be included if an environment is free of legacy devices.

MAC Enhancements As the data rate of a physical layer increases, the effective throughput of a protocol is still limited by its overhead. 802.11 overhead involves protocol header bits, backoffs, and IFS times.

802.11n provides some MAC enhancements. The most significant change is to aggregate multiple MAC frames into a single block for transmission. Once a station acquires the medium for transmission, it is allowed to transmit long packets without significant delays between transmissions. Throughput is affected if every frame requires an ACK, along with the DIFS and SIFS times between every frame. Instead, with 802.11n the receiver can send a single block acknowledgment. The physical header associated with transmission is sent only at the beginning of the aggregated frame, rather than one physical header per individual frame. Frame aggregation can result in significantly improved efficient use of the transmission capacity. Each frame no longer requires its own ACK and the associated IFS times.

The 802.11n specification includes three forms of aggregation, illustrated in Figure 11.16 [CISC14]. For simplicity, the 4-octet MAC trailer field is not shown. Aggregation either combines MSDUs, MPDUs, or both. Recall that MSDUs come down from the LLC layer and MPDUs from the MAC layer. A-MSDU aggregation combines multiple MSDUs into a single MPDU. Thus there is a single MAC header and single FCS for all of the MSDUs rather than for each of the MSDUs. This provides a certain amount of efficiency because the 802.11 MAC header is potentially quite lengthy. However, if a bit error occurs in one of the MSDUs, all of the aggregated MSDUs must be retransmitted, as seen in Figure 11.16b. A-MPDU aggregation combines multiple MPDUs in a single physical transmission. Thus, as with A-MSDU, only a single physical-layer header is needed. This approach is less efficient because each MPDU includes the MAC header and FCS. However, if a bit error occurs in one of the MPDUs, only that MPDU needs to be retransmitted. Finally, the two forms of aggregation can be combined (A-MPDU of A-MSDU).

If aggregation is not used, 802.11n can use a new 2 μs reduced interframe space (RIFS) between packets when transmitted in a group, instead of an SIFS of 10 μs for 2.4 GHz or 16 μs for 2.4 GHz. This feature, however, did not prove as useful as aggregation and was not carried forward into the later 802.11 enhancements discussed next.

11.6 GIGABIT WI-FI

Just as there has been a need to extend the Ethernet wired LAN standard to speeds in the gigabit per second range, the same requirement exists for Wi-Fi. Accordingly, IEEE 802.11 has recently introduced two new standards, 802.11ac and 802.11ad, which provide for Wi-Fi networks that operate at well in excess of 1 Gbps. We look at these two standards in turn.

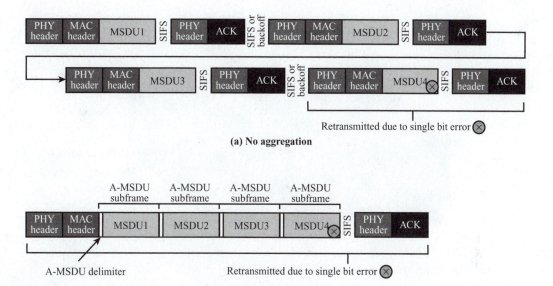

(a) No aggregation

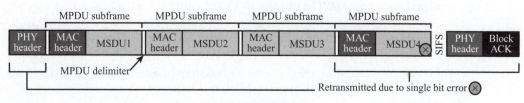

(b) A-MSDU aggregation

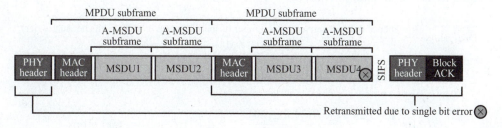

(c) A-MPDU aggregation

(d) A-MPDU of A-MSDU aggregation

Figure 11.16 Forms of Aggregation

IEEE 802.11ac

IEEE 802.11ac operates in the channels in the 5 GHz band as illustrated in Figure 11.14, as does 802.11a and 802.11n. It is designed to provide a smooth evolution from 802.11n. The new standard achieves much higher data rates than 802.11n by means of enhancements in three areas (as seen in the three axes of Figure 11.17):

* **Bandwidth:** The maximum bandwidth of 802.11n is 40 MHz; the maximum bandwidth of 802.11ac is 160 MHz.

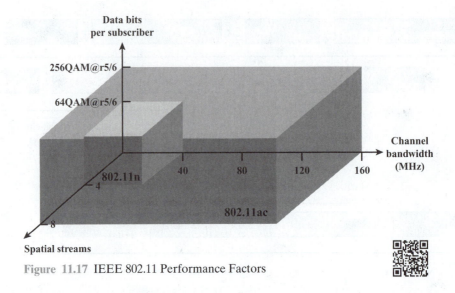

Figure 11.17 IEEE 802.11 Performance Factors

- **Signal encoding:** 802.11n can use 64 QAM with OFDM, and 802.11ac can use 256 QAM with OFDM. Thus, more bits can be encoded per symbol. Both schemes use forward error correction with a code rate of 5/6 (ratio of data bits to total bits).
- **MIMO:** With 802.11n, there can be a maximum of 4 channel input and 4 channel output antennas. 802.11ac increases this to 8×8.

We can quantify these enhancements using the following formula, which yields the physical layer data rate in bps:

$$\text{Data rate} = \frac{(\text{number of data subcarriers}) \times (\text{number of spatial streams}) \times (\text{data bits per subcarrier})}{(\text{time per OFDM symbol, in seconds})}$$

Using this equation, we have the following maximum data rates:

$$802.11\text{n:} \frac{108 \times 4 \times (5/6 \times \log_2 64)}{3.6 \times 10^{-6}} = 600 \times 10^6 \text{ bps} = 600 \text{ Mbps}$$

$$802.11\text{ac:} \frac{468 \times 8 \times (5/6 \times \log_2 256)}{3.6 \times 10^{-6}} = 6937 \times 10^6 \text{ bps} = 6.937 \text{ Gbps}$$

Increasing the channel bandwidth by a factor of 4 increases the data rate by a factor of 4.33, because the number of subcarriers expands from 108 to 468. The transmit power must now be spread over four times as many subcarriers, however, resulting in a slight reduction in range. Going from 64 QAM to 256 QAM increases the data rate by a factor of 1.33. However, 256 QAM is more sensitive to noise and thus is only effective at shorter ranges. Finally, the speed is directly proportional to the number of spatial streams. Of course, more spatial streams require more antennas, increasing the cost of the subscriber device.

Bandwidth Expansion Support for 80 MHz and 160 MHz channels requires extensions to CSMA techniques, spectrum considerations, and new RTS-CTS procedures.

- **CSMA Techniques:** 802.11ac devices set primary channels and perform standard clear channel assessment procedures over those channels. Then they use other procedures to see if additional secondary channels can be used to expand the bandwidth to up to 160 MHz. These procedures for secondary channels are less complex and use less overhead, but are more sensitive to signal energy that might be present. If the full bandwidth is not available, the device may restart the contention and backoff process. However, 802.11ac devices may also dynamically adjust their bandwidth allocations in every frame according to channels that are available.

- **Spectrum Considerations:** The 5 GHz ISM bands are less congested, which helps limit interference for 802.11ac. Figure 11.18 shows the channelization of possible frequency bands. Note that there are only two possible contiguous sets of frequencies for a 160 MHz channel. Therefore, 802.11ac supports an 80 + 80 MHz format where two noncontiguous 80 MHz bands can be combined.

- **RTS-CTS:** In order to test if, for example, the 80 MHz of a requested channel is available, the initiator senses for activity on each of those four 20 MHz channels and sends an RTS on each (so also 8 RTSs for 160 MHz). The 802.11ac RTS format that is used includes the requested bandwidth. The receiver of the RTS then also senses if anyone is actively using any of those channels. Figure 11.19 illustrates two possible scenarios that could result. The receiver will respond with CTSs to indicate available bandwidth (20, 40, or 80 MHz, but not 60 MHz); these CTSs will also be sent in 802.11a format on each free

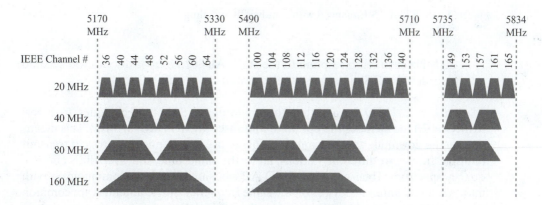

Figure 11.18 5 GHz 802.11ac Channel Allocations

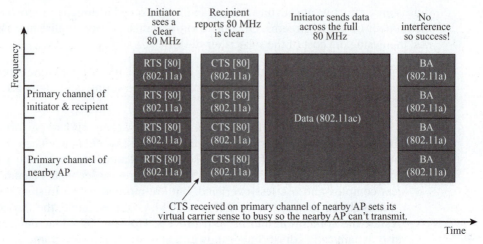

(a) No interference case

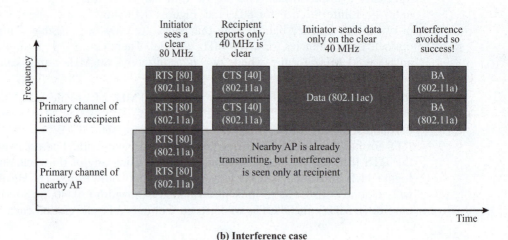

(b) Interference case

Figure 11.19 RTS/CTS Enhanced with Bandwidth Signaling

20 MHz channel to respond to the RTS. All 802.11a/n/ac devices will see and decode this CTS message so they can wait.

Multiuser MIMO In addition to expansion of 802.11n techniques to 8×8 MIMO, 802.11ac includes the option of multiuser MIMO (MU-MIMO). This means that on the downlink, the transmitter is able to use its antenna resources to transmit multiple frames to different stations, all at the same time and over the same frequency spectrum. Thus, an MU-MIMO AP can simultaneously communicate with multiple single-antenna devices on the same frequency. Single antennas are common on smartphones and tablets. This enables the AP to deliver significantly more data in many environments while keeping the complexity on the device side minimal.

Directional antennas not only can direct the signal but can also point antenna pattern nulls in other directions. For example, if MU-MIMO is directed toward three stations, the first beam might point strongly toward user 1 and with very little gain toward users 2 and 3. And the other two beams would be directed accordingly. The AP must know the quality of the wireless channel very accurately for this to work effectively, even as the channel is changing with time. This is especially challenging for moving mobile devices.

802.11n had a variety of possible mechanisms, but 802.11ac has a more consistent approach to ensure interoperability. Typically an AP sends a "Very High Throughput Null Data Packet Announcement" (VHT NDPA) that simply sends the address of the AP to intended recipients. After an SIFS, a "VHT Null Data Packet" (VHT NDP) is sent to perform *sounding*, which involves the AP sending training symbols that receivers use to measure channel conditions. The intended recipients use the preamble (a known sequence of bits at the beginning of the frame) of the VHT NDP to measure the RF channel. Then they respond with "VHT Compressed Beamforming" messages that are used to adjust the MIMO steering matrix (see Chapter 6). Ideally many measurements would be taken with a lot of detail in the measurements, but this creates high overhead. So the measurement information is compressed and an AP must send an appropriate number of messages.

Other PHY and MAC Enhancements FEC is implemented in 802.11ac using required PBCC or optional low density parity check (LDPC) codes. Space-time Block Coding can also be used along with MIMO as in 802.11n, but with fewer of those modes possible. Another difference for 802.11ac is that every transmission is required to be sent as an A-MPDU aggregate. This was introduced in 802.11n (see above) and was made mandatory in 802.11ac along with a larger maximum frame size. Other than the RTS/CTS modifications, this is the only significant modification to the MAC layer from 802.11n.

The Wi-Fi Alliance has taken a two-phase process in certification of 802.11ac products, related to which features are required and optional. "Wave 1" products provide rates up to 1.3 Gbps using 256 QAM, 80 MHz channels, and 3 spatial streams. "Wave 2" products are likely to additionally provide 160 MHz channels, 4 spatial streams, and MU-MIMO [CISC14].

IEEE 802.11ad

IEEE 802.11ad, using the name *WiGig*, is a version of 802.11 operating in the 60 GHz frequency band. This band offers the potential for much wider channel bandwidth than the 5 GHz band, enabling high data rates up to 7 Gbps with relatively simple signal encoding and antenna characteristics. This enables a series of high bandwidth applications; WiGig also supplies *Protocol Adaptation Layers* (*PALs*). There are audio/visual PALs to support HDMI and DisplayPort, and there are input/output PALs for SD, USB, and PCIe.

Few devices operate in the 60 GHz band, which means communications would experience less interference than in the other bands used by 802.11. However, at

60 GHz, 802.11ad is operating in the millimeter range, which has some undesirable propagation characteristics:

1. Free space loss increases with the square of the frequency [Equation (5.1)]; thus losses are much higher in this range (20 dB more from 6 GHz and 60 GHz) than in the ranges used for traditional microwave systems.

2. Multipath losses can be quite high. Reflection occurs when an electromagnetic signal encounters a surface that is large relative to the wavelength of the signal; scattering occurs if the size of an obstacle is on the order of the wavelength of the signal or less; diffraction occurs when the wavefront encounters the edge of an obstacle that is large compared to the wavelength.

3. Millimeter-wave signals generally don't penetrate solid objects.

For these reasons, 802.11ad is likely to be useful only within a single room. Because it can support high data rates and, for example, could easily transmit uncompressed high-definition video, it is suitable for applications such as replacing wires in a home entertainment system, or streaming high-definition movies from your cell phone to your television. It could also be used in an office environment for streaming video to a projector or between laptops and tablets in a conference room.

Adaptive beamforming of high gain directional antennas is used in 802.11ad to overcome the propagation loss. As seen in Chapter 6, directional beams can greatly increase antenna gain using MIMO. The 802.11ad beamforming process is supported through the MAC and PHY layers to establish basic course level communication through the sector level sweep (SLS) and then to fine-tune the settings through the beam refinement process (BRP). Because 60 GHz transmission is highly dependent on line-of-sight, a person walking in between the two stations can disrupt the communication. But the 802.11ad devices can quickly adapt their beams to an alternate path, even finding paths off reflections from walls or other objects.

The striking difference between 802.11ac and 802.11ad is the channel bandwidth. Instead of a 160 MHz maximum, 802.11ad has a huge channel bandwidth of 2160 MHz, centered at 58.32, 60.48, 62.64, and 64.8 GHz (not all channels are available depending on the country).

802.11ad PHY Layer IEEE 802.11ad defines four physical layer modulation and coding schemes (Table 11.7). Each type has a distinct purpose and supports a different range of data rates.

Control PHY (CPHY) is by far the most robustly coded (and consequently, lowest throughput) mode, with a code rate of only 1/2. Its purpose is exclusively to transmit control channel messages. The CPHY robustness is evident from its use of differential encoding, code spreading, and BPSK modulation. Differential encoding eliminates the need for carrier tracking, 32× spreading contributes a theoretical 15 dB gain to the link budget, and BPSK is very noise tolerant.

As with CPHY, *single carrier PHY (SCPHY)* uses the powerful LDPC code for robust forward error correction and provides three options for modulation. The set of options for code rate and modulation density allow for a trade-off between throughput and robustness to be determined operationally. Rates up to 4.62 Gbps can be achieved.

OFDM PHY (OFDMPHY) employs multicarrier modulation, which can provide higher modulation densities and hence higher data throughput than the

Table 11.7 IEEE 802.11ad Modulation and Coding Schemes

Physical Layer	Coding	Modulation	Raw Bit Rate
Control (CPHY)	1/2 LDPC, 32 × spreading	$\pi/2$-DBPSK	27.5 Mbps
Single carrier (SCPHY)	1/2 LDPC 1/2 LDPC, 5/8 LDPC 3/4 LDPC 13/16 LDPC	$\pi/2$-BPSK, $\pi/2$-QPSK, π 2-16 QAM	385 Mbps to 4.62 Gbps
OFDM (OFDMPHY)	1/2 LDPC, 5/8 LDPC 3/4 LDPC 13/16 LDPC	OFDM-OQPSK OFDM-QPSK OFDM-16 QAM OFDM-64 QAM	693 Mbps to 6.76 Gbps
Low-power single carrier (LPSCPHY)	RS(224,208) + Block Code(16/12/9/8,8)	$\pi/2$-BPSK, $\pi/2$-QPSK	636 Mbps to 2.5 Gbps

BPSK = binary phase-shift keying
DBPSK = differential binary phase-shift keying
LDPC = low density parity check code
OFDM = orthogonal frequency-division multiplexing
OQPSK = offset quadrature phase-shift keying
QAM = quadrature amplitude modulation
QPSK = quadrature phase-shift keying
RS = Reed-Solomon

single-carrier options, up to 6.756 Gbps. As with SCPHY, OFDMPHY provides a choice of error protection ratio and the depth of modulation applied to the OFDM data carriers, again to provide operational control over the robustness/throughput trade-off. The choice between SCPHY and OFDMPHY depends on several factors. OFDM modulation will generally impose greater power requirements than SCPHY, but is more robust in the presence of multipath distortion.

The LDPC error-correcting coding technique that is common to the CPHY, SCPHY, and OFDMPHY is based on a common codeword length of 672 bits carrying 336, 504, 420, or 546 payload bits to achieve a code rate of 1/2, 3/4, 5/8, or 13/16 as required.

Low-power single carrier (LPSCPHY) employs single-carrier modulation to minimize power consumption. It also uses either Reed-Solomon or Hamming block codes, which require less IC area and hence less power than LDPC, at the expense of less robust error correction. Small battery-powered devices could benefit from the extra power savings.

802.11ad MAC Layer The 802.11ad/WiGig MAC layer provides a series of necessary new and enhanced features.

- Network architecture: Instead of going through an AP, a new network architecture called the ***Personal BSS*** (***PBSS***) is provided that easily enables devices to talk directly with each other. Peer-to-peer 802.11 communication is also possible through an IBSS, but in the PBSS one node assumes the role of a PBSS control point to provide basic timing and allocation of service periods and contention-based access periods. This PBSS usage model would be common in WiGig, for example, between multimedia distribution and display devices.

- Seamless multiband operation: Allow seamless switching to and from 60 and 2.4/5 GHz operation to adapt to availability of 60 GHz channels.
- Power management: 802.11ad provides a new scheduled access mode to reduce power consumption. Devices can schedule between themselves when they are to communicate, then sleep otherwise.
- Advanced security: WiGig devices will use Galois/Counter mode, which supports higher speed communication through highly efficient calculations.

11.7 OTHER IEEE 802.11 STANDARDS

In addition to the standards so far discussed, which provide specific physical layer functionality, a number of other 802.11 standards have been issued or are in the works. Refer to Table 11.1 for the complete list.

IEEE 802.11e makes revisions to the MAC layer to improve quality of service and address some security issues. It accommodates time-scheduled and polled communication during null periods when no other data are being sent. In addition, it offers improvements to the efficiency of polling and enhancements to channel robustness. These enhancements should provide the quality required for such services as IP telephony and video streaming. Any station implementing 802.11e is referred to as a QoS station, or QSTA. In a QSTA, the DCF and PCF (Figure 11.9) modules are replaced with a hybrid coordination function (HCF). The HCF consists of enhanced distributed channel access (EDCA) and HCF controlled channel access (HCCA). EDCA is an extension of the legacy DCF mechanism to include priorities. As with the PCF, HCCA centrally manages medium access, but does so in a more efficient and flexible manner.

IEEE 802.11i defines security and authentication mechanisms at the MAC layer. This standard is designed to address security deficiencies in the wire equivalent privacy (WEP) mechanism originally designed for the MAC layer of 802.11. The 802.11i scheme uses stronger encryption and other enhancements to improve security and is discussed in Section 11.8.

IEEE 802.11k defines Radio Resource Measurement enhancements that provide mechanisms available to higher protocol layers for radio and network measurements. The standard defines what information should be made available to facilitate the management and maintenance of wireless and mobile LANs. Among the data provided are the following:

- To improve roaming decisions, an AP can provide a site report to a station when it determines that the station is moving away from it. The site report is an ordered list of APs, from best to worst service that a station can use in changing over to another AP.
- An AP can collect channel information from each station on the WLAN. Each station provides a noise histogram that displays all non-802.11 energy on that channel as perceived by the station. The AP also collects statistics on how long a channel is used during a given time. These data enable the AP to regulate access to a given channel.

- APs can query stations to collect statistics, such as retries, packets transmitted, and packets received. This gives the AP a more complete view of network performance.

- 802.11k extends the transmit power control procedures defined in 802.11h to other regulatory domains and frequency bands, to reduce interference and power consumption and to provide range control.

IEEE 802.11m is an ongoing task group activity to correct editorial and technical issues in the standard. The task group reviews documents generated by the other task groups to locate and correct inconsistencies and errors in the 802.11 standard and its approved amendments.

802.11p provides wireless access for the vehicular environment. It allows for communication between devices moving up to 200 km/hr (124.3 mi/hr). Devices do not need to associate or authenticate with each other. Instead, they just join the overall WAVE (Wireless Access in Vehicular Environments) network in the area. Lower data rates are used, because movement can cause more packet errors. 802.11p also allows for greater output power to accommodate longer distances.

IEEE 802.11r provides a fast roaming capability. Devices may register in advance with a neighbor AP, so security and quality of service settings can be negotiated before the device needs to switch to a new AP. The duration of connectivity loss can be substantially reduced.

IEEE 802.11s defines MAC procedures for 802.11 devices to use multi-hop communication to support a wireless LAN mesh topology. Devices mutually serve as wireless routers. The amendment supports unicast, multicast, and broadcast packet delivery.

IEEE 802.11z provides Tunneled Direct Link Setup, which allows devices to avoid the delays and contention process for going through an AP. Higher order modulation schemes could also be used if the devices are closer to each other than with an AP. 802.11z is an extension of features in 802.11e and defines a special Ethertype frame to tunnel setup messages through a legacy AP. Frequency offloading can also be used to switch to empty frequencies.

IEEE 802.11aa provides improved multimedia performance to enhance 802.11e capabilities. The enhancements include groupcast with retries for new transmission policies for group addressed frames and intra-access category prioritization to further clarify and create subcategories. It also includes a stream classification service to arbitrarily map streams to queues and solutions to overlapping BSS management problems by performing channel selection and cooperative resource sharing.

11.8 IEEE 802.11I WIRELESS LAN SECURITY

Wireless networks, and the wireless devices that use them, introduce a host of security problems over and above those found in wired networks. Some of the key factors contributing to the higher security risk of wireless networks compared to wired networks include the following [MA10]:

- **Channel:** Wireless networking typically involves broadcast communications, which is far more susceptible to eavesdropping and jamming than wired networks. Wireless networks are also more vulnerable to active attacks that exploit vulnerabilities in communications protocols.

- **Mobility:** Wireless devices are, in principal and usually in practice, far more portable and mobile than wired devices. This mobility results in a number of risks, described subsequently.

- **Resources:** Some wireless devices, such as smartphones and tablets, have sophisticated operating systems but limited memory and processing resources with which to counter threats, including denial of service and malware.

- **Accessibility:** Some wireless devices, such as sensors and robots, may be left unattended in remote and/or hostile locations. This greatly increases their vulnerability to physical attacks.

In simple terms, the wireless environment consists of three components that provide point of attack.

- **Client:** The wireless client can be a cell phone, a Wi-Fi-enabled laptop or tablet, a wireless sensor, a Bluetooth device, and so on.

- **Access Point:** The wireless access point provides a connection to the network or service. Examples of access points are cell towers, Wi-Fi hotspots, and wireless access points to wired local or wide area networks.

- **Wireless Medium:** The transmission medium, which carries the radio waves for data transfer, is also a source of vulnerability.

There are two characteristics of a wired LAN that are not inherent in a wireless LAN.

1. In order to transmit over a wired LAN, a station must be physically connected to the LAN. On the other hand, with a wireless LAN, any station within the radio range of the other devices on the LAN can transmit. In a sense, there is a form of authentication with a wired LAN in that it requires some positive and presumably observable action to connect a station to a wired LAN.

2. Similarly, in order to receive a transmission from a station that is part of a wired LAN, the receiving station also must be attached to the wired LAN. On the other hand, with a wireless LAN, any station within the radio range can receive. Thus, a wired LAN provides a degree of privacy, limiting reception of data to stations connected to the LAN.

These differences between wired and wireless LANs suggest the increased need for robust security services and mechanisms for wireless LANs. The original 802.11 specification included a set of security features for privacy and authentication that were quite weak. For privacy, 802.11 defined the **Wired Equivalent Privacy (WEP)** algorithm. The privacy portion of the 802.11 standard contained major weaknesses. Subsequent to the development of WEP, the 802.11i task group has developed a set of capabilities to address the WLAN security issues. In order to accelerate the introduction of strong security into WLANs, the Wi-Fi Alliance promulgated **Wi-Fi Protected Access (WPA)** as a Wi-Fi standard. WPA is a set of security mechanisms that eliminates most 802.11 security issues and was based on the current state of the 802.11i standard. The final form of the 802.11i standard is referred to as *Robust Security Network (RSN)*. The Wi-Fi Alliance certifies vendors in compliance with the full 802.11i specification under the WPA2 program.

The RSN specification is quite complex, and occupies 145 pages of the 2012 IEEE 802.11 standard. In this section, we provide an overview.

IEEE 802.11i Services

The 802.11i RSN security specification defines the following services:

- **Authentication:** A protocol is used to define an exchange between a user and an **authentication server (AS)** that provides mutual authentication and generates temporary keys to be used between the client and the AP over the wireless link.
- **Access control[4]:** This function enforces the use of the authentication function, routes the messages properly, and facilitates key exchange. It can work with a variety of authentication protocols.
- **Privacy with message integrity:** MAC-level data (e.g., an LLC PDU) are encrypted along with a message integrity code that ensures that the data have not been altered.

Figure 11.20 indicates the security protocols used to support these services.

IEEE 802.11i Phases of Operation

The operation of an IEEE 802.11i RSN can be broken down into five distinct phases of operation as seen in Figure 11.21. The exact nature of the phases will depend on the configuration and the end points of the communication. Possibilities include (referencing the ESS architecture in Figure 11.8) the following:

1. Two wireless stations in the same BSS communicating via the access point (AP) for that BSS.

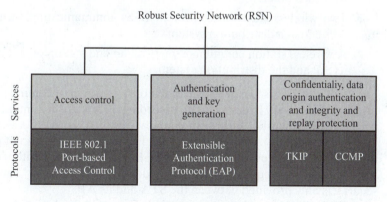

CCMP = Counter Mode with Cipher Block Chaining MAC Protocol
TKIP = Temporal Key Integrity Protocol

Figure 11.20 Elements of IEEE 802.11i

---

[4]In this context, we are discussing access control as a security function. This is a different function than MAC as described in Section 11.4. Unfortunately, the literature and the standards use the term access control in both contexts.

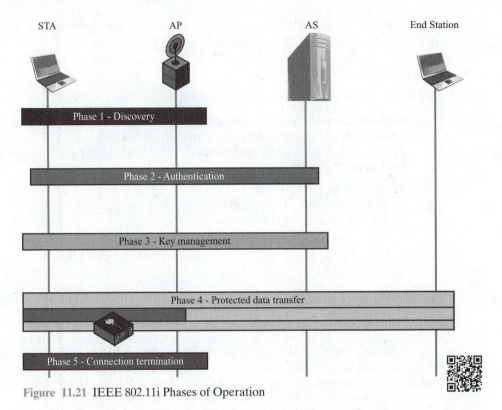

STA   AP   AS   End Station

Phase 1 - Discovery

Phase 2 - Authentication

Phase 3 - Key management

Phase 4 - Protected data transfer

Phase 5 - Connection termination

Figure 11.21 IEEE 802.11i Phases of Operation

2. Two wireless stations (STAs) in the same ad hoc IBSS communicating directly with each other.

3. Two wireless stations in different BSSs communicating via their respective APs across a distribution system.

4. A wireless station communicating with an end station on a wired network via its AP and the distribution system.

IEEE 802.11i security is concerned only with secure communication between the STA and its AP. In case 1 in the preceding list, secure communication is assured if each STA establishes secure communications with the AP. Case 2 is similar, with the AP functionality residing in the STA. For case 3, security is not provided across the distribution system at the level of IEEE 802.11, but only within each BSS. End-to-end security (if required) must be provided at a higher layer. Similarly, in case 4, security is only provided between the STA and its AP.

With these considerations in mind, Figure 11.21 depicts the five phases of operation for an RSN and maps them to the network components involved. One new component is the AS. The rectangles indicate the exchange of sequences of MPDUs. The five phases are defined as follows:

- **Discovery:** An AP uses messages called Beacons and Probe Responses to advertise its IEEE 802.11i security policy. The STA uses these to identify an AP for a WLAN with which it wishes to communicate. The STA associates with the AP, which it uses to select the cipher suite and authentication mechanism when the Beacons and Probe Responses present a choice.

- **Authentication:** During this phase, the STA and AS prove their identities to each other. The AP blocks non-authentication traffic between the STA and AS until the authentication transaction is successful. The AP does not participate in the authentication transaction other than forwarding traffic between the STA and AS.

- **Key generation and distribution:** The AP and the STA perform several operations that cause cryptographic keys to be generated and placed on the AP and the STA. Frames are exchanged between the AP and STA only.

- **Protected data transfer:** Frames are exchanged between the STA and the end station through the AP. As denoted by the shading and the encryption module icon, secure data transfer occurs between the STA and the AP only; security is not provided end-to-end.

- **Connection termination:** The AP and STA exchange frames. During this phase, the secure connection is torn down and the connection is restored to the original state.

Discovery Phase We now look in more detail at the RSN phases of operation, beginning with the discovery phase. The purpose of this phase is for an STA and an AP to recognize each other, agree on a set of security capabilities, and establish an association for future communication using those security capabilities.

The discovery phase consists of three exchanges.

- **Network and security capability discovery:** During this exchange, STAs discover the existence of a network with which to communicate. The AP either periodically broadcasts its security, indicated by RSN IE (Robust Security Network Information Element), in a specific channel through the Beacon frame, or it responds to a station's Probe Request through a Probe Response frame. A wireless station may discover available access points and corresponding security capabilities by either passively monitoring the Beacon frames or actively probing every channel.

- **Open system authentication:** The purpose of this frame sequence, which provides no security, is simply to maintain backward compatibility with the IEEE 802.11 state machine, as implemented in existing IEEE 802.11 hardware. In essence, the two devices (STA and AP) simply exchange identifiers.

- **Association:** The purpose of this stage is to agree on a set of security capabilities to be used. The STA then sends an Association Request frame to the AP. In this frame, the STA specifies one set of matching capabilities from among those advertised by the AP. If there is no match in capabilities between the AP and the STA, the AP refuses the Association Request. The STA blocks it too, in case it has associated with a rogue AP or someone is inserting frames illicitly on its channel.

Authentication Phase As was mentioned, the authentication phase enables mutual authentication between an STA and an AS located in the DS. Authentication is designed to allow only authorized stations to use the network and to provide the STA with assurance that it is communicating with a legitimate network.

IEEE 802.11i makes use of another standard that was designed to provide access control functions for LANs. The standard is IEEE 802.1X, Port-Based Network Access Control. The authentication protocol that is used, the Extensible Authentication Protocol (EAP), is defined in the IEEE 802.1X standard. IEEE 802.1X uses the terms *supplicant*, *authenticator*, and *authentication server*. In the context of an 802.11 WLAN, the first two terms correspond to the wireless station and the AP. The AS is typically a separate device on the wired side of the network (i.e., accessible over the DS) but could also reside directly on the authenticator.

Before the AS authenticates a supplicant using an authentication protocol, the authenticator only passes control or authentication messages between the supplicant and the AS; the 802.1X control channel is unblocked, but the 802.11 data channel is blocked. Once a supplicant is authenticated and keys are provided, the authenticator can forward data from the supplicant, subject to predefined access control limitations for the supplicant to the network. Under these circumstances, the data channel is unblocked.

We can think of authentication phase as consisting of the following three phases:

- **Connect to AS:** The STA sends a request to its AP (the one with which it has an association) for connection to the AS. The AP acknowledges this request and sends an access request to the AS.

- **EAP exchange:** This exchange authenticates the STA and AS to each other. A number of alternative exchanges are possible.

- **Secure key delivery:** Once authentication is established, the AS generates a master session key (MSK), also known as the Authentication, Authorization, and Accounting (AAA) key, and sends it to the STA. All the cryptographic keys needed by the STA for secure communication with its AP are generated from this MSK. IEEE 802.11i does not prescribe a method for secure delivery of the MSK but relies on EAP for this. Whatever method is used, it involves the transmission of an MPDU containing an encrypted MSK from the AS, via the AP, to the STA.

Key Management Phase During the key management phase, a variety of cryptographic keys are generated and distributed to STAs. There are two types of keys: pairwise keys used for communication between an STA and an AP and group keys used for multicast communication. Discussion of these keys is provided in [STAL13b].

Protected Data Transfer Phase IEEE 802.11i defines two schemes for protecting data transmitted in 802.11 MPDUs: the **Temporal Key Integrity Protocol (TKIP)** and the **Counter Mode-CBC MAC Protocol (CCMP)**.

TKIP TKIP is designed to require only software changes to devices that are implemented with the older wireless LAN security approach called wired equivalent privacy. TKIP provides two services:

- **Message integrity:** TKIP adds a message integrity code (MIC) to the 802.11 MAC frame after the data field. The MIC is generated by an algorithm, called Michael, which computes a 64-bit value using as input the source and destination MAC address values and the Data field, plus key material.

- **Data confidentiality:** Data confidentiality is provided by encrypting the MPDU plus MIC value using the RC4 encryption algorithm.

CCMP CCMP is intended for newer IEEE 802.11 devices that are equipped with the hardware to support this scheme. As with TKIP, CCMP provides two services:

- **Message integrity:** CCMP uses the cipher-block-chaining message authentication code (CBC-MAC).

- **Data confidentiality:** CCMP uses the CTR block cipher mode of operation and the AES algorithm for encryption. The same 128-bit AES key is used for both integrity and confidentiality.

11.9 RECOMMENDED READING

A brief but useful survey of 802.11 is [MCFA03]. [GEIE01] has a good discussion of OFDM in IEEE 802.11a. [CISC07] and [PERA08] are technical treatments of IEEE 802.11n. [HALP10] and [PAUL08] examine the 802.11n MIMO scheme. [ALSA13], [CISC14], and [VERM13] are good technical introductions to 802.11ac. [CORD10] and [PERA10] provide good technical overviews of 802.11ad. [HIER10] summarizes all 802.11 activity, and [XIAO04] discusses 802.11e. [STAL13] provides a thorough treatment of 802.11i security.

ALSA13 Alsabbagh, E.; Yu, H.; and Gallagher, K. "802.11ac Design Consideration for Mobile Devices." *Microwave Journal,* February 2013.

CISC07 Cisco Systems, Inc. "802.11n: The Next Generation of Wireless Performance." Cisco White Paper, 2007. cisco.com

CORD10 Cordeiro, C.; Akhmetov, D.; and Park, M. "IEEE 802.11ad: Introduction and Performance Evaluation of the First Multi-Gbps Wi-Fi Technology." *Proceedings of the 2010 ACM international workshop on mmWave communications: from circuits to networks,* 2010.

GEIE01 Geier, J. "Enabling Fast Wireless Networks with OFDM." *Communications System Design,* February 2001.

HALP10 Halperin, D., et al. "802.11 with Multiple Antennas for Dummies." *Computer Communication Review,* January 2010.

HIER10 Hiertz, G.R.; Denteneer, D.; Stibor, L.; Zang, Y.; Costa, X.P.; and Walke, B. "The IEEE 802.11 universe." *Communications Magazine, IEEE,* vol. 48, no. 1, pp. 62, 70, January 2010.

MCFA03 McFarland, B., and Wong, M. "The Family Dynamics of 802.11." *ACM Queue,* May 2003.

PAUL08 Paul, T., and Ogunfunmi, T. "Wireless LAN Comes of Age: Understanding the IEEE 802.11n Amendment." *Circuits and Systems Magazine, IEEE,* vol. 8, no. 1, pp. 28, 54, First Quarter 2008.

PERA08 Perahia, E. "IEEE 802.11n Development: History, Process, and Technology." Communications Magazine, IEEE, vol. 46, no. 7, pp. 48, 55, July 2008.

PERA10 Perahia, E., et al. "IEEE 802.11ad: Defining the Next Generation Multi-Gbps Wi-Fi." *Proceedings, 7th IEEE Consumer Communications and Networking Conference,* 2010.

STAL13 Stallings, W. *Cryptography and Network Security: Principles and Practice, Sixth Edition.* Upper Saddle *River*, NJ: Prentice Hall, 2013.

VERM13 Verma, L.; Fakharzadeh, M.; and Sunghyun Choi. "Wi-Fi on steroids: 802.11AC and 802.11AD." *Wireless Communications, IEEE,* vol. 20, no. 6, pp. 30, 35, December 2013.

XIAO04 Xiao, Y. "IEEE 802.11e: QoS Provisioning at the MAC Layer." *IEEE Communications Magazine,* June 2004.

11.10 KEY TERMS, REVIEW QUESTIONS, AND PROBLEMS

Key Terms

access point (AP)	extended service set (ESS)	service set identifier (SSID)
ad hoc networking	independent BSS (IBSS)	spread spectrum wireless
authentication server (AS)	Kiviat graph	LAN
basic service set (BSS)	logical link control (LLC)	Temporal Key Integrity
binary exponential backoff	MAC protocol data unit	Protocol (TKIP)
complementary code keying	(MPDU)	wired equivalent privacy
(CCK)	MAC service data units	(WEP)
counter mode-CBC MAC	(MSDUs)	Wi-Fi
protocol (CCMP)	medium access control (MAC)	Wi-Fi protected access (WPA)
distributed coordination func-	open system authentication	wireless LAN (WLAN)
tion (DCF)	point coordination function	
distribution system (DS)	(PCF)	

Review Questions

11.1 List and briefly define the IEEE 802 protocol layers.

11.2 What is a Kiviat graph?

11.3 What is the difference between a MAC address and an LLC address?

11.4 Is a distribution system a wireless network? Why or why not?

11.5 List and briefly define IEEE 802.11 services.

11.6 How is the concept of an association related to that of mobility?

11.7 What is the difference between a single-cell and a multiple-cell WLAN?

11.8 What characteristics of a wireless LAN present unique security challenges not found in wired LANs?

11.9 On the Wi-Fi Alliance Web site (www.wi-fi.org), investigate Wi-Fi Direct technology. How is this technology useful? What features does it add to the base 802.11 ad hoc WLAN functionality illustrated in Figure 11.3?

Problems ·

11.1 Answer the following questions about your wireless network:
   a. What is the SSID?
   b. Who is the equipment vendor?
   c. What standard are you using?
   d. What is the size of the network?

11.2 For IEEE 802.11n, determine the data rate for 16 QAM using a 2/3 coding rate with 2 parallel data streams.
   a. For a 20 MHz channel.
   b. For a 40 MHz channel.

11.3 For IEEE 802.11ac, determine the data rate over a 160 MHz channel for 64 QAM using a 1/2 coding rate with 8 parallel data streams.

11.4 There are many free tools and applications available for helping decipher wireless networks. One of the most popular is Netstumbler. Obtain the software at www .netstumbler.com and follow the links for downloads. The site has a list of supported wireless cards. Using the Netstumbler software, determine the following:
   a. How many access points in your network have the same SSID?
   b. What is your signal strength to your access point?
   c. How many other wireless networks and access points can you find?

11.5 Most wireless cards come with a small set of applications that can perform tasks similar to Netstumbler. Using your own client software, determine the same items you did with Netstumbler. Do they agree?

11.6 Try this experiment: How far can you go in different directions and still be connected to your network? This will depend to a large extent on your physical environment.

11.7 Compare and contrast wired and wireless LANs. What unique concerns must be addressed by the designer of a wireless LAN network?

11.8 For the 802.11 scrambler and descrambler described in Appendix 11A,
   a. Show the expression with exclusive-or operators that corresponds to the polynomial definition.
   b. Draw a figure similar to Figure 11.22.

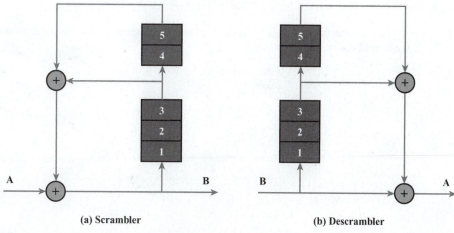

(a) Scrambler   (b) Descrambler

Figure 11.22 Scrambler and Descrambler

APPENDIX 11A SCRAMBLING

For some digital data encoding techniques, a long string of binary zeros or ones in a transmission can degrade system performance. Also, other transmission properties, such as spectral properties, are enhanced if the data are more nearly of a random nature rather than constant or repetitive. A technique commonly used to improve signal quality is scrambling and descrambling. The scrambling process tends to make the data appear more random.

The scrambling process consists of a feedback shift register, and the matching descrambler consists of a feedforward shift register. An example is shown in Figure 11.22. In this example, the scrambled data sequence may be expressed as follows:

$$B_m = A_m \oplus B_{m-3} \oplus B_{m-5}$$

where $\oplus$ indicates the exclusive-or operation. The descrambled sequence is

$$C_m = B_m \oplus B_{m-3} \oplus B_{m-5}$$
$$= (A_m \oplus B_{m-3} \oplus B_{m-5}) \oplus B_{m-3} \oplus B_{m-5}$$
$$= A_m (\oplus B_{m-3} \oplus B_{m-3}) \oplus (B_{m-5} \oplus B_{m-5})$$
$$= A_m$$

As can be seen, the descrambled output is the original sequence.

We can represent this process with the use of polynomials. Thus, for this example, the polynomial is $P(X) = 1 + X^3 + X^5$. The input is divided by this polynomial to produce the scrambled sequence. At the receiver, the received scrambled signal is multiplied by the same polynomial to reproduce the original input. Figure 11.23 is an example using the polynomial $P(X)$ and an input of 101010100000111. The scrambled transmission, produced by dividing by $P(X)$ (100101), is 101110001101001. When this number is multiplied by $P(X)$, we get the original input. Note that the input sequence contains the periodic sequence 10101010 as well as a long string of zeros. The scrambler effectively removes both patterns.

For 802.11, the scrambling equation is

$$P(X) = 1 + X^4 + X^7$$

In this case, the shift register consists of seven elements, used in the same manner as the five-element register in Figure 11.22.

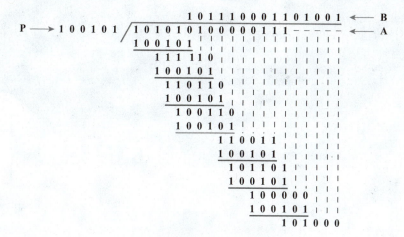

(a) Scrambling

```
               1 0 1 1 1 0 0 0 1 1 0 1 0 0 1  ⟵  B
                          1 0 0 1 0 1  ⟵  P
               1 0 1 1 1 0 0 0 1 1 0 1 0 0 1
             1 0 1 1 1 0 0 0 1 1 0 1 0 0 1
           1 0 1 1 1 0 0 0 1 1 0 1 0 0 1
C = A ⟶    1 0 1 0 1 0 1 0 0 0 0 0 1 1 1
```

(b) Descrambling

Figure 11.23 Example of Scrambling with $P(X) = 1 + X^{-3} + X^{-5}$

CHAPTER 12

BLUETOOTH AND IEEE 802.15

LEARNING OBJECTIVES

After studying this chapter, you should be able to:

- Describe the vision and purpose for the Internet of Things.
- Explain the roles of the Bluetooth protocol stack and core protocols.
- Describe the enhancements to Bluetooth in Bluetooth 3.0 and 4.0 (Bluetooth Smart).
- Compare the purposes of IEEE 802.15.3 and IEEE 802.15.4.
- Describe the various enhancements to 802.15.4.
- Explain the architecture of ZigBee and how it relates to IEEE 802.15.4.
- Describe the roles of ZigBee coordinator, router, and end device nodes.

This chapter provides an overview of technologies designed for short-range communication (over a few meters). Several standards have been provided by the IEEE 802.15 working group and have also been extended by industry consortiums. These short-range technologies tend to focus on being low-cost and low-energy to provide long battery life. These networks provide two services. The first is a **personal area network (PAN)** capability where a series of devices within a person's working space, especially on their bodies, work together to share information and provide communications to the user. The second is called the **Internet of Things (IoT)** in which devices engage in device-to-device communications to collaborate on data collection, data analysis, and automation applications. This chapter focuses on technologies related to IEEE 802.15, but there are several other viable alternatives in this expanding technology arena.

12.1 THE INTERNET OF THINGS

The future Internet will involve large numbers of objects that use standard communications architectures to provide services to end users. It is envisioned that tens of billions of such devices will be interconnected in a few years. This will provide new interactions between the physical world and computing, digital content, analysis, applications, and services. This resulting networking paradigm is called the Internet of Things (IoT), which will provide unprecedented opportunities for users, manufacturers, and service providers in a wide variety of sectors. Areas that will benefit from IoT data collection, analysis, and automation capabilities include health and fitness, health care, home monitoring and automation, energy savings and smart grid, farming, transportation, environmental monitoring, inventory and product management, security, surveillance, education, and many others.

Technology development is occurring in many areas. Not surprisingly, wireless networking research is being conducted and actually has been conducted for quite a while now, but under previous titles such as mobile computing, pervasive computing, wireless sensor networks, and cyber-physical systems. Many proposals and products have been developed for low power protocols, security and privacy, addressing, low cost radios, energy-efficient schemes for long battery life, and reliability for networks of unreliable and intermittently sleeping nodes. In addition, areas of development have also involved giving IoT devices social networking capabilities, taking advantage of machine-to-machine communications, storing and processing large amounts of real-time data, and application programming to provide end users with intelligent and useful interfaces to these devices and data.

Many have provided a vision for the IoT. In [STAN14], the author suggests personal benefits such as digitizing daily life activities, patches of bionic skin to communicate with surrounding smart spaces for improved comfort, health and safety, smart watches, and body nodes that optimize access to city services. City-wide benefits could include efficient, delay-free transportation with no traffic lights and 3-D transportation vehicles. Smart buildings could not only control energy and security, but also support health and wellness activities. Similar to the ways people have been provided new ways of accessing the world through smart phones, the IoT will create a new paradigm in the ways we have continuous access to needed information and services. Regardless of the level of positivity in one's view of the IoT or predictions about how soon this will be realized, it is certainly exciting to consider this future.

12.2 BLUETOOTH MOTIVATION AND OVERVIEW

Bluetooth[1] is an always-on, short-range radio hookup that resides on a microchip. It was initially developed by Swedish mobile phone maker Ericsson in 1994 as a way to let laptop computers make calls over a mobile phone. Since then, over 20,000 companies have signed on to make Bluetooth the low-power short-range wireless standard for a wide range of devices. Originally published as IEEE 802.15.1 standards, now an industry consortium known as the Bluetooth SIG (special interest group) publishes Bluetooth standards. The next few sections provide an overview.

The concept behind Bluetooth is to provide a universal short-range wireless capability. Key attributes are robustness, low power consumption, and low cost. Using the 2.4 GHz band, available globally for unlicensed low-power uses, two Bluetooth devices within 10 m of each other can share up to 2.1 Mbps or 24 Mbps of capacity. Bluetooth is intended to support an open-ended list of applications, including data (e.g., schedules and telephone numbers), audio, graphics, and even video. For example, audio devices can include smartphones, headsets, cordless and standard phones, and home stereos. The following are some examples of the capabilities that Bluetooth can provide consumers:

- Make calls from a wireless headset connected remotely to a cell phone.
- Control communication between a smartphone and a car stereo system.
- Control of peripherals such as a keyboard, mouse, or speaker from a computer or tablet.

---

[1]The name comes from King Harald Blaatand (Bluetooth) of Denmark, who lived in the tenth century A.D. Unlike his Viking counterparts, King Harald had dark hair (thus the name Bluetooth, meaning a dark complexion) and is credited with bringing Christianity to Scandinavia along with uniting Denmark and Norway. The blue logo that identifies Bluetooth-enabled devices is derived from the runes of his initials.

- Set up home networks so that a couch potato can remotely monitor air conditioning, the oven, and children's Internet surfing.
- Call home from a remote location to turn appliances on and off, set the alarm, and monitor activity.

Top uses in order of volume are for the following devices [DECU14a]:

- Mobile handsets
- Voice handsets
- Stereo headsets and speakers
- Personal computers and tablets
- Human interface devices, such as mice and keyboards
- Wireless controllers for video game consoles
- Cars
- Machine-to-machine applications: credit-card readers, industrial automation, and so on.

Bluetooth Applications

Bluetooth is designed to operate in an environment of many users. Up to eight devices can communicate in a small network called a **piconet**. Ten of these piconets can coexist in the same coverage range of the Bluetooth radio. To provide security, each link is encoded and protected against eavesdropping and interference.

Bluetooth provides support for three general application areas using short-range wireless connectivity:

- **Data and voice access points:** Bluetooth facilitates real-time voice and data transmissions by providing effortless wireless connection of portable and stationary communications devices.
- **Cable replacement:** Bluetooth eliminates the need for numerous, often proprietary, cable attachments for connection of practically any kind of communication device. Connections are instant and are maintained even when devices are not within line of sight. The range of each radio is approximately 10 m but can be extended to 100 m with an optional amplifier.
- **Ad hoc networking:** A device equipped with a Bluetooth radio can establish instant connection to another Bluetooth radio as soon as it comes into range.

Table 12.1 gives some examples of Bluetooth uses.

Bluetooth Standards Documents

The Bluetooth standards present a formidable bulk—over 2500 pages, divided into two groups: core and profile. The **core specifications** describe the details of the various layers of the Bluetooth protocol architecture, from the radio interface to link control. Related topics are covered, such as interoperability with related technologies, testing requirements, and a definition of various Bluetooth timers and their associated values. In the next few sections, we will first focus on what are known as

Table 12.1 Bluetooth Uses

Handsfree Headset Communication between a smartphone and a headset. This is one of the most popular applications, and is required in some jurisdictions when driving, for safety reasons.	**Low Data Rate Data Transfer** Instead of plugging in a USB device, files can be transferred wirelessly.
Car Stereo Communication with and control of a car stereo system.	**Bridges** Interconnection of Ethernet networks. **Game Consoles** Bluetooth is used for wireless game controllers.
PC Input and Output Input and output communication between a PC and devices like a mouse, keyboard, or printer.	**Medical Devices** Short range transmission between health-monitoring devices and a smartphone or a device that collects and sends health data.
Synchronization Automatic synchronization of calender information and contact details between smartphones and PCs.	**Security** Prevention of theft of smartphones if a Bluetooth connection is broken, indicating the smartphone is no longer in proximity to another wearable device on the person. This loss of connection could also indicate other dangerous conditions or falls.
Cable Replacement Substitution for previously wired RS-232 serial connections, such as in measurement equipment, medical equipment, and traffic control devices.	
Infrared Remote Replacement Controllers to use Bluetooth as a replacement for infrared remote controls.	

the **Basic Rate/Enhanced Data Rate (BR/EDR)** standards up through Bluetooth 2.1. The enhancement to Bluetooth for *High Speed (HS)* in Bluetooth 3.0 that uses the **Alternative MAC/PHY (AMP)** (actually an 802.11 connection) is covered in Section 12.4. **Bluetooth Low Energy** (also called **Bluetooth Smart**) in Bluetooth 4.0 is also covered in Section 12.4.

The **profile specifications** are concerned with the use of Bluetooth technology to support various applications. Each profile specification discusses the use of the technology defined in the core specifications to implement a particular **usage model**. The profile specification includes a description of which aspects of the core specifications are mandatory, optional, and not applicable. The purpose of a profile specification is to define a standard of interoperability so that products from different vendors that claim to support a given usage model will work together.

Protocol Architecture

Bluetooth is defined as a layered protocol architecture (Figure 12.1) consisting of core protocols, cable replacement and telephony control protocols, and adopted protocols.

The **core protocols** form a five-layer stack consisting of the following elements:

- **Radio:** Specifies details of the air interface, including frequency, the use of frequency hopping, modulation scheme, and transmit power.

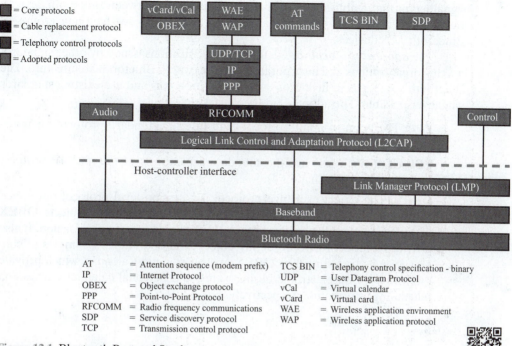

Figure 12.1 Bluetooth Protocol Stack

- **Baseband:** Concerned with connection establishment within a piconet, addressing, packet format, timing, and power control.

- **Link manager protocol (LMP):** Responsible for link setup between Bluetooth devices and ongoing link management. This includes security aspects such as authentication and encryption, plus the control and negotiation of baseband packet sizes.

- **Logical link control and adaptation protocol (L2CAP):** Adapts upper-layer protocols to the baseband layer. L2CAP provides both connectionless and connection-oriented services.

- **Service discovery protocol (SDP):** Device information, services, and the characteristics of the services can be queried to enable the establishment of a connection between two or more Bluetooth devices.

Radio frequency communication (RFCOMM) is the **cable replacement protocol** included in the Bluetooth specification. RFCOMM presents a virtual serial port that is designed to make replacement of cable technologies as transparent as possible. Serial ports are one of the most common types of communications interfaces used with computing and communications devices. Hence, RFCOMM enables the replacement of serial port cables with the minimum of modification of existing devices. RFCOMM provides for binary data transport and emulates EIA-232 control signals over the Bluetooth baseband layer. EIA-232 (formerly known as RS-232) is a widely used serial port interface standard.

Bluetooth specifies a ***telephony control protocol***. TCS BIN (telephony control specification—binary) is a bit-oriented protocol that defines the call control signaling for the establishment of speech and data calls between Bluetooth devices. In addition, it defines mobility management procedures for handling groups of Bluetooth TCS devices.

The ***adopted protocols*** are defined in specifications issued by other standard-making organizations and incorporated into the overall Bluetooth architecture. The Bluetooth strategy is to invent only necessary protocols and use existing standards whenever possible. The adopted protocols include

- **PPP:** The point-to-point protocol is an Internet standard protocol for transporting IP datagrams over a point-to-point link.
- **TCP/UDP/IP:** These are the foundation protocols of the TCP/IP protocol suite (described in Chapter 4).
- **OBEX:** The object exchange protocol is a session-level protocol developed by the Infrared Data Association (IrDA) for the exchange of objects. OBEX provides functionality similar to that of HTTP, but in a simpler fashion. It also provides a model for representing objects and operations. Examples of content formats transferred by OBEX are vCard and vCalendar, which provide the format of an electronic business card and personal calendar entries and scheduling information, respectively.

Profiles

Over 40 different profiles are defined in Bluetooth profile documents. In essence, a profile is a set of protocols that implement a particular Bluetooth-based application. Each profile defines the protocols and protocol features supporting a particular usage model. All Bluetooth nodes support the Generic Access Profile, plus profiles may be dependent on other profiles.

For example, the File Transfer Profile supports the transfer of directories, files, documents, images, and streaming media formats. It also includes the capability to browse folders on a remote device. The File Transfer Profile depends on the Generic Object File Exchange, Serial Port, and Generic Access Profiles. It uses OBEX functions within the Generic Object File Exchange. Then it interfaces with L2CAP and RFCOMM protocols.

Piconets and Scatternets

As was mentioned, the basic unit of networking in Bluetooth is a ***piconet***, consisting of a master and from one to seven active slave devices. The radio designated as the master makes the determination of the channel (frequency-hopping sequence) and phase (timing offset, i.e., when to transmit) that shall be used by all devices on this piconet. The radio designated as master makes this determination using its own device address as a parameter, while the slave devices must tune to the same channel and phase. A slave may only communicate with the master and may only communicate when granted permission by the master. A device in one piconet may also exist as part of another piconet and may function as either a slave or master in each piconet (Figure 12.2). This form of overlapping is called a **scatternet**. Figure 12.3 contrasts the piconet/scatternet architecture with other forms of wireless networks.

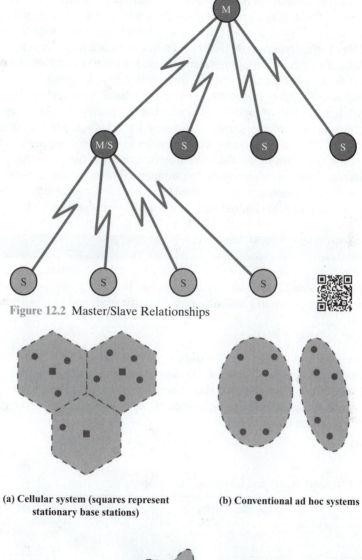

Figure 12.2 Master/Slave Relationships

**(a) Cellular system (squares represent
stationary base stations)**

(b) Conventional ad hoc systems

(c) Scatternets

Figure 12.3 Wireless Network Configurations

The advantage of the piconet/scatternet scheme is that it allows many devices to share the same physical area and make efficient use of the bandwidth. A Bluetooth system uses a frequency-hopping scheme with a carrier spacing of 1 MHz. Typically, up to 80 different frequencies are used for a total bandwidth of 80 MHz. If frequency hopping were not used, then a single channel would correspond to a single 1-MHz band. With frequency hopping, a logical channel is defined by the frequency-hopping sequence. At any given time, the bandwidth available is 1 MHz, with a maximum of eight devices sharing the bandwidth. Different logical channels (different hopping sequences) can simultaneously share the same 80-MHz bandwidth. Collisions will occur when devices in different piconets, on different logical channels, happen to use the same hop frequency at the same time. As the number of piconets in an area increases, the number of collisions increases, and performance degrades. In summary, the physical area and total bandwidth are shared by the scatternet. The logical channel and data transfer are shared by a piconet.

12.3 BLUETOOTH SPECIFICATIONS

Specifications for the various layers of the Bluetooth protocol stack are discussed in the following, starting with the radio specification and moving upward.

Radio Specification

The Bluetooth radio specification gives the basic details of radio transmission for Bluetooth devices. Some of the key parameters are summarized in Table 12.2. Bluetooth consists of Basic Rate and Enhanced Data Rate PHY layer options.

One aspect of the radio specification is a definition of three classes of transmitters based on output power:

Table 12.2 Bluetooth Radio and Baseband Parameters

	Basic Rate (BR)	**Enhanced Data Rate (EDR)**
Topology	Up to 7 simultaneous links in a logical star	Up to 7 simultaneous links in a logical star
Modulation	GFSK	$\pi/4$-DQPSK and 8DPSK
Peak data rate	1 Mbps	2 Mbps and 3 Mbps
RF bandwidth	220 kHz (-3 dB), 1 MHz (-20 dB)	220 kHz (-3 dB), 1 MHz (-20 dB)
RF band	2.4 GHz, ISM band	2.4 GHz, ISM band
RF carriers	23/79	23/79
Carrier spacing	1 MHz	1 MHz
Transmit power	0.1 W	0.1 W
Piconet access	FH-TDD-TDMA	FH-TDD-TDMA
Frequency hop rate	1600 hops/s	1600 hops/s
Scatternet access	FH-CDMA	FH-CDMA

- **Class 1:** Outputs 100 mW (+20 dBm) for maximum range, with a minimum of 1 mW (0 dBm). In this class, power control is mandatory, ranging from 4 to 20 dBm. This mode provides the greatest distance.

- **Class 2:** Outputs 2.5 mW (+4 dBm) at maximum, with a minimum of 0.25 mW (−6 dBm). Power control is optional.

- **Class 3:** Lowest power. Maximum output is 1 mW.

Bluetooth makes use of the 2.4 GHz band within the industrial, scientific and medical (ISM) band. In most countries, the bandwidth is sufficient to define 79 1-MHz physical channels (Table 12.3). Power control is used to keep the devices from emitting any more RF power than necessary. The power control algorithm is implemented using the link management protocol between a master and the slaves in a piconet.

Bluetooth makes use of Basic Rate (BR) and Enhanced Data Rate (EDR) connections. Modulation for BR is Gaussian frequency-shift keying (FSK), with a binary one represented by a positive frequency deviation and a binary zero represented by a negative frequency deviation from the center frequency. One million symbols/second are sent with one bit per symbol to produce 1 Mbps. The minimum deviation is 115 kHz.

EDR was introduced in Bluetooth Version 2.0 and uses the same 1 million symbols/second, but with $\pi/4$-DQPSK and 8DPSK which send 2 or 3 bits per symbol to produce 2 Mbps and 3 Mbps, respectively. The practical data rate for a raw 3 Mbps ends up 2.1 Mbps after protocol overheads.

Baseband Specification

One of the most complex of the Bluetooth documents is the baseband specification. In this section we provide an overview of the key elements.

Frequency Hopping **Frequency hopping (FH)** in Bluetooth serves two purposes:

1. It provides resistance to interference and multipath effects.

2. It provides a form of multiple access among co-located devices in different piconets.

The FH scheme works as follows. The total bandwidth is divided into 79 (in almost all countries) *physical channels*, each of bandwidth 1 MHz. FH occurs by jumping from one physical channel to another in a pseudorandom sequence. The

Table 12.3 International Bluetooth Frequency Allocations

Area	Regulatory Range	RF Channels
U.S., most of Europe, and most other countries	2.4 to 2.4835 GHz	$f = 2.402 + n$ MHz, $n = 0, \ldots, 78$
Japan	2.471 to 2.497 GHz	$f = 2.473 + n$ MHz, $n = 0, \ldots, 22$
Spain	2.445 to 2.475 GHz	$f = 2.449 + n$ MHz, $n = 0, \ldots, 22$
France	2.4465 to 2.4835 GHz	$f = 2.454 + n$ MHz, $n = 0, \ldots, 22$

same hopping sequence is shared by all of the devices on a single piconet; we will refer to this as an **FH channel**.[2] The hop rate is 1600 hops per second, so that each physical channel is occupied for a duration of 0.625 ms. Each 0.625-ms time period is referred to as a slot, and these are numbered sequentially.

Bluetooth radios communicate using a time division duplex (TDD) discipline. TDD is a link transmission technique in which data are transmitted in one direction at a time, with transmission alternating between the two directions. Because more than two devices share the piconet medium, the access technique is time division multiple access (TDMA). Thus, piconet access can be characterized as FH-TDD-TDMA. Figure 12.4 illustrates the technique.[3] In the figure, k denotes the slot number and $f(k)$ is the physical channel selected during slot period k.

Transmission of a packet starts at the beginning of a slot. Packet lengths requiring 1, 3, or 5 slots are allowed. For multislot packets, the radio remains at the same frequency until the entire packet has been sent (Figure 12.5). In the next slot after the multislot packet, the radio returns to the frequency required for its hopping sequence, so that during transmission, two or four hop frequencies have been skipped.

Using TDD prevents crosstalk between transmit and receive operations in the radio transceiver, which is essential if a one-chip implementation is desired. Note that because transmission and reception take place at different time slots, different frequencies are used.

The FH sequence is determined by the master in a piconet and is a function of the master's Bluetooth address. A rather complex mathematical operation involving permutations and exclusive-OR (XOR) operations is used to generate a pseudorandom hop sequence.

Because different piconets in the same area will have different masters, they will use different hop sequences. Thus, most of the time, transmissions on two devices on different piconets in the same area will be on different physical channels. Occasionally, two piconets will use the same physical channel during the same time slot, causing a collision and lost data. However, because this will happen

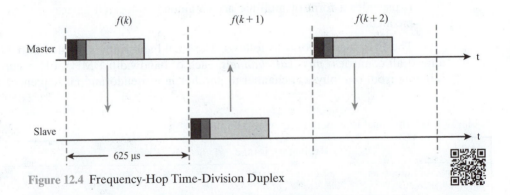

Figure 12.4 Frequency-Hop Time-Division Duplex

[2]The term *FH channel* is not used in the Bluetooth documents but is introduced here for clarity.
[3]The three regions indicated in each packet (dark gray, light gray, white) depict the three major subdivisions of each packet (access code, header, payload), as explained subsequently.

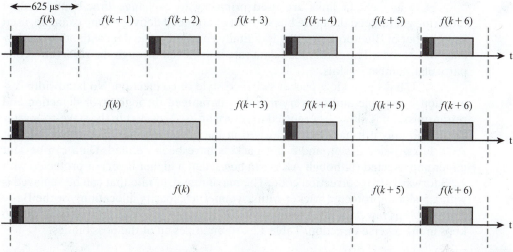

Figure 12.5 Examples of Multislot Packets

infrequently, it is readily accommodated with forward error correction and error detection/ARQ techniques. Thus, a form of code division multiple access (CDMA) is achieved between devices on different piconets in the same scatternet; this is referred to as FH-CDMA.

Piconets may also use *adaptive frequency hopping*, where metrics about the qualities of different hopping frequencies are obtained from many sources. Then the hopping sequence avoids the poor channels, especially those which are occupied by other devices. Thus, less than 79 channels may be used, but the size of the set must be at least 20.

User Logical Links Three types of links can be established between a master and a slave for the purposes of transmitted user data.

- **Synchronous connection oriented (SCO):** Allocates a fixed bandwidth between a point-to-point connection involving the master and a single slave. The master maintains the SCO link by using reserved slots at regular intervals. The basic unit of reservation is two consecutive slots (one in each transmission direction) so the connection is considered symmetric. The master can support up to three simultaneous SCO links while a slave can support three SCO links to a single master or two SCO links to different masters. SCO packets are never retransmitted.

- **Extended synchronous connection oriented (eSCO):** The eSCO reserves slots just like SCO. But these can be asymmetric. And retransmissions are supported.

- **Asynchronous connectionless (ACL):** A point-to-multipoint link between the master and all the slaves in the piconet. In slots not reserved for SCO or eSCO links, the master can exchange packets with any slave on a per-slot basis, including a slave already engaged in an SCO link. Only a single ACL link can exist. For most ACL packets, packet retransmission is applied.

SCO and eSCO links are used primarily to exchange time-bounded data requiring guaranteed data rate but without guaranteed delivery. One example, used in a number of Bluetooth profiles, is digitally encoded audio data with built-in tolerance to lost data. The guaranteed data rate is achieved through the reservation of a particular number of slots.

ACL links provide a packet-switched style of connection. No bandwidth reservation is possible and delivery may be guaranteed through error detection and retransmission. A slave is permitted to return an ACL packet in the slave-to-master slot if and only if it has been addressed in the preceding master-to-slave slot. For ACL links, 1-slot, 3-slot, and 5-slot packets have been defined. Data can be sent either unprotected (although ARQ can be used at a higher layer) or protected with a 2/3 forward error correction code. The maximum data rate that can be achieved is with a 5-slot unprotected packet with asymmetric capacity allocation, for the Basic Rate (1 Mbps raw data rate) resulting in 721 kbps in the forward direction and 57.6 kbps in the reverse direction. Table 12.4 summarizes all of the possibilities.

Packets The packet format for all Bluetooth packets is shown in Figure 12.6. It consists of three fields:

- **Access code:** Used for timing synchronization, offset compensation, paging, and inquiry.
- **Header:** Used to identify packet type and to carry protocol control information.
- **Payload:** If present, contains user voice or data and, in most cases, a payload header.

Table 12.4 Achievable Data Rates on the ACL Link

Type	Symmetric (kbps)	Asymmetric (kbps)	
DM1	108.8	108.8	108.8
DH1	172.8	172.8	172.8
DM3	258.1	387.2	54.4
DH3	390.4	585.6	86.4
DM5	286.7	477.8	36.3
DH5	433.9	723.2	57.6
AUX1	345.6	345.6	345.6
2-DH1	345.6	345.6	345.6
2-DH3	782.9	1174.4	172.8
2-DH5	869.1	1448.5	115.2
3-DH1	531.2	531.2	531.2
3-DH3	1177.6	1766.4	235.6
3-DH5	1306.9	2178.1	177.1

DMx = x-slot FEC-encoded
DHx = x-slot unprotected
2-Dxx = 2 Mbps Enhanced Data Rate
3-Dxx = 3 Mbps Enhanced Data Rate

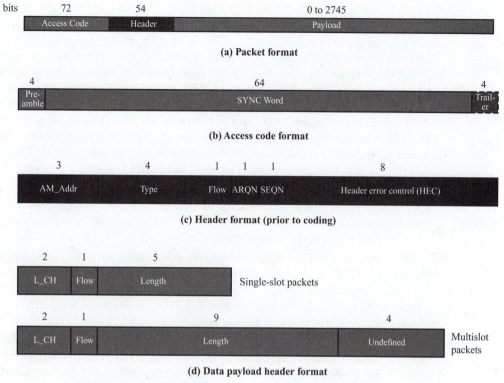

Figure 12.6 Bluetooth Baseband Formats

Access Code There are three types of access codes:

- **Channel access code (CAC):** Identifies a piconet (unique for a piconet).
- **Device access code (DAC):** Used for paging and its subsequent responses.
- **Inquiry access code (IAC):** Used for inquiry purposes.

An access code consists of a preamble, a sync word, and a trailer. The ***preamble*** is used for DC compensation. It consists of the pattern 0101 if the least significant (leftmost) bit in the sync word is 0 and the pattern 1010 if the least significant bit in the sync word is 1. Similarly, the ***trailer*** is 0101 if the most significant bit (rightmost) of the sync word is 1 and 1010 if the most significant bit is 0.

Packet Header The header format for all Bluetooth packets is shown in Figure 12.6c. It consists of six fields:

- **AM_ADDR:** Recall that a piconet includes at most seven active slaves. The 3-bit AM_Addr contains the "active mode" address (temporary address assigned to this slave in this piconet) of one of the slaves. A transmission from the master to a slave contains that slave's address; a transmission from a slave contains its address. The 0 value is reserved for a broadcast from the master to all slaves in the piconet.

- **Type:** Identifies the type of packet. Four type codes are reserved for control packets common to both SCO and ACL links. The remaining packet types are used to convey user information. For SCO links, multiple types of packets carry 64 kbps voice. The difference is the amount of error protection provided, which dictates how frequently a packet must be sent to maintain the 64 kbps data rate. Other types of packets carry both voice and data. For ACL links, 13 different packets are defined as we saw in Table 12.4. These carry user data with different amounts of error protection and different data rates. There is another packet type common to both physical links; it consists of only the access code, with a fixed length of 68 bits (does not include trailer). This is referred to as the ID packet and is used in the inquiry and access procedures.

- **Flow:** Provides a 1-bit flow control mechanism for ACL traffic only. When a packet with Flow = 0 is received, the station receiving the packet must temporarily halt the transmission of ACL packets on this link. When a packet with Flow = 1 is received, transmission may resume.

- **ARQN:** Provides a 1-bit acknowledgment mechanism for ACL traffic protected by a CRC. If the reception was successful, an ACK (ARQN = 1) is returned; otherwise a NAK (ARQN = 0) is returned. When no return message regarding acknowledge is received, a NAK is assumed implicitly. If a NAK is received, the relevant packet is retransmitted.

- **SEQN:** Provides a 1-bit sequential numbering schemes. Transmitted packets are alternately labeled with a 1 or 0. This is required to filter out retransmissions at the destination; if a retransmission occurs due to a failing ACK, the destination receives the same packet twice.

- **Header error control (HEC):** An 8-bit error detection code used to protect the packet header.

Payload Format For some packet types, the baseband specification defines a format for the payload field. For voice payloads, no header is defined. For all of the ACL packets and for the data portion of the SCO DV packet, a header is defined. For data payloads, the payload format consists of three fields:

- **Payload header:** An 8-bit header is defined for single-slot packets, and a 16-bit header is defined for multislot packets.

- **Payload body:** Contains user information.

- **CRC:** A 16-bit CRC code is used on all data payloads except the AUX1 packet.

The payload header, when present, consists of three fields (Figure 12.6d):

- **L_CH:** Identifies the logical channel (described subsequently). The options are LMP message (11); an unframented L2CAP message or the start of a fragmented L2CAP message (10); the continuation of a fragmented L2CAP message (01); or other (00).

- **Flow:** Used to control flow at the L2CAP level. This is the same on/off mechanism provided by the Flow field in the packet header for ACL traffic.

- **Length:** The number of bytes of data in the payload, excluding the payload header and CRC.

Error Correction At the baseband level, Bluetooth makes use of three error correction schemes:

- 1/3 rate FEC (forward error correction)
- 2/3 rate FEC
- ARQ (automatic repeat request)

These error correction schemes are designed to satisfy competing requirements. The error correction scheme must be adequate to cope with the inherently unreliable wireless link but must also be streamlined and efficient.

The *1/3 rate FEC* is used on the 18-bit packet header and also for the voice field in an HV1 packet. The scheme simply involves sending three copies of each bit. A majority logic is used: Each received triple of bits is mapped into whichever bit is in the majority.

The *2/3 rate FEC* is used in all DM packets, in the data field of the DV packet, in the FHS packet, and in the HV2 packet. The encoder is a form of Hamming code with parameters (15, 10). This code can correct all single errors and detect all double errors in each codeword.

The *ARQ scheme* is used with DM and DH packets, and the data field of DV packets. The scheme is similar to ARQ schemes used in data link control protocols (Section 10.4). Recall that ARQ schemes have the following elements:

- **Error detection:** The destination detects errors and discards packets that are in error. Error detection is achieved with a CRC error-detecting code supplemented with the FEC code.
- **Positive acknowledgment:** The destination returns a positive acknowledgment to successfully received, error-free packets.
- **Retransmission after timeout:** The source retransmits a packet that has not been acknowledged after a predetermined amount of time.
- **Negative acknowledgment and retransmission:** The destination returns a negative acknowledgment to packets in which an error is detected. The source retransmits such packets.

Bluetooth uses what is referred to as a *fast ARQ* scheme, which takes advantage of the fact that a master and slave communicate in alternate time slots. Figure 12.7 illustrates the technique and the animation is especially helpful. When a station receives a packet, it determines if an error has occurred using a 16-bit CRC. If so, the ARQN bit in the header is set to 0 (NAK); if no error is detected, then ARQN is set to 1 (ACK). When a station receives a NAK, it retransmits the same packet as it sent in the preceding slot, using the same 1-bit SEQN in the packet header. With this technique, a sender is notified in the next time slot if a transmission has failed and, if so, can retransmit. The use of 1-bit sequence numbers and immediate packet retransmission minimizes overhead and maximizes responsiveness.

Logical Channels Bluetooth defines six types of logical data channels designated to carry different types of payload traffic.

- **Link control (LC):** Used to manage the flow of packets over the link interface. The LC channel is mapped onto the packet header. This channel carries

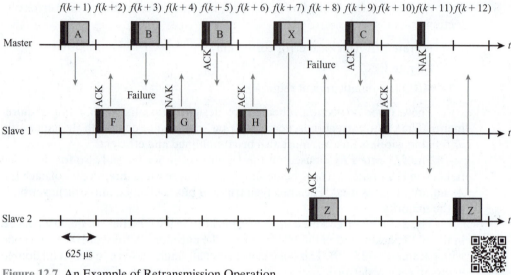

Figure 12.7 An Example of Retransmission Operation

low-level link control information like ARQ, flow control, and payload characterization. The LC channel is carried in every packet except in the ID packet, which has no packet header.

- **ACL Control (ACL-C):** Carries control information for the link managers in the master and slave(s).

- **Link manager (LM):** Transports link management information between participating stations. This logical channel supports LMP traffic and can be carried over either an SCO or ACL link.

- **User asynchronous/isochronous (ACL-U):** Carries asynchronous and isochronous[4] user data. This channel is normally carried over the ACL link but may be carried in a DV packet on the SCO link.

- **User synchronous (SCO-S):** Carries synchronous user data. This channel is carried over the SCO link.

- **User extended synchronous (eSCO-S):** Carried over the extended SCO link.

- **Profile broadcast data (PBD):** Carries profile broadcast data from a connectionless slave broadcast transmitter to one or more connectionless slave broadcast receivers.

Link Manager Specification

LMP manages various aspects of the radio link between a master and a slave. The protocol involves the exchange of messages in the form of LMP protocol data units (PDUs) between the LMP entities in the master and slave. Messages are always sent as single slot packets with a 1-byte payload header that identifies the message type and a payload body that contains additional information pertinent to this message.

---

[4]The term *isochronous* refers to blocks of data that recur with known periodic timing.

The procedures defined for LMP are grouped into 24 functional areas, each of which involves the exchange of one or more messages. These areas include authentication, pairing, encryption, clock offset request, switch master/slave, name request, hold or park or sniff mode, etc.

Logical Link Control and Adaptation Protocol (L2CAP)

Like Logical Link Control (LLC) in the IEEE 802 specification, L2CAP provides a link-layer protocol between entities across a shared-medium network. As with LLC, L2CAP provides a number of services and relies on a lower layer (in this case, the baseband layer) for flow and error control.

L2CAP makes use of ACL links; it does not provide support for SCO links. Using ACL links, L2CAP provides two alternative services to upper-layer protocols:

- **Connectionless service:** This is a reliable datagram style of service.
- **Connection-mode service:** This service is similar to that offered by HDLC. A logical connection is set up between two users exchanging data, and flow control and error control are provided.

L2Cap Channels L2CAP provides three types of logical channels:

- **Connectionless:** Supports the connectionless service. Each channel is unidirectional. This channel type is typically used for broadcast from the master to multiple slaves.
- **Connection oriented:** Supports the connection-oriented service. Each channel is bidirectional (full duplex). A quality-of-service (QoS) flow specification is assigned in each direction.
- **Signaling:** Provides for the exchange of signaling messages between L2CAP entities.

Quality of Service The QoS parameter in L2CAP defines a traffic flow specification based on RFC 1363.[5] In essence, a **flow specification** is a set of parameters that indicate a performance level that the transmitter will attempt to achieve.

The flow specification consists of the following parameters:

- Service type
- Token rate (bytes/second), which sets an average long-term data rate
- Token bucket size (bytes), which allows for burstiness in the traffic flow, within limits
- Peak bandwidth (bytes/second)
- Latency (microseconds)
- Delay variation (microseconds)

The **service type** parameter indicates the level of service for this flow. A value of 0 indicates that no traffic will be transmitted on this channel. A value of 1

---

[5]A *Proposed Flow Specification*, RFC 1363, September 1992.

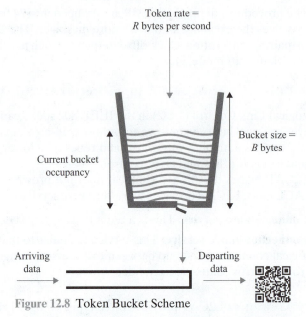

Figure 12.8 Token Bucket Scheme

indicates a best effort service; the device will transmit data as quickly as possible but with no guarantees about performance. A value of 2 indicates a guaranteed service; the sender will transmit data that conform to the remaining QoS parameters.

The *token rate* and *token bucket size* parameters define a **token bucket** scheme that is often used in QoS specifications. See Figure 12.8. The analogy is of a bucket where tokens are deposited on a regular basis (bytes/second). Every time a packet transmits, it takes some of the tokens from the bucket. If not enough tokens are present, the packet must wait until there are enough. If tokens arrive and the bucket is already full, then those tokens are lost. A burst of packets can be transmitted at the peak bandwidth until the bucket empties.

This token bucket mechanism manages long-term average transmission data rate, since it must be less than or equal to the token rate. But the token bucket scheme also allows for bursts of traffic, but packets afterward will experience a bucket close to empty.

12.4 BLUETOOTH HIGH SPEED AND BLUETOOTH SMART

Bluetooth specifications made significant advancements with releases 3.0 and 4.0. Bluetooth 3.0 created an alternative technique to achieve up to a 24 Mbps data rate. Bluetooth 4.0 created a capability known as Bluetooth Low Energy.

Bluetooth 3.0+HS

In addition to other enhancements, Bluetooth 3.0 provided a mechanism to achieve higher data rates, up to 24 Mbps. This involves the operation of a new additional controller that is compliant with the 2007 edition of the IEEE 802.11 standard. This in essence adds a Wi-Fi connection capability when higher data rates are necessary. This is known as the **Alternative MAC/PHY (AMP)**, which is an optional capability. The Bluetooth radio is still used for device discovery, association, initial connection setup, profile configuration, and connection maintenance. This allows the more power efficient Bluetooth modes to be used, except when higher data rates are needed. Each AMP uses a Protocol Adaptation Layer (PAL), which works above the MAC and PHY layers to map Bluetooth protocols and behavior to the MAC and PHY.

Bluetooth Smart, Bluetooth 4.0

Bluetooth Smart, previously known as Bluetooth Low Energy, was introduced with Bluetooth 4.0. It provides an intelligent, power-friendly version of Bluetooth. This enables Bluetooth to run long periods of time on a single battery or to scavenge for energy. Bluetooth Smart devices have an especially useful capability compared to other low energy device technologies because they can also communicate with other Bluetooth-enabled devices, such as legacy Bluetooth devices or Bluetooth-enabled smartphones. This is positioned as a possible successful technology for the Internet of Things. For example, health monitoring devices can easily integrate with existing smartphones.

Bluetooth Smart operates in the same 2.4 GHz ISM bands, just as Bluetooth BR/EDR, but uses 40 channels spaced 2 MHz apart (3 advertising and 37 data channels) instead of 79 channels spaced 1 MHz apart. Devices can implement a transmitter, a receiver, or both. Devices can also decide to implement only single-mode Bluetooth Smart functionality or dual-mode to also have the Bluetooth BR/EDR capability. Single-mode chips can be produced at reduced cost and can be integrated into compact devices.

Bluetooth Smart also provides the following design features:

- 10 mW output power
- 150 m range in an open field
- New advertising mechanism for efficient device discovery
- New asynchronous connectionless MAC to provide low delay and fast transactions
- New generic attribute protocol to provide a simple client/server model
- New generic attribute profile to efficiently collect data from sensors

12.5 IEEE 802.15

The IEEE 802.15 working group for *Wireless Personal Area Networks (WPANs)* was formed to develop standards for short-range wireless PANs. A PAN is a communications network within a small area in which all of the devices on the network are typically owned by one person or perhaps a family. Devices on a PAN may include portable and mobile devices, such as PCs, smartphones, tablets, health-monitoring devices, smart glasses, or computer peripherals. The first effort by the working group was to develop 802.15.1, with the goal of creating a formal standard of the MAC and

PHY layers of the Bluetooth specification; this standard was approved in 2002 and updated in 2005. The Bluetooth SIG developed the rest of the entire specification and has developed all parts of subsequent releases instead of the IEEE.

Following the 802.15.1 standard, the 802.15 work went in two directions. The 802.15.3 task group is interested in developing standards for devices that are of low cost and low power compared to 802.11 devices, but with significantly higher data rates than 802.15.1. An initial standard for 802.15.3 was issued in 2003, and the latest 802.15.3c standard provides gigabit rates in the 60 GHz band. Work continues on 802.15.3d, which will provide 100 Gbps data rates.

Meanwhile, the 802.15.4 task group developed a standard for very low cost, very low power devices at data rates lower than 802.15.1, with a standard issued in 2003. Since then, several new PHY layers were specified in subsequent standards, and a variety of other application area requirements are being addressed by 802.15.4 task groups.

Figure 12.9 shows the current status of the 802.15 work in 802.15.1, 802.15.3, and 802.15.4. Each of the three wireless PAN standards has not only different physical layer specifications but different requirements for the MAC layer. Accordingly, each has a unique MAC specification. Figure 12.10 gives an indication of the relative scope of application of the wireless LAN and PAN standards. As can be seen, the 802.15 wireless PAN standards are intended for very short range, up to about 10 m, which enables the use of low power, low cost devices.

This section provides an overview of 802.15.3 and 802.15.4. It also discusses work on IEEE 802.15.5 through 802.15.7.

IEEE 802.15.3

The 802.15.3 task group is concerned with the development of high data rate WPANs. Examples of applications that would fit a WPAN profile but would also require a relatively high data rate include

- Connecting digital cameras or smartphones to printers or kiosks
- Laptop to projector connection
- Speakers in a 5:1 surround-sound system connecting to the receiver

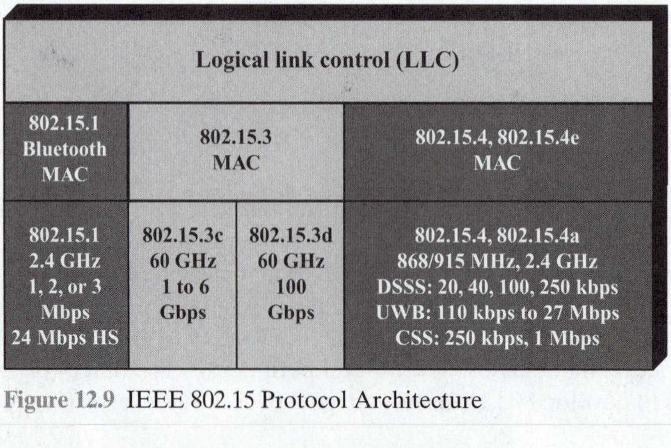

Logical link control (LLC)			
802.15.1 Bluetooth MAC	802.15.3 MAC		802.15.4, 802.15.4e MAC
802.15.1 2.4 GHz 1, 2, or 3 Mbps 24 Mbps HS	802.15.3c 60 GHz 1 to 6 Gbps	802.15.3d 60 GHz 100 Gbps	802.15.4, 802.15.4a 868/915 MHz, 2.4 GHz DSSS: 20, 40, 100, 250 kbps UWB: 110 kbps to 27 Mbps CSS: 250 kbps, 1 Mbps

Figure 12.9 IEEE 802.15 Protocol Architecture

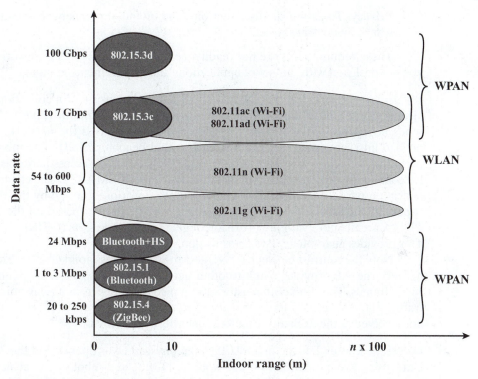

Figure 12.10 Wireless Local Networks

- Video distribution from a set-top box or cable modem
- Sending music to headphones or speakers
- Video camera display on television
- Remote view finders for video or digital still cameras

These applications are mainly in the consumer electronics area and generate the following requirements:

- **Short range:** On the order of 10 m.
- **High throughput:** Greater than 20 Mbps to support video and/or multichannel audio.
- **Low power usage:** To be useful in battery-powered portable devices.
- **Low cost:** To be reasonable for inexpensive consumer electronic devices.
- **QoS capable:** To provide guaranteed data rate and other QoS features for applications sensitive to throughput or latency.
- **Dynamic environment:** Refers to a piconet architecture in which mobile, portable, and stationary devices enter and leave the piconet often. For mobile device, a speed of less than 7 km/hr is addressed.
- **Simple connectivity:** To make networking easy and eliminate the need for a technically sophisticated user.

- **Privacy:** To assure the user that only the intended recipients can understand what is being transmitted.

These requirements are not readily met with an IEEE 802.11 network, which was not designed with this set of applications and requirements in mind.

Medium Access Control An 802.15.3 network consists of a collection of devices (DEVs). One of the DEVs also acts as a *piconet coordinator (PNC)*. The PNC sends beacons so DEVs can know when and how to access the network. Time is divided into sequential superframes, each with a beacon period, contention access period, and channel time allocation period. The contention access period is mainly for command and control communication, and it uses CSMA/CA. The channel time allocation period is composed of channel time allocations granted by the PNC between DEVs. This QoS feature of the 802.15.3 MAC layer is based on the use of a TDMA architecture with the provision of guaranteed time slots (GTSs). This provides guaranteed data transmission.

Note the contrast between a PNC and an 802.11 access point (AP) or Bluetooth master. The AP provides a link to other networks and acts as a relay point for all MAC frames. The Bluetooth master sets up piconets and acts as a relay point for all traffic. The PNC is used to control access to the time resources of the piconet but is not involved in the exchange of data frames between DEVs.

Physical Layer For the first 802.15.3, the physical layer operated in the 2.4 GHz band, using five modulation formats with an 11 Mbaud symbol rate to achieve data rates from 11 to 55 Mbps. The most significant aspect of the scheme is the use of trellis-coded modulation (TCM). TCM is an old technique, used in voice-grade telephone network modems.

IEEE 802.15.3c The latest ratified standard for IEEE 802.15.3 is 802.15.3c. This standard is the first 802.15.3 standard to utilize the 60 GHz band. The benefits of the 60 GHz unlicensed band were mentioned in the 802.11ad discussion in the previous chapter. Throughout the world, there is a commonly available band of 5 GHz available around 60 GHz, so large data rates are possible. Such frequencies, however, require higher transmission power and do not penetrate objects well, such as floors and walls. Beamforming can overcome some of these deficiencies, however. Four 2160 MHz channels are available worldwide through international agreements on 60 GHz unlicensed operation.

The 802.15.3c task group performed detailed analysis and found the following usage models for high bit rate wireless services:

- **Usage Model 1:** Uncompressed high definition video streaming, eliminating the need for video cables from video players and display devices. An uncompressed 1920 × 1080 pixel resolution at 24 bits/pixel and 60 frames per second would require over 3.5 Gbps, when also including protocol overheads.
- **Usage Model 2:** Uncompressed multivideo streaming for display of multiple video streams on the same screen.
- **Usage Model 3:** Office desktop communication with peripherals.
- **Usage Model 4:** Conference ad hoc services where computers communicate with each other.

- **Usage Model 5:** Kiosk file downloading to download music or video files.

To support the various usage models, three PHY modes have been specified.

- Single carrier with rates of 1.5 Gbps and 3 Gbps for Usage Models 3 and 5.
- High-speed interface using OFDM up to 5.775 Gbps for Usage Model 4.
- Audio/visual mode using OFDM with rates of 0.952, 1.904, and 3.807 Gbps for Usage Models 1 and 2.

The MAC layer for 802.15.3c was enhanced to provide support for coexistence of the three PHY modes. It also provided frame aggregation. We saw the benefits of frame aggregation to reduce overhead in the discussions of IEEE 802.11n and 802.11ac. IEEE 802.15.3c specifies an optional beamforming protocol. It does not require estimation of angles of arrival or departure or of channel state estimation. Beamforming is performed in three stages: sector-level coarse searching, then beam-level fine searching, and then an optional tracking phase to adjust the beam throughout the connection.

IEEE 802.15.3d IEEE 802.15.3d is intended for 100 Gbps operation for low cost and low power consumption devices. It is in development at the time of this writing. It is to enable the applications mentioned above for 802.15.3c, but also opens new possibilities for having entirely wireless offices where fiber optic networks would not be cost-effective. The IEEE project authorization for 802.15.3d mentions support for wireless switched point-to-point applications for data centers, as well as wireless backhaul and intra-device communication. The ranges are from a few centimeters to 100 m.

IEEE 802.15.4

The WPAN Low Rate Task Group (TG4) is chartered to investigate a low data rate solution with multimonth to multiyear battery life and very low complexity. Standards have evolved through two 802.15.4 releases then an 802.15.4a release. The standards specify several physical layers:

- 868 MHz/915 MHz direct sequence spread spectrum PHY to support over-the-air data rates of 20, 40, 100, and 250 kbps.
- 2.4 GHz direct sequence spread spectrum PHY to support 250 kbps.
- **Ultra wideband (UWB)** impulse radio that uses very short pulses that have high bandwidth but low spectral density over any narrowband range of frequencies. It operates in the unlicensed UWB sub-gigahertz (249.6 to 749.6 MHz), low band (3.1 to 4.8 GHz), and high band (5.8 to 10.6 GHz). Even though many other users occupy these bands, UWB signals have such low power spectral density that they minimally interfere; as a matter of fact they are usually weaker than the thermal noise. The PHY supports 851 kbps and optionally 110 kbps, 6.81 Mbps, or 27.234 Mbps. UWB impulses also support precision ranging, so devices can know their distance from each other within 1-meter accuracy.
- 2.4 GHz **chirp spread spectrum (CSS)** PHY to support 1 Mbps and optionally 250 kbps. Chirp spread spectrum uses sinusoidal signals that change frequency with time. This creates another form of spreading a signal across a wide bandwidth (i.e., spread spectrum).

The physical layer chosen depends on local regulations and user preference. Potential applications are sensors, interactive toys, smart badges, remote controls, and home automation.

Low data rate wireless applications have been largely ignored until recently because of the lack of standards and appropriate technology to develop transmitters and receivers of very low cost, very low power consumption, and very small size. At the physical and MAC layers, IEEE 802.15.4 is designed to address the need for such devices. The IEEE 802.15.4 MAC layer includes CSMA-CA channel access, automatic network establishment from a coordinator node, and a fully handshaked protocol to make sure packets are delivered reliably.

Above the LLC layer, the ZigBee Alliance and other groups are producing specifications to operate over 802.15.4 implementations. The ZigBee specification addresses the network, security, and application interface layers and is covered in Section 12.6.

The 802.15.4 Task Group is conducting a series of other creative and practical activities. Some are as follows.

- IEEE 802.15.4c and 802.15.4d have specified other PHY layers, including those for 780 and 950 MHz bands.

- IEEE 802.15.4e redesigned the 802.15.4 MAC protocol to better support industrial applications. It provides high reliability by using time synchronization and channel hopping. It also can maintain the low duty cycles needed for power efficient operation.

- IEEE 802.15.4f provides a standard for active **radio frequency identification (RFID)** and sensor applications that is low cost, has ultra low energy consumption, and is flexible and highly reliable. An RFID tag is typically attached to an asset such as a package, animal, or person with the purposes of identifying the object. Active RFID tags produce their own signal from a battery or other harvested energy source, whereas passive RFID tags use an external radio signal to produce an identification signal. Active RFIDs are the focus on 802.15.4f.

- IEEE 802.15.4g supports **smart utility networks** by providing a standard for very large-scale process control applications, such as the utility smart grid (discussed also in Section 16.5). Of particular interest are networks of sensors for smart meter reading with targeted data rates in ranges from 40 to 1000 kbps.

- IEEE 802.15.4j defines PHY layer meets requirements for a **medical body area network (MBAN)** in the 2.4 GHz band. Multiple low cost sensors are deployed on or around a patient to take readings of patient physiological information. A hub device is located near or on the patient to collect and transmit the information. It may also process the collected data locally to look for certain conditions to trigger a treatment procedure. Three major categories of MBANs have particular requirements. In-hospital patient monitoring and emergency ambulance applications require 1 to 3 m range with duty cycles less than 20%. Home-monitoring applications, however, need longer range (up to 10 m) with much longer battery life (i.e., a duty cycle less than 2%).

- IEEE 802.15.4k is defined by the ***Low Energy Critical Infrastructure (LECIM)*** task group. Its role is to facilitate communication with multi-thousands of devices. This is to be used for critical infrastructure monitoring devices, such as sensors on roads and bridges, which require low energy operation for multiyear battery life. The application requires minimal network infrastructure and should enable collection of regularly scheduled or event-driven data from end points that may be numerous, highly dispersed, or in challenging propagation environments. 802.15.4k minimizes network maintenance traffic and device wake durations.

- IEEE 802.15.4m specifies a PHY layer for meeting **TV white space** regulatory requirements. TV white space refers to spectrum that is underutilized (i.e., white), in particular those frequencies for analog television. Recently, the United States Federal Communications Commission (FCC) made unlicensed TV frequencies available for use. This amendment makes 802.15.4 wireless networks compliant with regulations so they can take advantage of this spectrum for large-scale device command and control applications.

- IEEE 802.15.4p expands the 802.15.4 standard for rail and rail transit. This provides ***Positive Train Control*** for four main components: equipment on locomotive/train, equipment trackside, network access points, and bidirectional wireless data links to wirelessly connect all these elements.

Other 802.15 Standards

In addition to the work in 802.15.1, 802.15.3, and 802.15.4, the following work has been produced:

- **IEEE 802.15.2:** Because most or all of the planned 802.15 standards would operate in the same frequency bands as used by 802.11 devices, both the 802.11 and 802.15 working groups were concerned about the ability of these various devices to successfully coexist. The 802.15.2 Task Group was formed to develop recommended practices for coexistence.

- **IEEE 802.15.5:** Going beyond the coverage of a personal area, 802.15.5 provides recommended practices for multihop ***mesh networking*** technology. It combines the 802.15.3 MAC and the 802.15.4 MAC to create high-rate or low-rate mesh networks. The objectives are interoperable, stable, and scalable mesh topologies.

- **IEEE 802.15.6:** ***Body area networks*** are highly reliable, miniaturized sensor networks using lightweight and low power sensor nodes to provide comfort and cost-efficient care healthcare. The IEEE 802.15.6 standard defines short-range wireless devices and networks for in-body, on-body, and around-the-body communication. Several frequency bands are used and three physical layers have been defined: narrowband, ultra-wideband, and body channel communication.

- **IEEE 802.15.7:** ***Visible light communication*** uses light wavelengths from 380 to 780 nm. Advances in LED technology have enabled this short-range communication approach. Its two main challenges are flicker mitigation and dimming support to make coexistence with humans tolerable. It has been standardized by IEEE 802.15.7, which provides data rates from 11.67 kbps to 96 Mbps with three PHY options.

12.6 ZIGBEE

The ZigBee Alliance has developed a suite of protocols based on IEEE 802.15.4 that creates a capability for small, low-power radios. These radios are simpler than wireless personal area networks such as Bluetooth. ZigBee is well suited for applications that require low data rate, long battery life, and secure networking. ZigBee provides data rates from 20 to 250 kbps, depending on the implementation and frequency, and it is best suited for periodic or intermittent communication. The name "ZigBee" refers to the waggle dance of honey bees when they return to a beehive. ZigBee standards first appeared in 2003.

Technical Overview

ZigBee has the following features:

- Low cost to be deployed for wireless control and monitoring.
- Low power to produce longer life with smaller batteries.
- Networking: Nodes connect with nearest neighbors and some nodes route each other's messages. The architecture provides high reliability and more extensive range.
- Operates in unlicensed (ISM) bands—868 MHz (Europe), 915 MHz (USA and Australia), 2.4 GHz (worldwide).
- Network topologies can be star, tree, and general mesh structures.
- One coordinator device creates, controls, and maintains the network.
- It has quick awake from sleep, going from sleep to active in 30 ms or less, compared to Bluetooth wake-up delays which could be 3 s. This means ZigBee nodes can sleep most of the time, even during communications, keeping average power consumption low.

ZigBee complements the IEEE 802.15.4 standard by adding four main components, as seen in Figure 12.11.

- Network layer provides routing.
- Application support sublayer supports specialized services.
- **ZigBee device objects (ZDOs)** are the most significant improvement. They keep device roles, manage requests to join the network, discover devices, and manage security.
- Manufacturer-defined application objects allow customization.

ZigBee Alliance

ZigBee-style networks began to be conceived around 1998, when installers realized Wi-Fi and Bluetooth were likely to be unsuitable. The IEEE 802.15.4 standard was first published in 2003 and later updated in IEEE 802.15.4-2006.

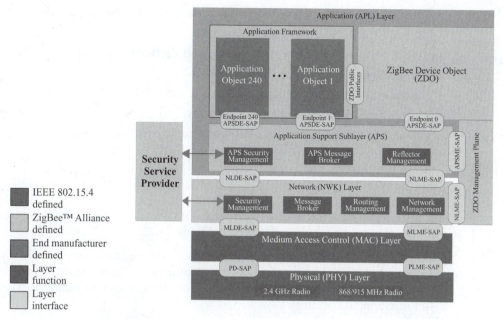

Figure 12.11 ZigBee Architecture

The ZigBee Alliance now maintains and publishes the ZigBee standard. ZigBee specifications were first ratified in December 2004, and then Enhanced ZigBee, called ZigBee PRO, was completed in 2007. This provides two stack profiles that can be implemented.

- Profile 1 (simply called ZigBee) for home and light commercial use.
- Profile 2 (called ZigBee PRO) with more features such as multicasting and higher security.

In addition, there are two other ZigBee specifications.

- **ZigBee IP Specification:** This provides an IPv6-based full wireless mesh for Internet connections to control ZigBee devices.
- **ZigBee RF4CE (Radio Frequency for Consumer Electronic Devices):** This provides a solution for control of products and supports the ZigBee Remote Control and ZigBee Input Device profiles discussed below.

The ZigBee Alliance also publishes application profiles to allow equipment vendors to create interoperable products if they implement the same profile. Certification processes make sure a profile is implemented properly. One expectation is that devices must have a battery life of at least 2 years. The following profiles have been released:

- ZigBee Building Automation (efficient commercial spaces)
- ZigBee Health Care (health and fitness monitoring)
- ZigBee Home Automation (smart homes)

- ZigBee Input Device (easy-to-use touchpads, mice, keyboards, wands)
- ZigBee Light Link (LED lighting control)
- ZigBee Network Devices (assist and expand ZigBee networks)
- ZigBee Retail Services (smarter shopping)
- ZigBee Remote Control (advanced remote controls)
- ZigBee Smart Energy 1.1 (home energy savings)
- ZigBee Smart Energy Profile 2 (IP-based home energy management)
- ZigBee Telecom Services (value-added services)

Device Types

The ZigBee network will consist of three types of devices. These can be organized in a variety of network topologies as seen in Figure 12.12.

1. The **ZigBee Coordinator** is the most capable device, and there is only one coordinator in each network. The coordinator starts the network and serves at the root if a tree topology is used. The coordinator also maintains network information, like security keys.
2. The **ZigBee Router** can pass data on to other ZigBee devices.
3. The **ZigBee End Device** contains only enough functionality to talk to a router or coordinator, but it cannot relay information to other devices. This allows it to sleep a significant amount of the time, saving energy. It also requires the least amount of memory, so it is much less expensive to manufacture.

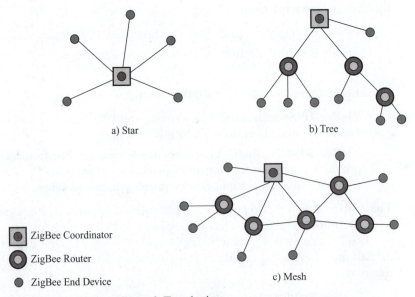

a) Star

b) Tree

ZigBee Coordinator

ZigBee Router

ZigBee End Device

c) Mesh

Figure 12.12 ZigBee Network Topologies

Protocols

The main goals of ZigBee protocols are to automatically construct low-speed ad hoc networks by using routing protocols to forward the packets across multiple hops. Ad hoc On-demand Distance Vector (AODV) and other routing protocols are used. AODV sends out route requests and either responds or forwards the messages to other nodes until someone responds. Nodes in the network store and use information about the routes they discover. The nodes can form into smaller clusters.

ZigBee can form two types of networks. ***Non-beacon-based networks*** use unslotted CSMA/CA. There is no time synchronization between devices. ZigBee routers have their receivers continuously active, so there is usually a need for a permanent power supply. But other nodes spend most of their time sleeping.

Beacon-based networks transmit periodic beacons for nodes to confirm their presence to other nodes. Time is divided into superframes. There is a Contention Access Period (CAP), which uses CSMA/CA using 16 equally sized slots. The Contention Free Period (CFP) is an optional period that uses guaranteed time slots (GTS) which are allocated by the coordinator for urgent real-time applications. There can also be an inactive period. Nodes may sleep between beacons, with intervals that may range from 15.36 ms to 251.65824 s when using 250 kbps.

Beacon-based access is typically used in star or tree network structures. Non-beacon-based access is more common for mesh structures. Virtually all commercially available systems use non-beacon-based access, since it is difficult to implement time synchronization within ZigBee low cost expectations.

Radio Hardware

Radio design has been carefully optimized for low cost in large-scale production, with few analog stages and digital circuits wherever possible. ZigBee operates in three frequency bands.

- 2.4 GHz band—16 ZigBee channels, each with 5 MHz of bandwidth. This provides up to 250 kbps, with lower actual throughput after packet overhead and processing delays. Offset QPSK modulation is used.
- 915 MHz band—Up to 40 kbps, BPSK modulation.
- 868 MHz band—Up to 20 kbps, BPSK modulation.

Transmission range is between 10 and 75 m, up to 1500 m with ZigBee PRO.

Application Layer ZigBee device objects (ZDOs) are responsible for defining the role of the device, as coordinator, end device, or router. A ZDO discovers new devices and what services they offer. Then it establishes secure links. The ZigBee Application Support Sublayer (APS) bridges between the network layer and other components of the application layer. There is also support for communication models where some applications may distribute work among many different nodes to carry out a task. For example, distributed control could occur for energy management in a home with several devices carrying out their tasks.

Zigbee Security ZigBee provides strict key management and distribution rules, which are the most important functions of the network. A network will designate one special device to be a trust center, which all devices trust for distribution of keys. Nodes manage internally how they encrypt information between layers. The layer that creates a frame is responsible for its security. ZigBee uses 128-bit keys, which can be associated either to a network or a link.

12.7 RECOMMENDED READING

[STAN14] provides one of many good discussions of IoT. [BRAY01] provides good treatment of Bluetooth 1.0. [DECU14a] and [DECU14b] provide overviews of Bluetooth Smart. [GILB04] is a thorough treatment of 802.15.3, and [BAYK11] discusses 802.15.3c.

[GUTI03] thoroughly covers the first 802.15.4, [KARA10] discusses 802.15.4a, and [PALA13] provides a comprehensive survey of PHY, MAC, and routing issues for 802.15.4 low power networks. IEEE task group Web sites for 802.15.4 also provide useful information. [WHEE07] and [WANG08] provide good overviews of ZigBee and the ZigBee Alliance Web site provides the latest updates on standards.

BAYK11 Baykas, T., et. al., "IEEE 802.15.3c: the first IEEE wireless standard for data rates over 1 Gb/s." *Communications Magazine, IEEE,* vol. 49, no. 7, pp. 114, 121, July 2011.

BRAY01 Bray, J., and Sturman, C., *Bluetooth: Connect Without Cables.* Upper Saddle River, NJ: Prentice Hall, 2001.

DECU14a Decuir, J., "Introducing Bluetooth Smart: Part 1: A look at both classic and new technologies." *Consumer Electronics Magazine, IEEE,* vol. 3, no. 1, pp. 12, 18, January 2014.

DECU14b Decuir, J., "Introducing Bluetooth Smart: Part II: Applications and updates." *Consumer Electronics Magazine, IEEE,* vol. 3, no. 2, pp. 25, 29, April 2014.

GILB04 Gilb, J., *Wireless Multimedia: A Guide to the IEEE 802.15.3 Standard.* New York: IEEE Press, 2004.

GUTI03 Gutierrez, J.; Callaway, E.; and Barrett, R. *Low-Rate Wireless Personal Area Networks: Enabling Wireless Sensors with IEEE 802.15.4.* New York: IEEE Press, 2003.

KARA10 Karapistoli, E.; Pavlidou, F.-N.; Gragopoulos, I.; and Tsetsinas, I., "An Overview of the IEEE 802.15.4a Standard." *Communications Magazine, IEEE,* vol. 48, no. 1, pp. 47, 53, January 2010.

PALA13 Palattella, M.R., et al., "Standardized Protocol Stack for the Internet of (Important) Things." *Communications Surveys & Tutorials, IEEE*, vol. 15, no. 3, pp. 1389, 1406, Third Quarter 2013.

STAN14 Stankovic, J.A., "Research Directions for the Internet of Things." *Internet of Things Journal, IEEE,* vol. 1, no. 1, pp. 3, 9, February 2014.

WANG08 Wang, C., et al., "Voice Communications over ZigBee Networks." *IEEE Communications Magazine*, January 2008, p. 121.

WHEE07 Wheeler, A., "Commercial Applications of Wireless Sensor Networks Using ZigBee." *IEEE Communications Magazine*, April 2007, p. 70.

12.8 KEY TERMS, REVIEW QUESTIONS, AND PROBLEMS

Key Terms

alternative MAC/PHY (AMP)	flow specification	scatternet
asynchronous connectionless (ACL)	frequency hopping	service discovery protocol
basic rate (BR)	Internet of Things (IoT)	smart utility networks
Bluetooth	link manager (LM)	synchronous connection oriented (SCO)
Bluetooth Low Energy	logical link control and adaptation protocol (L2CAP)	token bucket
Bluetooth Smart	medical body area network (MBAN)	ultra wideband (UWB)
cable replacement protocol		usage model
chirp spread spectrum (CSS)	personal area network (PAN)	TV white space
core protocols	piconet	ZigBee coordinator
core specifications	profile specifications	ZigBee device object (ZDOs)
enhanced data rate (EDR)	RFCOMM	ZigBee end device
extended synchronous connection oriented (eSCO)	radio frequency identification (RFID)	ZigBee router

Review Questions

12.1 In general terms, what application areas are supported by Bluetooth?

12.2 What is the difference between a core specification and a profile specification?

12.3 What is the relationship between master and slave in a piconet?

12.4 How is it possible to combine frequency hopping and time division duplex?

12.5 How does FH-CDMA differ from DS-CDMA?

12.6 List and briefly define the types of links that can be established between a master and a slave.

12.7 How does Bluetooth 3.0 increase Bluetooth data rates to 24 Mbps?

12.8 What is the alternate name for Bluetooth Smart and what is this version of Bluetooth called by those names?

12.9 How are 802.15.3 and 802.15.4 similar and different?

12.10 What method is used by 802.15.3 to achieve higher data rates?

12.11 Compare and contrast the 802.15.4 PHY options.

12.12 Describe the types of applications for active RFIDs versus passive RFIDs. This will require some of your own research.

12.13 Describe the four main components of ZigBee that were added in higher layers above 802.15.4.

Problems

12.1 Describe, step by step, the activity in each of the 12 time slots of Figure 12.7.

12.2 Consider a Bluetooth scatternet consisting of 2 piconets. What is the probability of a collision between packets of the two piconets? Assume nodes are not using CSMA. Remember that a successful transmission requires both a successful polling message to be sent from the master to slave, and then a successful message sent from slave to master. Assume there are 80 frequencies possible. All piconets constantly have packets they are trying to send and they are not using CSMA.

12.3 Repeat Problem 12.2, now with 10 piconets in the scatternet. Find the probability that the two-way communication between one master and slave are successful. Assume all piconets have packets they are trying to send.

12.4 Show the results for the previous two problems on a plot, with a range from 2 to 15 piconets per scatternet. This gives insight into why there is a limit of 10 piconets per scatternet.

12.5 A Bluetooth scatternet consists of 2 piconets. Find the success probability of sending a 5-slot ACL packet. Assume the other piconet is only sending 1-slot packets.

12.6 A typical 1.5 V watch battery has a capacity of 28 mAh. A ZigBee node is to last 2 years on this battery.
  a. How much power (in watts) can the node consume if it operates continuously?
  b. If the node can turn off its transceiver, this reduces power consumption by 75%. This means the node only consumes 25% of the power when the transceiver is not operating. If the node can use sleep modes to keep the transceiver on only 10% of the time, how much longer will the battery life become?
  c. A manufacturer offers a 1 mW RF transceiver for a ZigBee device. Assume this same power is used when transmitting and receiving. How much power can the rest of the node use if the transceiver is on 5% of the time and the battery is to last 2 years? Assume the rest of the node uses its power continuously.

12.7 From your own research, list and describe at least five ways in which methods are being developed for nodes to harvest energy from the environment.

12.8 From Equation (6.4), compute the extra power in dB that an 802.15.3c node will need to use when transmitting the same distance using 60 GHz as an 802.15.3d node using 2.4 GHz over the same distance.

12.9 The token bucket scheme places a limit on the length of time at which traffic can depart at the maximum data rate. Let the token bucket be defined by a bucket size B octets and a token arrival rate of R octets/second, and let the maximum output data rate be M octets/s.
  a. Derive a formula for S, which is the length of the maximum-rate burst. That is, for how long can a flow transmit at the maximum output rate when governed by a token bucket?
  b. What is the value of S for $b = 250$ KB, $r = 2$ MB/s, and $M = 25$ MB/s? *Hint:* The formula for S is not so simple as it might appear, because more tokens arrive while the burst is being output.

PART FOUR

Wireless Mobile Networks and Applications

CHAPTER 13

CELLULAR WIRELESS NETWORKS

Of all the tremendous advances in data communications and telecommunications, perhaps the most revolutionary is the development of cellular networks. Cellular technology is the foundation of mobile wireless communications and supports users in locations that are not easily served by wired networks. Cellular technology is the underlying technology for mobile telephones, smartphones, tablets, wireless Internet and wireless applications, and much more.

The next two chapters look at all aspects of cellular networks, from basic wireless communications and systems principles, to the latest fourth-generation Long-Term Evolution (LTE)-Advanced standards. We begin this chapter with a look at the basic principles used in all cellular networks. Then we look at specific cellular technologies and standards, which are conveniently grouped into four generations. The first generation is analog-based and has essentially passed from the scene. **Second-generation (2G)** systems are still in use to carry voice, and **third-generation (3G)** systems were the first to carry sufficiently high-speed data to support truly mobile networking. The next chapter studies LTE and its enhancements in LTE-Advanced. These form a suite of capabilities for fourth-generation cellular systems.

13.1 PRINCIPLES OF CELLULAR NETWORKS

Cellular radio is a technique that was developed to increase the capacity available for **mobile radio** telephone service. Prior to the introduction of cellular communication, mobile radio telephone service was provided only by a high-power transmitter/receiver. A typical system would support about 25 channels with an effective radius of about 80 km. The way to increase the capacity of the system is to use low-power systems with shorter radius and to use numerous transmitters/receivers. We begin this section with a look at the organization of cellular systems and then examine some of the details of their implementation.

Cellular Network Organization

The essence of a **cellular network** is the use of multiple low-power transmitters, on the order of 100 W or less, even much less. Because the range of such a transmitter is small, an area can be divided into cells, each one served by its own antenna. Each cell is allocated a band of frequencies and is served by a **base station**, consisting of a transmitter, receiver, and control unit. Adjacent cells are assigned different frequencies to avoid interference or crosstalk. However, cells sufficiently distant from each other can use the same frequency band.

The first design decision to make is the shape of cells to cover an area. A matrix of square cells would be the simplest layout to define (Figure 13.1a). However, this geometry is not ideal. If the width of a square cell is d, then a cell has four neighbors at a distance d and four neighbors at a distance $\sqrt{2}d$. As a mobile user within a cell moves toward the cell's boundaries, it is best if all of the adjacent antennas are equidistant. This simplifies the task of determining when to switch the user to an adjacent antenna and which antenna to choose. A hexagonal pattern provides for equidistant antennas (Figure 13.1b). The radius of a hexagon is defined to be the radius of the circle that circumscribes it (equivalently, the distance from the center to each vertex; also equal to the length of a side of a hexagon). For a cell radius R, the distance between the cell center and each adjacent cell center is $d = \sqrt{3}R$.

In practice, a precise hexagonal pattern is not used. Certainly an antenna is not designed to have a hexagonal pattern. Variations from the ideal are also due to topographical limitations such as hills or mountains, local signal propagation conditions such as shadowing from buildings, and practical limitations in siting antennas.

Frequency Reuse In a cellular system, each cell has a base transceiver. The transmission power is carefully controlled (to the extent that it is possible in the highly variable mobile communication environment) to allow communication within the cell using a given frequency band while limiting the power at that frequency that escapes the cell into adjacent cells. In some cellular architectures, it is not practical

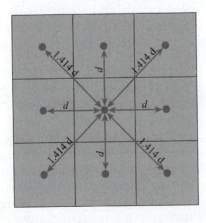

(a) Square pattern

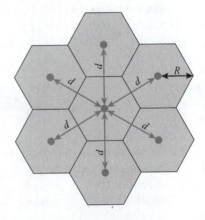

(b) Hexagonal pattern

Figure 13.1 Cellular Geometries

to attempt to use the same frequency band in two adjacent cells.[1] Instead, the objective is to use the same frequency band in multiple cells at some distance from one another. This allows the same frequency band to be used for multiple simultaneous conversations in different cells. Within a given cell, multiple frequency bands are assigned, with the number of bands depending on the traffic expected.

A key design issue is to determine the minimum separation between two cells using the same frequency band, so that the two cells do not interfere with each other. Various patterns of **frequency reuse** are possible. Figure 13.2 shows some

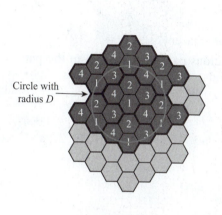

Circle with
radius D

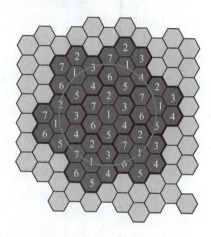

(a) Frequency reuse pattern for $N = 4$

(b) Frequency reuse pattern for $N = 7$

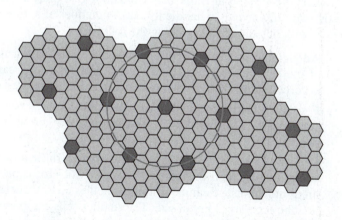

(c) Black cells indicate a frequency reuse for $N = 19$

Figure 13.2 Frequency Reuse Patterns

---

[1]Exceptions include CDMA systems and fourth-generation inter-cell interference coordination and coordinated multipoint transmission systems, described subsequently.

examples. If the pattern consists of N cells and each cell is assigned the same number of frequencies, each cell can have K/N frequencies, where K is the total number of frequencies allotted to the system. For one first-generation system, $K = 395$, and $N = 7$ is the smallest pattern that can provide sufficient isolation between two uses of the same frequency. This implies that there can be at most $395/7 \approx 57$ frequencies per cell on average.

In characterizing frequency reuse, the following parameters are commonly used:

D = minimum distance between centers of cells that use the same frequency band (called cochannels)

R = radius of a cell

d = distance between centers of adjacent cells ($d = \sqrt{3}R$)

N = number of cells in a repetitious pattern (each cell in the pattern uses a unique set of frequency bands), termed the **reuse factor**

In a hexagonal cell geometry, only the following values of N are possible:

$$N = I^2 + J^2 + (I \times J) \qquad I, \ J = 0, 1, 2, 3, \ldots$$

Hence, possible values of N are 1, 3, 4, 7, 9, 12, 13, 16, 19, 21, and so on. The following relationship holds:

$$\frac{D}{R} = \sqrt{3N}$$

This can also be expressed as $D/d = \sqrt{N}$.

Increasing Capacity Through Network Densification In time, as more customers use the system, traffic may build up so that there are not enough frequency bands assigned to a cell to handle its calls. A number of approaches have been used to cope with this situation, including the following:

- **Adding new channels:** Typically, when a system is set up in a region, not all of the channels are used, and growth and expansion can be managed in an orderly fashion by adding new channels from the unused set.

- **Frequency borrowing:** In the simplest case, frequencies are taken from adjacent cells by congested cells. The frequencies can also be assigned to cells dynamically.

- **Cell splitting:** In practice, the distribution of traffic and topographic features is not uniform, and this presents opportunities for capacity increase. Cells in areas of high usage can be split into smaller cells. Generally, the original cells are about 6.5 to 13 km in size. The smaller cells can themselves be split. Also, special small cells can be deployed in areas of high traffic demand; see the subsequent discussion of small cells such as picocells and femtocells. To use a smaller cell, the power level used must be reduced to keep the signal within the cell. Also, as the mobile units move, they pass from cell to cell, which requires transferring of the call from one base transceiver to another. This process is called a **handoff**. As the cells get smaller, these handoffs become much more frequent. Figure 13.3 indicates schematically how cells can be divided to

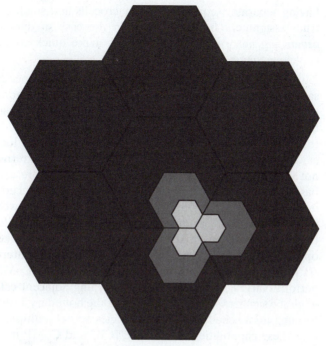

Figure 13.3 Cell Splitting

provide more capacity. A radius reduction by a factor of F reduces the coverage area and increases the required number of base stations by a factor of F^2.

- **Cell sectoring:** With cell sectoring, a cell is divided into a number of wedge-shaped sectors, each with its own set of channels, typically three sectors per cell. Each sector is assigned a separate subset of the cell's channels, and directional antennas at the base station are used to focus on each sector. This can be seen in the triangular shape of typical cellular antenna configurations, since the antennas mounted on each side of the triangle are directed toward their respective one of the three sectors.

- **Small cells:** As cells become smaller, antennas move from the tops of tall buildings or hills, to the tops of small buildings or the sides of large buildings, and finally to lampposts, where they form **picocells**. Each decrease in cell size is accompanied by a reduction in the radiated power levels from the base stations and the mobile units. Picocells are useful on city streets in congested areas, along highways, and inside large public buildings. If placed inside buildings, these are called **femtocells**, which might be open to all users or only to authorized users, for example only those who work in that building. If only for a restricted set of users, this is called a **closed subscriber group**. This process of increasing capacity by using small cells is called **network densification**. The large outdoor cells called **macrocells** are intended to support high-mobility users. There are a variety of frequency use strategies to share frequencies but avoid interference problems between small cells and macrocells, such as having separate frequencies for macrocells and small cells or dynamic spectrum assignment between them. In the case of dynamic assignment, **self-organizing networks** of base stations make quick cooperative decisions for channel assignment as **needs require**.

- Ultimately, the capacity of a cellular network depends on how often the same frequencies (or subcarriers in the case of orthogonal frequency division multiple access) can be reused for different mobiles. Regardless of their location, two mobiles can be assigned the same frequency if their interference is tolerable. Thus, interference is the limiting factor, not location. If interference can be addressed directly, then the channel reuse patterns in Figure 13.2 might not even be required. For example, if two mobiles are close to their respective base stations, transmit powers could be greatly reduced for each connection but still provide adequate service. This reduced power would limit interference to other users of the same frequency. Then the two mobiles could use the same frequencies even in adjacent cells. Modern systems take advantage of these opportunities through techniques such as **inter-cell interference coordination (ICIC)** and **coordinated multipoint transmission (CoMP)**. These techniques perform various functions, such as warning adjacent cells when interference might be significant (e.g., a user is near the boundary between two cells) or performing joint scheduling of frequencies across multiple cells. LTE-Advanced uses these capabilities extensively; ICIC and CoMP in LTE are discussed in Chapter 14.

Example 13.1   Assume a system of 32 cells with a cell radius of 1.6 km, a total of 32 cells, a total frequency bandwidth that supports 336 traffic channels, and a reuse factor of $N = 7$. If there are 32 total cells, what geographic area is covered, how many channels are there per cell, and what is the total number of concurrent calls that can be handled? Repeat for a cell radius of 0.8 km and 128 cells.

Figure 13.4a shows an approximately rectangular pattern. The area of a hexagon of radius R is $1.5R^2\sqrt{3}$. A hexagon of radius 1.6 km has an area of 6.65 km^2, and the total area covered is $6.65 \times 32 = 213$ km^2. For $N = 7$, the number of channels per cell is $336/7 = 48$, for a total channel capacity (total number of calls that can be handled) of $48 \times 32 = 1536$ channels. For the layout in Figure 13.4b, the area covered is $1.66 \times 128 = 213$ km^2. The number of channels per cell is $336/7 = 48$, for a total channel capacity of $48 \times 128 = 6144$ channels. A reduction in cell radius by a factor of ½ has increased the channel capacity by a factor of 4.

Operation of Cellular Systems

Figure 13.5 shows the principal elements of a cellular system. In the approximate center of each cell is a base station (BS). The BS includes an antenna, a controller, and a number of transceivers for communicating on the channels assigned to that cell. The controller is used to handle the call process between the mobile unit and the rest of the network. At any time, a number of mobile units may be active and moving about within a cell communicating with the BS. Each BS is connected to a mobile telecommunications switching office (MTSO), with one MTSO serving multiple BSs. Typically, the link between an MTSO and a BS is by a wire line,

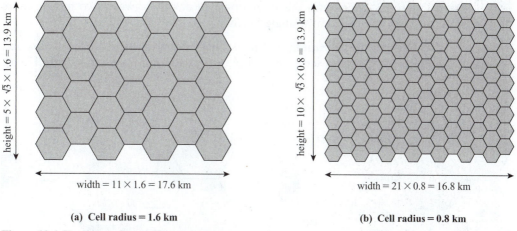

(a) Cell radius = 1.6 km   **(b) Cell radius = 0.8 km**

Figure 13.4 Frequency Reuse Example

although wireless links are becoming increasingly popular with technologies like WiMAX (discussed in Chapter 16). The MTSO connects calls between mobile units. The MTSO is also connected to the public telephone or telecommunications network and can make a connection between a fixed subscriber to the public network and a mobile subscriber to the cellular network. The mobile is also given access to the Internet. The MTSO assigns the voice channel to each call, performs handoffs (discussed subsequently), and monitors the call for billing information.

The use of a cellular system is fully automated and requires no action on the part of the user other than placing or answering a call. Two types of channels are available between the mobile unit and the base station: control channels and traffic channels. **Control channels** are used to exchange information having to do with setting up and maintaining calls and with establishing a relationship between a mobile unit and the nearest BS. **Traffic channels** carry a voice or data connection between

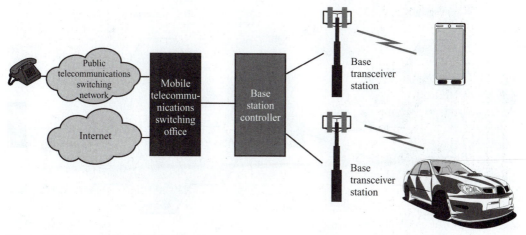

Figure 13.5 Overview of Cellular System

users. Figure 13.6 illustrates the steps in a typical call between two mobile users within an area controlled by a single MTSO:

- **Mobile unit initialization:** When the mobile unit is turned on, it scans and selects the strongest setup control channel used for this system (Figure 13.6a).

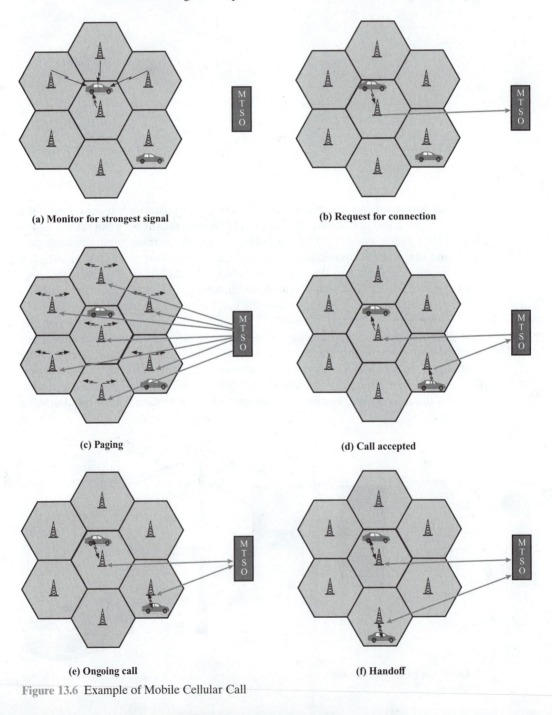

Figure 13.6 Example of Mobile Cellular Call

Cells with different frequency bands repetitively broadcast on different setup channels. The receiver selects the strongest setup channel and monitors that channel. The effect of this procedure is that the mobile unit has automatically selected the BS antenna of the cell within which it will operate.[2] Then a handshake takes place between the mobile unit and the MTSO controlling this cell, through the BS in this cell. The handshake is used to identify the user and register its location. As long as the mobile unit is on, this scanning procedure is repeated periodically to account for the motion of the unit. If the unit enters a new cell, then a new BS is selected. In addition, the mobile unit is monitoring for pages, discussed subsequently.

- **Mobile-originated call:** A mobile unit originates a call by sending the number of the called unit on the preselected setup channel (Figure 13.6b). The receiver at the mobile unit first checks that the setup channel is idle by examining information in the forward (from the BS) channel. When an idle state is detected, the mobile unit may transmit on the corresponding reverse (to BS) channel. The BS sends the request to the MTSO.

- **Paging:** The MTSO then attempts to complete the connection to the called unit. The MTSO sends a paging message to certain BSs to find the called mobile unit, depending on the called mobile unit number and the latest information on the unit's whereabouts (Figure 13.6c). The MTSO does not always know the location of every mobile if certain mobiles have been in idle modes. Each BS transmits the paging signal on its own assigned setup channel.

- **Call accepted:** The called mobile unit recognizes its number on the setup channel being monitored and responds to that BS, which sends the response to the MTSO. The MTSO sets up a circuit between the calling and called BSs. At the same time, the MTSO selects an available traffic channel within each BS's cell and notifies each BS, which, in turn, notifies its mobile unit (Figure 13.6d). The two mobile units tune to their respective assigned channels.

- **Ongoing call:** While the connection is maintained, the two mobile units exchange voice or data signals, going through their respective BSs and the MTSO (Figure 13.6e).

- **Handoff:** If a mobile unit moves out of range of one cell and into the range of another during a connection, the traffic channel has to change to the one assigned to the BS in the new cell (Figure 13.6f). The system makes this change without either interrupting the call or alerting the user.

Other functions performed by the system but not illustrated in Figure 13.6 include the following:

- **Call blocking:** During the mobile-initiated call stage, if all the traffic channels assigned to the nearest BS are busy, then the mobile unit makes a preconfigured number of repeated attempts. After a certain number of failed tries, a busy tone is returned to the user.

---

[2]Usually, but not always, the antenna and therefore the base station selected is the closest one to the mobile unit. However, because of propagation anomalies, this is not always the case.

- **Call termination:** When one of the two users hangs up, the MTSO is informed and the traffic channels at the two BSs are released.

- **Call drop:** During a connection, because of interference or weak signal spots in certain areas, if the BS cannot maintain the minimum required signal strength for a certain period of time, the traffic channel to the user is dropped and the MTSO is informed.

- **Calls to/from fixed and remote mobile subscriber:** The MTSO connects to the public switched telephone network. Thus, the MTSO can set up a connection between a mobile user in its area and a fixed subscriber via the telephone network. Further, the MTSO can connect to a remote MTSO via the telephone network or via dedicated lines and set up a connection between a mobile user in its area and a remote mobile user.

- **Emergency call prioritization and queuing:** If a user identifies the call as an emergency call, calls that may experience blocking due to a busy BS may be queued and given first access when a channel becomes available.

Mobile Radio Propagation Effects

Mobile radio communication introduces complexities not found in wired communication or in fixed wireless communication. Two general areas of concern are signal strength and signal propagation effects. These are discussed in detail in Chapter 6.

- **Signal strength:** The strength of the signal between the base station and the mobile unit must be strong enough to maintain signal quality at the receiver but not so strong as to create too much cochannel interference with channels in another cell using the same frequency band. Several complicating factors exist. Human-made noise varies considerably, resulting in a variable noise level. For example, automobile ignition noise in the cellular frequency range is greater in the city than in a suburban area. Other signal sources vary from place to place. The signal strength varies as a function of distance from the BS to a point within its cell. Moreover, the signal strength varies dynamically as the mobile unit moves due to shadowing from obstructions and geography.

- **Fading:** Even if the signal strength is within an effective range, signal propagation effects may disrupt the signal and cause errors. Section 6.4 discusses fading and various countermeasures.

In designing a cellular layout, the communications engineer must take account of these various propagation effects, the desired maximum transmit power level at the base station and the mobile units, the typical height of the mobile unit antenna, and the available height of the BS antenna. These factors will determine the size of the individual cell. Unfortunately, as just described, the propagation effects are dynamic and difficult to predict. The best that can be done is to come up with a model based on empirical data and to apply that model to a given environment to develop guidelines for cell size. One of the most widely used models was developed by Okumura et al. and subsequently refined by Hata. This is discussed in Section 6.3.

Handoff

Handoff[3] is the procedure for changing the assignment of a mobile unit from one BS to another as the mobile unit moves from one cell to another. Handoff is handled in different ways in different systems and involves a number of factors. Here we give a brief overview.

Handoff may be network initiated, in which the decision is made solely by the network measurements of received signals from the mobile unit. Alternatively, mobile unit assisted handoff schemes enable the mobile unit to participate in the handoff decision by providing feedback to the network concerning signals received at the mobile unit. In either case, the following different performance metrics may be used to make the decision:

- **Call blocking probability:** The probability of a new call being blocked, due to heavy load on the BS traffic capacity. In this case, the mobile unit is handed off to a neighboring cell based not on signal quality but on traffic capacity.
- **Call dropping probability:** The probability that, due to a handoff, a call is terminated.
- **Call completion probability:** The probability that an admitted call is not dropped before it terminates.
- **Probability of unsuccessful handoff:** The probability that a handoff is executed while the reception conditions are inadequate.
- **Handoff blocking probability:** The probability that a handoff cannot be successfully completed.
- **Handoff probability:** The probability that a handoff occurs before call termination.
- **Rate of handoff:** The number of handoffs per unit time.
- **Interruption duration:** The duration of time during a handoff in which a mobile unit is not connected to either base station.
- **Handoff delay:** The distance the mobile unit moves from the point at which the handoff should occur to the point at which it does occur.

The principal parameter used to make the handoff decision is measured signal strength from the mobile unit at the BS. Typically, the BS averages the signal over a moving window of time to remove the rapid fluctuations due to multipath effects. Figure 13.7a shows the average received power level at two adjacent base stations as a mobile unit moves from BS A, at L_A, to BS B, at L_B. The animation for this figure is especially helpful. This figure is useful in explaining various handoff strategies that have been used to determine the instance of handoff:

- **Relative signal strength:** The mobile unit is handed off from BS A to BS B when the signal strength at B first exceeds that at A. If the signal strength at B subsequently falls below that of A, the mobile unit is handed back to A. In

---

[3]The term *handoff* is used in U.S. cellular standards documents. ITU documents use the term **handover**, and both terms appear in the technical literature. The meanings are the same.

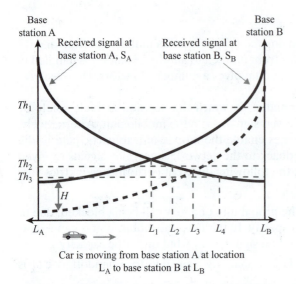

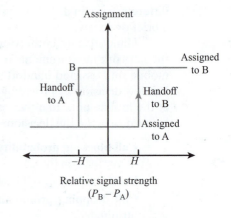

(a) Handoff decision as a function of handoff scheme

(b) Hysteresis mechanism

Figure 13.7 Handoff between Two Cells

Figure 13.7a, handoff occurs at point L_1. At this point, signal strength to BS A is still adequate but is declining. Because signal strength fluctuates due to multipath effects, even with power averaging, this approach can lead to a ping-pong effect in which the unit is repeatedly passed back and forth between two BSs.

- **Relative signal strength with threshold:** Handoff only occurs if (1) the signal at the current BS is sufficiently weak (less than a predefined threshold) and (2) the other signal is the stronger of the two. The intention is that so long as the signal at the current BS is adequate, handoff is unnecessary. If a high threshold is used, such as Th_1, this scheme performs the same as the relative signal strength scheme. With a threshold of Th_2, handoff occurs at L_2. If the threshold is set quite low compared to the crossover signal strength (signal strength at L_1), such as Th_3, the mobile unit may move far into the new cell (L_4) before handoff. This reduces the quality of the communication link and may result in a dropped call. A threshold should not be used alone because its effectiveness depends on prior knowledge of the crossover signal strength between the current and candidate base stations.

- **Relative signal strength with hysteresis:** Handoff occurs only if the new base station is sufficiently stronger (by a margin H in Figure 13.7a) than the current one. In this case, handoff occurs at L_3. This scheme prevents the ping-pong effect, because once handoff occurs, the effect of the margin H is reversed. The term *hysteresis* refers to a phenomenon known as relay hysteresis and can be appreciated with the aid of Figure 13.7b. We can think of the handoff mechanism as having two states. While the mobile unit is assigned to BS A, the mechanism will generate a handoff when the relative signal strength reaches or exceeds the *H*. Once the mobile unit is assigned to B, it remains so until the relative signal strength falls below –*H*, at which point it is handed back to A. The only disadvantage of this scheme is that the first handoff may still be unnecessary if BS A still has sufficient signal strength.

- **Relative signal strength with hysteresis and threshold:** Handoff occurs only if (1) the current signal level drops below a threshold, and (2) the target base station is stronger than the current one by a hysteresis margin *H*. In our example, handoff occurs at L_3 if the threshold is either Th_1 or Th_2 and at L_4 if the threshold is at Th_3.

- **Prediction techniques:** The handoff decision is based on the expected future value of the received signal strength.

Hard or Soft Handoff When the signal strength of a neighboring cell exceeds that of the current cell, plus a threshold, the mobile station is instructed to switch to a new frequency band that is within the allocation of the new cell. This is referred to as a **hard handoff**. In **soft handoff**, a mobile station is temporarily connected to more than one base station simultaneously. A mobile unit may start out assigned to a single cell. If the unit enters a region in which the transmissions from two base stations are comparable (within some threshold of each other), the mobile unit enters the soft handoff state in which it is connected to the two base stations. The mobile unit remains in this state until one base station clearly predominates, at which time it is assigned exclusively to that cell.

While in the soft handoff state, the transmissions from the mobile unit reaching the two base stations are both sent on to the mobile switching center, which estimates the quality of the two signals and selects one. The switch sends data or digitized speech signals to both base stations, which transmit them to the mobile unit. The mobile unit combines the two incoming signals to recover the information. Soft handoff not only increases the quality of the mobile's communication, especially at cell edges, but also increases its use of system capacity. For this example, separate frequencies from two base stations are both assigned to the mobile at once. Different technologies may or may not use soft handoff. Some may use hard handoff but have fast protocols for switching between base stations.

The handoff decision is complicated by the use of power control techniques, which enable the BS to dynamically adjust the power transmitted by the mobile unit. This topic is discussed in the following section.

Power Control

A number of design issues make it desirable to include a dynamic **power control** capability in a cellular system:

1. The received power must be sufficiently above the background noise for effective communication, which dictates the required transmitted power. As the mobile unit moves away from the transmitter, the received power declines due to normal attenuation. In addition, the effects of reflection, diffraction, and scattering can cause rapid changes in received power levels over small distances. This is because the power level is the sum from signals coming from a number of different paths and the phases of those paths are random,

sometimes adding and sometimes subtracting. As the mobile unit moves, the contributions along various paths change.

2. At the same time, it is desirable to minimize the power in the transmitted signal from the mobile unit, to reduce cochannel interference (interference with channels on the same frequency in remote cells), alleviate health concerns, and save battery power.

3. In spread spectrum (SS) systems using code division multiple access (CDMA), it is desirable to equalize the *received power level at the BS* from all mobile units when the signals arrive. This is crucial to system performance because all users have the same frequency allocation.

Cellular systems use the two kinds of power control. **Open-loop power control** depends solely on the mobile unit, with no feedback from the BS, and is used in some SS systems. In SS systems, the BS continuously transmits an unmodulated signal, known as a pilot. The pilot allows a mobile unit to acquire the timing of the forward (BS to mobile) CDMA channel and provides a phase reference for demodulation. It can also be used for power control. The mobile unit monitors the received power level of the pilot and sets the transmitted power in the reverse (mobile to BS) channel inversely proportional to it. This approach assumes that the forward and reverse link signal strengths are closely correlated, which is generally the case. The open-loop approach is not as accurate as the closed-loop approach. However, the open-loop scheme can react more quickly to rapid fluctuations in signal strength, such as when a mobile unit emerges from behind a large building. This fast action is required in the reverse link of a CDMA system where the sudden increase in received strength at the BS may suppress all other signals.

Closed-loop power control adjusts signal strength in the **reverse channel** (mobile to BS) based on some metric of performance in that reverse channel, such as received signal power level, received signal-to-noise ratio (SNR), received bit error rate, or received packet error rate. The BS makes the power adjustment decision and communicates a power adjustment command to the mobile unit on a control channel. Closed-loop power control is also used to adjust power in the **forward channel**. In this case, the mobile unit provides information about received signal quality to the BS, which then adjusts transmitted power.

Traffic Engineering

For an FDMA system, the capacity of a cell is equal to the number of frequency channels and subcarriers allocated to it. Ideally, the number of available frequencies in a cell would equal the total amount of demand that could be active at any time. In practice, it is not feasible to have the capacity to handle any possible load at all times. Fortunately, not all subscribers are active at the same time and so it is reasonable to size the network to be able to handle some expected level of load. This is the discipline of traffic engineering.

Traffic engineering concepts were developed in the design of telephone switches and circuit-switching telephone networks, but the concepts equally apply to cellular networks. Consider a cell that has L potential subscribers (L mobile units) and that is able to handle N simultaneous users (capacity of N channels). If $L \leq N$, the system is referred to as *nonblocking*; all calls can be handled all the time. If $L > N$, the system is *blocking*; a subscriber may attempt a call and find the capacity fully in use and therefore be blocked. For a blocking system, the fundamental performance questions we wish to answer are the following:

1. What is the degree of blocking; that is, what is the probability that a resource request will be blocked? Alternatively, what capacity (N) is needed to achieve a certain upper bound on the probability of blocking?

2. If blocked requests are queued for service, what is the average delay until that call is put into service? Alternatively, what capacity is needed to achieve a certain average delay?

In this subsection, we briefly introduce the relevant traffic engineering concepts and give an example of their use. Online Appendix A examines the subject in more detail.

Two parameters determine the amount of load presented to a system:

λ = the mean rate of calls (connection requests) attempted per unit time

h = the mean holding time per successful call

The basic measure of traffic is the **traffic intensity**, expressed in a dimensionless unit, the **Erlang**:

$$A = \lambda h$$

A can be interpreted in several ways. It is a normalized version of λ: A equals the average number of calls arriving during the average holding period. We can also view the cell as a multiserver queuing system where the number of servers is equal to the channel capacity N. The average service time at a server is h. A basic relationship in a multiserver queue is $\lambda h = \rho N$, where ρ is server utilization, or the fraction of time that a server is busy. Therefore, $A = \rho N$ and is a measure of the average number of channels required.

Example 13.2 If the calling rate averages 20 calls per minute and the average holding time is 3 minutes, then $A = 60$. We would expect a cell with a capacity of 120 channels to be about half utilized at any given time. A switch of capacity 50 would clearly be inadequate. A capacity of 60 would meet the average demand but, because of fluctuations around the mean rate A, this capacity would at times be inadequate.

Example 13.3 To clarify these concepts, consider Figure 13.8, which shows the pattern of activity in a cell with a capacity of 10 channels over a period of 1 hour. The rate of calls per minute is 97/60. The average holding time per call, in minutes, is 294/97. Thus $A = (97/60) \times (294/97) = 4.9$ Erlangs. Another way of viewing the parameter A is that it is the mean number of calls in progress. Thus, on average, 4.9 channels are engaged. The latter interpretation, however, is true only in the nonblocking case. The parameter λ was defined as the rate of calls attempted, not carried traffic.

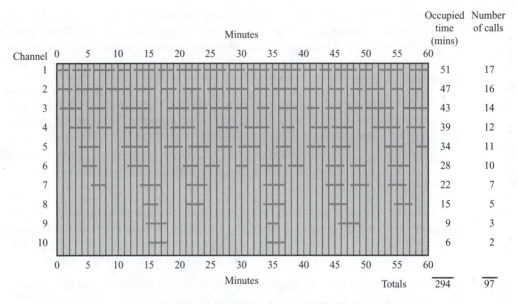

Channel	Occupied time (mins)	Number of calls
1	51	17
2	47	16
3	43	14
4	39	12
5	34	11
6	28	10
7	22	7
8	15	5
9	9	3
10	6	2
Totals	294	97

Note: horizontal lines indicate occupied periods to the nearest 1/2 minute

Figure 13.8 Example of Distribution of Traffic in a Cell with Capacity 10

Typically, a blocking system is sized to deal with some upper limit of traffic intensity. It is generally thought unreasonable to size for the highest surge of traffic anticipated; rather, the common practice is to size the system to meet the average rate encountered during a busy hour. The busy hour is the 60-minute period during the day when the traffic is highest, in the long run. ITU-T recommends taking the average of the busy hour traffic on the 30 busiest days of the year, called the "mean busy-hour traffic," and using that quantity to size the system. The North American practice is to take the average over the 10 busiest days. One of those busiest days in the United States is usually Mother's Day in the month of May. The measurements are typically of carried rather than offered traffic and can only be used to estimate the true load.

The parameter A, as a measure of busy-hour traffic, serves as input to a traffic model. The model is then used to answer questions such as those posed in the beginning of this subsection. There are two key factors that determine the nature of the model:

- The manner in which blocked calls are handled.
- The number of traffic sources.

Blocked calls may be handled in one of two ways. First, blocked calls can be put in a queue awaiting a free channel; this is referred to as **lost calls delayed (LCD)**, although in fact the call is not lost, merely delayed. Second, a blocked call can be rejected and dropped. This in turn leads to two assumptions about the action of the user. If the user hangs up and waits for some random time interval before another call attempt, this is known as **lost calls cleared (LCC)**. If the user repeatedly attempts calling, it is known as **lost calls held (LCH)**. For each of these blocking options, formulas have been developed that characterize the performance of the system. For cellular systems, the LCC model is generally used and is generally the most accurate.

The second key element of a traffic model is whether the number of users is assumed to be finite or infinite. For an infinite source model, there is assumed to be a fixed arrival rate. For the finite source case, the arrival rate will depend on the number of sources already engaged. In particular, if the total pool of users is L, each of which generates calls at an average rate of λ/L, then, when the cell is totally idle, the arrival rate is λ. However, if there are K users occupied at time t, then the instantaneous arrival rate at that time is $\lambda(L - K)/L$. Infinite source models are analytically easier to deal with. The infinite source assumption is reasonable when the number of sources is at least 5 to 10 times the capacity of the system.

Infinite Sources, Lost Calls Cleared For an infinite source LCC model, the key parameter of interest is the probability of loss, or **grade of service**. Thus a grade of service of 0.01 means that, during a busy hour, the probability that an attempted call is blocked is 0.01. Values in the range 0.01 to 0.001 are generally considered quite good.

The equation of infinite source LCC, known as Erlang B, has the following form:

$$P = \frac{\dfrac{A^N}{N!}}{\displaystyle\sum_{x=0}^{N} \dfrac{A^x}{x!}}$$

where

A = offered traffic, Erlangs

N = number of servers

P = probability of blocking (grade of service)

This equation is easily programmed, and tables of values are readily available. Table 13.1 is an extract from such a table. Given the offered load and number of servers, the grade of service can be calculated or determined from a table. More often, the inverse problem is of interest: determining the amount of traffic that can be handled by a given capacity to produce a given grade of service. Another problem is to determine the capacity required to handle a given amount of traffic at a given grade of service. For both these problems, tables or suitable trial-and-error programs are needed.

Two important points can be deduced from Table 13.1:

1. A larger-capacity system is more efficient than a smaller-capacity one for a given grade of service.

2. A larger-capacity system is more susceptible to an increase in traffic.

All of the preceding discussion deals with offered traffic. If sizing is done on the basis of system measurement, all that we are likely to have is carried traffic. A program can readily be developed that accepts carried traffic as input and then

Table 13.1 Erlang B Table

Number of Servers (N)	Capacity (Erlangs) for Grade of Service of:				
	$P = 0.02$ (1/50)	$P = 0.01$ (1/100)	$P = 0.005$ (1/200)	$P = 0.002$ (1/500)	$P = 0.001$ (1/1000)
1	0.02	0.01	0.005	0.002	0.001
4	1.09	0.87	0.7	0.53	0.43
5	1.66	1.36	1.13	0.9	0.76
10	5.08	4.46	3.96	3.43	3.09
20	13.19	12.03	11.10	10.07	9.41
24	16.64	15.27	14.21	13.01	12.24
40	31.0	29.0	27.3	25.7	24.5
70	59.13	56.1	53.7	51.0	49.2
100	87.97	84.1	80.9	77.4	75.2

Example 13.4 To illustrate the first point, consider two cells, each with a capacity of 10 channels. They have a joint capacity of 20 channels and can handle a combined offered traffic intensity of 6.86 (3.43 per cell) for a grade of service of 0.002. However, a single cell with a capacity of 20 channels will handle 10.07 Erlangs at a grade of service of 0.002. To illustrate the second point, consider a cell of 10 channels giving a grade of service of 0.002 for a load of 3.43 Erlangs. A 30% increase in traffic (up to 4.46 Erlangs) degrades the grade of service to 0.01. However, for a cell of capacity 70 channels, only a 10% increase in traffic (from 51.0 to 56.1 Erlangs) degrades the grade of service from 0.002 to 0.01.

performs a seeking algorithm to work backward to offered traffic. The relationship between carried traffic

C and offered traffic A is

$$C = A(1 - P)$$

For small values of P, A is a good approximation of C.

Effect of Handoff One complication in cellular traffic models not found in other such models is the effect of handoff. The arrival rate of calls at a cell has two components: new calls placed by mobile units in the cell (λ_1), and calls handed off to the cell for mobile units entering the cell while connected (λ_2). The total arrival rate is $\lambda = \lambda_1 + \lambda_2$. Similarly, the completion rate consists of calls being completed normally and calls being handed off. The model must be adjusted accordingly to obtain overall arrival rates and holding times.

13.2 FIRST-GENERATION ANALOG

The rest of the chapter provides an overview of first-, second-, and third-generation cellular systems. Only high-level discussion is provided, however; to learn details about a modern cellular system operates, detailed information is instead provided in Chapter 14 for fourth-generation LTE and LTE-Advanced systems.

The original cellular telephone networks provided analog traffic channels; these are now referred to as **first-generation (1G)** systems. Since the early 1980s the most common first-generation system in North America has been the **Advanced Mobile Phone Service (AMPS)** developed by AT&T. This approach is also common in South America, Australia, and China. Although it has been replaced, for the most part, by later-generation systems, AMPS is still in use. In this section, we provide an overview of AMPS.

Spectral Allocation

In North America, two 25-MHz bands are allocated to AMPS (Table 13.2), one for transmission from the base station to the mobile unit (869–894 MHz), the other for transmission from the mobile unit to the base station (824–849 MHz). Each of these bands is split in two to encourage competition (i.e., so that in each market two operators can be accommodated). An operator is allocated only 12.5 MHz in each direction for its system. The channels are spaced 30 kHz apart, which allows a total of 416 channels per operator. Twenty-one channels are allocated for control, leaving 395 to carry calls. The control channels are data channels operating at 10 kbps. The conversation channels carry the conversations in analog using frequency modulation. Control information is also sent on the conversation channels in bursts as data. This number of channels is inadequate for most major markets, so some way must be found either to use less bandwidth per conversation or to reuse frequencies. Both approaches have been taken in the various approaches to mobile telephony. For AMPS, frequency reuse is exploited.

Operation

Each AMPS-capable cellular telephone includes a *numeric assignment module* (NAM) in read-only memory. The NAM contains the telephone number of the phone, which is assigned by the service provider, and the serial number of the phone, which is assigned by the manufacturer. When the phone is turned on, it transmits its serial number and phone number to the MTSO (Figure 13.5); the MTSO maintains a database with information about mobile units that have been reported stolen and

Table 13.2 AMPS Parameters

Base station transmission band	869 to 894 MHz
Mobile unit transmission band	824 to 849 MHz
Spacing between forward and reverse channels	45 MHz
Channel bandwidth	30 kHz
Number of full-duplex voice channels	790
Number of full-duplex control channels	42
Mobile unit maximum power	3 watts
Cell size, radius	2 to 20 km
Modulation, voice channel	FM, 12-kHz peak deviation
Modulation, control channel	FSK, 8-kHz peak deviation
Data transmission rate	10 kbps
Error control coding	BCH (48, 36,5) and (40, 28,5)

uses serial number to lock out stolen units. The MTSO uses the phone number for billing purposes. If the phone is used in a remote city, the service is still billed to the user's local service provider.

When a call is placed, the following sequence of events occurs:

1. The subscriber initiates a call by keying in the telephone number of the called party and presses the send key.
2. The MTSO verifies that the telephone number is valid and that the user is authorized to place the call; some service providers require the user to enter a personal identification number (PIN) as well as the called number to counter theft.
3. The MTSO issues a message to the user's cell phone indicating which traffic channels to use for sending and receiving.
4. The MTSO sends out a ringing signal to the called party. All of these operations (steps 2 through 4) occur within 10 s of initiating the call.
5. When the called party answers, the MTSO establishes a circuit between the two parties and initiates billing information.
6. When one party hangs up, the MTSO releases the circuit, frees the radio channels, and completes the billing information.

AMPS Control Channels

Each AMPS service includes 21 full-duplex 30-kHz control channels, consisting of 21 reverse control channels (RCCs) from subscriber to base station, and 21 **forward channels** from the base station to subscriber. These channels transmit digital data using FSK. In both channels, data are transmitted in frames.

Control information can be transmitted over a voice channel during a conversation. The mobile unit or the base station can insert a burst of data by turning off the voice FM transmission for about 100 ms and replacing it with an FSK-encoded message. These messages are used to exchange urgent messages, such as change power level and handoff.

13.3 SECOND-GENERATION TDMA

This section begins our study of second-generation cellular systems. A large amount of voice traffic is still carried on 2G systems. Data traffic is primarily carried on 3G and 4G systems, and some Voice-over-IP (VoIP) traffic is carried on 3G and 4G systems either by carriers or through user apps. It is important to understand 2G systems, so we begin with an overview and then look in detail at one type of second-generation cellular system.

From First- to Second-Generation Cellular Systems

First-generation cellular networks, such as AMPS, quickly became highly popular, threatening to swamp available capacity even with frequency reuse. Second-generation systems were developed to provide higher-quality signals, higher data rates for support of digital services, and greater capacity. The following are the key differences between the two generations:

- **Digital traffic channels:** The most notable difference between the two generations is that the first-generation systems are almost purely analog, whereas the second-generation systems are digital. In particular, the first-generation systems are designed to support voice channels using FM; digital traffic is supported only by the use of a modem that converts the digital data into analog form. Second-generation systems provide digital traffic channels. These readily support digital data; voice traffic is first encoded in digital form before transmitting. Of course, for second-generation systems, the user traffic (data or digitized voice) must be converted to an analog signal for transmission between the mobile unit and the base station (e.g., see Figure 7.16).

- **Encryption:** Because all of the user traffic, as well as control traffic, is digitized in second-generation systems, it is a relatively simple matter to encrypt all of the traffic to prevent eavesdropping. All second-generation systems provide this capability, whereas first-generation systems send user traffic in the clear, providing no security.

- **Error detection and correction:** The digital traffic stream of second-generation systems also lends itself to the use of error detection and correction techniques, such as those discussed in Chapter 10. The result can be very clear voice reception. Or voice quality comparable to 1G can be provided but at a lower signal-to-noise ratio requirement.

- **Channel access:** In first-generation systems, each cell supports a number of channels. At any given time a channel is allocated to only one user. Second-generation systems also provide multiple channels per cell, but each channel is dynamically shared by a number of users using **time division multiple access (TDMA)** or **code division multiple access (CDMA)**. We look at TDMA-based systems in this section and CDMA-based systems in Section 13.4.

Beginning around 1990, a number of different second-generation systems were deployed. Table 13.3 lists some key characteristics of three of the most important of these systems.

Time Division Multiple Access

First-generation cellular systems provide for the support of multiple users with frequency division multiple access (FDMA). FDMA for cellular systems can be described as follows. Each cell is allocated a total of $2M$ channels of bandwidth δ Hz each. Half the channels (the reverse channels) are used for transmission from the mobile unit to the base station: $f_c, f_c + \delta, f_c + 2\delta, \ldots, f_c + (M-1)\delta$, where f_c is the center frequency of the lowest-frequency channel. The other half of the channels (the forward channels) are used for transmission from the base station to the mobile unit: $f_c + \Delta, f_c + \delta + \Delta, f_c + 2\delta + \Delta, \ldots, f_c + (M-1)\delta + \Delta$, where Δ is the spacing between the reverse and forward channels. When a connection is set up for a mobile user, the user is assigned two channels, at f and $f + \Delta$, for full-duplex communication. This arrangement is quite wasteful, because much of the time one or both of the channels are idle.

Table 13.3 Second-Generation Cellular Telephone Systems

	GSM	IS-136	IS-95
Year introduced	1990	1991	1993
Access method	TDMA	TDMA	CDMA
Base station transmission band	935 to 960 MHz	869 to 894 MHz	869 to 894 MHz
Mobile station transmission band	890 to 915 MHz	824 to 849 MHz	824 to 849 MHz
Spacing between forward and reverse channels	45 MHz	45 MHz	45 MHz
Channel bandwidth	200 kHz	30 kHz	1250 kHz
Number of duplex channels	125	832	20
Mobile unit maximum power	20 W	3 W	0.2 W
Users per channel	8	3	35
Modulation	GMSK	$\pi/4$ DQPSK	QPSK
Carrier bit rate	270.8 kbps	48.6 kbps	9.6 kbps
Speech coder	RPE-LTP	VSELP	QCELP
Speech-coding bit rate	13 kbps	8 kbps	8, 4, 2, 1 kbps
Frame size	4.6 ms	40 ms	20 ms
Error control coding	Convolutional 1/2 rate	Convolutional 1/2 rate	Convolutional 1/2 rate forward; 1/3 rate reverse

TDMA for cellular systems can be described as follows. As with FDMA, each cell is allocated a number of channels, half reverse and half forward. Again, for full duplex communication, a mobile unit is assigned capacity on matching reverse and forward channels. In addition, each physical channel is further subdivided into a number of logical channels. Transmission is in the form of a repetitive sequence of frames, each of which is divided into a number of time slots. Each slot position across the sequence of frames forms a separate logical channel.

Global System for Mobile Communications

Before the **Global System for Mobile Communications (GSM)** was developed, the countries of Europe used a number of incompatible first-generation cellular phone technologies. GSM was developed to provide a common second-generation technology for Europe so that the same subscriber units could be used throughout the continent. The technology was extremely successful. GSM first appeared in 1990 in Europe. Similar systems were implemented in North and South America, Asia, North Africa, the Middle East, and Australia. The GSM Association claimed 6.9 billion subscriber identity module (SIM) connections at the end of 2013, an average of 1.8 SIM cards per subscriber.

GSM Network Architecture Figure 13.9 shows the key functional elements in the GSM system. The boundaries at Um, Abis, and A refer to interfaces between

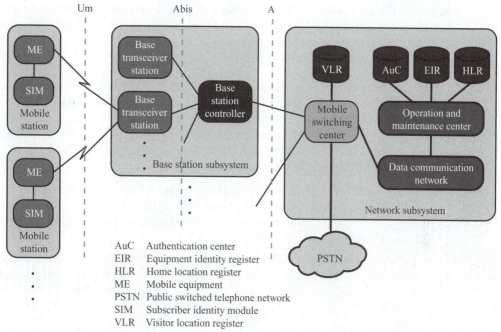

Um   Abis   A

AuC   Authentication center
EIR   Equipment identity register
HLR   Home location register
ME   Mobile equipment
PSTN   Public switched telephone network
SIM   Subscriber identity module
VLR   Visitor location register

Figure 13.9 Overall GSM Architecture

functional elements that are standardized in the GSM documents. Thus, it is possible to buy equipment from different vendors with the expectation that they will successfully interoperate.

Mobile Station A mobile station communicates across the Um interface, also known as the **air interface**, with a base station transceiver in the same cell in which the mobile unit is located. The **mobile equipment** (ME) refers to the physical terminal, such as a telephone or personal communications service (PCS) device, which includes the radio transceiver, digital signal processors, and the **subscriber identity module**. The SIM is a portable device in the form of a smart card or plug-in module that stores the subscriber's identification number, the networks the subscriber is authorized to use, encryption keys, and other information specific to the subscriber. The GSM subscriber units are totally generic until a SIM is inserted. Therefore, a subscriber need only carry his or her SIM to use a wide variety of subscriber devices in many countries simply by inserting the SIM in the device to be used. In fact, except for certain emergency communications, the subscriber units will not work without a SIM inserted. Thus, the SIMs roam, not necessarily the subscriber devices.

The SIM card approach by itself made GSM very popular in many parts of the world because of ease of traveling and moving to different devices.

Base Station Subsystem A base station subsystem (BSS) consists of a base station controller and one or more base transceiver stations. Each **base transceiver station (BTS)** defines a single cell; it includes a radio antenna, a radio transceiver, and a link to a base station controller. A GSM cell can have a radius of between 100 m and 35 km, depending on the environment. A **base station controller (BSC)** may be collocated with a BTS or may control multiple BTS units and hence multiple cells. The BSC reserves radio frequencies, manages the handoff of a mobile unit from one cell to another within the BSS, and controls paging.

Network Subsystem The network subsystem (NS) provides the link between the cellular network and the public switched telecommunications networks. The NS controls handoffs between cells in different BSSs, authenticates users and validates their accounts, and includes functions for enabling worldwide roaming of mobile users. The central element of the NS is the **mobile switching center** (MSC). It is supported by four databases that it controls:

- **Home location register (HLR) database:** The HLR stores information, both permanent and temporary, about each of the subscribers that "belongs" to it (i.e., for which the subscriber has its telephone number associated with the switching center).

- **Visitor location register (VLR) database:** One important, temporary piece of information is the location of the subscriber. The location is determined by the VLR into which the subscriber is entered. The visitor location register maintains information about subscribers that are currently physically in the region covered by the switching center. It records whether or not the subscriber is active and other parameters associated with the subscriber. For a call coming to the subscriber, the system uses the telephone number associated with the subscriber to identify the home switching center of the subscriber. This switching center can find in its HLR the switching center in which the subscriber is currently physically located. For a call coming from the subscriber, the VLR is used to initiate the call. Even if the subscriber is in the area covered by its home switching center, it is also represented in the switching center's VLR, for consistency.

- **Authentication center database (AuC):** This database is used for authentication activities of the system; for example, it holds the authentication and encryption keys for all the subscribers in both the home and visitor location registers. The center controls access to user data as well as being used for authentication when a subscriber joins a network. GSM transmission is encrypted, so it is private. A stream cipher, A5, is used to encrypt the transmission from the subscriber to the base transceiver. However, the conversation is in the clear in the landline network. Another cipher, A3, is used for authentication.

- **Equipment identity register database (EIR):** The EIR keeps track of the type of equipment that exists at the mobile station. It also plays a role in security (e.g., blocking calls from stolen mobile stations and preventing use of the network by stations that have not been approved).

Radio Link Aspects

The GSM spectral allocation is 25 MHz for base transmission (935–960 MHz) and 25 MHz for mobile transmission (890–915 MHz). Other GSM bands have also been defined outside Europe. Users access the network using a combination of FDMA and TDMA (both are discussed in the next section). There are radio-frequency carriers every 200 kHz, which provide for 125 full-duplex channels. The channels are modulated at a data rate of 270.833 kbps. As with AMPS, there are two types of channels: traffic and control.

TDMA Format GSM uses a complex hierarchy of TDMA frames to define logical channels. Fundamentally, each 200-kHz frequency band is divided into eight logical channels defined by the repetitive occurrence of time slots.

At the lowest level is the time slot, also called a burst period, which has a duration of 15/26 ms, or approximately 0.577 ms. With a bit rate of 270.833 kbps, each time slot has a length of 156.25 bits.

Moving up the frame format hierarchy, 8-slot TDMA frames are typically organized into a 26-frame multiframe. One of the frames in the multiframe is used for control signaling and another is currently unused, leaving 24 frames for data traffic. Thus, each traffic channel receives one slot per frame and 24 frames per 120-ms multiframe. The resulting gross data rate is

$$\frac{114\,\text{bits/slot} \times 24\,\text{slots/multiframe}}{120\,\text{ms/multiframe}} = 22.8\,\text{kbps}$$

The GSM specification also allows half-rate traffic channels, with two traffic channels each occupying one time slot in 12 of the 26 frames. With the use of half-rate speech coders, this effectively doubles the capacity of the system. There is also a 51-frame multiframe used for control traffic.

GPRS and Edge Phase 2 of GSM introduced the **Generalized Packet Radio Service (GPRS)**, which provides a datagram switching capability to GSM. Previously, sending data traffic required opening a voice connection, sending data, and closing a connection. GPRS allows users to open a persistent data connection. It also establishes a system architecture for carrying the data traffic. GPRS has different error control coding schemes, and the scheme with the highest throughput (no error control coding, just protocol overheads) produces 21.4 kbps from the 22.8 kbps gross data rate. GPRS can combine up to 8 GSM connections; so overall throughputs of up to 171.2 kbps can be achieved.

The next generation of GSM included **Enhanced Data Rates for GSM Evolution (EDGE)**. EDGE introduced coherent 8-PSK modulation, which creates a threefold increase in data rate up to 3 bits/symbol for 8-PSK from 1 bit/symbol for GMSK for GSM. This increased the gross max data rates per channel, depending on channel conditions, up to $22.8 \times 3 = 68.4$ kbps (including overhead from the protocol headers). Using all eight channels in a 200-kHz carrier, gross data transmission rates up to 547.2 kbps became possible. Actual throughput can be up to 513.6 kbps. A later release of EDGE, 3GPP Release 7, added even higher-order modulation and coding schemes that adapt to channel conditions. Downlink data rates over 750 kbps and uplink data rates over 600 kbps can be achieved in excellent channel conditions.

GSM Signaling Protocol Architecture A number of control messages are exchanged between the key entities that deal with mobility, radio resources, and connection management. The lowest layer of the architecture is tailored to the physical link between entities. At the link layer, a data link control protocol (see Figure 4.3) known as LAPDm is used. This is a modified version of the Link Access Protocol, D channel (LAPD) protocol designed to convert a potentially unreliable physical link into a reliable data link. Above the link layer are a number of protocols that provide specific functions. These include radio resource management, mobility management, connection management, mobile application part, and BTS management.

13.4 SECOND-GENERATION CDMA

CDMA is a spread spectrum–based technique for multiplexing, introduced in Section 9.4, that provides an alternative to TDMA for second-generation cellular networks. We begin this section with an overview of the advantages of the CDMA approach and then look at the most widely used scheme, IS-95.

Code Division Multiple Access

CDMA for cellular systems can be described as follows. As with FDMA, each cell is allocated a frequency bandwidth, which is split into two parts, half for reverse (mobile unit to base station) and half for forward (base station to mobile unit). For full duplex communication, a mobile unit uses both reverse and forward channels. Transmission is in the form of direct-sequence spread spectrum (DSSS), which uses a chipping code to increase the data rate of the transmission, resulting in an increased signal bandwidth. Multiple access is provided by assigning orthogonal chipping codes to multiple users, so that the receiver can recover the transmission of an individual unit from multiple transmissions.

CDMA has a number of advantages for a cellular network over TDMA:

- **Frequency diversity:** Because the transmission is spread out over a larger bandwidth, frequency-dependent transmission impairments, such as noise bursts and selective fading, have less effect on the signal.

- **Multipath resistance:** In addition to the ability of DSSS to overcome multipath fading by frequency diversity, the chipping codes used for CDMA not only exhibit low cross correlation but also low autocorrelation. Therefore, a version of the signal that is delayed by more than one chip interval does not interfere with the dominant signal as much as in other multipath environments.

- **Privacy:** Because spread spectrum is obtained by the use of noise-like signals, where each user has a unique code, privacy is inherent.

- **Graceful degradation:** With FDMA or TDMA, a fixed number of users can access the system simultaneously. However, with CDMA, as more users access the system simultaneously, the noise level and hence the error rate increases; only gradually does the system degrade to the point of an unacceptable error rate.

A number of drawbacks of CDMA cellular should also be mentioned:

- **Self-jamming:** Unless all of the mobile users are perfectly synchronized, the arriving transmissions from multiple users will not be perfectly aligned on chip boundaries. Thus the spreading sequences of the different users are not orthogonal and there is some level of cross correlation. This is distinct from either TDMA or FDMA, in which for reasonable time or frequency guard-bands, respectively, the received signals are orthogonal or nearly so.

- **Near-far problem:** Signals closer to the receiver are received with less attenuation than signals farther away. Given the lack of complete orthogonality, the transmissions from the more remote mobile units may be more difficult to recover. Thus, power control techniques are very important in a CDMA system.

- **Soft handoff:** As is discussed subsequently, a smooth handoff from one cell to the next requires that the mobile unit acquires the new cell before it relinquishes the old. This is referred to as a soft handoff and is more complex than the hard handoff used in FDMA and TDMA schemes.

Mobile Wireless CDMA Design Considerations

Before turning to the specific example of IS-95, it will be useful to consider some general design elements of a CDMA cellular system.

Rake Receiver In a multipath environment, which is common in cellular systems, if the multiple versions of a signal arrive more than one chip interval apart from each other, the receiver can recover the signal by correlating the chip sequence with the dominant incoming signal. This principle is used in the RAKE receiver and is discussed in Section 9.4.

Soft Handoff In an FDMA or TDMA system, neighboring cells use different portions of the available frequency spectrum (i.e., the frequency reuse factor N is greater than 1, typically 7). When the signal strength of a neighboring cell exceeds that of the current cell, plus a threshold, the mobile station is instructed to switch to a new frequency band that is within the allocation of the new cell. This is referred to as a hard handoff. In a typical CDMA cellular system, spatial separation of frequencies is not used (i.e., no frequency allocations like in Figure 13.2, frequency reuse factor $N = 1$), because most of the time the interference from neighboring cells will not prohibit correct reception of a DSSS signal.

For CDMA systems, soft handoff is more feasible. In soft handoff, a mobile station is temporarily connected to more than one base station simultaneously. It sends its packets to both base stations, using different spreading codes, and it receives packets from multiple base stations with the respective spreading codes. Since separate frequencies are not used in CDMA, soft handoff is simply a matter of using different codes for each base station instead of separate frequencies.

IS-95

The most widely used second-generation CDMA scheme is **IS-95**, which is primarily deployed in North America. Table 13.3 lists some key parameters of the IS-95 system. The transmission structures on the forward and reverse links differ and are described separately.

IS-95 Forward Link Table 13.4 lists forward link channel parameters. The forward link consists of up to 64 logical CDMA channels, each occupying the

Table 13.4 IS-95 Forward Link Channel Parameters

Channel	Sync	Paging		Traffic Rate Set 1				Traffic Rate Set 2			
Data rate (bps)	1200	4800	9600	1200	2400	4800	9600	1800	3600	7200	14400
Code repetition	2	2	1	8	4	2	1	8	4	2	1
Modulation symbol rate (sps)	4800	19,200	19,200	19,200	19,200	19,200	19,200	19,200	19,200	19,200	19,200
PN chips/ modulation symbol	256	64	64	64	64	64	64	64	64	64	64
PN chips/bit	1024	256	128	1024	512	256	128	682.67	341.33	170.67	85.33

same 1228-kHz bandwidth (Figure 13.10a). The forward link supports four types of channels:

- **Pilot (channel 0):** A continuous signal on a single channel. This channel allows the mobile unit to acquire timing information, provides phase reference for the demodulation process, and provides a means for signal strength comparison for the purpose of handoff determination. The pilot channel consists of all zeros.

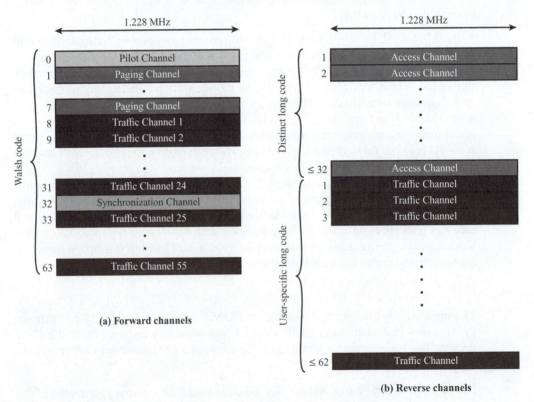

Figure 13.10 IS-95 Channel Structure

Table 13.5   IS-95 Reverse Link Channel Parameters

Channel	Access	Traffic Rate Set 1				Traffic Rate Set 2			
Data rate (bps)	4800	1200	2400	4800	9600	1800	3600	7200	14400
Code rate	1/3	1/3	1/3	1/3	1/3	1/2	1/2	1/2	1/2
Symbol rate before repetition (sps)	14,400	3600	7200	14,400	28,800	3600	7200	14,400	28,800
Symbol repetition	2	8	4	2	1	8	4	2	1
Symbol rate after repetition (sps)	28,800	28,800	28,800	28,800	28,800	28,800	28,800	28,800	28,800
Transmit duty cycle	1	1/8	1/4	1/2	1	1/8	1/4	1/2	1
Code symbols/ modulation symbol	6	6	6	6	6	6	6	6	6
PN chips/ modulation symbol	256	256	256	256	256	256	256	256	256
PN chips/bit	256	128	128	128	128	256/3	256/3	256/3	256/3

- **Synchronization (channel 32):** A 1200-bps channel used by the mobile station to obtain identification information about the cellular system (system time, long code state, protocol revision, etc.).
- **Paging (channels 1 to 7):** Contain messages for one or more mobile stations.
- **Traffic (channels 8 to 31 and 33 to 63):** The forward channel supports 55 traffic channels. The original specification supported data rates of up to 9600 bps. A subsequent revision added a second set of rates up to 14,400 bps.

Note that all of these channels use the same bandwidth. The chipping code is used to distinguish among the different channels.

IS-95 Reverse Link Table 13.5 lists reverse link channel parameters. The reverse link consists of up to 94 logical CDMA channels, each occupying the same 1228-kHz bandwidth (Figure 13.10b). The reverse link supports up to 32 access channels and up to 62 traffic channels.

The traffic channels in the reverse link are unique to each mobile unit. Each mobile unit has a unique long code mask based on its electronic serial number. The long code mask is a 42-bit number, so there are $2^{42} - 1$ different masks. The access channel is used by a mobile unit to initiate a call, to respond to a paging channel message from the base station, and for a location update.

13.5 THIRD-GENERATION SYSTEMS

The objective of the third generation of wireless communication is to provide fairly high-speed wireless communications to support multimedia, data, and video in addition to voice. The ITU's International Mobile Telecommunications for the year 2000 (IMT-2000) initiative has defined the ITU's view of third-generation capabilities as

- Voice quality comparable to the public switched telephone network.
- 144 kbps data rate available to users in high-speed motor vehicles over large areas.
- 384 kbps available to pedestrians standing or moving slowly over small areas.
- Support (to be phased in) for 2.048 Mbps for office use.
- Symmetrical and asymmetrical data transmission rates.
- Support for both packet-switched and circuit-switched data services.
- An adaptive interface to the Internet to reflect efficiently the common asymmetry between inbound and outbound traffic.
- More efficient use of the available spectrum in general.
- Support for a wide variety of mobile equipment.
- Flexibility to allow the introduction of new services and technologies.

More generally, one of the driving forces was the trend toward universal personal telecommunications and universal communications access. The first concept refers to the ability of a person to identify himself or herself easily and use conveniently any communication system in an entire country, over a continent, or even globally, in terms of a single account. The second refers to the capability of using one's terminal in a wide variety of environments to connect to information services (e.g., to have a portable terminal that will work in the office, on the street, and on airplanes equally well). This revolution in personal computing obviously involves wireless communication in a fundamental way. The GSM cellular telephony with its subscriber identity module, for example, is a large step toward these goals.

Personal communications services and personal communication networks (PCNs) are names attached to these concepts of global wireless communications, and they also formed objectives for third-generation wireless systems.

Both competing standards for 3G technology use code division multiple access to provide efficient use of the spectrum and high capacity.

Alternative Interfaces

Figure 13.11 shows the alternative schemes that were adopted as part of IMT-2000. The specification covers a set of radio interfaces for optimized performance in different radio environments. A major reason for the inclusion of five alternatives was to enable a smooth evolution from existing first- and second-generation systems.

The five alternatives reflect the evolution from the second-generation systems. Two of the specifications grow out of the work at the European Telecommunications Standards Institute (ETSI) to develop a **Universal Mobile Telecommunications System (UMTS)** as Europe's 3G wireless standard. UMTS includes two standards. One of these is known as **Wideband CDMA (WCDMA)**, for the air interface technology of UMTS. This scheme fully exploits CDMA technology to provide high data rates with efficient use of bandwidth. The other European effort under UMTS was known as IMT-TC, or TD-CDMA. This approach was a combination of WCDMA and TDMA technology. IMT-TC is intended to provide an upgrade path for the TDMA-based GSM systems.

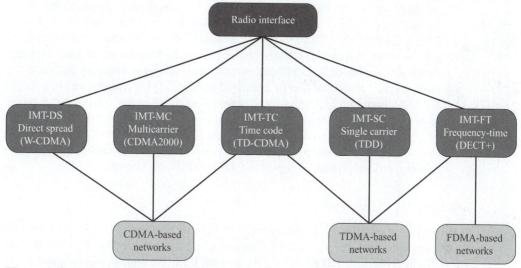

Figure 13.11 IMT-2000 Terrestrial Radio Interfaces

Another CDMA-based system, known as **CDMA2000**, has a North American origin. This scheme is similar to, but incompatible with, WCDMA, in part because the standards use different chip rates. Also, CDMA2000 uses a technique known as multicarrier, not used with WCDMA.

Two other interface specifications are shown in Figure 13.11. IMT-SC is primarily designed for TDMA-only networks. IMT-TC can be used by both TDMA and FDMA carriers to provide some 3G services; it is an outgrowth of the Digital European Cordless Telecommunications (DECT) standard.

In the remainder of this section, we present some general considerations for CDMA technology for 3G systems and then provide an overview of the UMTS/WCDMA and 1xEV-DO 3G systems.

CDMA Design Considerations

The dominant technology for 3G systems is CDMA. Although different CDMA schemes have been adopted, they share some common design issues as follows:

- **Bandwidth:** An important design goal for all 3G systems is to limit channel usage to 5 MHz. There are several reasons for this goal. On the one hand, a bandwidth of 5 MHz or more improves the receiver's ability to resolve multipath when compared to narrower bandwidths. On the other hand, available spectrum is limited by competing needs, and 5 MHz is a reasonable upper limit on what can be allocated for 3G.

- **Chip rate:** Given the bandwidth, the chip rate depends on desired data rate, the need for error control, and bandwidth limitations. A chip rate of 3 Mcps (mega-chips per second) or more is reasonable given these design parameters.

- **Multirate:** The term *multirate* refers to the provision of multiple fixed-data-rate logical channels to a given user, in which different data rates are provided on different logical channels. Further, the traffic on each logical channel can be switched independently through the wireless and fixed networks to different destinations. The advantage of multirate is that the system can flexibly support multiple simultaneous applications from a given user and can efficiently use available capacity by only providing the capacity required for each service. Multirate can be achieved with a TDMA scheme within a single CDMA channel, in which a different number of slots per frame are assigned to achieve different data rates. All the subchannels at a given data rate would be protected by error correction and interleaving techniques (Figure 13.12a). An alternative is to use multiple CDMA codes, with separate coding and interleaving, and map them to separate CDMA channels (Figure 13.12b).

3G Systems

Figure 13.13 shows the evolution of wireless cellular systems. 3G systems were the first to provide megabit per second data rates and went through several upgrades. **Long-Term Evolution (LTE)** 4G systems using LTE-Advanced (the original LTE did not meet 4G requirements) provide greater data rates and more flexible quality of service (QoS) capabilities.

Two 3G standards become prominent: UMTS/WCDMA and CDMA2000.

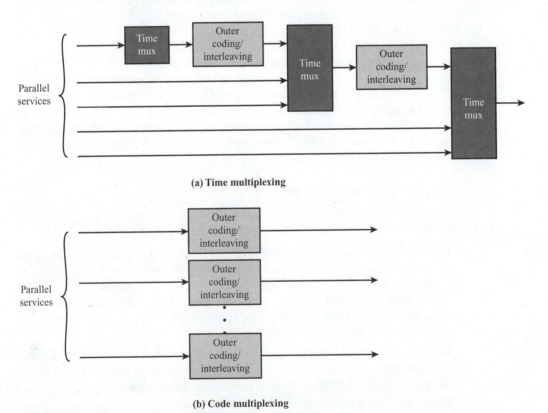

(a) Time multiplexing

(b) Code multiplexing

Figure 13.12 Time and Code Multiplexing Principles

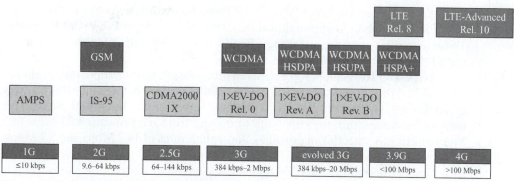

Figure 13.13 Evolution of Cellular Wireless Systems

Wideband CDMA and UMTS WCDMA is part of a group of standards from IMT-2000, UMTS, and also the **Third-Generation Partnership Project (3GPP)** industry organization. The 3GPP, which had previously released standards for GSM, released an original set of specifications known as "Release 99" in 1999 for WCDMA and UMTS. Its subsequent releases were labeled "Release 4" onwards. Many of the higher-layer core network functions of GSM were carried over from GSM to WCDMA; it was primarily the radio access technology that was changed.

WCDMA supports maximal data rates based on the speed of mobility of the user. At least 144 kbps is supported for speeds up to 500 km/h, 384 kbps for up to 120 km/h, and up to 2 Mbps for speeds up to 10 km/h using picocells. In most of the world, this is supported in frequencies from 1900 to 2025 MHz. 3GPP Release 5 introduced **High-Speed Downlink Packet Access (HSDPA)**, which improved downlink speeds to a range from 1.8 to 14.4 Mbps. HSDPA uses adaptive modulation and coding, hybrid ARQ, and fast scheduling. Release 6 then provided **High-Speed Uplink Packet Access (HSUPA)**, which increased uplink rates up to 5.76 Mbps.

High-Speed Packet Access Plus (HSPA+) was provided in Release 7 and successively improved through Release 11. Maximum data rates increased from 21 Mbps up to 336 Mbps by adding features such as 64 QAM, 2×2 and 4×4 MIMO, and dual or multicarrier combinations.

3GPP Release 8 specifications introduced LTE as a pathway to 4G. Releases 8 onward provided specifications for LTE, but also upgrades to HSPA+. For LTE, we discuss Release 8 and later 3GPP releases in Chapter 14.

CDMA2000 and EV-DO The CDMA2000 technology family first produced **CDMA2000 1xRTT** (radio transmission technology), where the name indicates that the technology operates using 1x (1 times) the 1.2288 Mcps spreading rate of a standard 1.25 MHz IS-95 CDMA channel (as opposed to the potential 3xRTT label for which the technology was never developed). Its intent was to offer near-broadband packet data speeds for wireless access to the Internet. The rates were not consistent with 3G objectives, so 1xRTT was considered a "2.5G" technology (as many also considered GPRS and EDGE).

The next step was to provide evolution of the air interface to the **Evolution-Data Only** format, **1xEV-DO**, and data/voice format, 1xEV-DV. The EV signifies that it is an evolutionary technology built on the IS-95 standard. The 1xEV-DV technology never succeeded, but 1xEV-DO was successfully deployed to provide 2.4 Mbps downlink and 153 kbps uplink data rates under the label **1xEV-DO Release 0**. These data rates are achieved using a bandwidth of only 1.25 MHz, one-quarter of the 5 MHz required for WCDMA.

1xEV-DO Revision A was approved four years later with improved maximum rates of 3.1 Mbps downlink and 1.8 Mbps uplink. Release A also supported quality of service for VoIP and advanced broadband applications. **1xEV-DO Revision B** implemented a multicarrier capability to expand from the previous 1.25 MHz to 5 MHz bandwidth, resulting in downlink and uplink rates of 14.7 Mbps and 5.4 Mbps, respectively.

What differentiates the EV-DO scheme from other 3G technologies is that it is designed for data only (DO) and is geared toward the use of IP for packet transmission and for Internet access. However, with VoIP technology, CDMA2000 1xEV-DO can support voice traffic.

This illustrates the benefits that can be provided from a data-only design. The 1xEV-DO design focuses on integration with IP-based networks. As a result, some vendors have built 1xEV-DO networks based entirely on IP technologies. Figure 13.14 shows the main elements in such an arrangement. Mobile users communicate with a base station in a nearby cell using the 1xEV-DO transmission scheme. Typically, the base station controller for a number of base stations is located in a central office to provide switching, handoff, and other services. An IP transport service is used to connect the base station to the central office. Using IP transport lowers connection costs by giving operators a choice of connection services, including frame relay, asynchronous transfer mode (ATM), broadband wireless links, and digitial

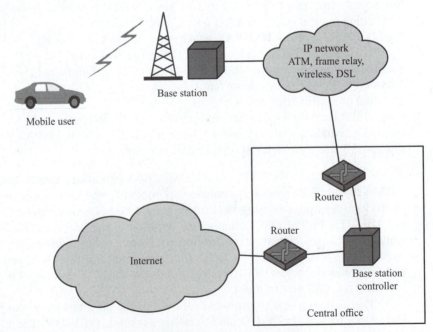

Figure 13.14 CDMA2000 1xEV-DO Configuration Elements

subscriber line (DSL). At the central office, the base station controller can route a call back out the IP network to another cellular subscriber or out over the Internet.

Because 1xEV-DO is specified as data-only, the transmission scheme can be optimized for data transfer and need not support voice requirements. Voice communications impose restrictions that inhibit efficient use of bandwidth. For example, a delay of 100 ms makes voice communication difficult. Longer delays make useful voice communication impractical. For this reason, voice frames are short, typically on the order of 20 ms, in order to minimize delays. But the use of short frames increases overhead, resulting in reduced efficiency since the headers have a large size relative to the data. In a data-only network, longer average delays can be tolerated, and QoS facilities can be used to accommodate a fraction of transmissions that require tight delay values. Accordingly, a data-only network can use longer frames, reducing overhead.

Another advantage to the longer frame is that it results in more efficient use of turbo codes (see Section 10.3). Whereas convolutional coding is well suited to the short voice frames, turbo coding is more powerful when frames are long (several hundred bits or more). Turbo coding with large frame sizes significantly improves performance by allowing the use of lower RF power while still achieving the same error rate.

In a typical data-only application, the amount of traffic from the network to the user significantly exceeds user-to-network traffic. Such applications include Web browsing and downloading e-mail. To optimize throughput and make the best use of the available bandwidth, 1xEV-DO sends and receives at different data rates.

A major difference in a data-only design as compared to a voice-optimized design is the technique used to maintain continuous communication in a noisy and variable RF environment. Voice-optimized systems use power control: users with weak signals increase their transmitting RF power to overcome path loss and/or fading while users close to the base station reduce power. In contrast, 1xEV-DO alters the data rate rather than the power when signal levels change. This is done in both directions (forward and reverse channels).

Let us consider the forward channel first. The base station always sends at full power, to assure that the mobile unit achieves the highest possible received SNR. If path loss increases, the resulting reduction in SNR yields a lower effective link capacity (using Shannon's formula) or, put another way, a higher error rate. The errors are reduced not by increasing RF power but by reducing the data rate. The data rate is reduced by increasing redundancy and altering the modulation method. Increasing the number of check bits reduces the effective rate of actual data since more bits are used for coding. Use of lower-order modulation methods (e.g., 16-QAM versus QPSK) lowers the data rate by improving the error performance. Table 13.6 shows some of the forward channel data rates for 1xEV-DO Revision B. Lower data rates increase the number of 1.67-ms time slots used, or change the code rate or modulation scheme. When using more time slots, the additional time slots provide redundant information. If the mobile unit can successfully decode a packet before all slots are sent, it sends an acknowledgment to the base station. This causes an early termination of the transmission, increasing effective throughput. The mobile unit provides continuous information about SNR conditions so that the base station can adjust its data rate.

Table 13.7 shows the data rates for the reverse channel. Because of the limited signal power on the reverse channel and poorer channel conditions when the signal

Table 13.6 CDMA2000 1xEV-DO Revision B Per-carrier Link Parameters: Forward Link[1]

Data rate (kbps)	Number of slots	Packet size (bytes)	Packet duration (ms)	Code rate	Modulation
38.4	16	128	26.67	1/5	QPSK
76.8	8	128	13.33	1/5	QPSK
153.6	4	128	6.67	1/5	QPSK
307.2	2	128	3.33	1/5	QPSK
614.4	2	256	3.33	1/3	QPSK
921.6	2	384	3.33	1/3	8PSK
1228.8	2	512	3.33	1/3	16QAM
1843.2	1	384	1.67	1/3	8 PSK
2457.6	1	512	1.67	1/3	16QAM
3686.4[2]	1	768	1.67	1/3	64QAM
4300.8[2]	1	896	1.67	1/3	64QAM
4915.2[2]	1	1024	1.67	1/3	64QAM

[1]Not a comprehensive list of all standardized options
[2]Optional

Table 13.7 CDMA2000 1xEV-DO Revision B Per-carrier Link Parameters: Reverse Link

Data rate (kbps)	Number of slots	Packet size (bytes)	Packet duration (ms)	Effective Code rate	Modulation
4.8	16	16	26.67	1/5	BPSK
9.6	16	32	26.67	1/5	BPSK
19.2	16	64	26.67	1/5	BPSK
28.8	16	96	26.67	1/5	BPSK
38.4	16	128	26.67	1/5	BPSK
57.6	16	192	26.67	1/5	QPSK
76.8	16	256	26.67	1/5	QPSK
115.2	16	384	26.67	1/5	QPSK
153.6	16	512	26.67	1/5	QPSK
230.4	16	768	26.67	1/5	QPSK
307.2	16	1024	26.67	1/5	QPSK
460.8	16	1536	26.67	1/3	8 PSK

is transmitted (since the antenna is much closer to the ground), only lower-order modulation schemes are used, which are less affected by RF channel conditions than more complex modulation schemes.

13.6 RECOMMENDED READING

[POLL96] covers the handoff problem in depth. [EVER94] and [ORLI98] provide good accounts of cellular traffic analysis. [BLAC99] is one of the best technical treatments of second-generation cellular systems. A good survey of GSM concepts is [RAHN93]; for more detail see [GARG99].

[OJAN98] provides an overview of key technical design considerations for 3G systems. Another useful survey is [ZENG00]. [PRAS00] is a much more detailed analysis. For a discussion of CDMA2000 1xEV-DO, see [BI03]. [BHUS06] and [ATTA06] provide good discussions of 1xEV-DO Revisions A and B.

ATTA06 Attar, R., et al. "Evolution of CDMA2000 Cellular Networks: Multicarrier EV-DO." *Communications Magazine, IEEE,* vol. 44, no. 3, pp. 46, 53, March 2006.

BHUS06 Bhushan, N., et al. "CDMA2000 1×EV-DO Revision a: A Physical Layer and MAC Layer Overview." *Communications Magazine, IEEE,* vol. 44, no. 2, pp. 37, 49, February 2006.

BI03 Bi, Q., et al. "Performance of 1xEV-DO Third-Generation Wireless High-Speed Data Systems." *Bell Labs Technical Journal,* vol. 7, no. 3, 2003.

BLAC99 Black, U. *Second-Generation Mobile and Wireless Networks.* Upper Saddle River, NJ: Prentice Hall, 1999.

EVER94 Everitt, D. "Traffic Engineering of the Radio Interface for Cellular Mobile Networks." *Proceedings of the IEEE,* September 1994.

GARG99 Garg, V., and Wilkes, J. *Principles and Applications of GSM.* Upper Saddle River, NJ: Prentice Hall, 1999.

OJAN98 Ojanpera, T., and Prasad, G. "An Overview of Air Interface Multiple Access for IMT-2000/UMTS." *IEEE Communications Magazine,* September 1998.

ORLI98 Orlik, P., and Rappaport, S. "Traffic Performance and Mobility Modeling of Cellular Communications with Mixed Platforms and Highly Variable Mobilities." *Proceedings of the IEEE,* July 1998.

POLL96 Pollini, G. "Trends in Handover Design." *IEEE Communications Magazine,* March 1996.

PRAS00 Prasad, R.; Mohr, W.; and Konhauser, W., eds. *Third-Generation Mobile Communication Systems.* Boston: Artech House, 2000.

RAHN93 Rahnema, M. "Overview of the GSM System and Protocol Architecture." *IEEE Communications Magazine,* April 1993.

ZENG00 Zeng, M.; Annamalai, A.; and Bhargava, V. "Harmonization of Global Third-Generation Mobile Systems." *IEEE Communications Magazine,* December 2000.

13.7 KEY TERMS, REVIEW QUESTIONS, AND PROBLEMS

Key Terms

1xRTT	forward channel	picocells
1xEV-DO Release 0	frequency reuse	power control
1xEV-DO Revision A	Generalized Packet Radio	reuse factor
1xEV-DO Revision B	Service (GPRS)	reverse channel
Advanced Mobile Phone	Global System for Mobile	second-generation (2G)
Service (AMPS)	Communications (GSM)	network
base station	handoff	self-organizing networks
CDMA2000	handover	soft handoff
cell sectoring	hard handoff	third-generation (3G)
cellular network	High-Speed Downlink Packet	network
closed-loop power control	Access (HSDPA)	Third-Generation Partnership
closed subscriber group	High-Speed Packet Access	Project (3GPP)
code division multiple access	Plus (HSPA+)	time division multiple access
(CDMA)	High-Speed Uplink Packet	(TDMA)
control channels	Access (HSDPA)	traffic channels
coordinated multipoint	IS-95	traffic intensity
transmission (CoMP)	inter-cell interference	Universal Mobile
Enhanced Data Rates for	coordination (ICIC)	Telecommunications
GSM Evolution (EDGE)	macrocells	System (UMTS)
Erlang	mobile radio	Wideband CDMA
femtocells	network densification	(WCDMA)
first-generation (1G) network	open-loop power control	

Review Questions

13.1 What geometric shape is used in cellular system design?

13.2 What is the principle of frequency reuse in the context of a cellular network?

13.3 List five ways of increasing the capacity of a cellular system.

13.4 Explain the paging function of a cellular system.

13.5 List and briefly define different performance metrics that may be used to make the handoff decision.

13.6 As a mobile unit in communication with a base station moves, what factors determine the need for power control and the amount of power adjustment?

13.7 Explain the difference between open-loop and closed-loop power control.

13.8 What is the difference between traffic intensity and the mean rate of calls in a system?

13.9 What are the key differences between first- and second-generation cellular systems?

13.10 What are the advantages of using CDMA for a cellular network?

13.11 What are the disadvantages of using CDMA for a cellular network?

13.12 Explain the difference between hard and soft handoff.

13.13 What are some key characteristics that distinguish third-generation cellular systems from second-generation cellular systems?

13.14 What are the two predominant families of third-generation cellular systems?

13.15 What are the names of the technologies associated with third-generation systems? With which family of standards are each associated?

Problems

13.1 Consider four different cellular systems that share the following characteristics. The frequency bands are 825 to 845 MHz for mobile unit transmission and 870 to 890 MHz for base station transmission. A duplex circuit consists of one 30-kHz channel in each direction. The systems are distinguished by the reuse factor, which is 4, 7, 12, and 19, respectively.

    a. Suppose that in each of the systems, the cluster of cells (4, 7, 12, 19) is duplicated 16 times. Find the number of simultaneous communications that can be supported by each system.

    b. Find the number of simultaneous communications that can be supported by a single cell in each system.

    c. What is the area covered, in cells, by each system?

    d. Suppose the cell size is the same in all four systems and a fixed area of 100 cells is covered by each system. Find the number of simultaneous communications that can be supported by each system.

13.2 A cellular system is composed of both macrocells and femtocells. There are a total of 200 voice channels available. Suppose a network engineer decided to implement frequency reuse by using a fixed partition of frequencies, some to the macrocells and the rest to femtocells. Macrocells use cluster sizes of 4 and 3 sectors per cell. Femtocells use cluster sizes of 1 and no sectoring; this assumes femtocells do not interfere with neighboring femtocells.

    a. If 20 channels are assigned to each femtocell, how many channels (both macrocell and femtocell channels) are potentially available to a mobile at every location?

    b. From part a, if there are 20 macrocells and 20 femtocells in the area, what is the total system capacity?

    c. From part a, if the femtocells are assigned to closed subscriber groups, how many channels are available to those who are not in the closed subscriber groups?

    d. Instead of the results from part a, how should the channels be distributed if at least 68 channels should be available to a mobile in a femtocell?

13.3 Describe a sequence of events similar to that of Figure 13.6 for

    a. a call from a mobile unit to a fixed subscriber.

    b. a call from a fixed subscriber to a mobile unit.

13.4 In the discussion of the handoff procedure based on relative signal strength with threshold, it was pointed out that if the threshold is set quite low, such as Th_3, the mobile unit may move far into the new cell (L_4). This reduces the quality of the communication link and may result in a dropped call. Can you suggest another drawback of this scheme?

13.5 Hysteresis is a technique commonly used in control systems. As an example, describe the hysteresis mechanism used in a household thermostat.

13.6 A telephony connection has a duration of 23 minutes. This is the only connection made by this caller during the course of an hour. How much is the amount of traffic, in Erlangs, of this connection?

13.7 Using Table 13.1, approximate the answers to the following. Also, in each case, give a description in words of the general problem being solved. *Hint:* straight-line interpolation is adequate.

    a. Given $N = 20$, $A = 10.5$, find P.

    b. Given $N = 20$, $P = 0.015$, find A.

    c. Given $P = 0.005$, $A = 6$, find N.

13.8 An analog cellular system has a total of 33 MHz of bandwidth and uses two 25-kHz simplex (one-way) channels to provide full duplex voice and control channels.

    a. What is the number of channels available per cell for a frequency reuse factor of (1) 4 cells, (2) 7 cells, and (3) 12 cells?

    b. Assume that 1 MHz is dedicated to control channels but that only one control channel is needed per cell. Determine a reasonable distribution of control channels and voice channels in each cell for the three frequency reuse factors of part (a).

13.9 As was mentioned, the one-way bandwidth available to a single operator in the AMPS system is 12.5 MHz with a channel bandwidth of 30 kHz and 21 control channels. We would like to calculate the efficiency with which this system utilizes bandwidth for a particular installation. Use the following parameters:
- Cell area = 8 km^2
- Total coverage area = 4000 km^2
- Frequency reuse factor = 7
- Average number of calls per user during the busy hour = 1.2
- Average holding time of a call = 100 s
- Call blocking probability = 2%
  a. How many voice channels are there per cell?
  b. Use Table 13.1 and a simple straight-line interpolation to determine the total traffic carried per cell, in Erlangs/cell. Then convert that to Erlangs/km2.
  c. Calculate the number of calls/hour/cell and the number of calls/hour/km2.
  d. Calculate the number of users/hour/cell and the number of users/hour/channel.
  e. A common definition of spectral efficiency with respect to modulation, or modulation efficiency, in Erlangs/MHz/km^2, is

$$\eta_m = \frac{\text{(Total traffic carried by the system)}}{\text{(Bandwidth)(Total coverage area)}}$$

Determine the modulation efficiency for this system.

13.10 A cellular system uses FDMA with a spectrum allocation of 12.5 MHz in each direction, a guard band at the edge of the allocated spectrum of 10 kHz, and a channel bandwidth of 30 kHz. What is the number of available channels?

13.11 For a cellular system, FDMA spectral efficiency is defined as $\eta_a = \dfrac{B_c N_T}{B_w}$ where

B_c = channel bandwidth
B_w = total bandwidth in one direction
N_T = total number of voice channels in the covered area
  a. What is an upper bound on η_a?
  b. Determine η_a for the system of Problem 13.8.

13.12 Consider a seven-cell system covering an area of 3100 km^2. The traffic in the seven cells is as follows:

Cell number	1	2	3	4	5	6	7
Traffic (Erlangs)	30.8	66.7	48.6	33.2	38.2	37.8	32.6

Each user generates an average of 0.03 Erlangs of traffic per hour, with a mean holding time of 120 s. The system consists of a total of 395 channels and is designed for a grade of service of 0.02.
  a. Determine the number of subscribers in each cell.
  b. Determine the number of calls per hour per subscriber.
  c. Determine the number of calls per hour in each cell.
  d. Determine the number of channels required in each cell. *Hint:* you will need to extrapolate using Table 13.1.
  e. Determine the total number of subscribers.
  f. Determine the average number of subscribers per channel.
  g. Determine the subscriber density per km^2.
  h. Determine the total traffic (total Erlangs).
  i. Determine the Erlangs per km^2.
  j. What is the radius of a cell?

FOURTH GENERATION SYSTEMS AND LTE-ADVANCED

LEARNING OBJECTIVES

After studying this chapter, you should be able to:

- Describe the purpose and motivation for 4G.
- Describe the roles of the Evolved Packet Core and the Evolved-UTRAN in LTE.
- Explain the roles of the entities of the EPC.
- Define the roles of bearers and resource blocks in LTE resource allocation.
- Describe and compare FDD and TDD frame structures.
- Explain the full LTE power-on procedure.
- Describe the major improvements in the LTE-Advanced releases.

Fourth-generation (4G) cellular technology provides a high-speed, universally accessible wireless service capability. This is creating a revolution of the same proportion for networking at all locations as the development of user-friendly tablets, smartphones, and widespread deployment of Wi-Fi 802.11 networks provided for indoor wireless networking.

The focus of this chapter is on Long-Term Evolution (LTE) and its 4G enhancement, LTE-Advanced. The chapter first considers the goals and requirements for 4G systems. Then the architecture of LTE-Advanced is presented from a complete wireless system architecture perspective. After that, the core network called the Evolved Packet System is discussed, followed by the LTE channel and physical layer structures. The technologies of LTE Release 8 are first discussed, then the enhancements in Releases 9 through 12.

14.1 PURPOSE, MOTIVATION, AND APPROACH TO 4G

The evolution of smartphones and cellular networks has ushered in a new generation of capabilities and standards, which is collectively called 4G. 4G systems provide ultra-broadband Internet access for a variety of mobile devices including laptops, smartphones, tablets, and device-to-device communications. 4G networks support Mobile Web access and high-bandwidth applications such as high-definition mobile TV, mobile video conferencing, and gaming services.

These requirements have led to the development of a 4G mobile wireless technology that is designed to maximize bandwidth and throughput while also maximizing spectral efficiency. The International Telecommunication Union (ITU) has issued directives for 4G networks. According to the ITU, an IMT-Advanced (or 4G) cellular system must fulfill a number of minimum requirements, including the following:

- Be based on an all-IP packet-switched network.
- Support peak data rates of up to approximately 100 Mbps for high-mobility mobile access and up to approximately 1 Gbps for low-mobility access such as local wireless access.
- Dynamically share and use the network resources to support more simultaneous users per cell.

Table 14.1 Wireless Network Generations

Technology	1G	2G	2.5G	3G	4G
Design began	1970	1980	1985	1990	2000
Implementation	1984	1991	1999	2002	2012
Services	Analog voice	Digital voice	Higher capacity packetized data	Higher capacity, broadband	Completely IP based
Data rate	1.9. kbps	14.4 kbps	384 kbps	2 Mbps	200 Mbps
Multiplexing	FDMA	TDMA, CDMA	TDMA, CDMA	CDMA	OFDMA, SC-FDMA
Core network	PSTN	PSTN	PSTN, packet network	Packet network	IP backbone

- Support smooth handovers across heterogeneous networks, including 2G and 3G networks, small cells such as picocells, femtocells, and relays, and WLANs.
- Support high quality of service for next-generation multimedia applications.

In contrast to earlier generations, 4G systems do not support traditional circuit-switched telephony service, providing only IP telephony services known as Voice over LTE (VoLTE). As may be observed in Table 14.1, the spread spectrum radio technologies that characterized 3G systems are replaced in 4G systems by orthogonal frequency division multiple (OFDM) multicarrier transmission and frequency-domain equalization schemes.

Figure 14.1 illustrates some major differences between 3G and 4G cellular networks. As shown in Figure 14.1a, the connections between **base stations** and switching offices in 3G networks are typically cable-based, either copper or fiber wires. Circuit switching is supported to enable voice connections between mobile users and phones connected to the PSTN. Internet access in 3G networks may also be routed through switching offices. By contrast, in 4G networks, IP telephony is the norm as are IP packet-switched connections for Internet access. These are enabled by wireless connections, such as fixed broadband wireless access (BWA) WiMAX, between base stations and switching offices (Figure 14.1b). Connections among mobile users with 4G-capable smartphones may never be routed over cable-based, circuit-switched connections—all communications between them can be IP-based and handled by wireless links. This setup facilitates deployment of mobile-to-mobile video call/video conferencing services and the simultaneous delivery of voice and data services (such as Web browsing while engaged in a phone call). 4G mobile users can still connect with 3G network users and PSTN subscribers over cable/fiber circuit-switched connections between the switching offices.

14.2 LTE ARCHITECTURE

Two candidates emerged for 4G standardization. One is known as **Long-Term Evolution (LTE)**, which has been developed by the Third Generation Partnership Project (3GPP), a consortium of Asian, European, and North American telecommunications

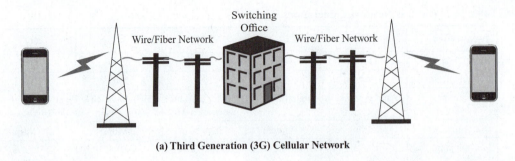

(a) Third Generation (3G) Cellular Network

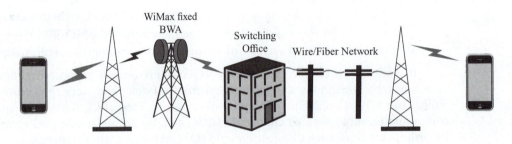

(b) Fourth Generation (4G) Cellular Network

Figure 14.1 Third versus Fourth Generation Cellular Networks

standards organizations. The other effort is from the IEEE 802.16 committee, which has developed standards for high-speed fixed wireless operations known as WiMAX (described in Chapter 16). The IEEE 802.16 committee specified an enhancement of WiMAX to meet mobile 4G needs. The two efforts are similar in terms of both performance and technology. Both are based on the use of orthogonal frequency division multiple access (OFDMA) to support multiple access to network resources. WiMAX uses a pure OFDMA approach of both uplink (UL) and downlink (DL). LTE uses pure OFDMA on the DL, but instead a single-carrier orthogonal frequency-division multiplexing (SC-OFDM) technique based on OFDMA offers enhanced power efficiency for the uplink. While WiMAX retains a role as the technology for fixed broadband wireless access, LTE has become the universal standard for 4G wireless. For example, all of the major carriers in the United States, including AT&T and Verizon, have adopted a version of LTE based on **frequency division duplex (FDD)**, whereas China Mobile, the world's largest telecommunication carrier, has adopted a version of LTE based on **time division duplex (TDD)**.

Development of some features of LTE began in the 3GPP 3G era and initial LTE releases provided data rates similar to 3G or enhanced 3G. 3GPP Release 8, LTE, however, was a *clean slate* approach with a completely new air interface that implemented OFDM, OFDMA, and multiantenna transmission and reception

(MIMO) from the beginning. The radio interface aims for LTE of the cellular system, hence the appropriateness of the name.

Beginning with Release 10, LTE provides a 4G service, known as **LTE-Advanced**. Table 14.2 compares the performance goals of LTE and LTE-Advanced. LTE has further been improved with Releases 11 and 12, which will be discussed.

The specifications for LTE releases are immense. This section provides a discussion of the architecture. Figure 14.2 illustrates the principal elements in an LTE network. The heart of the system is the base station, designated **evolved NodeB (eNodeB)**. Mobile devices connect into the network through an eNodeB. In previous 3GPP standards, the base station was referred to as the NodeB. The key differences between the two base station technologies are:

- The NodeB station interface with subscriber stations (referred to as **user equipment (UE)**) is based on CDMA, whereas the eNodeB air interface is based on OFDMA.

- eNodeB embeds its own control functionality, rather than using an RNC (Radio Network Controller) as does a NodeB. This means that the eNodeB now supports radio resource control, admission control, and mobility management, which was originally the responsibility of the RNC.

The simpler structure without an RNC results in simpler operation and higher performance.

Evolved Packet System

3GPP standards divide the network standards between the radio access network (RAN) and the core network (CN), which allow each to evolve independently. LTE is called the **Evolved UMTS Terrestrial Radio Access (E-UTRA)** and its enhancement of 3GPP's 3G RAN is called the **Evolved UMTS Terrestrial Radio Access Network (E-UTRAN)**. As seen in Figure 14.2, the eNodeB is the only logical node in the E-UTRAN since the RNC has been removed from the architecture.

The operator, or carrier, core network that interconnects all of the base stations of the carrier is referred to as the **Evolved Packet Core (EPC)**. Together LTE and

Table 14.2 Comparison of Performance Requirements for LTE and LTE-Advanced

System Performance		LTE	LTE-Advanced
Peak rate	Downlink	100 Mbps @20 MHz	1 Gbps @100 MHz
	Uplink	50 Mbps @20 MHz	500 Mbps @100 MHz
Control plane delay	Idle to connected	<100 ms	<50 ms
	Dormant to active	<50 ms	<10 ms
User plane delay		<5 ms	Lower than LTE
Spectral efficiency (peak)	Downlink	5 bps/Hz @2 × 2	30 bps/Hz @8 × 8
	Uplink	2.5 bps/Hz @1 × 2	15 bps/Hz @4 × 4
Mobility		Up to 350 km/hr	Up to 350–500 km/hr

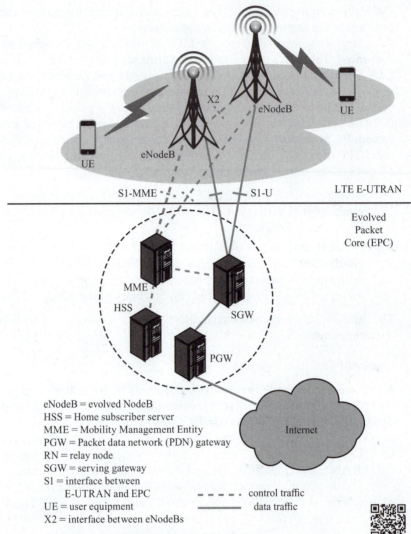

eNodeB = evolved NodeB
HSS = Home subscriber server
MME = Mobility Management Entity
PGW = Packet data network (PDN) gateway
RN = relay node
SGW = serving gateway
S1 = interface between
       E-UTRAN and EPC
UE = user equipment
X2 = interface between eNodeBs

- - - - - control traffic
———— data traffic

Figure 14.2 Overview of the EPC/LTE Architecture

the EPC form the **Evolved Packet System (EPS)** as shown in Figure 14.2. Because the purpose of this text is both to understand wireless networks and the complete wireless systems within which they operate, we will study both LTE and the EPC. It is certainly the goal of the EPS to provide everything needed to support a 4G communication session, from session management, accounting, and security to physical layer resource allocations, quality of service, delay bounds, and packet error control.

Design Principles

The following design principles were foundational to the design of the EPC and LTE.

- Clean slate design.
- Packet-switched IP core network.

- Minimum numbers of interfaces and network elements.
- Packet-switched transport for traffic belonging to all Quality of Service (QoS) classes, including conversational, streaming, real-time, non-real-time, and background traffic.
- Maximum performance or minor degradation for mobility speeds up to 120 km/hr. Sustained connections up to 500 km/hr for LTE-Advanced.
- Other performance requirements listed in Table 14.2.
- Radio resource management for the following: end-to-end QoS, transport for higher layers, load sharing/balancing, and policy management/enforcement across different radio access technologies.
- Integration with existing 3GPP 2G and 3G networks.
- Flexibility of spectrum deployment depending on geographic regions.
- Support for broadcast and multicast services, especially for emergency situations.
- Scalable bandwidth from 1.4 to 20 MHz.
- Carrier aggregation for overall bandwidths up to 100 MHz.
- FDD and TDD modes.
- Reduced cost: high spectral efficiency, reuse of existing spectrum allocations, flat architecture with fewer network components, base stations with lower power and space requirements, self-configuration and self-optimization.

High Level Functions of the EPS

The following functions are performed by the EPS.

- Network access control, including network selection, authentication, authorization, admission control, policy and charging enforcement, and lawful interception.
- Packet routing and transfer.
- Security, including ciphering, integrity protection, and network interface physical link protection.
- Mobility management to keep track of the current location of the UE.
- Radio resource management to assign, reassign, and release radio resources taking into account single and multicell aspects.
- Network management to support operation and maintenance functions.
- Selection of packet gateways, serving gateways, and mobility management entities for a UE session (more details follow).
- IP networking functions, connections of eNodeBs to the multiple mobility management entities, E-UTRAN sharing, emergency session support, among others.

The next section discusses the Release 8 EPC and then this chapter in successive sections works its way down through Release 8 LTE resource management functions and channel structures to the LTE physical layer. Concluding this chapter is a discussion of the innovations of LTE-Advanced in Release 10 (carrier aggregation, enhanced MIMO, heterogeneous environments, relaying) and the other enhancements in Releases 9, 11, and 12.

It is best to first understand the features of the Release 8 EPC and LTE E-UTRAN (called simply LTE), because many of today's deployments are Release 8. Therefore, the chapter first discusses Release 8. After that the chapter shows how the subsequent releases move to LTE-Advanced to change, enhance, and substantially add to those features. Such enhancements include carrier aggregation, support for **heterogeneous networks (HetNets)** using small cells such as picocells and femtocells, MIMO expansion, interference cancellation, coordinated multipoint transmission, and relaying.

14.3 EVOLVED PACKET CORE

Traditionally, the core cellular network was circuit switched, but for 4G the core is entirely packet switched. It is based on IP and supports voice connections using voice over IP (VoIP). Within 3GPP, the work on the evolved core network was first called the *System Architecture Evolution (SAE)*. The core network is interchangeably called the SAE or the EPC.

EPC Components

Figure 14.2 illustrates the essential components of the EPC:

- **Mobility Management Entity (MME):** Supports user equipment context, identity, authentication, and authorization.
- **Serving Gateway (SGW):** Receives and sends packets between the eNodeB and the core network.
- **Packet Data Network Gateway (PGW):** Connects the EPC with external networks.
- **Home Subscriber Server (HSS):** Database of user-related and subscriber-related information.
- **S1 interface:** Creates communication between the E-UTRAN and the EPC. For control purposes, the eNodeBs communicate with the MMEs through the S1-MME interface. The S1-U is for user plane data traffic between the eNodeB and the SGW.
- **X2 interface:** The X2 interface is used for eNodeBs to interact with each other. Although not shown in Figure 14.2, there are actually two X2 interfaces, the X2-U for user plane and the X2-C for control plane protocols.

Figure 14.2 shows two eNodeBs and only a single instance of each other configuration element. In practice, there are multiple eNodeBs and multiple instances of each of the EPC elements. And there are many-to-many links between eNodeBs and MMEs, between MMEs and SGWs, and between SGWs and PGWs. Each of these has defined interfaces. Now, the components of the EPC are examined in more detail.

Mobility Management Entity (MME) The MME manages control signaling related to UE mobility and security. This involves managing UE access to network connections and network resources. When a UE requires a handover into a cell in a new area, the MME initiates the transfer. This transfer can occur to another LTE U-TRAN area or to 2G or 3G access networks. The MME is responsible for the tracking and the paging of a UE in idle-mode. The MME provides security functions including temporary identities for user terminals, interacting with home subscriber servers for authentication, and negotiation of security algorithms. It also selects the appropriate SGWs and PGWs and gateways to other 2G and 3G networks.

The MME implements EPS Mobility Management (EMM) and EPS Session Management (ESM) protocols. EMM protocols support connection management, control of security, and mobility of the UE in the U-TRAN. A UE can stay registered with an MME or deregister, in which case the MME has no knowledge of the location of the MME until it attaches again.

The MME coordinates with the HSS to retrieve subscription information and with the SGW to establish communication session bearers. The HSS information is also used to generate the security keys used to protect control plane messages.

Serving Gateway (SGW) The SGW deals with user data transmitted and received by UEs in packet form, using IP. The Serving GW is the point of interconnect between the radio side and the EPC. As its name indicates, this gateway serves the UE by routing the incoming and outgoing IP packets. It is the anchor point for the intra-LTE mobility (i.e., in case of handover between eNodeBs under the same MME). Thus packets can be routed from an eNodeB to an eNodeB in another area via the SGW, and can also be routed to external networks such as the Internet via the PGW. The SGW also performs packet buffering, transport-level packet marking for UL and DL, and accounting functions.

Packet Data Network Gateway (PGW) The PGW is the point of interconnect between the EPC and the external IP networks such as the Internet. The PGW routes packets to and from the external networks. It also performs various functions such as routing, IP address/IP prefix allocation, policy control, deep packet inspection for filtering purposes, lawful interception, transport level packet marking, accounting for inter-operator charging, and access to non-3GPP access networks.

Home Subscriber Server (HSS) The HSS maintains a database that contains user-related and subscriber-related information. It also provides support functions in mobility management, call and session setup, user authentication, and access authorization.

S1 Interfaces The S1 interfaces involve both the S1-MME and S1-U interfaces. The S1-MME interface is defined for the control plane between the eNodeB and the MME. It has functions to establish, maintain, and release E-UTRAN radio access bearers (more details on bearers later in this chapter). It supports mobility functions for handovers intra-LTE, with other 3GPP technologies, and with CDMA2000 3G systems. The S1-MME also has paging procedures for the EPC to find the location of a UE.

The S1-U interface is for the user plane data transmission to connect with an SGW for each bearer. Multiple S1-U logical interfaces may exist between the eNodeB and the SGW.

X2 Interfaces The X2 interface is used for eNodeBs to interact with each other. The architecture is open so that there can be interconnections between different manufacturers. There is a control plan X2-C interface that supports mobility management, handover preparation, status transfer, UE context release, handover cancel, inter-cell interference coordination, and load management. The X2-U interface is the user plane interface used to transport data during X2 initiated handover.

Non-Access Stratum Protocols

The LTE E-UTRAN implements protocols are part of the **Access Stratum** that carries data across the wireless part of the network; these are discussed in Section 14.5. In addition to these protocols for management of connections within the LTE E-UTRAN, other protocols exist for the *Non-Access Stratum*. These involve interaction between the UE and the EPC core network and are as follows:

- **EPS Mobility Management (EMM):** Manage the mobility of the UE.
- **EPS Session Management (ESM):** Activate, authenticate, modify, and deactivate user-plane channels for connections between the UE, SGW, and PGW.

14.4 LTE RESOURCE MANAGEMENT

Now we elaborate on the functions that these entities and interfaces accomplish for management of LTE resources. This section discusses Release 8 LTE quality of service, handover, and interference coordination functions. The sections after this one work their way down to the LTE physical layer.

Quality of Service

LTE uses the concept of **bearers** for QoS control in its protocol architecture. Because LTE is packet switched from end to end, a bearer is LTE's central element of QoS control instead of a circuit. Each *EPS bearer* is defined between the PGW and the UE. It maps to specific QoS parameters such as data rate, delay, and packet error rate. Traffic flowing between applications on a client and a service can be differentiated by separate **Service Data Flows (SDFs)**. These SDFs must be mapped to EPS bearers for QoS treatment.

Applications such as voice or video might have fairly stringent data rate and delay requirements, whereas others such as e-mail might not. As discussed in Chapter 3, data applications might have a data rate expectation and some loss requirements, but would be elastic, meaning they could tolerate variations in data rate during transmissions as long as they are completed expeditiously. Voice and video traffic, however, has a much stronger expectation of steady packet delivery but can tolerate some level of packet loss. If voice or video streams are highly compressed, packet loss would have a more significant impact but in general an end user may not notice a few missed audio samples or erroneous pixels.

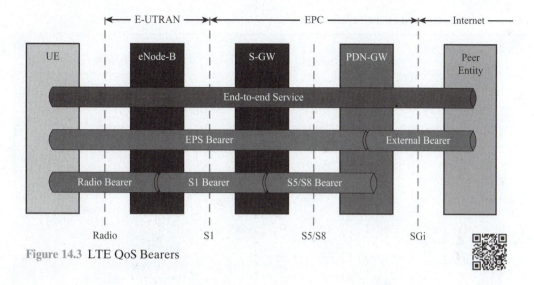

Figure 14.3 LTE QoS Bearers

Therefore, LTE allows these traffic types to be placed on separate bearers for different treatment and priority by the EPS through the different interfaces. End-to-end service between applications on different networks of course cannot be completely controlled by LTE, but inside the EPS (between the UE and the PGW) an EPS bearer is defined as illustrated in Figure 14.3. Across different interfaces, this EPS bearer is also bound to a bearer for that type of interface, whether it is an E-UTRAN radio access bearer, S1 bearer, or S5/S8 bearer.

Bearers are broadly categorized into two classes:

- **Guaranteed Bit Rate (GBR) bearers:** These are guaranteed a minimum bit rate and possibly higher bit rates if system resources are available. These would be most useful for voice, interactive video, or real-time gaming.

- **Non-Guaranteed Bit Rate (non-GBR) bearers:** These are not guaranteed a minimum bit rate. Performance is more dependent on the number of UEs served by the eNodeB and the system load. Non-GBR bearers are more useful for e-mail, file transfer, and P2P file sharing. Web browsing might also be appropriate here as long as web page response times are acceptable.

Each bearer is assigned a **QoS class identifier (QCI)** that refers to a priority, packet delay budget, maximum packet error loss rate, and GBR or non-GBR classification. Nine standard QCIs have been defined by LTE as shown in Table 14.3. Each QCI is given a set of standard forwarding treatments by an operator. These can include scheduling policy, admission thresholds, rate-shaping policy, queue management thresholds, and link layer protocol configuration. Operators pre-configure the set of QCIs and how they are handled by each network element. Because all traffic is ultimately mapped to this small set of nine QCI values, processing is greatly simplified and scalability is improved so that many bearers can be supported.

Table 14.3 Standardized QCI Characteristics

QCI	Resource Type	Priority	Packet Delay Budget	Packet Error Loss Rate	Example Services
1	GBR	2	100 ms	10^{-2}	Conversational Voice
2		4	150 ms	10^{-3}	Conversational Video (live streaming)
3		3	50 ms	10^{-3}	Real-Time Gaming
4		5	300 ms	10^{-6}	Nonconversational Video (buffered streaming)
5	Non-GBR	1	100 ms	10^{-6}	IMS Signalling
6		6	300 ms	10^{-6}	Video (buffered streaming) TCP-based (e.g., www, e-mail, chat, ftp, p2p file sharing, progressive video, etc.)
7		7	100 ms	10^{-3}	Voice, Video (live streaming) Interactive Gaming
8		8	300 ms	10^{-6}	Video (buffered streaming) TCP-based (e.g., www, e-mail, chat, ftp, p2p file sharing, progressive video, etc.)
9*		9			

*QCI value typicaly used for the default bearer

For each bearer the following information is associated:

- QoS class identifier (QCI) value.
- Allocation and Retention Priority (ARP): Used by call admission control to decide if a bearer request should be accepted or rejected. It is also used when networks are overloaded to decide which bearers to release and which can preempt others.

Additionally for GBR bearers:

- Guaranteed Bit Rate (GBR): minimum rate expected from the network.
- Maximum Bit Rate (MBR): bit rate not to be exceeded from the UE into the bearer.

3GPP additionally defines the following for groups of bearers:

- UE-Aggregate Maximum Bit Rate (UE-AMBR): Upper limit on the aggregate bit rate across all non-GBR bearers for a UE. This is enforced by the eNodeB.
- APN-Aggregate Maximum Bit Rate (APN-AMBR): Upper limit on the aggregate bit rate across all non-GBR bearers over all packet data network connections in the same network.

When a UE connects to the EPS, an EPS bearer is established that persists through the lifetime of the connection. This is called the **default bearer** and has a standard configuration established by the core network. This provides always-on connectivity. An additional bearer for special treatment can be established with the same network and is denoted as a **dedicated bearer**.

LTE uses a user plane protocol stack and a control plane protocol stack. The user plane transports IP packets between the PGW and UE. IP packets are encapsulated in an EPC-specific protocol, then tunneled using the ***GPRS Tunneling Protocol (GTP)***, and then from eNodeB to UE by the ***Packet Data Convergence Protocol (PDCP)***. The control plane protocols involve interactions between the MME and UE for bearer management, QoS management, and mobility management for handovers and paging. These protocols are discussed in more detail in Section 14.5.

Details on bearer binding between EPS bearers for assignment of physical resources (time slots and OFDM subcarriers in units of resource blocks) are discussed in a subsequent section after the details of the physical layer are introduced.

Mobility Management

The EPC supports mobility within the LTE system and mobility to other 3GPP systems. When moving within the LTE system, the X2 interface can be used if moving within the same RAN with nodes all coordinated under the same MME and if an X2 interface exists between the eNodeBs. If moving to an eNodeB that belongs to a different RAN that is using different MMEs, the S1 interface is used. The S1 is also used if eNodeBs are not connected with X2 interfaces or UEs moving to a different radio access technology. Both the X2 and S1 options are discussed here. Within LTE Release 8, all handovers are *hard handovers*; the UE can only be connected to one eNodeB at a time.

S1 Mobility The following steps are involved with S1 mobility:

1. **Preparation:** A decision has been made for handover and the destination MME and eNodeB have been identified, so the network needs to allocate resources at the destination. The MME sends a handover request to the destination eNodeB. Once this eNodeB has allocated resources, it responds with an acknowledgement (ACK) to the MME. The MME then sends the handover command to the UE.

2. **Execution:** Then the UE performs RAN-related procedures for the handover. While the UE is executing these procedures, the source eNodeB transfers the PDCP context of the UE to the destination eNodeB. The source eNodeB also sends the data in its PDCP buffer to the target eNodeB. Once all is completed and the UE has established a new Radio Access Bearer (RAB) with the destination eNodeB, the source eNodeB sends the handover confirmation message.

3. **Completion:** The target eNodeB notifies the MME. The MME then directs the source eNodeB to release the resources that had been used by the UE.

X2 Mobility The following steps are involved with X2 mobility when source and destination eNodeBs can work together directly through the X2 interface.

1. **Preparation:** A decision has been made for handover, so the source eNodeB sends a handover request message to the destination eNodeB. Then the

destination eNodeB works with the MME and SGW to establish resources for the UE. It is possible for the UE to continue to use the same RAB on the destination eNodeB with the same resources and QoS. This enables quick and seamless handover, because the UE is not required to set up a new RAB. The destination eNodeB responds with an ACK once it is ready.

2. **Execution:** The source eNodeB then signals the UE, and in response the UE performs RAN-related procedures for the handover. While the UE is working, the source eNodeB transfers status and data to the destination eNodeB on a per-RAB basis.

3. **Completion:** Once the handover is completed, the UE sends a handoff complete message to the MME/SGW and the SGW switches the GTP tunnel to the destination eNodeB. When the data path is established, the destination eNodeB sends a message for the source eNodeB to release the resources for the UE.

For X2 mobility, lossless handover can be performed between one or more RABs, by having the source eNodeB send all packets to the destination eNodeB that have not been sent or have been sent but not yet acknowledged by the UE. The destination eNodeB, however, may use *selective retransmission*, in which it may choose not to retransmit the unacknowledged packets.

Radio Access Network Procedures for Mobility The previous discussion assumed decisions had already been made about whether a handover should occur and about the selection of a destination eNodeB. Here are the RAN procedures that support these determinations. RAN-related mobility management procedures happen between UE and eNodeB or between UE and MME. Mobility occurs in two distinct cases, either in RRC_IDLE state or in RRC_CONNECTED state. The mobility management procedures are designed to be consistent during changes in these two states and in a host of other different scenarios (e.g., network sharing, country border, femtocells).

Information that might be included in different types of handover decision scenarios include radio link quality, UE capability, call type, QoS requirements, and policy-related aspects. The Reference Signal Received Power (RSCP) indicates radio link quality for a connection in an LTE cell. The UE prepares the *measurement report* which contains the RSCP for the neighboring eNodeBs; this is used to trigger and control the handover procedure. The serving eNodeB provides a list of neighboring cells and frequencies on which a report is requested from the UE.

For intra-LTE handover between eNodeBs in the same EPC, there are five events that trigger measurement reporting:

- **Event A1:** Serving cell radio link quality goes above an absolute threshold.
- **Event A2:** Serving cell radio link quality goes below an absolute threshold.
- **Event A3:** A neighbor cell radio link quality becomes better by an amount relative to the serving cell.
- **Event A4:** A neighbor cell radio link quality goes above an absolute threshold.
- **Event A5:** Serving cell radio link quality goes below an absolute threshold and a neighbor radio link quality goes above a different absolute threshold.

There are similar events for handovers between LTE and 2G or 3G 3GPP networks.

For all of these events, the E-UTRAN uses a *TimeToTrigger* parameter, which determines how long these events must be satisfied before a measurement report is to be sent. This prevents the UE from ping-ponging between eNodeBs due to temporary multipath fading dips or shadows. In the RRC_IDLE state, the UE decides when to conduct handover and the target cell and frequency. In RRC_CONNECTED state, the E-UTRAN determines the optimum cell and frequency.

Inter-Cell Interference Coordination

A UE will suffer from Inter-cell Interference (ICI) when the same frequency is used for a UE in a neighboring cell. This ICI limits the capacity of cellular systems. There are several ICI mitigation techniques that can be used as follows. Subsequent LTE releases have enhanced these capabilities.

To meet LTE spectrum efficiency targets, LTE uses universal **frequency reuse**, that is, all frequencies are reused in each cell. This is equivalent to using a cluster size of $N = 1$ and a **reuse factor** of 1, according to the discussion in Section 13.1 of the previous chapter. This means that two mobiles on the edges of cells could be using the same frequencies in close proximity to each other. At the same time, however, LTE has specific targets for cell edge throughput. Therefore, ICI control techniques are used in Release 8 using three major methods.

- **ICI randomization:** Scrambling the codeword with a cell-specific pseudo-random sequence after error control channel coding. If a neighboring cell uses the same frequency, its codeword will be scrambled differently. Similar to the direct sequence approach for spread spectrum, with the proper code the decoder will only decipher the intended codeword and the effect of others using the same frequency will be reduced.

- **ICI Cancellation:** If the UE can decode the interfering signal, it can recreate that signal and subtract it from the arriving signal. To do this, however, it would require the knowledge of the modulation and coding format of that interfering signal, but this is not usually available.

- **ICI Coordination and Avoidance:** If cells coordinate their use of time/frequencies and transmit power, ICI can be avoided. This can be done statically during the cell planning process, or it can be done semistatically to reconfigure (on time scales of seconds) transmission power and/or traffic loads on resource blocks. The eNodeBs use the X2 interface to share this information.

For LTE Release 8, indicators are included to assist ICI coordination/avoidance. For the DL, eNodeBs can send a **Relative Narrowband Transmit Power (RNTP)** indicator to tell where frequencies are going to be used, but with limited power. Therefore, neighboring cells might also be able to use those frequencies. For the UL, LTE sends two indicators between eNodeBs. The **High Interference Indicator (HII)** tells neighboring cells which parts of the channel bandwidth are being allocated to cell-edge users. A neighboring cell might wish to avoid those frequencies for cell-edge users in the area. An eNodeB can use an **Overload Indicator (OI)** to tell neighbor cells about interference levels experienced in parts of the cell bandwidth. A neighbor eNodeB receiving such an indication may help its neighbor reduce its interference by changing its scheduling to reduce the interference that the neighboring cell is experiencing from this cell.

Later in the chapter, more advanced ICI control schemes from the later LTE releases will be discussed, especially Coordinated Multi-Point Transmission (CoMP). In CoMP, eNodeBs can implement tight coordination of scheduling, beamforming, or multicell joint transmission.

14.5 LTE CHANNEL STRUCTURE AND PROTOCOLS

LTE implements a hierarchical channel structure between the layers of its protocol stack. This provides efficient support for QoS. This section first provides understanding of the radio interface protocols, and then the logical, transport, and physical channel structures are presented.

Radio Interface Protocols

The LTE radio interface protocol stack is divided into control plane and user plane stacks and is illustrated in Figure 14.4. More details on the protocols are shown in Figures 14.5 and 14.6 where the various EPC entities and interfaces are also shown in relation to the protocols. As we have seen for protocol layering elsewhere in previous chapters, each protocol adds a header for its own purposes to carry out its own functions. The user plane protocols in Figure 14.5 are part of the ***Access Stratum*** that carries data across the wireless part of the network. The user plane transports IP packets between the UE and PGW. The PDCP transports packets from UE to eNodeB, then IP packets are encapsulated in an EPC-specific protocol and tunneled

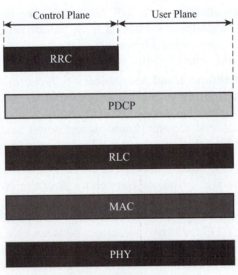

Figure 14.4 The LTE Radio Interface Protocol Stack

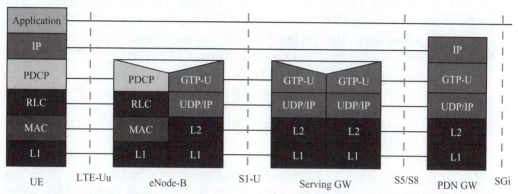

Figure 14.5 User Plane Protocol Stack

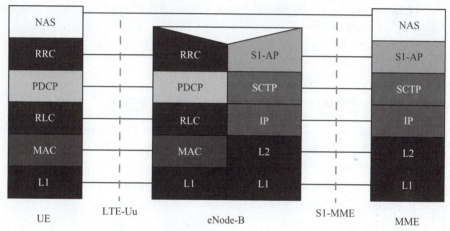

Figure 14.6 Control Plane Protocol Stack

using the GTP through the interfaces to the PGW. The top of the control plane in Figure 14.6 shows the NAS, which corresponds to the Non-Access Stratum for communication between the MME and the UE for bearer management, QoS management, and mobility management. The protocol layers are as follows:

Radio Resource Control (RRC) The RRC layer performs control plane functions for reliable and efficient control of the radio resource. It supervises management of RRC connections, radio bearers, mobility, and UE measurement reporting. Functionality also includes broadcasting system information. Important aspects of the RRC layer are as follows:

- **Two connection states:** LTE has two states for a UE, **RRC_IDLE** and **RRC_CCONNECTED**, in contrast to UMTS, which had four states. In RRC_IDLE state, a UE can receive system information and paging, but does not transmit or receive data. UEs control their own mobility in RRC_IDLE state by performing measurements of neighboring cells and cell selection. In RRC_CONNNECTED state, the UE has an E-UTRAN RRC connection and can transmit and/or receive data. The UE monitors PDCCH channels to see if data are ready to be sent to it. In this state, the network controls mobility/handover decisions.

- **Signaling Radio Bearers (SRBs):** SRBs are radio bearers used only for transmission of RRC and NAS messages. There are three different types of SRBs.

- **System control information:** LTE uses the Master Information Block (MIB) and System Information Block (SIB). The MIB provides the most essential information and parameters that UEs need to know about a cell and how to demodulate the SIB. The SIB contains more parameters to determine if a cell is suitable for cell selection, such as downlink system bandwidth, antenna configuration, and reference signal power.

- IP packet header compression, ciphering of data, and integrity protection for signaling. This supports interaction between higher layers of the protocol stack (e.g., RRC, RTP, TCP, UDP) and the RLC. It supports lossless handovers by sharing data with a destination eNodeB during a handover so no packets are lost.

Packet Data Convergence Protocol (PDCP) Packets are delivered to the UE from the eNodeB using PDCP. The following functions are provided:

- Header compression using the Internet Engineering Task Force Robust Header Compression (ROHC) framework. LTE services are based on IP protocols, but these bring large headers with repetitive information in the IP, TCP, UDP, and RTP protocols (see Chapter 4). ROHC provides various header compression algorithms.

- Ciphering and deciphering of user and control plane data.

- Integrity protection and verification of control plane data.

- In-sequence delivery.

- Buffering and forwarding of data packets to serving eNodeBs during handover.

Radio Link Control (RLC) The RLC will segment or concatenate data units. Segmentation is needed when service data units (SDUs) from upper layers are too large for the MAC layer. Concatenation allows multiple smaller packets to be combined and share header information to reduce system overhead. RLC also performs ARQ retransmission functions for error correction when H-ARQ at the MAC layer has failed (i.e., all H-ARQ transmissions are exhausted). RLC also delivers packets in sequence at the receiver to higher layers. An RLC entity can operate in one of three modes.

- **Transparent Mode (TM):** Simple mode with no header with no RLC functions for segmentation or concatenation. This is used to broadcast system information messages and paging messages, not for user plane data transmission.

- **Unacknowledged Mode (UM):** Provides in-sequence delivery of data, but no retransmission. This can be used for delay-sensitive applications that can tolerate some data loss, for example VoIP.

- **Acknowledged Mode (AM):** Most complex mode which has the same functions as UM but also retransmits missing PDUs. This is best for error-sensitive but delay tolerant applications.

Figure 14.7 shows the formats of the RLC PDUs for the three different modes, either a TM Data PDU (TMD), UM Data PDU (UMD), AM Data PDU (AMD), or AM Data PDU segment. There are different fields for each format as follows:

- **Framing Info (FI):** Segmentation information.
- **Length Indicator (LI):** Length in bytes of corresponding data field.
- **Extension Bit (E):** Indicates whether data follows or another E-LI combination follows. This supports concatenation so multiple PDUs are carried in the data field.
- **Sequence Number (SN):** This is used for in-sequence delivery.
- **Data/Control (D/C):** To indicate the presence of a control or data PDU.
- **Re-segmentation Flag (RF):** Indicates if this is a full AMD or AMD segment.
- **Polling bit (P):** Indicates if a transmitter requests a STATUS report from the receiver.
- **Segment Offset (SO):** For AMD segment to indicate the position of this PDU within the overall PDU before it was segmented.
- **Last Segment Flag (LSF):** Indicates whether this is the last of the segments.

Medium Access Control (MAC) The MAC layer performs H-ARQ procedures to complete the implementation of a two-layer retransmission scheme. The MAC layer performs a fast H-ARQ protocol with low latency and low overhead; then highly reliable ARQ is performed at the RLC layer if H-ARQ is unsuccessful.

The MAC layer also multiplexes and demultiplexes data from logical channels and transport channels (more on channels below in this section); multiple packets can be delivered in a MAC protocol data unit. The eNodeB MAC layer prioritizes and decides which UEs and radio bearers will send or receive data on which shared physical resources. The eNodeB MAC layer also decides the transmission format, that is, the modulation format, code rate, MIMO rank, and power level.

Physical Layer (PHY) PHY functions primarily involve actual transmission of data. Also included are control mechanisms, such as signaling of H-ARQ feedback, power control, signaling of scheduling allocations, and channel measurements.

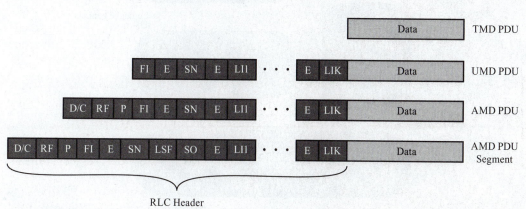

Figure 14.7 Formats of RLC Data PDUs

Channel Structure

There are three types of channels in LTE, and these are defined at the *Service Access Points (SAPs)* between protocol layers as shown in Figure 14.8. To simplify the architecture from previous 3GPP standards, LTE consists entirely of shared and broadcast channels; there are no dedicated transport or physical channels to carry data to specific UEs. By understanding the channel structure, one can understand the data flow for various LTE services and be ready to understand more detailed processing procedures in the physical layer.

Logical Channels Logical channels provide MAC services to the RLC, either for control purposes or traffic delivery. Logical control channels are as follows:

- **Broadcast Control Channel (BCCH)**: Downlink common channel to broadcast system control information to UEs, such as system bandwidth, antenna configuration, and reference signal power.
- **Multicast Control Channel (MCCH):** For UEs receiving broadcast or multicast services.
- **Paging Control Channel (PCCH):** Searching for a UE not connected to the network in idle mode.
- **Common Control Channel (CCCH):** Bidirectional channel for control information when a UE is not attached to the network.

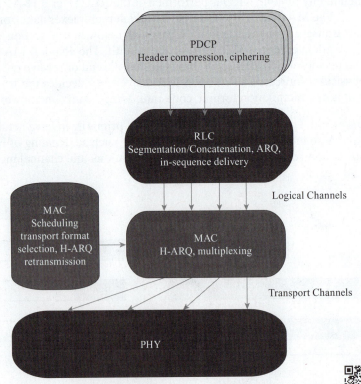

Figure 14.8 The Radio Interface Protocol Architecture and the SAPs between different Layers

- **Dedicated Control Channel (DCCH):** Point-to-point bidirectional channel for dedicated control information when the UE is attached to the network.

Logical traffic channels are as follows:

- **Dedicated Traffic Channel (DTCH):** Dedicated point-to-point channel between a UE and the network.
- **Multicast Traffic Channel (MTCH):** One-way channel from the network to multicast or broadcast to groups of UEs.

Transport Channels The PHY layer offers services to the MAC layer through transport channels. These define the methods and characteristics of data transfer over the radio interface, such as modulation, coding, and antenna configurations.

Downlink Transport Channels:

- **Downlink Shared Channel (DL-SCH):** Transmits downlink data, including control and traffic data, used by both the logical control and traffic channels.
- **Broadcast Channel (BCH):** Broadcasts system information.
- **Multicast Channel (MCH):** Supports the *Multicast/Broadcast Single Frequency Network (MBSFN)* to transmit the same information from multiple base stations on the same radio resource to multiple UEs.
- **Paging Channel (PCH):** Associated with the logical PCCH to broadcast paging over the entire coverage area.

Uplink Transport Channels:

- **Uplink Shared Channel (UL-SCH):** Uplink counterpart to the DL-SCH.
- **Random Access Channel (RACH):** Not mapped to any channel, intended to transmit small amounts of data.

Physical Channels The physical channel defines the set of time and frequency resources used to carry information to the upper layers.

Downlink Physical Channels:

- **Physical Downlink Control Channel (PDCCH):** Carries information about the format and resources related to DL-SCH and PCH transmissions.
- **Physical Downlink Shared Channel (PDSCH):** Carries the user data and signaling for higher layers.
- **Physical Broadcast Channel (PBCH):** Carries the BCH transport channel.
- **Physical Multicast Channel (PMCH):** Carries information for the MBMS multicast service.
- **Physical Hybrid ARQ Indicator Channel (PHICH):** Carries H-ARQ ACK/NACKs for uplink transmissions.
- **Physical Control Format Indicator Channel (PCFICH):** Informs UE about number of OFDM symbols used by the PDCCH.

Uplink Physical Channels:

- **Physical Uplink Control Channel (PUCCH):** Carries control information using Channel Quality Indicators (CQIs).

- **Physical Uplink Shared Channel (PUSCH):** Carries the user data and signaling for higher layers. Supports the UL-SCH transport channel.

Besides the physical channels themselves, there are extra signals included in the downlink and uplink. The ***Reference Signal (RS)*** is used for channel quality measurements. This is especially important for MIMO. Later 3GPP releases have defined various special RSs for this purpose. The ***Synchronization Signal*** is on the downlink to acquire symbol timing and the precise frequency.

Based on this discussion of the channel structure, Figure 14.9 shows the relationships between the logical, transport, and physical channels.

14.6 LTE RADIO ACCESS NETWORK

LTE relies on two key technologies to achieve high data rates and spectral efficiency: OFDM and MIMO antennas. Both of these technologies are explored in summary in Chapter 5 and in more detail in Chapter 6.

For the downlink, LTE uses OFDMA and for the uplink SC-OFDM (single-carrier OFDM). OFDM signals have a high peak-to-average power ratio (PAPR), requiring a linear power amplifier with overall low efficiency and high cost. This is acceptable for base station transmitters on the downlink, but this is poor for battery-operated handsets. While complex, using SC-FDMA instead for the uplink has a lower PAPR and is better suited to implementation in mobiles.

Frame Structure

OFDM provides many benefits over the CDMA technologies used by 3G. It combats frequency-selective fading by using long symbol times. OFDMA provides further benefits by allowing multiple users to schedule transmission on the subcarriers

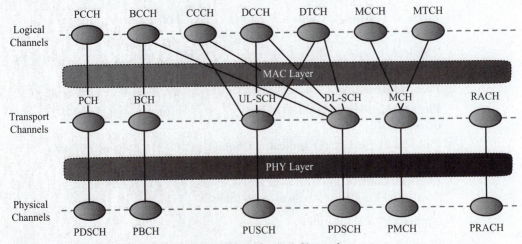

Figure 14.9 Mapping of Logical, Transport, and Physical Channels

which are best for them at the time. OFDM also has a low complexity transceiver structure by using FFT operations.

LTE uses subcarriers 15 kHz apart. The maximum FFT size is 2048, so this sets up a basic time unit in LTE of $T_s = 1/(15{,}000 \times 2048) = 1/30{,}720{,}000$ s. The downlink and uplink are organized into *radio frames* with duration 10 ms, which corresponds to $307{,}200 T_s$.

LTE has been defined to accommodate both paired spectrum for FDD and unpaired spectrum for TDD operation. Both LTE TDD and LTE FDD are being widely deployed as each form of the LTE standard has its own advantages and disadvantages. Table 14.4 compares key characteristics of the two approaches.

FDD systems allocate different frequency bands for UL and DL transmissions. The UL and DL channels are usually grouped into two blocks of contiguous channels (paired spectrum) that are separated by a guard band of a number of vacant radio frequency (RF) channels for interference avoidance. Figure 14.10a illustrates

Table 14.4 Characteristics of TDD and FDD for LTE

Parameter	LTE-THD	LTE-FDD
Paired spectrum	Does not require paired spectrum as both transmit and receive occur on the same channel.	Requires paired spectrum with sufficient frequency separation to allow simultaneous transmission and reception.
Hardware cost	Lower cost as no diplexer is needed to isolate the transmitter and receiver. As cost of the UEs is of major importance because of the vast numbers that are produced, this is a key aspect.	Diplexer is needed and cost is higher.
Channel reciprocity	Channel propagation is the same in both directions which enables transmit and receive to use one set of parameters.	Channel characteristics are different in the two directions as a result of the use of different frequencies.
UL/DL asymmetry	It is possible to dynamically change the UL and DL capacity ratio to match demand.	UL/DL capacity is determined by frequency allocation set out by the regulatory authorities. It is therefore not possible to make dynamic changes to match capacity. Regulatory changes would normally be required and capacity is normally allocated so that it is the same in either direction.
Guard period/guard band	Guard period required to ensure uplink and downlink transmissions do not clash. Large guard period will limit capacity. Larger guard period normally required if distances are increased to accommodate larger propagation times.	Guard band required to provide sufficient isolation between uplink and downlink. Large guard band does not impact capacity.

(Continued)

Table 14.4 (*Continued*)

Parameter	LTE-THD	LTE-FDD
Discontinuous transmission	Discontinuous transmission is required to allow both uplink and downlink transmissions. This can degrade the performance of the RF power amplifier in the transmitter.	Continuous transmission is required.
Cross slot interference	Base stations need to be synchronized with respect to the uplink and downlink transmission times. If neighboring base stations use different uplink and downlink assignments and share the same channel, then interference may occur between cells.	Not applicable.

a typical spectrum allocation in which user i is allocated a pair of channels U_i and D_i with bandwidths W_U and W_D. The frequency offset, W_O, used to separate the pair of channels should be large enough for the user terminal to avoid self-interference among the links because both links are simultaneously active.

For TDD, the UL and DL transmissions operate in the same band but alternate in the time domain. Capacity can be allocated more flexibly than with FDD. It is a simple matter of changing the proportion of time devoted to UL and DL within a given channel.

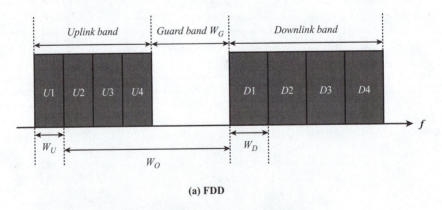

(a) FDD

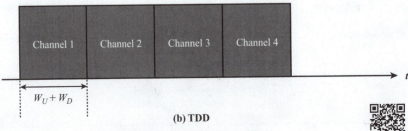

(b) TDD

Figure 14.10 Spectrum Allocation for FDD and TDD

Virtually all physical layer processing in LTE is the same for FDD and TDD, so that there can be low-cost implementation of terminals that support TDD and FDD modes. The difference lies mainly in the frame structures.

In addition to the benefits of OFDM at combating multipath-induced frequency selective fading due to its long symbol times, the cyclic prefix (CP) adds extra time to overcome multipath effects. LTE uses a cyclic prefix of $144 \times T_s = 4.7$ μs. For worse environments, a CP of $512 \times T_s = 16.7$ μs could instead be used. Using the speed of light, 4.7 μs corresponds to a maximum path length difference for multipath components of $(4.7 \times 10^{-6})(3 \times 10^8) = 1.41$ km. The 16.7 μs CP allows for 5.0 km.

Frame Structure Type 1, FDD For FDD, the frame structure is shown in Figure 14.11. Three different time units are applicable.

- The *slot* equals $T_{slot} = 15,360 \times T_s = 0.5$ ms.
- Two consecutive slots comprise a *subframe* of length 1 ms. Channel dependent scheduling and link adaptation (otherwise known as adaptive modulation and coding) occur on the time scale of a subframe (1000 times/second).
- 20 slots (10 subframes) equal a *radio frame* of 10 ms. Radio frames schedule distribution of more slowly changing information, such as system information and reference signals.

The **normal CP** fills 4.7 μs of the 500 μs frame, 144 of the 15,360 samples. An OFDM symbol is $1/15,000 = 66.67$ μs, 2048 samples. Thus 7 OFDM symbols and 7 CPs will fit in a slot, with the first CP made slightly longer, 160 samples. This results in $160 + 6 \times 144 + 7 \times 2048 = 15,360$ samples per 0.5 ms. If the longer **extended CP** is used, only 6 OFDM symbols will fit. The CP is 512 samples, which results in $6 \times (512 + 2048) = 15,360$ samples per 0.5 ms. All else being equal, this means that ratio of extended CP throughput to normal CP throughput is 6/7, a 14.3% reduction.

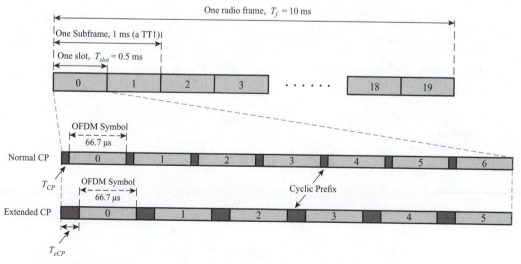

Figure 14.11 FDD Frame Structure, Type 1

For FDD, UL and DL use separate carrier frequencies, so each uses the same structure of 10 subframes and 20 slots per 10 ms.

Frame Structure Type 2, TDD For TDD, the frame structure is shown in Figure 14.12. All transmission occurs on a single carrier frequency. The frame structure is designed to be compatible with 3GPP legacy 3G systems. Each radio frame is again of length 10 ms, which has two half-frames of 5 ms each. There are special subframes to accommodate the switch downlink-to-uplink with the three following fields.

- **Downlink Pilot TimeSlot (DwPTS):** Ordinary but shorter DL subframe for data transmission. It can be 3 to 12 OFDM symbols.
- **Uplink Pilot TimeSlot (UpPTS):** Short duration of one or two OFDM symbols which can be used for sounding reference signals or random access preambles.
- **Guard Period (GP):** Remaining symbols in the special subframe in between to provide time to switch between DL and UL. This is used to overcome propagation delays and interference; LTE supports a guard period ranging from 140 to 667 μs (2 to 10 OFDM symbols), depending on the distance between UEs and eNodeBs.

The total length of these three fields together is 1 ms. Table 14.5 shows seven configurations for sharing of TDD uplink and downlink slots ("S" denotes the special frames). Downlink-to-uplink ratios vary from 2:3 to 9:1.

Resource Blocks

A time-frequency grid is used to illustrate the LTE allocation of OFDM physical resources. This is called a *resource grid* and the downlink structure is shown in Figure 14.13. Each column corresponds to the 6 or 7 OFDM symbols per slot.

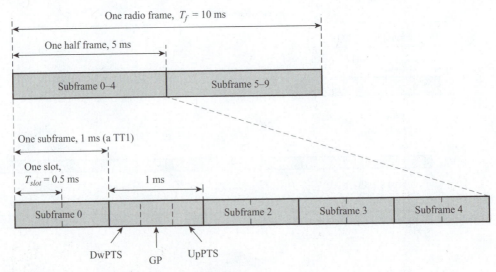

Figure 14.12 TDD Frame Structure, Type 2

Table 14.5 Uplink-Downlink Configurations for LTE TDD

Uplink-Downlink Configuration	Downlink-Uplink Switch-Point Periodicity	Subframe Number									
		0	1	2	3	4	5	6	7	8	9
0	5 ms	D	S	U	U	U	D	S	U	U	U
1	5 ms	D	S	U	U	D	D	S	U	U	D
2	5 ms	D	S	U	D	D	D	S	U	D	D
3	10 ms	D	S	U	U	U	D	D	D	D	D
4	10 ms	D	S	U	U	D	D	D	D	D	D
5	10 ms	D	S	U	D	D	D	D	D	D	D
6	5 ms	D	S	U	U	U	D	S	U	U	D

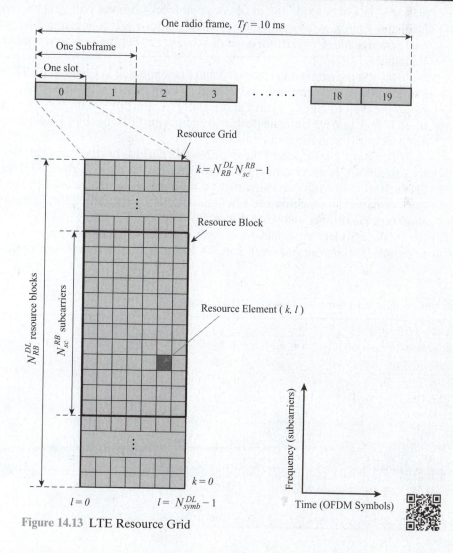

Figure 14.13 LTE Resource Grid

Each row corresponds to the allocated subcarriers. LTE uses 15 kHz subcarriers and allocates blocks of 12 subcarriers, a total of 180 kHz per allocation. The combination of 6 or 7 OFDM symbols over 12 subcarriers results in an allocation of 72 or 84 **resource elements** (i.e., OFDM symbols) over a **resource block.**

Table 14.6 shows the possible channel bandwidths and the number of resource blocks for each. For the larger bandwidth 3 MHz and above, 10% of the bandwidth is used for guard band, leaving 90% for resource blocks. For a 20 MHz channel, therefore, 18.0 MHz is available for 1200 15 MHz subcarriers. This corresponds to 100 resource blocks.

For the UL, carrier frequencies must be contiguously allocated because single-carrier OFDM is used. SC-OFDM is discussed in Chapter 8. Therefore, this contiguous block of 180 MHz for the resource block is also called the *physical resource block (PRB)* because it corresponds to a set of contiguous frequencies.

For the DL, however, frequencies are not required to be contiguous. As a matter of fact, the option to not be contiguous provides the potential for frequency diversity. Therefore, a resource block allocated for a DL connection is called a *virtual resource block (VRB)* for a set of subcarriers, but the subcarriers need not be consecutive.

MIMO is described in Chapter 5 and in more detail in Chapter 6. LTE Release 8 supports up to four transmit and four receive antennas. LTE-Advanced in Release 10 supports up to eight transmit and eight receive antennas. In such cases, there is one resource grid per antenna port. An antenna port is defined by a reference signal, not necessarily a physical antenna.

For both the DL and UL, the eNodeB decides on the resource blocks and uses the PDCCH to communicate these decisions to the UEs. In the UL case, the eNodeB will also communicate different timing advances to be used by the UEs so the signals will be synchronized when they reach the eNodeB. This synchronization preserves the orthogonality of OFDM.

The eNodeB dynamically assigns resources based on channel-dependent scheduling. *Multiuser diversity* can be exploited to increase bandwidth usage

Table 14.6 Typical Parameters for Downlink Transmission

Transmission bandwidth (MHz)	1.4	3	5	10	15	20
Occupied bandwidth (MHz)	1.08	2.7	4.5	9.0	13.5	18.0
Guardband (MHz)	0.32	0.3	0.5	1.0	1.5	2.0
Guardband, % of total	23	10	10	10	10	10
Sampling Frequncy (MHz)	1.92 $1/2 \times 3.84$	3.84	7.08 2×3.84	15.36 4×3.84	23.04 6×3.84	30.72 8×3.84
FFT size	128	256	512	1024	1536	2048
Number of occupied subcarriers	72	180	300	600	900	1200
Number of resource blocks	6	15	25	50	75	100
Number of CP samples (normal)	9×6 10×1	18×6 20×1	36×6 40×1	72×6 80×1	108×6 120×1	144×6 160×1
Number of CP samples (extended)	32	64	128	256	384	512

efficiency by assigning resource blocks for UEs with favorable qualities on certain time slots and subcarriers. These decisions can also include fairness considerations, understanding of UE locations, and typical channel conditions versus fading, and other user and QoS priorities.

Physical Transmission Formats

LTE uses the following physical transmission formats.

- **Channel coding:** For transport blocks, LTE first adds CRC codes of 8, 16, or 24 parity bits. Blocks larger than 6144 bits are then segmented into smaller blocks and CRC is added to each one. These segmented blocks are encoded using either 1/3 rate tail-biting convolutional codes or 1/3 rate convolutional turbo codes. Tail-biting convolutional coding is a special approach for the starting state of the convolutional encoder.

- **Modulation:** LTE supports downlink and uplink QPSK, 16QAM, and 64QAM, depending on channel conditions and UE capabilities. Choices are based on CQI and various other parameters. Of course, both transmitter and receiver need to use the same format, so this is communicated in the Downlink Control Information (DCI). The UE determines a CQI index that will provide the highest throughput while maintaining at most a 10% block error rate on the first H-ARQ transmission. The LTE CQI table is provided in Table 14.7. Then a modulation and coding scheme along with block size is chosen to meet packet error rate targets. H-ARQ will then correct errors. The efficiency

Table 14.7 4-Bit CQI Table

CQI Index	Modulation	Code Rate × 1024	Efficiency
0	Out of Range		
1	QPSK	78	0.1523
2	QPSK	120	0.2344
3	QPSK	193	0.3770
4	QPSK	308	0.6016
5	QPSK	449	0.8770
6	QPSK	602	1.1758
7	16QAM	378	1.4766
8	16QAM	490	1.9141
9	16QAM	616	2.4063
10	64QAM	466	2.7305
11	64QAM	567	3.3223
12	64QAM	666	3.9023
13	64QAM	772	4.5234
14	64QAM	873	5.1152
15	64QAM	948	5.5547

column shows the number of bps/Hz that can be achieved. For example, on a 20 MHz channel with CQI 14:

$$\text{Total bit rate} = (20 \text{ MHz}) \times (5.1152 \text{ bps/Hz}) = 102.3 \text{ Mbps}$$

- **Scrambling:** Each codeword is mixed with a pseudo-random code that depends on physical cell ID and the mobile's radio network temporary identifier. This reduces interference with transmissions in nearby cells using the same resource block.

- **Reference Signals:** Reference signals are used to measure channel conditions. It is not practical to measure every frequency at every time slot, nor is it necessary because coherence times and coherence bandwidths dictate that there will be similarities in closely spaced times and frequencies. Reference signals are inserted at scattered points in the time, frequency, and antenna resources to achieve a balance of overhead and estimation accuracy. They are used to perform coherent demodulation and channel measurement. Later releases of LTE increase the types and usefulness of these reference signals, especially to enhance MIMO and expand to 8×8 MIMO and multiuser-MIMO.

- **H-ARQ:** Turbo coding is first applied to the code block. If there is a retransmission, Hybrid ARQ at the receiver will combine the new data with the previously received block. If no error, an ACK is sent on the PUCCH physical channel. For each retransmission, the same turbo-encoded block is sent by H-ARQ, but with different puncturing. There is typically an 8 ms delay for a retransmission, so LTE allows other blocks to be transmitted in the meantime with an N-channel Stop-and-Wait protocol. The maximum number of retransmissions of each transport block is determined by the RRC layer.

Power–On Procedures

Now that full descriptions of LTE Release 8 have been provided, it is helpful to consider how everything works together to create a communication session for a UE [COX14]. This is commonly considered the power-on sequence, because it involves all activities from the time a UE is completely disconnected until it is successfully communicating. Here is the sequence.

1. Power on the UE.
2. **Network selection:** The UE selects a public land mobile network (PLMN). It first attempts to register with the PLMN to which it was previously registered. If the UE cannot find this PLMN, it scans all of its known LTE carrier frequencies to find another network. If the mobile supports legacy technologies such as UMTS, GSM, or CDMA2000, it will try those as well.
3. **Cell selection:** The UE selects a suitable cell that belongs to the PLMN. It can scan its last known set of potential LTE frequencies or scan all frequencies it supports. For a cell to be suitable, the UE must be able to successfully hear downlink transmissions, the base station must be able to successfully hear the UE on the uplink, and interference levels must not be high.

4. **Contention-based random access:**
   a. The mobile transmits a random access preamble on the physical random access channel (PRACH). If it receives no response, it will keep retransmitting with increasing power until it receives a response or reaches a maximum number of retransmissions.
   b. The base station will provide a random access response. There may be contention with other mobiles and the base station may tell the mobile to randomly back off and try again later. The base station provides a C-RNTI (cell radio network temporary identifier), timing advance, and resources on the PUSCH.
5. **RRC connection establishment:** The mobile then sends an RRC Connection Request to move to RRC_CONNECTED state. The eNodeB responds with an RRC connection setup that configures the mobile's physical layer, MAC protocols, and signaling radio bearer. The mobile responds with the confirmation message *RRC Connection Setup Complete* that is also forwarded to the MME to serve as an EPS mobility management exchange with the MME.
6. **Attach procedure:** Four main objectives are accomplished. The UE registers its location with the MME, the network configures a radio bearer for non-access stratum signaling messages, the network gives an IP address, and the network sets up a default EPS bearer.
7. **Packet Transmission:** Then the UE transmits and receives data. It is now in EMM-REGISTERED, ECM-CONNECTED, and RRC_CONNECTED states and will stay there as long as it is communicating.

   For downlink transmission:
   a. The base station begins by sending a *scheduling command* that uses the DCI on the PDCCH. The scheduling command specifies parameters such as the amount of data, resource block allocation, and modulation scheme. This is repeated for each packet to be sent, unless *semi-persistent scheduling* is used, which allows the BS only to send one scheduling command for a set of messages. This is useful to reduce overhead for services like VoIP.
   b. Then the base station uses the downlink shared channel (DL-SCH) and the PDSCH to send the data.
   c. In response, the mobile sends a hybrid ARQ acknowledgment on the PUCCH. Alternatively, it may use the PUSCH if it is also transmitting uplink data on the same subframe.

   For uplink transmission, the mobile must first indicate to the BS that it wishes to send. If in RRC_IDLE mode, it can use the random access procedure above in Step 4. If RRC_CONNECTED, it can send a scheduling request on the PUCCH. If already transmitting other packets, the mobile can keep the BS updated about its buffer status (i.e., letting the BS know it has other packets to send) using buffer status reports.
   a. The base station begins by sending a *scheduling grant* that uses the DCI on the PDCCH. The scheduling grant specifies parameters such as the amount of data, resource block allocation, and modulation scheme.
   b. The mobile sends data on the UL-SCH and the PUSCH.
   c. If unsuccessful, the base station can respond either on the PHICH for a simple NACK to request a retransmission in the same format, or the BS

can respond on the PDCCH. A NACK on the PDCCH can include a new scheduling grant for resource block allocation or modulation.

8. **Improve quality of service:** If the user needs better QoS than the default bearer can provide, it sends an *ESM Bearer Resource Allocation Request* to the MME. It requests parameters such as QCI, guaranteed and maximum bit rates. It can also give further information about service data flows with IP addresses and TCP/UDP port numbers. The SGW, MME, and PGW share messages, and the PGW usually establishes a dedicated bearer. If the user already has a suitable dedicated EPS bearer, it may modify that bearer.

More details on these procedures are provided in the 3GPP standards and in [COX14].

14.7 LTE-ADVANCED

Since 3GPP LTE Release 8, Releases 9–11 have subsequently been issued and, at the time of this writing, Release 12 is close to being finalized. With Release 10, LTE was able to meet the requirements of IMT-Advanced for true 4G and took on the name LTE-Advanced. Many important technology advances have been published in these releases, but we will focus on those that have had the greatest impact on capacity and quality improvements for LTE-Advanced. These are the following:

- carrier aggregation
- MIMO enhancements to support higher dimensional MIMO
- relay nodes
- heterogeneous networks involving small cells such as femtocells, picocells, and relays
- cooperative multipoint transmission and enhanced intercell interference coordination
- voice over LTE

Carrier Aggregation

The ultimate goal of LTE-Advanced is to increase bandwidth to 100 MHz. **Carrier aggregation (CA)** is used in LTE-Advanced to increase the bandwidth, and thereby increase the bit rates. Because it is important to keep backward compatibility with LTE, the aggregation is of LTE carriers. Carrier aggregation can be used for both FDD and TDD. Each aggregated carrier is referred to as a component carrier, CC. The CC can have a bandwidth of 1.4, 3, 5, 10, 15, or 20 MHz and a maximum of five component carriers can be aggregated, hence the maximum aggregated bandwidth is 100 MHz. These CCs can come from multiple cells, for example, two different macro cells and maybe one small cell. One is named the primary cell and others the secondary cells. In FDD the number of aggregated carriers can be different in DL and UL. However, in FDD the number of UL component carriers is always equal to or lower than the number of DL component carriers. The individual component carriers can also be of different bandwidths. When TDD is used the number of CCs and the bandwidth of each CC are the same for DL and UL. Up through Release 11, the CCs need to have the same mode of operation (FDD or TDD), but in Release 12 this restriction is removed.

Figure 14.14a illustrates how three carriers, each of which is suitable for a Release 8 station, are aggregated to form a wider bandwidth suitable for a 4G LTE-Advanced station. As Figure 14.14b suggests, there are three approaches used in LTE-Advanced for aggregation:

- **Intra-band Contiguous:** This is the easiest form of LTE carrier aggregation to implement. Here, the carriers are adjacent to each other. The aggregated channel can be considered by the terminal as a single enlarged channel from

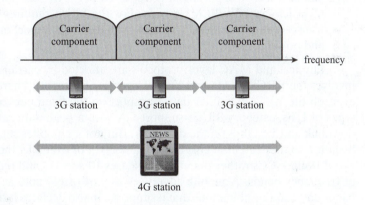

(a) Logical view of carrier aggregation

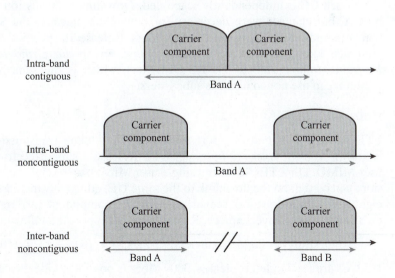

(b) Types of carrier aggregation

Figure 14.14 Carrier Aggregation

the RF viewpoint. In this instance, only one transceiver is required within the subscriber station. The drawback of this method is the need to have a contiguous spectrum band allocation.

- **Intra-band noncontiguous:** Multiple CCs belonging to the same band are used in a noncontiguous manner. In this approach, the multicarrier signal cannot be treated as a single signal and therefore multiple transceivers are required. This adds significant complexity, particularly to the UE where space, power, and cost are prime considerations. This approach is likely to be used in countries where spectrum allocation is noncontiguous within a single band or when the middle carriers are in use by other subscribers.

- **Inter-band noncontiguous:** This form of carrier aggregation uses different bands. It will be of particular use because of the fragmentation of bands—some of which are only 10 MHz wide. For the UE it requires the use of multiple transceivers within the single item, with the usual impact on cost, performance, and power.

Physical and MAC layer protocols are affected by carrier aggregation, so this involves the RRC, S1-AP, and X2-AP signaling protocols. There is no impact, however, on the RLC, PDCP, or data transport on the fixed network. Of the different types of UEs, category 8 UEs support CA with a peak data rate of 3 Gbps on the downlink and 1.5 Gbps on the downlink. But not all mobiles support every category 8 feature so they can limit cost and complexity. For example, they may only support two downlink CCs rather than five (Releases 10 and 11) and only a limited number of frequency bands. A mobile advertises as part of its radio access capabilities the bands and band combinations that it supports. It also declares its *bandwidth class* that states the number of CCs and resource blocks it can handle. Bandwidth classes A, B, C, and D have 1, 2, 2, or 3 CCs, respectively and 100, 100, 200, or 300 maximum RBs.

Each CC is independently scheduled. Downlink transmission is not affected by CA, but changes were necessary for the uplink, because the SC-FDMA format required a contiguous set of subcarriers. Release 10 specified a more general approach known at *Discrete Fourier Transform Spread Orthogonal Frequency Division Multiple Access* (DFT-S-OFDMA), which is the same as SC-FDMA, except it can use noncontiguous subcarriers.

Enhanced MIMO

LTE-Advanced extends support for downlink antenna transmission using what is known as *eight layer multiplexing*. LTE Release 8 supported four layer single-user MIMO. For LTE-Advanced single-user MIMO, up to eight separate transmissions can be sent on the downlink to the same UE, effectively increasing throughput eight times. In a downlink scenario where two component carriers are used with eight transmission layers apiece, Release 10 can support the following.

$$(75 \text{ Mbps per 20 MHz carrier}) \times (2 \text{ CCs}) \times (8 \text{ layers}) = 1200 \text{ Mbps}$$

If 5 CCs are used in later releases, 3000 Mbps is possible in ideal conditions.

If multiuser MIMO is used instead, up to four mobiles can receive signals simultaneously. And the eNodeB can switch between single-user and multiuser techniques every subframe without needing more RRC signaling.

Downlink references signals are keys to MIMO functionality. Reference signals are used widely within 3GPP releases. The UE measures the downlink channel using measurement reference signals, prepares recommendations for the eNodeB, and sends back the following recommendations in channel state information (CSI).

- **Rank Indicator (RI):** Recommended number of layers for SU-MIMO transmission.
- **Precoding matrix indicator (PMI):** Index into a codebook of matrices used at the eNodeB.
- **Channel Quality Indicator (CQI):** Index to table of recommended modulation and coding schemes.

LTE Release 8 uses the common reference signal (CRS) for data demodulation. LTE Release 10 adds the CSI-RS reference signal. These signals are sent on dynamically assigned subframes and resource blocks. The measurement interval can be 5 to 80 ms, depending on the mobile's speed. This reduces overhead by not using resource blocks for channel measurements unless they are needed.

LTE-Advanced uplink MIMO supports multiple antennas. In Release 8, MU-MIMO was supported, because it only required a single antenna on a mobile. This allowed the eNodeB to simultaneously send signals to multiple mobiles. With multiple antenna support on the UE in LTE-Advanced, SU-MIMO is also supported, so that up to four transmission layers are supported between a single UE and an eNodeB. By also adding the ability to use two component carriers on the uplink, the uplink maximum throughput was increased by a factor of 8 from 75 to 600 Mbps.

Relaying

Another key element of an LTE-Advanced cellular network is the use of **Relay Nodes (RNs)**. As with any cellular system, an LTE-Advanced base station experiences reduced data rates near the edge of its cell, due to lower signal levels and higher interference levels. Rather than use smaller cells, it is more efficient to use small relay nodes, which have a reduced radius of operation compared to an eNodeB, distributed around the periphery of the cell. A UE near an RN communicates with the RN, which in turn communicates with the eNodeB.

An RN is not simply a signal repeater that amplifies a received signal, amplifying both the signal and noise. Instead the RN receives, demodulates, and decodes the data and applies error correction as needed, and then transmits a new signal to the base station, referred to in this context as a **donor eNodeB**. See Figure 14.15. The RN functions as a base station with respect to its communication with the UE and as a UE with respect to its communication with the eNodeB.

- The eNodeB $\rightarrow$ RN transmissions and RN $\rightarrow$ eNodeB transmissions are carried out in the DL frequency band and UL frequency band, respectively, for FDD systems.
- The eNodeB $\rightarrow$ RN transmissions and RN $\rightarrow$ eNodeB transmissions are carried out in the DL subframes of the eNodeB and RN and UL subframes of the eNodeB and RN, respectively, for TDD systems.

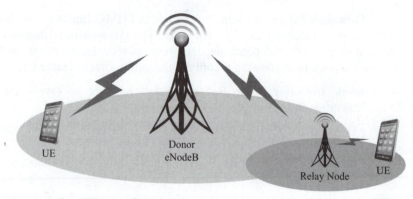

Figure 14.15 Relay Nodes

RNs can use out-of-band communication using microwave links or inband communication. Inband communication means that the RN–eNodeB interface uses the same carrier frequency as the RN–UE interface. This creates an interference issue that can be described as follows. If the RN receives from the eNodeB and transmits to the UE at the same time, it is both transmitting and receiving on the downlink channel. The RN's transmission will have a much greater signal strength than the DL signal arriving from the eNodeB, making it very difficult to recover the incoming DL signal. The same problem occurs in the uplink direction. To overcome this difficulty frequency resources are partitioned as follows:

- eNodeB → RN and RN → UE links are time division multiplexed in a single frequency band and only one is active at any one time.
- RN → eNodeB and UE → RN links are time division multiplexed in a single frequency band and only one is active at any one time.

The relay's non-access stratum in controlled by the MME, and its access stratum is controlled by the eNodeB. In this sense, the relay acts as a mobile to the eNodeB and EPC. But it also acts as a base station to a mobile node. It handles the access stratum for the mobile and can interact with other base stations using the X2 interface for handovers.

Release 10 assumes relays to be stationary, so they cannot be handed over to other eNodeBs. Multihop **relaying** is also not supported.

Heterogeneous Networks

Industry has responded to the increasing data transmission demands from smartphones, tablets, and similar devices by the introduction of 3G and now 4G cellular networks. As demand continues to increase, it becomes increasingly difficult to satisfy this requirement, particularly in densely populated areas and remote rural areas. An essential component of the 4G strategy for satisfying demand is the use of **picocells** and femtocells.

A **femtocell** is a low-power, short range, self-contained base station. Initially used to describe consumer units intended for residential homes, the term has expanded to encompass higher capacity units for enterprise, rural, and metropolitan areas. Key attributes include IP backhaul, self-optimization, low power consumption, and ease of deployment. Femtocells are by far the most numerous types of small cells.

The term *small cell* is an umbrella term for low-powered radio access nodes that operate in licensed and unlicensed spectrum that have a range of 10 m to several hundred meters indoors or outdoors. These contrast with a typical mobile **macrocell**, which might have a range of up to several tens of kilometers. Macrocells would best be used for highly mobile users, and small cells for low speed or stationary users. Femtocells now outnumber macrocells, and the proportion of femtocells in 4G networks is expected to rise dramatically. Deployment of these cells is called **network densification** and the result is a heterogeneous network of large and small cells called a *HetNet*.

Figure 14.16 shows the typical elements in a network that uses femtocells. The femtocell access point is a small base station, much like a Wi-Fi hotspot base station, placed in a residential, business, or public setting. It operates in the same frequency band and with the same protocols as an ordinary cellular network base station. Thus, a 4G smartphone or tablet can connect wirelessly with a 4G femtocell with no change. The femtocell connects to the Internet, typically over a DSL, fiber, or cable landline. Packetized traffic to and from the femtocell connects to the cellular operator's core packet network via a femtocell gateway.

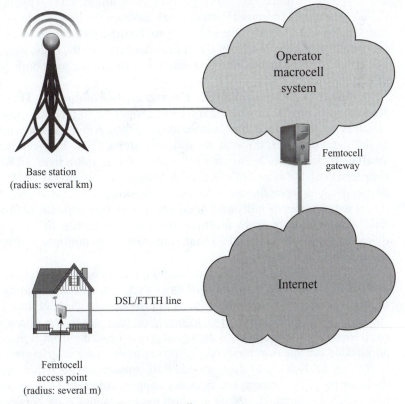

Figure 14.16 The Role of Femtocells

Coordinated Multipoint Transmission and Reception

Interference coordination between cells has been a topic for several LTE releases. Release 8 specified Inter-cell Interference Coordination (ICIC) as discussed in Section 14.4. LTE is designed for all cells to reuse all frequencies, but this can cause interference at cell edges. The X2 interface was enhanced so eNodeBs could coordinate their use of resource blocks. In one approach, cells could avoid using the same resource blocks, but this would reduce overall spectral efficiency. Cells could also reuse some RBs for UEs near the base stations, but avoid using the same RBs for mobiles near the cell edges. This could also be enhanced by also reducing power levels for mobiles near base stations. Release 8 introduced the RNTP indicator, HII, and OI for these purposes.

Interference between small cells and macrocells can be significant. Release 10 provided some solutions, called enhanced ICIC. On one hand, a deployment may expect that a mobile will connect with a nearby small cell, but the macrocell signal could be stronger and the mobile would attempt to connect to the macrocell instead. This effectively unnecessarily reduces the range of the small cell. Conversely, a small cell may implement a closed subscriber group. For example, a femtocell may be deployed in a business and only the employees are authorized to connect to it. An outside mobile would need to connect to a macrocell instead, but would be unable to do so because of the femtocell interference. This would effectively create a hole in the macrocell coverage area. As solution, LTE-Advanced introduces the *almost blank subframe*. Each cell has subframes where minimal information is transmitted (i.e., they are almost blank) so the other cell can be heard with reduced interference. These subframes are not reused between the cells, which means spectral efficiency is reduced, but this coexistence function allows both cells to operate effectively.

Release 11 implemented **Coordinated Multipoint Transmission and Reception (CoMP)**. In CoMP, antennas cooperate to increase power to mobiles at cell edges and reduce interference at cell edges. Antennas may come from those at the same eNodeB, those at separate eNodeBs, those between macro cells and small cells, and those between a cell and a **remote radio head (RRH)**, which is a simple set of antennas deployed away from a base station. CoMP may use techniques such as *coordinated scheduling/coordinated beamforming* (CS/CB) that steers antenna beam nulls and mainlobes, *joint transmission* (JT) that transmits data simultaneously from multiple transmission points to the same UE, and *dynamic point selection* (DPS) that transmits from multiple transmission points but only one at a time.

Release 11 supports these techniques (actually only a noncoherent form of JT) and defines the *CoMP measurement set* as a set of nodes participating in these techniques. The main LTE enhancement is to provide new channel state information to support CoMP. The channel state information provides the set of resource elements to be used for measurement of the signal power (as came from Release 10) and also an interference measurement configuration to measure interference, which is new to Release 11. Release 11 does not add RRC measurements to help determine eNodeBs for the measurement set, does not support coherent JT, and does not change S1 and X2 interfaces. Therefore, it is best to implement CoMP between antennas on the same eNodeB or between an eNodeB and remote radio head, because an RRH is under direct control of an eNodeB.

Other Enhancements

The following other enhancements are provided in LTE-Advanced Releases 10 and 11, and are also likely to be issued in Release 12.

- Traffic offload techniques to divert traffic onto non-LTE networks.
- Enhanced Physical Downlink Control Channel to enable adjustable capacity and interference coordination.
- Enhancements for machine-type communications—overload control, device triggering so an application service can call devices into action, a new device identity known as the external identifier to tackle number shortages, proximity services for device-to-device communications, and enhancements for machine-type data and mobile data.
- Support for dynamic adaptation of TDD configuration so traffic fluctuations can be accommodated, which are especially common in small cells.
- Release 12 also conducted studies for future requirements on enhancements to small cells and heterogeneous networks, such as higher order modulation like 256-QAM, a new mobile-specific reference signal, dual connectivity (for example, simultaneous connection with a macrocell and a picocell), and a lean carrier for use as a secondary cell.
- Also in Release 12, studies were conducted on two-dimensional arrays that could create beams on a horizontal plane and also at different elevations for user-specific elevation beamforming. This would be supported by *massive MIMO* or *full dimension MIMO* that is created by a two-dimensional array with many more antenna elements than previous deployments.

In addition to these enhancements, the cellular industry's main trade association, the **GSM Association**, has defined profiles and services for what is known as **Voice over LTE (VoLTE)**. The GSM Association documents provide additional specifications for issues that 3GPP specifications left as implementation options. The GSM Association also specifies services beyond voice, such as video calls, instant messaging, chat, and file transfer in what is known as the **Rich Communication Services (RCS)**. The IP Multimedia Subsystem (IMS) is used to control the delivery of VoIP streams. IMS is not part of LTE; it is a separate network, the same way the Internet is a separate network. IMS is mainly concerned with signaling. It provides a higher layer capability to use LTE for voice transport.

14.8 RECOMMENDED READING

[GHOS10] provides a thorough background to LTE. Worthwhile introductions to LTE-Advanced include [FREN13], [BAKE12], [PARK11]. [DAEW12], [LING12], and [IWAM10] provide introductions to CoMP, MIMO, and carrier aggregation in LTE-Advanced. [COX14] provides an excellent detailed coverage of LTE-Advanced and Releases 11 and 12.

BAKE12 Baker, M. "From LTE-Advanced to the Future." *IEEE Communications Magazine,* February 2012.

COX14 Cox, C. *An Introduction to LTE: LTE, LTE-Advanced, SAE, VoLTE, and 4G Communications,* Second Edition. United Kingdom: John Wiley & Sons, Ltd, 2014.

DAEW12 Daewon L., et al. "Coordinated multipoint transmission and reception in LTE-advanced: deployment scenarios and operational challenges." *Communications Magazine, IEEE,* vol. 50, no. 2, pp. 148, 155, February 2012.

FREN13 Frenzel, L. "An Introduction to LTE-Advanced: The Real 4G." *Electronic Design,* February 2013.

GHOS10 Ghosh, A., et al. "LTE-Advanced: Next-Generation Wireless Broadband Technology." *IEEE Wireless Communications,* June 2010.

IWAM10 Iwamura, M., et al. "Carrier Aggregation Framework in 3GPP LTE-Advanced." *IEEE Communications Magazine,* August 2010.

LING12 Lingjia Liu; Runhua Chen; Geirhofer, S.; Sayana, K.; Zhihua Shi; Yongxing Zhou. "Downlink MIMO in LTE-advanced: SU-MIMO vs. MU-MIMO." *Communications Magazine, IEEE,* vol. 50, no. 2, pp. 140, 147, February 2012.

PARK11 Parkvall, S.; Furuskar, A.; and Dahlman, E. "Evolution of LTE toward IMT-Advanced." *IEEE Communications Magazine,* February 2011.

14.9 KEY TERMS, REVIEW QUESTIONS, AND PROBLEMS

Key Terms

access stratum	femtocell	Packet Data Network
base station	fourth-generation (4G)	Gateway (PGW)
bearers	network	picocells
carrier aggregation (CA)	frequency division duplex	QoS class identifier (QCI)
coordinated multipoint	(FDD)	radio link control
transmission and reception	frequency reuse	radio resource control (RRC)
(CoMP)	GSM Association	relay nodes (RNs)
dedicated bearer	guaranteed bit rate (GBR)	relaying
default bearer	bearers	remote radio head (RRH)
donor eNodeB	heterogeneous networks	resource block
EPS mobility management	(HetNets)	resource elements
(EMM)	home subscriber server (HSS)	reuse factor
EPS session management	Long Term Evolution (LTE)	rich communication services
(ESM)	LTE-Advanced	(RCS)
evolved NodeB (eNodeB)	macrocells	service data flows (SDFs)
evolved packet core (EPC)	mobility management entity	S1 interface
evolved packet system (EPS)	(MME)	Serving Gateway (SGW)
evolved UMTS terrestrial	network densification	Time division duplex (TDD)
radio access (E-UTRA)	non-guaranteed bit rate	user equipment (UE)
evolved UMTS terrestrial	bearers	voice over LTE (VoLTE)
radio access network	packet data convergence pro-	X2 interface
(E-UTRAN)	tocol (PDCP)	

Review Questions

14.1 What are the major reasons for 4G?

14.2 Which 3GPP releases are related to LTE-Advanced?

14.3 What are the main components of the Evolved Packet Core (EPC)? What are their main functions?

14.4 What are the roles of the RRC, PDCP, and RLC protocols?

14.5 What are logical, transport, and physical channels?

14.6 What two types of cyclic prefixes are supported by LTE?

14.7 What is the difference between the LTE FDD and TDD frame structures?

14.8 What is a resource block? What does it consist of?

14.9 What types of modulation are supported by LTE?

14.10 List and describe the steps in the power-on procedure.

14.11 What is carrier aggregation? What are the different types of carrier aggregation?

14.12 How does LTE-Advanced enhance MIMO?

14.13 What is relaying?

14.14 What is a femtocell?

14.15 What is the difference between eICIC and CoMP?

Problems

14.1 For which generation of cellular wireless network was a >5 Mbps data rate achieved?

14.2 According to Table 14.2, if LTE-Advanced provides 1 Gbps for a 100 MHz channel whereas LTE provides 100 Mbps over a 20 MHz channel, by what factor has the channel efficiency (bps/Hz) improved?

14.3 Table 14.2 shows how LTE-Advanced can use 8×8 MIMO, or 8 parallel streams. By what factor is per-stream bandwidth efficiency higher for LTE-Advanced?

14.4 By what factor does Table 14.2 show that the uplink has lower channel efficiency than the downlink?

14.5 What would be the expected packet delay budget when a user is watching a movie from an online video service?

14.6 Why do conversational forms of voice and video have smaller packet delay budgets in LTE?

14.7 From Table 14.5, what are the maximum and minimum proportions of the subframe used for uplink traffic?

14.8 From Table 14.6, for 15 MHz transmission bandwidth, show how to compute the total occupied bandwidth of 13.5 MHz from the values in the table.

14.9 From Tables 14.6 and 14.7, show the expected data rate to be achieved for CQI 9 on a 15 MHz channel.

14.10 Based on Figure 14.11, show how 7 OFDM symbols fit within a slot time of 0.5 ms for the normal CP and only 6 OFDM symbols for the extended CP.

14.11 Based on Table 14.7, if a user is experiencing a CQI of index 6, how many resource blocks should be assigned if the user requires at least 3.0 Mbps?

14.12 From Problem 14.11, if the CQI index improves to 13, then how many resource blocks should be assigned?

14.13 Given LTE system parameters, what was likely assumed in the system design concerning the coherence time (see Chapter 6) of the environments in which LTE was designed to operate?

CHAPTER 15

MOBILE APPLICATIONS AND MOBILE IP

492

Several of the major developments in wireless networking have come not just in wireless communication, networks, or systems themselves, but also in the applications (or "apps" as they are simply called) supported on wireless devices. A variety of platforms and free or low-cost apps have captured the attention of potential consumers of wireless services. These apps have made mobile computing on small devices very easy to accomplish. Mobile device hardware designers have also included many types of sensors such as location, temperature, light, acceleration, magnetic field, and so on that are used in innovative ways.

This chapter first looks at two of the leading mobile device operating systems: **Android** and **iOS**. It describes the platforms for application development, and then shows the processes for app development and deployment. Then the remainder of the chapter considers an important Internet Protocol (IP) standard that provides application-level support for wireless networking: Mobile IP.

15.1 MOBILE APPLICATION PLATFORMS

Operating systems for mobile platforms are fundamentally quite similar to those for traditional desktop environments, with the addition of lower level drivers and middleware to talk to hardware components, such as audio I/O and cameras. Mobile platforms require the same core systems facilities as desktops: memory management, process scheduling, device drivers, and security. Because of this, many operating systems used on today's modern mobile systems (such as Android) actually derive common source and systems principles from previous systems (such as Linux).

While mobile environments share core systems facilities, their environment and use cases dictate very different needs. For example, mobile platforms will typically have limited computing power and do not run batch programs same as a server would. Mobile platforms also have very different interaction styles. Rather than a graphical user interface (GUI) based on a mouse and window system, mobile devices typically include a touchscreen guided by touch or voice command, and user interfaces (UIs) are typically vastly different. Because of this, most mobile platforms pair a traditional OS for operating hardware abstractions (such as memory, devices, and the network) and provide additional abstractions to tailor to the special needs of mobile platforms.

Today, mobile platforms typically run a core system (such as Android or iOS) and allow third parties to extend the platform with applications that run on top of the framework (sometimes simply called "apps"). Systems typically provide many mechanisms, which separate the apps from core functionality to make programming easier (e.g., so that the app does not have to manually read location from a driver), to ensure a unified user interface (e.g., by providing a single set of GUI elements), and to maintain security guarantees that might not have been present in previous systems (e.g., Android's permissions system).

Resource Constraints

A modern desktop computer or server will have a large amount of RAM and a powerful processor, operating while connected to a large power supply. By contrast, mobile platforms have limited resources. Specifically, mobile systems are powered almost exclusively by batteries and have a much smaller amount of RAM and internal memory, with limited computing power for graphics and computation. As such, many mobile platforms provide mainly user interfaces to applications that interface to remote cloud services. As an example, consider many popular apps, such as social networking, banking, or chat platforms. All of these applications are front ends to applications that are run on remote servers in the cloud, where heavy computation runs.

As an example, an application might use the location sensors on the platform to determine the user's location, and then forward it to a remote service, which does the computation (a database query, perhaps) to determine which restaurants are near the user, and display the results that are most likely to appeal to the user. Expensive computation (such as looking up nearby restaurants and correlating it to the user's preferences) is done on the server, which has much higher amounts of computing power. After the computation is executed, the results are relayed back to the mobile device, and the application displays the results to the user, providing a user interface that allows the user to visualize the results in a helpful way.

The Interaction Layer

Mobile platforms require a much different user interface than traditional desktop computers. Instead of using a mouse and manipulating windows and text, the user interacts with mobile devices primarily by touch or sometimes voice input. As such, the windowing environments for mobile platforms are very different than windowing environments for desktop computers.

Along with input from hardware buttons, users also typically interact with a device by touch (gestures, for example) or voice command. A user input layer should also account for various accessibility utilities for users, which cannot or prefer not to interact with the device via touch alone. These include voice and vibration, for example, which may be helpful for users that are visually or otherwise impaired, and should also account for situations in which traditional input is difficult (e.g., while the user is driving).

Two Example Hardware Stacks

The two largest **mobile application platforms** are Apple's iOS (running on iPads and iPhones) and Google's Android. (The principles discussed in this chapter are similar for other popular platforms, such as Windows phone and BlackBerry.)

iOS runs on a limited set of devices manufactured by Apple. Because of this, developers can be certain about various device characteristics such as display density and amount of RAM available (at least to a certain extent). In iOS, programmers target their applications to a specific operating system version. The operating system version can only be installed on compatible phones. Because Apple controls the hardware running iOS, developers can also tailor their applications to a fixed aspect ratio and sensory inputs.

iOS applications are written in Objective C and Swift, and compiled using Apple's compiler. Applications make use of the iOS application framework, through which they display GUI output, access sensory (touch, location, voice) input, and communicate with the network. These happen using Objective C and Swift libraries, meaning that programmers acquainted with Objective C and Swift desktop programming can move to developing for iOS simply by learning new system libraries and best practices unique to iOS. However, programmers must learn new techniques that allow robust programming for a mobile environment. As an example, a programmer must gracefully handle the case when an application has only intermittent network access.

By contrast, Google's Android operating system may be installed on a range of devices. This means that the range of hardware configurations for Android devices is much larger. To run Google Play, a device must meet certain standards required by Google, allowing the developer to make some assumptions about the hardware, but ultimately the set of configurations is much larger. Because Google does not control the hardware, many third-party manufacturers build Android devices and apply for certification from Google. If the device passes the requisite test suite, it can run Android.

Device manufacturers also compile a unique version of Android called a ROM, which literally means Read Only Memory but now also means the main firmware/OS and system apps. Manufacturers create a ROM specific to their device and include a set of standard applications (such as applications unique to the mobile carrier on which the device will be used). Because of the much larger set of configurations, along with unique differences between individual devices (e.g., a bug appearing in a popular ROM), developers frequently test on a much larger range of devices (e.g., the most popular phones and tablets in use at the time of production).

With respect to programming, both Android and iOS share a similar design. They both include a core operating system, which handles processes (apps), coordinates access to resources, and manages core concerns (e.g., security). Programmers write apps that run on top of the frameworks, and take the place of desktop processes. When an application needs access to a resource (such as the network, location, etc.), it uses the application framework to call into the underlying system, which performs an action on behalf of the application.

15.2 MOBILE APP DEVELOPMENT

Application Development Fundamentals

Mobile platforms and operating systems share many common design challenges with traditional desktop computers, but the differences impact the design of the operating systems along with application development. Application development for mobile platforms typically happens in the same languages as for desktops (e.g., Java for Android, Objective C for iOS). This allows programmers to work with familiar toolsets. To access the mobile-specific features, mobile platforms also provide application frameworks: application programming interfaces (APIs) that allow programmers to access features unique to mobile devices. These frameworks typically allow the programmer to access

- GUI interaction with the user
- Sensor data available (GPS, acceleration, etc.)
- Authentication and account access
- Interaction with remote servers

The rich amount of input available to the programmer (such as location and social media account access) enables applications on mobile platforms to be highly context aware. For example, an application might suggest restaurants nearby the user, tailored to their preferences retrieved from a social media account. The use of this context-specific information not only provides a unique interaction style and allows the design of applications, which present rich interaction mechanisms, but it also provides its own set of challenges (such as security and privacy concerns). The degree of input also differentiates mobile applications from Web services, and explains why many Web sites also provide applications to access their services: the range of application functionality (such as data persistence, sensory input) provided by the framework usually offers more flexibility than a Web-based implementation of the same technology.

Mobile platforms typically use different hardware than traditional desktop computers. In the early days of mobile computing, this meant that applications for mobile platforms were very customized and specific. To write applications for a mobile device, the programmer would have to learn the specific APIs provided by the manufacturer and typically program in a hardware-dependent way. As a consequence, it was difficult for a programmer to write applications for a specific device: they would have to learn many low-level details such as internals of the processor or cater their application to a foreign operating system. As the mobile landscape has evolved, modern platforms utilize high-level languages (such as Objective C and Java) and provide access to system utilities via libraries. This is making mobile application development much more accessible to programmers familiar with traditional desktop or Web-based settings, as they can take their knowledge about these languages and use it to guide their design of applications for mobile platforms.

Many mobile platforms use familiar languages, but provide custom toolchains to run code on the device. As an example, the Android system allows programmers to write in Java, but the Java bytecode (emitted by the Java compiler) is translated to **Dalvik virtual machine (DVM)** bytecode. Dalvik is a virtual machine for Android, which is similar to the Java virtual machine. The virtual machine is implemented to optimize for the mobile platforms on which Android applications run by handling resources in a way tailored to mobile platforms. Similarly, on iOS, the LLVM cross compiler compiles Objective C code to compile to native code that runs on the device's processor.

Development Environments

Developing applications for mobile platforms means managing potentially large source projects. Projects are not simply limited to application code, but include GUI layouts, device configurations (specifying the requirements for the application), and documentation. To develop and maintain large applications, programmers typically use Interactive Development Environments (IDEs). This allows a programmer to organize projects, write code, and debug applications in a unified environment. Just as programmers would use an IDE for desktop or Web applications, mobile platforms provide custom versions of IDEs for developing mobile applications.

Android development allows for a number of development environments. Google supports Android Studio and Eclipse, both IDEs tailored to Java-based development that include custom extensions tailored to Android development. Both IDEs include support for testing and debugging code on an emulator, allowing programmers to interactively design GUI layouts, and manage build systems and source control. While developers are encouraged to use one of these tools, the Android ecosystem also supports using custom builds via traditional java build systems (via ant or gradle, both of which are used by the aforementioned IDEs) and code managed by any other editor (such as Emacs).

iOS applications are written using XCode, an IDE for developing applications in Apple frameworks that includes support for designing for iOS devices. XCode provides similar functionality to Eclipse, but for Objective C projects that target iOS devices. XCode also provides facilities for app distribution.

A Look Inside Android

Initial Android OS development was done by Android, Inc., which was bought by Google in 2005. The first commercial version, Android 1.0, was released in 2008. As of this writing, the most recent version is Android 5.0 (Lollipop). In 2007, the Open Handset Alliance (OHA) was formed. OHA is a consortium of 84 firms to develop open standards for mobile devices. Specifically, OHA is responsible for the Android OS releases as an open platform. The open-source nature of Android has been key to its success.

Android System Architecture It is useful to illustrate Android from the perspective of an application developer, as shown in Figure 15.1. We examine each of the architecture layers in turn.

Application developers are primarily concerned with the *Applications and Framework* layer and the APIs that allow access to lower-layer services. This layer provides high-level building blocks, accessible through standardized APIs, that programmers use to create new apps. The architecture is designed to simplify the reuse of components. In addition, all the applications that the user interacts with directly are part of the application layer. This includes a core set of general-purpose applications, such as an e-mail client, SMS program, calendar, maps, browser, contacts, and other applications commonly standard with any mobile device. Applications are typically implemented in Java.

The *Binder Inter-Process Communication (IPC)* mechanism allows the application framework to cross process boundaries and call into the Android system

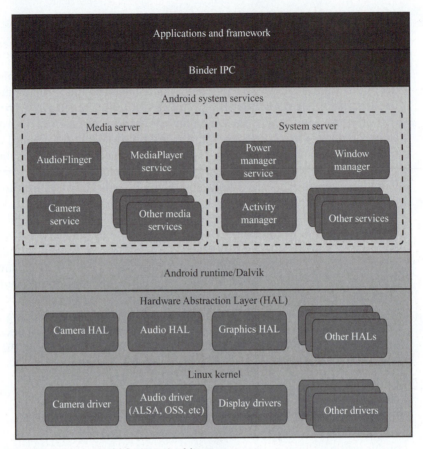

Figure 15.1 Android System Architecture

services code. This basically allows high-level framework APIs to interact with Android's system services.

Most of the functionality exposed through the application framework APIs invokes **Android system services** that in turn access the underlying hardware and kernel functions. Services are codes that run in the background, not attached to a user. Services can be seen as being organized in two groups. Media services deal with playing and recording media. System services deal with system functions visible to the application. The latter include:

- **Activity Manager:** Manages the lifecycle of applications. It is responsible for starting, stopping, and resuming the various applications. This is discussed further subsequently.

- **Window Manager:** Java abstraction of the underlying Surface Manager. The Surface Manager handles the frame buffer interaction and low-level drawing, whereas the Window Manager provides a layer on top of it, to allow applications to declare their client area, and use features like the status bar.

- **Content Providers:** These functions encapsulate application data that need to be shared between applications, such as contacts. A content provider is an extensible interface that allows other applications to access resources in a clearly defined way (similar to a database).

- **View System:** Provides the user interface primitives, such as buttons, list boxes, date pickers, and other controls, as well as UI events (such as touch and gestures).

- **Notification Manager:** Manages events, such as arriving messages and appointments.

- **Power Manager:** Provides an interface to features added to the Linux kernel to enhance the ability to perform power management.

The ***Android Runtime/Dalvik*** layer provides two components. The Android Runtime component includes a set of core libraries that provides most of the functionality available in the core libraries of the Java programming language. Every Android application runs in its own process, with its own instance of the Dalvik virtual machine.

The ***Hardware Abstraction Layer (HAL)*** provides a standard interface to kernel-layer device drivers, so that upper-layer code need not be concerned with the details of the implementation of specific drivers and hardware. The HAL is virtually unchanged from that in a standard Linux distribution.

The ***Linux kernel*** for Android is similar to, but not identical with, the standard Linux kernel distribution. One noteworthy change is that the Android kernel lacks drivers not applicable in mobile environments, making the kernel smaller. In addition, Android enhances the Linux kernel with features that are tailored to the mobile environment and generally not as useful or applicable on a desktop or laptop platform.

Android relies on its Linux kernel for core system services such as security, memory management, process management, network stack, and driver model. The kernel also acts as an abstraction layer between the hardware and the rest of the software stack and enables Android to use the wide range of hardware drivers that Linux supports.

Developing an Application As an example, we may wish to develop an application, which allows users to stream Internet radio stations from links they have downloaded. The app would need to accept input from the user as to which station should be played, stream the station and play the music to the headphones, and allow other applications to query the user's favorite stations. The input code would take place in an Activity, which would allow the programmer to specify a layout (e.g., a textbox or spinner allowing the user to choose a station, and buttons for play, stop, and next station). This code would communicate with a background service, which would maintain a connection to the Internet and decode music, sending it to the output channel (headphones). The application could also allow other applications to query the user's favorite radio stations by using a content provider.

Each Android application comprises a set of the aforementioned components. When developers construct applications, they structure their logic based on using these components as building blocks. The components are implemented in code as Java classes, and declared in a manifest file. The manifest file contains the application metadata, such as the name, icon to be used, set of permissions the application requires, and the main activity (which will be the entry screen to the app). Unlike many desktop applications, there is not a clear notion of application closing. Many traditional batch applications process some input, produce an output, and then close. By contrast, Android applications live in memory, so the user can go back to them at any point. The Android system retains a stack of activities within an application, so the user retains a notion of where they are in the application.

Android applications run in separate OS processes to isolate components and enforce security properties of the system. Because of this isolation, applications must frequently communicate across processes to perform actions (e.g., an application will call into the location provider process to access location information). Android provides a fast remote procedure call (RPC) mechanism based on the **Binder** system, which acts as a conduit for fast message passing and communication between processes. A large portion of the functionality in the Android framework is built on top of this lightweight but fast interprocess communication mechanism.

Android Applications An Android application is the software that implements an app. Each Android application consists of one or more instances of one or more of four types of application components. Each component performs a distinct role in the overall application behavior, and each component can be activated individually within the application and even by other applications. The following are the four types of components:

- **Activities:** An activity corresponds to a single screen visible as a user interface. For example, an e-mail application might have one activity that shows a list of new e-mails, another activity to compose an e-mail, and another activity for reading e-mails. Although the activities work together to form a cohesive user experience in the e-mail application, each one is independent of the others. Android makes a distinction between internal activities and exported activities. Other apps may start exported activities, which generally include the "main" screen of the app. However, other apps cannot start the internal activities. For example, a camera application can start the activity in the e-mail application that composes a new mail, in order for the user to share a picture.

- **Services:** Services are typically used to perform background operations that take a considerable amount of time to finish. This ensures faster responsiveness, for the main thread (aka UI thread) of an application, with which the user is directly interacting. For example, a service might create a thread or process to play music in the background while the user is in a different application, or it might create a thread to fetch data over the network without blocking user interaction with an activity. A service may be invoked by an application. Additionally, there are system services that run for the entire lifetime of the Android system, such as Power Manager, Battery, and Vibrator services. These system services create threads inside the System Server process.

- **Content providers:** A content provider acts as an interface to application data that can be used by the application. One category of managed data is private data, which is used only by the application containing the content provider. For example, the Notepad application uses a content provider to save notes.

The other category is shared data, accessible by multiple applications. This category includes data stored in file systems, an SQLite database, on the Web, or any other persistent storage location your application can access.

- **Broadcast receivers:** A broadcast receiver responds to system-wide broadcast announcements. A broadcast can originate from another application, such as to let other applications know that some data has been downloaded to the device and is available for them to use, or from the system, for example a low-battery warning.

Each application runs on its own dedicated virtual machine and its own single process that encompasses the application and its virtual machine (Figure 15.2). This approach, referred to as the sandboxing model, isolates each application. Thus, one application cannot access the resources of the other without permission being granted. Each application is treated as a separate Linux user with its own unique user ID, which is used to set file permissions.

The Activity Lifecycle Each component in the Android system structures its behavior around a state machine called a lifecycle (Figure 15.3). Activities form the part of Android applications that interact with the user. Activities are implemented by extending the Activity class of the Android API. While an application comprises multiple activities, only one is on screen (active) at any time. Navigating between activities happens by the user performing actions (such as clicking the "back" button on the device) and the application sending requests (e.g., to start a new activity) via Intents (messages sent to the Android system that trigger certain action). The

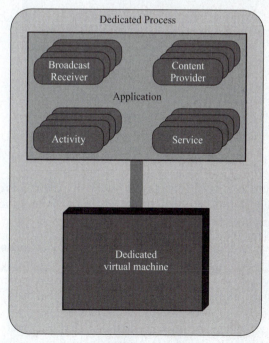

Figure 15.2 Android Application

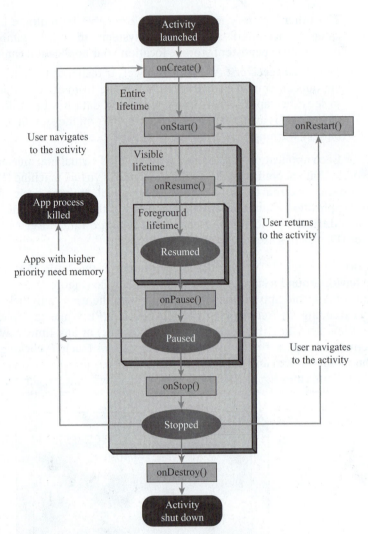

Figure 15.3 Activity State Transition Diagram

Activity class has methods (such as onCreate(), which is called when the activity is first created) that the developer extends to implement the desired application logic (such as displaying buttons on the screen).

GUI Input Interacting with the user happens via **Android activities**. Unlike many desktop applications, Android applications occupy the entire screen of the device. Each activity specifies the GUI layout for what the user sees on the screen. An application may comprise many activities. As an example, in our streaming app, we may have a main screen that presents the list of streams that can be played, a screen to add a new stream to the database, and a screen to set preferences (e.g., quality of the music, volume controls, etc.). In Android, screen navigation follows a stack: when the user goes to a new activity (taking over the screen), they can press the back button, and move back to their previous activity.

To interact with the Android operating system, an application developer will send various messages to the system. These messages are called Intents, and allow the programmer to change the currently active activity, start a new service, query a content provider, and more.

Accessing Sensors Mobile platforms allow highly context-aware computing because of the rich amount of information available to the programmer. Sensor data and user information are accessed by content providers and application interfaces. For example, the user's location is accessed by the LocationProvider. This is a Java class that contains hooks to obtain user location information at varying intervals. The programmer registers a callback with a piece of code that will be run each time a location fix is acquired (which happens at an interval determined in part by hardware constraints). Other sensor and device information is accessed in a similar fashion.

Security By default, applications cannot perform any operations other than displaying graphical interfaces to the user. To access user data (such as their contacts and text message history) and perform privileged operations (such as sending text messages and writing on the Internet), the user must explicitly grant access to the application. In Android, this happens via permissions. Each privileged operation or API will be guarded by a permission declared in the manifest (e.g., READ_CONTACTS or INTERNET). When the application is installed, the user is presented with a list of these permissions, and decides whether to install the app. Application developers should only request access to resources explicitly needed by the application (e.g., the application should never request for contact information if it isn't necessary to the application's performance).

While the permission-based security architecture works for access control, it still has flaws, and application developers must be careful to ensure that data does not leak the application in an inappropriate way. As an example, many ad services require the user's location to provide targeted ads to the user based on stores nearby their geographic location. The developer must carefully think about what information is leaking to what parties, and inform the user when information is being used.

15.3 MOBILE APPLICATION DEPLOYMENT

When a developer completes construction of an application, there are a variety of ways to distribute the application. One possibility is simply to distribute the application as a package and have users install the application (e.g., by hosting their app on a personal Web site). This practice, typically called *sideloading*, is potentially dangerous (e.g., if the developer is untrusted, their potentially malicious code could access the user's private information) and may require devices to be modified.

Because of the problems associated with trusting an application from an unknown developer, most mobile platforms have specific markets for distributing apps in a trusted way, along with the infrastructure to report suspicious apps and maintain quality control within the market. Two popular markets include Google

Play (for Android), and Apple's App Store. Third-party markets (such as Amazon Appstore) also exist and offer different options for users and developers (such as different selections of apps, ways apps are marketed, payment processes, and developer submission procedure).

Deployment to Markets

Each market has a procedure through which developers identify themselves and apply to have their apps available for purchase (or for free). Developers must first register (sometimes paying a fee) and submit various identifying information (such as tax information or encryption keys). Developer accounts act as a point of contact if users report that an app is behaving incorrectly, and having to pay a registration fee can help avoid developers submitting malicious apps that will quickly be revoked from the market (because, e.g., they break the user's privacy).

After a developer registers with a market, there is typically a process to upload their application, typically signed with a cryptographic key that ties the application to the developer that registered on the market (to prevent a malicious app distributor from masquerading as the developer). Next, the market will typically review the app, scan it for viruses, and make sure that it performs the intended function and does not violate any terms of service. As an example, many markets require that purchase in applications happen through the market rather than a third-party service and that an application does perform malicious operations on the user's behalf. After an application passes this phase, it is released on the market and users may install it on their device.

User Reviews and Marketing

Once an app is deployed on the market, users will see it appear on the market associated with the developer's account. Users may install the application and leave the developer feedback in the form of ratings. Because a market will include many applications (Google Play, e.g., includes over a million apps), there is frequent competition between developers to have high reviews and a good relationship with their user base.

Because of the large number of applications in most markets, it can be difficult for new developers to get traction and establish a user base. Because most markets do not have a mechanism for advertising new applications, developers have to rely on third-party advertising mechanisms to market their applications, such as ads on social media (Twitter and Facebook), third-party advertising services, and word of mouth.

Quality Control

App developers must take care to ensure that once their app is deployed, they continue to be responsive to user needs. Developers can help to improve their ratings by responding in a timely manner to bug reports and feature requests, along with informing users of updates to applications and making sure that their application is up-to-date with respect to new system features. Because platforms continually become more powerful, frameworks add new features and applications using old layouts or themes will appear aged. Developers must keep in mind to update their applications to account for current themes of popular applications.

Testing an application can never identify all of the bugs potentially present. Because of this, there will always be errors in deployed apps. As a developer, employing defensive strategies such as unit and regression testing can help to identify bugs early, but there are many factors that developers cannot always plan for. For example, a new device may ship with a unique screen configuration for which the application developer may not have accounted. It is important that when bugs do crop up in applications, developers can reproduce and isolate them in a systematic way, and release an update to users in a timely fashion.

One tool for doing this on Android is Automated Crash Reporting for Android (ACRA). This tool allows developers to detect and isolate errors, and gives detailed reports as to which errors are most important to allow developers to triage bugs. Similar crash reporting systems exist for other systems, and developers should have a strategy for assessing the sources of bugs and determining which can be easily reproduced and fixed in subsequent application versions.

15.4 MOBILE IP

In response to the increasing popularity of mobile computers, **Mobile IP** was developed to enable computers to maintain Internet connectivity while moving from one Internet attachment point to another. Although Mobile IP can work with wired connections, in which a computer is unplugged from one physical attachment point and plugged into another, it is particularly suited to wireless connections.

The term *mobile* in this context implies that a user is connected to one or more applications across the Internet, that the user's point of attachment changes dynamically, and that all connections are automatically maintained despite the change. This is in contrast to a user, such as a business traveler, with a portable computer of some sort who arrives at a destination and uses the computer to connect into an Internet service provider (ISP). In this latter case, the user's Internet connection is terminated each time the user moves and a new connection is initiated when the user connects again. Each time an Internet connection is established, software at the point of attachment (typically an ISP) is used to obtain a new, temporarily assigned IP address. This temporary IP address is used by the user's correspondent for each application-level connection (e.g., FTP, Web connection). A better term for this kind of use is *nomadic*.

We begin with a general overview of Mobile IP and then look at some of the details.

Operation of Mobile IP

As was described in Chapter 4, routers make use of the IP address in an IP datagram to perform routing. In particular, routers use the ***network portion*** of an IP address (Figure 4.11) to move a datagram from the source computer to the network to which the target computer is attached. Then the final router on the path, which is attached to the same network as the target computer, uses the ***host portion*** of the IP address to deliver the IP datagram to the destination. Further, this IP address is known to the next higher layer in the protocol architecture (Figure 4.1). In particular, most applications over the Internet are supported by TCP connections. When a TCP connection is set up, the TCP entity on each side of the connection knows the IP address of the correspondent host. When a TCP segment is handed down to the IP layer for delivery, TCP provides the IP address, and IP creates an IP datagram with that IP address in the IP header and sends the datagram out for routing and delivery. However, with a mobile host, the IP address may change while one or more TCP connections are active.

Two approaches can be used to handle the problem of dynamic addresses. The mobile node can manage the process using a ***client-based*** approach, or the network can manage the changes in IP addresses using a ***network-based*** approach. In a network-based approach, such as Mobile IPv6 standardized in Internet Engineering Task Force Request for Comments RFC 5213, many of the same procedures are followed as the client-based approach, except that different actors are involved and procedures are largely hidden to the mobile node. We focus our discussion on the client-based approach, but again the procedures are similar for both.

Figure 15.4 shows in general terms how Mobile IP deals with the problem of dynamic IP addresses. A mobile node is assigned to a particular network, known as its **home network**. Its IP address on that network, known as its **home address**, is static. When the mobile node moves its attachment point to another network, that network is considered a **foreign network** for this host. Once the mobile node is reattached, it makes its presence known by registering with a network node, typically a router, on the foreign network known as a **foreign agent**. The mobile node then

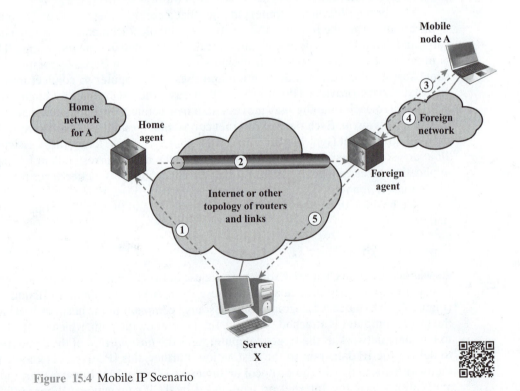

Figure 15.4 Mobile IP Scenario

communicates with a similar agent on the user's home network, known as a **home agent**, giving the home agent the **care-of address** of the mobile node; the care-of address identifies the foreign agent's location. Typically, one or more routers on a network will implement the roles of both home and foreign agents.

When IP datagrams are exchanged over a connection between the mobile node and another host (a server in Figure 15.4), the following operations occur:

1. Server X transmits an IP datagram destined for mobile node A, with A's home address in the IP header. The IP datagram is routed to A's home network.

2. At the home network, the home agent intercepts the incoming IP datagram. The home agent encapsulates the entire datagram inside a new IP datagram that has A's care-of address in the header, and retransmits the datagram. The use of an outer IP datagram with a different destination IP address is known as **tunneling**. This IP datagram is routed to the foreign agent.

3. The foreign agent strips off the outer IP header, encapsulates the original IP datagram in a network-level PDU (e.g., a LAN LLC frame), and delivers the original datagram to A across the foreign network.

4. When A sends IP traffic to X, it uses X's IP address. In our example, this is a fixed address; that is, X is not a mobile node. Each IP datagram is sent by A to a router on the foreign network for routing to X. Typically, this router is also the foreign agent.

5. The IP datagram from A to X travels directly across the Internet to X, using X's IP address.

To support the operations illustrated in Figure 15.4, Mobile IP includes three basic capabilities:

- **Discovery:** A mobile node uses a discovery procedure to identify prospective home agents and foreign agents.

- **Registration:** A mobile node uses an authenticated registration procedure to inform its home agent of its care-of address.

- **Tunneling:** Tunneling is used to forward IP datagrams from a home address to a care-of address.

Figure 15.5 indicates the underlying protocol support for the Mobile IP capability. The registration protocol communicates between an application on the mobile node and an application in the home agent and hence uses a transport-level protocol. Because registration is a simple request-response transaction, the overhead of the connection-oriented TCP is not required, and therefore UDP is used as the transport protocol. Discovery makes use of the existing **Internet Control Message Protocol (ICMP)** by adding the appropriate extensions to the ICMP header. ICMP, which is described in Appendix 15A, is a connectionless protocol well suited for the discovery operation. Finally, tunneling is performed at the IP level.

Mobile IP is specified in a number of RFCs. The basic defining document is RFC 5944 for IPv4. Table 15.1 lists some useful terminology from RFC 5944. Mobile IPv6 is described in RFCs 5213 and 6275.

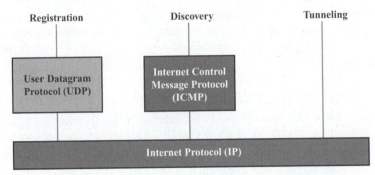

Figure 15.5 Protocol Support for Mobile IP

Table 15.1 Mobile IP Terminology (RFC 5944)

Mobile node	A host or router that changes its point of attachment from one network or subnetwork to another. A mobile node may change its location without changing its IP address; it may continue to communicate with other Internet nodes at any location using its (constant) IP address, assuming link-layer connectivity to a point of attachment is available.
Home address	An IP address that is assigned for an extended period of time to a mobile node. It remains unchanged regardless of where the node is attached to the Internet.
Home agent	A router on a mobile node's home network, which tunnels datagrams for delivery to the mobile node when it is away from home and maintains current location information for the mobile node.
Home network	A network, possibly virtual, having a network prefix matching that of a mobile node's home address. Note that standard IP routing mechanisms will deliver datagrams destined to a mobile node's home address to the mobile node's home network.
Foreign agent	A router on a mobile node's visited network which provides routing services to the mobile node while registered. The foreign agent detunnels and delivers datagrams to the mobile node that were tunneled by the mobile node's home agent. For datagrams sent by a mobile node, the foreign agent may serve as a default router for registered mobile nodes.
Foreign network	Any network other than the mobile node's home network
Care-of address	The termination point of a tunnel toward a mobile node, for datagrams forwarded to the mobile node while it is away from home. The protocol can use two different types of care-of address: a "foreign agent care-of address" is an address of a foreign agent with which the mobile node is registered, and a "co-located care-of address" is an externally obtained local address which the mobile node has associated with one of its own network interfaces.
Correspondent node	A peer with which a mobile node is communicating. A correspondent node may be either mobile or stationary.
Link	A facility or medium over which nodes can communicate at the link layer. A link underlies the network layer.
Node	A host or a router.
Tunnel	The path followed by a datagram while it is encapsulated. While it is encapsulated, a datagram is routed to a knowledgeable decapsulating agent, which decapsulates the datagram and then correctly delivers it to its ultimate destination.

Discovery

The discovery process in Mobile IP is very similar to the router advertisement process defined in ICMP (see Appendix 15A). Accordingly, agent discovery makes use of ICMP router advertisement messages, with one or more extensions specific to Mobile IP.

The mobile node is responsible for an ongoing discovery process. It must determine if it is attached to its home network, in which case IP datagrams may be received without forwarding, or if it is attached to a foreign network. Because handoff from one network to another occurs at the physical layer, a transition from the home network to a foreign network can occur at any time without notification to the network layer (i.e., the IP layer). Thus, discovery for a mobile node is a continuous process.

For the purpose of discovery, a router or other network node that can act as an agent periodically issues a router advertisement ICMP message (see Figure 15.9d in Appendix 15A) with an advertisement extension. The router advertisement portion of the message includes the IP address of the router. The advertisement extension includes additional information about the router's role as an agent, as discussed subsequently. A mobile node listens for these *agent advertisement messages*. Because a foreign agent could be on the mobile node's home network (set up to serve visiting mobile nodes), the arrival of an agent advertisement does not necessarily tell the mobile node that it is on a foreign network. The mobile node must compare the network portion of the router's IP address with the network portion of its own home address. If these network portions do not match, then the mobile node is on a foreign network.

The *agent advertisement extension* follows the ICMP router advertisement fields. The extension includes the following 1-bit flags:

- **R:** Registration with this foreign agent is required (or another foreign agent on this network). Even those mobile nodes that have already acquired a care-of address from this foreign agent must reregister.
- **B:** Busy. The foreign agent will not accept registrations from additional mobile nodes.
- **H:** This agent offers services as a home agent on this network.
- **F:** This agent offers services as a foreign agent on this network.
- **M:** This agent can receive tunneled IP datagrams that use minimal encapsulation, explained subsequently.
- **G:** This agent can receive tunneled IP datagrams that use generic routing encapsulation (GRE) encapsulation, explained subsequently.
- **r:** reserved.
- **T:** Foreign agent supports reverse tunneling.

In addition, the extension includes zero or more *care-of addresses* supported by this agent on this network. There must be at least one such address if the F bit is set. There may be multiple addresses.

Agent Solicitation Foreign agents are expected to issue agent advertisement messages periodically. If a mobile node needs agent information immediately, it can issue an ICMP router solicitation message (see Figure 15.9e in Appendix 15A). Any agent receiving this message will then issue an agent advertisement.

Move Detection As was mentioned, a mobile node may move from one network to another due to some handoff mechanism, without the IP level being aware of it. The agent discovery process is intended to enable the agent to detect such a move. The agent may use one of two algorithms for this purpose:

- **Use of lifetime field:** When a mobile node receives an agent advertisement from a foreign agent that it is currently using or that it is now going to register with, it records the lifetime field as a timer. If the timer expires before the mobile node receives another agent advertisement from the agent, then the node assumes that it has lost contact with that agent. If, in the meantime, the mobile node has received an agent advertisement from another agent and that advertisement has not yet expired, the mobile node can register with this new agent. Otherwise, the mobile node should use agent solicitation to find an agent.

- **Use of network prefix:** The mobile node checks whether any newly received agent advertisement is on the same network as the node's current care-of address. If it is not, the mobile node assumes that it has moved and may register with the agent whose advertisement the mobile node has just received.

Co-Located Addresses The discussion so far has involved the use of a care-of address associated with a foreign agent; that is, the care-of address is an IP address for the foreign agent. This foreign agent will receive datagrams at this care-of address, intended for the mobile node, and then forward them across the foreign network to the mobile node. However, in some cases a mobile node may move to a network that has no foreign agents or on which all foreign agents are busy. As an alternative, the mobile node may act as its own foreign agent by using a co-located care-of address. A co-located care-of address is an IP address obtained by the mobile node that is associated with the mobile node's current interface to a network.

The means by which a mobile node acquires a co-located address is beyond the scope of Mobile IP. One means is to dynamically acquire a temporary IP address through an Internet service such as Dynamic Host Configuration Protocol (DHCP). Another alternative is that the co-located address may be owned by the mobile node as a long-term address for use only while visiting a given foreign network.

Registration

Once a mobile node has recognized that it is on a foreign network and has acquired a care-of address, it needs to alert a home agent on its home network and request that the home agent forward its IP traffic. The registration process involves four steps:

1. The mobile node requests the forwarding service by sending a registration request to the foreign agent that the mobile node wants to use.
2. The foreign agent relays this request to the mobile node's home agent.
3. The home agent either accepts or denies the request and sends a registration reply to the foreign agent.
4. The foreign agent relays this reply to the mobile node.

If the mobile node is using a co-located care-of address, then it registers directly with its home agent, rather than going through a foreign agent.

The registration operation uses two types of messages, carried in UDP segments (Figure 15.6). The ***registration request message*** consists of the following fields:

- **Type:** 1, indicates that this is a registration request.

- **S:** Simultaneous bindings. The mobile node is requesting that the home agent retain its prior mobility bindings. When simultaneous bindings are in effect, the home agent will forward multiple copies of the IP datagram, one to each care-of address currently registered for this mobile node. Multiple simultaneous bindings can be useful in wireless handoff situations, to improve reliability.

- **B:** Broadcast datagrams. Indicates that the mobile node would like to receive copies of broadcast datagrams that it would have received if it were attached to its home network.

- **D:** Decapsulation by mobile node. The mobile node is using a co-located care-of address and will decapsulate its own tunneled IP datagrams.

- **M:** Indicates that the home agent should use minimal encapsulation, explained subsequently.

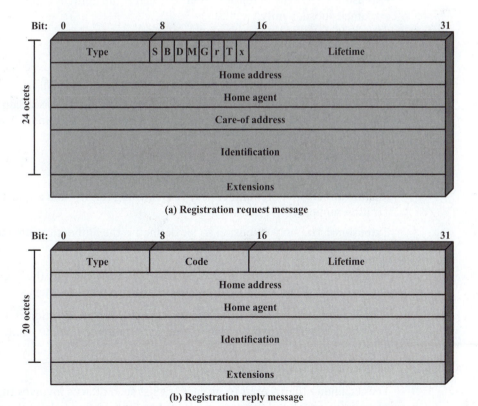

(a) Registration request message

(b) Registration reply message

Figure 15.6 Mobile IP Registration Messages

- **G:** Indicates that the home agent should use GRE encapsulation, explained subsequently.
- **r:** Reserved.
- **T:** Reverse tunneling requested.
- **x:** Reserved.
- **Lifetime:** The number of seconds before the registration is considered expired. A value of zero is a request for de-registration.
- **Home Address:** The home IP address of the mobile node. The home agent can expect to receive IP datagrams with this as a destination address, and must forward those to the care-of address.
- **Home Agent:** The IP address of the mobile node's home agent. This informs the foreign agent of the address to which this request should be relayed.
- **Care-of Address:** The IP address at this end of the tunnel. The home agent should forward IP datagrams that it receives with mobile node's home address to this destination address.
- **Identification:** A 64-bit number generated by the mobile node, used for matching registration requests to registration replies and for security purposes, as explained subsequently.
- **Extensions:** The only extension so far defined is the authentication extension, explained subsequently.

The *registration reply message* consists of the following fields:

- **Type:** 3, indicates that this is a registration reply.
- **Code:** Indicates result of the registration request (see Table 15.2).
- **Lifetime:** If the code field indicates that the registration was accepted, the number of seconds before the registration is considered expired. A value of zero indicates that the mobile node has been de-registered.
- **Home Address:** The home IP address of the mobile node.
- **Home Agent:** The IP address of the mobile node's home agent.
- **Identification:** A 64-bit number used for matching registration requests to registration replies.
- **Extensions:** The only extension so far defined is the authentication extension, explained subsequently.

Securing the Registration Procedure A key concern with the registration procedure is security. Mobile IP is designed to resist two types of attacks:

1. A node may pretend to be a foreign agent and send a registration request to a home agent so as to divert traffic intended for a mobile node to itself.

2. A malicious agent may replay old registration messages, effectively cutting the mobile node from the network.

The technique that is used to protect against such attacks involves the use of message authentication and the proper use of the identification field of the registration request and reply messages (Figure 15.6).

Table 15.2   Code Values for a Mobile IP Registration Reply[1]

Registration successful	Registration denied by the foreign agent
0 Registration accepted	64 Reason unspecified
1 Registration accepted, but simultaneous mobility bindings unsupported	65 Administratively prohibited
	66 Insufficient resources
2 Concurrent registration (pre-accept)	67 Mobile node failed authentication
Registration denied by the home agent	68 Home agent failed authentication
	69 Requested lifetime too long
128 Reason unspecified	70 Poorly formed request
129 Administratively prohibited	71 Poorly formed reply
130 Insufficient resources	72 Requested encapsulation unavailable
131 Mobile node failed authentication	73 Reserved and unavailable
132 Foreign agent failed authentication	74 Request reverse tunnel unavailable
133 Registration identification mismatch	75 Reverse tunnel is mandatory and 't' bit not set
134 Poorly formed request	76 Mobile node too distant
135 Too many simultaneous mobility bindings	77 Invalid care-of address
136 Unknown home agent address	78 Registration timeout
137 Request reverse tunnel unavailable	79 Delivery style not supported
138 Reverse tunnel is mandatory and 't' bit not set	80 Home network unreachable (icmp error received)
	81 Home agent host unreachable (icmp error received)
139 Requested encapsulation unavailable	82 Home agent port unreachable (icmp error received)
	88 Home agent unreachable (other icmp error received)

[1]For the complete list, see http://www.iana.org.

For purposes of message authentication, each registration request and reply contains an *authentication extension* which includes the following fields:

- **Security Parameter Index (SPI):** An index that identifies a security context between a pair of nodes. This security context is configured so that the two nodes share a secret key and parameters relevant to this association (e.g., authentication algorithm).

- **Authenticator:** A code used to authenticate the message. The sender inserts this code into the message using a shared secret key. The receiver uses the code to ensure that the message has not been altered or delayed. The authenticator protects the entire registration request or reply message, any extensions prior to this extension, and the type and length fields of this extension.

The default authentication algorithm is HMAC-MD5, defined in RFC 2104, which produces a 128-bit message digest. HMAC-MD4 is an example of what is known as a keyed hash code. Appendix 15B describes such codes. The digest is computed over a shared secret key, and the protected fields from the registration message.

Three types of authentication extensions are defined as follows:

- **Mobile-home:** This extension must be present and provides for authentication of the registration messages between the mobile node and the home agent.

- **Mobile-foreign:** The extension may be present when a security association exists between the mobile node and the foreign agent. The foreign agent will strip this extension off before relaying a request message to the home agent and add this extension to a reply message coming from a home agent.

- **Foreign-home:** The extension may be present when a security association exists between the foreign agent and the home agent.

Note that the authenticator protects the identification field in the request and reply messages. As a result, the identification value can be used to thwart replay types of attacks. As was mentioned earlier, the identification value enables the mobile node to match a reply to a request. Further, if the mobile node and the home agent maintain synchronization, so that the home agent can distinguish between a reasonable identification value from a suspicious one, then the home agent can reject suspicious messages. One way to do this is to use a timestamp value. As long as the mobile node and the home agent have reasonably synchronized values of time, the timestamp will serve the purpose. Alternatively, the mobile node could generate values using a pseudorandom number generator. If the home agent knows the algorithm, then it knows what identification value to expect next.

Tunneling

Once a mobile node is registered with a home agent, the home agent must be able to intercept IP datagrams sent to the mobile node's home address so that these datagrams can be forwarded via tunneling. The standard does not mandate a specific technique for this purpose but references Address Resolution Protocol (ARP) as a possible mechanism. The home agent needs to inform other nodes on the same network (the home network) that IP datagrams with a destination address of the mobile node in question should be delivered (at the link level) to this agent. In effect, the home agent steals the identity of the mobile node in order to capture packets destined for that node that are transmitted across the home network.

For example, suppose that R3 in Figure 15.7 is acting as the home agent for a mobile node that is attached to a foreign network elsewhere on the Internet. That is, there is a host H whose home network is LAN Z that is now attached to some foreign network. If host D has traffic for H, it will generate an IP datagram with H's home address in the IP destination address field. The IP module in D recognizes that this destination address is on LAN Z and so passes the datagram down to the link layer with instructions to deliver it to a particular MAC-level address on Z. Prior to this time, R3 has informed the IP layer at D that datagrams destined for that particular address should be sent to R3. Thus, D inserts the MAC address of R3 in the destination MAC address field of the outgoing MAC frame. Similarly, if an IP datagram with the mobile node's home address arrives at router R2, it recognizes that the destination address is on LAN Z and will attempt to deliver the datagram to a MAC-level address on Z. Again, R2 has previously been informed that the MAC-level address it needs corresponds to R3.

For traffic that is routed across the Internet and arrives at R3 from the Internet, R3 must simply recognize that for this destination address, the datagram is to be captured and forwarded.

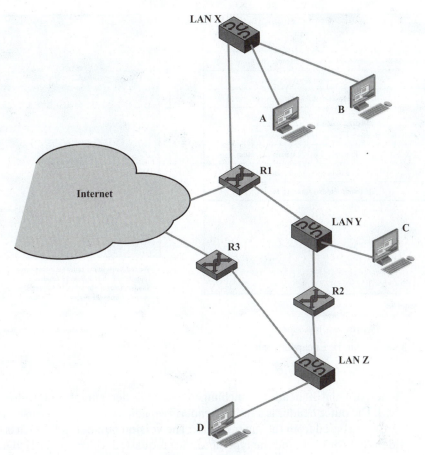

Figure 15.7 A Simple Internetworking Example

To forward an IP datagram to a care-of address, the home agent puts the entire IP datagram into an outer IP datagram. This is a form of **encapsulation**, just as placing an IP header in front of a TCP segment encapsulates the TCP segment in an IP datagram. Three options for encapsulation are allowed for Mobile IP:

- **IP-within-IP encapsulation:** This is the simplest approach, defined in RFC 2003.
- **Minimal encapsulation:** This approach involves fewer fields, defined in RFC 2004.
- **Generic routing encapsulation:** This is a generic encapsulation procedure that was developed prior to the development of Mobile IP, defined in RFC 1701.

We review the first two of these methods.

IP-Within-IP Encapsulation With this approach, the entire IP datagram becomes the payload in a new IP datagram (see IPv4 example in Figure 15.8a). The

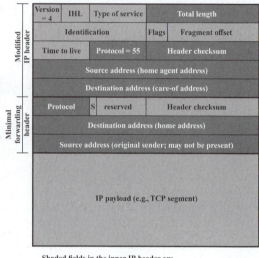

Figure 15.8 Mobile IP Encapsulation

inner, original IP header is unchanged except to decrement time-to-live (TTL) field by 1. The outer header is a full IP header. Two fields (indicated as unshaded in the figure) are copied from the inner header: The version number is 4, which is the protocol identifier for IPv4, and the type of service requested for the outer IP datagram is the same as that requested for the inner IP datagram.

In the inner IP header, the source address refers to the host that is sending the original datagram, and the destination address is the home address of the intended recipient. In the outer IP header, the source and destination addresses refer to the entry and exit points of the tunnel, respectively. Thus, the source address typically is the IP address of the home agent, and the destination address is the care-of address for the intended destination.

Example 15.1 Consider an IP datagram that originates at server X in Figure 15.4 and that is intended for mobile node A. The original IP datagram has a source address equal to the IP address of X and a destination address equal to the IP home address of A. The network portion of A's home address refers to A's home network, and so the datagram is routed through the Internet to A's home network, where it is intercepted by the home agent. The home agent encapsulates the incoming datagram with an outer IP header, which includes a source address equal to the IP address of the home agent and a destination address equal to the IP address of the foreign agent on the foreign network to which A is currently attached. When this new datagram reaches the foreign agent, it strips off the outer IP header and delivers the original datagram to A.

Minimal Encapsulation Minimal encapsulation results in less overhead and can be used if the mobile node, home agent, and foreign agent all agree to do so. With minimal encapsulation, the new header is inserted between the original IP header and the original IP payload (Figure 15.8b). It includes the following fields:

- **Protocol:** Copied from the destination address field in the original IP header. This field identifies the protocol type of the original IP payload and thus identifies the type of header than begins the original IP payload.
- **S:** If 0, the original source address is not present, and the length of this header is 8 octets. If 1, the original source address is present, and the length of this header is 12 octets.
- **Header Checksum:** Computed over all the fields of this header.
- **Original Destination Address:** Copied from the destination address field in the original IP header.
- **Original Source Address:** Copied from the source address field in the original IP header. This field is present only if the S bit is 1. The field is not present if the encapsulator is the source of the datagram (i.e., the datagram originates at the home agent).

The following fields in the original IP header are modified to form the new outer IP header:

- **Total Length:** Incremented by the size of the minimal forwarding header (8 or 12).
- **Protocol:** 55; this is the protocol number assigned to minimal IP encapsulation.
- **Header Checksum:** Computed over all the fields of this header; because some of the fields have been modified, this value must be recomputed.
- **Source Address:** The IP address of the encapsulator, typically the home agent.
- **Destination Address:** The IP address of the exit point of the tunnel. This is the care-of address and may either be the IP address of the foreign agent or the IP address of the mobile node (in the case of a co-located care-of address).

The processing for minimal encapsulation is as follows. The encapsulator (home agent) prepares the encapsulated datagram with the format of Figure 15.8b. This datagram is now suitable for tunneling and is delivered across the Internet to the care-of address. At the care-of address, the fields in the minimal forwarding header are restored to the original IP header and the forwarding header is removed from the datagram. The total length field in the IP header is decremented by the size of the minimal forwarding header (8 or 12) and the header checksum field is recomputed.

15.5 RECOMMENDED READING

A variety of references on Android and iOS development are provided on this book's Web site at corybeardwireless.com. RFC 5213 describes Mobile IPv6 and [ALI09] provides a discussion of Mobile IP and the interaction with the LTE Evolved Packet Core.

ALI09 Ali, I; Casati, A; Chowdhury, K.; Nishida, K.; Parsons, E.; Schmid, S.; and Vaid-ya, R. "Network-based mobility management in the evolved 3GPP core network," *Communications Magazine, IEEE,* vol. 47, no. 2, pp. 58, 66, February 2009.

15.6 KEY TERMS, REVIEW QUESTIONS, AND PROBLEMS

Key Terms

Android	foreign agent	Internet Control Message
Android activity	foreign network	protocol (ICMP)
binder	hash function	iOS
care-of address	home address	mobile application platform
Dalvik	home agent home	Mobile IP
encapsulation	network	tunneling

Review Questions

15.1 List some commonalities between mobile platform OSs and traditional desktop/laptop OSs.

15.2 What features unique to mobile devices are typically accessible via APIs by programmers?

15.3 List and briefly define the architecture layers of Android.

15.4 List and briefly define some of the key Android system services.

15.5 What is Dalvik?

15.6 Describe the Android activity lifecycle.

15.7 Explain the distinction between a mobile user and a nomadic user.

15.8 What is tunneling?

15.9 List and briefly define the capabilities provided by Mobile IP.

15.10 What is the relationship between Mobile IP discovery and ICMP?

15.11 What are the two different types of destination addresses that can be assigned to a mobile node while it is attached to a foreign network?

15.12 Under what circumstances would a mobile node choose to use each of the types of address referred to in Question 15.11?

Problems

15.1 This problem refers to Figure 15.7. Suppose that LAN Z is the home network for host E and that D sends a block of data to E via IP.

    a. Show the PDU structure, including the fields of the IP header and the lower-level headers (MAC, LLC) with the contents of address fields indicated for the case in which E is on its home network.

    b. Repeat part a for the case in which E is on a foreign network reachable via the Internet through R3. Show formats for the MAC frame leaving D and the IP datagram leaving R3. Assume that IP-to-IP encapsulation is used.

    c. Repeat part b for the IP datagram leaving R3, but now assume that minimal encapsulation is used.

15.2 Again referring to Figure 15.7, assume that A is a mobile node and that LAN X is a foreign network for A. Assume that an IP datagram arrives at R1 from the Internet to be delivered to A. Show the format of the IP datagram arriving at R1 and the MAC frame leaving R1 (include the IP header or headers) for the following cases:
    a. IP-to-IP encapsulation is used and R1 is the care-of address.
    b. Minimal encapsulation is used and R1 is the care-of address.
    c. IP-to-IP encapsulation is used and A is the care-of address.
    d. Minimal encapsulation is used and A is the care-of address.

15.3 In a typical Mobile IP implementation in a home agent, the agent maintains a mobility-binding table to map a mobile node's home address to its care-of address for packet forwarding. What entries are essential for each row of the table?

15.4 In a typical Mobile IP implementation in a foreign agent, the agent maintains a visitor table that contains information about the mobile nodes currently visiting this network. What entries are essential for each row of the table?

APPENDIX 15A INTERNET CONTROL MESSAGE PROTOCOL

The IP standard specifies that a compliant implementation must also implement ICMP (RFC 792, RFC 950, RFC 1256). ICMP provides a means for transferring messages from routers and other hosts to a host. In essence, ICMP provides feedback about problems in the communication environment. Examples of its use are when a datagram cannot reach its destination, when the router does not have the buffering capacity to forward a datagram, and when the router can direct the station to send traffic on a shorter route. In most cases, an ICMP message is sent in response to a datagram, either by a router along the datagram's path or by the intended destination host.

ICMP is a user of IP. An ICMP message is constructed and then passed down to IP, which encapsulates the message with an IP header and then transmits the resulting datagram in the usual fashion. Because ICMP messages are transmitted in IP datagrams, their delivery is not guaranteed and their use cannot be considered reliable.

Figure 15.9 shows the format of the various ICMP message types. An ICMP message starts with a 64-bit header consisting of the following:

- **Type (8 bits):** Specifies the type of ICMP message.
- **Code (8 bits):** Used to specify parameters of the message that can be encoded in one or a few bits.
- **Checksum (16 bits):** Checksum of the entire ICMP message. This is the same checksum algorithm used for IP.
- **Parameters (32 bits):** Used to specify more lengthy parameters.

For some message types, these fields are followed by additional information fields that further specify the content of the message.

In those cases in which the ICMP message refers to a prior datagram, the information field includes the entire IP header plus the first 64 bits of the data field of the original datagram. This enables the source host to match the incoming ICMP message with the prior datagram. The reason for including the first 64 bits of the data field is that this will enable the IP module in the host to determine which upper-level protocol or protocols were involved. In particular, the first 64 bits would include a portion of the TCP header or other transport-level header.

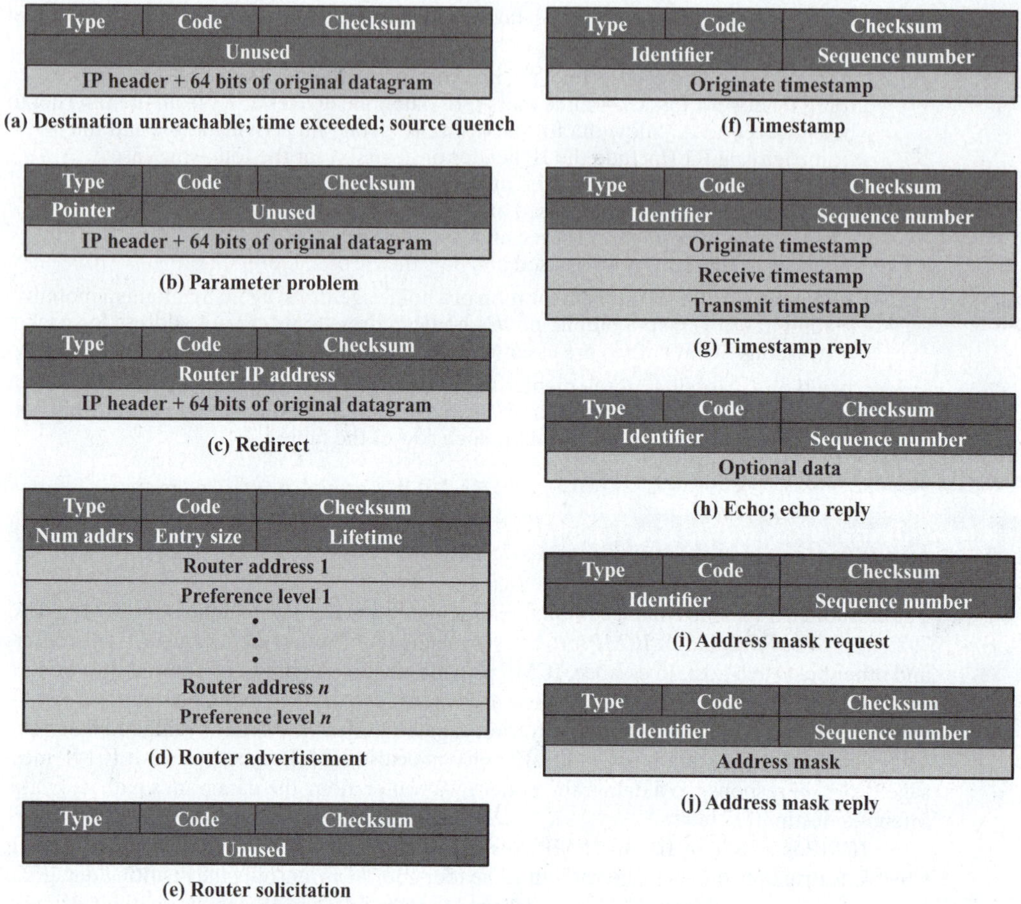

Type	Code	Checksum
Unused		
IP header + 64 bits of original datagram		

(a) Destination unreachable; time exceeded; source quench

Type	Code	Checksum
Pointer	Unused	
IP header + 64 bits of original datagram		

(b) Parameter problem

Type	Code	Checksum
Router IP address		
IP header + 64 bits of original datagram		

(c) Redirect

Type	Code	Checksum
Num addrs	Entry size	Lifetime
Router address 1		
Preference level 1		
•		
•		
•		
Router address *n*		
Preference level *n*		

(d) Router advertisement

Type	Code	Checksum
Unused		

(e) Router solicitation

Type	Code	Checksum
Identifier		Sequence number
Originate timestamp		

(f) Timestamp

Type	Code	Checksum
Identifier		Sequence number
Originate timestamp		
Receive timestamp		
Transmit timestamp		

(g) Timestamp reply

Type	Code	Checksum
Identifier		Sequence number
Optional data		

(h) Echo; echo reply

Type	Code	Checksum
Identifier		Sequence number

(i) Address mask request

Type	Code	Checksum
Identifier		Sequence number
Address mask		

(j) Address mask reply

Figure 15.9 ICMP Message Formats

The ***destination unreachable*** message covers a number of contingencies. A router may return this message if it does not know how to reach the destination network. In some networks, an attached router may be able to determine if a particular host is unreachable and return the message. The destination host itself may return this message if the user protocol or some higher-level service access point is unreachable. This could happen if the corresponding field in the IP header was set incorrectly. If the datagram specifies a source route that is unusable, a message is returned. Finally, if a router must fragment a datagram but the Don't Fragment flag is set, the datagram is discarded and a message is returned.

A router will return a ***time exceeded*** message if the lifetime of the datagram expires. A host will send this message if it cannot complete reassembly within a time limit.

A syntactic or semantic error in an IP header will cause a ***parameter problem*** message to be returned by a router or host. For example, an incorrect argument may be provided with an option. The parameter field contains a pointer to the octet in the original header where the error was detected.

The ***source quench*** message provides a rudimentary form of flow control. Either a router or a destination host may send this message to a source host, requesting that it reduce the rate at which it is sending traffic to the Internet destination. On receipt of a source quench message, the source host should cut back the rate at which it is sending traffic to the specified destination until it no longer receives source quench messages. The source quench message can be used by a router or host that must discard datagrams because of a full buffer. In that case, the router or host will issue a source quench message for every datagram that it discards. In addition, a system may anticipate congestion and issue source quench messages when its buffers approach capacity. In that case, the datagram referred to in the source quench message may well be delivered. Thus, receipt of a source quench message does not imply delivery or nondelivery of the corresponding datagram.

A router sends a *redirect* message to a host on a directly connected router to advise the host of a better route to a particular destination. The following is an example, using Figure 15.7. Router R1 receives a datagram intended for D from host C on network Y, to which R1 is attached. R1 checks its routing table and obtains the address for the next router, R2, on the route to the datagram's Internet destination network, Z. Because R2 and the host identified by the Internet source address of the datagram are on the same network, R1 sends a redirect message to C. The redirect message advises the host to send its traffic for network Z directly to router R2, because this is a shorter path to the destination. The router forwards the original datagram to its Internet destination (via R2). The address of R2 is contained in the parameter field of the redirect message.

The *echo* and *echo reply* messages provide a mechanism for testing that communication is possible between entities. The recipient of an echo message is obligated to return the message in an echo reply message. An identifier and sequence number are associated with the echo message to be matched in the echo reply message. The identifier might be used like a service access point to identify a particular session, and the sequence number might be incremented on each echo request sent.

The *timestamp* and *timestamp reply* messages provide a mechanism for sampling the delay characteristics of the Internet. The sender of a timestamp message may include an identifier and sequence number in the parameters field and include the time that the message is sent (originate timestamp). The receiver records the time it received the message and the time that it transmits the reply message in the timestamp reply message. If the timestamp message is sent using strict source routing, then the delay characteristics of a particular route can be measured.

The *address mask request* and *address mask reply* messages are useful in an environment that includes subnets. The address mask request and reply messages allow a host to learn the address mask for the LAN to which it connects. The host broadcasts an address mask request message on the LAN. The router on the LAN responds with an address mask reply message that contains the address mask.

Router Discovery

A router discovery capability was added to ICMP with RFC 1256. The objective of the router discovery capability is to automate the process by which a host determines a router address. In order for a host to send an IP datagram beyond the network to which it is attached, the host must have the address of at least one router attached to that network. These router addresses can be preconfigured in the host, but this approach has limitations. In particular, for newly attached hosts, including mobile hosts, such configuration files may not be available. RFC 1256 provides a way by which hosts may discover router addresses. It is applicable on networks that provide a multicast and/or broadcast capability.[1]

---

[1] A multicast address is an address that designates a group of entities within a domain (e.g., network, Internet). A broadcast address is an address that designates all entities within a domain. Multicast and broadcast are easily done on a local area network, because all stations share the same transmission medium. Multicast and broadcast are also available on a number of wireless and switched network technologies.

RFC 1256 defines two new ICMP message types: router advertisement and router solicitation. Periodically, each router that conforms to RFC 1256 issues a *router advertisement* message. The message includes the following fields:

- **Num Addrs:** The number of router addresses advertised in this message.

- **Addr Entry Size:** The number of 32-bit words per each router address; the value must be 2.

- **Lifetime:** The maximum number of seconds that the router advertisement may be considered valid; the default value is 1800 (30 minutes).

- **Router Address *i*, for $1 \le i \le$ Num Addrs:** The sending router's IP address(es) on the interface from which the message was sent.

- **Preference Level *i*, for $1 \le i \le$ Num Addrs:** The preferability of each router address *i* as a default router address, relative to other router addresses on this network. This is a signed value in twos complement representation; a higher value indicates more preferable.

Typically, a router will have a single IP address on a network, but multiple IP addresses are allowed. There will be multiple IP addresses for a router if the router has multiple physical connections (interfaces) to the network. Multiple IP addresses may also be assigned to a single interface to serve multiple subnets; this latter use need not concern us here. The preference level is used by a host to determine a default router to use when the host does not have sufficient routing information to determine which router is best for a given destination address. For example, in Figure 12.6, an IP datagram from host D addressed to host C is best sent through router R2, whereas a datagram addressed to a remote host elsewhere in the network should be sent through R3. But initially, if D has no information about which router to use, it needs to send the datagram to a default router. In this example, if the network administrator determines that most Internet traffic from LAN Z is local (to other LANs at this location), then R2 should be assigned a higher preference level; and if most of the traffic is remote, then R3 should be assigned a higher preference level.

As a default, routers should issue router advertisement messages once every 7 to 10 minutes. If all hosts on this network support the IP multicast feature, then the messages should be sent on the all-systems multicast address of 224.0.0.1. Otherwise the broadcast address of 255.255.255.255 must be used.

If a host is just becoming active on a network, it can solicit router advertisements from all attached routers by issuing a *router solicitation* message. Note from Figure 15.9e that this message contains no information other than identifying the type of message. Its purpose is simply to stimulate all routers to issue advertisements; hence no additional information is needed. If all routers on this network support the IP multicast feature, then the messages should be sent on the all-routers multicast address of 224.0.0.2. Otherwise the broadcast address of 255.255.255.255 must be used.

APPENDIX 15B MESSAGE AUTHENTICATION

One of the requirements for the Mobile IP registration protocol is message authentication. This appendix provides a brief overview. For more detail, see [STAL14].

A message, file, document, or other collection of data is said to be authentic when it is genuine and comes from its alleged source. Message authentication is a procedure that allows communicating parties to verify that received messages are authentic. The two important aspects are to verify that the contents of the message have not been altered and that the source is authentic. We may also wish to verify a message's timeliness (it has not been artificially delayed and replayed) and sequence relative to other messages flowing between two parties.

A common technique used for message authentication is based on a keyed one-way hash function.

One-Way Hash Function

A **hash function** maps a variable-length block of data into a smaller fixed-length block. The purpose of a hash function is to produce a "fingerprint" of a file, message, or other block of data. To be useful for message authentication, a hash function H must have the following properties:

1. H can be applied to a block of data of any size.
2. H produces a fixed-length output.
3. $H(x)$ is relatively easy to compute for any given x, making both hardware and software implementations practical.
4. For any given code h, it is computationally infeasible to find x such that $H(x) = h$.
5. For any given block x, it is computationally infeasible to find $y \neq x$ with $H(y) = H(x)$.
6. It is computationally infeasible to find any pair (x, y) such that $H(x) = H(y)$.

The first three properties are requirements for the practical application of a hash function to message authentication. The fourth property is the "one-way" property: it is easy to generate a code given a message but virtually impossible to generate a message given a code. This property is important if the authentication technique involves the use of a secret value, as described subsequently.

The fifth property guarantees that it is impossible to find an alternative message with the same hash value as a given message.

A hash function that satisfies the first five properties in the preceding list is referred to as a *weak hash function*. If the sixth property is also satisfied, then it is referred to as a *strong hash function*. The sixth property protects against a sophisticated class of attack known as the birthday attack.

In addition to providing authentication, a message digest also provides error detection. It performs the same function as an error detection code such as cyclic redundancy check (CRC): If any bits in the message are accidentally altered in transit, the message digest will be in error.

A widely used hash function is MD5, which produces a 128-bit message digest. MD5 is the default hash function for Mobile IP.

Keyed Hash Code

Figure 15.10 shows a technique that uses a hash function for message authentication. This technique assumes that two communicating parties, say A and B, share a common secret value S_{AB}. When A has a message to send to B, it calculates the hash function over the concatenation of the secret value and the message: $MD_M = H(S_{AB}||M)$.[2] It then sends $[M||MD_M]$ to B. Because B possesses S_{AB}, it can recompute $H(S_{AB}||M)$ and verify MD_M. Because the secret value itself is not sent, it is not possible for an attacker to modify an intercepted message. As long as the secret value remains secret, it is also not possible for an attacker to generate a false message.

---

[2] || denotes concatenation.

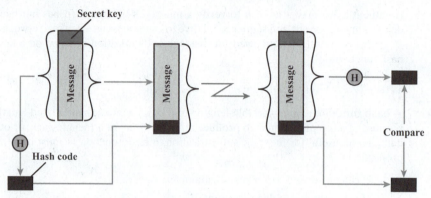

Figure 15.10 Message Authentication Using a One-Way Hash Function

The keyed hash code approach depends on the hash function being one way. If the hash function is not one way, an attacker can easily discover the secret value: If the attacker can observe or intercept a transmission, the attacker obtains the message M and the hash code $MD_M = H(S_{AB}||M)$. The attacker then inverts the hash function to obtain $S_{AB}||M = H^{-1}(MD_M)$. Because the attacker now has both M and $S_{AB}||M$, it is a trivial matter to recover S_{AB}.

CHAPTER 16

LONG RANGE COMMUNICATIONS

> **LEARNING OBJECTIVES**
>
> After studying this chapter, you should be able to:
>
> - Describe the satellite communication process.
> - Identify the distinctions between orbital heights and purposes.
> - Understand the issues involved and requirements for fixed broadband wireless access.
> - Compare WiMAX with Wi-Fi and LTE-Advanced.
> - Present an overview of the IEEE 802.16 network reference model and protocol architecture.
> - Describe the architecture of IEEE 802.16 WiMAX.
> - Define the utility smart grid and the ways it uses wireless communication.

Wireless communication has a rich history and vital current usage for long range communications. These include satellite communications, fixed wireless communication, and applications for monitoring and control of critical infrastructure like the electric power grid, pipelines, and roadways.

This chapter begins with a discussion of satellite technology principles and current technologies. IEEE 802.16 WiMax is then discussed as an example of fixed wireless communication. And finally, the chapter discusses the topic of *smart grid*, which is an innovation of intelligence, control, and communication technologies for control and monitoring of the electric power **transmission** and **distribution** grid. Smart grid is an excellent example of a vital application of long distance wireless communication.

16.1 SATELLITE PARAMETERS AND CONFIGURATIONS

Satellite communications is comparable in importance to optical fiber in the evolution of telecommunications and data communications. This section provides an introduction to key concerns and parameters related to the use of satellite antennas in wireless communications. Subsequent sections explore satellite capacity allocation and applications.

The heart of a satellite communications system is a satellite-based antenna in a stable orbit above the earth. In a satellite communications system, two or more stations on or near the earth communicate via one or more satellites that serve as relay stations in space. The antenna systems on or near the earth are referred to as **earth stations**. A transmission from an earth station to the satellite is referred to as **uplink**, whereas transmissions from the satellite to the earth station are referred to as **downlink**. The component in the satellite that takes an uplink signal and converts it to a downlink signal is called a **transponder**.

There are a number of different ways of categorizing communications satellites:

- **Coverage area:** Global, regional, or national. The larger the area of coverage, the more satellites must be involved in a single networked system.
- **Service type:** Fixed service satellite (FSS), broadcast service satellite (BSS), and mobile service satellite (MSS). This chapter is concerned with FSS and BSS types.
- **General usage:** Commercial, military, amateur, experimental.

There are a number of differences between satellite-based and terrestrial wireless communications that affect design:

- The area of coverage of a satellite system far exceeds that of a terrestrial system. In the case of a geostationary satellite, a single antenna is visible to about one-fourth of the earth's surface.
- Spacecraft power and allocated bandwidth are limited resources that call for careful tradeoffs in earth station/satellite design parameters.
- Conditions between communicating satellites are more time invariant than those between satellite and earth station or between two terrestrial wireless antennas. Thus, satellite-to-satellite communication links can be designed with great precision.
- Transmission cost is independent of distance, within the satellite's area of coverage.
- Broadcast, multicast, and point-to-point applications are readily accommodated.
- Very high bandwidths or data rates are available to the user.
- Although satellite links are subject to short-term outages or degradations, the quality of transmission is normally extremely high.
- For a geostationary satellite, there is an earth-satellite-earth propagation delay of about one-fourth of a second.
- A transmitting earth station can in many cases receive its own transmission.

Satellite Orbits

Satellite orbits may be classified in a number of ways:

1. The orbit may be circular, with the center of the circle at the center of the earth, or elliptical, with the earth's center at one of the two foci of the ellipse.

2. A satellite may orbit around the earth in different planes. An *equatorial orbit* is directly above the earth's equator. A *polar orbit* passes over both poles. Other orbits are referred to as *inclined orbits*.

3. The altitude of communications satellites is classified as **geostationary orbit (GEO)**, **medium earth orbit (MEO)**, and **low earth orbit (LEO)**, as explained subsequently.

Distance Figure 16.1 illustrates the geometry that dictates satellite coverage. A key factor is the *elevation angle* θ of the earth station, which is the angle from the horizontal (i.e., a line tangent to the surface of the earth at the antenna's location) to the point on the center of the main beam of the antenna when the antenna is pointed directly at the satellite. To obtain maximum satellite coverage, we would like to use an elevation angle of 0°, which would enable the satellite's coverage to extend to the optical horizon from the satellite in all directions. However, three problems dictate that the *minimum elevation angle* of the earth station's antenna be somewhat greater than 0° [INGL97]:

1. Buildings, trees, and other terrestrial objects that would block the line of sight. These may result in attenuation of the signal by absorption or in distortions due to multipath reflection.

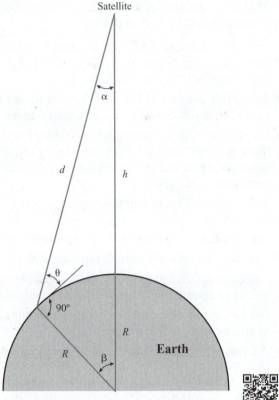

Figure 16.1 Coverage and Elevation Angles

2. Atmospheric attenuation is greater at low elevation angles because the signal traverses the atmosphere for longer distances the smaller the elevation angle.

3. Electrical noise generated by the earth's heat near its surface adversely affects reception.

For downlinks, current design practice is to use a minimum elevation angle of from 5° to 20° depending on frequency. For uplinks, the FCC requires a minimum elevation angle of 5°.

The *coverage angle* β is a measure of the portion of the earth's surface visible to the satellite taking into account the minimum elevation angle; β defines a circle on the earth's surface centered on the point directly below the satellite. The following equation holds:[1]

$$\frac{R}{R + h} = \frac{\sin(\alpha)}{\sin\left(\theta + \dfrac{\pi}{2}\right)} = \frac{\sin\left(\dfrac{\pi}{2} - \beta - \theta\right)}{\sin\left(\theta + \dfrac{\pi}{2}\right)} = \frac{\cos(\beta + \theta)}{\cos(\theta)}$$

---

[1]The first equation uses the law of sines, which states that in any triangle the sides are proportional to the sines of the opposite angles. The second equation uses that fact that the sum of the angles of a triangle equals π. The third equation uses the trigonometric identity $\sin(x) = \cos(x - \pi/2)$.

where

R = earth's radius, 6370 km
h = orbit height (altitude from point on earth directly below satellite)
β = coverage angle
θ = minimum elevation angle

The distance from the satellite to the furthest point of coverage is calculated as follows:

$$\frac{d}{R+h} = \frac{\sin\beta}{\sin\left(\theta + \dfrac{\pi}{2}\right)} = \frac{\sin\beta}{\cos(\theta)}$$

$$d = \frac{(R+h)\sin\beta}{\cos\theta} = \frac{R\sin\beta}{\sin\alpha}$$

(16.1)

The round-trip transmission delay is therefore in the range:

$$\frac{2h}{c} \leq t \leq \frac{2(R+h)\sin\beta}{c(\cos\theta)}$$

where c is the speed of light, approximately 3×10^8 m/s.

The coverage of a satellite is typically expressed as the diameter of the area covered, which is just $2\beta R$, with β expressed in radians.

Figure 16.2 shows the satellite period of rotation, coverage (in terms of terrestrial radius of coverage), and the maximum round-trip propagation delay.

Geostationary Satellites Table 16.1, based on one in [ITU02], classifies satellites on the bases of their altitude range. The most common type of communications satellite today is the **geostationary (GEO)** satellite, first proposed by the science fiction author Arthur C. Clarke, in a 1945 article in *Wireless World*. If the satellite is in a circular orbit 35,863 km above the earth's surface and rotates in the equatorial plane of the earth, it will rotate at exactly the same angular speed as the earth and will remain above the same spot on the equator as the earth rotates.[2] Figure 16.3 depicts the GEO orbit in scale with the size of the earth; the satellite symbols are intended to suggest that there are many satellites in GEO orbit, some of which are quite close together.

The GEO orbit has several advantages to recommend it:

- Because the satellite is stationary relative to the earth, there is no problem with frequency changes due to the relative motion of the satellite and antennas on earth (Doppler effect).

- Tracking of the satellite by its earth stations is simplified.

---

[2]The term *geosynchronous* is often used in place of *geostationary*. For purists, the difference is that a geosynchronous orbit is any circular orbit at an altitude of 35,863 km, and a geostationary orbit is a geosynchronous orbit with zero inclination, so the satellite hovers over one spot on the earth's equator.

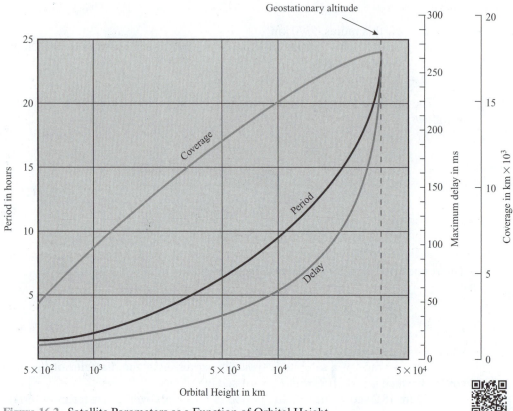

Figure 16.2 Satellite Parameters as a Function of Orbital Height

Table 16.1 Orbital Comparison for Satellite Communications Applications

ORBITS	LEO	MEO	GEO
Orbital period	1.5 to 2 h	5 to 10 h	24 h
Altitude range	500 to 1500 km	8000 to 18,000 km	35,863 km
Visibility duration	15 to 20 min/pass	2 to 8 hr/pass	Permanent
Elevation	Rapid variations; high and low angles	Slow variations; high angles	No variation; low angles at high latitudes
Round-trip propagation delay	Several milliseconds	Tens of milliseconds	≈ 250 ms
Instantaneous ground coverage (diameter at 10° elevation)	≈ 6000 km	≈ 12,000 to 15,000 km	16,000 km
Examples of systems	Iridium Globalstar Teledesic Skybridge Orbcomm	Odyssey Inmarsat	Intelstat Interspoutnik Inmarsat

Figure 16.3 Geostationary Earth Orbit (GEO)

- At 35,863 km above the earth the satellite can communicate with roughly a fourth of the earth; three satellites in geostationary orbit separated by 120° cover most of the inhabited portions of the entire earth excluding only the areas near the north and south poles.

On the other hand, there are problems:

- The signal can get quite weak after traveling over 35,000 km.
- The polar regions and the far northern and southern hemispheres are poorly served by geostationary satellites.
- Even at the speed of light, about 300,000 km/s, the delay in sending a signal from a point on the equator beneath the satellite to the satellite and back is substantial.

The delay of communication between two locations on earth directly under the satellite is in fact $(2 \times 35{,}863)/300{,}000 \approx 0.24$ s. For other locations not directly under the satellite, the delay is even longer. If the satellite link is used for telephone communication, the added delay between when a person speaks and when that person receives a response is almost 0.5 s. This is definitely noticeable. Another feature of geostationary satellites is that they use their assigned frequencies over a very large area. For point-to-multipoint (PMP) applications such as broadcasting TV programs, this can be desirable, but for point-to-point communications it is very wasteful of spectrum. Special spot and steered beam antennas, which restrict the area covered by the satellite's signal, can be used to control the "footprint" or signaling area. To solve some of these problems, orbits other than geostationary have been designed for satellites. Low-earth-orbiting satellites (LEOSs) and medium-earth-orbiting satellites (MEOSs) are important for third-generation personal communications.

LEO Satellites LEOs (Figure 16.4a) have the characteristics listed in Table 16.1. Because the motion of the satellite relative to a fixed point on earth is high, the system must be able to cope with large Doppler shifts, which change the frequency of the signal. The atmospheric drag on a LEO satellite is significant, resulting in gradual orbital deterioration.

Practical use of this system requires the multiple orbital planes be used, each with multiple satellites in orbit. Communication between two earth stations typically will involve handing off the signal from one satellite to another.

LEO satellites have a number of advantages over GEO satellites. In addition to the reduced propagation delay mentioned previously, a received LEO signal is much stronger than that of GEO signals for the same transmission power. LEO coverage can be better localized so that spectrum can be better conserved. For this reason, this technology is currently being proposed for communicating with mobile terminals and with personal terminals that need stronger signals to function. On the other hand, to provide broad coverage over 24 hours, many satellites are needed.

A number of commercial proposals have been made to use clusters of LEOs to provide communications services. These proposals can be divided into two categories:

- **Little LEOs:** Intended to work at communication frequencies below 1 GHz using no more than 5 MHz of bandwidth and supporting data rates up to 10 kbps. These systems are aimed at paging, tracking, and low-rate messaging. Orbcomm is an example of such a satellite system. It was the first (little) LEO in operation; its first two satellites were launched in April of 1995. It is designed for paging and burst communication and is optimized for handling small bursts of data from 6 to 250 bytes in length. It is used by businesses to track trailers, railcars, heavy equipment, and other remote and mobile assets. It can also be used to monitor remote utility meters and oil and gas storage tanks, wells, and pipelines. It can be used to stay in touch with remote workers anywhere in the world as well. It uses the frequencies 148.00 to 150.05 MHz to the satellites, and 137.00 to 138.00 MHz from the satellites. It has well over 30 satellites in LEO. It supports subscriber data rates of 2.4 kbps to the satellite and 4.8 kbps down.

- **Big LEOs:** Work at frequencies above 1 GHz and support data rates up to a few megabits per second. These systems tend to offer the same services as those of small LEOs, with the addition of voice and positioning services.

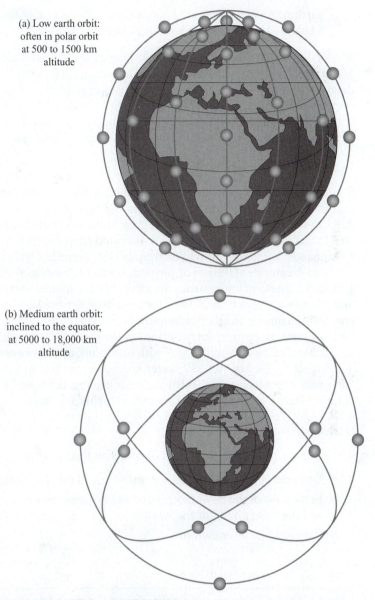

(a) Low earth orbit:
often in polar orbit
at 500 to 1500 km
altitude

(b) Medium earth orbit:
inclined to the equator,
at 5000 to 18,000 km
altitude

Figure 16.4   LEO and MEO Orbits

Globalstar is one example of a big LEO system. Its satellites are fairly rudimentary. Unlike some of the little LEO systems, it has no onboard processing
or communications between satellites. Most processing is done by the system's
earth stations. It uses CDMA as in the CDMA cellular standard. It uses the
S band (about 2 GHz) for the downlink to mobile users. Globalstar is tightly
integrated with traditional voice carriers. All calls must be processed through

earth stations. The satellite constellation consists of 48 operating satellites and 8 spares. They are in 1413-km-high orbits.

MEO Satellites MEOs (Figure 16.4b) have the characteristics listed in Table 16.1. MEO satellites require much fewer handoffs than LEO satellites. While propagation delay to earth from such satellites and the power required are greater than for LEOs, they are still substantially less than for GEO satellites. A prime example of MEOs is the Global Positioning System (GPS). This is discussed in a separate subsection below related to example applications of satellite technology.

Frequency Bands

Table 16.2 lists the frequency bands available for satellite communications. Note that increasing bandwidth is available in the higher-frequency bands. However, in general, the higher the frequency, the greater the effect of transmission impairments. The mobile satellite service (MSS) is allocated frequencies in the L and S bands. In these bands, compared to higher frequencies, there is a greater degree of refraction and greater penetration of physical obstacles, such as foliage and nonmetallic structures. These characteristics are desirable for mobile services. However, the L and S bands are also heavily used for terrestrial applications. Thus, there is intense competition among the various microwave services for L and S band capacity.

For any given frequency allocation for a service, there is an allocation of an uplink band and a downlink band, with the uplink band always of higher frequency. The higher frequency suffers greater spreading, or free space loss, than its lower-frequency counterpart. The earth station is capable of higher power, which helps to compensate for the poorer performance at higher frequency.

Transmission Impairments

The performance of a satellite link depends on three factors:

- Distance between earth station antenna and satellite antenna.
- In the case of the downlink, terrestrial distance between earth station antenna and the "aim point" of the satellite.
- Atmospheric attenuation.

Table 16.2 Frequency Bands for Satellite Communications

Band	Frequency Range	Total Bandwidth	General Application
L	1 to 2 GHz	1 GHz	Mobile satellite service (MSS)
S	2 to 4 GHz	2 GHz	MSS, NASA, deep space research
C	4 to 8 GHz	4 GHz	Fixed satellite service (FSS)
X	8 to 12.5 GHz	4.5 GHz	FSS military, terrestrial earth exploration, and meteorological satellites
Ku	12.5 to 18 GHz	5.5 GHz	FSS, broadcast satellite service (BSS)
K	18 to 26.5 GHz	8.5 GHz	BSS, FSS
Ka	26.5 to 40 GHz	13.5 GHz	FSS

We look at each of these factors in turn.

Distance Recall from Equation (5.2) that free space loss can be expressed as:

$$L_{dB} = 10\log\frac{P_t}{P_r} = 20\log\left(\frac{4\pi d}{\lambda}\right) = -20\log(\lambda) + 20\log(d) + 21.98 \text{ dB} \quad (16.2)$$

where

P_t = signal power at the transmitting antenna
P_r = signal power at the receiving antenna
λ = carrier wavelength
d = propagation distance between antennas

and d and λ are in the same units (e.g., meters).

The higher the frequency (shorter the wavelength), the greater the loss. For a GEO satellite, the free space loss at the equator is

$$L_{db} = -20\log(\lambda) + 20\log(35.863 \times 10^6) + 21.98 \text{ dB}$$

$$= -20\log(\lambda) + 173.07 \text{ dB}$$

Losses at points on the surface of the earth away from the equator but still visible from the satellite will be somewhat higher. The maximum distance (from the satellite to the horizon) for a GEO satellite is 42,711 km. At this distance, the free space loss is

$$L_{db} = -20\log(\lambda) + 174.59 \text{ dB}$$

Figure 16.5 plots the attenuation as a function of frequency and orbital height.

Satellite Footprint At microwave frequencies, which are used in satellite communications, highly directional antennas are used. Thus, the signal from a satellite is not isotropically broadcast but is aimed at a specific point on the earth, depending on which area of coverage is desired. The center point of that area will receive the highest radiated power, and the power drops off as you move away from the center point in any direction. This effect is typically displayed in a pattern known as a **satellite footprint**; an example is shown in Figure 16.6. The satellite footprint displays the effective radiated power of the antenna at each point, taking into account the signal power fed into the antenna and the directionality of the antenna. In the example figure, the power for Arkansas is +36 dBW and for Massachusetts is +32 dBW. The actual power received at any point on the footprint is found by subtracting the free space loss from the effective power figure.

Atmospheric Attenuation The primary causes of atmospheric attenuation are oxygen, which is of course always present, and water. Attenuation due to water is present in humid air and is more pronounced with fog and rain. Another factor that affects attenuation is the angle of elevation of the satellite from the earth station (angle θ in Figure 16.1). The smaller the angle of elevation, the more of the atmosphere that the signal must travel through. Finally, atmospheric attenuation depends on frequency. In general, the higher the frequency, the greater the effect. Figure 16.7 shows the typical amount of attenuation as a function of angle of elevation for

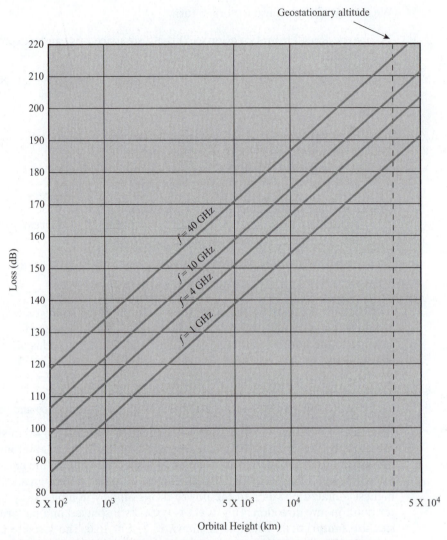

Figure 16.5 Minimum Free Space Loss as a Function of Orbital Height

frequencies in the C band. Of course, the attenuation due to fog and rain only occurs when those elements are present in the atmosphere.

Satellite Network Configurations

Figure 16.8 depicts in a general way two common configurations for satellite communication. In the first, the satellite is being used to provide a point-to-point link between two distant ground-based antennas. In the second, the satellite provides communications between one ground-based transmitter and a number of ground-based receivers.

A variation on the second configuration is one in which there is two-way communication among earth stations, with one central hub and many remote stations.

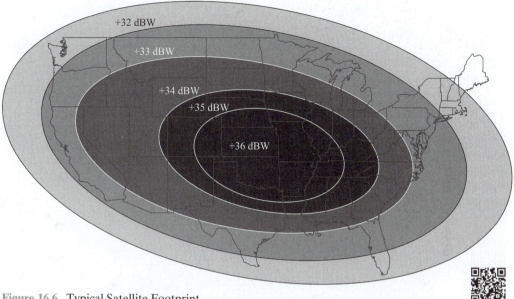

Figure 16.6 Typical Satellite Footprint

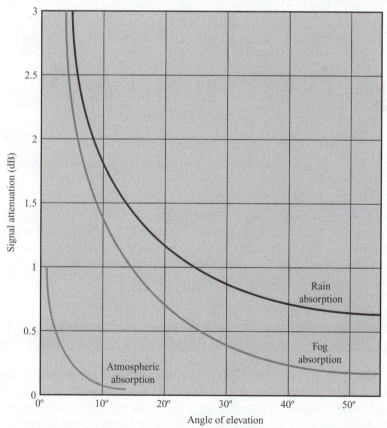

Figure 16.7 Signal Attenuation Due to Atmospheric Absorption (C Band)

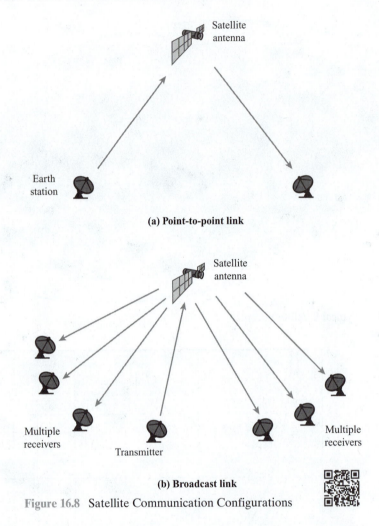

Figure 16.8   Satellite Communication Configurations

This type of configuration, depicted in Figure 16.9, is used with the very small aperture terminal (VSAT) system. A number of subscriber stations are equipped with low-cost VSAT antennas. Using some discipline, these stations share a satellite transmission capacity for transmission to a hub station. The hub station can exchange messages with each of the subscribers and can relay messages between subscribers.

16.2 SATELLITE CAPACITY ALLOCATION

Typically, a single GEO satellite will handle a rather large bandwidth (e.g., 500 MHz) and divide it into a number of channels of smaller bandwidth (e.g., 40 MHz). Within each of these channels, there is a capacity allocation task to be performed. In some instances, such as TV broadcasting or a single 50-Mbps digital data stream, the entire

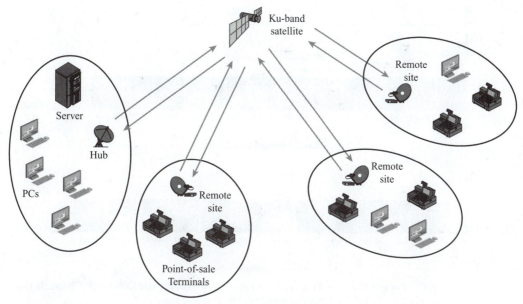

Figure 16.9 Typical VSAT Configuration

channel is dedicated to a single user or application. With these exceptions, however, the cost-effective use of the satellite requires that many users share each channel. Hence, the task is fundamentally one of multiplexing, which is a concept introduced in Chapter 2. In some cases, the allocation is carried out by centralized control, usually by the satellite; but in other cases, the allocation is a distributed function carried out by the earth stations.

All of the allocation strategies fall into one of three categories:

- Frequency division multiple access (FDMA)
- Time division multiple access (TDMA)
- Code division multiple access (CDMA)

In this section we examine FDMA and TDMA. CDMA was discussed in Chapter 9.

Frequency Division Multiplexing

As was mentioned, the overall capacity of a communications satellite is divided into a number of channels. This is a top level of FDM, with further capacity allocation carried out within each channel. Figure 16.10 is an example of an FDM scheme, which is typical of GEO communications satellites; this particular allocation is used in the Galaxy satellites from INTELSAT.[3] The satellite uses C-band frequencies

---

[3]Intelsat is the largest satellite operator in the world. It is a private corporation providing satellite communications capacity worldwide.

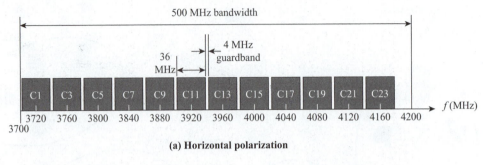

(a) Horizontal polarization

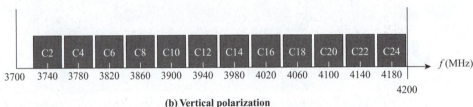

(b) Vertical polarization

Figure 16.10 Typical Satellite Transponder Frequency Plan for the Downlink Channels (for the uplink plan, add 2225 MHz to the numbers given above)

and provides a 500-MHz bandwidth, which is broken up into 24 40-MHz channels. The satellite is able to squeeze 24 channels into the 500 MHz by means of *frequency reuse*: each frequency assignment is used by two carriers with orthogonal polarization. Each 40-MHz channel includes a 4-MHz guardband, so each channel is actually 36-MHz wide. When used in a point-to-point configuration (Figure 16.8a), each channel could be used for one of a number of alternative purposes. Examples include:

- 1200 voice-frequency (VF) voice channels
- One 50-Mbps data stream
- 16 channels of 1.544 Mbps each
- 400 channels of 64 kbps each
- 600 channels of 40 kbps each
- One analog video signal
- Six to nine digital video signals

The bandwidth for an analog video signal may seem surprisingly high. To determine it, we need to use Carson's rule [Equation (7.15)], discussed in Chapter 7. The bandwidth of the video signal combined with the audio signal is approximately 6.8 MHz. This is then translated to a carrier at 6 GHz using frequency modulation (FM). The peak deviation of the signal using this process turns out to be $\Delta F = 12.5$ MHz. The transmission bandwidth is

$$B_T = 2\Delta F + 2B = 2(12.5 + 6.8) = 38.6 \text{ MHz}$$

which is accepted by the 36-MHz transponder.

For digital video, the use of compression can result in a data rate for a single channel in the range of 3 to 5 Mbps, depending on the amount of motion in the video.

Frequency Division Multiple Access

The discussion in the preceding subsection suggests that the satellite is used as in intermediate device providing, in effect, a point-to-point link between two earth stations. Because of the wide area coverage of the satellite, this is not necessarily the case. For example, the Intelsat series satellites allow a single 36-MHz channel to be divided using FDM into a number of smaller channels, each of which uses FM. Each of the smaller channels in turn carries a number of VF signals using FDM. Multiple earth stations access the same channel using FDMA.

The number of subchannels provided within a satellite channel via FDMA is limited by three factors:

- Thermal noise
- Intermodulation noise
- Crosstalk

These terms are defined and discussed in Chapter 6. The first two factors work in opposite directions. With too little signal strength, the transmitted signal will be corrupted by background noise. With too much signal strength, nonlinear effects in the satellite's amplifiers result in high intermodulation noise. Crosstalk stems from a desire to increase capacity by reusing frequencies, and limits but does not eliminate that practice. A frequency band can be reused if antennas that can radiate two polarized signals of the same frequency (cochannels) in orthogonal planes are employed. Again if signal strength is too high, cochannel interference becomes significant.

Figure 16.11 is a specific example of FDMA, with seven earth stations sharing the 36-MHz uplink capacity; a similar downlink diagram can be drawn. Station A is assigned the 5-MHz bandwidth from 6237.5 to 6242.5 MHz, in which it can transmit 60 VF channels using FDM-FM. That is, FDM is used to carry the 60 channels, and FM is used to modulate the channels onto the carrier frequency of 6240 MHz. Figure 16.11b indicates that station A has traffic for other stations as follows: 24 channels to B, 24 channels to D, and 12 channels to E. The remaining spectrum of the 36-MHz channel is divided among the other earth stations according to their traffic needs.

Time Division Multiple Access

Although FDM techniques are still quite common in satellite transmission, TDM techniques are in increasingly widespread use. The reasons include:

- The continuing drop in the cost of digital components.
- The advantages of digital techniques, including the use of error correction.
- The increased efficiency of TDM due to the lack of intermodulation noise.

TDMA is in essence the same as synchronous TDM (Section 2.5). Transmission is in the form of a repetitive sequence of frames, each of which is divided into a number of time slots. Each slot position across the sequence of frames is dedicated to a particular transmitter. Frame periods range from 100 μs to over 2 ms and consist of from 3 to over 100 slots. Data rates range from 10 Mbps to over 100 Mbps.

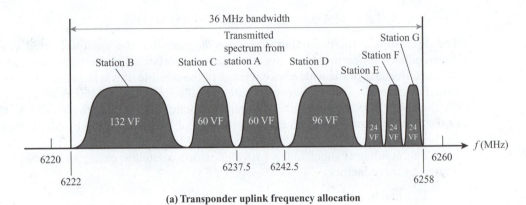

(a) Transponder uplink frequency allocation

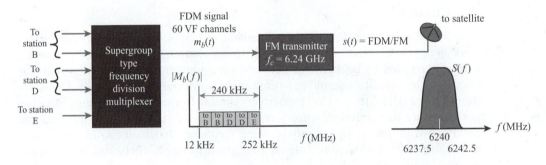

(b) Station A ground transmitting equipment

Figure 16.11 Fixed-Assignment FDMA Format for Satellite Communication

Figure 16.12 depicts a typical frame format (compare Figure 2.13b). Typically, a frame begins with two reference bursts to define the beginning of the frame. Two bursts are used, provided by two different earth stations, so that the system can continue to function even if one reference station is lost due to malfunction. Each reference burst begins with a carrier and bit timing recovery pattern, which is a unique pattern that allows all stations to synchronize to a master clock. Each of the N stations is assigned one or more slots in the frame. The station uses an assigned slot to transmit a burst of data, consisting of a preamble and user information. The preamble contains control and timing information, plus the identification of the destination station. The individual bursts are separated by guard times to ensure that there is no overlap.

Figure 16.13 depicts the operation of TDMA. Individual earth stations take turns using the uplink channel and may put a burst of data in the assigned time slot. The satellite repeats all incoming transmissions, which are broadcast to all stations. Thus, all stations must know not only which time slot to use for transmission, but also which time slot to use for reception. The satellite also repeats the reference burst, and all stations synchronize on the reception of that burst.

Each of the repetitive time slots is a channel and is independent of the other channels. Hence it can be used in any way that is required by the transmitting station.

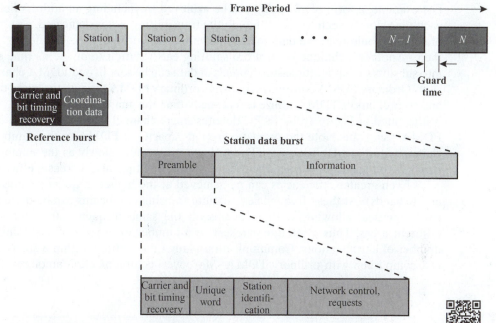

Figure 16.12 Example of TDMA Frame Format

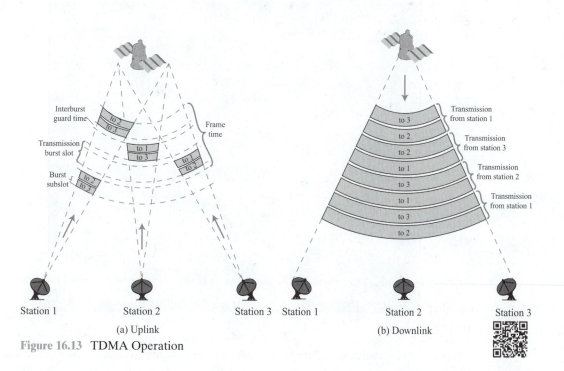

Figure 16.13 TDMA Operation

For example, a form of switching can be achieved by including an address field in each time slot. In such a case, although the transmitting slot is dedicated, a number of stations could read the data in each downlink slot looking for data addressed to them. Another technique is for a transmitting earth station to divide its time slots into subslots so that multiple subchannels of data can be sent in one TDMA channel.

Ordinary TDMA is more efficient than ordinary FDMA because the guard times and control bits of TDMA utilize less capacity than the guard bands of FDMA. This is illustrated in Figure 16.14. SCPC denotes single channel per carrier, which is an FDMA technique. Note the dramatic drop in capacity of FDMA as the number of channels increase. By contrast, TDMA drops much more slowly as the number of time slots (channels) increase. The use of a long frame time also increases efficiency.

Even greater efficiencies can be achieved at the higher frequency bands (K_u and K bands). At these frequencies, satellite transmission beams can be quite narrowly focused, allowing multiple beams on the same frequency transmitted to different areas. Thus a satellite can service a number of areas, each containing a number of earth stations. Communication among the stations within a single area is accomplished with ordinary TDMA. Moreover, communication among stations

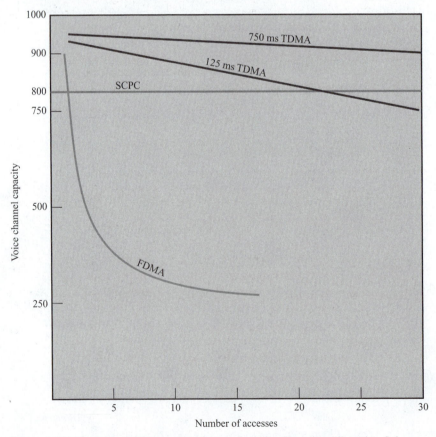

Figure 16.14 Relative Efficiency for Various Satellite Capacity Allocation Schemes

in different areas can be achieved if the satellite has the ability to switch time slots from one beam to another. This is known as **satellite-switched TDMA (SS/TDMA)**.

Figure 16.15 shows a simple SS/TDMA system serving two areas, each with two stations. As with ordinary TDMA, only one station at a time may transmit within an area. Thus, within area A, either station 1 or 2 may transmit in any given time slot. Similarly, either station 3 or station 4 may transmit in area B at any one time. Stations from the two areas do not interfere either through the use of polarized signals or different frequencies. At the satellite, data that are received are immediately retransmitted on a downlink frequency. Two separate downlink beams are used. The satellite contains a switch for interconnecting input beams and output beams. The connections through the switch may change over time. In the figure, downlink beam A repeats uplink beam A during periods 1 and 3 and repeats uplink beam B during period 2. Thus any station in any area can send data to any other station in any area.

For a satellite serving N areas, there are N TDM input streams. At any given time, the switch is configured to route these uplink beams in a particular fashion to the N downlink beams. Each configuration is referred to as a *mode* and $N!$ different modes are required for full connectivity. Table 16.3 shows the modes for a three-area system. For example, stations in area A can communicate with each other during modes 1 and 2, then those stations in area A communicate with stations in area B during modes 3 and 5, and so on. The satellite will change from mode to mode periodically. At most, a mode change would occur once per slot time. The mode pattern and duration are normally adjustable by ground command to meet changing traffic requirements.

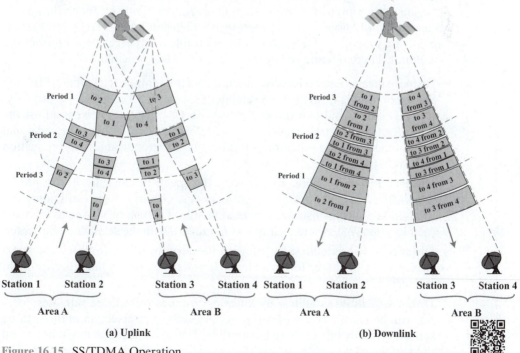

Figure 16.15   SS/TDMA Operation

Table 16.3 SS-TDMA Modes (Three Beams)

Input	Output					
	Mode 1	Mode 2	Mode 3	Mode 4	Mode 5	Mode 6
A	A	A	B	C	B	C
B	B	C	C	A	C	B
C	C	B	A	B	A	A

16.3 SATELLITE APPLICATIONS

Many different types of satellite applications exist, but two are familiar to everyday consumers: Global Positioning System (GPS) and Satellite Television applications.

Global Positioning System

The **Global Positioning System** was first developed by the United States Department of Defense in the 1970s to overcome weaknesses with other navigation approaches. A constellation of 24 MEO satellites was launched throughout the 80s and early 90s. Since then, GPS modernization has continually been occurring. The United States government is committed to 95% availability of these 24 satellites; therefore, 31 operational GPS satellites have been flying for the past few years.

GPS satellites operate in six orbital planes at a height of 20,350 km (12,600 mi) and provide service anywhere on Earth as illustrated in Figure 16.16. Each satellite orbits the earth in 12 hours. Signals operate at 1.2276 and 1.57542 GHz. For the service to operate properly, a GPS receiver must be able to observe at least four of the GPS satellites. These operate according to the following principles.

- **Distance measurement:** Receivers generate a pseudonoise code that will match the signal coming from the GPS satellite. This is a direct sequence spread spectrum (DSSS) signal like those discussed in Chapter 9. Receivers adjust the time offset between the locally generated PN sequence and the received signal until both signals are synchronized. The time offset indicates the propagation time from the satellite.

- **Distance to one satellite:** By knowing the speed of electromagnetic propagation from the satellites and their locations, GPS receivers can know their location as a certain distance d from a satellite. This can be viewed as knowing their location somewhere on a sphere of radius d with the satellite at the center.

- **Distance to two satellites:** By knowing distance from two satellites, the intersection of two spheres forms a circle, anywhere on which the receiver might be located.

- **Distance to three satellites:** By knowing distance from three satellites, location can be known as one of two possible points of intersection of those three spheres. Usually one of those locations is absurd; the location might not be on the surface of the earth or might indicate impossibly high receiver velocity.

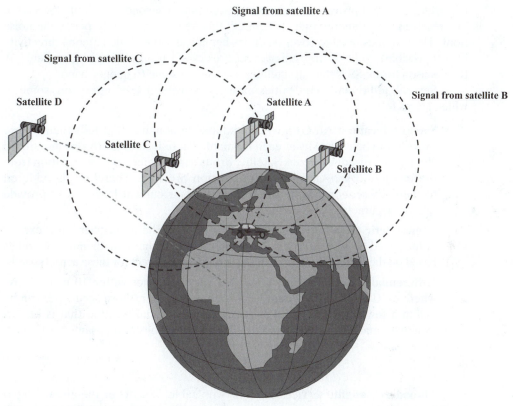

Figure 16.16 Global Positioning System

The receiver then would choose the other option as the solution; the result is a longitude, latitude, and elevation.

- **Fourth satellite signal:** There will be a timing bias between the GPS clock and the receiver clock. The fourth signal is used to detect that timing offset. This will correct the distance calculations.

- **Clock synchronization:** In addition to distance measurements, the GPS receiver is now also wirelessly synchronized with the highly accurate atomic clocks on the GPS satellites. This accurate clock can be useful on its own for a wide variety of purposes.

Once the location (and velocity and direction based on history of locations) is known, a variety of uses exist, for example, disaster recovery, automotive, maritime, fleet tracking, geoscience observation, and aviation purposes. GPS by itself only provides location information; mapping data is provided separately by the devices and through other wireless networks.

The DSSS approach allows for three benefits. First, signals can be kept from unauthorized use. Until May 2, 2000, a policy called *Selective Availability* was in place where a GPS signal (called the C/A coarse acquisition signal) was provided, but with intentionally degraded quality for public use. GPS encrypted another signal exclusively for military use that provided much greater accuracy. A second benefit of DSSS is the low received signal energy that is required; this signal can even be below the noise floor. The satellites need to cover an entire hemisphere (i.e., little antenna directivity gain is possible), so DSSS transmission reduces power transmission requirements. A third reason for DSSS is that all satellites can use the same frequency band.

Several additional complexities exist for successful GPS operation, some of which are as follows.

- **Satellite location:** All GPS receivers have an almanac that tells them where they should be in the sky at each moment. These locations are also monitored closely for any adjustments. Satellite orbits can be affected by gravitation from the moon and sun, and by solar radiation pressure. Therefore, in addition to their PN sequences, the satellites send their current locations to provide greater accuracy for use by the receivers.

- **Atmospheric effects:** GPS signals travel through the atmosphere, not exactly at the speed of light. GPS receivers can use atmospheric mathematical models based on the inclination angles of the satellites to correct for these actual speeds.

- **Differential GPS:** GPS signals can provide accuracies within 10 meters anywhere on Earth. If **differential GPS** is used, however, those accuracies can be within a few centimeters. DGPS uses one terrestrial position that is known exactly to make corrections to the GPS computations at that same location.

Direct Broadcast Systems

Direct broadcast satellite services compete with cable, DSL, over-the-air, and fixed broadband wireless access technologies to provide television services. These services can be provided through analog or digital formats, although digital formats have certainly become predominant due to the benefits of digital transmission that we have introduced previously. Early analog satellite television broadcasted in the **C-band** (4–8 MHz) and now digital television uses the K_u **band** (12–18 GHz). Receiving dishes in the C-band require diameters of 3 m or greater while K_u-band dishes can be much smaller, from 0.5 to 1.0 m across. But one consequence of the higher frequencies is outages due to heavy snow or rain. The International Telecommunication Union calls this the **Broadcast Satellite Service (BSS)** and refers only to specific frequency bands in different regions, for example, 10.7–12.5 GHz in Europe, Russia, and Africa or 12.2–12.7 GHz in North and South America.

Programming providers, such as DirecTV or DISH network, send signals up to the satellites over very large satellite dishes, 9 to 12 meters in diameter as shown in Figure 16.17. Then the satellites rebroadcast the signals on different frequencies back down to earth. Receivers will process the signals, typically decrypting them by permission of the service provider based on user subscriptions. Some programming sources themselves broadcast their programming over satellites back down to programming providers. Other programming sources, such as local channels, are received by the programming provider through some other means, such as through fiber-optic cable. The suite of programs is then highly compressed to make best use of the channel. Most DBS systems use MPEG-2 compression over the Digital Video Broadcasting-Satellite (DVB-S) standard.

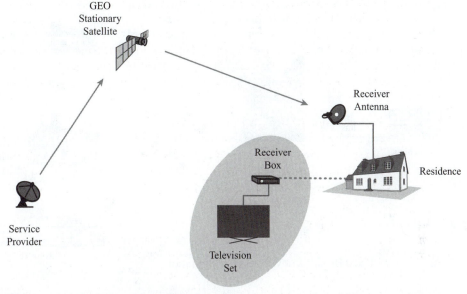

Figure 16.17 Direct Broadcast Satellite

16.4 FIXED BROADBAND WIRELESS ACCESS

Traditionally, the provision of voice and data communications to the end user, over the local loop, or subscriber loop, has been provided by wired systems. As the demand for broadband Internet access has grown, providers of wired local loop service have responded with increasing reliance on optical fiber and coaxial cable.

However, increasing interest is being shown in competing wireless technologies for subscriber access. These approaches are generally referred to as *wireless local loop (WLL)*, or *fixed wireless access*. The most prominent **fixed broadband wireless access** (fixed BWA) system is referred to as WiMAX, based on the IEEE 802.16 standard. We examine WiMAX in the next section. In this section, we provide an overview of the concept of fixed BWA.

Figure 16.18 illustrates a simple fixed BWA configuration. A BWA provider services one or more cells. Each cell includes a base station (BS) antenna, mounted on top of a tall building or tower. In earlier systems, subscribers used a fixed antenna mounted on a building or pole that has an unobstructed line of sight to the BS antenna. The technology has evolved so that indoor wireless access points are possible. From the BS, there is a link, which may either be wired or wireless, to a switching center. The switching center is typically a telephone company local office, which provides connections to the local and long-distance telephone networks. An Internet service provider (ISP) may be collocated at the switch or connected to the switch by a high-speed link.

Figure 16.18 shows what amounts to a two-level hierarchy. More complex configurations have also been implemented, in which a BS may serve a number of subordinate BS antennas, each of which supports a number of subscribers.

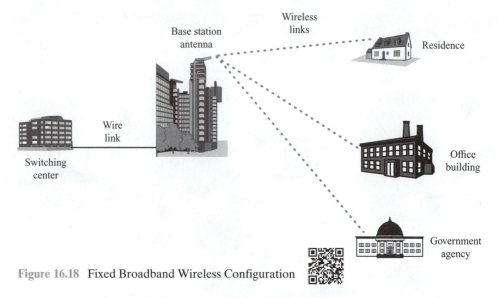

Figure 16.18 Fixed Broadband Wireless Configuration

The fixed BWA has a number of advantages over a wired approach to subscriber loop support:

- **Cost:** Wireless systems are less expensive than wired systems. Although the electronics of the wireless transmitter/receiver may be more expensive than those used for wired communications, with BWA the cost of installing kilometers of cable, either underground or on poles, is avoided, as well as the cost of maintaining the wired infrastructure.

- **Installation time:** BWA systems typically can be installed rapidly. The key stumbling blocks are obtaining permission to use a given frequency band and finding a suitable elevated site for the BS antennas. Once these hurdles are cleared, a BWA system can be installed in a small fraction of the time required for a new wired system.

- **Selective installation:** Radio units are installed only for those subscribers who want the service at a given time. With a wired system, typically cable is laid out in anticipation of serving every subscriber in a local area.

BWA needs to be evaluated with respect to two alternatives:

- **Wired scheme using existing installed cable:** A large fraction of the earth's inhabitants do not have a telephone line. For high-speed applications, many subscribers with telephone lines do not have a line of sufficient quality or are too far from the central office to effectively use Digital Subscriber Line (DSL). Many of these same subscribers also do not have cable TV or their cable provider does not offer two-way data services. Finally, because WLL has become cost-competitive with wired schemes, new installations face a genuine choice between the wired and wireless approaches.

- **Mobile cellular technology:** 4G cellular systems provide broadband support. The primary advantages of a fixed BWA scheme are that the fixed BWA BS can cover a larger area, and that higher data rates can be achieved.

With the growing interest in BWA services, a need was recognized within the industry to develop standards for this service. In response to this need the IEEE 802 committee set up the 802.16 working group in 1999 to develop broadband wireless standards. The charter for the group was to develop standards that:

- Use wireless links with microwave or millimeter wave radios.
- Use licensed spectrum (typically).
- Are metropolitan in scale.
- Provide public network service to fee-paying customers (typically).
- Use PMP architecture with stationary rooftop or tower-mounted antennas.
- Provide efficient transport of heterogeneous traffic supporting quality of service (QoS).
- Are capable of broadband transmissions (>2 Mbps).

In essence, **IEEE 802.16** standardizes the air interface and related functions associated with BWA. In addition, an industry group, the **WiMAX** (Worldwide Interoperability for Microwave Access) Forum, was formed to promote the 802.16 standards and to develop interoperability specifications. Initially targeted at fixed BWA, IEEE 802.16 and the associated WiMAX specification now deal with both fixed and mobile BWA. In this section, we provide an overview of the 802.16 and WiMAX specifications, with an emphasis on the fixed BWA application. This section is based on the 2012 version of IEEE 802.16.

IEEE 802.16 Architecture

Network Reference Model The WiMAX Forum has developed a logical representation of the architecture of a network that implements WiMAX, called the network reference model [WIMA12]. The model is useful in determining interface points between logical functional entities that can be used as a guide for developing interoperability standards. Figure 16.19 illustrates key elements of this model, which include the following:

- **Access Service Network (ASN):** The set of network functions needed to provide radio access to WiMAX subscribers.
- **Network Access Provider (NAP):** A business entity that provides WiMAX radio access infrastructure to one or more WiMAX Network Service Providers.
- **Connectivity Service Network (CSN):** A set of network functions that provide IP connectivity services to WiMAX subscribers. These functions include Internet access, authentication, and admission control based on user profiles.
- **Network Service Provider (NSP):** A business entity that provides IP connectivity and WiMAX services to WiMAX subscribers.
- **ASN Gateway:** Provides connectivity from an ASN to an NSP. The gateway performs such functions as routing and load balancing.

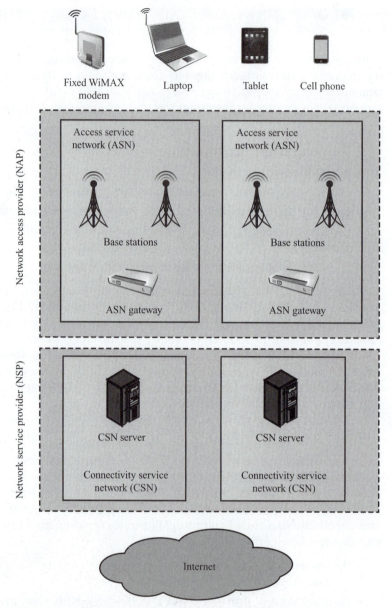

Figure 16.19 Elements of the WiMAX Network Reference Model

The network architecture logically divides into three parts: subscriber stations (SSs), the access service network, and the connectivity service networks. Subscribers may be fixed or mobile. Fixed subscribers are at a fixed geographic location and connect using a fixed WiMAX modem for broadband access. Fixed locations include residential, business, and government entities. An ASN consists of one or more BSs that are interconnected by a core network and connect to an ASN gateway. The gateway connects to one or more CSNs, which provide broadband access to the Internet. IEEE 802.16 standards are concerned with the air interface between the subscriber's transceiver station and the base transceiver station. The standards specify all the details of that interface, as discussed subsequently in this section. The system reference model also shows interfaces between the transceiver stations and the networks behind them. The details of these interfaces are beyond the scope of the 802.16 standards. The reason for showing these interfaces in the system reference model is that the subscriber and core network technologies (such as voice, ATM, etc.) have an impact on the technologies used in the air interface and the services provided by the transceiver stations over the air interface.

Protocol Architecture Figure 16.20 illustrates the IEEE 802.16 protocol reference model. The *physical layer* includes the following:

- Encoding/decoding of signals
- Preamble generation/removal (for synchronization)
- Bit transmission/reception
- Frequency band and bandwidth allocation

The medium access control (MAC) layer is divided into three sublayers. The *security sublayer* includes authentication, secure key exchange, and encryption. Note that this sublayer is concerned with secure communication between the SS and the ASN base station. Secure communication between the SS and the CSN is handled at a higher layer.

The ***MAC common part sublayer*** includes the basic functions of any MAC layer:

- On transmission, assemble data into a protocol data unit (PDU) with address and error detection fields.
- On reception, disassemble PDU, and perform address recognition and error detection.
- Govern access to the wireless transmission medium.

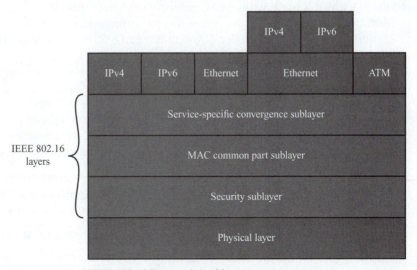

Figure 16.20 IEEE 802.16 Protocol Architecture

This sublayer, between the BS and the SS, is responsible for sharing access to the radio channel. Specifically, the MAC protocol defines how and when a BS or SS may initiate transmission on the channel. Because some of the layers above the MAC layer, such as ATM, require specified service levels (QoS), the MAC protocol must be able to allocate radio channel capacity so as to satisfy service demands. In the downstream direction (BS to SS), there is only one transmitter and the MAC protocol is relatively simple. In the upstream direction, multiple SSs are competing for access, resulting in a more complex MAC protocol.

The service-specific convergence sublayer provides functions specific to the service being provided. A convergence layer protocol may do the following:

- Encapsulate PDU framing of upper layers into the native 802.16 MAC PDUs.
- Map an upper layer's addresses into 802.16 addresses.
- Translate upper layer QoS parameters into native 802.16 MAC format.
- Adapt the time dependencies of the upper layer traffic into the equivalent MAC service.

IEEE 802.16 MAC Layer

Data transmitted over the 802.16 air interface from or to a given subscriber are structured as a sequence of MAC PDUs. The term **MAC PDU** as used in this context refers to the PDU that includes MAC protocol control information and higher-level data. This is not to be confused with a ***TDMA burst***, which consists of a sequence of time slots, each dedicated to a given subscriber. A TDMA time slot may contain exactly one MAC PDU, a fraction of a MAC PDU, or multiple MAC PDUs. The sequence of time slots across multiple TDMA bursts that is dedicated to one subscriber forms a logical channel, and MAC PDUs are transmitted over that logical channel.

Connections and Service Flow The 802.16 MAC protocol is connection oriented. That is, a logical connection is set up between peer entities (MAC users) prior to the exchange of data between those entities. Each MAC PDU includes a connection ID, which is used by the MAC protocol to deliver incoming data to the correct MAC user. In addition, there is a one-to-one correspondence between a connection ID and service flow. The service flow defines the QoS parameters for the PDUs that are exchanged on the connection.

The concept of a service flow on a connection is central to the operation of the MAC protocol. Service flows provide a mechanism for upstream and downstream QoS management. In particular, they are integral to the bandwidth allocation process. The BS allocates both upstream and downstream bandwidth on the basis of the service flow for each active connection. Examples of service flow parameters are latency (maximum acceptable delay), jitter (maximum acceptable delay variation), and throughput (minimum acceptable bit rate).

PDU Format A good way to get a grasp of the MAC protocol is to examine the PDU format (Figure 16.21). The MAC PDU consists of three sections:

- **Header:** Contains protocol control information needed for the functioning of the MAC protocol.

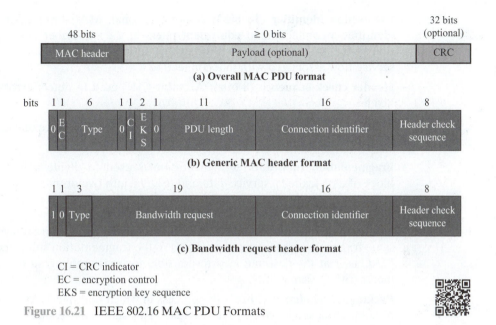

CI = CRC indicator
EC = encryption control
EKS = encryption key sequence

Figure 16.21   IEEE 802.16 MAC PDU Formats

- **Payload:** The payload may be either higher-level data (e.g., an ATM cell, an IP packet, a block of digital speech) or a MAC control message.
- **CRC:** The cyclic redundancy check field contains an error-detecting code. This optional CRC covers both the header and the payload and is applied after the payload is encrypted, if encryption is used.

Two types of headers are defined: the generic MAC header and the bandwidth request header. The *generic MAC header* is used in both the downlink (BS to SS) and uplink (SS to BS) directions. A MAC PDU with a generic header contains either MAC management messages or convergence sublayer data. The generic MAC header consists of the following fields:

- **Header type (1 bit):** This bit is set to zero indicating the header type is generic MAC PDU.
- **Encryption control (1 bit):** Indicates whether the payload is encrypted.
- **Type (6 bits):** Indicates the subheaders and special payload types present in the message payload.
- **Reserved (1 bit):** Reserved bit, set to zero.
- **CRC indicator (1 bit):** Indicates whether there is a 32-bit CRC after the payload.
- **Encryption key sequence (2 bits):** An index into a vector of encryption key information, to be used if the payload is encrypted.
- **Reserved (1 bit):** Reserved bit, set to zero.
- **PDU length (11 bits):** Length in bytes of the entire MAC PDU.

- **Connection identifier (16 bits):** A unidirectional, MAC-layer address that identifies a connection to equivalent peers in the subscriber and base station MAC. A CID maps to an SFID, which defines the QoS parameters to the service flow associated with that connection.
- **Header check sequence (8 bits):** An 8-bit CRC used to detect errors in the header.

The type field contains bits that indicate the presence or absence of each of the following subheaders at the beginning of the payload:

- **Fragmentation subheader:** Fragmentation is used to divide a higher-level block of data [called a service data unit (SDU)] into two or more fragments in order to reduce the size of MAC frames. This is done to allow efficient use of available bandwidth relative to the QoS requirements of a connection's service flow. If fragmentation is used, then all of the fragments are assigned the same fragment sequence number (FSN) in the fragmentation subheader. The MAC user at the destination is responsible for reassembling all of the fragments with the same FSN.
- **Packing subheader:** Packing is the process in which multiple MAC SDUs are packed into a single MAC PDU payload. This subheader contains the information needed for the receiving MAC entity to unpack the individual SDUs.
- **Fast feedback allocation subheader:** Only used in the downlink direction. It requests feedback from a SS with an advanced antenna system.
- **Grant management subheader:** Only used in the uplink direction. It conveys various information related to bandwidth management, such as polling request and additional-bandwidth request.

The ***bandwidth request header*** is used by the subscriber to request additional bandwidth. This header is for a MAC frame with no payload. As shown in Figure 16.21, this header includes many of the fields in the generic MAC header. The 19-bit bandwidth request field indicates the number of bytes of capacity requested for uplink transmission. The type field allows the SS to request bandwidth for this connection only or aggregate bandwidth for all connections on this uplink.

Scheduling Service and QOS An IEEE 802.16 network is designed to be able to transfer many different types of traffic simultaneously, including real-time flows such as voice, video, and bursty TCP flows. Although each such traffic flow is handled as a stream of PDUs traveling through a connection, the way in which each data flow is handled by the BS depends on the characteristics of the traffic flow and the requirements of the application. For example, real-time video traffic must be delivered within minimum variation in delay. See Section 3.5 for more discussion on traffic types and QoS requirements.

To accommodate the requirements of different types of traffic, IEEE 802.16 defines a number of different service classes. Each class is defined by certain general characteristics and a particular service flow is defined by assigning values to a set of QoS parameters. The most important of these parameters are the following:

- **Maximum sustained traffic rate:** The peak information rate, in bits per second of the service. The rate pertains to the SDUs at the input to the system. The parameter is 6 bits in length and includes values in the range from 1200 bps to 1.921 Mbps.

- **Minimum reserved traffic rate:** The minimum rate, in bits per second, reserved for this service flow. The BS shall be able to satisfy bandwidth requests for a connection up to its minimum reserved traffic rate. If less bandwidth than its minimum reserved traffic rate is requested for a connection, the BS may reallocate the excess reserved bandwidth for other purposes. Values range from 1200 bps to 1.921 Mbps.

- **Maximum latency:** The maximum interval between the reception of a packet at the convergence sublayer of the BS or the SS and the forwarding of the SDU to its air interface. Values range from 1 ms to 10 s.

- **Tolerated jitter:** The maximum delay variation (jitter) for the connection. Values range from 1 ms to 10 s.

- **Traffic priority:** The priority of the associated service flow. Given two service flows identical in all QoS parameters besides priority, the higher-priority service flow should be given lower delay and higher buffering preference. For otherwise nonidentical service flows, the priority parameter should not take precedence over any conflicting service flow QoS parameter. Eight priority levels are used.

Table 16.4 lists the principal QoS parameters used for each of the five service classes defined in IEEE 802.16. The standard designates separate uplink and downlink services. Corresponding services use the same QoS parameter set. The principal

Table 16.4 IEEE 802.16 Service Classes and QoS Parameters

Scheduling Service (uplink)	Data Delivery Service (downlink)	Applications	QoS Parameters
Unsolicited grant service (UGS)	Unsolicited grant service (UGS)	VoIP	• Minimum reserved traffic rate • Maximum latency • Tolerated jitter
Real-time polling service (rtPS)	Real-time variable-rate (RT-VR) service	Streaming audio or video	• Minimum reserved traffic rate • Maximum sustained traffic rate • Maximum latency • Traffic priority
Non-real-time polling service (nrtPS)	Non-real-time variable-rate (NRT-VR) service	FTP	• Minimum reserved traffic rate • Maximum sustained traffic rate • Traffic priority
Best effort (BE) service	Best effort (BE) service	Data transfer, Web browsing, etc.	• Maximum sustained traffic rate • Traffic priority
Extended rtPS	Extended real-time variable-rate service (ERT-VR)	VoIP (voice with activity detection)	• Minimum reserved traffic rate • Maximum sustained traffic rate • Maximum latency • Tolerted jitter • Traffic priority

difference is that for two of the service classes, polling is involved in the uplink transmission. Downlink transmission from the BS does not use polling, as there is a single transmitter, the BS.

The **unsolicited grant service (UGS)** is intended for real-time applications that generate fixed-rate data. A service flow with a data delivery service of UGS gets uplink resources assigned at uniform periodic intervals without requesting them each time (Figure 16.22). UGS is commonly used for uncompressed audio and video information. On the downlink, the BS generates fixed-rate data as a uniform stream of PDUs. Examples of UGS applications include videoconferencing and distance learning.

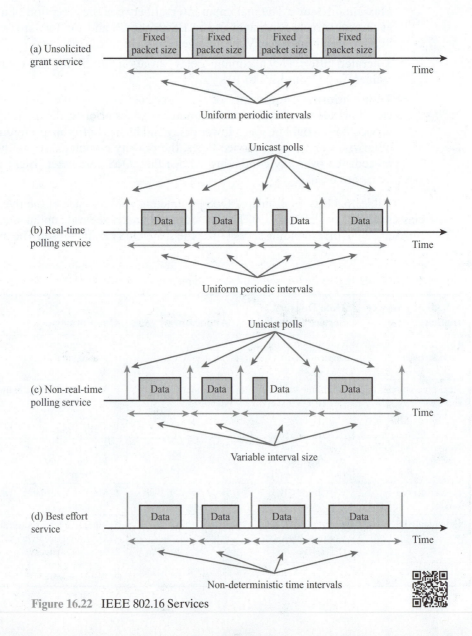

Figure 16.22 IEEE 802.16 Services

The **real-time variable rate (RT-VR)** downlink service is intended for time-sensitive applications, that is, those requiring tightly constrained delay and delay variation. The principal difference between applications appropriate for RT-VR and those appropriate for UGS is that RT-VR applications transmit at a rate that varies with time. For example, the standard approach to video compression results in a sequence of image frames of varying sizes. Because real-time video requires a uniform frame transmission rate, the actual data rate varies. On the downlink, RT-VR is implemented by transmitting the available data at uniform periodic intervals. On the uplink, the service is called **real-time polling service (rtPS)**. The BS issues a unicast poll (poll directed at a SS station) at periodic intervals, enabling the SS to transmit a block of data in each interval (Figure 16.22b). The RT-VR/rtPS service allows the network more flexibility than UGS. The network is able to statistically multiplex a number of connections over the same dedicated capacity and still provide the required service to each connection.

The *extended real-time variable rate (ERT-VR)* service is to support real-time applications with variable data rates, which require guaranteed data and delay, for example, VoIP with silence suppression. On the uplink, this service is called *extended rtPS*. As with UGS, the BS provides unicast grants of bandwidth in an unsolicited manner, thus saving the latency of a bandwidth request. However, in this case the allocations are variable in size, based on the amount of traffic so far carried. On the downlink side, the BS transmits PDUs over the service flow in varying sizes and at varying intervals, to keep up with the service flow QoS.

The **non-real-time variable-rate (NRT-VR)** service is intended for applications that have bursty traffic characteristics, do not have tight constraints on delay and delay variation, but for which it is possible to characterize the expected traffic flow and therefore set QoS parameters. An example is file transfer. On the downlink, the BS transmits data at variable intervals, to satisfy the minimum and maximum data rate requirements of the service flow. On the uplink, the service is called **non-real-time polling service (nrtPS)**. The BS issues polls at varying intervals, depending on how much data has so far been transferred, so as to keep up with the required flow (Figure 16.22c).

At any given time, a certain amount of capacity between the BS and SSs is unused by the four classes of service so far discussed. This capacity is available for the **best effort (BE)** service. This service is suitable for applications that can tolerate variable delays and rates. Most applications running over TCP exhibit such tolerance. On the uplink, the SS sends requests for bandwidth in either random access slots (time slots in which SSs contend for access) or using dedicated transmission opportunities.

IEEE 802.16 Physical Layer

The IEEE 802.16 physical layer set of standards is still evolving, but is sufficiently stable to form the basis of widespread WiMAX implementation and deployment. The 2012 standard devotes almost 600 pages to the physical layer specification. Here we provide a brief overview.

The 802.16 specification defines three principal air interfaces, summarized in Table 16.5. All of these operate in licensed frequency bands. In addition, there are modifications to these specifications for operation in unlicensed bands below 11 GHz.

Table 16.5 IEEE 802.16 Physical Layer Modes

	WirelessMAN-SC	WirelessMAN-OFDM	WirelessMAN-OFDMA
Frequency band	10 to 66 GHz	≤ 11 GHz	≤ 11 GHz
LOS limitation	LOS	NLOS	NLOS
Duplexing technique	TDD, FDD	TDD, FDD	TDD, FDD
Uplink access	TDMA, DAMA	OFDM	OFDMA
Downlink access	TDM, TDMA	OFDM	OFDMA
Downlink modulation	QPSK, 16-QAM, 64-QAM	QPSK, 16-QAM, 64-QAM, BPSK	QPSK, 16-QAM, 64-QAM, BPSK
Uplink modulation	QPSK, 16-QAM, 64-QAM	QPSK, 16-QAM, 64-QAM, BPSK	QPSK, 16-QAM, 64-QAM, BPSK
Channel size	20 to 28 MHz	1.75 to 20 MHZ	1.25 to 20 MHZ
Subcarrier spacing	N/A	11.16 kHz	11.16 kHz
Data rate	32 to 134 Mbps	≤ 70 Mbps	≤ 70 Mbps
Downlink FEC	Reed-Solomon	Reed-Solomon	Convolutional
Uplink FEC	Reed-Solomon	Reed-Solomon	Convolutional

WirelessMAN-SC The *WirelessMAN-SC* interface is intended for use in the 10–66 GHz bands. In this region, due to the short wavelength, line of sight (LOS) is required and multipath is negligible. This environment is well suited for PMP access serving applications from small office/home office (SOHO) through medium- to large-office applications. Thus, this standard is suited for fixed wireless broadband access but does not support mobile stations.

Uplink transmission, from SSs, is based on a combination of **time-division multiple access (TDMA)** and *demand-assignment multiple access (DAMA)*. TDMA employs a single, relatively large, uplink frequency band that is used to transmit a sequence of time slots. Repetitive time slots are assigned to an individual subscriber station to form a logical subchannel. When DAMA is employed, the time-slot assignment is changed as needed to respond optimally to demand changes among the multiple stations.

Downlink transmission from the BS is TDM, with the information for each SS multiplexed onto a single stream of data and received by all SSs within the same sector. To support SSs that operate in a half-duplex mode with frequency-division duplex (FDD), the standard makes provision for a TDMA portion of the downlink. With TDMA, the downlink time slots are scheduled to coordinate the interchange with specific SSs.

WirelessMAN-OFDM The *WirelessMAN-OFDM* interface operates below 11 GHz. In this region, due to the short wavelength, LOS is not necessary and multipath may be significant. The ability to support near-LOS and non-LOS (NLOS) scenarios requires additional physical-layer functionality, such as the support of advanced power management techniques, interference mitigation/coexistence, and MIMO antennas. Both uplink and downlink transmission use OFDM. Both

Table 16.6 Data Rates Achieved at Various WirelessMAN-OFDM Bandwidths

Modulation	QPSK	QPSK	16-QAM	16-QAM	64-QAM	64-QAM
Code Rate	1/2	3/4	1/2	3/4	2/3	3/4
1.75 MHz	1.04	2.18	2.91	4.36	5.94	6.55
3.5 MHz	2.08	4.37	5.82	8.73	11.88	13.09
7.0 MHz	4.15	8.73	11.64	17.45	23.75	26.18
10.0 MHz	8.31	12.47	16.63	24.94	33.25	37.40
20.0 MHz	16.62	24.94	33.25	49.87	66.49	74.81

WirelessMAN-OFDM and WirelessMAN-OFDMA are suitable for an environment that includes mobile SSs.

WirelessMAN-OFDM supports a range of channel bandwidths. Table 16.6 shows likely data rates achievable for various bandwidths.

WirelessMAN-OFDMA *WirelessMAN-OFDMA* is an enhanced version of WirelessMAN-OFDM that provides added flexibility and efficiency by the use of OFDMA. Figure 16.23 is an example of how WirelessMAN-OFDMA operates using time-division duplex (TDD). Transmission is structured as a sequence of frames, each of which includes a downlink (DL) subframe followed by an uplink (UL) subframe. In each frame, a time gap is inserted between the DL and UL subframes and at the end of each frame to allow for transmission turnaround. Each DL subframe begins with a preamble used to synchronize all stations. This is followed by a DL-MAP pattern, which indicates how all of the subchannels are allocated in the DL

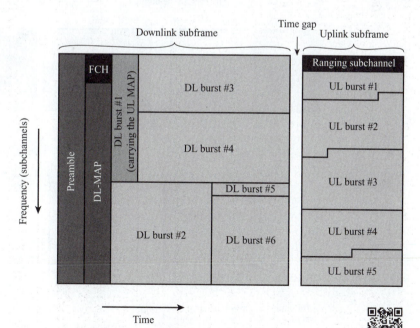

Figure 16.23   IEEE 802.16 OFDMA Frame Structure in TDD Mode

subframe and a frame control header (FCH). The FCH provides frame configuration information, such as the MAP message length, the modulation and coding scheme, and the usable subcarriers. The remainder of the DL subframe is divided into bursts, with each burst occupying a contiguous set of subchannels for a contiguous set of time intervals. One of these bursts is the UL-MAP pattern. The remaining bursts contain data, each burst intended for a specific SS. The UL subframe is similarly divided into bursts. One of these bursts is the ranging subchannel, which is allocated for SSs to perform closed-loop time, frequency, and power adjustment as well as bandwidth requests. The remaining bursts are allocated to SSs for transmission to the BS.

TDD, by its structure, readily supports half-duplex transmission, because UL and DL transmissions must alternate in time. This is not the case with FDD. Figure 16.24 shows how the structure of FDD WirelessMAN-OFDMA supports half-duplex operation. The FDD frame structure supports both full-duplex and half-duplex SS types. The frame structure supports a coordinated transmission arrangement of two groups of half-duplex SSs (Group-1 and Group-2) that share the frame at distinct partitions of the frame. In each frame, one portion of the frequency band is devoted to DL transmission and one portion to UL transmission. The DL transmission consists of two subframes, the first for Group-1 and the second for Group-2. The UL transmission consists of a Group-2 subframe followed by a Group-1 subframe. Time gaps are inserted between subframes to enable both turnaround and half-duplex operation.

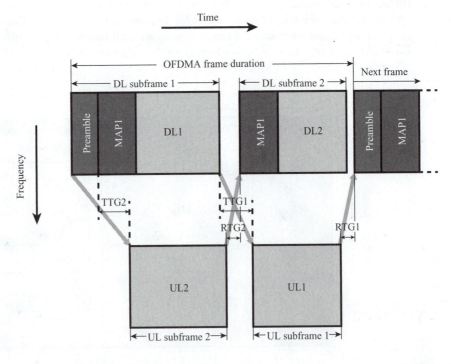

TTG = transmitter-to-receiver gap
RTG = receiver-to-transmitter gap

Figure 16.24 IEEE 802.16 OFDMA Frame Structure in FDD Mode

16.6 SMART GRID

As society becomes increasingly aware of and adept at energy efficiency, the electric power grid is becoming increasingly complex. The traditional issues of efficient control of the electric power grid, such as fault isolation, voltage control, and reactive power control now are more important than ever. But communications technologies are increasingly helpful as the grid becomes increasingly "smart" to become the *smart grid* The term "*smart*," however, is somewhat of a misnomer, as the electric power grid has already been very smart for a long time. See Figure 16.25 for an overview of the electric power grid. Generation systems are highly efficient with myriads of optimized controls. And transmission systems have used a combination of complex relaying with supervisory control and data acquisition (SCADA) systems efficiently for decades.

The *generation*, transmission, and distribution networks, however, can no longer be seen as logical trees with power flowing from the roots of the trees out to their branches. High power **distributed generation** can be located on the transmission grid through wind and solar stations, and distributed generation sources are increasingly common on the distribution networks as homes and businesses generate their own energy and seek to push and sell unneeded energy back into the power grid. Additionally, the advent of increasing numbers of batteries in electric vehicles adds new types of demands, but also brings opportunities to make use of those batteries to send power back into the grid when demand is high.

Increasingly "smart" distribution, secondary, and home electric networks provide much promise. Distribution networks may not have automated devices to monitor and control voltage, capacitance, or switching/relaying, and they may not be adept at handling distributed generation. Communications and distributed control

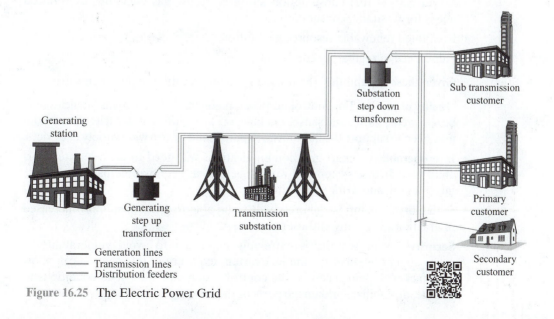

Figure 16.25 The Electric Power Grid

can help in many ways. Inside homes, home area networks not only could help consumers manage their home energy usage, but they may also communicate with utility companies about special **rate incentives**.

Many of the opportunities for this functionality require effective communications technology. In addition to wireless, there are options for powerline, fiber optic, etc., technologies to communicate control of the power grid. And there are also a variety of technologies such as cable modem, fiber to the home, fixed wireless, and DSL to get into the home.

Nonetheless, wireless technology provides much of the potential backbone for the **smart grid**. Many of the home network concepts were explored in Chapter 12 when discussing the Internet of Things (IoT). Energy management possibilities exist when the devices within the home can communicate with each other and provide helpful information to home dwellers. This will capitalize on the IoT.

Smart Grid Communication Requirements

Using a more precise definition, Smart Grid can refer to a *power grid that uses advanced two-way communication and pervasive computing to improve control, efficiency, reliability, and safety*. Smart grids may use power line, fiber optic, wireless communications, etc. Wireless communication will most effectively be used in the distribution and home environments, but can even be useful for transmission and power plant networks.

Smart grid technologies are driven by the following motivations [YAN13].

- Enhanced customer experience through improved service reliability, better power quality, and reduced outage times.
- Increased productivity of utility personnel.
- Improved power grid utilization.
- Lower carbon fuel consumption and greenhouse gas emissions by reduced needs for fossil fuel consumption.
- Facilitated renewable resource generation.
- Adherence to regulatory constraints.

Given these capabilities, the following communication requirements exist.

- **Quality of service:** For control purposes, highly reliable 12–20 ms latencies may be required. Alarms and sensor readings will have different latencies. Bandwidth may need to support 100,000 messages per second from a wide variety of devices.
- **Interoperability:** Smart grid communications will need to provide interoperability for diverse systems to work together, use compatible parts, exchange information, and work cooperatively.
- **Scalability:** The infrastructure needs to be able to grow to support increased interaction with many end-user devices.
- **Security:** Cyber security is extremely important to avoid vulnerability to cyber attacks. Deliberate and inadvertent exposure of information can allow an attacker to gain access to the control system and alter load conditions to disable, destabilize, or damage parts of the power grid.

- **Standardization:** Transitioning toward advanced sensing/automation requires standardized protocols and interfaces to convert vendor equipment offerings away from their traditionally proprietary communication platforms. The IEEE P2030 group, the International Society of Automation (ISA), and the International Electrotechnical Commission (IEC) are all working on standards and different layers of communication and information exchange.

Implementation of smart grid communications involves several challenges, including addressing the extreme complexity of the power grid, fail proof and nearly instantaneous two-way communications, reliability, and security.

Smart Grid Wireless Technology

A variety of smart grid industry projects have utilized the wireless technologies presented in this book. A potential combination of WiMAX/Cellular and ZigBee technologies for smart grid communication is seen in Figure 16.26.

One project utilized WiMAX IEEE 802.16 communications to create a smart community automated meter reading infrastructure. Thousands of houses communicated using WiMAX between meters and IT systems. Information was collected regarding measurements, events, and faults, along with information provided by appliances equipped with intelligent communication chips that allowed remote monitoring and control. This information was analyzed and used to better diagnose problems on the primary and secondary distribution networks, as well as guide planning for system improvements. Another project utilized a network of ZigBee coordinators and ZigBee end devices to perform several of these same automated meter reading functions [YAN13].

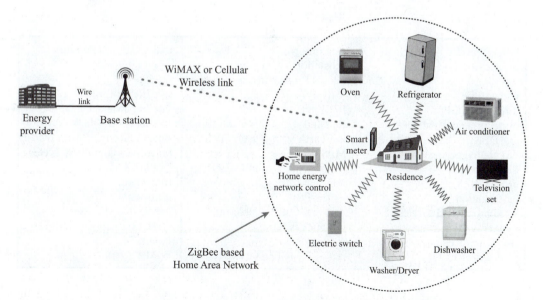

Figure 16.26 Use of WiMAX/Cellular and ZigBee for Smart Grid Applications

16.7 RECOMMENDED READING

[ELBE08] provides technical details on satellite communications. [PARE12] is an informative history of the evolution of IEEE 802.16 and WiMAX. [EKLU02] is a good technical overview of IEEE 802.16 developments up to 2002. [YAN13] discusses Smart Grid communications.

ELBE08 Elbert, B. *Introduction to Satellite Communication.* Boston: Artech House, 2008.

EKLU02 Elkund, C., et al. "IEEE Standard 802.16: A Technical Overview of the WirelessMAN™ Air Interface for Broadband Wireless Access." *IEEE Communications Magazine,* June 2002.

INGL97 Inglis, A., and Luther, A. *Satellite Technology: An Introduction.* Boston: Focal Press, 1997.

PARE12 Pareit, D.; Moerman, I.; and Demester, P. "The History of WiMAX: A Complete Survey of the Evolution in Certification and Standardization for IEEE 802.16 and WiMAX." *IEEE Communications Surveys and Tutorials,* Fourth Quarter 2012.

PRAT03 Pratt, T.; Bostian, C.; and Allnutt, J. *Satellite Communications.* New York: Wiley, 2003.

YAN13 Ye Yan; Yi Qian; Sharif, H.; and Tipper, D. "A Survey on Smart Grid Communication Infrastructures: Motivations, Requirements and Challenges." *Communications Surveys & Tutorials, IEEE,* vol. 15, no. 1, pp. 5, 20, First Quarter 2013.

16.8 KEY TERMS, REVIEW QUESTIONS, AND PROBLEMS

Key Terms

best effort (BE)	generation	real-time variable rate
broadcast service satellite	geostationary (GEO)	(RT-VR)
(BSS)	Global Positioning System	satellite
C-band	(GPS)	satellite footprint
differential GPS	IEEE 802.16	satellite-switched TDMA
direct broadcast satellite	K_u-band	(SS/TDMA)
(DBS)	low earth orbit (LEO)	smart grid
distributed generation	MAC PDU	time division multiple access
distribution	medium earth orbit (MEO)	(TDMA)
downlink	non-real-time polling service	transmission
earth station	(nrtPS)	transponder
fixed broadband wireless	non-real-time variable-rate	unsolicited grant service
access	(NRT-VR)	(UGS)
frequency division multiple	rate incentives	uplink
access (FDMA)	real-time polling service (rtPS)	WiMAX

Review Questions

16.1 List three different ways of categorizing communications satellites.

16.2 What are some key differences between satellite-based and terrestrial wireless communications?

16.3 List three different ways of classifying satellite orbits.

16.4 Explain what GEO, LEO, and MEO satellites are (including what the acronyms stand for). Compare the three types with respect to factors such as size and shape of orbits, signal power, frequency reuse, propagation delay, number of satellites for global coverage, and handoff frequency.

16.5 Under what circumstances would you use GEO, LEO, and MEO satellites, respectively?

16.6 What are three key factors related to satellite communications performance?

16.7 What are the primary causes of atmospheric attenuation for satellite communications?

16.8 What are three factors that limit the number of subchannels that can be provided within a satellite channel via FDMA?

16.9 Describe how GPS uses each of the four satellites it needs to be able to connect with.

16.10 What types of orbits do GPS satellites use?

16.11 Define fixed broadband wireless access.

16.12 List and briefly define IEEE 802.16 service classes.

16.13 List and briefly describe the three IEEE 802.16 physical layer options.

Problems

16.1 Using Kepler's laws of planetary motion, we can derive the following expression for a circular orbit:

$$T^2 = \frac{4\pi^2 a^3}{\mu}$$

where

T = orbital period
a = orbital radius in km = distance from the center of the earth to the orbit
μ = Kepler's constant = 3.986004418×10^5 km^3/s^2

The earth rotates once per sidereal day of 23 h 56 min 4.09 s.
a. Determine the orbital radius of a GEO satellite.
b. Assuming an earth radius of 6370 km, what is the orbit height h (Figure 16.1) of a GEO satellite? *Note:* your answer should differ slightly from the figure used in the chapter. Different sources in the literature give slightly different values.

16.2 The Space Shuttle is an example of a LEO satellite. Sometimes, it orbits at an altitude of 250 km.
a. Using a mean earth radius of 6378.14 km, calculate the period of the shuttle orbit.
b. Determine the linear velocity of the shuttle along this orbit.

16.3 You are communicating between two satellites. The transmission obeys the free space law. The signal is too weak. Your vendor offers you two options. The vendor can use a higher frequency that is twice the current frequency or can double the effective area of both of the antennas. Which will offer you more received power or will both offer the same improvement, all other factors remaining equal? How much improvement in the received power do you obtain from the best option?

16.4 A satellite at a distance of 40,000 km from a point on the earth's surface radiates a power of 10 W from an antenna with a gain of 17 dB in the direction of the observer. The satellite operates at a frequency of 11 GHz. The receiving antenna has a gain of 52.3 dB. Find the received power.

16.5 For the transponder scheme of Figure 16.10, what is the percentage bandwidth used for the guardbands?

16.6 For the TDMA frame of Figure 16.12, assume the following parameters. The frame length is 2 ms. Data are encoded using QPSK with a signal element rate of 60.136 Mbaud. All traffic bursts are of equal length of 16,512 bits. The reference burst has length of 576 bits, the preamble is 560 bits, and the guard interval is 24 bits. Assume that there are two participating reference stations, so that two reference bursts are required.

   a. Determine the maximum number of earth stations the system can serve.

   b. What is the frame efficiency (fraction of frame carrying user data rather than overhead bits)?

16.7 A TDMA network of 5 earth stations shares a single transponder equally. The frame duration is 2 ms, the preamble time per station is 20 μs, and guard bands of 5 μs are used between bursts. Transmission bursts are QPSK at 30 Mbaud.

   a. Calculate the number of 64-kbps voice channels that each TDMA earth station can transmit.

   b. If the earth stations send data rather than digital speech, what is the transmission rate of each earth station?

   c. What is the efficiency of the TDMA system expressed as Efficiency = (message bits sent)/(maximum number of possible bits that could have been sent)?

16.8 Three identical large earth stations access a 36-MHz bandwidth transponder using TDMA, with a frame length of 1 ms, a preamble tie of 10 μs, and a guard time of 2 μs. There is no reference burst in the TDMA frame. The signals are transmitted using QPSK, and within the earth stations, the bit rates of the signals are:

     Station A: $R = 15$ Mbps
     Station B: $R = 10$ Mbps
     Station C: $R = 5$ Mbps

Calculate the burst bit rate and burst symbol rate for each earth station.

16.9 In Figure 16.23, the DL subframe contains both DL-MAP and UL-MAP. Why not make UL-MAP a preamble in the UL subframe?

REFERENCES

ABBREVIATIONS

ACM   Association for Computing Machinery
IEEE   Institute of Electrical and Electronics Engineers

ADAM91   Adamek, J. *Foundations of Coding.* New York: Wiley, 1991.

ALI09   Ali, I.; Casati, A.; Chowdhury, K.; Nishida, K.; Parsons, E.; Schmid, S.; and Vaidya, R. "Network-Based Mobility Management in the Evolved 3GPP Core Network." *Communications Magazine, IEEE*, vol. 47, no. 2, pp. 58, 66, February 2009.

ALSA13   Alsabbagh, E.; Yu, H.; and Gallagher, K. "802.11ac Design Consideration for Mobile Devices." *Microwave Journal*, February 2013.

ANDE95   Anderson, J.; Rappaport, T.; and Yoshida, S. "Propagation Measurements and Models for Wireless Communications Channels." *IEEE Communications Magazine*, January 1995.

ASH90   Ash, R. *Information Theory.* New York: Dover, 1990.

ATTA06   Attar, R., et al. "Evolution of cdma2000 Cellular Networks: Multicarrier EV-DO." *Communications Magazine, IEEE,* vol. 44, no. 3, pp. 46, 53, March 2006.

BAKE12   Baker, M. "From LTE-Advanced to the Future." *IEEE Communications Magazine*, February 2012.

BAYK11   Baykas, T., et al. "IEEE 802.15.3c: The First IEEE Wireless Standard for Data Rates over 1 Gb/s." *Communications Magazine, IEEE,* vol. 49, no. 7, pp. 114, 121, July 2011.

BEAR79   Beard, Charles L., Jr. *Recognition of Chest, Head and Falsetto Registers of Isoparametric Tones of Tenor Voices*, Ph.D. Dissertation, University of Missouri-Kansas City, 1979.

BELL00   Bellamy, J. *Digital Telephony.* New York: Wiley, 2000.

BEND00   Bender, P., et al. "CDMA/HDR: A Bandwidth-Efficient High-Speed Wireless Data Service for Nomadic Users." *IEEE Communications Magazine*, July 2000.

BERA08   Beradinelli, G., et al. "OFDMA vs. SC-FDMA: Performance Comparison in Local Area IMT-A Scenarios." *IEEE Wireless Communications*, October 2008.

BERL80   Berlekamp, E. "The Technology of Error-Correcting Codes." *Proceedings of the IEEE*, May 1980.

BERL87   Berlekamp, E.; Peile, R.; and Pope, S. "The Application of Error Control to Communications." *IEEE Communications Magazine,* April 1987.

BERR96   Berrou, C., and Glavieux, A. "Near Optimum Error Correcting Codes and Decoding: Turbo Codes." *IEEE Transactions on Communications,* October 1996.

BERT00   Bertoni, H. *Radio Propagation for Modern Wireless Systems.* Upper Saddle River, NJ: Prentice Hall, 2000.

BERT92   Bertsekas, D., and Gallager, R. *Data Networks.* Englewood Cliffs, NJ: Prentice Hall, 1992.

BERT94   Bertoni, H.; Honcharenko, W.; Maciel, L.; and Xia, H. "UHF Propagation Prediction for Wireless Personal Communications." *Proceedings of the IEEE*, September 1994.

BHAR83   Bhargava, V. "Forward Error Correction Schemes for Digital Communications." *IEEE Communications Magazine*, January 1983.

BHUS06   Bhushan, N., et al. "CDMA2000 1×EV-DO Revision a: A Physical Layer and MAC Layer Overview." *Communications Magazine, IEEE*, vol. 44, no. 2, pp. 37, 49, February 2006.

BI03   Bi, Q., et al. "Performance of 1xEV-DO Third-Generation Wireless High-Speed Data Systems." *Bell Labs Technical Journal*, vol. 7, no. 3, 2003.

BLAC99   Black, U. *Second-Generation Mobile and Wireless Networks*. Upper Saddle River, NJ: Prentice Hall, 1999.

BOLC01   Bolcskei, H., et al. "Fixed Broadband Wireless Access: State of the Art, Challenges, and Future Directions." *IEEE Communications Magazine*, January 2001.

BRAY01   Bray, J., and Sturman, C. *Bluetooth: Connect Without Cables*. Upper Saddle River, NJ: Prentice Hall, 2001.

CARN99   Carne, E. *Telecommunications Primer: Data, Voice, and Video Communications*. Upper Saddle River, NJ: Prentice Hall, 1999.

CHEU04   Cheung, D. "WLAN Security & Wi-Fi Protected Access." *Dr. Dobb's Journal*, June 2004.

CISC07   Cisco Systems, Inc. "802.11n: The Next Generation of Wireless Performance." Cisco White Paper, 2007. cisco.com

COME13   Comer, D. *Internetworking with TCP/IP, Volume I: Principles, Protocols, and Architecture*. Upper Saddle River, NJ: Pearson, 2013.

CORD10   Cordeiro, C.; Akhmetov, D.; and Park, M. "IEEE 802.11ad: Introduction and Performance Evaluation of the First Multi-Gbps WiFi Technology." *Proceedings of the 2010 ACM International Workshop on mmWave Communications: From Circuits to Networks*, 2010.

COTT00   Cottrell, R.; Langhammer, M.; and Mauer, V. "Turbo Decoding for Comm Apps." *Communication Systems Design*, August 2000.

COUC13   Couch, L. *Digital and Analog Communication Systems*. Upper Saddle River, NJ: Pearson, 2013.

COX14   Cox, C. *An Introduction to LTE: LTE, LTE-Advanced, SAE, VoLTE, and 4G Communications*, Second Edition. United Kingdom: John Wiley & Sons, Ltd, 2014.

DAEW12   Daewon, L., et al. "Coordinated multipoint transmission and reception in LTE-advanced: deployment scenarios and operational challenges." *Communications Magazine, IEEE*, vol. 50, no. 2, pp. 148, 155, February 2012.

DALK96   Dalke, R.; Hufford, G.; and Ketchum, R. *Radio Propagation Considerations for Local Multipoint Distribution Systems*. National Telecommunications and Information Administration Publication PB97116511, August 1996.

DAUM82   Daumer, W. "Subjective Evaluation of Several Efficient Speech Coders." *IEEE Transactions on Communications*, April 1982.

DECU14a   Decuir, J. "Introducing Bluetooth Smart: Part 1: A Look at Both Classic and New Technologies." *Consumer Electronics Magazine, IEEE*, vol. 3, no. 1, pp. 12, 18, January 2014.

DECU14b   Decuir, J. "Introducing Bluetooth Smart: Part II: Applications and Updates." *Consumer Electronics Magazine, IEEE,* vol. 3, no. 2, pp. 25, 29, April 2014.

DINA98   Dinan, E., and Jabbari, B. "Spreading Codes for Direct Sequence CDMA and Wideband CDMA Cellular Networks." *IEEE Communications Magazine,* September 1998.

DIXO94   Dixon, R. *Spread Spectrum Systems with Commercial Applications.* New York: Wiley, 1994.

ECON99   "The World in Your Pocket." *The Economist,* October 1999.

EDNE04   Edney, J., and Arbaugh, W. *Real 802.11 Security: Wi-Fi Protected Access and 802.11i.* Reading, MA: Addison-Wesley, 2004.

EKLU02   Elkund, C., et al. "IEEE Standard 802.16: A Technical Overview of the WirelessMAN™ Air Interface for Broadband Wireless Access." *IEEE Communications Magazine,* June 2002.

ELBE08   Elbert, B. *Introduction to Satellite Communication.* Boston: Artech House, 2008.

ENGE00   Engelmann, R. "The Origins of Radio." *IEEE Potentials,* October/November 2000.

EVAN98   Evans, J. "New Satellites for Personal Communications." *Scientific American,* April 1998.

EVER94   Everitt, D. "Traffic Engineering of the Radio Interface for Cellular Mobile Networks." *Proceedings of the IEEE,* September 1994.

EYUB02   Eyuboglu, V. "CDAM2000 1xEV-DO Delivers 3G Wireless." *Network World,* February 25, 2002.

FREE04   Freeman, R. *Telecommunication System Engineering.* New York: Wiley, 2004.

FREE07   Freeman, R. *Radio System Design for Telecommunications.* New York: Wiley, 2007.

FREE98   Freeman, R. "Bits, Symbols, Baud, and Bandwidth." *IEEE Communications Magazine,* April 1998.

FREE99   Freeman, R. *Fundamentals of Telecommunications.* New York: Wiley, 1999.

FREN13   Frenzel, L. "An Introduction to LTE-Advanced: The Real 4G." *Electronic Design,* February 2013.

FROD01   Frodigh, M., et al. "Future Generation Wireless Networks." *IEEE Personal Communications,* October 2001.

FUNG98   Fung, P. "A Primer on MMDS Technology." *Communication Systems Design,* April 1998. Available at csdmag.com.

GARG99   Garg, V., and Wilkes, J. *Principles and Applications of GSM.* Upper Saddle River, NJ: Prentice Hall, 1999.

GEIE01   Geier, J. "Enabling Fast Wireless Networks with OFDM." *Communications System Design,* February 2001.

GHOS10   Ghosh, A., et al. "LTE-Advanced: Next-Generation Wireless Broadband Technology." *IEEE Wireless Communications,* June 2010.

GHOS11   Ghosh, A.; Zhang, J.; Andrews J.; and Muhamed, R. *Fundamentals of LTE.* Upper Saddle River, NJ: Prentice Hall, 2011.

GIBS93   Gibson, J. *Principles of Digital and Analog Communications.* New York: Macmillan, 1993.

GILB04   Gilb, J. *Wireless Multimedia: A Guide to the IEEE 802.15.3 Standard.* New York: IEEE Press, 2004.

GUNT00   Gunther, N. *The Practical Performance Analyst*. Lincoln, NE: Authors Choice Press, 2000.

GUTI01   Gutierrez, J., et al. "IEEE 802.15.4: A Developing Standard for Low-Power Low-Cost Wireless Personal Area Networks." *IEEE Network*, September/October 2001.

GUTI03   Gutierrez, J.; Callaway, E.; and Barrett, R. *Low-Rate Wireless Personal Area Networks: Enabling Wireless Sensors with IEEE 802.15.4*. New York: IEEE Press, 2003.

HALP10   Halperin, D., et al. "802.11 with Multiple Antennas for Dummies." *Computer Communication Review*, January 2010.

HATA80   Hata, M. "Empirical Formula for Propagation Loss in Land Mobile Radio Services." *IEEE Transactions on Vehicular Technology*, March 1980.

HIER10   Hiertz, G.R.; Denteneer, D.; Stibor, L.; Zang, Y.; Costa, X.P.; and Walke, B. "The IEEE 802.11 Universe." *Communications Magazine, IEEE,* vol. 48, no. 1, pp. 62, 70, January 2010.

INGL97   Inglis, A., and Luther, A. *Satellite Technology: An Introduction*. Boston: Focal Press, 1997.

ITU02   International Telecommunications Union. *Handbook on Satellite Communications*. New York: Wiley, 2002.

IWAM10   Iwamura, M., et al. "Carrier Aggregation Framework in 3GPP LTE-Advanced." *IEEE Communications Magazine*, August 2010.

JAIN90   Jain, Y. "Convolutional Codes Improve Bit-Error Rate in Digital Systems." *EDN*, August 20, 1990.

JAME01   James, J. *A Student's Guide to Fourier Transforms*. Cambridge, England: Cambridge University Press, 2001.

JAYA84   Jayant, N., and Noll, P. *Digital Coding of Waveforms*. Englewood Cliffs, NJ: Prentice Hall, 1984.

JOHN04   Johnston, D., and Yaghoobi, H. "Peering into the WiMAX Spec." *Communications System Design,* January 2004. Available at www.commsdesign.com.

KAMM00   Kammler, D. *A First Course in Fourier Analysis*. Upper Saddle River, NJ: Prentice Hall, 2000.

KARA10   Karapistoli, E.; Pavlidou, F.N.; Gragopoulos, I.; and Tsetsinas, I. "An Overview of the IEEE 802.15.4a Standard." *Communications Magazine, IEEE,* vol. 48, no. 1, pp. 47, 53, January 2010.

KELL00   Keller, T., and Hanzo, L. "Adaptive Multicarrier Modulation: A Convenient Framework for Time-Frequency Processing in Wireless Communication." *Proceedings of the IEEE,* May 2000.

KOFF02   Koffman, I., and Roman, V. "Broadband Wireless Access Solutions Based on OFDM Access in IEEE 802.16." *IEEE Communications Magazine,* April 2002.

KROO86   Kroon, P., and Deprettere, E. "Regular Pulse Excitation—A Novel Approach to Effective Multipulse Coding of Speech." *IEEE Transactions on Acoustics, Speech, and Signal Processing,* no. 5, 1986.

LATH09   Lathi, B. *Modern Digital and Analog Communication Systems*. New York: Oxford University Press, 2009.

LAYL04   Layland, R. "Understanding Wi-Fi Performance." *Business Communications Review,* March 2004.

LEBO98   Lebow, I. *Understanding Digital Transmission and Recording.* New York: IEEE Press, 1998.

LING12   Lingjia Liu; Runhua Chen; Geirhofer, S.; Sayana, K.; Zhihua Shi; and Yongxing Zhou. "Downlink MIMO in LTE-advanced: SU-MIMO vs. MU-MIMO." *Communications Magazine, IEEE,* vol. 50, no. 2, pp. 140, 147, February 2012.

MACW76   Macwilliams, F., and Sloane, N. "Pseudo-Random Sequences and Arrays." *Proceedings of the IEEE,* December 1976. Reprinted in [TANT98].

MART94   Martine, R. *Basic Traffic Analysis.* Upper Saddle River, NJ: Prentice Hall, 1994.

MCFA03   McFarland, B., and Wong, M. "The Family Dynamics of 802.11." *ACM Queue,* May 2003.

METT99   Mettala, R., et al. *Bluetooth Protocol Architecture Version 1.0.* Bluetooth Whitepaper 1.C.120/1.0, 25 August 1999. www.bluetooth.com.

MILL01   Miller, B., and Bisdikian, C. *Bluetooth Revealed.* Upper Saddle River, NJ: Prentice Hall, 2001.

MOLI11   Molisch, A. *Wireless Communications,* Second Edition. West Sussex, UK: John Wiley & Sons, Ltd.

MYUN06   Myung, H.; Lim, J.; and Goodman, D. "Single Carrier FDMA for Uplink Wireless Transmission." *IEEE Vehicular Technology,* September 2006.

NIST97   Stone, W. C. "NIST Construction Automation Program Report No. 3: Electromagnetic Signal Attenuation in Construction Materials." NIST, tech. rep., October 1997.

NORD00   Nordbotten, A. "LMDS Systems and Their Application." *IEEE Communications Magazine,* June 2000.

OJAN98   Ojanpera, T., and Prasad, G. "An Overview of Air Interface Multiple Access for IMT-2000/UMTS." *IEEE Communications Magazine,* September 1998.

OKUM68   Okumura, T., et al. "Field Strength and Its Variability in VHF and UHF Land Mobile Radio Service." *Review of the Electrical Communications Laboratories,* 1968.

ORLI98   Orlik, P., and Rappaport, S. "Traffic Performance and Mobility Modeling of Cellular Communications with Mixed Platforms and Highly Variable Mobilities." *Proceedings of the IEEE,* July 1998.

ORTI00   Ortiz, S. "Broadband Fixed Wireless Travels the Last Mile." *Computer,* July 2000.

PALA13   Palattella, M. R., et al. "Standardized Protocol Stack for the Internet of (Important) Things." *Communications Surveys & Tutorials, IEEE,* vol. 15, no. 3, pp. 1389, 1406, Third Quarter 2013.

PARE12   Pareit, D.; Moerman, I.; and Demester, P. "The History of WiMAX: A Complete Survey of the Evolution in Certification and Standardization for IEEE 802.16 and WiMAX." *IEEE Communications Surveys and Tutorials,* Fourth Quarter 2012.

PARK11   Parkvall, S.; Furuskar, A.; and Dahlman, E. "Evolution of LTE toward IMT-Advanced." *IEEE Communications Magazine,* February 2011.

PARK88   Park, S., and Miller, K. "Random Number Generators: Good Ones are Hard to Find." *Communications of the ACM,* October 1988.

PASU79   Pasupathy, S. "Minimum Shift Keying: A Spectrally Efficient Modulation." *IEEE Communications Magazine,* July 1979.

PAUL08   Paul, T., and Ogunfunmi, T. "Wireless LAN Comes of Age: Understanding the IEEE 802.11n Amendment." *Circuits and Systems Magazine, IEEE,* vol. 8, no. 1, pp. 28, 54, First Quarter 2008.

PEAR92   Pearson, J. *Basic Communication Theory.* Englewood Cliffs, NJ: Prentice Hall, 1992.

PERA08   Perahia, E. "IEEE 802.11n Development: History, Process, and Technology." *Communications Magazine, IEEE,* vol. 46, no. 7, pp. 48, 55, July 2008.

PERA10   Perahia, E., et al. "IEEE 802.11ad: Defining the Next Generation Multi-Gbps Wi-Fi." *Proceedings, 7th IEEE Consumer Communications and Networking Conference,* 2010.

PETE61   Peterson, W., and Brown, D. "Cyclic Codes for Error Detection." *Proceedings of the IEEE,* January 1961.

PETE95   Peterson, R.; Ziemer, R.; and Borth, D. *Introduction to Spread Spectrum Communications.* Englewood Cliffs, NJ: Prentice Hall, 1995.

PETR00   Petrick, A. "IEEE 802.11b - Wireless Ethernet." *Communications System Design,* June 2000. www.commsdesign.com.

PHIL98   Phillips, J., and Namee, G. *Personal Wireless Communications with DECT and PWT.* Boston: Artech House, 1998.

PICK82   Pickholtz, R.; Schilling, D.; and Milstein, L. "Theory of Spread Spectrum Communications—A Tutorial." *IEEE Transactions on Communications,* May 1982. Reprinted in [TANT98].

POLL96   Pollini, G. "Trends in Handover Design." *IEEE Communications Magazine,* March 1996.

POOL98   Polle, I. *Your Guide to Propagation.* Potters Bar, Herts, UK: Radio Society of Great Britain, 1998.

PRAS98   Prasad, R., and Ojanpera, T. "An Overview of CDMA Evolution: Toward Wideband CDMA." *IEEE Communications Surveys,* Fourth Quarter 1998. Available at www.comsoc.org.

PRAS00   Prasad, R.; Mohr, W.; and Konhauser, W., eds. *Third-Generation Mobile Communication Systems.* Boston: Artech House, 2000.

PRAT03   Pratt, T.; Bostian, C.; and Allnutt, J. *Satellite Communications.* New York: Wiley, 2003.

PROA01   Proakis, J. *Digital Communications.* New York: McGraw-Hill, 2001.

PROA02   Proakis, J. *Communication Systems Engineering.* Upper Saddle River, NJ: Prentice Hall, 2002.

PROA14   Proakis, J. *Fundamentals of Communication Systems.* Upper Saddle River, NJ: Pearson, 2014.

RABI95   Rabiner, L. "Toward Vision 2001: Voice and Audio Processing Considerations." *AT&T Technical Journal,* March/April 1995.

RAHN93   Rahnema, M. "Overview of the GSM System and Protocol Architecture." *IEEE Communications Magazine,* April 1993.

RAMA88   Ramabadran, T., and Gaitonde, S. "A Tutorial on CRC Computations." *IEEE Micro,* August 1988.

RAPP02   Rappaport, T. *Wireless Communications: Principles and Practice.* Upper Saddle River, NJ: Prentice Hall, 2002.

RODB00   Rodbell, M. "Bluetooth: Wireless Local Access, Baseband and RF Interfaces, and Link Management." *Communications System Design,* March, April, May 2000. www.csdmag.com.

RODR02   Rodriguez, A., et al. *TCP/IP Tutorial and Technical Overview.* Upper Saddle River, NJ: Prentice Hall, 2002.

ROSH04   Roshan, P., and Leary, J. *802.11 Wireless LAN Fundamentals.* Indianapolis: Cisco Press, 2004.

SAIR02   Sairam, K.; Gunasekaran, N.; and Reddy, S. "Bluetooth in Wireless Communication." *IEEE Communications Magazine,* June 2002.

SCHI00   Schiller, J. *Mobile Communications.* Reading, MA: Addison-Wesley, 2000.

SKLA01   Sklar, B. *Digital Communications: Fundamentals and Applications.* Upper Saddle River, NJ: Prentice Hall, 2001.

SKLA93   Sklar, B. "Defining, Designing, and Evaluating Digital Communication Systems." *IEEE Communications Magazine,* November 1993.

SKLA97a   Sklar, B. "A Primer on Turbo Code Concepts." *IEEE Communications Magazine,* December 1997.

SKLA97b   Sklar, B. "Rayleigh Fading Channels in Mobile Digital Communication Systems." *IEEE Communications Magazine,* July 1997.

SPOH02   Spohn, D. *Data Network Design.* New York: McGraw-Hill, 2002.

STAL02   Stallings, W. "The Advanced Encryption Standard." *Cryptologia,* July 2002.

STAL13   Stallings, W. *Cryptography and Network Security: Principles and Practice,* Sixth Edition. Upper Saddle River, NJ: Pearson, 2013.

STAL14   Stallings, W. *Data and Computer Communications,* Tenth Edition. Upper Saddle River, NJ: Pearson, 2014.

STAN14   Stankovic, J.A. "Research Directions for the Internet of Things." *Internet of Things Journal, IEEE,* vol. 1, no. 1, pp. 3, 9, February 2014.

TANT98   Tantaratana, S., and Ahmed, K., eds. *Wireless Applications of Spread Spectrum Systems: Selected Readings.* Piscataway, NJ: IEEE Press, 1998.

TERP00   Terplan, K., and Morreale, P. eds. *The Telecommunications Handbook.* Boca Raton, FL: CRC Press, 2000.

THUR00   Thurwachter, C. *Data and Telecommunications: Systems and Applications.* Upper Saddle River, NJ: Prentice Hall, 2000.

UNGE87   Ungerboeck, G. "Trellis-Coded Modulation with Redundant Signal Sets, Part 1: Introduction." *IEEE Communications Magazine,* February 1987.

VERM13   Verma, L.; Fakharzadeh, M.; and Sunghyun Choi. "Wifi on Steroids: 802.11AC and 802.11AD." *Wireless Communications, IEEE,* vol. 20, no. 6, pp. 30, 35, December 2013.

VITE89   Viterbi, A., et al. "A Pragmatic Approach to Trellis-Coded Modulation." *IEEE Communications Magazine,* July 1989.

VUCE00   Vucetic, B., and Yuan, J. *Turbo Codes: Principles and Applications.* Boston: Kluwer Academic Publishers, 2000.

WANG08   Wang, C., et al. "Voice Communications over ZigBee Networks." *IEEE Communications Magazine,* January 2008, p. 121.

WEBB00   Webb, W. *Introduction to Wireless Local Loop: Broadband and Narrowband Systems.* Boston: Artech House, 2000.

WILS00   Wilson, J., and Kronz, J. "Inside Bluetooth: Part I and Part II." *Dr. Dobb's Journal,* March, April 2000.

XION94   Xiong, F. "Modem Techniques in Satellite Communications." *IEEE Communications Magazine,* August 1994.

XIAO04   Xiao, Y. "IEEE 802.11e: QoS Provisioning at the MAC Layer." *IEEE Communications Magazine,* June 2004.

XION06   Xiong, F. *Digital Modulation Techniques.* Boston: Artech House, 2006.

YAN13   Ye Yan; Yi Qian; Sharif, H.; and Tipper, D. "A Survey on Smart Grid Communication Infrastructures: Motivations, Requirements and Challenges." *Communications Surveys & Tutorials, IEEE,* vol. 15, no. 1, pp. 5, 20, First Quarter 2013.

ZENG00   Zeng, M.; Annamalai, A.; and Bhargava, V. "Harmonization of Global Third-Generation Mobile Systems." *IEEE Communications Magazine,* December 2000.

ZHEN04   Zhent, J., and Lee, M. "Will IEEE 802.15.4 Make Ubiquitous Networking a Reality?: A Discussion on a Potential Low Power, Low Bit Rate Standard." *IEEE Communications Magazine,* June 2004.

INDEX

THE WILLIAM STALLINGS BOOKS ON COMPUTER

DATA AND COMPUTER COMMUNICATIONS, TENTH EDITION

A comprehensive survey that has become the standard in the field, covering (1) data communications, including transmission, media, signal encoding, link control, and multiplexing; (2) communication networks, including circuit- and packet-switched, frame relay, ATM, and LANs; (3) the TCP/IP protocol suite, including IPv6, TCP, MIME, and HTTP, as well as a detailed treatment of network security. **Received the 2007 Text and Academic Authors Association (TAA) award for the best Computer Science and Engineering Textbook of the year.**

WIRELESS COMMUNICATION NETWORKS AND SYSTEMS (WITH CORY BEARD)

A comprehensive, state-of-the art survey. Covers fundamental wireless communications topics, including antennas and propagation, signal encoding techniques, spread spectrum, OFDM, and error correction techniques. Examines cellular systems, wireless LANs, personal area networks, satellite and other long range wireless communications, and the Internet of Things. Technologies include LTE-Advanced, Bluetooth, ZigBee and 802.11. Covers wireless mobile networks and applications.

COMPUTER SECURITY, THIRD EDITION (WITH LAWRIE BROWN)

A comprehensive treatment of computer security technology, including algorithms, protocols, and applications. Covers cryptography, authentication, access control, database security, cloud security, intrusion detection and prevention, malicious software, denial of service, firewalls, software security, physical security, human factors, auditing, legal and ethical aspects, and trusted systems. **Received the 2008 TAA award for the best Computer Science and Engineering Textbook of the year.**

OPERATING SYSTEMS, EIGHTH EDITION

A state-of-the art survey of operating system principles. Covers fundamental technology as well as contemporary design issues, such as threads, SMPs, multicore, real-time systems, multiprocessor scheduling, embedded OSs, distributed systems, clusters, security, and object-oriented design. **Third, fourth and sixth editions received the TAA award for the best Computer Science and Engineering Textbook of the year.**

AND DATA COMMUNICATIONS TECHNOLOGY

CRYPTOGRAPHY AND NETWORK SECURITY, SIXTH EDITION

A tutorial and survey on network security technology. Each of the basic building blocks of network security, including conventional and public-key cryptography, authentication, and digital signatures, are covered. Provides a thorough mathematical background for such algorithms as AES and RSA. The book covers important network security tools and applications, including S/MIME, IP Security, Kerberos, SSL/TLS, network access control, and Wi-Fi security. In addition, methods for countering hackers and viruses are explored. **Second edition received the TAA award for the best Computer Science and Engineering Textbook of 1999.**

NETWORK SECURITY ESSENTIALS, FIFTH EDITION

A tutorial and survey on network security technology. The book covers important network security tools and applications, including S/MIME, IP Security, Kerberos, SSL/TLS, network access control, and Wi-Fi security. In addition, methods for countering hackers and viruses are explored.

BUSINESS DATA COMMUNICATIONS, SEVENTH EDITION (WITH TOM CASE)

A comprehensive presentation of data communications and telecommunications from a business perspective. Covers voice, data, image, and video communications and applications technology and includes a number of case studies. Topics covered include data communications, TCP/IP, cloud computing, Internet protocols and applications, LANs and WANs, network security, and network management.

MODERN NETWORKING WITH SDN AND QOE FRAMEWORK

A comprehensive and unified survey of modern networking technology and applications. Covers the basic infrastructure technologies of software defined networks, OpenFlow, and Network Function Virtualization (NVF), the essential tools for providing Quality of Service (QoS) and Quality of Experience, and applications such as cloud computing and big data.

COMPUTER NETWORKS WITH INTERNET PROTOCOLS AND TECHNOLOGY

An up-to-date survey of developments in the area of Internet-based protocols and algorithms. Using a top-down approach, this book covers applications, transport layer, Internet QoS, Internet routing, data link layer and computer networks, security, and network management.